INSIDE THE FASHION BUSINESS

Text and Readings

2ND EDITION

INSIDE THE FASHION BUSINESS

TEXT AND READINGS

JEANNETTE A. JARNOW

Edwin Goodman Professor,
Fashion Merchandising,
Fashion Institute of Technology

BEATRICE JUDELLE

Research Consultant

JOHN WILEY AND SONS, INC., New York • London • Sydney

Library of Congress Cataloging in Publication Data:

Jarnow, Jeannette A   ed.
  Inside the fashion business.

  Includes bibliographies.
  1. Fashion.   2. Clothing trade—United States.
I. Judelle, Beatrice, 1908–   joint ed.   II. Title.

HD9940.U4J3   1974   338.4'7'6870973   73–9855
ISBN 0–471–44066–3

Printed in the United States of America

10 9 8 7 6 5 4

*To the readers whose acceptance of the first edition
encouraged us to undertake this new version*

PREFACE

This book is for people who have a particular interest in what is called "the fashion business"—that complex of enterprises concerned with the design, production, and distribution of apparel and accessories for men, women, and children. Our objectives are twofold: to develop an understanding of the workings of an industry that is an important segment of our economy, and to expose the newcomer to the viewpoints of persons actively engaged in the fashion business.

Fashion, in its broadest sense, touches nearly every business today. Those businessmen who believed that fashion influenced women's clothes exclusively were rudely awakened in the final years of the 1960s. Style consciousness, along with a greater acceptance of design innovation, appeared in almost every sector of consumer goods. The result was to put almost every industry squarely in the fashion business. Here, however, we necessarily have limited ourselves to apparel and accessories for men and women, and to the industries and services involved in the production and distribution of this kind of merchandise.

Inside the Fashion Business is designed to meet the needs of the career-oriented student of fashion. It provides a comprehensive up-to-date presentation of the many different industries and services involved in the business of fashion. Although the text and readings are intended for use in an introductory course in a fashion program, the book may also be used, in whole or in part, in courses dealing with any of the varied activities that constitute the fashion business: fashion merchandising, fashion design, apparel production, fashion sales promotion, and fashion coordination, for instance. It also may be used as the text for a final course in a specialized fashion program, following some of the courses mentioned above.

Behavioral Objectives

This volume gives the fashion-career student the facts and awareness necessary for greater job satisfaction and faster career advancement among the widely varying opportunities in the field. If one is to progress in any segment of the fashion business, it is essential to have a knowledge of the workings of the many industries and services that comprise the business and to understand the relationships among them.

Inside the Fashion Business enables the student to:

- Understand the dynamics of fashion.
- Identify and recognize the economic and social factors that influence consumer fashion demand.
- Know the nature, activities, and relationships of the different types of enterprises involved in the production and distribution of fashion goods.
- Become familiar with the many different career opportunities in the world of fashion.

The best way to learn what makes the wheels turn in the fashion business is to consult the people who have achieved success and recognition as leaders in that business. From them come the most vivid analyses and the most penetrating insights into this fascinating field. These people usually write articles that appear in business periodicals with limited life and circulation, or speak before groups of business people. A collection of the most illuminating, diverse, and provocative material of this kind is presented here.

The readings repeated from the first edition have become classics. The basis for our selection of material was not the newness alone of a talk or article but its ability to illuminate an aspect of the fashion business or its history.

New York, N.Y. 1973

Jeannette A. Jarnow
Beatrice Judelle

FOREWORD

A hundred, perhaps even fifty years ago, "fashion" was directed toward the few—a leisured few to be elegantly adorned in the moments of tranquility which the calm pace of life afforded. Today we move in a larger world, and a faster one, and the fashion industry has become as complex as that world itself. The eloquent but mild postures of Poiret have given way to the lively, study-in-motion clothes of current American and European designers. For fashion is simply the most attractive front to the spirit of the times; and if experiment, change, and motion are the characteristics of our times, then they, too, are the ingredients of fashion.

With this change in the speed of life there has come an equally enormous change in the scale and scope of the fashion industry. Fashion for the few was ordained, cultivated, and handled by the few, in small shop operations. Yet the business that began as an enterprise of small shops now caters to millions of people, accepts a great diversity of talents, and offers a multitudinous array of products. The fashion industry is, on the one hand, the pleasant air of a Fifth Avenue salon, presenting a carefully edited collection of high-priced originals; and, on the other, it is factories that dispatch "blue jeans" in endless dozens to seaports, cities, and prairie towns across America. It is at one time the custom fitting room *and* the mail-order warehouse: a curious and exciting contrast.

More vast than the sheer size of the industry is the number of human resources that it calls into play. The citizens of the fashion world are designers and salesmen, seamstresses and accountants, merchandisers and markers, models and publicity experts. Together, they represent a wealth of contrary and complementary talents, feeding and fostering each other. In their cooperative endeavors fashion employs an incredible number of technical skills, a great deal of financial acumen, remarkable inventiveness, and occasionally a touch of what we can only call "genius." It is always astonishing, for example, to consider the demands that we put upon our fashion creators. In a society that expects from its authors and playwrights one or two great works in a lifetime, we take it in stride when a designer does a magnificent collection each season. And no less astonishing are the skill and enterprise that can adapt, promote, and sell these collections to meet the fast-changing demands of people throughout the world.

Of course there is glamour in the fashion industry and amazing vitality, which make it intriguing to the romantic and to the ambitious. But between the sketches in the margin of a schoolgirl's notebook and the order blank in a New York showroom—between the first imaginative interest and the real business of fashion—lies a vast terrain. And the young pioneer who sets out to chart this territory will need more than imagination, although that is a prerequisite, and more than ambition, although that is essential.

The troika of speed, scale, and scope has made the fashion industry a formidable subject for study. New tools are needed to bridge the gap between simple theories and the complex world of fashion that exists today. Providing some of these tools is the task that Jeannette Jarnow and Beatrice Judelle have set for themselves in this book. Professor Jarnow, as the Edwin Goodman Professor of the Fashion Institute of Technology, founded the Fashion Buying and Merchandising program under the Edwin Goodman Chair, which was established in 1955 in my father's memory. Prior to joining FIT, she had a long and successful merchandising career in fashion retailing. Miss Judelle has been associated with a variety of publications and the National Retail Merchants Association as a writer and a research specialist. From their collective experience they have compiled a book that will introduce the fashion aspirant to the many facets of our worlds, its insights and intrigues, its colorful personalities, and its calculated costs. This comprehensive survey set before the newcomer can only make the challenge of that world even more intriguing.

Andrew Goodman
President, Bergdorf Goodman Company

ORGANIZATION OF THE BOOK

The plan that we have followed is simple. Each section deals with a particular aspect of the fashion business. Within each section, there is, first, an introductory text, designed to give an organized body of facts and principles. This is followed in each case by a collection of readings, chosen to complement, supplement, and illustrate the subject matter of the text. Next, there are a bibliography for each section, a list of related trade periodicals and trade associations, and end-of-section activities. An appendix containing a fashion-business language guide follows the final section. Within this framework, the newcomer will be better able to understand the industry, its workings, and its people.

A brief summary of the sections is given below.

Section 1 (The Socioeconomics of Fashion) discusses the nature of fashion, how it moves, how it can be predicted, and the scope of the fashion business.

Section 2 (The Materials of Fashion) covers the industries that provide the raw materials of fashion, such as fibers, fabrics, leathers, and furs, along with their influence upon and response to fashion.

Section 3 (Women's Apparel and Accessories, U.S.A.) traces the history, development and character of the domestic industries producing apparel and accessories for women and examines particularly their reaction to fashion and the nature of the apparel-producing process.

Section 4 (Foreign Fashion Producers—Couture and Ready-to-Wear) traces the development of the couture in Paris and other centers abroad, its impact upon domestic fashion industries, and its advent into ready-to-wear.

Section 5 (The Retailers of Fashion) discusses the history, development, and present position of each of the many types of fashion retailers upon the American scene.

Section 6 (Auxiliary Fashion Enterprises) deals with fashion magazines, newspapers, trade publications, fashion advisory services, advertising agencies, publicity and public relations firms, and others that contribute to the functioning of the fashion business.

Section 7 (The Men's Wear Industry) explains the operation of the industries that produce men's wear and shows how they have changed in response to the awakening of a vigorous fashion demand among men.

Section 8 (Directions in the Fashion Business) is concerned with the changing demographics and dimensions of the fashion market and with how the broadening demand for fashion is changing the pattern of production and distribution in the fashion business.

Each section concludes with a series of suggested student-learning experiences that require review, interpretation, and application of knowledge. These learning activities consist of: "Fashion Business Terminology," a listing of meaningful words or names that students are asked to explain or identify; "Topics for Review," a series of questions reviewing the content of the section; and "Applications with Examples," a series of three topics that require the student to utilize factual content and illustrate its application by citing current industry practices, and illustrating with examples.

J.A.J.
B.J.

ACKNOWLEDGMENTS

This book reflects the work and thought of many people. We are grateful to the publications, organizations, and business leaders who shared their experience and observations with us, and who granted reprint permissions for readings. Also we thank the faculty members and students of the Fashion Institute of Technology for their continuing support and suggestions, and so many friends in the academic and fashion worlds who gave advice and counsel. These are the people who helped us shape the first edition and who encouraged and guided us in this new edition.

J.A.J.
B.J.

CONTENTS

SECTION 1 **THE SOCIOECONOMICS OF FASHION 2**

The Meaning of Fashion 2
How Fashion Moves 5
What Determines Fashion 8
The Consumer's Role in Fashion 12
The Prediction of Fashion 14
The Business of Fashion 17
Readings 21
Nature of Fashion, *Alfred H. Daniels* **22**
Fashion Cycles, *Kenneth Collins* **24**
Fashion: A Detective Story, *James Laver* **25**
The Meaning of Fashion, *Dwight E. Robinson* **27**
What Were They Wearing? 1910–1970, *Women's Wear Daily* **30**
Fashion Closes the Gaps, *Daisy Goldsmith* **35**
Clothes Now, *Estelle Hamburger* **37**
Analyzing Fashion Trends, *Rita A. Perna* **42**
Life-Style, Fashion, and the Economy, *Carl Priestland* **45**
Bibliography 47
Section Review and Activities 49

SECTION 2 **THE MATERIALS OF FASHION 53**

The Textile Industry 54
Other Primary Markets 70
Relationship to Apparel and Accessories 74
Readings 75
Burlington Industries: A Total World of Textiles, *Clothes* **76**
The Durable Threads of J.P. Stevens, *Richard J. Whalen* **81**
Merge No More, *Forbes* **85**
A Fabric Designer's Philosophy, *Pola Stout* **86**
The Fiber Producer in Marketing: Activating the Consumer Market, *American Fabrics* **88**
Can We Take the Gamble Out of Fashion?, *American Fabrics* **89**
Forward Looking Marketing Techniques at the Fiber, Mill, and Manufacturing Levels, *Louis F. Laun* **90**
Fifty Landmark Years for Fabrics, *Women's Wear Daily* **95**
Bibliography 97
Section Review and Activities 99

SECTION 3 **WOMEN'S APPAREL AND ACCESSORIES–U.S.A. 103**

Economic Importance 104
History and Development 105

Geographical Locations   109
Nature of Apparel Firms   112
Patterns of Operations   117
Marketing Activities   123
Fashion Design Activities   126
Fashion Accessories   129
Readings   137
    The Development of American Creativity in Fashion, *Virginia Pope*   138
    Seventh Avenue's New, Corporate Look, *Isadore Barmash*   141
    "Going Public". . ., *Henry Bach*   145
    Jonathan Logan, King of the Jungle, *Clothes*   147
    Fashion—A Very Hot Tin Roof, *Harry Serwer*   154
    The World of the Designer, *Evelyn Portrait*   156
    American Couture: Toujours Trigère, *Clothes*   158
    One Cornerstone of American Couture Is A Man Named Ben Shaw, *Stores*   162
    A Daniel Boone on Seventh Avenue, *Eugenia Sheppard*   165
    Research Spears Levi Strauss' Fashionable March into Europe, *Advertising Age*   166
Bibliography   168
Section Review and Activities   171

SECTION 4   FOREIGN FASHION PRODUCERS—COUTURE AND
READY-TO-WEAR   175
Paris   176
Other Foreign Fashion Centers   192
American Imports of Ready-To-Wear and Accessories   196
Readings   199
    Backstage at Paris' Fashion Drama, *Françoise Giroud*   200
    Style Piracy, *Kenneth Collins*   203
    Meet Manhattan, *Marilyn Hoffman*   204
    First De Gaulle—Now Couture, *Clothes*   205
    Paris Couture: More RTW, *Bernardine Morris*   207
    Subject: Buy American, *Dorothy Coleman Seeman*   209
    Apparel Firms Ring Bell in Big Hong Kong Year, *J.W. Cohn*   211
    The Import Apparel Wonderland—A Guide for Discounters, *Aeta Salba*   212
    These Designers Made Fifty Years of Fashion History, *Women's Wear Daily*   219
Bibliography   227
Section Review and Activities   228

SECTION 5   THE RETAILERS OF FASHION   231
Fashion Retailing in the Past   232
Diversity of Fashion Retailing Today   235
Current Trends in Retailing   248

Retailing Changes With Customers   255
Readings   257
   Lord & Taylor: Serendipity on Fifth Avenue, *Faye Hammel*   258
   Bloomingdale's: "First the Idea, Then the Merchandise," *Susan Margetts*   260
   We'd Like to Tell You about Lane Bryant, *Lane Bryant, Inc.*   261
   Lerner Shops—More Than Just Window Changing, *Clothes*   262
   Alexander's—Underselling New York, *Clothes*   268
   The Drugstore of the 60s—Boutiques, *Thomas Isbell*   272
   Fashion, the Heartbeat of Retailing, *Hector Escobosa*   274
   Fashion Merchandising, *Alfred H. Daniels*   277
   Merchandising Fashion, *Stanley Marcus*   285
   The Changing Face of Retailing, *Stanley J. Goodman*   286
Bibliography   289
Section Review and Activities   291

SECTION 6   **AUXILIARY FASHION ENTERPRISES   295**
   Fashion in Print   296
   Advertising and Publicity Agencies   302
   Fashion Consultants   306
   Resident Buying Offices   307
   Other Fashion Enterprises   310
   Readings   313
      The Role of the Fashion Magazine in the Business of Fashion, *Edith Raymond Locke*   314
      How American Fashion Got There, *New York Couture Business Council*   315
      The Fashion Role of an Ad Agency, *Arthur A. Winters*   316
      Costumers' Nightmare: Minis, Midis, Hot Pants!, *Marketing-Communications*   319
      A Jaunt with Fashion, *Jean Cameron*   321
      Polka Dots Are Poison in Georgia, *Sonia Arcone*   323
      How to Select A Resident Buying Office, *Ernest A. Miller*   326
      What is "The Fashion Group"?, *Sarah Tomerlin Lee*   329
   Bibliography   330
   Section Review and Activities   332

SECTION 7   **THE MEN'S WEAR INDUSTRY   335**
   History and Development   336
   Geographical Centers   340
   Nature of the Industry   342
   Marketing and Distribution   347
   Fashion Revolution in Men's Wear   349
   Readings   355
      The Peacock Revolution, *Dr. Ernest Dichter*   356
      The Terrible Trouble with Men, *Forbes*   358

Male Plumage '68, *Newsweek* **363**
The Last Convert to Marketing, *Ralph Leezenbaum* **368**
The IACD Designer States His Case, *Apparel Manufacturer* **373**
The American Designer: The New Face of Malewear, *Clothes* **374**
The Designer Shop, *Department Store Management* **379**
Bibliography 382
Section Review and Activities 383

SECTION 8   DIRECTIONS IN THE FASHION BUSINESS 387
Developing Markets for Fashion 388
Changing Dimensions of the Fashion Market 390
The Marketing Concept 397
The Business of Fashion Is Change 401
Readings 409
Looking Ahead in Fashion, *E.B. Weiss* **410**
Bibliography 413
Section Review and Activities 413

APPENDIX   FASHION INDUSTRY LANGUAGE GUIDE 417

CREDIT LIST 423

INDEX 425

INSIDE THE FASHION BUSINESS

Text and Readings

THE FASHION EXPLOSION

SECTION 1
THE SOCIO-ECONOMICS OF FASHION

Fashion is as old as time and as new as tomorrow. In its most general sense fashion is expressed not only in what people wear but in what they eat, the way they talk, what they do, how they live, and the things they use. The intensity with which changes in fashion are followed by people everywhere on all levels of society is evidence of its social significance and its impact on human activities.

The influence of fashion is felt not only throughout the social world but in all categories of business activities. Its impact is most clearly demonstrated, however, in the multibillion dollar complex of industries dedicated to the design, production, and distribution of apparel and accessories for men, women, and children. The women's branch of this great business complex was once caricatured as "suffering from a form of schizophrenia because it manufactures clothing but it really doesn't sell clothing. What it sells is fashion."[1] This description, once applicable only to women's apparel, is now equally applicable to men's wear.

What is fashion? This section discusses the generally accepted definitions of fashion and the theories of its origins and dynamics. It also indicates the economic importance of the fashion business and the vital role that the consumer plays in determining which fashions will be developed and at what speed. The readings that follow give the fashion philosophies of successful professionals in the world of fashion.

THE MEANING OF FASHION

Few words in any language have as many different implications as the word "fashion." To the layman, it implies a mysterious force that makes a particular style of dress or behavior acceptable in one year but quite the reverse in another. Economists view fashion as an element of artificial obsolescence that impels people to replace articles that still retain much of their original usefulness even though the new articles may not greatly differ from the old ones. To sociologists, fashion represents an expression of social interaction and of status seeking;[2] psychiatrists find indications of sex impulses in patterns of dress.[3] But whatever fashion may mean to others, it represents billions of dollars in sales to the group of enterprises concerned with the production and distribution of apparel and accessories. As one fashion student said, "Everything that matters, everything that gives their trade its nature and place in the world must be ascribed to fashion."[4]

[1]"The Rag Business: 7th Avenue Goes to Wall Street," *Forbes Magazine*, July 1, 1964, pp. 24–29.

[2]See Bernard Barber and Lyle Lobel, "Fashion in Women's Clothes and the American Social System," *Social Forces*, December 1952. Also see R. K. Merton, *Social Theory and Social Structure*, The Free Press, Glencoe, Ill., 1949, Chapter 1.

[3]See Edmund Bergler, *Fashion and the Unconscious*, R. Brunner, New York, 1953, for a provocative work based on his psychoanalysis of many persons connected with the fashion industry.

[4]Dwight E. Robinson, "The Economics of Fashion Demand," *Quarterly Journal of Economics*, Vol. LXXV, August 1961, p. 377.

Terminology of Fashion

Among the countless definitions of fashion the one from Webster's latest unabridged dictionary comes very close to what professionals mean when they use the word: "The prevailing or accepted style or group of styles in dress or personal decoration established or adopted during a particular time or season." A widely recognized and often quoted fashion economist, Dr. Paul H. Nystrom, defined fashion in similar words as being "nothing more nor less than the prevailing style at any given time."[5]

Frequently the word *fashion* is used interchangeably with the word *style*, and people will ask, "Isn't it stylish?" when they really mean, "Isn't it fashionable?" A *style* of clothing is considered to be a product with specific characteristics that distinguish it from another product of the same type. For example, all jeans have a common characteristic that makes them different from other types of pants. Jeans, however, can have many individual variations in materials and trimming details; these variations are called *designs*. For instance, the fashion may be for jeans; the most popular type or style might be flare-bottomed jeans; the individual designs might include front pockets or back pockets, matching or contrasting stitching, corduroy or denim, and so on.

A few other key words should be explained here to facilitate further discussion of fashion principles. A *fashion trend* refers to the direction in which fashion is moving; the styles that are gaining in favor constitute the trend. A *fad* is a style of unusually short life, characterized by a sudden sweep of popularity and followed by an abrupt decline. *High fashion*, a term in common use, has a number of meanings, all of which imply a fashion of limited appeal. Some styles are limited because their high cost keeps them permanently out of reach of all but the people in top income brackets, because of expensive materials, intricate design, and elaborate workmanship, for example; other styles are limited because they are too sophisticated to be attuned to the needs of the average man or woman or too extreme for the person who must wear last year's coat with this year's new slacks or dress. Still other styles are limited only temporarily until their newness wears off or the price drops, and they then become generally acceptable. High price alone does not make a garment high fashion, but it can keep an otherwise widely acceptable fashion from reaching all the people who would enjoy it. The term *high fashion* is most commonly used to describe the very new styles and designs that have been adopted only by a limited group of consumers—referred to as fashion leaders—who are first to accept fashion change; these styles and designs are usually high in price. Because high fashions are so well publicized, people are likely to lose sight of the fact that they account for only a small portion of the total fashion business.

Fashion Means Consumer Acceptance

Although fashion feeds on new designs and styles, it is not the producers or designers of these styles who determine fashion. No style or group of styles and no

[5]Paul H. Nystrom, *Economics of Fashion*, Ronald Press, New York, 1928, p. 4.

manner of dress can be considered to be a fashion unless it is accepted—that is, bought—by a substantial portion of the public. This element of public acceptance of a style is the very essence of fashion; and of the many styles that are created, only those that are followed by sufficient numbers of consumers can be called fashions. Designers who acquire a reputation for "creating" fashion are simply those who have been outstandingly successful in giving tangible expression to the shapes, colors, lines, or looks wanted by a considerable segment of the consuming public. Fashions are not business creations; they are essentially socioeconomic in their origin.

Fashion Means Change

Also to be considered in the concept of fashion is its changeable nature. Fashion is not static, although a style is. An individual style remains a style, such as peasant blouses, turtleneck sweaters, and blazer jackets, whether it is rising or falling in popularity. Fashion, however, is always changing, sometimes rapidly, sometimes slowly. The only thing constant about fashion is change. This element of change is recognized in the definitions cited earlier by the use of such words as a "given" or "particular" time. Fashion changes are not purposeful, nor are they directed by one or many designers. They spring from changes in socioeconomic conditions that affect the public's needs, wants, and receptivity to the style offerings of designers and producers.

An obvious example of such change occurred in the early decades of the twentieth century when women sought, gained, and enjoyed new political and economic freedom. Their altered activities and concepts of themselves encouraged them to discard the constricting garments that had been in fashion for centuries, and to adopt shorter skirts, relaxed waistlines, bobbed hair, and other fashions more appropriate to their more active lives. Similarly, in the decades following World War II, both men and women responded to increased leisure, suburban life, and a more varied and casual way of living by adopting a more varied and casual way of dressing.

Change arises also from less dramatic and worldshaking causes. People grow bored with what they have; the eye wearies of the same colors, lines, and textures after a time; what is new and different appears refreshing; and what has been on the scene for a while appears dull and unattractive. Thorstein Veblen, writing at the beginning of the present century, made this clear in his *Theory of the Leisure Class.* As he pointed out:

"We readily and for the most part with utter sincerity find those things pleasing that are in vogue. Shaggy dress-stuffs and pronounced color effects, for instance, offend us at times when the vogue is goods of a high, glossy finish and neutral colors. A fancy bonnet of this year's model unquestionably appeals to our sensibilities today more forcibly than an equally fancy bonnet of the model of last year; although when viewed in the perspective of a quarter of a century, it would, I apprehend, be a

matter of the utmost difficulty to award the palm for intrinsic beauty to one rather than to the other."[6]

Fashion Involves Places and People

Consider also the element of places and people. Obviously, what may be considered fashionable in the Orient or in the Australian bush may be simply outlandish on a New York street, and what New York women wear is very often unacceptable in parts of the United States which have markedly different climate, terrain, or mores.

Finally, consider the group of people by whom a style or manner of dress must be accepted before we may call it a fashion. What is adopted by those who are venturesome or who seek distinction may be anything but acceptable to those of more conservative tastes. Furthermore, what is used by a particular age or occupational group may not be appropriate for those of a different age or occupational group.

Definition of Fashion

Our concept of fashion, then, emerges as a *continuing process of change in the styles of dress* (or behavior, if one is interested in the broadest aspects of the term) *that are accepted or followed by substantial groups of people at any given time and place.* A specific "fashion," however, would be the particular style that is popular at a given time.

HOW FASHION MOVES

In studying the tempo and direction of fashion change, not merely over the past few decades but over several centuries, scholars have observed that fashions follow an evolutionary development, and that each individual fashion experiences a steadily increasing acceptance until it reaches the greatest popularity to which it is susceptible; thereafter its acceptance wanes.

Fashions Change Gradually

Styles shift constantly, and minor innovations appear every season, but a full-scale changeover is never completed at any one time. Fashions usually evolve gradually unless some momentous event induces an abrupt switch. There was one such dramatic change in 1947 when the government curbs on the use of fabric during

---

[6]Thornstein Veblen, *The Theory of the Leisure Class,* Mentor Edition, New American Library of World Literature, Inc., New York, 1963, p. 97.

HEMLINES RISE GRADUALLY

1950	1955	1960	1965	1970

World War II were rescinded and the much publicized "New Look" by Dior was launched. The natural shoulder line, cinched-in waist, and full, long skirts changed the look of fashion almost overnight and made up in one season for the many years of wartime "freezing" of fashions. Had there been no war to require fabric economies, there probably would have been a gradual rather than dramatic abandonment of the skimpy short skirts and padded shoulders that had endured for most of the decade.

Trends do reverse themselves eventually, of course. Fashions usually move so steadily in one direction that revulsion seems to set in and the trend begins to move in an opposite direction. It is only in retrospect that changes in fashion seem sudden and drastic; actually they are cumulative and come about as a result of a series of gradual shifts over a period of time. For example, when women's skirts in the 1960s began inching up from midcalf, the change was not particularly noticed at first; it was only when the skirts became mini and moved toward micro-mini that people took notice of the approaching extreme. Similarly, when men in the late 1960s began abandoning very narrow ties in favor of ties that were somewhat wider, and gradually moved into styles that were wide indeed, the change was not noticed at first. People often mistake their belated recognition of gradual change for a sudden, dramatic change in the fashions. Even when the rate of fashion change accelerates rapidly, as it did in the 1960s, the pace is slower than it appears to be to the casual observer who has failed to notice the early, tentative movements in some new direction.

Fashion Cycles

The process by which fashions rise, peak, and decline was described in the 1920s by Professor Melvin Copeland in a way that still applies to most developments on the fashion scene.[7] People of prominence, taste, and affluence do not want to dress as everyone else does. Each year, the fashion leaders among them shop the new styles offered by designers who have a reputation for great style sense. The leaders' selections are copied at progressively lower prices until the styles appear in cheaper materials in low-priced stores. At that point, the original fashion leaders have already selected different styles that are more distinctive, and the process repeats itself.

Academically minded students of fashion have described this rise, peak, and eventual decline of accepted styles as the fashion cycle.[8] Some have even sought to chart the ups and downs of fashions in an effort to determine the length of time a fashion movement takes to run its course. The time intervals, however, elude measurement. The spread of fashion, as of every new idea, is a complicated social phenomenon. The public's needs and interests, which affect its receptivity to new styles or its boredom with an old one, do not change by clockwork.

The problem of applying the stopwatch technique to an analysis of fashion movements is also complicated by the fact that price differentials, which at one time tended to mark the different stages of style acceptance, have virtually disappeared. Furthermore, it is rare nowadays for a single style to dominate the scene at any particular time. While some cycles are in their peaks, their successors are already in the growing stage. Many new fashions often reach full growth without ever entirely displacing those that preceded them. A further complicating factor is that, owing to the evolutionary nature of changes, clearly definable shifts in fashion do not occur at a given time, and it is impossible to pinpoint the exact beginning or end of a specific fashion.

The more one studies fashion, in theory and in practice, the more apparent it becomes that the term "fashion cycle" is a misnomer. The very word "cycle" implies a repetitive rise and fall, as if a wheel had turned and the fashions that were "in" had to go "out" for a time and then reappear at predictable intervals. There are revivals of styles from time to time but the fashions of another day never quite come back in their entirety; neither history nor fashion ever plays itself back to us unchanged.

Fashions are cyclical, however, to the extent that they do go through stages of increasing and decreasing popularity. They also vary in duration and in degree of acceptance. As an overall rule, broad, general trends have the longest life: for example, the fashion of casual clothes. Those that are narrow and more specific, such as particular styles of casual apparel, are usually of shorter duration. Occasionally an individual style so satisfies a basic need that it remains in fashion almost indefinitely; this is called a *classic.* Typical are simple cardigan sweaters for women and white shirts with button down collars for men.

Dr. Paul Nystrom, in his theory on the life cycles of fashions, noted that cycles in accessory fashions such as scarfs, handbags, costume jewelry, and the like tend to run for a season, whereas fashions in color, design, and materials usually require a year, and silhouette cycles tend to run much longer.[9]

---

[7]Melvin T. Copeland, *Principles of Merchandising,* A. W. Shaw, New York, 1924, pp. 100, 165, 166, 304.
[8]Nystrom, *op. cit.* p. 19.
[9]*Ibid.* p. 29.

A reading in this section has aptly compared the rise and decline of a particular fashion to the rise and fall of waves in the surf.[10] No mathematical formula governs their formation, cresting and breaking, but the experienced swimmer learns to study them and to time the individual waves that concern him. So it is in the fashion business. Like experienced swimmers and navigators, fashion firms evaluate the rise and fall in the popularity of styles by their own curve of sales and develop a fairly good idea of where their particular organization stands in relation to fashion movements.

WHAT DETERMINES FASHIONS

It is far easier to recognize what is fashionable than to say why or how it became a fashion. When we search for the influences that bring forth fashions such as the crinolines of the past or the more natural silhouettes of the present, we are confronted with a complex question indeed. One thing we do know: esthetic appeal does not produce a fashion. Veblen made this point when he observed that there is no intrinsic difference between the gloss of a patent leather shoe and the shine of a threadbare garment. People, he observed, are ready to find beauty in what is in vogue; therefore the shine on the shoe is beautiful and the garment's shine is repulsive.[11]

A modern illustration may be found in the changing concept of what constitutes beautiful hair among women. Before the 1960s, wavy hair was considered beautiful and women with straight hair submitted themselves to curlers and permanent wave treatments to induce curls and waves. During the 1960s, the reverse was true; straight, smooth hair was considered beautiful, and women with wavy hair submitted to straightening treatments.

Imitation Makes Fashion

Styles become fashions through a follow-the-leader process, as was explained earlier in the discussion of fashion cycles. Widespread imitation of the styles worn by admired individuals or groups results in the development of a fashion. That great fashion designer, the late Coco Chanel, said this very clearly: "If there is no copying, how are you going to have fashion?"[12] Social scientists explain the element of imitation in fashion in terms of the individual's desire to achieve status by associating himself through his choice of apparel with an admired person or group; it is a means of bridging the gap between a social class and the one above it.[13]

---

[10]Kenneth Collins, *Fashion Cycles*, included in this volume on page 24.

[11]Veblen, *op. cit.*, p. 97.

[12]*Women's Wear Daily*, November 16, 1964, p. 1.

[13]Edward Sapir, "Fashion," *Encyclopedia of the Social Sciences*, Vol. VI, The Macmillan Co., New York, 1931, pp. 139–144; and Gabriel Tarde, *The Laws of Imitation*, Henry Holt & Co., New York, 1903, p. 313.

Imitation and conformity in dress are also explained in terms of insecurity, since it takes more social courage than most of us possess to be conspicuously different from others in the appearance we present to the public. Thus fashion gives expression to two basic needs: the craving for social recognition and the desire to conform.[14]

Centuries ago the leaders and setters of fashion were royalty. The nobility copied royalty and were then copied by people in the middle class who had the means. The lower classes, of course, had neither the means nor the temerity to copy, or they were prohibited by law from doing so. In time, royalty went out of fashion in many countries and their position as fashion leaders was assumed by outstanding individuals at the top of the economic and social ladder. Many such people made it their business to dress well, and their activities and appearance were highly publicized and reported. The large majority of the public, with more restricted social activities and more limited budgets, were necessarily cautious in their spending and, in fashion, this caution expressed itself in imitating what "they" wore and in avoiding experimentation. Fashion thus *trickled down* from higher to lower echelons. Meantime, new ideas were being introduced at the top.

This *trickle-down theory* of fashion adoption was grasped and widely accepted by such nineteenth century economists as John Roe, Caroline R. Foley, and Thorstein Veblen[15] and by such sociologists as George Simmel, who spelled it out, step by step, in a 1904 paper.[16]

As the twentieth century progressed, however, it became clear that fashion was no longer a matter of imitating any particular social or economic class but of choosing one's own heroes and heroines of fashion—and not necessarily from among individuals with glittering genealogy or fabulous wealth. Fashions have been given impetus by movie stars, television personalities, big men on campus, and other public figures who capture the imagination.

Another theory of fashion emulation was advanced: the *trickle-across theory*, enunciated by Charles W. King in 1963.[17] He observed that each group or segment of society has its own leader or leaders whose approval is required for a fashion to be adopted within the group.

A third and more recent theory, espoused by many students of the fashion process and by many fashion professionals, is that the traditional trickle-down process has reversed itself and that fashions now *filter-up*, not down. Says designer Rudi Gernreich, "New fashion starts in the street. What I do is watch what the kids are putting together for themselves. I formalize it, give it something of my own, perhaps, and that is fashion. But St. Laurent and other designers must pick it up at

---

[14]Elizabeth B. Hurlock, *The Psychology of Dress*, The Ronald Press, New York, 1929, p. 181.

[15]Veblen, *op. cit.;* John Roe, *The Sociological Concept of Capital*, The Macmillan Co., London, 1834, Chapter 13; Caroline R. Foley, *Economic Journal*, London, Vol. 3, 1893, p. 458.

[16]George Simmel, "Fashion", *American Journal of Sociology*, Vol. 62, May, 1957, pp. 541–558, reprinted from the *International Quarterly*, Vol. X, October 1904, pp. 130–155.

[17]Charles W. King, "Fashion Adoption: A Rebuttal to the 'Trickle Down' Theory," Reprint Series 119, reprinted from American Marketing Association Winter Conference, 1963 by Purdue University, Krannert School of Business Administration.

the same time I do. No one person invents anything today and then sends it out to the rest of the world. It's got to be in the air. That's why I watch the kids."[18]

This *bottom-up theory,* as enunciated by Greenberg and Glynn,[19] maintains that fashions filter up, not merely from youth to age, but from the lower economic classes to the upper. Typical of fashions initiated by the young and less than affluent are the miniskirts of the 1960s, which started with young girls of modest means in London and spread to well-to-do grandmothers. The male espousal of flowing locks and beard similarly started with the young and spread to gray-haired, balding men. The boots bought in low-priced chain stores by motorcycle gangs in New York and Los Angeles were featured, in time, by prestige shoe stores for men. The Edwardian influence on men's fashions in the 1960s and early 1970s traces back to clothes worn by Teddy boys, or young London toughs, in the early 1950s. "Granny" dresses and eyeglasses, old military uniforms, and fringed frontier jackets all started with the scavenging of young hippies in junk shops and attics and, in time, won acceptance among the mature and financially secure sectors of society.

New Technical Developments Make Fashions

Some fashions also seem to have their origins in the development of new fibers and fabrics, new processes for utilizing familiar ones, and other fruits of the chemist's genius—plus, perhaps, a waiting need for the new or a weariness with the old. For example, the synthetic fibers that made wash-and-wear fabrics possible, and thus influenced fashion, might not have received such a rousing welcome if they had come upon the scene at a time when domestic help was plentiful and when the stiffly starched, beautifully ironed garment was a symbol of the well-run household. Other examples abound. The development of stretch fabrics made possible a fashion for skintight slacks in the early 1960s. Improved knitting methods brought knit fabrics into an enormous range of men's and women's apparel in the late 1960s and early 1970s. Pile fabrics employing man-made fibers achieved a furlike effect and opened new avenues of styling to coats of modest price. The zipper not only changed the construction of clothing but, at various times, provided a decorative note in women's dresses. Plastics, in their infinite variety, at different periods made possible such fashions as "wet look" women's apparel, transparent shoe uppers, raincoats in gay colors, and thigh-high boots for indoor wear.

The Times Make Fashions

A glance at the past makes it apparent that many fashions grow out of the interaction of different factors that serve as sources of inspiration and also appear to trigger both the trends and their acceptance by the public. During this century, for example, fashion has been influenced by two world wars and by the social and

---

[18] "The Youthquake," *Fortune,* January 1969.

[19] Allan Greenberg and Mary Joan Glynn, *A Study of Young People,* Doyle, Dane, Bernbach, Inc., New York, 1966.

economic currents that caused and were stimulated by the exodus to the suburbs, by the impact on society of a huge, independent, and well-educated younger generation, and by a resurgence among blacks of interest and pride in their racial inheritance. Reflections of such events include the importance gained by casual clothes in the 1950s and 1960s, the miniskirts, love beads, headbands, and bright colors of the late 1960s, and the "Afro" hair styles of the late 1960s that told the white world, "Black is beautiful."

Fashions have been made by major events and outstanding personalities in the worlds of science, entertainment, politics, art, and sports. To cite some examples: Egyptian motifs inspired by the discovery of the tomb of King Tut-Ankh-Amen; Hawaiian prints gaining impetus when the territory became a state; the fashion for ballet slippers, pony tails, and other ballerina influences inspired by the popularity of the Russian ballet; colors and print designs that sprang from modern paintings; the growing enthusiasm for boating and the resultant popularity of sailing denims for city wear; the impact of a young and lovely first lady like Jacqueline Kennedy on hair and dress styles; and the influence of the Beatles, not only on music but also on men's hair styles.

Creative designers are alert to such stimuli. People and events in the news suggest to them new silhouettes, new fabric textures, new colors, and new accessories. If the designer is successful in translating the outside happenings into styles that reflect the public's own enthusiasm for the person or place concerned, then a new fashion is "created."

Even though it may seem that the fashion grows out of the news, actually the news is only the catalyst. A fashion must be ready to be born, just as soil must be fertile if seed is to grow. No one factor alone—people, places, events, inventions, or creative designer—can make a fashion. Each influences the other, but in the final analysis it is the customer's acceptance or rejection that makes or breaks a fashion idea.

Life-Styles Make Fashion

Fashions in clothing have always been more than merely a manner of dressing; they are social expressions that reflect a period's ideals and life-styles. Fashions document the taste and values of their time in the same manner as paintings, sculpture, and other art forms. They have been called "a kind of psychic weathercock which shows which way the wind blows."[20] Fashion's constant change is simply a reflection of the constant change in our way of life.

There is, of course, no one universal way of life in America today; our values are varied. Some of us are hedonistic; others are antimaterialistic. Some are "establishment"; some trust no one over 30. Whatever the life-style one chooses, the dress reflects that choice—often consciously. As one commentator points out, clothes nowadays are viewed "sometimes with almost mystical fervor, as the most basic expression of life style, indeed of identity itself."[21]

[20]James Laver, *Taste and Fashion*, George C. Harrap & Company Ltd., London, 1937, p. 266.
[21]Charles E. Silberman, "Identity Crisis in the Consumer Markets," *Fortune*, March 1971, p. 95.

Thus the young who wear jeans, T-shirts, granny dresses, long hair, and headbands are often consciously confronting their elders with a rejection of establishment standards. Thus the bra burners of 1970 expressed a rejection of woman's traditional role just as surely as the draft-card burners a few years earlier expressed their rejection of man's traditional responsibility to serve in the military. The wearing of pants, slacks, and shorts on many relatively formal occasions expresses the life-style of women who free themselves of some of the physical and conventional restraints that their mothers and grandmothers accepted. The understated fashions of the very wealthy, and their rejection of garments made from the furs of endangered species, are expressions of their social and ecological awareness. A generation or two earlier, the immensely wealthy flaunted their money, rank, and privileges in their dress and in their entire life-style, with no concern for the impact of their fashions on the poor or on nature itself.

THE CONSUMER'S ROLE IN FASHION

The goal of everyone in the fashion business is to have the ultimate consumer buy his merchandise. There is much that can be done to stimulate consumer buying, but in order to do this effectively, one must first understand people and their buying motivation. This need to understand why and how customers buy is not uniquely a fashion industry problem. Every business that serves the public has to guide its operations in the light of consumer demand. The fashion industry, however, moves at a fast tempo. The rewards of success are great and the cost of failure correspondingly high. As Dr. Nystrom put it:

"Consumer demand is the guide to intelligent production and merchandising. . . . A knowledge of the fundamental facts of what consumers want and why, is clearly of the first importance . . . to those who plan the policies, design the product, determine the price lines, prepare the advertising and sales promotion, sell the goods and make the collections, in fact all who deal with the problems of the consumer." [22]

Why People Buy Fashion

In an effort to achieve an understanding of the consumer in relation to her buying response to fashion, we find ourselves joining the social scientists and marketing experts in a continuing search for answers to a few basic questions: Why do people buy apparel? What factors influence their choice?

There are some commentators on buying behavior who would have us believe that almost every fashion purchase we make is in search of status. Edward Sapir, the social scientist, saw people's fondness for new clothes an "an outward emblem of

[22]Paul H. Nystrom, *Economics of Consumption*, The Ronald Press, New York 1929, p. 111.

personal display" and a desire to impress others with their spending power.[23] Veblen's "conspicuous consumption" value was, in his eyes, the major buying motive.[24]

Not all students of buying motivation, however, see the picture in such simple terms. A consumer study sponsored by the University of Michigan concluded that many elements condition what and why a purchase is made, among them "habits, background, individual caprice, quality and price."[25] Steuart Henderson Britt, long an authority on marketing, pointed out in *The Spenders* that every purchase involves a balancing of three factors: what one likes, what one needs, and what one can afford.[26] Decisions on any points are bound to be colored by emotional reactions—even the question of what is needed, unless one lives at the bare subsistence level. Thoreau tried that at Walden Pond more than a century ago, and found that he needed very little—so little, in fact, that he came to think it childish and savage for people to want new clothes or to follow the fashions of their day. He found it difficult, when he lived so austerely, to understand why other people wanted and worked for variety in their wardrobes, or why they cast aside garments that were not utterly worn out.[27]

The wellsprings of these wants that he did not share lie deep in human nature. Men and women are complex creatures whose actions are seldom governed by reason alone. Some people are always interested in change—as a relief from boredom with what they own, or as a means of differentiating themselves from others. They see in new styles a chance for distinction or self-assertion. The attention attracted by wearing a new style may be attention the individual wants but is unable to obtain readily in any other socially acceptable manner. Youth, particularly, tends to express its rebellion against existing social conventions by adopting different styles of dress. For the large majority of people, however, fashion buying is strongly motivated by the natural desire to imitate others or to identify with a group.

Fashion buying motives, then, are seldom either rational or simple, nor do they spring purely from physical needs. Emotional needs and the natural human wants and desires must also be taken into account.

The Power of the Consumer

The role of the ultimate consumer in the fashion business is an important one and, in the final analysis, controlling. This is a fact recognized by successful fashion

[23] Sapir, *op. cit*, pp. 139–144; also J. C. Flugel, *The Psychology of Clothes*, International Psychoanalytic Library, London, 1950, p. 15.

[24] Veblen, *op. cit.*, for a discussion of conspicuous consumption.

[25] Dr. Eva Mueller, reporting on the results of a consumer buying study conducted by the University of Michigan, in "Buying Habits of Women Found to be Inconsistent," *The New York Times*, May 1, 1964.

[26] McGraw-Hill Co., New York, 1960.

[27] Henry David Thoreau, *Walden and Other Writings*, Modern Library, Random House, New York 1950, pp. 21–22.

professionals and repeatedly stated in their own words throughout the readings in this book.

Ordinarily the part that consumers play is a passive one. People do not actually demand new products and designs of which they have little or no knowledge; neither do they demand change. Their individual and collective power is exercised in the selections they make on one hand and in their refusals to buy, on the other. It is by their acceptance or rejection that they influence the goods which will be presented for their favor and even the methods of presentation.

The history of the fashion business is dotted with examples of unsuccessful efforts to make the consumer buy what she did not want. One classic example was the promotional campaign by producers of millinery trimmings to arrest a buying trend towards simpler millinery. They received the cooperation of Paul Poiret in their efforts to bring back hats "smothered with leaves, fruit, flowers, feathers, and ribbons" but even the sponsorship of the great Poiret could not make customers buy the decorated hats of earlier years.[28]

A second classic case was the failure of textile manufacturers to persuade women to purchase fuller skirts requiring more yardage than the tight hobble skirts which they were buying in 1912. In the course of their promotional activities they secured the endorsement of Paris couturiers, fashion editors, and retail distributors. The whole campaign was a failure. Consumers continued to buy hobble skirts almost as though the different business groups were backing this style instead of fighting it.[29]

There is no question that the promotional activities of the industry can influence what people buy. There is a big question, however, as to whether such activities could succeed in creating fashions that consumers do not want. The high ratio of markdowns in the apparel business[30] is evidence enough that consumers are not "pawns in the hands of advertisers"[31] but rather the voters in the marketplace of fashion.

THE PREDICTION OF FASHION

Predicting which styles will become the fashions at a particular time has been called an occupational guessing game for the fashion industry with millions of dollars at stake. Actually, prediction is neither guesswork nor a game. The makers and sellers of fashion merchandise have their own methods for studying trends in consumer preferences. They examine their past experience for clues as to what will succeed today, and they watch today's activity for indications of what may happen tomorrow.

[28]Quentin Bell, *On Human Finery*, A. A. Wyn, New York, 1949, pp. 48–49.

[29]Paul H. Nystrom, *Economics of Fashion*, pp. 11–12.

[30]The median markdown rate of women's apparel departments in department stores is usually 14 percent or more of net sales in a given year, whereas the storewide figure is likely to be only 6 or 8 percent. Source: *Department Merchandising and Operating Results*, compiled and published annually by the Controllers Congress, National Retail Merchants Association, New York, N.Y. 10001.

[31]Mueller, *loc. cit.*

Analyzing Customers' Purchases

There is in the fashion industry a constant flow, back and forth, of information about what the customer is buying. In most retail stores, some record is kept as to the styles, colors, fabrics, and so on, that have been purchased for resale. On this record are also entered the day-to-day sales. Every garment bought by a consumer thus becomes a ballot cast by the customer for the wanted size, color, fabric, silhouette, and style.

From the records of an individual store, the retailer can discern sudden or gradual changes in the preferences of his own customers. These changes become apparent whether the same customers are turning to different fashions, or whether there is a change in the kind of people who make up the store's clientele. In either case, the proprietor or buyer sees that there is less demand for this, and more for that.

These variations in what consumers are buying at that store are reflected in what the store buys from the manufacturers of fashion merchandise. Multiply that store's experience by the hundreds or even thousands of stores that buy from one manufacturer, and you see that the producer has a pretty broad spectrum of consumer response represented in the rate at which his various styles are sold. If he has country-wide distribution, he may see that certain areas are buying certain colors, styles, or fabrics faster or more slowly than others. If he has no reason to believe that this is due to special effort (or lack of effort) on the part of his retail outlets in those areas, he can assume that a regional difference is influencing his sales. Typical of such differences are the West Coast's quickness to accept what is new, and especially what is casual and relaxed, or the Middle West's fondness for shades of blue, to go with the blue eyes that predominate among the German and Scandinavian groups who have settled there.

From the manufacturer of the finished garment, information about customer preferences, as expressed in customer purchases, flows in several directions. One flow is back to the retail stores, via the manufacturer's salesmen, to alert them to trends they may not have noticed for themselves. Another flow is to the fabric producers, in the form of the garment-maker's reorders for the most accepted materials and shades.

Information about the customer and the balloting that he or she does from day to day at the retail cash register is also collected by other people in the fashion field. Editors of consumer magazines, for instance, check regularly on trends with manufacturers of raw materials and finished products. They do this to see whether their own previous editorial judgments of fashion trends have been right, and to establish a basis on which to select styles to be featured in future issues. What the customer does or does not buy is watched as closely in the fashion industry as stockbrokers watch the ticker tape.

Often the customer is a guinea pig on whom the experts test their judgment. Sometimes he or she is a member of a committee formed by retailers or editors to represent a particular section of the public, and to be available for consultation on reaction to new ideas, or just to sound off on subjects that interest her. Typical are the teen-age committees and teen-age clubs that many retail stores sponsor for boys and girls. Consumer surveys are also used by stores, producers, and publications.

More often, the customer serves unknowingly as a test subject. When a new style, color, fabric, or silhouette is introduced, makers and retailers usually proceed on a "sample, test, reorder" system. This means that only small quantities are made up and placed on sale in retail stores. At the first inkling of customer reaction, the retailer reorders the acceptable styles and discontinues whatever other styles may have evoked little customer enthusiasm. The garment manufacturer, meanwhile, is watching the retail reorders to see which styles he should cut in quantity and which ones he should drop.

No one, least of all the customer, may fully understand why one style is chosen in preference to another, but everyone in the fashion industry is observing the selection and thus deciding the fate of the individual styles among the infinite number created each season.

Forecasting Fashions

People in the fashion business seem to develop almost a sixth sense for weighing various factors and judging the probable ups and downs of trends. They learn to study signs that may escape the untrained observer and to predict which styles are most likely to succeed, just as a weatherman becomes adept at forecasting the weather.

Forecasting errors can be costly, however, and guiding rules and principles are used to keep these errors to a minimum, in fashion as in weather. The meteorologist arms himself with data about wind velocity and air pressure and the known results of certain combinations when they occur; the fashion professional arms himself with information about customers, trends, and modifying factors.

Whether one is designing, producing, or selling, the first step is to have a clear picture of the customer group that constitutes one's target. A noted economist has said that "the central function of the entrepreneur in a fashion industry is far less the efficient organization of the production of a given commodity and much more the shrewd anticipation of the changing preferences of his numerically restricted clientele—his own small niche in 'the great neighborhood of women.' "[32] Just as there can be no universal weather forecast, but only one that is pinned down as to time and area, so it is with fashion prediction. There is no universal group of customers: there is city, suburban, or rural; there is young or not-so-young; there is the blue-collar or white-collar background; there is the middle-income or well-to-do; there is the conservative or the *avant garde*; and so on. What one forecasts for, say, the young juniors in a wealthy suburb of the West may be all wrong for the same age group in a poor neighborhood of an Eastern city.

With a specific customer group in mind, the next principle is to collect all the facts one can get. How numerous are these customers? What are they buying from day to

[32] Robinson, *op. cit*, pp. 395–396.

day this season? What are the activities and occasions for which they dress? What people, periodicals, or other influences will affect their choice? The more answers one has to such questions, the clearer the picture becomes, and the easier to forecast.

The fact-gathering procedure also includes weighing present observations in the light of possible future developments. In predicting weather, the meteorologist not only examines local indicators but also studies the satellite picture for conditions beyond the horizon that may ultimately affect his area. Similarly, in fashion, the observer studies the life-style and dress of those men and women most likely to influence what his own customers will ultimately adopt. In this way, it is possible to make tentative judgments of the growth potential of a current trend or to anticipate a downturn in a currently popular fashion.

Thus a forecaster—whose official title may be designer, fashion coordinator, magazine editor, or department store buyer, but whose work requires an awareness of fashion currents—may decide that ruffles have run their course for the time being, that sleek hairdos are coming in, or that brighter and gayer colors will be better received than they were last year, and so on.

This fact gathering process, to pursue the analogy to weather forecasting, is like preparing a meteorological map, with isobars, temperature readings, wind indicators, and everything else that is needed to evaluate the current situation. A fashion forecast, once made, whether in one's own mind or in print, is seldom final and immutable. The unexpected often happens when some new factor enters the picture. In fashion, as in weather, the study of conditions and influencing forces is essential at all times if one is to succeed or even to survive.

THE BUSINESS OF FASHION

The more one understands the dynamics of fashion, the more obvious it becomes that fashion is not imposed on the public by industry but instead is a phenomenon that must be analyzed and interpreted into the shapes and looks of clothes. Thousands of styles and designs are created and produced each year by designers and manufacturers of fabrics, apparel, and accessories. Styles that are widely purchased by retail distributors and then by a substantial group of ultimate consumers are considered to constitute a fashion. The fact that a new style may be highly publicized as a new fashion does not make it so; furthermore, a style is not a fashion because it is worn by one or a few individuals, no matter who they may be. Fashion is not a matter of opinion but of actual count.

The late Norman Norell, one of America's most successful designers, underscored the importance of this point some time ago when he said, "I'm more interested in launching a fashion than in creating beautiful things. Fashion is what is accepted and worn by the general public. When it reaches that point, you know the design is a good one."[33]

[33]*Business Week*, September 12, 1964, pp. 64ff.

Fashion Is Big Business

Fashion plays an important role in our economy. Americans spend over $62 billion a year for clothing, shoes, and accessories—an amount that constitutes more than $1 in every $12 that they spend.[34] Millions of people are employed in producing the apparel and accessories and in staffing the retail stores that sell this merchandise. Of the nearly 19 million people employed in manufacturing industries in the United States in 1972, practically 1 out of 8 persons was employed either in the industries that produce apparel for men, women, and children or the textile industries that produce the materials from which clothing is made. Apparel manufacturing alone employs more people than the entire printing and publishing field and more people than the chemical and drug industries.[35]

Complexity of the Fashion Industry

Unlike industries such as tobacco or automobile manufacturing, the fashion industry is not a clearly defined entity. It is a complex of many different industries, not all of which appear to have anything of fashion among their products.

Plainly recognizable as part of the fashion business are industries devoted to the making of dresses, coats, skirts, and similar articles of women's apparel; those devoted to the production of men's wear; and those that make accessories such as scarfs, millinery, costume jewelry, handbags, wallets, gloves, shoes, and hosiery. Some of these industries serve one sex or the other; some serve both sexes and children as well.

When one moves back to an earlier stage of production, to the fabrics, leathers, and plastics from which the finished products are made, the line between what is and what is not the fashion business becomes harder to draw. Some textile mills that produce dress and coat fabrics also produce bed sheets, carpets, or industrial fabrics. Some chemical companies that produce fibers that are eventually spun and woven to make garments are also producers of explosives, fertilizers, and photographic film. Some producers and processors in fields normally remote from fashion find themselves temporarily with one foot in the fashion business when prevailing styles demand such items as industrial zippers, decorative chain belts, paper dresses, and lucite heels, for example. A season or two later, these people may be as far removed from the fashion business as ever but, for the time being, they too are part of it.

The fashion business also includes stores that sell apparel and accessories, and mail-order catalogues from which many consumer purchases are made. It includes businesses that neither produce nor sell merchandise but render advice, assistance, or information to those that do.

In this last category are consumer publications that disseminate news of fashion, ranging from the women's page of the daily newspaper to magazines devoted

[34]*Survey of Current Business,* April 1973, p. 14.

[35]*Ibid.,* p. S–13.

FASHION INDUSTRY FLOW CHART: APPAREL AND TEXTILES

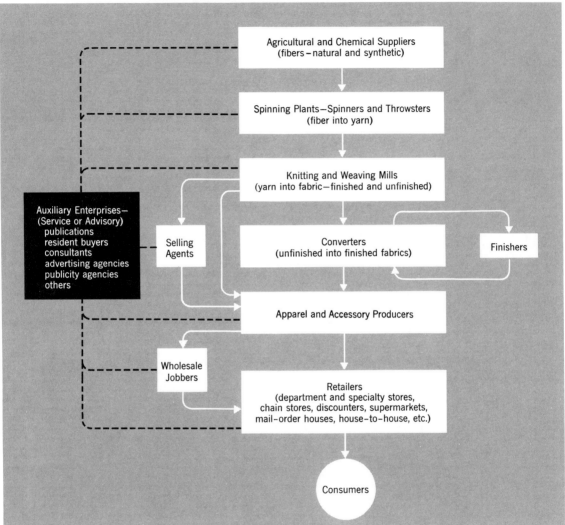

primarily to that one subject, such as *Vogue, Harper's Bazaar,* or *Gentlemen's Quarterly*. Also included in this category are trade periodicals that carry news of fashion and information on production and distribution techniques to retailers, apparel manufacturers, and textile mills. It includes also publicists and advertising specialists, fashion consultants, and buying offices that represent retail stores in the vast wholesale centers.

All these and more are part of the business—farms and mills and factories, union labor and white-collar workers, tycoons, and creative artists. All play their parts in the business of fashion.

READINGS

The readings in this section present the fashion philosophies of professionals of established reputation in a variety of fields—retailing, fashion history, journalism, economics, fashion coordination, consulting, and research. Notice that these experts base their opinions solidly on their analyses of what the public accepts instead of on their own individual ideas or intuition. Notice, too, how carefully they observe socioeconomic conditions and human behavior in all its many facets, in order to determine what is acceptable—and why—at given times and places, and in given segments of society.

NATURE OF FASHION

Alfred H. Daniels

This is a field where the only good place to begin is with a definition of the subject. Much of the mystery of fashion merchandising is simply a matter of not knowing what fashion is.

There are a host of definitions, many by erudite men and women. For instance, Ambrose Bierce has said that "fashion is a despot whom the wise ridicule—and obey." And according to Thoreau, "Every generation laughs at the old fashions but follows religiously the new." In Oscar Wilde's opinion, "Fashion is a form of ugliness so intolerable that we have to alter it every six months." Shakespeare philosophized that "the fashion wears out more apparel than the man."

In each of these observations—and there are countless others equally appropriate—there is something germane. But the definition which best seems to sum up the essential characteristics of fashion is a much more mundane one: "Fashion is a conception of what is currently appropriate." The report from which this quotation is taken goes on to say:

"Fashion influences human activities and shapes the forms of our possessions. It affects the things we do, the things we say, the things we wear, and the things we use. Times and conditions largely affect fashion and may be looked upon as a subtle reflection of our composite feelings and reactions to life at any given period. Fashion is not necessarily high fashion, the latter being the expression of a limited number of people with above-normal means or taste to enjoy it. Mass fashions are the most widely accepted versions of high fashion trends."[1]

Definition

Our definition of fashion as a conception of "what is currently appropriate" means, in simpler language, a conception of what the customer wants. This idea will be popping up again and again in the subsequent discussion. Once the concept is well understood, it will be seen that the fashion merchant need only look at the facts and rarely at the reasons behind the facts. If he can jump this hurdle, he is over the hurdle of inferiority complex in his business. Since this point is such a vital one, let me break it down into its four essential components.

1. There are psychological and biological drives involved in fashion, and these drives remain pretty constant. Hence, what is wanted is constant: glamour and a sense of belonging or security; the desire to keep up with the Joneses, on the one hand, and the attempt to become Mrs. Jones on the other.

2. *General* fashions change slowly. For instance, emancipation of women had to be reflected in women's clothes, but that was a long, historical process. Suburban and casual living has increased the importance of sportswear, but that too did not happen overnight. The increasing number of working women has brought about many new fashions, including the basic dress that can change its look at 7:00 P.M. by the addition of an accessory, but this has not been a quick development either. The fact is that *general*

SOURCE: Excerpted and reprinted with permission from "Fashion Merchandising," *Harvard Business Review*, May, 1951. Mr. Daniels was Vice-President of Abraham and Straus, Brooklyn, N. Y. when he wrote this article. Later, he was Group President of I. Magnin, California.

[1]Associated Merchandising Corporation Committee Report on "The Significance of Fashion Leadership to Our Stores."

fashions change slowly. The specific causes of a general fashion change are not necessarily of concern to the fashion merchant. For example, there is an Oriental influence taking place in women's apparel. The fashion merchant will know this—he cannot escape it—but he does not need to know how it came about. If he is curious, he can call up some fashion expert, who may tell him that it is the result of pressure by Mongolian idiots or of the decision of women in Bali finally to dress themselves. He would find this very fascinating and proceed about his business, reassured that the development was going to stay on for a while.

3. Fashion no longer refers to price. Students of marketing used to talk about the fashion cycle as having three phases—a conveniently divided Tinkers-to-Evers-to-Chance sort of affair—with different price characteristics for each phase. By contrast, the fact today is that the fashion cycle moves so quickly that it is a blur. Almost everyone instantaneously wants the same thing. The differential price characteristic has virtually disappeared. Radio, TV, the theater, and the press can be thanked for this.

4. If fashion in the broad sense changes slowly, specific manifestations of fashion can and do change quickly—very quickly. This point is a crucial one. To make the distinction, some people have called general fashion merely "fashion," and specific fashion "style," or vice versa.

Let me illustrate the distinction by an example previously referred to: the growing importance of sportswear. This is a general fashion trend, and its course will not be altered except in the space of a long period. At the moment, however, within sportswear there can be a demand for white sweaters. Tomorrow this demand may change to purple skirts; the next day, to something else. These are the changes involved in Professor Melvin T. Copeland's fashion cycle theory, where emulation becomes the pivotal drive. The nub of the whole thing is right here. William Hazlett's definition, "Fashion is gentility running away from vulgarity and afraid of being overtaken," is just another way of stating Copeland's thesis that there are "distinctive," "emulation," and "mass emulation" stages (however momentary) of every specific fashion.

Going back to our illustration, certain social leaders, a distinguished campus, or the "international set" will decide to wear white sweaters. Why is unimportant. Then other persons in the next social stratum down begin to emulate—and there we go. It should be clear, though, that the distinguished group, no matter how distinguished, cannot bring about a fundamental change in fashion. The roots have to be deeper than that. Given a general fashion trend, what the distinguished group does is to try to be different within it. That is all. As has been indicated, because of improved methods of communication and because of economic competition on the part of manufacturers, this difference remains momentary. So the process to gain prestige starts again. It is like perpetual motion.

Let me summarize the foregoing points about fashion, now, very briefly:

1. Women buy fashion to look pretty and glamorous and to be "in the swing" or to belong.
2. Long-range fashions change slowly.
3. Fashion does not refer to price.
4. Specific fashions or styles change quickly because certain people want to look unique within the general fashion trend.

FASHION CYCLES

Kenneth Collins

A young woman writes: "From your experience, is there any way to foresee the beginning of a new fashion? How does one estimate or guess its duration? What are the signs that it is about to die?"

I shall, of course, not attempt to answer these questions. They go far beyond my knowledge. But they do give me an excuse to present an analogy between ocean waves and style trends that has been in my mind so many years. I should like to air it even if only to have it laughed at. Please bear with me.

If you have ever sat idly watching the surf, you must have noted that each wave rolls in with a curve, a crest, and a crash. To me, this general pattern seems identical to that of fashions which certainly curve, crest, and crash.

But the similarity appears to go much further. Some waves race headlong for a shallow beach, swell rapidly to a tremendous foaming top, then drop abruptly with a thud. Is this not precisely what happens with fads? But other waves move gradually upwards, curl over in a quiet, leisurely way, then break with little or no force. Is this not precisely the movement of sane, properly conceived style cycles? They are slow to develop, hold their own for a time, then subside rather than collapse.

You may now say: Your analogy is amusing and is no doubt a useful way to describe the emergence and disappearance of fashions. But that is all it is—a bit of description.

Probably so. But people who have done much swimming or boat handling in the surf might see more to the comparison than something merely pictorial. They know it is great fun to time a wave and to ride over it. They also know it is a very different matter to miss one's timing and to get caught just as the crest topples. That can be annoying. And in some circumstances it can be exceedingly dangerous—just as dangerous, for example, as taking disastrous markdowns after badly miscalculating the appeal of a freak style.

Oh well, I must not go on with the analogy. It may simply be a pleasant conceit on my part. But if it does not make at least a little sense, I wish someone would tell me why.

SOURCE: Reprinted by permission of *Women's Wear Daily*, June 19, 1957. Copyright 1957, Fairchild Publications, Inc. Upon retirement from a long and distinguished retailing career, Mr. Collins became a feature columnist for *Women's Wear Daily*.

FASHION: A Detective Story

James Laver

As soon as fashion crops up, some hard-headed fellow who takes pride in having no illusions is sure to say: "It's all a romp. Half a dozen men in Paris get together and decide to change the fashion. They want to sell their goods. It's as simple as that."

It is not as simple as that, for if it were, fashion would be arbitrary and meaningless. But that is just what fashion never is, and one can see this quite plainly when looking at the fashions of the past. Every style seems completely appropriate to its epoch. We can not imaging Madame de Pompadour, or the Empress Josephine, or the early Victorian lady in anything but the clothes she actually wore. Each represents completely the ideals of her time: elegant artificiality, or post-Revolutionary morals, or the prudery of the rising middle class. When seen in retrospect fashions seem to express their era. Although it is more difficult to draw conclusions from contemporary clothes, the same principles which hold for the clothes of the past must hold for clothes of the present and the future.

I am a social historian, if I may call myself that, a museum official, and my interest in fashion began in a round-about way. At the Victoria and Albert Museum, we have, I suppose, the largest collection of miniatures in the world, and people are constantly bringing in their family heirlooms for an opinion. "This is my great-, great-aunt Augusta who danced at the Waterloo Ball," one might say. I would reply, with growing confidence as the years went by, "I'm afraid there must be something wrong with the family records. This portrait

SOURCE: Reprinted with permission from *Vogue*, January 1959. Copyright © 1958 by the Conde Nast Publications, Inc. James Laver, noted fashion historian was Keeper of Prints and Drawings of the Victoria and Albert Museum, London, England for almost forty years.

represents a woman of about twenty wearing the clothes of 1840. She couldn't have danced at the Waterloo Ball in 1815."

For this purely utilitarian purpose I began to assemble a file of fashion. I found that I could date any picture to within a year in the nineteenth century, to within two years in the eighteenth century, to within ten years in the seventeenth. I could, that is, if there was a fashionable woman in the picture.

Men won't do, for men's clothes perpetually formalize themselves and do not follow the principle of fashion. Peasants won't do, because peasant, or regional costume as it is properly called, changes by place and not by time. Until the fourteenth century, that was how all fashion changed. During the greater part of human history, if you stayed where you were nothing altered. If you went into the next village, however, everything was different. Today, if you travel the world, everything is the same. If you stay in one spot for a year, however, practically all the women change their hats. We have exchanged the tyranny of place for the tyranny of time. We have the Time Disease.

When I had assembled my file of fashion, I began to make such curious discoveries as the strange relationship which seems to exist between clothes, especially women's clothes, and architecture. It is generally agreed, for example, that the dominant architectural shape of the Middle Ages was the sharply pointed lancet arch. Sharpened still further, it is the pinnacle or the steeple on a church. Similarly, in the fifteenth century, men's shoes were so long they sometimes had to be turned back and tied to the knees. The female headdress, the hennin, was correspondingly steeple-shaped. By 1500 the lancet arch was blunted, and became what we call the Tudor Arch. When Henry VIII came to the throne in 1509, his shoes were not sharp and pointed like those of his father

Henry VII, but blunted. The headdress of his wife, Catherine of Aragon, was blunted too—just like the Tudor Arch.

In the eighteenth century, the dominant architectural motif of the period the French call Louis Seize and the English, Adam Brothers, was the neoclassical pilaster. One can see the same motif as it was interpreted in fashion, in the costumes of the Empress Josephine. Simple, straight, her dress is typical of what I call the post-crisis style. After a great social upheaval like the French Revolution women have a burst of emancipation, sometimes only momentary. When about ten years have elapsed and fashion settles down into a post-crisis style, women's clothes become "little girl" clothes. They are subsconsciously designed to "do down" the older woman.

If we take the dress of 1925, another post-crisis period, we find that, different as the dresses of 1800 and 1925 are, they have certain things in common. The lines are as straight as nature will allow, or even straighter; the waist is in the wrong place: very high in 1800, very low in 1925. In both years, the hair was worn short. It seemed to me that in the next post-crisis epoch we would see something similar and therefore, after World War II, I predicted that in approximately ten years we would have a dress with straight lines and a wandering waist. Just about that time Dior introduced his H-line and his A-line. I think it fair to say that this style, with the chemises that followed, had a definite resemblance to the clothes of 1800 and 1925.

In violent contrast to these post-crisis styles was the full-skirted dress of the relatively placid mid-nineteenth century. The skirt was swelled by what might be called a machine age triumph, a steel hoop that substituted for a prodigious number of petticoats. Its size said: "This is an age of male domination, expanding population, social stability, and 'hard' money," just as the skimpy clothes of 1800 and 1925 said, "This is an age of female emancipation, declining birthrate, social instability, and inflation." (Incidentally, the frame of the hoop bore a curious resemblance to the butt-end of the Crystal Palace, which was erected in 1851). The hoop was hollow and if you are looking for a symbol of mid-Victorian hypocrisy you could hardly find a better. The hoop seemed

to say, "You cannot come near enough to touch my hand," and yet it swayed in every wind. It was also uncontrollable, and a deplorable number of young women were burned to death when their clothes caught in open fires.

Nothing is more revealing of an age than its hypocrisies and perhaps analysing them can help us to understand how fashion works. There seem to me to be three principles: The hierarchical principle, or dressing for class. The seduction principle, or dressing to attract the opposite sex. The utility principle, or dressing for warmth, et cetera.

Women's clothes follow, on the whole, the seduction principle (slightly modified by the utility principle) because men largely select their wives by their attractiveness as women. The object of women's clothes is, therefore, to make their wearers attractive to men. Many women say, "I dress to please myself," or even, "I dress to displease other women." Perhaps this is the formula: Women dress, in competition with other women, to please themselves by attracting men.

Women, on the other hand, select their husbands with the hope that they will be able to support a family. Men's clothes, therefore, are essentially hierarchical, or class-conscious. Compared to the constant mutations of women's dress, men's fashions are like fossils.

The psychologists have invented something they call "the shifting erogenous zone." In other words, woman as a whole is a desirable object, but the mind of man is too weak to take it all in at once. He must be persuaded to concentrate on one bit of this object, and it is the function of fashion to emphasize and exaggerate that little bit until the whole thing becomes a bore causing the erogenous zone to shift. In 1925 I wrote in my diary that I found the newly exposed legs of women rather exciting. By 1930 legs were a bore, and attention had to be directed elsewhere. In 1915, however, a woman in 1925 clothes would have been arrested for indecent exposure. This is the game which seduction plays with prudery. Prudery in fact might be called a necessary psychological device for keeping up the temperature of eroticism in cold climates.

We can therefore draw up a chart and say:

The same dress is indecent ten years before its

time; daring one year before its time; chic (contemporarily seductive) in its time; dowdy five years after its time; hideous twenty years after its time; amusing thirty years after its time; romantic one hundred years after its time; beautiful one hundred and fifty years after its time. It would have been quite impossible to revive the fashions of the mid-twenties until thirty years had elapsed. Thirty years elapsed and behold! Those fashions or modes very like them, came back again.

If we could understand the full significance of a woman's hat we could prophesy her clothes for the next year, the interior decoration of the next ten years, the architecture of the next ten years, and we would have a fairly accurate notion of the pressures, political, economic, religious, that go to make the shape of an age. Properly evaluated, fashion is never a frivolity.

THE MEANING OF FASHION

Dwight E. Robinson

The behavioral complex underlying all stylistic innovation—by this I mean all changes in design which are not purely the results of engineering advances—can conveniently be summed up under the single word *fashion*. And fashion, defined in its most general sense, is the pursuit of novelty for its own sake. Every market into which the consumer's fashion sense has insinuated itself is, by that very token, subject to this common, compelling need for unceasing change in the styling of its goods.

The reason for this is that the stimuli of fashion derive solely from the *comparisons* that consumers draw between new designs and the old designs they replace. No single style of design, no matter how brilliantly it is conceived, can claim any independent fashion significance at all, nor can it possess more than a fugitive lease on life.

RULE OF EXCESS

Paul Poiret, the top Paris couturier of the 1920's, once summed up his credo by declaring "All

SOURCE: Excerpted by permission from "Fashion Theory and Product Design," *Harvard Business Review*, November-December, 1958, Vol. 36, No. 6. Professor Robinson is widely recognized as one of the few business historians who has done research in the field of fashion.

fashions end in excess"—a principle which is the beginning of wisdom for all who are concerned with style policy. He was aware that the overriding responsibility of the designer in a fashion market is the unending provision of novelty. Implicitly he recognized that one of the most exacting problems the stylist ever faces is that of deciding what to do when he has exhausted the possibilities of a current direction in styling emphasis. What does he do, for example, when the waistline, hemline, or any other line has been carried as far as it will go? It is here that the couturier must exercise to the utmost every ounce of his insight into the meaning of fashion.

As a couturier Poiret knew that the appetite for novelty, arising from the twofold insistence of the lady of fashion on preserving her inimitability from the onslaught of the vulgar and on demonstrating her affluence through unrelenting expenditure on newly cut costumes, is never satisfied with any one mode of presenting the figure. Fashions in dress design subsist on measures to transform or to distort, whether through exaggeration or minimization, the shape and features of the human figure. To illustrate:

The hoop skirts of the eighteenth century and the crinoline of the nineteenth ballooned to diameters of eight feet. As the hip line was exaggerated beyond the point of simply imperiling navigation to the point of making it literally impossible, the waistline was tightened to the point of suffocation and interference with digestion.

In the interim, in the Directoire and Empire periods around 1800, a contrary tendency toward undress was exploited. *La Parisienne's* test of the suitability of a pseudoclassical gown of transparent silk was to see whether she could easily draw it through a ring taken from her little finger. The last resort of modesty was fleshcolored tights.

The flapper of the Jazz Age, though she was in her turn the despair of her late-Victorian parents, never dashed about in quite the dishabille of Mme. Récamier, but what she missed in transparency she made up for with leg display.

Whether, at a given time, the particular form of emphasis is toward padding out or constricting, toward concealment or exposure, once such a movement is launched it must be intensified each season, ensuring that the ultrafashionable will be able to disport themselves in more of a good thing than their less-favored contemporaries. Indeed, this recurrent pattern can be traced back to even earlier centuries. The style of European costume associated with the French Regency (1715–1730) emphasized delicacy and restraint. Its graceful, free-flowing costume is best remembered in the airy, idyllic scenes depicted in the paintings of Watteau. Yet it fell between the ornate periods of the stately Baroque and the frivolously extravagant Rococo.

COROLLARY OF REVERSAL

The most important corollary of Poiret's axiom is this: a fashion can never retreat gradually and in good order. Like a dictator it must always expand its aggressions—or collapse. Old fashions never just fade away; they die suddenly and arbitrarily.

The reason for this is simple and logically inescapable. The one thing fashion cannot stand is to repeat the recently outmoded style, the *passé*. Better for the lady of fashion to look like a freak than to be mistaken for her grocer's wife dolled up in a cheap version of something she herself sported a year or two ago. For instance:

The hoop skirts of the French court and the crinoline of a century later did not gradually contract: they both exploded in a fragmentation of trains, loops, and bustles.

Within a decade after court ladies found it necessary to crouch on the floor of their coaches so as to accommodate their soaring headdresses, Lady Hamilton (Nelson's Emma) was enthralling the court of Naples and eminent visitors such as Goethe with her "classical attitudes," for which her main props were no more than her own silky curls, a few yards of gauze and a pet dove or two. And it was not long before thousands of less notorious ladies were taking her cue.

Again, a couple of generations later, after such devices as the bustle and the leg-of-mutton sleeve exhausted the expansionist tendencies of late-Victorian days, the shirt-waist and hobble skirt were suddenly introduced, clearing the way for the boyish skimpiness of the 1920's. . . .

CLASSIC COMPROMISE

What lies behind these swift and extreme changes? If functional criteria could be more precisely defined, the game of fashion change might be interpreted as a series of departures from, and returns to, the norm of function. Unfortunately, this is not the case. Function is permissive. Even nature's experiments in animals—on land, in the sea, and in the air—reveal that the laws of locomotion or mechanics permit a kaleidoscopic variety of anatomical forms.

The designer has learned that the usefulness of a garment—together with all the functional criteria surrounding utility—is a consideration of only incidental relevance to his purposes. Naturally, he is more than willing to play up the merits of a new design by claiming that it permits greater freedom of movement, better accentuates the feminine figure, or is more suitable to modern living. But he does this with tongue in cheek. He is only too aware that, judging by results, the aims of feminine coquetry have been as well served by the dress designs of one era as by those of another.

The safest thing that can be said of costume variation is that it veers between extremes of overdressing and underdressing, although there are many other variables. Perusal of the fashion journals suggests that when one of these extremes has been reached, the recourse that has typically proved most successful is swift return to a form of compromise, or golden mean, which lies about halfway between overdress and underdress. Such norms are somewhat loosely referred to as "classical" styles in the dress trade. In turn, they serve as points of departure toward an alternative extreme.

The couturier is then likely to visit the art galleries or museums to seek inspiration from the designs of past eras. (The Metropolitan Museum of Art in New York, for instance, maintains a Costume Institute, where thousands of dresses going back several centuries are carefully preserved, catalogued, and made available for inspection by qualified visitors from the garment district.) He will also, of course, give careful heed to technological advances in the form of new materials or new mechanical dressmaking aids, as well as to arising needs of contemporary living, in shaping his patterns to present-day conditions.

As Christian Dior puts it, "There is room for audacity in the framework of tradition." It is an arresting thought that relics of the past, together with fruits of industrial progress, so frequently form the chief supports of the game of novelty which is fashion. . . .

CONCLUSION

My aim has been to provide a springboard to a better understanding of a fascinating but perplexing area of decision making. I have sought to point out that fashion—the impulse underlying the dynamics of style—is both a less mystifying and a more profound force in social behavior than is commonly supposed. Most authorities on fashion consider it an evolutionary process. In this I join them. Yet evolution relies on sudden mutations as much as, if not more than, small changes. For this reason, I have emphasized the sharply pronounced reactions which always seem to follow the extremes of styling.

Of course, I do not intend to put forward a formula or nostrum for the automatic prediction of style trends. History does not repeat itself any more neatly and prettily in styles than it does in any other sphere—business fluctuations, for example. My objective has been only to present a systematic exposition of a few of the insights that have long been the guideposts of fashion's most adept practitioners.

Nobody's crystal ball can show up the fashion future in complete detail. If it could, a lot of brain power would be unemployed; a lot of fun would go out of life. But this much is certain: the fact that an industry invests billions of dollars in equipment is no guarantee of a continued market for its products. Fashion is absolutely and callously indifferent to any monumental achievements in manufacturing proficiency. If anything, she takes capricious delight in nullifying man's industry—or pretenses to rationality. All of the fame and bulk of a leading textile, appliance, construction, or automobile company will not save it from fashion's dustbin if she so wills. She, and not the so-called fashion dictator—as Paul Poiret always professed—is the true autocrat; and only in a totalitarian state, where the consumer's taste is legislated by government edict, does she meet her match.

WHAT WERE THEY WEARING? 1910–1970

1910–1920

The Gibson girl was departing, even as *Women's Wear Daily* was making its entry on the 1910 scene. The dress silhouette was changing: Skirts were straighter, narrower at the hem, sometimes draped and crossed at front (see sketch). Clothes generally had a more sophisticated look. *Ensembles* were tremendously significant. There were many elaborate dresses with matching coats, for all seasons. The simple tailored suit, often bound with silk braid and worn with ruffled white blouse, became generally popular about 1913, and on. This same year was known for the exaggerated dressmaker suit which simulated a dress. . . . About this time the first *fur-lined* coats were introduced, usually lined with squirrel and with large fur collar. By 1915 coat silhouettes had changed and fur bands now accented voluminous, swirling hemlines. Within four years, design interest had again shifted: Bulk was at the top, capes in all lengths were important, as was the dolman coat. By 1919 Paris was striving for shorter skirts, but most Americans still clung to lower hems. The *large fur muff* worn with single fox scarf or long stole came into its own about 1912. White fox was among the long-haired furs immensely popular then. This decade in furs also produced the long, fitted black ponyskin coat, frequently with black lynx collar. Older women favored black caracul coats. . . . It was in 1912 that *the toque* was launched by milliners, a then radical departure from the large merry widow or lacy lingerie hats of earlier years. By 1919, wide

1910–1920

SOURCE: The sections from 1910 to 1960 are reprinted by permission of *Women's Wear Daily*, July 13, 1960. Copyright 1960, Fairchild Publications, Inc. The 1960–1970 section was added by the authors.

The capsule review of fashion change has been digested from material in the Fairchild Costume Library. Nucleus of the library is a collection of books on the history of costume. Supplementing this are more than 2000 scrapbooks of current material, which keep references up to date.

brimmed trimmed models with smallish flat crowns were an important adjunct to the many soft dressy afternoon costumes. . . . Women had been going down to the sea in heavy wool serge sailor-dress bathing styles, and when at the turn of the century Annette Kellerman popularized the one-piece knit suit it was as much of a shocker as today's bikini, although it provided neck-to-toe coverage. . . . The average city women spent $64 for her wardrobe in 1917.

1920–1930

The 20's brought in a new era in dress designing. The Poiret-inspired, unlined, uncorseted dress of soft Oriental contour was generally adopted early in the decade. Lanvin's ageless robe de style was introduced in the early 20's, was still going strong at the start of World War II. Chanel first launched her two-piece jerseys and untrimmed chiffon evening gowns in this period. By 1926, skirts were knee high for the first time in the twentieth century. For evening, the beaded sheath credited to Callot had won wide popularity. When World War I badly damaged France's cotton and woolen mills, a radical change in style resulted as the couture turned to the ensemble, popularized the little straight wool coat which could be worn over several silk dresses. It was the great era of silk crepe de chine, flat crepe and satin dresses for all ages. Suits, as such, all but disappeared, instead taking on the characteristics of the dominant ensemble: Soft skirt plus dressy overblouse, jacket lined to match (see sketch). . . . The luxurious 20's brought in the sumptuous long *wraparound fur coat*, and by 1926 the short ermine evening wrap, bulky at top. This was also the start of the mink coat as known today. 1926 furs for people of modest income included natural muskrat, often in three-quarter length, the pelts seamed without being worked into strips. The affinity of the 1920's coed for the casual raccoon coat hardly bears repetition here. . . . Hats were untrimmed and *the cloche* became a uniform, varying only in material used and manipulation. Growing interest in spectator sports led to development of simple felt or straw hats, shielding the eyes and turned up in back. Berets appeared in great variety. . . . The 20's witnessed the *birth of sportswear.* Stars like Suzanne Lenglen and Helen Wills popularized knee-length tennis dresses. Riding skirts were abandoned for breeches, worn with long jacket and high boots. Long trousers and knickers, combined with heavy sweater and high socks on the ski slopes. Covered legs persisted even with the slim above-knee bathing dress of 1924. . . . Average wardrobe expenditure in 1929 was $76.

1930–1940

Longer skirts and bias cuts came in with the 30's as Patou succeeded in bringing the hem down again.

1920–1930

Vionnet was still doing the dress depending entirely on bias cut for its appeal, devoid of trim and needing no fastenings, which was a hallmark of the 1930's (see sketch of 1932 model). Coats capitalized on the overwhelming fashion for *silver fox* bringing in full length fitted wool coats with large face-framing fox collars extending to the waistline. In mid-decade, Schiaparelli did a collarless dressmaker coat accenting large sleeves, very different from the later simpler coat cuts associated with the collarless neckline. The 30's also revived simple suits with longer skirts, the short jacket often in contrasting color. In 1937, Schiaparelli was the first to use *padding* in suit shoulders, borrowing her idea from the London Guardsman's uniform. . . . Subtle tailoring in furs came in by

1930-1940

1940-1950

1934 with the fitted broadtail full-length coat. This was also the year of the *collarless fox jacket,* beloved of women for both day and evening wear. The 30's were famous, too, for the many black and gray persian lamb coats, which continued significantly into the 40's. . . . The manipulated hat body offered many unusual hat shapes at the start of the decade. In 1931 *the bonnet* associated with Sally Victor appeared. By 1934, off-face types were popular. Suzanne Talbot created for the Duchess of Windsor the Pompadour hat whose wide appeal continued right through World War II. 1936 brought the pointed clown hat of Schiaparelli, and 1938 her "doll" hat. . . . The divided skirt, or *culotte,* returned to favor in 1936. The riding habit of this decade was jodhpurs and tweed jacket. On the ski slopes, the snow suit with full trousers and matching jacket dominated. On the beach, the dressmaker suit shared honors with the sleek *one-piece maillot* made popular with the invention of elasticized yarns. . . . The city woman in 1939 spent an average of $55 for her wardrobe.

1940–1950

World War II brought restrictions to the fashion industries, chiefly L-85 which fixed the outside measurements of garments. The influence of the shirtwaist dress was very strong in the war period. Along about 1942 came a tendency toward severity in dress which produced many masculine coat styles, including the officer's coat and the *Chesterfield* (see sketch). Adrian's square-shouldered, long-jacketed suit clicked with the general public, and women for a long time after resisted the many serious attempts to woo them from heavily padded shoulders. Suits were often topped with simple tailored coats, including the fur-lined model of 1943, popular for the first time in over 25 years. *The short coat* of 1945, sometimes belted, had a long life, toward the end of this decade becoming the shortie or topper, so adaptable with sportswear. Style curbs finally disappeared, opening the gate to the *new look* which made up in one deluge for all wartime fabric pinching, with its nipped waist, padded hips, long full skirts, and over all the voluminous tent coat. In 1945 Balenciaga had shown a suit with padded hips and tiny waist but with a short skirt. However, it was Dior's long-skirted 1947 version which caught on in America. . . . Even before the war's end the first French influence to filter across the seas was the large, elaborate *"more hat"* which few people wore but which tended to restore more trimming on millinery. . . . The 40's also witnessed the introduction of informal western riding rigs made up of levi, cotton shirt, and casual jacket. Skiers adopted the more practical slope fashion of slim tapered trouser and separate jacket. Bare midriff swimsuits made an appearance followed by the two-piece bra and shorts. The strapless top of the late 40's extended corsetiere techniques of wiring and boning to swimwear. . . . In 1949, the average woman spent $136 on apparel.

1950–1960

1950–1960

Casual and relaxed were key words in the 1950s, when sportswear truly came into its own, in part reflecting the new emphasis on suburban living, in part, the maturing of this comparatively young industry. It was helped by Chanel's decision to reactivate her design career, and the warm reception of her styles by a new generation of Americans. Italian designers, taking a leaf from California's book, found their niche in this branch of style, contributing much to knitwear and to color palettes, and pioneering the *tight tapered pants* which many women gradually adopted for everything from beach to street wear (see sketch). In this decade, Bohemia's beatnik added a new word and new look to the fashion lexicon. Coats and suits decided to compete with sportswear on its suburban battlefield, where the uniform was largely the camel boycoat or classic tweeds. With a

TV set in every ranch house and apartment, *at-home clothes* flourished, as did teen fashions which were nurtured by a fashion-conscious crop of former war babies. Dress designers, bored with the pretty-doll aspect of many styles, launched a drive toward a looser silhouette which, had it followed the logical sequence of "filtering down" from couture to basement levels, might have made progress. But in this quick-copying period, there were immediately *sacks on the racks* in cheaply made versions which diverted what might have been a new style direction into an abortive fiasco. Immediate aftermath was a sharp swing to classics, although some influential designers were still much attuned to eased, unwaisted styles, a possible augury for the future. There was but one story in furs: *mink.* Many deplored this lopsided development and sparked a move to revive non-mink furs in youthful styles, going outside the industry for the design talent to blueprint the revival. This was the decade that spawned "togetherness," but milliners and hairdressers somehow missed the cue and embarked on separate paths signpointed to the spread of hatlessness as the widely copied Hepburn shingle, Italian boycut, and Bardot scrambled coiffure defied the milliners' best efforts. Another imponderable: The acceptance of dyed hair, women's pleasure with their new locks, and reluctance to cover their handiwork. . . . The average woman budgeted $169 for wardrobe needs in 1959.

1960–1970

The decade of the 1960s was one in which youth was sovereign, in which new fashions came from anywhere and everywhere—astronauts, the African jungle, Liverpool, grandma's attic, and American Indian culture. It was a decade in which elegance yielded to contemporaneity and in which fashion reporters showed that, for the "beautiful people," youth was a look rather than an age. It was a period in which black became beautiful, in which men rediscovered fashion, and in which the center of fashion gravity shifted from the garment itself to the accessorized body beautiful, from Paris *haute couture* to boutiques everywhere. It was a decade during which the Paris couture turned enthusiastically to ready-to-wear, in which many designers of women's wear moved into the men's wear field as well, and in which Seventh Avenue manufacturers moved up and down the price scale.

At the beginning of the 1960s, the then first lady, Jacqueline Kennedy, became the Pied Piper of fashion for the masses. Women adopted her bouffant hairdo, pill-box hats, and "little nothing" dresses. Later, when she wore her hair flowing, went hatless, adopted mammoth sunglasses, and eventually hiked her skirts above the knee, even truly cautious matrons followed her lead.

The young adopted the miniskirts of London's Mary Quant. Hemlines moved to midthigh and above; sleeves were dispensed with. André Courrège's fashion for boots, worn indoors and out on

1960–1970

all occasions, was firmly launched and accepted. As skirts grew shorter, boots grew longer, reaching even to the hips.

Look-alike fashions for men and women appeared. Op and Pop art had their day and were promptly reflected in fashion. Hair grew longer for both sexes—among men, this possibly was a Beatle influence at first. Wigs became big business, not only for women but, in time, also for men. Body worship replaced prudishness in women's fashions. Miniskirts yielded to micro-minis. The bikini, introduced in European resorts, finally won acceptance in the United States. Rudi Gernreich made the news with a topless bathing suit for women. Yet at the same time, women had begun to wear pants for evening and daytime,—in elegant restaurants, on the streets, and in business offices. By the end of the decade, fashion was very much a matter of doing one's own thing.

FASHION CLOSES THE GAPS

Daisy Goldsmith

GAP I . . . Place to Place

At one time you could tell where you were because of what the natives were wearing. But the natives are restless these days, they move around a lot and they have crossed many boundaries. Geography is out of style. It's been replaced with sociology, and the new Rosetta Stone is fashion. Fashion is sociology on the hoof. As the geologist reads rocks to understand ages past, the fashionist can read the people on the street as a clue to what's happening now. While the late late shows have dragged back some of the aura of the 20s, 30s, and 40s, it becomes increasingly apparent as we crowd the 70s that fashion as we used to know it is no longer a separate thing, but inextricably bound up in a churning society. By definition fashion is custom, usage, accommodation, acceptance—all designates of society itself.

London revisited. It's a sign of the times that people in London looked the same as people in New York . . . or San Francisco . . . or any city. That is to say, the cool cats there looked like the cool cats here, and the squares there looked like the squares here, with a vast indeterminate area between. London swings, but the rhythm is seismic; wherever it starts, the shock waves are universal.

There are two mainstreams of fashion today. One starts at the top, from the couture showings in Paris which are picked up by manufacturers in New York, Hamburg, and Tokyo for translation into the local idiom. This goes to the upper age and upper money groups. The other source is the geyser-like eruption of style trends from the lively and

ingenious young, mostly British and American. Because of very effective underground communication among the young, styles spread with astonishing rapidity. As a protest against the uptight adult world they started buying their wearables from the Salvation Army and army navy surplus stores. They cultivated a ragbag thrift shop look of such gaiety and nonchalance that it caught the imagination of many and quickly percolated upward. Even Yves St. Laurent purchased a peacoat from a famous army navy store in Times Square when he visited the U.S., which inspired his subsequent collection.

GAP II . . . Sex to Sex

Unisex . . . trans-sex . . . intersex . . . ambisex . . . nonsex . . . the lines are blurring in the concepts of what was once thought of as strictly masculine or feminine attire. All this he/she, boy/girl, mama/papa (in Honolulu the middle-aged tourists wear matching muumuu and shirt in shrieking prints) interchangeable wearing apparel has changed only one thing . . . wearing apparel. Don't for one minute think that sex has changed. Far from it. Sex appeal is the same good old-fashioned brand and the boys and the girls never make a mistake. They like each others' company and they like to do many things together. For these same activities they like the same clothing and they shop for it together, hand in hand. The new breed of retail shops doesn't separate the merchandise, whoever it fits buys it. What's dressing for the goose is dressing for the gander and these new feathered birds are a whole new flock.

Close-fitting clothing is bringing back a glorification of the body that Western culture took

SOURCE: Reprinted by permission from October, 1968 issue of *Color Engineering*. Daisy Goldsmith is a fashion coordinator specializing in color and fabrics in Montgomery Wards's New York fashion office.

centuries to kill off. This change is showing up all over. A case in point is the Nehru, taken off the back of the Indian ruler. This is the tunic jacket shaped from narrow shoulders with high set-in skinny sleeves to a gentle flare at the hip. Word has it that this was Nehru's prison garb when he was the unwilling guest of England and he continued to wear it as a constant reminder to himself and his people. Now you hear all sorts of "I told you it couldn't last" comments from the hidebound who say it is a fading fad. Well, the word "Nehru" may leave the fashion lexicon but the breakaway from the traditional shape for men's clothing remains. Popular waist suppression moves upward into chest suppression. Sack the sack is the attitude of the man who is trimming down to his former fighting weight and finds it socially acceptable to show it.

GAP III . . . People to People

In Mexican Hat, Utah, Navajos are stringing cedarberries to make beads for the fashion-bearing animal, both male and female. They brighten up the necklaces with glass beads from Czechoslovakia so they're hoping the political situation there cools before they're put out of business. The whole Indian kick in fashion is tremendous. Cochise country is where it's at and everybody into the wigwam for fringed leather, braids and headbands, wampum, soft moccasins and boots, and laced shirts (these showed up in collections, too). How much more 100% American can you get?

But it's not only the American Indian who has reached fashion stature. Ethnic groups of all kinds add their distinctive flavor and color. Think of the long acceptance of the Scandinavian sweater, Irish and Portuguese fisherman sweaters, the Basque beret, the Scottish kilt; add to them the current craze for flowing African kaftan and djellabah, Indian beads and medallions, Mexican and South American gaucho pants, Spanish matador hats and boleros, Afghanistan sheep jackets and vests, mittel European laced bodices and embroidery, gypsy blouses and petticoats, Russian cossack shirts and boots. All of these retain their native indigenous colors. Travelling in the other direction, our western gear is universal in its appeal.

Levis, cowboy neckerchiefs, snapped and yoked plaid shirts are popular everywhere.

Gilbert and Sullivan sang, "Never mind the why and wherefore/love will level ranks and therefore . . ." Today it's fashion that levels the ranks and obliterates the why and wherefore; not only in where it comes from and where it is worn, but in who buys it. According to the U.S. Bureau of Statistics, black urban consumers have about the same spending habits at the same income level as white consumers. Smart advertising now recognizes that all consumers buy for the same reasons and is moving in the direction of broader product appeal and purchase motivation.

GAP IV . . . Product to Product

To revive a rather passé word, the clue to current merchandising is kook. What's kooking today started with the milk-and-kookie set a handful of years back. The sharp edges have rubbed off, the kids are older and more sophisticated now with a lot more to spend for lots more big ticket products. Their determinined preferences have made dents in high-placed thinking, as high as Ford Motor Company management.

Early sales of foreign automobiles could be ignored and deprecated. Now that they account for 10% of the American market the industry has adopted the "join 'em" point of view. A Ford veep, in an interview with a men's retailing magazine, says there is a rub-off from fashion to the car business, that new colors in cars are a direct outgrowth of the colors of ladies' dresses. Lively greens, pumpkin, and red with orange trim, that's the way they see their new Mustang. True, these colors follow a geographical trend line. While fashion starts on the East Coast, leaps to the West Coast, lopes into the Midwest, then limps into the South, automobile trends start in the turned-on areas of San Francisco and Los Angeles, then go from the Southwest diagonally northeast, ending in New England, with Boston being the last to accept change.

And that's what makes the business go 'round — clockwise or counterclockwise; just keep closing those gaps to keep that healthy green color.

CLOTHES NOW

Estelle Hamburger

Clothes-Now are no longer "a look" but a language. They communicate self-identity and group-identity with instant impact, needing no translation. They speak to the eye, the body, the life, the values. They express the "me" and the "us" of People-Now. Me-not-you. Us-not-them.

Clothes-Now are not the same as clothes before now. Change is more than fashion change. Changes in clothes are part of the ferment in our culture and ourselves. Clothes-Now have become part of the second American Revolution, which is nothing less than revolution in the only true sense of the word: transformation in people. It is a voluntary, vigorous, articulate breaking away from the past, with many breaks by many people in many ways and new definitive purposes in embracing the present, commitment to the future, many purposes by many people in many ways.

Change and the speed of change, quality of change and quantity of change, numbers of people affected by all the changes in all the people in a nation grown to 205 million people (comprising 50 million family units), including both sexes, all ages and sizes, all colors, all backgrounds and degrees of have and have-not. All are questioning as never before who they are, what they are, their goals and satisfactions, the way they want to live, and the values that make life worth living. All of which are profoundly changing the clothes that serve life, express life, and enhance life. No longer a look, but a language—that is what Clothes-Now are all about.

Now, here is the anatomy of two periods: spring to spring 1970–1971 and then spring 1972. You can make your own comparison. I will draw a tentative conclusion.

SOURCE: Estelle Hamburger, fashion consultant, delivered this address to a Workshop in Fashion Merchandising, on January 26, 1972, at the Fashion Institute of Technology, New York, N. Y.

FIRST, SPRING 1970 TO SPRING 1971

The wild year, when change took on the momentum of change faster than changes in people, faster than need, faster than desire, the year when an industry called clothes "A Look" and they lost their meaning as language.

From Longuette to Hotpants

(DATELINE FEBRUARY 16, 1970) You are present at the creation and the christening: THE LONGUETTE. You are reading about it in a 72-page special section published by *Women's Wear Daily*. It is a report of the just-completed presentations of the Paris couture spring 1970 collections, repeating collectively the pictures and reportage that had been covered daily as news during the previous two weeks. Why? Because something had happened that had not happened before. Out of the diversity that marks the collections of these creative individualists of the Paris couture, a message had emerged, a force of change with the momentum of a movement. *Women's Wear* called it THE LONGUETTE.

Here was the challenger to the MINI, which was then not only the prevailing fashion but the *Zeitgeist*—that saucy, audacious, leg-liberating, male-enticing MINI, love of the young around the world, imitated by the youth-pursuing, self-deluding, no-longer-young.

In a front-page box explaining this phenomenal issue—"The Longuette is the biggest fashion news in years, THE NEW LENGTH REVOLUTION. The Paris spring collections will go down in fashion history. The overall dominant direction is the NEW LONG LENGTH. Everything goes down, coats, suits, dresses.

(DATELINE MARCH 13, 1970: Ohrbach's, 34th Street, New York, U.S.A. The New York Times) A full page advertisement invites the public to their

semiannual fashion show of line-for-line couturier copies: "Paris, Rome, Madrid say, 'THE KNEE IS DEAD' and that was the message in the clothes. Something died that day, but not the knee. Six months passed, to August 1970. Hear from Macy's in a full-page ad. "MEN, are you distraught about the disappearance of the beautiful American knee? Macy's has good news for you. Just relax. Close your eyes. Breathe deeply and think positively. Think words like slink, slender, smooth. Think cling, close-fit. Think of shape, soft, feminine. Fashion news is more than length. IT'S NOT HOW LONG YOU MAKE IT, BUT HOW YOU MAKE IT LONG!"

The battle was joined. Women's Lib, newly militant, found its fighting issue. To the streets, to the barricades, to the television cameras with shouts and placards. G-A-M-S, Girls Against More Skirt. F-A-D-D, Fight Against Dictating Designers. You know the rest. The attempt to murder the American knee resulted in the death of American business. The young made it shorter, see-knee, thigh-high, low-buttock. The not-so-young sulked in pants or that middle-aged mini, the pants-suit.

HOW DID WE GET OUT OF IT?

With a bad dream. By starting all over where Eve began, with a snake. The snake-repulsive became the snake-embraced. The symbol of evil became the fashion of love. Snakes crawled out of the earth and shed their skins for the cause. Real snake, fake snake, fake snake prints on Ban-Lon dresses, on chiffon dresses, and on poplin raincoats. Snake bags, shoes, belts. Snake-under-glass was the patent version. Don't try to explain it. Not a matter for sociologists, psychologists, or philosophers. Just clothes flirting with a look, not yet having realized that they are a language. Soon came the revulsion, and the snakes slithered back into the earth. But not until they had spawned a weird generation of reptile prints, animal prints, butterflies, hearts, and cult symbols, including the Spiro Agnew watch.

HOW DID WE GET OUT OF THAT?

By having a party, a big nationwide binge of a costume party, in the clothes-language of LOVE.

Dress real, like real people, in real-people clothes, but not too real to be fun. Out of the mountains and prairies the real people came: the gypsies and the peasants, the American Indians, and the India Indians with the embroidered festival dresses of European villagers and the patchwork dresses of American pioneer settlers. On came the Indian suedes swinging fringe: fringed jackets, bags, belts, beaded wampum headbands, and silver amulets on chains. On came the India-Indian tie-dyes in dark colors making long wrapped skirts worn with tiny choli blouses, leaving midriffs bare.

THEN, WITH THE FIERY FERVOR OF A NEW GOSPEL, BLACK IS BEAUTIFUL

Protest shouted with pride, declared in clothes language, reaching its supreme moment at the Mohammed Ali-Joe Frazier fight-of-of-the-century in Madison Square Garden in winter 1970, when patched fur maxicoats and striped satin pants, with chains and amulets gleaming on ebony skin, outdid, outshone, and outcost any clothes worn by any people at any public event, ever before. Counterculture, soul-culture, in the vocabulary of Clothes-Now. We were learning to talk Clothes language.

CAME THE MORNING AFTER, AND THE SOBERING UP

Why larger than life when life is large enough, getting too large for most of us? Life is earnest, life is labor, serious, and tough. Life is construction workers, truck drivers, trainmen, dock workers, (when they worked), and sanitation men, in denim overalls. Suddenly, as the year turned to 1971, DENIMANIA struck, a contagious clothes epidemic. Denim solid or pinstriped in suspendered overalls. Brushed denim in trench coats with white double-stitched edges. Jacquard denim in suits with buttonfront skirts and battle jackets. Denim bags, luggage, sneakers. Batik denim jeans. And while we were digging denim we dug canvas, corduroy, suede and suede cloth, anything tough! Tough life, talking clothes language.

THEN, SUDDENLY, THEY WERE THERE, HOTPANTS!

From the streets of London, from the streets and boutiques of Paris, from the sharp-eyed, quick-witted American designers and manufacturers (recovering from a nightmare and regaining their sharp eyes and quick wits), and from the quick pounce of American stores (which by now would pounce on anything that would bring a buck), HOTPANTS, for the girls who will gladly make money talk when clothes talk the international eye language of Clothes-Now. Satisfaction of a longing, fulfillment of a desire, for leg show; long, beautiful legs, up to there, to there, in HOTPANTS. The sound in the land was the wolf call of the hardhats, and hotpants had it made.

Not only for the young who could and did, but for the not-so-young who shouldn't and would, and for all who saw a hundred ways to wear hotpants under an overskirt with a parting of the ways. Printer's ink flowed like wine through the news press. Hotpants on covers and featured in living color. To *Women's Wear Daily* it was bacchanale. In every edition the HOTSIES. In a special edition, just HOTPANTS, their own impudent name. It stuck. On they came, brief and brassy, in suede and denim, corduroy and velvet, sweater knit and double knit, fake fur and real fur, covered in jet paillettes or twinkling nailheads, edged in rhinestones.

Smarty-pants, mini-pants, short-stops, shorts; the stores tried to refine the name, but they should have known better. Clothes language talks, it isn't talked to. And so, they just tripled and quadrupled their orders and added all the magnetic attractions: little sleeveless sweaters in bang-bang colors with symbols or stripes over white shirts. Long skinny sweaters with low-slung belts. Little knit-caps, suede ghillies, body stockings, knee socks, long hair blowing in the wind. Hotpants brought fashion, brought joy, brought business. Happy Days are here again. Clothes had learned clothes-language, people-language, Clothes-Now.

There was more to say than anyone had believed; that was the year when deep elemental forces in ourselves and our culture surfaced, erupted, exploded, until we wondered who we were and what we had become. It all became articulated in our clothes.

YOUTHCULT

That was the year. Never before in human history was a whole generation so probed, dissected, analyzed, publicized, and televised in its own time as the young at the turn of 1970s. They revolted on the campuses of France, Italy, Mexico, Japan, Berkeley, and Columbia, U.S.A. They revolted against the draft, the war, the government, the establishment, pollution, killing baby seals, and against anything they chose to call hypocritical or phony in the generation of their parents. They revolted with sound, songs, sex, hair, and anti-clothes. We-Not-They clothes, Me-Mini. He-She jeans, T-shirts, sandals, sunglasses. Us-ethnics. Down with word-language; up with body-language. First they were frowned on, then feared by their elders, and then imitated by adults in a frenzied search for their own lost youth. Then given the vote from age 18 by swiftly passed constitutional amendment. Now vote-courted for the 1972 elections. Youthcult became, is becoming, and will continue to become a primary force in culture and clothes.

HAIR

This was the generation gap declaration of independence. Long straight hair blowing free. Hair tossing in a tumble of curls. Hair squeaky clean or matted and unwashed. Hair electrically charged like an Afro-sphere. Hair bobbed like a page boy. Grow it yourself if you're young. Or have it instantly in a wig of Modacrylic, Elura, Venicelon, Kanekelon, or Tiejin fiber. The GUYS got the message. They grew it on cheeks, chins, and upper lips. Those who could grew it on heads and let it grow and grow until they looked as if they slept in trees. For the no longer young, the sign in the Rockefeller Center barber shop told them off: "Your hair? Just forget it, and it will go away." Hair became a primary force in our culture, leading to the clothes that went with the hair.

CULT OF THE BODY

Fat is out. Slim is in. The beautiful body is weightless, willowy, supple, sexy, lean, and stretched out between its fore and aft curves. It is narrow-thighed, long-legged, healthy, suntanned, young, and gorgeous. For this, or any reasonable facsimile thereof, any sacrifice, any diet, any exercise, action sport, or pill that promises devaluation of the pound. I can be it. I can wear it. Often the ultimate self-delusion, because clothes-language tells the truth about a body. The cult-of-the-body is THE ELEMENTAL FORCE in Clothes-Now. Lane Bryant cultivates the business of women whose Cult-of-the Body is overfeeding it. Ohrbach's believes in truth-in-advertising, "IT'S IN, but maybe you shouldn't be IN IT!"

SEX

Liberated, written about, talked about, four-lettered, staged, filmed, sold, published, practiced with candor, battled in the courts to draw the fine line between sex and pornography, and battled in the streets to shut it out of sight as a trade, "Everything you always wanted to know" became the all-time best seller. Sex-into-fashion became elemental: slinky, slithery, seductive, plunging in front, naked in back . . . indeed if it wasn't sexy, why should I buy it? OK, dear, start with a bodystocking and take it from there, or have you seen the one-piece swimsuit that takes less fabric than a bikini?

SAVE THE SPECIES

March for the baby seals, organize protests with shouts and placards against fashion shows of furs. Keep the animals alive and fake the pelts of those threatened with extinction. Love the ones that look like black seal. Don't look too hard if they have borders of real wolf, raccoon, and opossum, or if the suede coats are lined with shaggy lamb that spills over at the edges.

NATURE FOODS

Eat bean sprouts. Eat wheat germ. Drink carrot juice. Flavor it with sea kelp. Wear righteous clothes of nature people: hair unlimited, frayed jeans, sandals on feet that have never known shoes. Or project your nature loving with innocent prints of berries, flora and fauna, on shirts, on little sweaters.

THE GOOD EARTH

Love it. Stop polluting it. Take action against those who do. Take back your beer cans and glass bottles for recycling. Sing earth songs to a plaintive guitar. Wear earth colors: the gold of its sunshine, the russet of its autumn leaves, the brown of its soil, and the purplish reds of its red onions and red cabbages. In everything, from polyester knits to suede shoes and belts.

ACTION SPORTS

Don't just stand there. Play the game. Water is for swimming, water skiing, sailing. Snow is for skiing, snow-mobiling. Courts are for tennis. Roads are for cycling. Get out there where the action is. The action sports. Buy the right equipment. Wear the right clothes. Go to the right places every weekend. Bring your racquet, skis, underwater gear, or maybe just your bikini and sun oil. Learn judo, you may need it. Bring money. If you haven't any left, bring your credit cards.

DO IT YOURSELF

Sew it. Crochet it. Knit it, Do it in needlepoint. Make it yours. Wear it with joy. "I did it myself!" I embroidered it, quilted it, put rows and rows of braid on it. I bought the pattern, the fabric, the trimmings, the etceteras. I paid for a sewing course, bought an instruction book, subscribed to *Seventeen's* Make-It," Singer's *How*, and renewed my *Glamour* subscription. Do it yourself is big business now, $3 billion worth last year, 44 million who are making it.

LA DOLCE VITA

This takes time, money, and two. The places are there now. Go to the Costa Smerelda of Sardinia, the luxury-with-simplicity domain of the Aga Khan. Here, on the little ivory crescent beaches, washed by the emerald sea, under the azure sky, is the new life-without-words, *la dolce vita*. He and She. She oils him. He oils her. Their golden bodies stretch out in the sun. Silence. Then a swim, sunbathing, more oiling. A basket lunch with sandwiches, fruit, cheese and wine. Late dining in flowered courtyards under the stars, to native music. Faintly, from a distance, the rock beat from discos of the together-young. Clothes? A minimal bikini, pants and a T-shirt, a body sling with jewelry at night. Go by private plane or yacht. Or go on a student bargain-fair to the campsites of Yugoslavia. *La dolce vita* is now and next.

THEY, THE GUYS

They got the message in clothes-language. "Oh, the gorgeousness of me with this hair. Oh, the manliness of me in these show-my-body clothes. This skinny shirt left unbuttoned, these amulets on my sun tanned chest, these uptight pants with a big bold belt. Where have I been all my life?"

ON MAY 2, 1970

Charlotte Curtis, editor of women's interests for *The New York Times*, took to the streets of New York, and reported all the news that's fit to print about what she saw. "The streets are filled with cotton T-shirts, denim maxi-coats, Chanel suits, Italian ready-to-wear, suede mini-skirts, crocheted mini-dresses, Kimberly knits, printed nylon pants-suits, trench coats, white vinyl boots, blue jeans, picture hats, mink jackets, and hotpants." James Reston called it "the best free show on earth." The American fashion business called it disaster.

IN FALL 1971

We tried to pick up the pieces, multi-pieces . . . in layers. Blazers, pants, shirts, shrinks, shrugs, over body-suits. We sought solace in the past, nostalgia, from "Love Story" and "No, No, Nanette" and in the time remembered by Proust. Still looking for A LOOK, while women yearned for clothes with a language, vitalized by life news, action, attitudes, realities.

And so, we swing into spring 1972, and what are Clothes-Now, just one year later?

Clothes have come to terms with life and, in the process of reaching for reality, have discovered that validity has its own vitality. Sharpened awareness of world news by instant communication. Heightened consciousness of America revolutionizing its values. Candor of the body: exercise it, slenderize it, enjoy its health, and bare it. These are the dynamics of clothes now.

EYES-EAST

World news coverage by satellite of the American president's unprecedented trip to the Republic of China next month will stimulate an upsurge of interest in all that is different and beautiful in the land so old in time, so new in history.

China-in-the-news was registered in that original male-female Chinese blue cotton worker's suit, imported by Bloomingdale's via Paris, a sellout as soon as it was advertised. Now come the variations in stripes, prints, and solid colors. Then, China-of-the-centuries, in the design and mood of clothes, subtle in styling, strong in patterns and colors. Band necks, side closings, contrast pipings, frog fastenings. Serene silk shantungs, honans, silk linens. Flowering prints on crepe de chine and silky jersey, inspired by the flowers on Chinese vases and screens.

And, in spite of the tragic events of recent weeks on the Indian subcontinent, many heads of American firms and designers have been traveling in the Far East. We will see a new wave of sophisticated American fashions from many Eastern arts and cultures. Altman's "Gateway to India" and Lord & Taylor's "Far East Odyssey" last fall are only the preface of things-to-come. Clothes-language will talk Far East, its news, art, culture, and beauty transformed into life-enhancing American fashion.

EYES U.S.A.

The scene shifts to America. 1972 is the year when we will elect a president. 1972 is the year when 25 million new young voters have been enfranchised by constitutional amendment. (The figure includes those older than the 18- to- 21-year-olds who have not yet been able to participate in a presidential election.) 1972 is the year of new priorities, new self-searching, to define who we are, what we are, what we want, and where we are going as a nation. We seek a new American-ness in ourselves, in our clothes. That's what started the U.S. Navy wave: the red-white-blue scheme, the stars, stripes and ship prints, and the anchors insignia. Then, American sportsmanship, not only to watch on a television screen, but to play and enjoy. Winter Olympics next week in Sapporo, Japan. Summer Olympics next August in Munich, Germany. In the United States 67 hours of satellite telecasting will stimulate action sports participation, in tennis, cycling, swimming, boating, skiing, demanding clothes for gamesmanship, in which the action-function generates the fashion.

EYES ON ME

Not daring now, but baring as total acceptance of the body as part of the design. Body-and-clothes together. Little baretops with pants. Baretops under open shirt-jackets or cardigans. Bare-on-the-beach with swim suits barely there. Halters, straps, drawstrings, barebacks, one bare shoulder. Day and night. Short and long. Eyes on me, my body, my clothes, my freedom.

In a single year, a total switch. From clothes for escape to clothes for belonging. Fashion validity to express life reality. Participation, action, candor now, life aware of the world, seeking a new America, lifting standards of quality, taste, simplicity, honesty, beauty. America is in revolution now, nothing less, changing how it lives, what it does, where it goes, what it values, determined that its clothes will be life-expressing and life-enhancing, clothes-language of the new realities.

Finally, remember that in America clothes are Big Business. $58-1/2 billion worth of clothes, shoes and cosmetics bought by men, women and children in 1970, nearly $29 billion worth of which was female clothes alone. Only food uses more of the budget than clothes. More is spent for clothes than for cars. There are 5,792 department stores in the United States, but the four chains—Sears, Penney's, Ward's and Gamble's—do half the department store business. Sears will exceed the $10 billion mark when the figures for 1971 are published, the largest corporate volume for a single business in the United States. Big business, fascinating business, Clothes business, now to next. Aren't you glad you made it your business?

ANALYZING FASHION TRENDS

Rita A. Perna

Let's dispel some of the fiction associated with fashion straight-away. Fiction about forecasting, prophesying, having a "fashion feeling" being an

SOURCE: Rita Perna, Fashion Director and Vice-President of Montgomery Ward and Co., Inc., wrote this article especially for this book.

expert, a seer, or omnipotent in a fashion decree. All of us have been in the position of looking with awe to someone who is reputed to have these special occult qualities. If I can but shorten the learning period of others by stripping away the mystery—by reducing the steps to their simplest terms—I will at least have made the growing pains a little easier to bear.

RESEARCH

Although fashion is not considered a science many scientific steps are applied. The number one step being that of *good hard research*— which means *leg work* and consultation with the primary sources of information. The *mills* and *tanners* working months and years ahead of the market are in the best position to guide you on basic facts. Their information will include the approaching season's *promotional plans* plus ideas in the incubator stage that you can look forward to in the future seasons. Remember that they have *had to take a position* on raw goods and machinery well in advance. Their research should be of benefit to you. Next, the *magazines* whose fashion editors have also tread the same steps of basic research. Consult with them, tossing ideas back and forth searching out their convictions.

Let us not forget the *trade magazines* and newspapers, again, whose expert staff mulled over the very same problems—check *again!* If you are lucky enough to be a member of or have access to any special fashion services, such as Color Card Association, Tobé Reports, etc., once again you have *another pipeline* of information on basic research at your command.

ANALYSIS

If you have the fortitude, stamina, strong legs, and unbending spirit to have completed a thorough job of research then you are in a perfect position to analyze this knowledge. In scrutinizing the facts it is important that you first put the information in *order of importance;* for example, let's talk about color. You may have learned that beige, pink, and yellow are slated for promotion. How will you determine their *degree of importance?*

TIMING

It is not possible for all three colors to be equally strong at the same time. One color is probably right as a cruise color in January; a second color might be right as an early spring color; the third one might be perfectly timed for the summer. After seasonal timing, another question to ask your-self—what is the timing for *your* particular store or company? Are you a high-fashion specialty shop, a volume department store, an exclusive boutique, a window chain or mail-order catalog? Is your store located in New York, Kansas, California, or Texas? Are *you* the *best store* in town or the price promoter in town? The reply to these questions will determine *how timely you* should or must be. Being early or first is just as destructive as being late.

CLASSIFICATIONS

Determining the *one, two, three colors* is step number one. Determining the *correct timing* for the image of your store is step number two. Determining the *kinds of goods* that are right in the selected color for a particular time of year in a *particular climatic* and *geographic* location is step number three. For example, the color beige as an early spring color would be adaptable for *all classifications* of goods, but, obviously the depth and breadth of stock behind yellow would be much shallower than the classic beige. The *degree of newness* would also be a factor in determining the *risk element* for your store. Purple is far riskier than pink; therefore, you would put it into short-lived fashion garments that would move in and out of your stock quickly rather than investing the color in merchandise of a relatively long life and basic character.

NEWNESS

Newness is the blood of fashion business. It is absolutely necessary to take calculated risks in new ideas whether it be color, silhouette, length, or fabric. Investing wisely in newness will pay dividends. By exposing any new idea to the consumer you are *bound to learn the degree of acceptance* or the problems caused by the change. This enables you to take action based on your *own* findings. Allowing someone else to experiment for you may seem wise, but since you cannot always apply someone else's experience to your company you will still have to go through the experimental pains. This makes you *late* because you are a *follower* and *not a leader.* This mars your fashion image because *customers* will *not look to you* for newness. This lateness *destroys the momentum* that you would have gained had you been in at the inception of the trend and *ready* when it reached its crest.

SENSITIVITY

Basically we are pleading for the development of a *sensitivity* to the changing currents of fashion. This sensitivity comes through an awareness of what is going on at the mill level, manufacturer level, retail level, and consumer level. With this sensitivity and knowledge of what is eminent on the fashion horizon, you should be able to jump on the bandwagon at the proper time.

DAY-TO-DAY

So far we have dealt with some methods used in fashion analysis in its early or beginning stages. What happens on a *day-to-day basis?* Once you have set your plans for the promotion of certain colors, silhouettes, categories of merchandise, you must then watch with a keen eye and ear for those ideas that have met with customer acceptance. This is obtained very simply in *reading sales records.* Did it *sell; how well* did it sell; *how fast* did it sell; *when* did it sell? Based on the responses you are able to add *strength to your convictions* or delete the ideas that have not won customer sales. Remember, it is the customer who sets the trend by parting with her disposable fashion dollars. No matter how you personally love a fashion feature you must abandon it *in depth* until you see evidence of a customer's change of heart. You will

keep it alive through repeated investments in newness where they have refined the original idea. How long has it taken the majority to accept loose-fitting clothes since the advent of the chemise? How long did it take the majority to accept short skirts? How long did it take the majority of the women to accept the understated look? These ideas were *not abandoned* along the way, but were tried repeatedly with a new disguise—with better fit, better construction, better understanding on the part of the customer and manufacturer. Some trends take hold like a whirlwind, others maintain a slow and steady growth. Let us look ahead—how long will it take for the return of the fitted clothes and the longer skirts? It will be interesting to watch!

PERSONAL ATTITUDES

The personal qualities that I am about to speak of are applicable to everyone from the president to a lonely stock boy. I speak of:

1. *A Sense of Urgency.* Demanding *Immediate* delivery, lugging merchandise from the receiving room now, sending the report out *immediately.* In other words, *action!*

2. *Dedication.* A sense of perfection that is not fanatic, but simply a matter of personal pride of *doing* something *now* and *well.* In other words, *thoughtfully!*

3. *Self-Evaluation.* You will always hear the blame and hardly ever the praise, that is the nature of our business. You should be able to determine if the job was A plus, good, or only fair. Get into the habit of *rating yourself* after every job assignment. Compare yourself with *best people,* not the mediocre characters around you. In this way you will be pulling yourself up to the higher standard. In other words, be *self-critical!*

LIFE-STYLE, FASHION, AND THE ECONOMY

Carl Priestland

Fashion is the customary mode of dress which is in use at a particular time. The difference between fashion today and in the early 1900's is related to the ability to be fashionable. Being fashionable at the turn of the century was a luxury. Relatively few people could afford fashionable apparel. Today fashionable apparel is within the budget of most Americans. Unlike earlier periods, fashionable garments are offered at many price points, from the very expensive specialty shop garments to the discounter's inexpensive copy.

For the purposes of this discussion, style is defined as the various forms which a fashion can take, depending on the manufacturer's execution of the fashion. A firm's choice of fabric, trim, color, and cut of a garment differentiates it from other styles of the same garment.

ECONOMIC TRENDS AND APPAREL

There is a saying that the length of women's skirts varies with economic fluctuations. At the bottom of an economic downturn there is a trend to more liberal use of fabric and a lowering of the skirt length. The reason for this is that as the price of fabric declines, apparel producers want to create additional consumption. They use more cloth and create a new longer length garment which, if accepted, makes shorter skirts less acceptable. This creates new demand. As economic activity increases, inflationary pressures push up prices. This would make it more difficult to remain in the same price point and use as much of the higher priced fabric. One way to retain the price point is to reduce the use of fabric. Less fabric use is made possible by shortening the skirt length.

SOURCE: Reprinted from *Apparel Manufacturer*, April 1972, Copyright 1972, Forge Association Publications, Inc. Carl Priestland is economic consultant to The American Apparel Manufacturers Association.

How much of this is fact and how much is myth is difficult to ascertain. During the inflation of the 1920's skirts were short. In the depression of the 1930's they were long. World War II inflation and limited fabric availability resulted in a rise of the skirt length by 1945. By 1949, along with the recession, skirts were long again. The latest try at changing the skirt length—the midi—did not work. There is a feeling that the relationship between skirt length and economic fluctuations has become a myth, if it was not one already.

Economic fluctuations affect the purchase of large ticket apparel items, mostly tailored clothing. During each recession since World War II the demand for suits and coats has declined far more than the demand for low priced apparel, such as dresses or shirts. Expenditures for these high priced items are delayed until better times. Last year's coat or suit generally will do for one more year. There are less radical changes in the styling of these garments because people tend to be conservative when purchasing a suit or coat that is expected to last for several years.

Manufacturers also react to economic fluctuations. They try to create a unique product to encourage the consumer to buy. As economic activity increases and consumers are spending freely, apparel producers take more chances to try to capture a larger market share. As things get tight, unemployment is increasing, and additional income from overtime declines, consumer purchases decline. Retailers get more conservative, there is a trend to more basic styles, etc.

As the economy starts to grow, firms add to their advertising budgets once again. Apparel producers will restyle within the current fashion and even offer something new just to see consumer acceptance. If it goes, a new fashion may be started.

ECONOMIC AND SOCIAL FORCES

The changing pace of economic activity is not the

only force that influences fashion and the styling of that fashion. Basic long run economic trends affect the consumer and, in turn, his acceptance of fashion and ability and willingness to purchase fashionable apparel. The importance of these economic trends cannot, in many cases, be separated from the sociological trends taking place at the same time. The interaction of these trends, economic and sociological, affect our life style. It is our life style that dictates what is fashionable.

The decade of the 1960's saw major changes in life style. The youth movement dominated the decade. Attitudes toward "the establishment" changed radically from the more conservative 1950's. In an attempt to demonstrate their anti-establishment attitude, young people in the 1960's made blue jeans and work shirts the fashion. The unkempt look was in.

The concept of a wardrobe has become a thing of the past for many Americans. Less expensive, more comfortable apparel has become fashionable. Knits were accepted for their comfort and easy care. With the acceptance of more body exposure, clinging knits became more important.

TRENDS THAT HAVE PROMOTED

Mass Media has shortened the incubation period of a new fashion. The time between introducing and general acceptance of a fashion has been shortened enormously. Copies of expensive, fashionable garments show up in the stores of the mass merchandisers as soon as the fashion has been accepted. Television is particularly important in the wide dissemination of news and fashion changes.

Travel by everyone, but particularly the young, both in the U.S. and abroad has helped to change our life style. The ability to travel at very low cost has exposed millions of young people to many new ideas, including new fashions. Clothes good for travel as well as some foreign garments have become important items in American apparel.

Imports of apparel have created substantial competition in many apparel lines. To avoid price competition with imported apparel many manufacturers started to produce more high-style apparel. The woven dress shirt industry provides a good

example. As imports took more and more of the low end staple shirt market, shirt makers went to colored, deep dyed, striped, and printed shirts. Now knit dress shirts have been introduced. Much of this fashion trend was created by the imported shirt market. It must be said that it would not have gotten anywhere if the consumers did not want more high-style shirts. Emphasis on the young look and the more flamboyant attitude of the young helped stimulate acceptance of these shirts.

Retailers also have influenced fashion because of their desire to retain and add to their market share of the consumer's dollar. Retailers have developed more apparel "seasons." There are fewer staple apparel products in the market today. To sell apparel, the retailer believes he must continually have something new for the consumer. This has led to the development of greater amounts of less expensive fashionable goods, less inventory to hold and faster turnover of goods. More "seasons" have led to fewer reorders. These changes are not so much changes in fashion as in style. For each new "season" the apparel manufacturer hopes to come up with a new style of a going fashion.

Casual apparel has been accepted for comfort and easy care. Man-made fibers, permanent press, and the easy care of knits have influenced the acceptability of casual apparel. This trend in fashion is adversely affecting commercial home laundries. The laundry business in many areas of the country is declining. On the other hand, manufacturers of home washing machines and driers are promoting the replacement of old machines with one that will handle synthetic fabrics and permanent press garments.

Approval of slacks and jeans for school wear for both boys and girls affected the demand for these garments. While this is a sociological change, it also has economic importance and influences fashions.

It is difficult to say which comes first. The fashion trend is accepted and economic forces are set up to sustain this acceptance. Or an economic trend sets up forces that would influence manufacturer's decisions on what type of apparel to offer. Sometimes this goes wrong, as with the midi. There will be more experiences like the midi disaster if manufacturers and retailers do not see how acceptable a trend in fashion is before making a large commitment to it.

There has been a definite move toward individualism. The uniform dress of the young has given way to greater variety of dress to fit individual taste. A large variety of skirt lengths is now available. There is much greater latitude in the choice of fashionable apparel.

Fashion trends are filtering up from the young because there is a desire to look youthful. One reason for this emphasis is the economic importance of the 20 to 35 year olds in the population. The number of people in this age group will increase by more than one-third during the 1970's. Much of today's advertising is pointed toward influencing this group. Trends in fashion and style of apparel during this next decade will be greatly influenced by the economic and social changes of this group. Our life style has changed dramatically from the early 1960's.

The interaction of economic and sociological trends on our life style has influenced fashion in the past and will continue to do so in the future. The emphasis on youth and individualism will make it more difficult to meet the consumer's demand for apparel because of the variety of styles demanded within the fashion framework.

BIBLIOGRAPHY

Adburgham, Alison. *View of Fashion.* London, Allen and Unwin, 1966.

Anspach, Karlyne. *The Why of Fashion.* Ames, Iowa, Iowa State University Press, 1967.

Beaton, Cecil W. H. *The Glass of Fashion.* Garden City, N.Y., Doubleday, 1954.

Bell, Quentin. *On Human Finery.* New York, A.A. Wyn, 1949.

Bergler, Edmund. *Fashion and the Unconscious.* New York, R. Brunner, 1953.

Bigelow, Marybelle. *Fashion in History.* Minnesota, Burgess Pub. Co., 1970.

Binder, Pearl. *Muffs and Morals.* New York, Morrow, 1954.

Boehn, Max von. *Modes and Manners.* Philadelphia, Lippincott, 1932.

Boucher, Francois. *20,000 Years of Fashion.* New York, Harry N. Abrams, 1967.

Broby-Johansen, R. *Body and Clothes; An Illustrated History of Costume.* New York, Reinhold, 1968.

Burris-Meyer, Elizabeth. *This Is Fashion.* New York and London, Harper, 1943.

Contini, Mila. *Fashion; From Ancient Egypt to the Present Day.* New York, Odyssey, 1965.

Crawford, Morris De Camp. *One World of Fashion.* 3rd edition. New York, Fairchild, 1967.

Crawford, Morris De Camp. *The Ways of Fashion.* New York, Fairchild, 1948.

Cunningham, Cecil W. *Why Women Wear Clothes.* London, Faber and Faber, 1941.

D'Assailly, Gisele. *Ages of Elegance; Five Thousand Years of Fashion and Frivolity.* London, Macdonald, 1968.

Fairley, Roma. *A Bomb in the Collection: Fashion with the Lid Off.* Brighton, England, Clifton Books, 1969.

Flügel, John C. *The Psychology of Clothes.* New York, International Universities Press, 1966.

Fourt, Lyman. *Clothing: Comfort and Function.* New York, Marcel Dekker, 1970.

Garland, Madge. *The Changing Form of Fashion.* New York, Praeger, 1971.

Harris, Christie and Moira Johnston. *Figleafing through History: The Dynamics of Dress.* New York, Athenaeum, 1971.

Hill, Margot H. and Peter Bucknell. *The Evolution of Fashion.* New York, Reinhold, 1968.

Horn, Marilyn J. *The Second Skin: An Interdisciplinary Study of Clothing.* Boston, Houghton Mifflin, 1968.

Hurlock, Elizabeth, *The Psychology of Dress.* New York, The Ronald Press, 1929.

Ironside, Janet. *A Fashion Alphabet.* London, Joseph Pub., 1968.

Katona, George. *The Powerful Consumer.* New York, McGraw-Hill, 1960.

Kohler, Carl. *A History of Costume.* New York, Dover Publications, 1963.

Langner, Lawrence, *The Importance of Wearing Clothes.* New York, Hastings House, 1959.

Laver, James. *The Concise History of Costume and Fashion.* New York, Harry N. Abrams, Inc. 1969.

Laver, James. *Dress.* London, J. Murray, 1950.

Laver, James. *Modesty in Dress.* Boston, Houghton Mifflin, 1969.

Laver, James. *Women's Dress in the Jazz Age.* London, H. Hamilton 1964.

Laver, James. *Taste and Fashion.* New York, Dodd Mead, 1938.

Lynes, Russell. *The Tastemakers.* New York, Harper and Bros., 1954.

Nystrom, Paul H. *Economic Principles of Consumption.* New York, The Ronald Press, 1929.

Nystrom, Paul H. *Economics of Fashion.* New York, The Ronald Press, 1928.

Parsons, Frank. *The Psychology of Fashion.* Garden City, New York, Doubleday, 1920.

Pickens, Mary Brooks. *The Fashion Dictionary.* New York, Funk and Wagnalls, 1957.

Pistolese, Rosana and Ruth Horsting. *History of Fashions.* New York, Wiley, 1970.

Price, Julius. *Dame Fashion.* Paris and London, Marston Co., 1913.

Roach, Mary Ellen and Joanne B. Eicher. *Dress, Adornment and the Social Order.* New York, Wiley, 1965.

Rudofsky, Bernard. *Are Clothes Modern?* Chicago, P. Theobald, 1947.

Rudofsky, Bernard. *The Unfashionable Human Body.* New York, Doubleday, 1971.

Ryan, Mary S. *Clothing, A Study in Human Behavior.* New York, Holt, 1966.

Wilcox, R. Turner. *Five Centuries of American Costume.* New York, Chas. Scribner and Sons, 1963.

Wilcox, Ruth Turner. *The Dictionary of Costume.* New York, Scribner, 1969.

Women's Wear Daily. Sixty Years of Fashion. New York, Fairchild, 1963.

Young, Agnes Brooks. *Recurring Cycles of Fashion, 1760–1937.* New York, Harper, 1937.

TRADE ASSOCIATION

The Fashion Group, 9 Rockefeller Plaza, New York, N.Y. 10020.

SECTION REVIEW AND ACTIVITIES

FASHION BUSINESS TERMINOLOGY

Define, identify, or briefly explain the following:

Fashion
Fad
Style
High fashion
Trend
Design
Life-style

QUESTIONS FOR REVIEW

1. Give a current example of a fashion, a style, a fad, a design, a fashion trend, and a high fashion. Use your examples to explain the differences between each term.
2. Is it correct to say that designers create fashion? Explain.
3. Why do fashions change? Do you agree that changes in fashion are evolutionary in nature? Cite current examples to prove your answer.
4. Name and briefly explain the three different theories pertaining to the development of a fashion. Cite examples of current fashions that illustrate each theory.
5. What events and personalities in today's news are influencing current fashions? How?
6. Do you agree that fashion does not refer to price? Defend your answer by citing examples.

7. Why do people buy new clothing? Are their reasons largely emotional or rational? Explain.

8. Can new fashions come into being without consumers expressing an active desire for them? Why?

9. What techniques are used by fashion professionals to predict coming fashions?

10. Study the fashions described in the reading, "What Were They Wearing? 1910–1970," and explain how they reflected their times.

11. Name three industries, other than clothing or accessories, that are directly or indirectly affected by the apparel business. How?

12. When the average person thinks of styles and fashion, he or she probably relates them to apparel and accessories. What other products are produced and sold with the fashion element in mind? Give examples to prove your answer.

APPLICATIONS WITH EXAMPLES

1. In the reading, "Clothes–Now," Estelle Hamburger states that clothes are now a language that communicates self-identity and group identity. Discuss this and illustrate with examples.

2. Some people claim it is wasteful to urge customers to buy new fashions in clothing when plenty of wear remains in their present clothing. They criticize the emphasis on fashion in the marketing of apparel as a social and economic waste. Prove or disprove this viewpoint.

3. Discuss and/or visually illustrate the following statement: "The only thing constant about fashion is change."

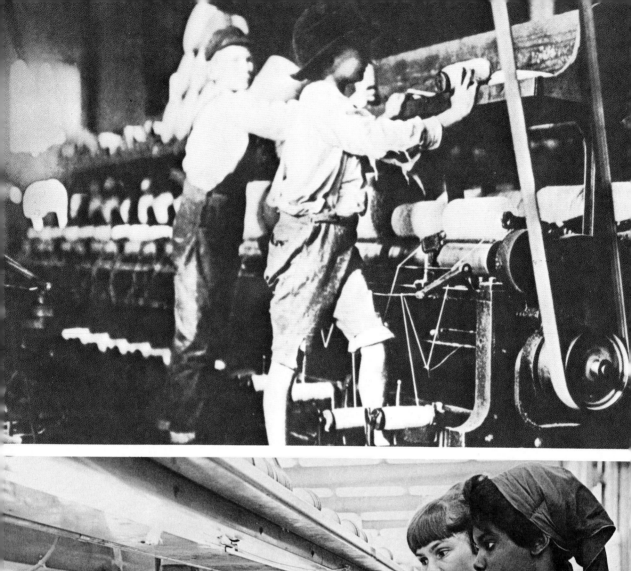

SECTION 2
THE MATERIALS
OF FASHION

Fashion is serious business, and its makings form the basis of a highly complex, multibillion dollar, many-faceted manufacturing industry. Its producers, of which there are many thousands, divide into two broad categories: (1) the primary markets that provide the raw materials of fashion, such as fibers, fabrics, and leathers; and (2) the cutting-up or needle trades that manufacture the finished articles of apparel.

This section is concerned with the primary fashion markets, whose designs, colors, and textures frequently pace a new fashion trend and provide apparel and accessories designers with the stuff that gives substance to their ideas. The text discusses the most important primary markets and indicates how each market influences fashion and is influenced by it. The readings that follow the text have been selected to illustrate and amplify points made in the discussion.

THE TEXTILE INDUSTRY

The largest and most important of fashion's primary markets is the textile industry, which transforms fibers—animal, vegetable, or man-made—into yarns and then into fabric.

Size and Scope

The textile industry is made up of thousands of widely scattered, heterogeneous companies engaged in producing or processing fibers, or in performing one or more of the steps through which fibers must pass before being transformed into fabrics suitable for fashion use. Technically, sheep herders and growers of cotton and flax are part of the textile industry but, for purposes of this discussion, these agricultural aspects are ignored, and the industry is considered to include the production of man-made fibers, the processing of natural fibers, and the succeedings stages of textile production. Even thus limited, the industry is huge. It is so large that it plays a vital role in the economy of the United States. It gives employment to nearly 1 million workers[1] and enjoys annual sales of over $28 billion.[2] Although the bulk of the manufacturing facilities is in the South and in New England, some phase of textile activity is carried on in nearly every state of the union. Styling and design activities are centered in New York City, and the sales and merchandising operations reach into almost every other major city. The output is used in such diverse products as tire cord, industrial filters, and artificial arteries, as well as fashion apparel and accessories.

In the fashion business, which absorbs much of its output, the basic responsibility of the textile industry is the conversion of raw fibers into finished fabrics. At one end of the industry spectrum are about 7000 textile manufacturing plants[3] that

[1]U.S. Department of Commerce, *U.S. Industrial Outlook, 1973*, p.145.
[2]U.S. Department of Commerce, *Survey of Current Business*, April, 1973, p. S5.
[3]U.S. Department of Commerce, *U.S. Industrial Outlook, 1973*, p. 147.

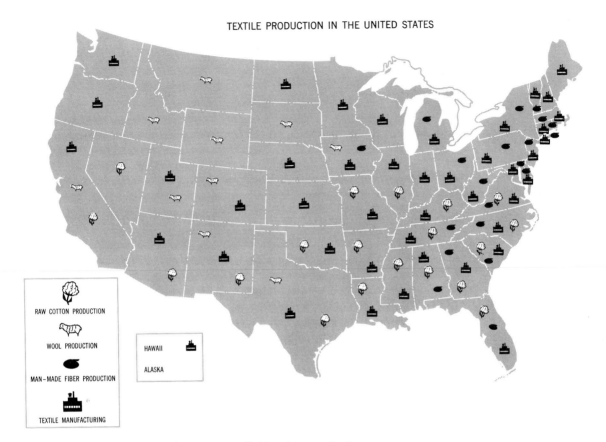

TEXTILE PRODUCTION IN THE UNITED STATES

RAW COTTON PRODUCTION

WOOL PRODUCTION

MAN-MADE FIBER PRODUCTION

TEXTILE MANUFACTURING

HAWAII

ALASKA

Source: Reprinted, courtesy of American Textile Manufacturers Institute.

perform one or more of the three major processes involved in the manufacture of textiles: the spinning of natural or synthetic fibers into yarn, the weaving or knitting of yarn into fabric, and the finishing of fabric to impart color, texture, pattern, ease of care, and the other characteristics. At the other end of the spectrum are the sales offices that market the finished cloth to the cutting-up trades. Some of these sales offices are owned by the mills; others own their own mills; and still others are independent selling agents that represent several mills and receive a commission for their services.

History and Development

Although the United States textile industry today is the largest in the world, textile production by factory methods had its beginnings in England. During the eighteenth century, while the United States was becoming aware of itself and struggling for its independence, a series of inventions, each a closely guarded trade secret, had mechanized both spinning and weaving in England and had moved production from the home to the factory in that country.[4]

Production in America began in the cabins of the settlers where, from home-grown fibers, the spinning, weaving, dyeing, cutting, and sewing were responsibilities of the womenfolk. The husbands supervised the tanning of leathers, made the shoes, and cured the furs that were to be used. Fabrics produced by these early household industries were crude homespuns and were far less attractive to prosperous citizens of the young country than those they could import from Europe.

FIRST MILL IN 1793.   The transition from handcraft to factory production of textiles had its start in the United States when the first cotton spinning mill was built in 1793 at Pawtucket, Rhode Island by Samuel Slater.[5] His mill (now a textile museum) was not only the first successful spinning or yarn-making plant in this country but was also considered the forerunner of mass production in the United States. Its contribution to the industrialization of the country was later recognized by President Andrew Jackson, who called Slater "The Father of American Manufacture."[6] For the first 20 years, the growth of the industry was quite slow, largely because of the competition from the more attractive imports. In 1808, there were only 15 more or less isolated little mills scattered about New England.[7] The War of 1812, however, led to a rapid expansion when blockades and embargoes cut off imports from abroad and forced the United States to satisfy its needs from domestic textile sources. More mills came into being and, protected by tariffs imposed when the war was over, the industry was able to exploit the growing domestic market and maintain a high rate of expansion. Substantial impetus was given to industry growth by Francis Cabot Lodge, who built the first successful power loom in this country in 1814, after having visited England and having memorized the system in factories there.[8] By the end of 1815, there were reported to be "according to a memorial presented to the United States Congress, 99 mills in Rhode Island, 57 in Massachusetts, and 14 in Connecticut, making a total of 170 mills."[9]

RAPID GROWTH IN NINETEENTH CENTURY.   The years preceding the Civil War saw a period of great development and manufacturing activity. The country was growing rapidly, and the continuing improvement of factory machines and methods made it increasingly economical to produce textiles and to process leathers and furs outside the home. More and more factories were built to supply the needs of a

[4]E. B. Alderfer and H. E. Michl, *Economics of American Industry,* Third Edition, McGraw-Hill & Co., New York, 1957, pp. 333-334.

[5]Frederick Lewton, "Samuel Slater and the Oldest Cotton Machinery in America," Smithsonian Report for 1926.

[6]*Textiles—An Industry, A Science, An Art,* American Textile Manufacturers Institute, Charlotte, N.C., p. 15.

[7]Frank Walton, *Tomahawks to Textiles,* Appleton-Century-Crofts, Inc., New York, 1953, p. 98.

[8]"Mankind's Magic Carpet," American Textile Manufacturers Institute, Charlotte, N. C.

[9]Lewton, *op. cit.*

growing nation. By 1831, there were 795 textile mills throughout New England, and in that year they produced 230 million yards of fabric.[10]

American textile producers were not yet in a position, however, to compete with the better grade textile products that were available from European sources, notably England and France. In 1858, broadcloth and other fine fabrics were entirely supplied from Europe, and the New York Chamber of Commerce reported "that American wool, when used alone, cannot produce cloth of equal quality and finish as that made of foreign wools."[11] The Civil War gave additional impetus to the development of the industry. The great demands on American mills for fabrics for soldiers' uniforms were added to normal requirements and, by the end of the war, the textile industry was firmly established and well on its way toward mass production of quality fabrics.

FROM NORTH TO SOUTH. Throughout the nineteenth century, the industry was located almost entirely in the North, principally New England. Toward the end of the century, however, Southern leaders, concerned by the lack of industrialization in their states, offered textile companies special inducements, such as low taxes and utility rates, if they would build plants in the South. The movement of cotton manufacturing plants gained momentum after World War I and by 1920, over half the spinning and weaving capacity of cotton textile manufacturing was found in the South.[12] Woolen and worsted plants, attracted by an improved spinning system

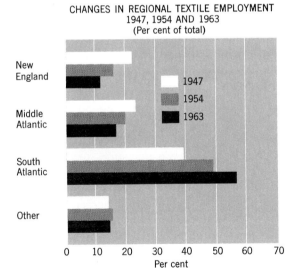

CHANGES IN REGIONAL TEXTILE EMPLOYMENT
1947, 1954 AND 1963
(Per cent of total)

New England

Middle Atlantic

1947
1954
1963

South Atlantic

Other

0 10 20 30 40 50 60 70
Per cent

Source: *Technology and Manpower in the Textile Industry of the 1970's,* U.S. Department of Labor, Bulletin 1578.

[10]"The Dress Industry," Market Planning Service of National Credit Office, New York, March 1948.

[11]Herbert Heaton, "Benjamin Gott and the Anglo-American Cloth Trade," *Journal of Economics and Business History,* Vol. II, November 1929, p. 147.

[12]Walter Adams, *Structure of American Industry,* revised edition, The Macmillan Co., New York, 1957, Chapter 2.

developed in the South for woolen manufacture, followed suit shortly after World War II. By 1970, the three Southern states of Georgia, North Carolina, and South Carolina employed 56 percent of the textile industry's labor force with the shift southward expected to continue.[13]

Along with the expansion of the industry came changes in the selling and distribution of its output. Merchants who had originally started as importers of European fabrics gradually became selling agents for the domestic mills or bought their goods outright for resale. The expansion of domestic output after the Civil War stimulated the establishment of a textile center in downtown Manhattan, on and near Worth Street, that became the heart of the textile trade. The name "Worth Street" became synonymous with the body of textile merchants on whom American mills depended for their orders and often for their financing.

ENTRANCE OF MAN-MADE FIBERS.   In the period between the two world wars, man-made fibers (rayon, acetate, and the earliest nylon) entered the textile picture and brought about many changes in the pattern of the industry's operation. As the use and popularity of these new fibers grew, agriculture diminished in importance as a source of fibers, and chemistry provided a larger share. Giant chemical corporations, such as E.I. duPont de Nemours and Company, Inc. and the Celanese Corporation of America, began to operate actively in the textile fiber field.

Another change that took place was that many of the textile firms that had formerly specialized in a single natural fiber began to work also with synthetic fibers or with combinations of natural and synthetic fibers—in spinning, in weaving or knitting, in finishing, and in selling. The traditional boundary lines that had divided the textile industry along lines of fiber specialization began to disappear.

INTEGRATION AND DIVERSIFICATION IN THE TWENTIETH CENTURY.   During and immediately after World War II, problems of scarcity and price made the prewar marketing procedures of the textile industry unfeasible. The industry began to integrate and diversify itself. In some cases, mills ceased to rely on independent converters and selling agents and set up their own finishing plants, converting operations, and sales organizations. Burlington Industries was one such organization. Until 1947, its plants in the south wove cotton and synthetic fabrics to be sold in the *greige* (unfinished) state to other firms. Today, the company functions at all levels of production, from the spinning of yarn to the sale of finished goods.

In other cases, converting firms like Cohn-Hall-Marx bought mills in order to be sure of having fabrics to sell. In still others, sales agents acquired textile mills and absorbed them into their corporate setup. A notable example of this latter method of expansion was J.P. Stevens & Co., then a leading selling house in the cotton and rayon fabrics field. In 1946 it united its selling house and its mill company with eight other companies.[14]

[13]U.S. Department of Labor, *Technology and Manpower in the Textile Industry of the 1970s*, Bulletin No. 1578.

[14]"The Merger Movement in the Textile Industry," U. S. House of Representatives, Committee on the Judiciary, January 1955, p. 14, and *Women's Wear Daily*, April 14, 1965, p. 1, report of study by Dr. John M. Blair, Chief Economist, Senate Judiciary Committee on Anti-Trust.

The process of integration speeded up in the 1950s and is still continuing. Between 1955 and 1966, about 365 textile companies, according to the Federal Trade Commission, were acquired by other companies through mergers and acquisitions.[15] For some companies, the objective was diversification, such as a company that acquired hosiery and carpet mills; for others, the objective was greater vertical integration through acquisition of spinning mills and retail clothing outlets.

FROM COTTON TO FABRIC

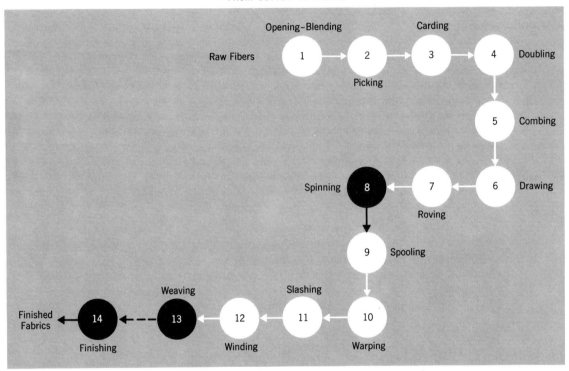

Many processes are required to transform raw fibers into yarn and yarn into fabric. They begin in the opening room where staple from many different bales of cotton are blended or where blends of natural and man-made fiber staple are made. In the picking room, the fiber is cleaned and foreign matter removed.

The carding and doubling processes further clean and begin to parallel the fibers. Through the combing, drawing and roving processes, the short fibers are removed and the remaining fibers are drawn out or lengthened, given a slight twist for strength, and readied for the spinning frames where the ropelike strands of loose fiber are spun into yarn.

From the spinning frame, the yarn is wound first onto "cheeses," then onto large warp beams. Slashing adds a starchlike substance called sizing to stengthen the yarn. In the winding process, the filling or crosswise yarns are transferred to bobbins which feed the yarn to the loom shuttle. The back-and-forth motion of the shuttle "weaves" the filling or "woof" yarn into the warp or vertical yarns to form the fabric.

The finishing process bleaches the fabric, and then adds color, texture, pattern, and, depending on the type of fabric, chemical and other finishes to impart ease-of-care characteristics to the finished fabric.

Note: Similar processes are followed for other natural fibers. For man-made fibers, the first 7 steps are omitted.

Source: Courtesy of American Textile Manufacturing Institute, Charlotte, N.C.

[15]U.S. Department of Labor, *op. cit.,* p. 10.

Nature of the Industry

The production of a textile fabric begins with the spinning of raw fiber—natural or man-made—into yarn. Yarn is then woven or knitted into fabric, which comes from the looms as *greige* (or unfinished) goods. *Greige* goods are then subjected to any number of processes such as bleaching, dyeing, and printing, which are called finishing operations.

HIGHLY SPECIALIZED. Historically, the United States textile industry has been highly fragmented, with each entrepreneur specializing in a single stage of production or in the processing of a single fiber. From its beginnings, the industry has been dominated by cotton, with other natural fibers, such as wool and silk, representing only a small portion of its output. In recent years, cotton's share has been declining but, even so, until the late 1960s this fiber represented approximately half the total poundage of fiber consumed by American mills. Man-made fibers now represent the major portion of total mill consumption.[16]

Especially in the case of cotton cloth, much of the fabric produced in the United States before World War II passed through many hands before reaching the garment producers or retail fabric shops. Weaving and knitting mills purchased yarn from spinners and produced fabric in the *greige*. At this point, independent selling agents, each serving one or more mills, entered the picture and sold *greige* goods to converters.

Today the textile industry includes many corporations whose operational scope encompasses every step in the production of fabrics from the purchase of natural and man-made fibers to the promotion and sale of finished cloth. Nevertheless, operations are specialized in the different plants in different locations and the products are distributed by different marketing divisions, all of which are owned by the same parent corporation. Two readings in this section, "Burlington Industries, A Total Textile World" and "The Durable threads of J. P. Stevens," describe the specialized divisions of two of the largest textile companies of the world.

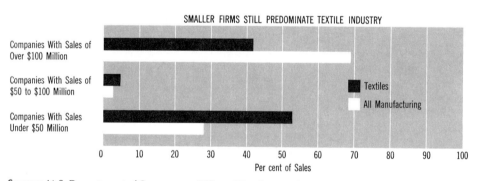

SMALLER FIRMS STILL PREDOMINATE TEXTILE INDUSTRY

Source: U.S. Department of Commerce, Office of Textiles, Market Analysis Division.

[16]U.S. Department of Commerce, *Statistical Abstract of the United States, 1971*, p. 703 and *U. S. Industrial Outlook, 1973*, p. 146.

Despite the consolidation of textile firms in the past 20 years, there are still many smaller firms that limit themselves to narrow product lines, such as velvets and velveteens, or to such dressy fabrics as chiffons, taffetas, and silk failles. There are also firms that produce only knits, brocades, metallics, or novelty fabrics. Their specializations seem, for the time being, to make them invulnerable to penetration by the large integrated firms.

ROLE OF THE CONVERTER.   The converter, who played a major role in the industry before World War II, and who still fulfills an important function, does not own facilities for production. Instead, he buys *greige* goods from the mills, contracts with finishing plants to have the goods processed to his order, and sells the finished product to apparel manufacturers. The typical converter, today as in the past, keeps in close contact with the apparel industry, seeking indications of colors, patterns, and finishes that are most likely to be wanted. Since he enters the process of production in its late stages, he can work quite close to the time of need and adjust quickly to any changes in demand. The successful converter is a keen student of fashion, studies trends, and anticipates demand. Many converters are small operators who "carry their business in their hats"; others are big names in the industry, such as Everfast, Cohn-Hall-Marx, and M. Lowenstein.

In branches of the textile industry other than cotton, the converter's role has been considerably less important. Woolen fabric producers have usually had to be completely integrated with respect to the spinning, weaving, and finishing processes. This has been a matter of necessity because the styling of a wool fabric often begins with the selection of fiber and yarn, and because a pattern is sometimes introduced into woolen cloth by dyeing some or all of the yarns before any weaving is done. Woolen mills, therefore, were never able to divorce themselves from the styling function, as was possible for cotton mills, nor could they wait for last-minute directives from garment producers. The silk textile industry, in the days before World War II, was also integrated for the most part. Plants were small and usually located in Paterson, New Jersey, close to their showrooms in the New York City garment manufacturing district. Quantities produced in each style were small. The management of a plant, with no great disruption of production schedules, could put into work a fabric or color wanted by its garment industry customers.

PUBLICLY OWNED GIANTS.   Mergers and acquisitions gave impetus to both diversification and integration and helped create the huge, publicly owned enterprises that dominate the textile industry. Largest of the giants is Burlington Industries, Inc., which began as a small mill in North Carolina in 1923, and which now ranks high, both in sales and in number of employees, on *Fortune's* list of the 500 largest corporations in the United States. Today, its 30-odd divisions produce and sell fabric from many fibers; make and sell yarn; sell *greige* goods to independent converters; finish *greige* goods for other textile firms; produce ribbons, hosiery, carpets, and vinyl-coated fabrics; act as selling agents; and are publicly owned. The second largest is J. P. Stevens Co., Inc., which celebrated its 150th anniversary in 1963. Highlights of Burlington's and Stevens's history,

Rise of the Textile Giants

COMPANY	ANNUAL SALES IN MILLIONS OF DOLLARS			
	1948	1960	1965	1972
Burlington Industries	288.2	913.0	1,313.3	1,816.1
J. P. Stevens & Co., Inc.	287.3	512.7	759.9	947.6
United Merchants & Manufacturers	211.5	468.2	559.7	787.0
Springs Mills, Inc.	154.0	200.0	252.0	398.9
Cone Mills Corp.	120.4	188.5	253.9	331.2
M. Lowenstein & Sons, Inc.	120.1	253.3	288.7	470.0
Dan River Mills, Inc.	103.6	156.9	246.3	366.6

Source: Published financial statements of these firms.

development, and present organization are discussed in the readings in this section.

The best available measure of the trend toward larger business organizations is the increasing proportion of the textile industry's output accounted for by the largest textile firms. Although relative to other major industries these ratios are still low, in 1972 the top four and eight firms accounted for 16 and 23 percent, respectively, of total industry sales. Another indication of the trend is that two-thirds of the industry's work force is employed in plants with at least 250 employees.[17] The textile industry, while still highly fragmented and competitive, is gradually emerging as an industry of fewer and larger firms. The rapid pace at which some of the industry's giants have grown is reflected in the published sales figures of some of the leading firms.

EMPHASIS ON BRAND NAMES.   A natural outgrowth of the trend to bigness in the textile industry is the emphasis on brand names, both in man-made fibers and in fabrics. A brand is a device, sign, symbol, or name that is used to identify and distinguish products as a means of building a market for them. The producers of man-made fibers have been especially aggressive in promoting their respective brand names. Each does this to build prestige and acceptance for his product, to differentiate it from other products in the customer's mind, to lessen price competition, and to pave the way for public acceptance of the next new fiber to emerge from its laboratory.

To accomplish these ends the chemical companies that produce man-made fibers advertise in consumer magazines and other public media in their own names, or in conjunction with fabric or finished-product makers. They also publicize fashion products in which their fibers are involved by other means, such as educational programs that include talks to women's clubs and retail salespeople. Frequently, they arrange elaborate fashion showings with retail stores, featuring merchandise made of fabrics in which their fibers are used. The impact of their publicity and

[17]U.S. Department of Commerce, *U.S. Industrial Outlook, 1972*, p. 13, and *1973*, p. 146.

advertising gives wide exposure not only to their brand names but also to the fashions with which their fibers are associated.

Similarly, the large textile firms— sometimes on their own, and sometimes in cooperation with fiber sources—will advertise their names and/or subsidize advertisements by garment makers in consumer fashion magazines and fashion sections of newspapers. It is not unusual to see magazine advertisements for dresses, coats, and suits that feature not only the name of the garment maker or designer and the retailer but also the name of the fabric producer and the fiber source. With such financial assistance from sources of supply, a dress or coat manufacturer can advertise more widely to the public than he could hope to do on his own.

In the process of promoting their brand names, fiber and fabric sources have used promotional methods undreamed of in the days when a mill's responsibility ended with the sale of the cloth. As recently as the 1940s, it was most unusual to find any name but that of the retail store of a garment. Today, promotions of the various fiber and fabric brand names reach all the way down to the consumer in the form of garment hangtags that carry the name of the garment manufacturer, the fabric source, the fiber source, and any special finish that has been applied to the fabric.

There is keen competition, too, among the suppliers of natural fibers, and this competition also gives impetus to the flow of fabric and fashion information to the consumer. Each natural fiber—wool, cotton, linen, and silk—has an industry association that makes itself a source of information about fibers, fabrics, and fashions in general, and keeps directing the public's attention to the desirable qualities of its own fiber. Typical is the Maid of Cotton program of the cotton industry. Each year, for many years, an attractive young woman has been selected as the Maid to travel widely in a wardrobe of cotton fabrics styled by well-known designers. In the course of her travels and the attendant publicity, designers, garment producers, and the consuming public have been reminded of the practical and fashionable virtues of cotton. The effort to hold the public's attention is unremitting.

The net effect upon the consumer is that she is more conscious of brand names in fibers and fabrics, and is exposed to infinitely more advertising and articles about fabrics than ever before. The more money the fiber and fabric producers pour into making the consumer aware of their brand names and the virtues of their products, the more it pays them to study the consumer in order to understand both her preferences and her response to their efforts.

Fashion's Impact on Textiles

Until well into the 1950s, fashion was more of a word than a directing force in the production of textiles. Color, texture, and design were not dictated so much by fashion trends as by the producer's equipment for certain types of weaving, printing, or finishing. In the period of economic expansion following World War II, however, the demand for fashion strengthened at all price levels, and the public's mass appetite for the new and the different encouraged the industry to develop new fibers, new ways to vary the properties of existing fibers, and new ways to make fabrics attractive. In turn, textile innovations influenced style trends and set new fashions in motion. Today, textile and apparel styling complement one another and each acts as a spur to the other.

INCREASING IMPORTANCE OF VARIETY AND CHANGE.   Before World War I, about 80 percent of the output of the textile industry in the United States consisted of fabrics in extremely staple weaves, weights, and colors.[18] Those were the days when the blue serge suit was the uniform of the white-collar male, and the good black silk or gabardine was his lady's Sunday best. Those were the days, too, when fashion was the prerogative of the wealthy Four Hundred, who bought much of their wardrobes abroad. Women at the opposite end of the income scale had very little to spend on anything but bare necessities. The ready-to-wear industry was still in its infancy, and the few apparel producers who were in existence selected from whatever the mills offered and then sought to make attractive, acceptable styles from them. With so docile and uncreative a market, mills needed to pay little attention to variety and change in design. They produced relatively few fabrics, each of which could look forward to a fairly long if unexciting fashion life. Even the seasonal factor that shifts demand from light to heavyweight fabrics and back again was not as important as it became decades later. In that age of long underwear, multiple petticoats, and shawls, a woman did not have to change her outer garments to adjust to colder weather. She simply added layers.

During the period between and after the two world wars, the buying power of middle and lower-income families grew. Studies of the U.S. Department of Commerce, Office of Business Economics, show, for example, that from 1935 to 1939, 45.4 percent of families in the United States had annual incomes of less than $2000 a year; in 1941, only 27.9 percent had less than $2000; and by 1972, only 3.5 percent were in that low-income bracket.[19]

As the buying power of the middle class and lower-income segments of the public grew, so did the ready-to-wear industry. Fashion and seasonal changes became elements for the textile industry to reckon with. Both garment and fabric producers found that they could not afford to separate the styling of the cloth from the conception of fashion. Textile operations had to be adjusted, not only to the most economical procedures but also to the procedures that would permit quick response to the demands of both the growing garment industry and the consumer for change and a wider variety of fabric choices. Even as the increasing variety in designs, colors, and textures stimulated the sales volume of the industry, the growing importance of fashion also made its operation more complex and costly. Unlike the garment manufacturer, who can use the same sewing machine to produce many different looks, the textile producer usually undergoes considerable expense in order to respond to fashion change. The development of new fabrics may require heavy investment in new equipment or in adjustments to existing

[18]Alderfer and Michl, *op. cit., p. 329.*

[19]U.S. Department of Commerce, Bureau of the Census, Current Population Reports, Series P-60, No. 87, June, 1973, and *Statistical Abstract of the United States, 1964,* p. 338.

equipment. A further complicating factor, according to one industry observer, is uncertainty as to what styles consumers will accept and how long they will continue to accept them.

FASHION AND TECHNOLOGY.   In the 1950s and 1960s, as the textile industries became more sensitive to the dynamic influence of fashion, fiber and fabric developments came in a flood. Man-made fibers, for example, endowed fabrics in which they were used with wash-and-wear qualities, provided warmth and bulk without weight, or locked color into the fiber in such a way that fading ceased to be possible. Meanwhile special treatments were developed to impart to natural fibers qualities that some of them had previously lacked, such as wrinkle resistance, crease retention, and durable press. Soil-resistant and soil-release qualities became possible with the addition of special finishes to fabrics made of almost any fibers or combinations of fibers, thus broadening the range of colors that could be practical and fashionable for the consumer. Techniques were developed for double knitting and also for bonding two different fabrics into one.

The interaction of fashion and technological advances on one another played a major role in introducing apparel and accessories in new styles and types. For example, sheer wool did not become fashionable for dresses until mechanization of the combing process made it possible for the worsted mills to produce suitable fabrics. The fashion for sheer and seamless stockings could not develop until there was the combination of nylon yarn in fine deniers and a knitting machine that could shape hosiery adequately without seaming. The development of easy-care fabrics helped to create an important new fashion category: a new type of raincoat styled for all-purpose wear instead of for rainy days alone. Fabrics designed to resemble fur or leather made possible mass-produced garments that looked as if they were made by painstaking, handcraft methods from expensive natural materials. The flexibility and color range of vinyl-coated fabrics made it possible for women to enjoy boots of any height, in almost any color, and at almost any price. Man-made yarns, available in short fibers or continuous filaments, in smooth or nubby form, gave impetus to the styling of knit fabrics and contributed to the spectacular growth of knitted fashions.

Through such developments as these, the fabric industry is able to lay before apparel designers an immense variety of materials with which to work. Sheer or opaque, soft or stiff, smooth or napped, shiny or dull, light or heavy—almost any quality or look that fashion may require rolls off the looms of the textile industries these days.

FASHION PLANNING IN FIBERS AND YARNS.   Before the textile mills or their fabric designers can set the creative process in motion and plan new fabrics, the fiber and yarn producers must develop their own early projections of the fabric colors, textures, and constructions that will receive public acceptance at the time they appear. The fibers offered to yarn producers each season present an immense variety: rough or smooth; continuous filament or short staple; possibly lofted or puffed into irregular thickness; or perhaps with colors already locked into the fiber by means of solution dyeing. Yarn houses select the fibers they wish to work with. These fibers, separately or in combinations, are then spun and dyed to present the fabric mills with an assortment of thicknesses, textures, and colors from which to choose.

Although fiber and yarn producers are many steps (and often several years) ahead of the production and sale of apparel, they nevertheless observe fashion trends closely and gear their operations to what they think consumers will want. For example, a color stylist for a yarn company described her fashion decisions as follows:

"I can only speak for Dixie . . . and to us the very world and the times we live in are grist for our mill: current events . . . world happenings . . . vacation spots . . . museums . . . the whole world of art . . . maybe a village craftsman's rug loom . . . perhaps a jaunt to far-off lands . . . a ballet . . . an opera. Everything looked at with the colorist's eye, ever on the alert for the newest nuance of color and tonality . . . offers fresh fields for fashion and inspiration.

"But let me say that, while we are always responsive to new sources of inspiration, we also pay strict heed and mind to the historical color patterns of selling and consumer acceptance with relation to a specific product. Color changes cannot always be sudden and startling at the consumer level, and acceptance may take several seasons."[20]

The hard facts of economics and consumer acceptance, and the fascinating aspects of fashion change, demand consideration from stylists, designers, and technicians alike at every step of the way.

FABRIC DESIGN.   Apparel designers say that "fabric is the designer's creative medium, just as pigment is the painter's. A good designer responds to new fabrics . . . and searches for the quality that will make it—and her design—come alive."[21] To make possible fabrics that will evoke such response, textile producers and converters maintain staffs of fabric designers and stylists or purchase designs from independently owned textile design studios in the field.

The fabric designer's problem is to select from the welter of possibilities before him the elements or combinations in yarn, weave, finish, and color that best interpret what he believes will be wanted by the segment of the apparel industry and the consuming public that his firm serves. Since from one to two years may elapse between the time a fabric designer starts work on a line and the time that garments of the fabrics involved are offered to consumers, a successful designer must be uniquely sensitive to fashion currents for a coming season. What such a designer selects and presents is the outgrowth of his taste, experience, and training, plus his assessment of the cultural climate of the time and his knowledge of what has been selling. He also must be thoroughly familiar with the kinds of clothes in which his apparel-manufacturing customers specialize.

From the trend of current demand, and from any other available straws in the fashion wind, fabric designers and stylists estimate what is likely to be in demand in

[20]Mabel Nolan, color stylist for Dixie Yarn Co., in address before Market Forum for Textile Executives, May 20, 1960.

[21]Rosalie Kolodny, *Fashion Design for Moderns*, Fairchild Publications, Inc., New York, 1968, p. 79.

the season for which they are working. If they believe that apparel fashions will be harsh and geometric, for instance, they may plan fabrics with little drape, with plenty of bulk, and in colors that are strong and that are used in bold combinations. If they believe that apparel will be romantic and feminine, they may create fabrics that drape softly, that are smooth and sheer, and that are in soft and subtly combined colors.

The fabric stylist in his effort to achieve the effects he considers salable, also considers the technical methods by which these effects can be achieved by the mill for which he is working. If a nubby texture is desired, for example, this may be imparted to the fabric in weaving or by using yarns of irregular thickness. Colors may be introduced into the yarns before weaving, as in the case of yarn-dyed wools and solution-dyed synthetics, or the fabric may be dyed in the piece. Also, both methods may be combined for subtle or dramatic juxtapositions of color. Crispness may be imparted to a fabric by the choice of fiber, the weave, or by a finish applied after the weaving process, for instance.

Only by weighing technical and fashion factors can a fabric designer or stylist work up a line that successfully anticipates the wants of the apparel industries.

FASHION AS A PROMOTIONAL TOOL. The rise of giant fiber and textile firms has provided important new sources of fashion information and new influences on fashion. If only to guide their own complex organizations, these firms need much longer-range fashion thinking than a plant that is concerned with only one of the many steps from fiber to fabric. Also, because of the dominant positions they occupy, the decisions of these huge firms as to what fabrics are to be made available may have a good deal to do with the interpretations that current fashions will be given by apparel designers.

Fiber and fabric firms have developed considerable skill in applying their fashion knowledge—not only of current trends but also of how fashion moves—in order to promote their products. An outstanding example was offered in 1968 when du Pont introduced its new, silk-like nylon fiber: Qiana. The firm, wise in the the ways of fashion, took its fiber to France where mills can accommodate (as mills in the United States cannot) short runs of high quality fabrics. Such mills were induced to prepare limited amounts of prestige fabrics from the new fiber. These fabrics were then offered to the couture houses. At the Paris openings for fall 1968, in the blaze of publicity that accompanies such occasions, the fashion world saw its first garments of Qiana.

Fabric mills will also occasionally take the lead and work with apparel designers, retail buyers, or both, to create and promote special groups of designs. An example of this was a fashion promotion based on the "gypsy look" theme initiated by Klopman Mills, a division of Burlington Industries. Its design staff came up with fabrics and garments to illustrate the look; its industry contact representatives worked with apparel manufacturers to help exploit the gypsy concept in blouses, dresses, loungewear, and lingerie. Its retail contact representatives worked with stores to prepromote the new fashions and pave the way for their acceptance at the consumer level.[22]

[22]"The Klopman Story," *Clothes*, April 15, 1967.

In addition to stimulating sales of fabrics and apparel, the textile industry's use of fashion as a promotional tool results in many other benefits. First, it makes all related branches of the industry aware of new design ideas and thus encourages creativity all along the line, from fiber production and processing to finished garment. Second, it contributes to the awareness and interest that precede the adoption of fashion change. At the same time, it coordinates and unifies the thinking of related areas within the industry, so that they change in phase with one another and facilitate the mass production that mass demand requires.

The planning that goes into fashion promotion when it involves all stages of production, from fiber to finished garment, was once described by an executive of the Celanese Corporation of America; as follows:

"Long and patient hours, stretching into days and months and years, go into planning by such a concern as Celanese of what it expects to be popular—which weight, thickness, finish; which colors and which combinations will catch the popular fancy; and which designs will be accepted and reordered. With it all goes promotional planning, checking, surveys of stores and individual consumers, market testing, and trade advertising, long before consumer copy appears in newspapers and magazines and on television and radio. Our task is to work out new uses for fabrics. That means we must decide at least a year ahead what the trend is going to be, in terms of color, construction, and appearance. Then we take trade advertising to spread the news of what is going to be advertised and what stores will have. . . . All the steps in the selling chain—from the yarn producer to the mill, to the converter, to the cutter, to the retailer, to the consumer—were as nothing, unless the consumer is sold."[23]

SPECIALIZED FASHION STAFFS.   All of the large companies have their own fashion staffs who research and report on trends. The recommendations of these staffs guide the production of their company's various units and also provide advice for the industry's customers, the garment producing trades. So sound is the fashion research of leaders in the textile industries that apparel and accessories manufacturers look to them for advice on coming trends. Many companies have design departments and technical staffs to show their customers how best to work with their fibers or fabrics Some of these companies maintain "fashion libraries" for the convenience and use of manufacturers and retailers alike. Some also stage clinics or fashion shows for the trade at the beginning of each season to present garments made up of their new fabrics. An outstanding example is the week-long series of breakfast meetings at which the Deering-Milliken company presents musical fashion shows each season.

Some of the many activities and job titles of fashion specialists working within the textile industry are described in the following quotation from *Mademoiselle* magazine:

[23]Paul H. White, general merchandise manager, Textile Division, Celanese Corp., in "News of the Advertising and Marketing Fields," *New York Times,* November 5, 1956.

"A really first-rate stylist must rely on a good bit more than what may be her own impeccable taste. She must be thoroughly familiar with fabric firms and their customers, the manufacturers. She must know the best end uses for fabrics—this for a daytime dress, that for a man's sport shirt. What will a shopper buy if she has $10.95 to spend on a blouse? Or $39.95? What print styles, inspired by French or Italian couture, can survive a descent to mass usage?. . . .

"An experienced woman named Billy Gordon, who works for the Brewster Finishing Company, which does the printing for Loomskill Fabrics (a converting firm), will spot a trend-print with a Persian motif, say, and will feed her ideas to design studio for execution. Or she may bring a Pucci blouse back from a trip to Europe. . . . The blouse has an interesting arrangement of male figures marching through the pattern. Knowing that the average woman who buys a medium-priced blouse made of Loomskill fabric 'wouldn't be caught dead wearing men' Miss Gordon works out with the design studio artists a pattern substituting seashells for men. . . .

"The firm names of the average-sized fabric house, like Loomskill, are little known to those outside of the fashion business. But even the fashion-ignorant know the big ones—big by virtue of their connections, since they are the finishing divisions of mills that produce gray goods. Galey and Lord, for example, is a well-known converting division of Burlington Industries. J.P. Stevens is another such giant mill-fabric house. . . .

"Within such fabric houses as these, you will find, besides stylists and staff designers, a woman fashion coordinator or director. Her responsibilities are indirectly concerned with getting the fabric sold to customers: manufacturers and their designers, and buyers of piece goods. (Store buyers of apparel must also be sold, in a sense, since they often get a manufacturer to use something they like.)

"The fabric-firm coordinator, whose salary can get to fifteen thousand dollars or more, organizes fashion shows to impress clients and the influentials—buyers and the press. The coordinator is in touch with manufacturers and their designers every day, too, and makes sure in this way that she knows which manufacturer has bought what fabrics—and how he intends to use them. She can make herself invaluable to these customers by telling them, 'Don't use this stuff for swimsuits—Joe Blow's already bought it for that.' Her knowledge is helpful, also, when she works with the fabric firm's advertising managers and the outside ad agency involved in plotting the resource to be used for an ad.

" 'I case the market', says Mary Ellen Fannon, fashion coordinator of Galey and Lord,' to find a designer like Trigère . . . . whose high-quality product—using our fabric—will work into an ad. The ad's snob appeal hooks the volume market into buying our merchandise.'

"Fabric coordinators also work closely with editors on fashion magazines, showing them swatches of new materials, and keeping them posted on resources."[24]

---

[24]"Are You Cut Out for Seventh Avenue?" *Mademoiselle,* March 1962, pp. 118–119, reprinted by permission.

CHANGE OF LOCATION.   A significant indicator of fashion's impact on the textile industry and the increasingly close relationship between the cutting-up trades and the mills is to be found in the geography of the textile market in New York City. Before World War II, only the major woolen and silk textile firms had sales offices in the midtown area referred to as "Seventh Avenue" or "Garmentown"—the region of Manhattan's West Side in which most of the women's garment makers have their offices and showrooms. Most of the textile trade made its headquarters in Worth Street, much farther downtown, where the textile trade formed a community of it own, with its charities, its luncheon clubs, and its opportunities for textile men to talk textiles without special emphasis on fashion.

After World War II, when fashion's full impact hit the industry, the showrooms began moving uptown. There are still great textile names in Worth Street, but these are likely to be only particular divisions of the various complex firms that are concerned with sheets, blankets, towels, and related fabrics. The fashion fabric "greats" now have their showrooms in midtown, on the West Side, and right on the doorstep of the women's garment industries. The textile producers have, indeed, woven themselves right into the fashion world.

OTHER PRIMARY MARKETS

The textile industry is not the only primary fashion market that has had to develop speed and flexibility to meet the demands of apparel and accessories designers; nor is it the only fashion market to develop materials with attributes that were undreamed of even a decade or two earlier. Fashion's quickening pace and broadening markets also have demanded change in leather, fur, plastic materials, metals, and gems—almost anything that can somehow be incorporated into a garment or accessory.

Furs and leathers especially have undergone great changes, requiring the industries that process them to develop ways to impart suppleness, colors, and weights that would have been impossible to achieve with the techniques used a generation ago.

The Leather Industry

An essential ingredient in the processing of leather is time. In spite of mechanization, automation, and the development of new chemicals for tanning purposes, it still takes weeks to soak and dry animal pelts, subject them to chemical baths and other treatments, and transform them into flexible leather of the color, texture, and weight required for specific end uses. Moreover, considerable amounts of time are needed to purchase and transport hides and skins from their places of origin to the tanneries. Leather, after all, is a by-product of the slaughter of meat animals; if goat and kid skins, for example, are wanted, they may have to be imported from distant countries whose peoples consider the meat of these animals more of a staple element in the diet than it is in the United States.

EARLY FASHION PLANNING.   Because of the length of time required to purchase and process its raw materials, the leather industry is among the earliest in the fashion field to research and anticipate trends. Its decisions as to colors, weights, and textures are reached early and disseminated early. As trained observers of fashion signals and long-range forecasters of trends, tanners are looked to for guidance by other segments of the fashion business. Apparel and accessory leathers can be dyed in perhaps 500 colors and can be prepared in weights and textures suitable for every fashion use from sturdy walking shoes to tissue-thin gloves, from supple skirts to heavy, windbreaker jackets. When leaders in the industry have made their commitments to a season's colors and textures, they publicize the ones that they sponsor, along with the reasons why they consider them important. In this way, they often help to shape the decisions of other primary fashion industries and the decisions of apparel and accessories producers.

Fashion, however, need not wait for the leather industry if it should falter in its response to trends, or if it can produce wanted materials only in limited supply or only at prices beyond the reach of an appreciable segment of the waiting market. Usually, a leatherlike effect can be produced in fabric or plastic, in quantities and at prices geared to mass markets. Thus, a wealthy man or woman may wear a beautifully hand-crafted jacket or pair of boots, while a person of modest means may wear similar garments that have been produced quickly and economically from fabric or plastic yard goods.

U.S. PRODUCERS OF LEATHER.   The tanning and finishing industry in the United States processes annually about 24 million hides (meaning pelts of large animals, such as cattle) and 11 million skins (meaning those of small animals, such as goat, kid, and calf), in addition to about 30 million sheet and lamb skins.[25] The United States has more than enough cattle hides for its needs and therefore exports some; it imports some of its calfskins, about half of its sheep and lamb skins, nearly all of its goat and kid skins, and whatever exotic skins—such as kangaroo, ostrich, and reptile—are in demand. The value of the industry's shipments, at the factory level, is close to $1 billion a year, of which very little is exported. Imports add 13 percent to the supply for domestic use.[26]

Production takes place in approximately 500 plants, located mostly in the Northeast and North Central states. Most of these plants are integrated; some are even allied financially with meat-packing firms from whom hides and skins are obtained. Other tanneries operate on a contract basis, owning the tools of production but processing hides and skins to order for converters. The latter serve a somewhat broader function than their counterparts do in the textile industry, since they not only market the finished products but also provide the raw hides and skins from which those products are made.

[25]Tanners Council of America, Inc.
[26]U.S. Department of Commerce, *U. S. Industrial Outlook, 1973*, pp. 134–136.

Essentially the industry, which employs fewer than 30,000 people, is one of small plants. Only one in every six plants employs 100 or more persons. Even so, the industry does a good deal of research into ways to improve its methods and its products, through a research facility it sponsors at the University of Cincinnati. One of its present aims is to find ways to impart machine washability to garment leathers—not a surprising objective, now that leather has been accepted for such indoor garments as skirts, slacks, and jumpsuits.[27]

The Fur Industry

The wearing of fur as a status symbol is a custom that goes back as far as the ancient Egyptians, if not further. Present-day use of fur for prestige and fashion is seen in the parades of sable, chinchilla, unusual breeds of mink, and other expensive varieties at inaugural balls, opera openings, and other gatherings of the socially and financially elite. Generally, the price and prestige of a fur vary in accordance with its rarity and with the difficulty involved in working the pelts. Providing outward signs of status is only one aspect of the fur industry's market, however. Nowadays, the wearing of "little" furs, such as fur hats, and the fashion for "fun" furs (relatively inexpensive types for all sorts of occasions, including casual and indoor wear) has broadened the industry's market considerably and has kept it very much in the fashion eye of middle-income as well as wealthy consumers.

SIZE OF INDUSTRY.   Total activity in the fur industry is estimated to exceed $1 billion a year. About 2 million trappers and thousands of fur farms produce 20 to 30 million pelts annually, depending on demand in world fur markets.[28] The manufacture of fur garments takes place in 1300 plants, principally in the New York area, and employs about 8500 persons. Output is valued at more than $300 million a year at wholesale, or easily double that amount at retail.[29] An important share of the fur business is done in custom retail shops, of which there are over 2300, distributed throughout the country and doing about $250 million in sales annually.[30] Wide fluctuations in demand are characteristic of the fur industry, however, and its activities expand and contract along with the economy of the country.

TRAPPING AND BREEDING.   The fur industry has two sources of pelts—trappers of wild animals and breeders of ranch animals. Because scarcity is an element of value in furs, breeders (especially of mink) seek constantly to develop new strains. Ranch mink has been developed in strains that produce light and even white furs, and one of the newer mutations is Kojah, extremely dark and much like sable. To secure desirable pelts, fur traders attend auctions all over the world. The United States

[27]U.S. Department of Commerce, *U. S. Industrial Outlook, 1969*, pp. 97–100, and *U. S. Industrial Outlook, 1972*, p. 126.

[28]U.S. Department of Commerce, Business and Defense Services Administration, *Fur Facts and Figures, A Survey of the United States Fur Industry*, Revised.

[29]U.S. Department of Commerce, *Census of Manufactures*.

[30]U.S. Department of Commerce, *Census of Business, Retail Trade*.

buys furs from countries as remote as Afghanistan and the Republic of South Africa; it sells furs to Canada, Europe and Australia.

PROCESSING AND MANUFACTURE.   A great deal of handwork on the part of highly skilled craftsmen is required at every step of the way traveled by pelts as they are converted into furs and then fabricated into garments. Pelts are soaked and then expertly cleaned by the flesher's knife, which removes any vestiges of tissue attached to the hide. Some skins are dyed; some are sheared or plucked; all are treated to enhance their natural beauty and softness or to alter their appearance and texture to conform with what is in fashion. In the making of a garment, each pelt is cut by hand, sometimes into many pieces in order to provide greater suppleness and more uniform color in the finished garment. The various sections of each garment, whether factory made or custom made, are separately sewn, then nailed wet to a board to dry into shape before the garment is finally put together. The smaller the animal whose fur is used, and the smaller the pieces into which a pelt may be cut, the slower and more expensive is the operation of constructing a garment.

Furs lend themselves to a variety of treatments, and the industry is quick to adopt new ways of coloring, shearing, and sewing its materials to conform to currently fashionable looks. By the way in which pelts are handled, garments may be made to yield a long, soft line or to break at the waist as fabric would, to be fluffy or smooth. Inexpensive furs in ample supply can be made to look like those that are rare and costly so that, for fashion purposes, a moderately priced fur garment will create an appearance substantially similar to that achieved by one that is very expensive. No deception is involved in this particular form of democratizing fashion because federal law requires furs to be labeled with the English name of the animal, its country of origin, and the processing to which it has been subjected.

TRENDS THAT BROADEN DEMAND.   Several fashion trends in recent years have broadened the market for furs. One of these trends is partly the fruit of the industry's own efforts through its Fur Information and Fashion Council. By working hard to disseminate fashion information, this organization helped to launch and encourage an interest in popular-priced furs, especially among younger women or women of any age whose means do not extend to expensive, full-length coats. And women of wealth, who already have their rare minks, their sable, and their chinchilla, have a reason to make additional fur purchases of little vests, jackets, or other articles for indoor and outdoor wear.

A more recent broadening of the market has been the attraction of fur for men. Fur hats for men have been on the fashion scene intermittently for a dozen or so winters. Fur coats for men did not really become well launched as a trend until the winter of 1968 and 1969, although demand began earlier.

Thus the fur industry has broadened its market by reaching down for the young as well as the mature, the middle-income person as well as the wealthy, the casual occasion as well as the formal one, and the male as well as the female wearer.

OTHER INFLUENCES.   Several other trends influence the course of the fur business. One is the tendency of the fashion world to go overboard for an exotic fur, to the point that the animal whose pelts have suddenly become desirable is threatened with extinction, or the industry is threatened with the wrath of conservationists. This has happened with leopard, which zoomed into prominence in the 1960s and caused such indiscriminate slaughter of the species that, by 1969, the animal was scarce indeed. Similarly, revulsion has set in against the use of certain types of seal, for which trappers kill very young pups.

Another influence on the fur business is the development of furlike fabrics of man-made fibers. Although these "fake furs" are below the price levels in which fur is normally used, and thus do not compete with fur garments, their presence tends to push the cycle of demand for a particular look more rapidly toward its decline than might otherwise be the case.

RELATIONSHIP TO APPAREL AND ACCESSORIES

The demand stimulated by fashion has influenced the primary markets to improve their technology and broaden the range of their products. Conversely, the availability of new materials and the greater variety of colors, weights, textures, and qualities have made it possible for apparel and accessories designers to foster new fashions and move existing ones along to their culminations at an even faster pace. The relationship is a reciprocal one. Without the materials, producers could not create styles to stimulate consumer demand; without that demand, the primary markets would have much less incentive than they now enjoy to continue to improve the materials that they provide.

READINGS

The problems, developments, and opportunities of the producer of materials for the fashion industries are discussed in the readings that follow. Although the subject is the textile industry in each case, the points made apply with almost equal force to every other industry serving producers of apparel and accessories. The pros and cons of bigness and the minimizing of the fashion gamble in designing and marketing are everyone's problems in fashion production.

BURLINGTON INDUSTRIES:
A Total World of Textiles

Twenty years ago the concept of one firm encompassing all areas of textile merchandising was as remote as the idea of one garment manufacturer servicing all consumers with his products. The textile world of that time was as fragmented as the customers it served and in many cases more so because of the complexity of the job. There were spinners and rovers and weavers and finishers. There were thousands of small mills spread throughout the southeastern United States while others still tried to till the harsh ground of New England in order to make a living.

Cotton and rayon were located basically in the south while woolens, worsteds and domestics were largely in the north. Tied in with all this activity, although not a part of the mill organization, were the thousands of converters located in New York and elsewhere who bought the greige goods from the mills and then fashioned it into the colors and prints that would titillate the American consumer.

The mills were on Worth Street in downtown Manhattan—their customers were uptown. But the gulf separating the two areas of the fashion business was more than a matter of street blocks—it was a mentality.

The mills of America had a long and difficult history behind them which seemed to indicate that only during war and early post-war years could they operate profitably and that in the intervening time the belt had to be pulled in and the risks kept to a minimum. They could smile tolerantly at their uptown neighbors with their frenetic activity and continual optimism. It was nice to talk about fashion and certainly Dior's New Look with its extra yardage had proven to be as much of a boon to the mills as to the manufacturers. But the important thing was to keep the looms rolling at capacity

SOURCE: *Clothes* Magazine, June 15, 1968. Reprint permission granted.

without creating a glut on the market which could depress prices.

THE PICNIC WAS OVER

And 20 years ago that glut was creeping all over the textile market—marking the fact that the halcyon days of the World War II era were over and the dog-eat-dog days were back.

But if this was the general state of mind in the textile industry at that period it was by no means universal. There were a few men who had the vision to see that the America of the late forties was beginning to shape up quite differently than that of previous decades. They also felt that the textile industry could only blossom if and when it became master of its total destiny—which meant not only spinning and weaving the greige goods but also finishing it, dyeing it and selling it to the cutter.

To a conservative industry which liked to pride itself on the fact that it was the oldest of all major American industries, the idea of one mill taking on all the functions of several mills and finishing plants would have been out and out heresy. For by doing this, one mill would in effect assume all the risks inherent in the business and become totally vulnerable to the vagaries of feast and famine which were considered a law of the textile business.

Of all those heretics who attempted to do the impossible, one man was to stand out far and away above all others in his desire to expand. For not only was he dreaming in terms of integrated mill operations within the framework of a particular fiber, he was just as anxious to expand into all fibers and finally into all areas of textiles—whether for the garment trade or for the home . . . whether for the consumer or for the trade.

One by one this man, J. Spencer Love, would lead his firm from rayon greige goods into cottons, woolens and worsteds, then into nylon and other synthetic blends, and finally into fiberglas. In a period of only 17 years he would make Burlington Mills, an $80 million producer of rayon greige goods, into a billion dollar complex with 35 autonomous divisions producing every conceivable kind of fabric for any end use.

By the time of his sudden death in January 1962, Love had already proved to his peers in the industry that by accepting the risk and burden of total responsibility for the finished cloth, textile manufacturing could be as profitable as any other major industry and that it didn't require a war to keep the looms operating at full capacity. In his last year in office, Burlington Industries' net profit was 4 per cent. The legacy he had left to his successors was considerable.

NEXT INTERNAL EXPANSION

While Love had laid the groundwork and helped create a successful textile empire, the new president and current chairman of the board, Charles F. Myers, Jr. was to take Burlington Industries on a course of internal rather than external expansion in order to obtain growth.

Early this year, in order to further strengthen its management team, it elevated Myers to chairman of the board and appointed Ely Calloway, formerly executive vice-president, to the presidency. Calloway, who has a strong background in merchandising and who launched the men's wear division of Deering Milliken years ago, is expected even more to further the Burlington concept of marketing textiles instead of just selling them.

Burlington in the last five years spent almost a half billion dollars on new equipment and the renovation of existing plants. It set up its own research center from which all the divisions could profit through scientific advancement in the textile industry. It was one of the leaders in opting for the Mali method of producing fabric by setting up a separate division with its own president rather than entrusting it as a sideline to another division.

Its Klopman division early this year opened the first American textile plant in the common market with complete spinning, weaving and finishing operations that would sell blends of Dacron and cotton not only in Italy, where the plant is located, but throughout western Europe. Finally, Burlington embarked on a major television advertising program to implant in the mind of the consumer the idea that there was a Burlington Industries whose products were used daily by all people in all walks of life. Next year Burlington will open its own building in New York in which all of its divisions will be quartered.

How does Burlington operate today? Burlington is 34 autonomous divisions, each of which is headed by its own president, who is also the marketing man. It is the president's job to plan the sales and profit increases for his division on a semi-annual basis over a five year period. Every six months the corporate executive committee, a nine-man team composed of the chairman of the board, the president and executive vice-presidents, reviews the six month results. It is the executive committee, of course, which controls the purse strings and decides how much money can be allotted to each division in the light of its sales projections.

In other words, corporate Burlington operates like most major corporations in the United States in that it allots both money and autonomy to its division heads. But most important of all, by placing the final decision in the hands of a merchandiser in the north rather than with the head of manufacturing in the south, Burlington had embarked upon what could be termed a marketing program—a true rarity in the textile business. In other words it was no longer the southern mill that made the decision as to what it could weave economically and then place the responsibility in the hands of the salesmen stationed in the north. Instead the north investigated potential markets for its products before it met with the heads of manufacturing to decide what fibers could best produce the desired products and how to adjust the costing of the production in order to obtain the largest potential market.

If this method seems a perfectly logical way to conduct one's business it is good to bear in mind that while few other mills operate on this basis, neither do the majority of retailers and manufacturers. Like the majority of mills, merchants and cutters buy what is available, manufacture it, advertise it—and then hope to sell it. There is rarely a question of what audience the particular product is for—the trade just follows the path of least resistance.

Thus if twills are coming into the forefront of men's wear as the new fashion weave, every mill will have twills and the winners will be those with the best price, reputation for delivery and quality, and color card.

But some of the Burlington divisions operate quite differently. Take Galey & Lord. Years ago it used to make up a $35 fabric for a top couturier and sell him about 5,000 yards for $2.75 a yard. This was obviously no way to get rich. But the following year the mill would take the fabric to Seventh Avenue as a "designer" fabric and sell it till the cows came home. That is marketing.

Or take the case of Klopman, which has done the most outstanding job of marketing in the industry. Klopman's retail marketing group works in conjunction with the mill and the sales force. This marketing group, which is continually touring the major stores of the country, will plant the idea for a new fabric in the minds of key merchandisers throughout the country long before the first garment has been manufactured. As a matter of fact, Klopman manufactures its own garments in an effort to show the industry possible applications for a new cloth.

Thus, long before the garment manufacturers' representatives take to the road with actual garments made from the new fabric, it has been partially pre-sold to key retailers either through direct contact or trade advertising. Naturally, not all promotions turn out to be smash successes. But the important thing for Klopman is that it has established itself as the only mill in America which is interested in helping to stimulate new fashions for the retailer.

As for what marketing generally means today to Burlington it can perhaps best be explained by the fundamental change that has taken place in the fashion market itself.

Up until the beginning of the sixties, the word, fashion, was more of a word . . . a mass dream . . . than an actual property of the garment. To further explain this one should separate clothes that are bought out of need from clothes that are bought for fun.

FASHION FOR EVERYONE

Until the mass affluence of today's society, fashion—or clothes for fun—was merely for a small minority of the population. Yes, the consumer of those days might have made a choice as to color or fabric—but the garment was still being purchased out of necessity and not out of frivolity.

But with the arrival of a mass affluent society one sees millions of people buying apparel for the mere fun of it. This changes all the ground rules of merchandising—particularly when the bulk of this audience is under 30 and has never known anything but prosperity.

And right in the middle of this fashion revolution was neither the manufacturer, retailer nor fiber producer but rather the conservative of the conservatives—the American mill. For the mills control three fourths of the elements which go into fashion—color, texture and pattern. Only the silhouette and trimmings are left in the hands of the designer and manufacturer.

And the market for fashion and its changes was not in the Carolinas or in Georgia or Alabama but in New York where the presidents of the 34 divisions of Burlington make their headquarters and plan their marketing strategies.

With the men's and women's garment industry vying with one another to come up with goodies that would stimulate the prosperous American male or female to buy, a mill had to be in on the ground floor in order to sense the changes and to know when to cut back. In addition, the mill, which has always had the most difficult manufacturing function of any American industry—it goes from a raw fiber to the dyed and finished piece goods—also had to face the problem of coming up with new ideas in fashion which could be exploited by the manufacturers.

The days of the looms running almost forever on the same construction in the same fiber had been brought to a close. Furthermore, there were now such a multiplicity of synthetic fibers on the market, along with durable press and soil-release that mills not only had to keep up with fashion but also with the new technology.

Obviously, the role of the marketing man had become paramount in the successful merchandising of fabrics. But there was another equally important factor in the successful operation of a mill—diversification—where one division might be in the fashion limelight while the other could be suffering from the doldrums or a change in consumer taste. And to successfully survive under these new fashion conditions nobody was as well prepared as Burlington Industries with its 34 divisions covering every facet of the apparel and home furnishings market.

In a sense Burlington was the precursor to what is now happening with garment center manufacturers and retailers as they hedge on their basic operations by adding new divisions which are capable of picking up any slack that takes place in the old ones.

This is Burlington! Marketing oriented through having the north control the south; geared to the new techniques in production by plowing a half billion dollars back into plant, machinery and expansion, and sufficiently diversified as an across-the-board textile producer to weather any sudden drop in one category of apparel or home furnishings. On the surface these three attributes would seem sufficient to account for Burlington being Number One among all other mills. And yet there is another reason, perhaps a little more subtle, which explains the unusual success story of this complex of mills. And that reason can best be termed a devotion to synthetics.

A PIONEER IN RAYON

When Spencer Love was to launch Burlington in 1923 it was not as another producer of cotton goods but as a manufacturer of rayon greige goods. At that time rayon was a novelty—it did not as yet have the proper hand and most of all it was something strange. And in the mill business anything strange both repels and attracts. And yet Love was to stick with rayon—bet his future on this synthetic fiber and finally reap the rewards of his judgment.

But in betting on rayon, Love was doing more than merely stacking his chips on a new blue chip fiber. Love was staking his future on the new technology and from there on in he would continue to place his bets on what came out of the test tube.

Thus Burlington, unlike any other major mill, was attuned to the new synthetics, made its living from them, and was not married in its pre-war history to either cotton or wool. As a matter of fact so synthetic-minded was Love that when he bought Galey & Lord in the mid-forties he wanted to convert the famous Cramerton plant to the manufacture of synthetics rather than cotton and

only the stubborness of William G. Lord prevented that.

Today, of course, Burlington is not only the largest user of synthetics but also the major user of raw cotton and wool. But it was the basic admiration for synthetics and the fact that Burlington was always ready to plunge in first that was, in large part, responsible for its top-dog position in the textile industry.

STILL SPLINTERED

What is the textile industry today? Despite the plaints of so many people that there are only a few mills left, the truth of the matter is that the ten top mills only account for about 25 per cent of the total textile production in this country or about $5 billion. The remaining business is still divided up among a myriad of small mills in their own way similar to the small manufacturers which people the garment center.

Despite the fact that literally thousands of mills have disappeared from the textile scene, the number that still remains in business is considerable. A good many of these cater to specific markets and so, for the time, seem invulnerable to penetration by the larger combines. But each year the percentage of the market owned by the big 10 increases as they alone are capable of making the capital investment in equipment and of marketing their wares long before they come to market.

How do the various divisions of Burlington decide on what piece goods to offer the market for the next season? To do this most effectively, the company maintains a market research organization which is continually probing the consumer's needs and wants in apparel and home furnishings. But while this offers a guide-line for the future, the day-to-day problems are resolved either through improvements in technology or by assessing last year's sales along with what the avant-garde is showing. Out of these findings selections are made which are then presented to volume customers such as the mass merchandisers and to fashion customers such as the exclusive stores and manufacturers of America.

Thus, in a sense, Burlington acts in the same fashion as its customers—it is testing reaction. And, on the basis of these reactions it is able to project its mill needs for the next six months or about three months before the retail market makes its commitments in men's wear or women's wear.

But almost as important in the decision to market new fabrics are the giant fiber companies which are not only introducing new blends and types of blends but are in their own way attempting to market fashions for the retailer and manufacturer. By working closely with the mills they have brought a degree of sophistication to the fabric business that never existed before.

FASHION BEGINS AT THE MILL

To the retailer, removed as he is from the company of fabric houses, all of these marketing plans, all of these efforts to prognosticate the future may seem to be straws in the wind ready to be blown astray by that lady called fashion. And yet, in truth, it is the efforts of the mills and fiber companies to come up with new fashions that have helped the fashion-apparel trades to continually forge with the new and the novel.

Burlington, of course, has been one of the prime movers in this direction of unfathoming the unfathomable of fashion.

But Burlington has done more than that. As the largest producer of carpeting, draperies, and sheets and pillow-cases it has helped to set the pace for the home furnishings market. Moreover, what it learns in the fashion market can be quickly applied to home furnishings. Nor has the North Carolina firm restricted itself solely to fabrics for the home. A few years ago it bought the Globe Furniture Co. and is now selling Burlington furniture as well as sheets, hosiery, socks and carpeting directly to the retailer.

It dominates the men's worsted suiting field with its Pacific and Raeford mills and takes a strong position in woolens with its Cleveland Woolens plant.

Its Burlington Men's Wear division is unusually strong in the synthetic blend field for men's and boys' suits and slacks. Its Klopman Mills is the number one producer of Dacron/cotton in the country and its Galey & Lord company has the reputation for producing the finest combed cotton and blended fabrics.

It is a tremendous factor in the men's and women's hosiery field and is also actively engaged in the tricot business and in the industrial fabrics field.

MAINLY IN APPAREL

Its total dollar volume is divided into 70 per cent for the apparel markets, 25 per cent for home furnishings and 5 per cent for industrial use. It also does a large overseas business of almost $100 million.

How good is Burlington and what are the projections for the future? Over the past 10 years its percentage of the total business of the textile industry has risen from 5.8 per cent in 1959 to an estimated 7.7 per cent in 1968. In profits, it does about 12.6 per cent of the industry's total of $750 million.

Does Burlington dominate the textile business today? Not really. While in many areas it has outstripped its competition both technologically and in fashion, Burlington's key customers are no more ready to depend totally on one division of Burlington as a sole source than a retailer wants to be dependent on a single manufacturer. And the key customers of Burlington are big—far bigger than the mill itself—in other words, the mail order chains and the mass merchandisers who, themselves, would not entrust their destinies to one source.

But Burlington is more than a top dog among textile mills. It is also a big business—a very big business—and like all big business it is looking for new horizons.

The purchase of any additional mills in America seems unlikely for Burlington just now because its total share of the market to date would seem to prohibit any additions at this time. So in all likelihood any future growth must come from either outside the United States or from industries within which Burlington is presently not doing business.

Already, Burlington is making use of its vast computer set-up to sell time on its computer machines to outside organizations. Last year it went into an arrangement with the Scott Paper Co. for the development of new processes in the handling of paper. And only last week it made a joint investment for the manufacture of jet airplanes.

CONGLOMERATE

From jets to paper to computers to a rayon greige goods mill—is Burlington truly becoming a conglomerate? There is no answer. At the present time it believes that every new field outside of textiles that it moves into is indirectly related to its own parent business and therefore the skills already in practice can be applied to it. It, like all other major organizations, believes its strength is in its management team and that these men can contribute to the growth of any new firms that may be acquired.

In other words Burlington, as conceived and built by Spencer Love and continued by his successors, is just a growing young child. It has to be fed a constant diet of new business in order to grow bigger and stronger but not all diets are available to it. Most of the growth will come from what it does itself but every now and then it is going to reach out for something new to give the growing organism new strength, and when it does there will always be a reason why. *Oh reason not the need.* . . . Who needs the reason? The important thing is—success—and at the moment Burlington Industries has plenty of that.

THE DURABLE THREADS OF J. P. STEVENS

Richard J. Whalen

In the whole history of United States business there has never been anything quite like Stevens. Its uniqueness goes beyond being the world's oldest diversified textile company. Over the century and a half, the management of the firm has passed from father to son in a direct line (even the du Ponts had to rely on an occasional son-in-law) from the founder, Captain Nathaniel Stevens, who began it all by weaving woolen broadcloth in a converted gristmill in North Andover, Massachusetts. Among some one hundred families who started woolen mills in the United States in the years 1800 to 1815, the Stevenses are the sole survivors.

Last year the company's 1,200,000 spindles and nearly 30,000 looms poured out more than 800 million linear yards of fabric, which almost defy

classification by end use. A billowing ocean of cloth, this output included luxurious woolens (at $6 a yard), lightweight cotton muslins (at 17-1/4 cents a yard), sheer dress fabrics of 65 per cent Dacron and 35 per cent cotton, fiberglass to be laminated and machined into missile nose cones and other components, snowy damask tablecloths and flower-bedecked printed sheets and a synthetic fabric for tents that will be pitched on the roof of the world this year, if the American climbers conquer Mount Everest. Also, Stevens sold 150 million yards of fabric for outside mills.

Handling nearly a billion yards of goods implies unusual size and scope in an industry commonly described as "fragmented" among some 5500 small companies. Stevens is big. In eight states from Maine to Georgia, the company employs some 35,000 workers in fifty-five plants. (The word "mill" is passing out of fashion among modern textile men.) With record sales of $586 million in fiscal 1962, the company boosted volume 18 per cent over 1961. Stevens is the second-largest textile company in the United States (and the world),

SOURCE: Excerpted and reprinted with permission from *Fortune*, April 1963. Copyright 1963, Time, Inc. J. P Stevens & Company is one of America's oldest and most respected textile firms as well as the second largest fabric organization in the country.

surpassed only by Burlington Industries, which last year became the first billion-dollar textile company. With a diversified base dating from before and immediately after World War II, Stevens has been on the leading edge of a glacial trend toward ever larger textile entities: there were fourteen $100-million textile companies in 1962, compared to ten a decade earlier. Large companies like Stevens, by transforming themselves, are gradually transforming the industry.

THE USES OF DIVERSITY

Stevens has propelled itself light-years away from the one-mill, one-fiber textile business because it meant to stay in the game. The old business of supplying staple goods to huge markets was production-obsessed; the new business lives by merchandising. "We're continually fitting equipment to fabric," says Harry Carter, a vice president of the synthetics division. "It's not the business it was ten years ago, when we ran crepes for five years in one mill. Now it's a style and merchandising business." Eighty-four Stevens selling departments in the New York City headquarters tailor the mills' output to the specialized wants of hundreds of distinct markets. An enormous 73 per cent of Stevens' production goes into the volatile apparel trade, which rips apart the familiar pattern every season.

A newcomer might lose his head (not to say his business) in the swings. In 1961 and 1962, Stevens' cotton and synthetics divisions each provided about two-fifths of the company's total volume, and the woolen and worsted division the remaining one-fifth. But consider the relative profitability of fibers in those years: in 1961 the cotton division was the leading money-maker contributing 44 per cent of company profits, followed by synthetics (29 per cent) and woolens (27 per cent). In 1962, however, synthetics, especially spun rayons and blends of natural and man-made fibers, made a strong comeback, and the synthetics division contributed 47 per cent of company profits. Meanwhile, the cotton and woolen divisions tailed off, contributing 32 per cent and 21 per cent of profits, respectively. The ups and downs from year to year, even quarter to quarter, are extreme. Since

1950, for example, the synthetics division has made as much as 75 cents of each dollar of company profit in a year—and as little as 18 cents. Despite the swing, 1962 was a good year for Stevens: the company's volume of $586 million produced a net income of $16 million.

Quiet, mild-mannered Chairman Stevens, the former Secretary of the Army under Eisenhower who did battle with the late Senator McCarthy before a television audience of millions, is frankly sentimental about the company founded by his great-grandfather. He is unsentimental about how his company spins a profit. "We go to the marketplace and attempt to find out what the public wants. If the public wants straw, we'll weave straw. We're not wedded to any particular product or fiber."

That philosophy has an oddly radical ring in an industry still composed largely of "cotton men," "wool men," and the like. Indeed, so deep is the attachment to a fiber (and so difficult the adjustment to new ones) that a Stevens executive, lecturing not long ago at Manhattan's Fashion Institute of Technology, was hissed by "silk men" in the audience after what they took to be a slur against their true love. But Nathaniel Stevens was nothing if not adaptable, and he would approve the trait in his heirs and their company.

THE BRIDE COULD WAIT

Nathaniel Stevens, known familiarly as "Captain Nat" in recognition of his rank in the Massachusetts militia, was typical of the early Yankee entrepreneurs. One of fourteen children of a farmer who fought the British at Concord and Lexington, Nathaniel shipped out at twenty-one on a merchant vessel, returned to clerk in a general store, and showed a talent for trading. War with Great Britain in 1812 decided young Nathaniel on his career. With the westward push of population, United States markets for cloth were expanding, and imports would be cut off for the duration. Borrowing money from his father, Nathaniel, with two friends as partners, took over the gristmill and converted it to woolens. Family lore provides an illustration of his diligence. On his wedding day, in 1815, while his bride-to-be waited at the church,

Captain Nat was discovered in his mill, absorbed in dyeing a piece of cloth.

Postwar resumption of imports drove many infant mills out of business and posed an early test of Captain Nat's flexibility. He converted from broadcloth to flannels, a daring diversification: up to then no one had successfully produced flannel in the United States. Captain Nat succeeded, and reinvested the profits. However, a Boston importer, Abbot Lawrence, advised Captain Nat to "shut down your mill and save what you have, for we can bring goods in here and sell them for less than it costs you to manufacture them." Unconvinced, Captain Nat chose instead to whip the invader.

He parted company with one partner and bought out the other to become sole proprietor, served a term in the Massachusetts legislature, and sired nine children. He kept on improving the mill. The Panic of 1837 hit New England hard and every mill closed down for a spell, except the one at North Andover, which kept running and was even expanded as Captain Nat took advantage of the scare to steal a march on the competition. He drove himself and his help through a six-day, seventy-six-hour week, for which he paid above-average wages: $4.50 a week, plus board of $2.

One of his sons, Moses Tyler, became a partner in 1850; his help was needed. For the Stevenses soon acquired a mill in Haverhill, Massachusetts, and became the first family owning more than one flannel mill. Sons were a blessing in the growing business. Captain Nat sent a second son, George, to Haverhill, summoning a third, Horace, from his studies at Harvard to assist Moses at North Andover. When the Civil War broke out, the mills worked overtime, under flickering whale-oil lamps, to supply the Union Army with blankets.

Captain Nat died a month before Lee's surrender, and Moses was his natural successor among the three sons who had become partners. Like their resourceful father, they were willing to experiment. They bought a bale of cotton and proceeded to whip up a blended fabric, an indigo-dyed mixture of 60 per cent wool and 40 per cent cotton. The blend sold well, and the Stevenses were in a position to ride out the collapse of the postwar boom in 1873. They acquired two mills. The deaths of Horace and George left Moses alone but, once again, there

was a son on hand. On the day the name of the firm was changed—from Nathaniel Stevens & Sons to M. T. Stevens—another Nathaniel Stevens, son of Moses, quit school and went to work for his father.

A SALESMAN IN THE FAMILY

However, one young Stevens, John P., the son of Horace, did *not* enter the family business, at least not in the usual way. Instead, he went (at a salary of $150 a year) into the commission house that handled the goods from the Stevens mills. He learned to sell and to sniff out a poor credit risk. A blood tie with a commission house being thus established, expansion from manufacturing into merchandising soon seemed an obvious move, so the family created its own selling house. On August 1, 1899, J. P. Stevens & Company, with capital of $25,000 and twenty-one employees, opened its doors on Thomas Street in lower Manhattan's textile district. True to the time-honored script, the day before it opened John P. had occasion to wire cousin Nathaniel in North Andover, announcing the arrival of a "new office boy," later christened Robert Ten Broeck.

While the selling house was gaining its feet, the mill company prospered. Like his father, Moses admitted his three sons to partnership early, and served in the state legislature and Congress, where he was pointed out as the largest individual woolen manufacturer in the country. But the Stevenses were also reaching out for cotton. John P. crisscrossed the rapidly developing South, lining up cotton mills for the selling house and investing in likely ones. When Moses died, in 1907, after sixty-four years in the business, the family already had laid the foundation of diversification.

By World War I, J. P. Stevens & Company from its New York office was selling the output of nine cotton mills and was doing the bulk of its business in that fiber. The usual bust after the war boom found the Stevenses shopping as usual; they acquired five mills. Experiments with the new-fangled synthetic, rayon, were begun in the Twenties. John P.'s son Robert served an apprenticeship in the mills, and got a start in his father's firm selling the handkerchief trade. He assumed command in the selling house when J. P. died two days before the crash in 1929. Over the next decade Bob and his older brother, John P. Jr., hustled the house to a volume of better than $100 million.

As a result of acquisitions and investments, the Stevens textile interests sprawled in all directions. The explosive expansion of World War II, and a death in the family, produced a crisis. Moses' son Nathaniel, "Mr. Nat," who had run the mill company since 1907, died in 1946 at the age of eighty-eight. His estate needed to sell stock to settle with the tax collector. The selling house, which now dwarfed the family's mill operations, needed access to the capital markets to continue growing. Everything pointed to the wisdom and necessity of going public.

In September 1946, after months of negotiations, a merger was arranged, uniting the Stevens selling house and mill company with eight other companies. J. P. Stevens & Company, Inc., with Bob Stevens as chairman and J. P. Stevens Jr. as president, was listed on the New York Stock Exchange, the ninth-oldest company on the big board. Within two years the family sold 375,000 shares. Going public brought only a passing twinge. "I think the change was a good thing," reflects Chairman Stevens. "The discipline of public ownership is a stimulus to management to do a better job. We wouldn't retrace our steps."

While J. P. Stevens was about rebuilding, it built a different kind of business, integrating such operations as finishing, which had formerly been done by outsiders. A cotton-finishing plant at Wallace, South Carolina, built in 1950, has been automated and expanded to five times its original size. In synthetics, Stevens used to sell its entire output of tricot as gray goods; now it finishes most of its tricot, and has seen sales grow from $10 million to $30 million. Vertical integration is profitable, but mainly it shortens the channel of trade between manufacturing a yard of goods and the final sale at the retail counter. This long channel, in which goods pass through the hands of the converter, the jobber, the cutter, the wholesaler, and other specialists, has been the grave of many a primary producer. For the message signaling the turn of the retail market from one product to another travels slowly along this complex network, usually not reaching the manufacturer until he is buried in unwanted inventory.

Stevens wants to control its goods through as many processes as are profitable, with the aim of getting closer to the consumer.

FASHION IS A FORM OF DIVORCE

Whatever Captain Nat might think of computers, he would doubtless applaud, and marvel at, his great-grandson's attention to style and fashion. With almost three-fourths of its yardage going into apparel markets, J. P. Stevens is goaded by the generally accepted estimate that half of the apparel fabrics in use in 1970 will be constructions now unknown. The firm employs 140 stylists. Some of their ideas are exuberant—e.g., the decision a few years ago to splash bright colors through the lingerie line. ("Fashion is the desire to change," says a stylist. "For a woman, it's a mild form of divorcing her husband.") Other style ideas are coldly practical, such as the application of a relatively underpriced fiber to an emerging trend. "We caught the market unaware on the development of mohair fabrics in the fashion cycle of luxury and style," says a Stevens man. "We bought mohair near the beginning of a rise from $1.50 to $2 a pound, and had a good thing going for a year and a half."

In today's textile markets, size, once it is under skilled management control, tends to attract sizable customers. In 1952, Stevens had about fifty million-dollar-plus accounts. Last year it had twice as many, and the ninety-nine largest among its 17,000 customers accounted for 40 per cent of Stevens' total volume. Large retailers, apparel manufacturers, and other customers, witnessing wholesale liquidation of primary textile producers, have given new weight to the continuity of supply offered by a large company, and relatively less to the lower price sometimes offered by a small company that may go under. The trend toward lean inventories in U.S. industry also favors the larger, more efficient supplier. Stevens' transportation fleet of 450 units, with headquarters at Greensboro, can make delivery to warehouses on the West Coast within seventy-two hours. In Kenosha, Wisconsin, American Motors operates on a three-day supply of auto carpets, depending on Stevens to deliver every fourth day. The interaction of large customers and large producers is an important force affecting the structure of the textile industry. Bigness breeds bigness.

Still, the more things change at Stevens, the more they remain the same, in at least one respect. When John P. Stevens Jr. retired a year ago, he turned the chairmanship over to brother Bob. But the role he had loved best was being chief woolen and worsted merchant for the company. Both John and Bob were particularly careful about filling that vacancy. Now selling a tough line in a tough business is thirty-six-year-old Whitney Stevens, one of Bob's four sons. And in the generation right behind are more sons, whose job it may be to stretch the durable Stevens threads from North Andover around the world.

MERGE NO MORE

Many a textile company has sought to ape Burlington and grow and diversify via mergers. Now the FTC has put up a roadblock on Acquisition Street.

For years textile companies have been urged to profit by the example of Burlington Industries, which merged its way to diversified, big-company status during the Fifties and early Sixties and so has been able to afford modern management and marketing techniques. Only thus, the thinking went, could small and middle-sized textile companies survive in an industry pressured by huge chemical fiber producers on one side and sharp-bargaining apparel-industry customers on the other.

But now it will be almost impossible for middle-sized textile firms to take the Burlington route. The Federal Trade Commission has laid down new merger guidelines for the industry that really are tough. The reason: Although textiles—with some 7,000 individual companies—is hardly the most concentrated of U.S. industries, "it was tending in the direction of concentration," says William Boyd, head of the mergers division of FTC.

The guidelines detail what kind of mergers the FTC will "examine" in the future—a polite way of saying what type of mergers the commission would feel called upon to investigate and bring antitrust complaints against.

SOURCE: *Forbes* magazine, Feb. 1, 1969. Reprinted by permission.

Mergers involving textile firms where the combined sales or assets would exceed $300 million lead the proscribed list. Also given the gimlet eye will be mergers within a textile market that increases market share to over 5% or acquisitions of suppliers or customers that result in a concentration of over 10% in any market.

In the last two years, FTC has issued similar guidelines, and followed up with action, in the cement, food distribution and grocery products manufacturing industries. Textile companies have only to look at FTC's five actions in recent years to prevent consolidations of cement producers with ready-mix concrete makers to see their fate.

TOP COMPANIES HIT

The $300-million limitation effectively stops the long-standing acquisition programs of such industry notables as J.P. Stevens, West Point-Pepperell, M. Lowenstein & Sons, Indian Head Inc., Cannon Mills, Cone Mills, Dan River Mills, and United Merchants & Manufacturers, all of which are at or over that sales volume. Springs Mills, Fieldcrest Mills and Collins & Aikman, now around $200 million each, cannot look to grow much by acquisitions.

The merger route has been especially appealing in the $20-billion textile industry because it is awash with small, family-owned firms turning out a single product line. The needs of emerging public companies for diversification into multiple product lines meshed nicely with the frequent desire of family firms to sell out for stock and avoid estate taxes.

Now the FTC is putting a crimp in this cozy situation. But, ironically, Burlington is not affected, because at the time the guidelines came out Burlington cleared up a legal contest of long standing over its 1962 acquisition of Erwin Mills by signing a consent decree with FTC. Burlington cannot make any domestic acquisitions in the textile industry for the next ten years. This doesn't bother Burlington. The company's last textile acquisition was in 1962. It has lately been expanding its horizons to other countries and other fields. One such new field is the fragmented furniture industry, where it has made one acquisition and has another in the works.

CONSENT DECREES LIKELY

Of course, guidelines are not law and FTC will still have to bring actions on each individual case. Since the resources of federal antitrust agencies become strained very quickly by lengthy court actions, the FTC probably will seek consent decrees like the one Burlington agreed to. However, a future prospect of consent decrees still puts a halt to the merger movement in textiles.

The industry, therefore, will have to devise ways to live with the guidelines. The FTC has said nothing about textile companies merging outside their own industry, and that, perhaps, will be the way the smarter ones eventually will go. After all, that again would simply be following Burlington Industries' example.

A FABRIC DESIGNER'S PHILOSOPHY

Pola Stout

The credo on which I was nurtured was beautifully expressed by an old friend in Vienna, who said, "The artist must learn only one thing in order to be creative—not resist himself, but to resist without exception, everything else that prevents him from being himself." More and more often during the past year I have been asked: "Is design fabrics an art? If you call designing an art, how do you define art?" To me art is perfectly defined when you say that it is intuition plus hard work. It is largely a matter of original concepts; no amount of training and education—necessary though they are—can

SOURCE: Excerpted and reprinted with author's permission from presentations at the Workshops of Color and Design of Textiles for Apparel, College of Household Arts and Sciences, Texas Woman's University (July 20-25, 1959; July 11-16, 1960, July 17-22, 1961). Pola Stout is particularly noted for her designs for woven fabrics.

substitute for the spontaneous expression of individuality of the creative worker. . . .

Another way to state an important aspect of my philosophy is to say that I never give up the search for *quality* in *quantity* production. My feeling about this is even stronger than it was at the time I designed the Botany Perennials. More than ever at this period of history, fashion cuts across all lines of economic status, and is gradually becoming part of the heritage of the whole world. . . .

CREATIVE DESIGNING VERSUS STYLING

The *designer* starts from scratch, evolving new concepts out of her own creative ability and experience. To be sure, it can be said that there is nothing new under the sun, but there are new ways and genuinely creative ways of reexpressing basic esthetic principles. The designer might be said to be an artist; the stylist an artisan. *Styling* might be said to be the fashion equivalent of editing in the literary field. The good stylist has a grounding in the history of art, the principles of design, and a knowledge of fibers and construction, so that she can "edit" fabrics, that is, change proportions, colors, checks, stripes, weights, etc., in adapting a design. But she starts with a fabric already completed by one or another designer. . . .

When people ask me how I design, I have to say that I approach design analytically and logically. I have to develop my ideas on a logical basis—but I also trust in intuition (which really can be defined as logic that operates more quickly.) As time goes on, one's work acquires greater and greater technical proficiency, and the creative person is liberated for a far greater range of creation when he has technical knowledge in his fingertips. . . .

It is also essential that the fabric designer be thoroughly familiar with the kind of clothes with which the apparel designer is identified, and then the designer of fabrics must search for the colors and weights and textures that would be most appropriate in styling these specific garments. The designer needs to have a solid understanding of the commercial side of her job; to have a general love for creative expression in textiles; to study merchandising problems; to constantly experiment with original design and to constantly strive for newer and clearer solutions to the problems

that exist in the manufacturing field. The textile designer needs to develop fundamental ideals and principles to stand up for those principles. And in order to achieve competence in self-expression, she must have a basic knowledge of the graphic arts. She must learn to be flexible, to adapt herself to economic and production necessities without permitting her designs to suffer as a result of changes, when changes are necessary. She must be a craftsman—that is, a patient, disciplined, concentrated worker in the field she has chosen because she loves it. She must have a sixth sense about the needs and tastes of living people—not only in terms of fashion, but in terms of the problems of the individual. She should take time to familiarize herself thoroughly with the intricacies of various styles—in a world-wide range, since this is in truth one world. . . .

It is regrettable but true that the consumer, by and large, is completely unaware of the contribution to the finished garment that has been made by the designer of fabrics. Consumers may be familiar with certain trade names attached to fabrics, such as Forstmann, Hockanum, Stroock and so forth; some may have heard of the late European fabric designer, Paul Rodier—but this is the exception that proves the rule. Actually, whether the consumer knows it or not, her acceptance or rejection of the designer's concepts is a decisive factor in gauging the public taste; and I believe it would be desirable to educate the public in the understanding of the designs and what has inspired the designer's concepts. . . .

THE FIBER PRODUCER IN MARKETING:
Activating The Consumer Market

There has been a good deal of murmuring on the mill and converter levels of the textile industry recently about the dominant role now played by the man-made fiber producer in the whole textile continuum. It begins to sound as though mill management feels a little sheepish about having —by its own inactivity—left much of the textile research and development function to the fiber producer. There is talk of mill and converter reasserting their creative roles, not only in the area of styling but also in advertising and promotion.

So much the better! No one—least of all the fiber producer—would quarrel with this. Such a development could only be a healthy one for the textile industry as a whole, provided the mill and the converter are able and willing to tackle the job in all its vast ramifications. Actually this is already taking place, for as mills grow larger and more diversified in their functions they are inevitably assuming greater responsibility for research and promotion activities.

But in the light of this seeming dissatisfaction, it is instructive to re-examine the role of the man-made fiber producer, to assess the contributions he has made to the total well-being of the textile industry, and to see with some perspective why he has taken on the broad functions he now performs in the design, production and marketing of fabrics and often of end products.

It was, after all, a logical development. When man-made fibers first came on the scene, few knew how to process them. The fiber producer was understandably faced with the task of teaching and guiding spinner, weaver, knitter, finisher and garment maker. Yet that, in itself, was not enough, for the textile producer could not at that time be

depended on to give the new man-made fibers the right kind of introduction. He had little understanding of modern marketing methods. With few exceptions he was unaccustomed to spending large sums of money for advertising and promotion. And as for research, that was the name of a guessing game in which he often found out he had made the wrong product only after it didn't sell.

The grower of cotton, wool and silk was not then in the marketing picture at all. His traditional role was to sell his raw material and depart from the scene. He did not consider it his responsibility to reach either the maker of garments or the consumer. Marketing, advertising and promotion as we know them today were beyond his ken.

But the man-made fiber producer was a different breed of cat. His offices were staffed with bright young men trained in business administration. The laissez-faire world of their fathers was not for them. They had been taught to plan, to think ahead, to chart the graph and plot the curve. They saw the possibility of replacing chaos with order and they leaped into the breach.

They were reaching for a planned and expanding economy in textiles.

And it was a possible objective, for one of the major distinctions between the natural and the man-made fibers was—and continues to be—the fact that production of man-mades can be controlled to meet demand. However, this very advantage brought another factor into the picture. In order to be able to plan production, the man-made fiber producers were faced with the need to create a demand for their new products. They had to inform and educate, as well as to research and develop. And they had the money to do the job. They literally launched a revolution in textile advertising which had never previously been more than minimal. The advertising and promotion power they thus unleashed has made

SOURCE: *American Fabrics* magazine, No. 74, Winter-Spring, 1967. Reprint permission granted.

the American consumer more aware of textiles, more knowledgeable about function and performance, than any consumer before in history.

It is not too much to say that the man-made fiber producers have brought the whole textile industry up to a new level of professionalism. They have given it the excitement of new ideas. They have the perspective and the money to work on new concepts in both technology and fashion without being pressed for immediate returns on research dollars invested. They can send their fashion scouts around the world to bring back fresh ideas which are made available to mill, converter and manufacturer. And they can then build a market for these new ideas through the power of their trade and consumer advertising. No small mill or converter could hope to finance a program of this scale.

What converter or mill or garment maker in the past, for example, would have contracted for a full collection of original designs by almost every leading name in the Paris haute couture and then presented this collection in a full-scale fashion show? A fiber company did this! And other fiber companies mount equally impressive promotions which are giving the whole textile-apparel community a cachet it never before enjoyed. Their power and their financial resources put even the small textile and apparel producer in a position to compete with the giants in his field in terms of world design trends, technology, directions in fashion and color.

The textile producer and the garment maker are not the the only ones who have been stimulated and stretched by this multi-faceted activity of the man-made fiber producer. The growers of natural fibers have also been influenced. The necessity to compete with the man-mades has forced both the cotton and wool groups into a new evaluation of their role in the total textile picture. They have been impelled to extend their function, to move out to reach the consumer through both improved technology and marketing.

The result has been a thorough revolution in the structure and function of the textile industry, the creation of a fully inter-connected progression from production to sales. Its objective is to reach and satisfy the needs of the ultimate consumer and thus to achieve a planned and expanding economy for textiles.

CAN WE TAKE THE GAMBLE OUT OF FASHION?

Maybe! The Big Mills May Do it Through Coordination.

A new and significant program has been launched at the management levels of our big textile mills.

It is an attempt to coordinate the fabric production of many separate divisions for a total fashion look in color, pattern, texture and construction.

The objective is to take the gamble out of fashion through pre-planning. Such attempts have been

SOURCE: *American Fabrics Magazine,* No. 82, Spring 1969. Reprint permission granted.

made before, notably by the fiber producers, but this current development is qualitatively different because it carries authority. It represents not simply a suggestion for fashion coordination but a powerful commitment by diversified producers who have seen the need and mean to fulfill it.

Symptomatic of the trend are the programs now underway at Burlington Industries and J. P. Stevens & Co.

The Stevens program takes the form of a "Fashion Workshop." In effect this is a seasonal school for fashion which gives Stevens customers overall guidance in their fashion planning. A typical Workshop session covers:

1. The latest fashion trends from European and American couture.
2. Color trends from the world fashion capitals.
3. Fashion directions in pattern and construction.
4. Coordinated groupings of fabrics made by many different Stevens divisions each of which has interpreted these advance fabric/fashion trends for the American market.

The Burlington program is called "Programmed Fashion" and is devoted entirely to menswear. Burlington's corporate management has coordinated the products of 12 different menswear divisions in an unusual presentation geared to trendsetting developments on the men's fashion scene. The presentation takes the form of a "fashion theatre" in which color slides, live models, manikins and fabric swatches are brought together through a witty and informative taped commentary by the ubiquitous Robert Green of Playboy. The format of the show is designed for viewing by limited numbers of Burlington customers on demand.

These two programs, we suspect, are the precursors of many more to come. They answer two pressing needs:

1. As the textile mill grows bigger and more diversified it tends to lose personal touch with its customers. Its image as a concerned supplier becomes submerged in the spread of its many divisions, some of them competing with each other. The coordination program is therefore a step on the road to humanizing the giant anonymous corporation.
2. The textile giant has now become supplier to manufacturing and retailing giants. All three must plan far in advance of the consumer selling season. They are therefore all gambling on their ability to anticipate fashion trends. But if such trends can be pre-planned on all three levels, if they can in some measure be controlled then the gamble is reduced. That is a major goal of these coordination programs.

Such programs are still very much in the trial stage. They are difficult to bring off with authority and style. And the effort involved is very great. But the Burlington and Stevens programs show it can be done. If they succeed, this will become a persuasive demonstration of our long-held conviction that the textile producer can be both big and interesting at the same time.

FORWARD LOOKING MARKETING TECHNIQUES AT THE FIBER, MILL, AND MANUFACTURING LEVELS

Louis F. Laun

The steps a fiber must go through from our machinery to the ultimate consumer are many, any

SOURCE: Talk by Louis F. Laun, President, Celanese Fibers Marketing Company, given to a special textile seminar at the Fashion Institute of Technology on November 17, 1969. Reprint permission given.

one of these steps has problems, and any one of these steps can be its last step.

I count 17 inventory steps alone in getting a pound of filament Fortrel into a double-knit dress worn by a consumer. Let me list them:

1. Fiber in our warehouse.
2. Warehouse of throwster.

3. In process at throwster.
4. Finished textured yarn of throwster.
5. Textured yarn in knitter's stock.
6. In process at knitter.
7. Greige knit fabric at knitter.
8. Greige knit fabric at finisher.
9. In process at finisher.
10. From finisher to finished fabric seller.
11. Finished fabric seller.
12. Finished fabric at garment manufacturer.
13. In process at garment manufacturer.
14. Finished garment at garment manufacturer.
We'll forget jobbers and wholesalers.
15. Finished garment at retailer.
16. Your closet inventory.
17. In use.

The fiber marketing job is not done if we get it satisfactorily through only 5 or 15 of these steps because until we have a satisfied consumer, and I accent the word "satisfied," we have not marketed our fiber. We have simply moved it into another inventory step on the way to the consumer, and the cost of death goes up at each inventory step.

At Celanese, (and I regret that there is no way I can make a speech about the techniques of fiber marketing without talking about my own company quite a lot) we call our concept of marketing "Total Marketing" and we describe it as follows:

Develop a product line that meets a consumer or intermediate customer need. Then make sure that all the forces that can impede the progress of that product toward the end are neutralized and the forces that can help its progress are stimulated. In other words, assist the mills, finishers, converters, manufacturers and retailers at every stage in creating and manufacturing products that are desirable to the consumer and then help to merchandise and sell these products through the textile distribution system to retailers and from retailers to consumers.

This requires us to exercise three broad areas of textile expertise: fashion, technology, and merchandising. The people in these three general areas must work closely together on a day-to-day basis to accomplish the objective: to increase the profitable sales of our Fortrel polyester, Arnel

triacetate, Celanese acetate, and Celanese nylon, each of which is wrapped in a different package of marketing strategies, requires different handling, and covers many different end uses.

The best way that I think there is to explain this interplay of fashion, technical knowledge, and merchandising is to start with our relationship with the consumer and then work our way back so you can see how this total marketing concept helps everyone using our fibers to get functional fashion into the consumers' hands.

The consumer—at least today's shopper—first looks at a product because it appeals to her aesthetically. Then, if the price is right, she takes a second look to see if she can determine if its good looks will last awhile, and how to take care of it.

This is where our hangtags or labels come in. The consumer learns to depend on some trademarks more than others—just as she depends on some stores more than others. That's where our total marketing story begins and ends: with the consumer and our fiber brands. Because even before technology could create the right fiber, yarn, fabrics, and finishes for that garment, Celanese people had to be at work to determine what kinds of fashions and performance characteristics would be desired by consumers.

Fashion experts in women's wear, men's wear, and home furnishings work two years ahead of the time a fabric comes out. Our stylists tour the world fashion centers looking for fabrics in the making. They talk to designers, decorators, editors, manufacturers, and experts from all areas of the international fashion field. Designers' collections are expertly critiqued. Our stylists try to spot a couture look that seems to be finding its way into more and more collections. They measure and analyze any indication of change because we have to be on the spot when changes begin if we are to be ready to benefit by them. At the same time we are analyzing consumer attitudes, their desires, and their changing tastes and preferences. Through consumer panels in market research surveys and through our consumer relations staff who are in touch with more than 20,000 consumer opinion leaders, we're learning what fashion changes are more important than others and what performance characteristics are becoming desirable.

So from one team of experts we may perhaps learn that a soft flowing look for women's dresses is becoming important and that a particular style of prints and a depth of color will be desired. And from the other team of experts we learn that we had better design fabrics that do not wrinkle or snag, that can be machine washed and that can be more easily handled on home sewing equipment. Then our technical people review the new styling and fabric performance ideas with the fashion and consumer relations staff. These white-coated people have the job of determining what fibers, fabric constructions, new shades, and dyeing and finishing techniques will be appropriate to achieve specific fashion looks and performance characteristics.

Together, this diverse team must determine what fibers will apply; whether they should be in combination with other fibers or used alone; whether the fabric should be bright, dull, coarse, stiff, or soft; what new characteristics will have to be engineered into what fiber; or what new finish can be developed to produce the desired qualities and effects.

This is all accomplished at our fibers technical center in Charlotte, South Carolina, one of the industry's largest centers dedicated entirely to the development of fibers and fabrics. This is the focal point of our worldwide research and development network. Fibers and yarns for every one of of our existing or potential markets—from lingerie to cigarette filters to tire cord—are developed here. And it contains a microcosm of the textile industry. Every operation—from fiber and yarn processing, to weaving, knitting, and the new non-woven techniques, to dyeing, printing, and finishing fabrics—all are operating in our fibers technical center as part of the fiber and fabric development effort.

When a new fiber variation is produced, whether its objective is to add a new fabric styling characteristic or provide an improvement to the knitting, weaving, or finishing process, it moves into the Celanese simulated mill. The new variation goes through all fabric processing steps to see what further improvements are required. Close to 1,000 new home furnishings and apparel fabrics are produced at the fibers technical center each year

to help meet fashion and fabric trends and consumer and industry needs.

Now the fiber is ready to start on the 17-step journey I talked about earlier.

At this point, account representatives take the new fiber and fabric developments to the spinners, throwsters, mills and converters. They are not only taking new products with them, they are taking along an entire package of new ideas that will supplement the development efforts of our direct customers. This is where that idea of service with sales comes in. Because we have been working up these ideas under duplicate mill conditions, we have eliminated most of the problems ahead of time and can now help our customers develop their own programs faster and more efficiently. We cannot afford to have our new ideas die on a plant's machinery for want of technical know-how.

We also keep them abreast of new equipment and new techniques in the industry, anything to help our customers save time and manpower in their own effort to stay ahead of upcoming fashion or technical developments.

Of course, next to helping create new products for our customers, the most important service is to make sure there is somebody out there that will buy these new products once they are produced. That is the real test for all the creative effort up to this point. Will the new fabrics complement the designers' new styles? At this point the fashion season for which the new fabric ideas are intended is still about six months to a year away and designers are making their first sketches of the new lines.

Our stylists present the fabric swatches to the designers. In many cases, they are returning to the very source where the new ideas first germinated. Designers select the fabric styles most important to their lines, find out what mills and converters are producing them, and begin manufacturing their products. Each year, hundreds of fabrics first made at our fiber technical center become commercial reality for scores of mills and converters.

We then present a broad cross section of designer collections using the new fabric concepts in fashion shows to help mills, manufacturers, and retailers in their search for the most popular looks for the forthcoming season.

As the new fabrics move into commercial production, the Celanese licensed trademark program swings into action. This is where our fiber brands suddenly become visible. Until now, they have been a hidden umbrella under which all our fashion and technical services have been working. Our fibers are not sold as Fortrel or Arnel. They are shipped as polyester from fiber industries or triacetate from Celanese Fibers Company. With licensed trademarks, converters and Celanese sign licensing agreements granting the use of a fiber trademark only when samples of the licensee's fabrics pass specific Celanese tests for their intended end use. This assures all users of our fibers—from mills and converters to manufacturers, retailers, and consumers—that the quality and performance of the fabric meet the consumer's needs. Celanese tests samples from many millions of yarns of finished fabric every month, using a range of some 40 tests designed to evaluate end-use performance requirements. These tests may run the gamut from back staining to tear strength, from pilling to light and wash fastness. Many of these tests were created by us. But we also recognize that fabric performance cannot be evaluated through laboratory tests alone. So we have hundreds of people wearing, washing, sleeping on, and walking on products containing our fibers, putting them through their normal paces to duplicate normal stress and strains of day-to-day wear.

Through our licensing program, we maintain a complete record of fabrics, even including the economic factors that affect its success in the market. The major licensing agreements require submission of samples for testing from every lot, batch, or 5000 yards, throughout the production life of the fabric.

Now and then—as with any test—a failure crops up, that's when our customer service goes into action again. Armed with the same package of technical know-how that was developed when we first created many of the fabrics, our customer service staff helps spinners, throwsters, knitters, weavers, dyers, printers, and finishers to correct whatever problem that particular fabric has. As fabrics continue to meet the performance levels, tags and labels are distributed to the manufacturers buying the fabrics. Hundreds of millions of tags and labels may be distributed in one year alone.

This is an enormously important part of total marketing. Today's world demands innovation; we spend countless hours satisfying the fashion explosion we are living in. But the consumer is no longer willing to let us experiment on her while we are doing the innovating. If our innovations are at the expense of quality, we are innovating ourselves right into government controls.

But our job of total marketing does not stop here. We must continually stimulate demand for the products containing our branded fibers. To do this, we help the manufacturers sell their new lines to the nation's retailers and the retailers to consumers through a continous flow of advertising and publicity on television and radio, and in magazines and newspapers. Our fabric libraries, at our New York headquarters and in field offices, are visited constantly by apparel designers, home fashion decorators, and retail buyers that want to see samples of all the most recently developed commercial products in our fibers. And, as our home furnishing counterpart of the apparel fashion show, we have created Celanese House—an historical New York brownstone open each day for customers and consumers to see new products and home decorating ideas brought to life in our fibers.

Then we work directly with retailers to create customized programs and sales promotion activities to meet the sales needs of department stores, specialty shops, and chains. All the fabric development and merchandising efforts that began up to two years before this moment only pay off if the consumer comes into the stores, buys the products, *and keeps them.* So we continue our efforts by helping retailers to present special traffic-building promotions, by helping them train sales personnel and by the constant stream of advertising and publicity I mentioned before.

Fiber producers have contributed new techniques to consumer advertising of apparel and home furnishings. Newspapers once were the only advertising medium for retailers. Fiber producers have made it possible for them to now participate in television—too expensive until now because of the high cost of producing quality commercials. TV specials, both network and syndicated, have been used to carry fiber producers' brand messages to the consumer. And now fiber brands are being featured in local spot TV commercials produced in a retailer's own image: a message tailored to attract consumers into a specific store. We are also helping retailers gain greater local advertising impact through the use of metropolitan issues of major consumer magazines.

We also do our share in helping the shopper recognize quality and to select her purchases wisely. The performance assurance story behind our licensed trademarks is the central theme of our consumer education program. Those same 20,000 consumer opinion leaders who help keep us informed about the consumers' needs, are also using our educational material and our guest speakers to help inform the consumers about the quality assurance behind our licensed fiber trademarks. Home economics teachers, extension agents, consumer officials of government, political agency representatives, and legislative leaders in the consumer movement are all contacted regularly through our educational materials or directly by our consumer relations staff—to be assisted in their own efforts to be informed and to inform others about new textile developments.

And, throughout the year, our representatives are constantly reinforcing the flow of information throughout the textile industry by communicating the many new ideas and developments as they occur.

All the way back and forth within the textile distribution network—with mills and converters, dyers and finishers, end-product manufacturers, retailers, and the consumer—the total marketing service is at work—helping to create the supply to meet the consumer's needs, helping to stimulate the consumer's desire for the products, and providing fiber brands that carry more and more selling power as the consumer's satisfactory experience with them continues to grow. And the times are with us. The consumer movement is well under way. Demands for quality are becoming more vocal and more powerful every day, and this favors good brands—not cheap merchandise from unknown sources. Frankly, I am glad to see it happening. It is an added plus for our fiber brands. What marketer does not recognize the selling advantage of satisfied consumers?

What is the main, new technique I have been talking about here? Really, it is total concern for the opportunities and pitfalls that occur at every level in the marketing chain and the willingness to "get involved," not to say it is the other fellow's problem. We will have new fibers and we will have hundreds and thousands of new fiber variations, but none are worth anything unless they are properly marketed to satisfied consumers. "Oversell" is dated, and only stupid or frightened companies do it today. Innovation and satisfaction are the key words.

FIFTY LANDMARK YEARS FOR FABRICS

1910–1920

The United States already had flourishing mass production mills (whose styling ideas were European) but much fabric and 90 percent of all dyes were imported, mostly from Germany. National textile unions versus existing craft and company unions came into being, did away with child labor, improved wages.

When World War I that started in Europe in 1914 embroiled U.S.A. in 1917 and 1918, development of a national dye industry began. Silk hosiery then was $3.65 per pair for service types plus tax. Today nylon hose runs 99c to $1.95.

Vol. 1 No. 1 WWD quoted cotton gray goods 64x64 at 4c and 39-inch 68x72 (returned to popularity today as a base for wash-wear finished goods) at 5-3/4c. It was news that American Printing Co. (now vanished) had reduced prints from 6c to 5-1/2c.

During 1910 the first rayon fiber mill was started in Marcus Hook, Pa., a beginning of a new era in fabrics that did not ripen until the late twenties when mills learned to concoct the popular crepes of the period and dye them properly. It was not until the thirties that the cheaper prices of rayon and acetate goods gave rayon mills a boom period during what was depression time for all other textile markets.

1920–1930

Historically "mad." Soaring stock market after brief depression in 1921 and 1924. Sharp changes in women's fashions, behavior, and lives.

The Flapper, shingled heads, the Charleston, boyish form, dieting, waistlines dropped to the hips, knee-length skirts, corsets abandoned, (leading to a big flurry in rubber reducers in the mid-twenties), sports for women, more women in business, demands for sports, and career girl clothes.

Big spurt in ready-to-wear and fabrics that would "cut," beginning of the eclipse of the private dressmaker. But Macy's carried French handmade and ready-to-wear at less than $50. Stenographers wore "from Paris hats" or a $15 Fortnum & Mason British cloche.

There were crazes . . . sunbathing, tennis, golf, nightclub life, cruises in the winter, all with special fabric requirements. Every European and Asian fabric-producing nation had branches in New York. American firms expanded to meet the demand for silks, Kaska (invented by French Rodier), white flannels, plushy coatings topped by long-haired furs that framed shingled heads concealed by cloches.

Rayon and acetate trade was plodding, came up with transparent velvet, later crepe, and Schiaparelli serpentine crepe.

Some of the crazes that made special fabric demands were not only crepes, prints, and embroideries, but "King Tut" motifs (following the discovery of King Tutankhamen's tomb in Egypt).

Rodier's discovery of the United States Southwest Indian art which he translated into cottons, woolens, and silks, and Vionnet's bias cuts that made a fashion for "balance" crepes.

Loads of beads, spangles, and Chanel-inspired costume jewelry came into being, influenced the fabrics styled for fashion trades, built a demand for glittering metal brocades (now having a renascence). Poiret's introduction of effete harem pants were the forerunners of the shorts, beach pajamas, and playsuits of the thirties, "Rosie the Riveter" garb and jump suits in war-time forties, skin-fitting "crazy" pants, suburbanite dungarees, and the bifurcated skirts for street wear introduced by American designer, Norell, for this fall.

SOURCE: Reprinted by permission of Women's Wear Daily, July 13, 1960. Copyright 1960, Fairchild Publications, Inc.

1930-1940

Financially depressed years all over the world. Stock market crashes in 1929 and 1930, failures of banks and insurance companies, declines in tourist business and cruises, apple sellers on corners in cities, bread lines, soup kitchens, overproduction of unpurchasable edibles . . . importers folded and many mills faded. The National Recovery Act began to operate to stem the unnecessary devastation in a growing country.

It was opportunity time for the rayon and acetate fabricators. With a lot to gain (from investments in previous decades), fiber companies such as Du Pont, Celanese, American Viscose, and Eastman floated mills and converters who would play. Silk had gyrated in price so much that mills were afraid of it.

When everyone buckled down to work, some of the prettiest, most becoming clothes in years succeeded the short straight lines of the twenties—floor-length evening dresses, coordinated sheers and heavy fabrics, revivals of matelasses, satins, taffetas, and laces, all contributing to the growth of rayons and acetates. Toward the end of the decade, war had begun in Europe and the first sensational nylon hosiery and lace had been introduced.

1940-1950

World War II removed France as a fashion source, removed silk and nylon from civilian uses, imposed restrictions on uses of cottons and woolens, on lengths and widths of skirts, cuts of sleeves and the composition of play clothes. As women moved into war work, pants became the daily uniform and sequin-trimmed rayon afternoon dresses the thing for the relaxed hours and the business girl.

Preoccupied with producing fabrics for the services and war uses, mills reduced their civilian output to a minimum number of quick weaving fabrics made of rayons and acetates. Cottons became so scarce that many retail stores closed down counters where cotton yardage, sheets, pillowcases, and towels had been sold. This went on for two years after the war ended while world-wide needs for American cottons were being served.

During this period with a war-depleted staff, *Women's Wear Daily* followed and interpreted all the many government regulations on fabric uses and pricing, and the rationing of goods into the most needed channels.

Meanwhile, the cotton industry had become aware of the threat of highly washable nylon and pushed war-built research departments into intensified efforts to develop the wash-wear cottons that have become basic in sales.

1950-1960

A ten-year period of mergers, big fabric firms growing bigger, diversifying into metals, plastics, chemicals. The shift of mill locations from North to South intensified, Government control of cotton and wool, establishment of a minimum wage law, appearance of strong, machine-washable rayons, Federal Trade Commission recognition of acetates as separate from rayons, legislation barring flammable fabrics, a wealth of new trademarked fibers, and a sharp rise in imports marked the years.

There are now sixteen separate generic classes of man-made fibers, including stretch, rubber, glass, and metal types, fibers with new molecular structures, expensive fibers, cheap fibers, processes that protect against flame, mildew, moths, stain and water spotting, germs. Finishes that make fabrics crush-resistant and wash-wear and whiter-than-white are taken for granted, so are fast colors.

Big mills' research departments are headed toward more improvements in a big way. Coming are wash-wear woolens, and possibly silks.

Techniques in handling yarns to make pleasant textures advanced notably in the fifties. Stretch yarns, for example, have given rise to a new type of ski-pants cloth, a market for half-leotards, and new lightweight corsetry. Fluffed-up man-made fibers invaded the sweater field, and compete strongly with woven woolen goods.

Meanwhile, mills have gone "on steam" in buildings, machinery, and merchandising, reaching through all manufacturing and retailing levels.

During the last five years controversies between textile producers and government have sharpened. Japan is on a self-imposed quota of cotton goods and cotton articles to export to the United

States. The whole wool-supplying world tries to get in on the quota of goods that may be imported into United States at a low rate of duty. Makers of velveteen and silks are vocal about foreign competition and cotton goods manufacturers (although Japan has been curbed) are complaining about rises in exports by Hong Kong and India, both countries that have such low-cost production that the higher-geared American economy cannot hope to compete with it, as is. However, they are already taking steps in cost cutting through more efficient machinery, development of perfection in quality for the masses, on-time deliveries, and creation of goods and merchandising especially suited to the American public—all things in which foreign countries lag more or less.

BIBLIOGRAPHY

Alderfer, E. B. and H. E. Michl. "The Textile Industries," *Economics of American History*, 3rd ed. New York, McGraw-Hill and Co., 1957.

Allen, Edw. L. "The Cotton Textile Industry," *Economics of American Manufacturing*. New York, Henry Holt, 1952.

Barnhardt, Robert. *Opportunities in the Textile Industry*. New York, Universal Publishers, 1966.

Clarke, Leslie J. *The Craftsman in Textiles*. New York, Praeger, 1968.

Collier, Ann M. *A Handbook of Textiles*. New York, Pergamon Press, 1970.

Cone, Sidney M. *Aim for a Job in the Textile Industry*. New York, Richards Rosen, 1969.

Cox, Reavis. *The Marketing of Textiles*. The Textile Foundation, Washington, D.C., 1938.

Dutton, Wm. Sherman. *DuPont: One Hundred and Forty Years*. New York, Chas. Scribner Sons, 1949.

Fuchs, Victor R. *The Economics of the Fur Industry*. New York, Columbia University Press, 1957.

Glover, John George and William Cornell. *The Development of American Industries*. New York, Prentice-Hall, 1955.

Hammond, J. L. *The Rise of Modern Industry*. New York, Harper and Row, 1969.

Howell, L. D. *The American Textile Industry*. Economic Research Report No. 58, Department of Agriculture, 1964.

Kopycinski, Joseph V. *Textile Industry: Information Sources*. Detroit, Gale Research, 1964.

Landsberg, Hans H., Leonard Fischmann, and Joseph L. Fisher. "Clothing and Textiles," *Resources in America's Future*. Baltimore, John Hopkins Press, 1963.

Little, Arthur D. "The Textile Industry," *Patterns and Problems of Technical Innovation in American Industry*. National Science Foundation, September 1963.

Long, Richard. *The Textile and Apparel Industries: A View through the Inter-Industry Tables*. Federal Reserve Bank of Atlanta, May 1966.

Robson, R. *The Man-Made Fibers Industry*. London, Macmillan, 1958.

Ruhm, Herman D. *Marketing Textiles*. New York, Fairchild Publications, 1970.

Seidel, Leon E. *Applied Textile Marketing*. Atlanta, Ga., W. R. C. Smith Publishing Co., 1971.

Sinclair, John L. *The Production, Marketing and Consumption of Cotton*. New York, Praeger, 1968.

Walton, Frank. *Tomahawks to Textiles: The Fabulous Story of Worth Street*. New York, Appleton-Century-Crofts, 1953.

Walton, Perry. *The Story of Textiles*. Boston, John S. Lawrence, 1912.

Ware, Caroline F. *The Early New England Cotton Manufacture*. New York, Johnson Reprint Corporation, 1966.

Weiss, Leonard W. "Competitive Manufacturing Textiles," *Economics and American Industry*. New York, Wiley, 1961.

TRADE PUBLICATIONS

American Fabrics, 24 East 38th St., New York, N.Y. 10016.
America's Textile Reporter, 211 East 43rd St., New York, N.Y. 10017.
Daily News Record, 7 East 12th St., New York, N.Y. 10013
Fur Age Weekly, 127 West 30th St., New York, N.Y. 10001
Knitted Outerwear Times, 51 Madison Ave., New York, N.Y. 10010
Modern Textiles, 303 Fifth Ave., New York, N.Y. 10016
Textile Industries, 1760 Peachtree Rd., Atlanta, Ga. 30309

TRADE ASSOCIATIONS

American Textile Manufacturers Institute, 1501 Johnston Building, Charlotte, N.C. 28202
American Printed Fabrics Council, 909 3rd Ave., New York, N.Y. 10022
Cotton, Incorporated, 350 Fifth Ave., New York, N.Y. 10001
Fur Information and Fashion Council, 101 West 30th St., New York, N.Y. 10001
International Silk Association USA, 185 Madison Ave., New York, N.Y. 10016
Irish Linen Guild, 36 West 40th St., New York, N.Y. 10018
National Cotton Council, 1918 Parkway, Memphis, Tenn.
Tanners' Council, 411 Fifth Ave., New York, N.Y. 10016
Textile Fabrics Association, 373 Park Ave. South, New York, N.Y. 10016
Textile Distributors Association, 1040 Avenue of the Americas, New York, N.Y. 10018
Wool Bureau Inc., 386 Lexington Ave., New York, N.Y. 10017

SECTION REVIEW AND ACTIVITIES

FASHION BUSINESS TERMINOLOGY

Define, identify, or briefly explain the following:
  Primary market
  Converter
  Brand name
  Burlington Industries
  Needle trades
  Samuel Slater
  Worth Street

QUESTIONS FOR REVIEW

1. What is the major function of the textile industry in the business of fashion?
2. What social and economic events in U.S. history influenced the development of the domestic textile industry? Explain when, how, and why. What current factors, if any, are affecting the industry?
3. Burlington Industries and J. P. Stevens are examples of vertically integrated textile firms. What does this mean? Do vertically integrated firms have an advantage? Why?
4. What is the function of a converter?
5. Find the names of three "giant" textile firms that are listed on the New York Stock Exchange. What does this listing mean in terms of ownership? What is the current price of their stocks?
6. Are fabric "names" or brands important to customers when they buy clothing? Why? How many fabric brands can you name and by what textile firms are they promoted?
7. In what products, other than wearing apparel and accessories, do fabrics play a "fashion role?" Cite specific examples.
8. From current apparel advertisements, cite or show examples of "tie-ins" by textile producers, apparel producers, and retail stores.
9. If you were employed as a "fashion specialist" in a fabric or leather firm, how could you contribute to its success?
10. Why is the leather industry among the earliest to research and anticipate fashion trends?
11. Do you believe that the consumer's acceptance or rejection of a designer's concepts should be the decisive factor that Pola Stout claims it is? (See the

reading, "A Fabric Designer's Philosophy.") Considering that professional designers may be better qualified to judge good design than the average customer, do you think that this is fair to designers? Why?

APPLICATIONS WITH EXAMPLES

1. Discuss the statement, "Fabric is the (apparel) designer's creative medium, just as pigment is the painter's." Cite or show examples of apparel and/or fabrics that prove your discussion points.

2. Discuss the ways and means used by textile producers to "take the gamble out of fashion."

3. The reading, "Fifty Landmark Years for Fabrics," suggests that apparel styles and fabric developments influence one another. Research current fabric developments and suggest or show how they might influence future apparel fashions.

IF YOU DON'T
COME IN
SUNDAY
DON'T COME
IN MONDAY.

THE
MANAGEMENT

SECTION 3
WOMEN'S APPAREL AND ACCESSORIES -U.S.A.

Although the idea of ready-to-wear did not originate in the United States, this country has brought mass production of fashionable clothing to its highest development and leads the world in the quality, quantity, and variety of its output. The apparel industry is relatively young in the industrial history of America, but its growth has been rapid. A little more than a century ago there were fewer than 100 manufacturers of women's wear, and their combined output amounted to a scant two and a quarter million dollars worth of cloaks and mantillas.[1] Today, the production of fashionable ready-to-wear garments for women in all walks of life is the function of a multibillion dollar industry—dynamic, mechanized, and ferociously competitive. Known by many names—such as the apparel industry, the garment trades, the cutting-up trades, the needle trades, the "rag" business, and even characterized as the "Wild West of United States industrial society,"[2]—the production of women's apparel is a sizable force in our nation's economy.

This section deals with the development, operation, and economics of the women's branch of the American apparel industry, and the related industries that produce fashion accessories. The selected readings give the reader a deeper insight into the unique nature of one of this country's major industries.

ECONOMIC IMPORTANCE

Whatever yardstick is used to measure the size and scope of the apparel business, its importance becomes clear. In terms of the amount of money American consumers spend each year for their personal wants, clothing, jewelry and other accessories for both sexes account for more than 10 percent of the total dollar outlay. For women's and children's clothing and accessories alone, exclusive of footwear, consumer expenditures in 1972 were over $34 billion.[3]

In terms of the value of factory output, the industry also ranks high. Using 1972 as a yardstick year, factory shipments of major items of apparel for women and children exceeded $10 billion.[4] By way of comparison, the entire tobacco industry's shipments in that same year were $6.2 billion.[5]

Employment in the major divisions of the women's and children's garment trade was above 600,000 in 1972, or more than 3 percent of all manufacturing employment.[6] The apparel industry as a whole (men's, women's and children's wear combined) employs 1.3 million people in its factories, or 7 percent of total manufacturing employees.[7] Numbers alone, however, do not tell the full story of

[1]"Fifty Years of Women's Fashion Industries," *Women's Wear Daily*, August 28, 1950, p. 2.
[2]S. Freedgood, "$100 Million in Rags," *Fortune*, May 1963, p. 151.
[3]U.S. Department of Commerce, annual estimates of personal consumption expenditures by type of product, and authors' estimates.
[4]Research Department, ILGWU, *Conditions in the Women's Garment Industry*, February, 1973.
[5]U.S. Department of Commerce, *Survey of Current Business*, April 1973, p. S–5.
[6]Research Department, ILGWU, *op. cit.*
[7]U.S. Department of Commerce, *Survey of Current Business*, April 1973, p. S–13.

Dollar Volume of Shipments of Women's and Children's Garments and Unit Production of Selected Categories of Women's and Misses' Garments, 1966–1972 (all figures in millions)

| | | | UNIT PRODUCTION | | | | | | |
PERIOD	COATS	SUITS	DRESSES, UNIT-PRICES	DRESSES, DOZEN-PRICED	BLOUSES	SKIRTS	SWEATERS[a]	SLIPS AND PETTICOATS	TOTAL DOLLAR VOLUME
1966	27.7	10.7	202.8	112.1	223.3	131.1	144.5	150.8	$8,667
1967	26.0	10.0	207.0	118.3	192.8	115.8	135.0	151.2	8,942
1968	25.9	9.6	204.1	116.4	206.9	110.2	140.7	157.2	9,423
1969	25.2	8.4	194.9	112.7	191.5	113.1	131.8	139.0	9,680
1970	25.3	8.2	186.2	103.8	175.9	94.8	114.8	122.6	9,470
1971	24.1	7.4	172.5	97.5	167.8	95.6	117.7	98.2	10,003
1972	23.4	6.2	155.6	110.6	217.5	102.2	144.5	81.2	10,222

Source: International Ladies' Garment Workers' Union, New York, *Conditions in the Women's Garment Industry*, June 27, 1973.
[a] Sweaters for men and women.

the importance of the fashion industry as an employer. Historically, the industry has been a haven for the foreign born and the ghetto resident in search of work; it is a vast source of jobs in all parts of the country for semiskilled labor; and it is notable for hiring and training unskilled workers.

The women's apparel industry, with which we are primarily concerned here, is not only of considerable size itself, but its activities have had great influence on many other business areas. Its productive facilities, as will be discussed later in this section, are distributed throughout the United States. It provides an outlet for the talent of gifted, creative individuals and employment for workers who are happiest at routine jobs. In addition, it is an industry that has changed fashion from what was once the privilege of the Four Hundred to something within reach of all but the most deprived women in this country. And, as its influence and its methods spread to other countries, so does the idea that, thanks to factory production of apparel, women of modest means can be well and becomingly dressed.

HISTORY AND DEVELOPMENT

Less than a century ago, when fashionable clothing was something that relatively few people in the United States could afford, the wants of these few were supplied by imports (usually from England or France) or by the products of the hand labor of a small number of custom tailors and dressmakers. The dressmakers worked at home, in the homes of their customers or in small craft shops. The fabrics they used were generally imported from Europe. The majority of Americans, from colonial times to the end of the nineteenth century, wore clothes made at home by the women of the house; every home in modest circumstances was its own clothing factory. Ready-made clothing was virtually nonexistent, and what little was available was of the poorest quality and completely lacking in design. Home dressmaking continued to prevail into the early twentieth century and it was not until well into the 1900s that the term "store clothes" was used in other than a derogatory manner.

Men's Wear First

The development of the garment industry started with men's ready-to-wear. It was born in the early 1800s in the port cities of New England, almost half a century before the women's apparel industry had its beginnings. A few enterprising merchants, notably Brooks Brothers[8] conceived the idea of producing and selling cheap ready-to-wear trousers and shirts for sailors who needed to replenish their wardrobes inexpensively and quickly during their brief stays in port. The market for ready made clothing soon expanded to serve bachelors who had no one at home to sew clothing for them, and to fill orders for cheap clothing for plantation slaves. Other merchants followed suit, and established men's clothing plants in Chicago and St. Louis in response to the demand generated by the Gold Rush. Apparel manufacturing had begun in earnest and in a way typical of American frontier life—with work clothes for laborers. The clothes were poorly made and sewn by hand. They certainly were not fashionable. The designing—such as it was—and the cutting of this early ready-to-wear clothing was done in the dealers' shops; the garments were "put out" to local women for hand sewing.

Two events in the mid-nineteenth century opened the way to expanded production. The first was the perfection of the sewing machine by Elias Howe in 1846. This invention revolutionized clothes making in America by making possible volume production in machine-powered factories. The second was the Civil War, which created an unprecedented demand for ready-made Army clothing and hastened the change from homemade, hand-sewn garments. A further development was the standardization of sizes, developed by the government for military uniforms. After the war, these sizes were converted to civilian needs, and helped to place the men's ready-to-wear trade on a firm basis.

Women's Wear in 1860

Meantime, the production of women's ready-to-wear was also developing, but more slowly. The first official report of a women's clothing industry appeared in the U.S. Census of 1860, covering products such as hoop skirts, cloaks, and mantillas. Once started, the industry grew rapidly. From 1860 to 1880, the wholesale volume of production increased from $2 million to $32 million; the number of manufacturers

---

[8]Brooks Brothers company booklet, *Established 1818*. Also, Egal Feldman, *FIT for Men*, Washington, D.C., Public Affairs Press, 1970.

GROWTH OF WOMEN'S APPAREL INDUSTRY

Source: Research Department, ILGWU.

from 96 to 562, and the number of employees from 5739 to 25,192.[9] Factory production, however, though stimulated by the invention of the sewing machine, was still in its infancy. Between 1890 and 1910, the pace of the industry's growth received additional impetus from the influx to America of immigrants from Central and Eastern Europe, many of whom brought with them traditional tailoring skills and a capacity for hard work. By 1900, the women's clothing industry reported 2070 manufacturers, employing 96,000 workers, with sales of $174 million and surpassing the combined efforts of all the custom tailors and dressmakers in America.[10]

1900 to 1950

The early years of the twentieth century saw the industry develop an awareness of fashion and a capacity for responding to it. At first, that response was little more than copying or adapting Paris originals at the urging of retail leaders and fabric producers. Inevitably, original design talent was attracted to the industry and, by the 1930s, many capable creators were at work in the trade. Neither producers nor retailers made capital of designers' names, however, until the 1940s when Lord & Taylor, a major New York fashion retailer, instituted a policy of promoting the names of young American designers and their work and thus gave impetus to a trend toward recognizing that design talent existed on both sides of the Atlantic Ocean.

By that time, the industry had recognized and begun to design for the then uniquely American fondness for casual, comfortable clothes—a field in which this country still holds the lead. Also developing in the 1930s and 1940s was an awareness of the need for precise fit in ready-to-wear garments. Instead of continuing to produce garments for that rarity, the tall, slender "model" figure, manufacturers began to study prevailing figure types among American women and to work out size ranges and size specifications that would keep the need for alterations to a minimum.

[9]*The Dress Industry*, Market Planning Service, National Credit Office, Dun & Bradstreet, New York, March 1948.
[10]*Ibid.*

As the twentieth century approached its midpoint, manufacturers of the principal categories of women's outerwear (dresses, suits, coats, skirts and blouses) employed more than a quarter of a million production workers, maintained nearly 10,000 plants, and shipped in excess of $3 billion a year of merchandise, at factory value.[11] Compared with the 1900 figure, the increase in annual output over the half century seems enormous. That increase seems even more spectacular, however, when it is measured against the country's growth in population and product during the same 50-year period. From 1900 to 1950, population in the United States doubled, and the gross national product increased almost five times. But the women's apparel industry registered an increase in annual output to more than 20 times what it produced in 1900.

Rise of Publicly Owned Giants in the 1960s

Until the 1950s, the women's apparel industry consisted almost entirely of privately owned businesses. Even the largest of them was small in comparison to the giants that dominated such manufacturing industries as steel, automobiles, tobacco, and chemicals. In the late 1950s and throughout the 1960s, however, a change took place: the rise of publicly owned giant apparel firms. Before 1960, the apparel manufacturing firm that was large enough to "go public" was relatively rare; in 1959, there were only 22 such firms. By the close of the 1960s, however, there were some 100 publicly owned firms producing women's and children's apparel. Corporations, listed on the stock exchange and inviting public investment capital, grew rapidly by means of mergers, acquisitions, and internal expansion to become giants in the industry. The industry's giants, however, do not compare in size or dominance with

The Rise of Six Fashion Giants: Growth Pattern of Publicly Owned Apparel Producing Firms

FIRM	MAJOR PRODUCTS	ANNUAL SALES IN MILLIONS		
		1960	1965	1972
Kayser-Roth	Men's, women's, and children's lingerie and accessories	$121	$240	$519
Jonathan Logan	Dresses, sportswear, knitwear	48	162	332
Bobbie Brooks	Junior sportswear	53	121	199
Russ Togs	Sportswear, dresses, girls' wear	16	57	127
Leslie Fay	Dresses, sportswear	12	52	124
Levi Strauss & Co.	Jeans and slacks (for men and women)	50	124	504

Source: Published financial statements of these firms.

[11]U.S. Department of Commerce, *Census of Manufactures 1958*, MC58(2)–23B, p. 5.

such firms as U.S. Steel or General Motors in their respective industries. The combined output of the eight largest producers of women's apparel represents only 17 percent of the industry's total output. By contrast, the eight largest producers of motor vehicles represent 98 percent of their industry's total output; the eight largest steel producers represent 66 percent of the total in their field; and the eight largest producers of cigarettes turn out their industry's entire total.[12]

Growth of Union

No history of the apparel industry would be complete without mention of its union and of that organization's unique contribution to its development. In the early days of the industry, working conditions were, as in so many industries of the period, extremely bad. Factory conditions were primitive and unhealthy; work was also carried on in tenements; hours were long; wages were low. Some workers provided their own machines, paid for thread and needles, for the water they drank, and sometimes even for the "privilege" of working in the shops. Sleeping overnight in the shop to gain an extra hour or two of working time was not unknown.

It was in this atmosphere that the ILGWU (International Ladies' Garment Workers' Union) was founded in 1900, with 2000 members, after a desperate struggle dating back to the 1880s. After two years of bitter conflict in an effort to achieve better working conditions and higher pay levels, industry and labor made common cause with one another. Since the 1920s, industry-wide strikes and lockouts have been all but nonexistent. Today, labor-management relations are characterized by cooperation in research, education, and industry development, and the apparel industry pattern is held up as a model for others to follow.

GEOGRAPHICAL LOCATIONS

Although some phase of apparel-industry activity is carried on in nearly every state of the Union, New York City is the unquestioned fashion capital of the country. Insofar as mass production of women's and children's wear is concerned, it is the world's capital.

Concentration in New York

It is not entirely an accident that New York occupies this dominant position. When Elias Howe first perfected his sewing machine, mass production of garments was not limited to any one city or area. But then came outside events that ensured New

[12]U.S. Department of Commerce, *Statistical Abstract of the United States, 1971*, pp. 699–700, and *U.S. Industrial Outlook 1973*, p. 164.

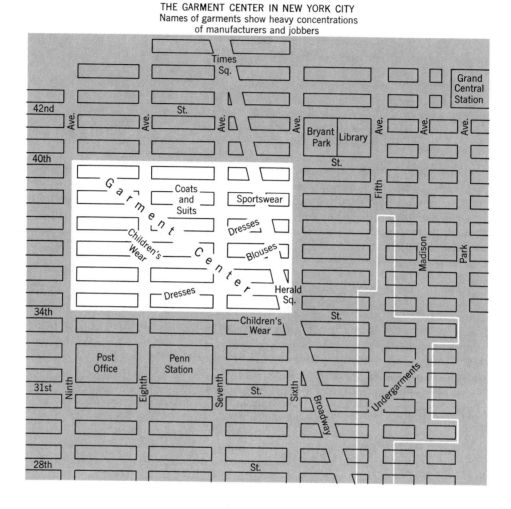

THE GARMENT CENTER IN NEW YORK CITY
Names of garments show heavy concentrations
of manufacturers and jobbers

York's dominance in women's fashions. From 1880 to 1910, as a result of Jewish persecutions throughout Eastern Europe, a great wave of immigrant Jews arrived at the port of New York. Since tailoring had been a Jewish occupation in Europe, many of these immigrants were skilled tailors, and they entered the then fledgling, ready-to-wear industry.[13] Others who were not skilled, but eager to find work in the city where they landed, were absorbed into the infant garment industry. It was also during this period that the ready-to-wear concept was catching on; American women were putting away their thimbles, needles, and patterns, and buying the "store-made" apparel. The coincidence of a bottomless pool of immigrant labor at

[13]Florence S. Richards, *The Ready-to-Wear Industry, 1900–1950*, Fairchild Publications, New York, 1951.

hand and the upsurge in American consumer demand was the circumstance that permitted New York City to leave all its rivals far behind in the production of apparel.

New York had the further advantage of being close to the woolen mills of New England and the cotton mills of the South. It was also the market to which retail buyers came for almost every kind of merchandise carried in their shops. Once New York had gained dominance, it became a magnet, attracting such auxiliary businesses as embroidery, pleating, stitching, trimmings, and the like. With these advantages, plus its traditional position as the nation's largest city and center of fashionable society, the city became, and still remains, the hub of the fashion industries. The New York garment industry presently accounts for over 60 percent of the wholesale sales of all women's and children's garments in the United States,[14] and is the largest industry in New York City and in New York State.

Seventh Avenue.   So much of New York City's garment business is concentrated within a distance of one block east or west of Seventh Avenue, from 40th Street south into the low 30s, that the term "Seventh Avenue" has become synonymous with the women's fashion industry. There are other centers elsewhere in the country, even in other parts of New York City where women's garments are produced, but to those in the fashion business, no other industrial center has the color, tension, or drama of Seventh Avenue.

A key factor in this concentration was the erection, in the 1920s of several tall, completely fireproofed buildings for showroom and factory use. Numbers 498 and 500 Seventh Avenue were the first such fireproof structures for the garment trades, and they were soon followed by 512, 530, and 550. Higher priced houses in the trade are almost all in 550, 530, 512, and 498—such firms as Norman Norell, Pauline Trigère, Donald Brooks, Bill Blass, and their peers. At the lower or southern end of the district, in a section that has been nicknamed Chinatown, are manufacturers of lower priced apparel whose names are generally unknown to the public. The large, mass-production houses are located on Broadway, just east of Seventh Avenue, at 1400, 1407, and 1411.

Originally, all the manufacturing operations of a garment firm took place under one roof. Now, many concerns locate their cutting and, to a larger extent, the actual sewing processes elsewhere. But the nerve center of their operations—the showrooms, designing, and shipping—remains quartered on Seventh Avenue. New York's vast supply of skilled labor and the availability of many supporting industries make it a desirable headquarters for fashion manufacturers. Equally important is the availability of designing talent and production know-how, plus the opportunity to exchange ideas with others. To creative people, this last element is usually vital.

Paris-born designer Pauline Trigère has said, "With the possible exception of Paris, New York is the only city in the world in which I could work. . . . I need the tempo of New York to create clothes for the women of the world; sensitive,

---

[14]Authors' estimate.

elegant, practical clothes. In New York, my mind never stays still. Inspiration comes from within, and New York feeds the 'within' constantly."[15]

Secondary Fashion Centers

There are other fashion centers outside New York, although none compares with it in the variety or quantity of its output. These centers are known in the trade as "markets" and they tend to be fairly specialized as to the types and price ranges of their products. *Los Angeles*, once a center for sportswear alone, now produces apparel and accessories in a broad range of categories and price levels. Attempts to draw retail buyers to that city for seasonal openings have not been too successful, however, since many of the Los Angeles firms have New York showings, thus diminishing the incentive for retailers to travel westward. *Chicago*, for generations a wholesale center for merchandise in the Middle West, has a giant Merchandise Mart, in which it is estimated that over 800 different companies in the infants', children's, and women's apparel field maintain showrooms—in addition to several hundred others in the men's and boys' apparel field. *Philadelphia* produces women's and misses' outerwear, millinery, and children's wear. *Boston* is known primarily for rainwear, although other apparel categories, notably sportswear, are produced there also. *Dallas*, a fast-growing center that made its name in sportswear, has moved into dresses and other apparel categories, principally in the medium- and popular-priced ranges. *St. Louis* is known for junior dresses. Other centers include Cleveland, Kansas City, Miami, Baltimore, and San Francisco.

Decentralization of Production Facilities

Even though New York is the headquarters for the designing and merchandising activities of the city's manufacturers, a number of New York firms have begun to produce their goods in other areas. Jonathan Logan, Inc., for example, operates several factories in different parts of the country, and shuttles raw and finished materials among these plants by means of a company owned airplane. So far, this trend toward decentralized operations has been more evident for the sewing stages of the cheaper and more standardized apparel operations. It remains to be seen, however, whether the production process of highly styled garments can be successfully separated from their design and marketing operations.

NATURE OF APPAREL FIRMS

Apparel producers vary widely as to size, product, and the nature of their operations. Tiny firms coexist with giants. Specialists rub shoulders with firms that,

---

[15]Jack Alexander, "New York's New Queen of Fashion", *Saturday Evening Post*, April 8, 1961, pp. 30ff.

LEADING PRODUCTION CENTERS IN WOMEN'S WEAR
(Womens, Misses, Juniors, Childrens Wear)
(As a per cent of total U.S. sales)

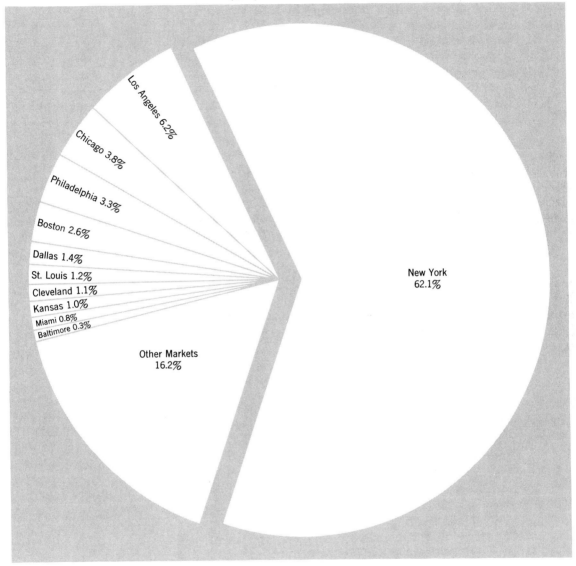

Los Angeles 6.2%
Chicago 3.8%
Philadelphia 3.3%
Boston 2.6%
Dallas 1.4%
St. Louis 1.2%
Cleveland 1.1%
Kansas 1.0%
Miami 0.8%
Baltimore 0.3%

New York
62.1%

Other Markets
16.2%

Source: International Ladies' Garment Workers' Union.

through their various divisions, can dress a woman from the skin out and for every conceivable occasion. Self-contained operations, plants that perform no more than a single step of the productive process, fashion creators, and flagrant copiers—all are found in the industry.

Types of Manufacturing Operation

The U.S. Census of Manufactures divides the industry's firms into three classifications, according to the comprehensiveness of their production activities: manufacturers, jobbers, and contractors. Classified as manufacturers are firms that buy the fabric and do the designing, sewing, cutting, and assembling of garments in factories of their own. The jobber is a firm that handles everything but the actual sewing, and sometimes the cutting, which it farms out to independently owned sewing factories. The independently owned sewing shops, employing operators and producing goods to the specifications of those that hire them, are classified as contractors.

Common trade usage, however, does not ordinarily make the distinction between jobbers and manufacturers that the Census does; any firm that buys fabrics, designs and cuts its own garments, and maintains a showroom to sell the finished product to retail store buyers is generally referred to as a manufacturer, regardless of where the sewing is done. The trade does make a distinction, however, between "inside" and "outside" shops. The "inside" shops produce garments from beginning to end in their own factories; "outside" shops farm out the sewing. The term "contractors" is used, in the trade and in the Census, for those firms that perform the sewing operation for hire.

The Contracting System

The contracting system evolved early in the history of the industry. Prior to 1880, the manufacture of women's apparel was generally completely integrated. During the expansion of the industry in the years between 1880 and 1890, manufacturers turned to contractors because the burden of seasonal idleness and the responsibility of dealing directly with labor could be shifted to these entrepreneurs, as could the problem of adjusting to increased or reduced production needs.

Today, contracting continues to play an important role. Contractors are used by both small and large firms and are found in every section of the country. Some firms use outside contractors exclusively; others with their own "inside" production facilities also hire independent contractors for extra capacity in busy periods; still others subsidize and/or own contracting shops. This system of using outside production facilities enables manufacturers to expand their output rapidly to meet upsurges in demand, but it causes contractors to bear the brunt of seasonal swings and any industry instability.

A Stronghold of Small Business

The apparel industry is unique among major manufacturing industries in that it is still a stronghold of small business. Because it takes comparatively little capital to

Manufacturers and Jobbers Classified by Sales Volume:
Selected Branches of Women's Garment Industry, 1969
(percent of total in each branch)

INDUSTRY	UNDER $500,000	$500,000 TO $1,000,000	$1,000,000 TO $2,500,000	$2,500,000 TO $5,000,000	$5,000,000 TO $10,000,000	$10,000,000 AND OVER
Coat and suit	24.7	21.8	30.9	14.4	6.3	1.9
Unit-priced dress	27.5	17.7	31.2	14.8	5.5	3.3
Blouse and sportswear	31.6	18.3	26.2	12.7	6.5	4.7
Housedress, uniform, and service apparel	36.5	13.2	23.3	13.8	9.0	4.2
Children's outerwear	34.1	17.7	27.6	10.9	6.7	3.0
Corset and brassiere	26.4	14.4	24.7	16.7	9.2	8.6
Lingerie	25.2	21.9	29.8	12.9	5.9	4.3
All branches	29.4	18.4	28.5	13.5	6.4	3.8

Sources: National Credit Office. ILGWU, *Trends and Prospects in the Women's Garment Industry 1968–1971*, May 1971, p. 18

open a shop, an enterprising person with a flair for fashion can set up business and hope to prosper. Basic equipment consists of a cutter, two sewing machines, and the operators to run them. The key to success is in producing styles that can find customer acceptance. In that respect, the small firm has an equal chance with the larger one. If the business prospers, a few more sewing machines and operators can be added, or the manufacturer can farm out the sewing to contractors. Sudden style shifts can often be more quickly exploited by a small manufacturer since he has greater flexibility in his operations. On the other hand, a single poor season can

SIZE OF WOMEN'S APPAREL INDUSTRY SHOPS

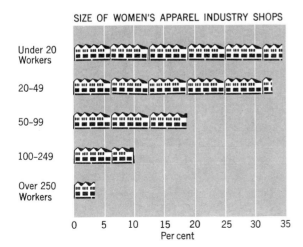

Source: *Trends and Prospects in the Women's Garment Industry 1968–1971*, p. 19. ILGWU, May, 1971.

wipe out a small, undercapitalized firm—and often does. There is a high failure rate in the industry. The ILGWU has estimated that business turnover, including discontinuances and transfers, as well as failures, is about 18 percent a year in the industry under normal conditions.[16] The rate is believed to have risen in the early 1970s.

In every major branch of the industry, close to half the manufacturers and jobbers have individual annual sales volumes of under $1 million.[17] Individual plants are quite small; 70 percent of those in the industry employ fewer than 50 people.[18]

Despite the rise of publicly owned giant apparel firms in the 1960s, the industry is still dominated by small firms. There are thousands of individually owned producing companies and partnerships that consider themselves fortunate whenever a few "runners" (numbers that are reordered by customers) bring their annual sales up to $1 million. Today, small reputable manufacturers and outstanding designers still continue to set the fashion pace for the industry in the higher-priced fields.

What the future will bring remains to be seen, but industry observers feel that there will always be a place in the apparel industry for the small firm. The reason they give is the continuing demand for highly specialized fashion items that can best be produced by smaller firms.

Highly Specialized

There is a high degree of product and price-line specialization in the industry. A typical producer specializes in a particular size range, such as juniors, and in a particular type of garment, such as coats or knit dresses, in a narrow range of prices. Once he has built his reputation for distinct types and prices, the producer has difficulty in winning acceptance for other types or price lines. A maker of coats at $16.75 to $22.75 wholesale, for example, could not readily switch to $29.75 to $39.75. He would be out of reach of his former customers and would have to make a fresh start among those who could patronize the new price lines. Similarly, a firm well established among stores and departments selling to young juniors could not readily switch to conservatively styled half-sizes. The effect would be the same as going out of business and starting all over again.

Firms in the industry that have diversified have recognized this situation and have either created separate divisions to handle each new field in which they wished to function or have acquired companies already active in that field. Under the corporate umbrella of an industry giant one may find separate divisions, each specialized in such fields as junior dresses, raincoats, beachwear, and so on. Each

[16]Milton Fried and Lazare Tepper, *Domestic Apparel Industry, Economic Background and Impact of Imports,* New York, ILGWU, 1968, p. 10.
[17]International Ladies' Garment Workers' Union, *Trends and Prospects in the Women's Garment Industry, 1968–1971,* May 1971.
[18]U.S. Department of Commerce, *U.S. Industrial Outlook, 1972,* pp. 146–147, and *1973,* p. 164.

division has its own identity, its own clearly marked-out field, its own designers, and its own selling organization.

PATTERNS OF OPERATION

Throughout the fashion industries, the pattern of operation is basically the same. It is geared to the need of retailers to offer their customers a broad range of styles at the start of each selling season and to reorder those styles that show signs of achieving strong acceptance. Thus producers prepare lines, or assortments of styles, well in advance of each consumer buying season and offer them to retail buyers. By custom and consensus, each branch of the industry establishes market periods, during which retailers visit producers' showrooms to make their initial selections.

Seasons and Lines

Seasonal factors and the periodic presentation of new lines, or collections of new styles, are fundamental in the operating pattern of the fashion industries. Although the number of seasonal showings varies from one branch to another, at the very minimum a firm must invest in fabric and present a new "line" twice yearly. In the women's apparel industry, three to five new collections a year are customary. A dress firm, for example, will bring out a spring, fall, summer, holiday, and often a special resort line. In addition to revising their lines seasonally, many firms continue to revise their offerings as the season progresses. Styles that win consumer acceptance may be produced in a wider range of fabrics than originally planned; new "hot" styles may come into demand; those that prove to have little or no consumer appeal may be dropped altogether.

  The showing of a new line is only the beginning. The reaction of retail buyers must be measured before styles are put into production, and those that do not win acceptance must be eliminated to avoid costly markdowns or "closeouts" later in the season.

Market Weeks

During periods known to the trade as "market weeks," buyers from retail stores all over the country converge on manufacturers' showrooms to shop and compare the different collections in preparation for placing their orders.

  The method of presenting new lines to buyers varies. Some firms present elaborate fashion shows on live models to open their collections; others simply have the garments ready for inspection on racks in their showrooms. Some firms stage previews of their new collections, to which they invite reporters from fashion

New York Couture Business Council, Inc.
Spring 1973 Opening Dates

ALDRICH	Wednesday, October 25th	2:30 P.M.
ALPER SCHWARTZ	Monday, October 16th	continuous
The ARKIN COLLECTIONS	Monday, October 23rd	continuous by appointment
ANDREW ARKIN PETITES	Monday, October 23rd	continuous by appointment
GEOFFREY BEENE COUTURE	Thursday, October 26th	12:00 NOON
GEOFFREY BEENE BOUTIQUE	Monday, October 23rd	4:00 P.M.
HOUSE OF BRANELL	Tuesday, October 24th	continuous by appointment
DONALD BROOKS	Tuesday, October 24th	4:00 P.M. by invitation
CARLYE	Monday, October 23rd	continuous by appointment
PETER CLEMENTS	Wednesday, October 25th	11: A.M. by invitation
DAVIDOW	Monday, October 16th	by appointment
DON LUIS de ESPANA	Monday, October 23rd	continuous
HALSTON	Thursday, November 9th	3:00 P.M.
KIKI HART NEW YORK	Monday, October 23rd	continuous by appointment
CHUCK HOWARD	Monday, October 23rd	continuous by appointment
IMAGES	Monday, October 16th	continuous by appointment
JAEGER	Monday, October 23rd	by appointment
JAMISON	Monday, October 16th	by appointment
JEREMY	Monday, October 30th	continuous by appointment
JEUNESSE	Monday, October 16th	continuous by appointment
JS LTD	Monday, October 23rd	continuous by appointment
NAT KAPLAN	Monday, October 23rd	by appointment
LANVIN COUTURE	Monday, October 23rd	continuous by appointment
LANVIN SPORTSWEAR	Thursday, November 2nd	continuous by appointment
KASPER FOR JOAN LESLIE	Wednesday, October 25th	time to be announced
HAROLD LEVINE	Monday, October 23rd	1:00 P.M.
M.S. COUTURE	Monday, October 16th	continuous by appointment
JOHN MAC DOUGALL	Tuesday, October 31st	continuous
MAISONETTE	Wednesday, October 18th	continuous by appointment
VERA MAXWELL	Monday, October 23rd	continuous by appointment
NANTUCKET	Wednesday, October 25th	continuous
OSCAR de la RENTA COUTURE	Tuesday, October 24th	10:30 A.M.
OSCAR de la RENTA BOUTIQUE	Thursday, October 26th	11:00 A.M.
SOMETHING BY OSCAR de la RENTA	Monday, October 23rd	1:30 P.M.
PARNES FEINSTEIN	Wednesday, October 25th	continuous by appointment
MOLLIE PARNIS COUTURE	Monday, October 23rd	12:00 NOON by invitation
MOLLIE PARNIS BOUTIQUE	Tuesday, October 31st	11:00 A.M. by invitation
BEN REIG	Monday, October 30th	11:15 A.M.
OLE BORDEN for REMBRANDT	Monday, October 23rd	4:00 P.M.
DOMINIC ROMPOLLO	Monday, October 23rd	continuous by appointment
ROYAL PARK COUTURE	Tuesday, October 31st	continuous
PAT SANDLER	Monday, October 23rd	continuous by appointment
ABE SCHRADER	Monday, October 23rd	continuous by appointment
SCHRADER SPORT	Monday, October 23rd	continuous by appointment
STEPHAN CASUALS	Monday, October 23rd	continuous by appointment
STUDIO SIX	Tuesday, October 24th	continuous by appointment
THE SIDNEY'S DESIGNS	Tuesday, October 24th	continuous by appointment
JERRY SILVERMAN	Monday, October 23rd	continuous by appointment
MALCOLM STARR	Monday, October 23rd	continuous by appointment
STARR BOUTIQUE	Tuesday, October 24th	continuous by appointment
TEAL TRAINA	Tuesday, October 24th	1:00 P.M.
TRAINA BOUTIQUE	Tuesday, October 24th	10:00 A.M.
TRAINA SPORT	Thursday, October 26th	10:00 A.M.
TRIGERE	Thursday, October 26th	by appointment
CHESTER WEINBERG		4:00 P.M.

Source: As advertised in *Women's Wear Daily*, October 10, 1972.

magazines and newspapers, in order to get publicity; others do not. But, although the method of showing may vary, the timing for a particular branch of the industry is fairly standardized. Customary business practices dictate the week or weeks of the year in which the largest number of buyers is likely to be in the market; the maker who is conspicuously early or late risks ringing up the curtain on an empty house.

Each branch of the fashion industry sets its market dates by balancing many factors against one another: the periods when it is convenient for retailers to come to market; the time required to produce goods after retail buyers have placed their orders; and the time needed for designers to assess the past season's experience for clues to the coming season's demand. Attempts to change market dates radically have been made in some branches of the industry but with no conspicuous success. Tradition usually prevails—not because it is tradition but simply because there are not too many periods of the year in which designers can be ready, retailers can be available, and enough lead time can be provided for production.

From Design to Finished Product

In order to be ready with their lines for the normal market weeks of their industries, apparel manufacturers must start working on their collections at least two or three months prior to the showings—or about six months before the consumer herself is ready to buy. In some branches of the fashion business, even longer preparation is required. For example, large producers of sportswear coordinates may work as much as a full year ahead to assemble the many kinds of materials they need for mix-and-match sweaters, blouses, pants, skirts, and jackets. The farther ahead the maker works, the more intensely must he analyze trends in fashion and study the consumers in order to foresee their needs and tastes with sufficient accuracy.

First of the many steps in the production of apparel is the designing process for the coming season. From one to three months before the openings, each firm's designer, or team of designers, is busy working up the styles that will fit into the price range and type of merchandise in which the firm specializes. Among the fashion leaders in the industry, the designs originate on the drawing board or in the muslin, but for many less-original manufacturers, a style will often start life in the form of someone else's merchandise that has been sketched or purchased for copying purposes. In many instances, because fashion is basically an evolutionary process, "new" designs will be slightly revised versions of the previous season's best sellers.

Once a design has crystallized, the next step is to execute an actual garment. This is generally done by an assistant, working closely with the designer and making revisions until a satisfactory sample emerges. For these early trials, some firms work in muslin; others, in the fabric of the garment. Next, company executives check the garment for costs, availability of materials, potential salability, and the possibility of profit. Some designs may be changed at this point; others may be discarded entirely.

If a design is to become part of a line, it is given a style number, and a highly skilled patternmaker makes a production pattern for it—in one size only (whatever size the firm uses for its samples). From this pattern, one garment at a time is made for testing and possible correction of the pattern. When the pattern is right, as many samples are made as are needed to show the line.

Production of Selected Women's Garments by Wholesale Price Ranges
(each price range as percent of total production)

PRODUCT AND PRICE RANGE	1966	1967	1968	1969	1970	1971
COATS, UNTRIMMED						
Under $16.00 per unit	47.9	37.2	36.9	36.1	39.1	33.2
$16.00–$38.99	43.5	50.0	50.1	48.9	48.9	53.2
$39.00 and over	8.6	12.8	13.0	15.0	12.0	13.6
SUITS						
Under $16.00 per unit	38.0	32.0	33.4	31.5	43.7	43.7
$16.00–$38.99	47.1	52.8	49.4	46.6	42.3	44.0
$39.00 and over	14.9	15.2	17.2	21.9	14.0	12.3
DRESSES, UNIT-PRICED						
Under $6.00 per unit	38.9	31.0	33.0	28.0	23.8	16.0
$6.00–$9.99	29.1	32.6	28.8	30.3	32.8	33.8
$10.00–$15.99	18.7	20.9	23.3	24.3	24.5	27.5
$16.00 and over	13.3	15.5	14.9	17.4	18.9	22.7
DRESSES, DOZEN-PRICED						
Under $26.00 per dozen	22.5	14.4	14.3	12.8	12.0	6.2
$26.00–$34.99	25.2	37.0	34.7	32.8	31.5	31.7
$35.00–$50.99	24.9	22.0	18.4	16.0	17.2	18.7
$51.00 and over	27.4	26.6	32.6	38.4	39.3	43.4
BLOUSES						
Under $23.00 per dozen	51.4	41.9	36.9	27.5	29.2	22.5
$23.00–$38.99	30.1	31.1	30.0	30.2	30.5	26.6
$39.00 and over	18.5	27.0	33.1	42.3	40.3	50.9
SKIRTS						
Under $39.00 per dozen	32.9	27.6	25.1	27.4	29.3	23.7
$39.00–$75.99	51.4	57.3	58.0	56.9	54.1	59.9
$76.00 and over	15.7	15.1	16.9	15.7	16.6	16.4

Source: International Ladies' Garment Workers' Union, New York, *Conditions in the Women's Garment Industry*, February 28, 1973. Based upon data from U. S. Bureau of the Census.

Going into Production

Large, confident producers decide at once which numbers they will produce. Innovators and those less sure of themselves await retail reaction before putting any number into production. From an initial collection of 200 designs, perhaps one-third will be eliminated after they have been shown; of the remainder, it may be that only about a dozen will develop into "runners" or reorder styles. The number of orders received or realistically anticipated that is considered sufficient to warrant production varies with each firm's needs and price levels. For example, producers whose dresses retail at from $75 to $200 each say that they require orders of from 100 to 500 pieces of a number before cutting. On the other hand, one producer whose coats employ carefully hand-cut leather in their designs and that retail at prices up to $750 each says that he will put a number into production even with orders for as few as 10 pieces.[19]

After it has been decided to produce a style in quantity the pattern for it is graded. This means that the pattern's various parts are "sloped" up and down to adjust for each size that is to be produced. The process can be done more or less mechanically by adding or subtracting the appropriate fraction of an inch; or it may be done with care, skill, and constant checking to insure excellent fit.

Next, after grading, comes the marker. This is a long paper guide that shows all of the various pieces and sizes of the pattern, as they should be laid out in order to cut the cloth economically and with bias and straight where each is needed. For the actual cutting, layers of fabric are rolled out on long tables. The marker is placed on top. Guided by the marker, the cutters use electrically powered knives that cut through a very substantial depth with speed and accuracy. The number of garments cut at one time varies with the thickness of the fabric, the cutter's skill, the price of the garment, the number of orders, and so forth. As many as 6000 garments of a style can be cut on a long table in one operation.

The cut parts of the garments are then collected, identified, and "bundled," to be passed along for the sewing operation. This may be done in the firm's own plant if it is an "inside" shop; more commonly, the bundles go by truck to a contractor's plant for the sewing. In some instances, contractors do the cutting, working from the marker and continuing from that point.

In many sections of the apparel industries, piecework prevails among the sewing operators. This requires a preview of the garment by an industry-union committee, which determines the precise price to be paid for each step in the sewing.

In some plants, a single operator does all of the machine sewing on a garment. This is the tailor system, still followed for better garments (notably coats and suits), and it requires highly skilled workers. More often, team or section work prevails, and each operator does just one part. Where different machines or different adjustments of one machine are needed for the various elements of the garment, the team system makes for speed. Any hand sewing that is required comes under

[19]Inquiry made by authors.

the heading of trimming, and is done by operators other than those who put together the main body of the garment.

Garments are then inspected, pressed, and readied for return from the contractor (if one is involved) to the original establishment, where they are finally inspected and distributed to the stores that bought them.

The period between design and delivery of a dress or similar fashion garment is a long one that the ultimate consumer knows little about. Yet the important decisions on what type of merchandise customers will find in the stocks of their favorite stores are made during this period.

Concentration on Best Sellers

The manufacturer's concern with the acceptance of his styles is not ended once the garment has been delivered to the retailer. Initial orders and production of a style often do not cover the costs of manufacturing, distribution, and overhead, and frequently, the margin of profit is dependent on the degree to which the firm receives reorders and can recut styles in large quantities. By discarding slow sellers and concentrating on reorder numbers, manufacturers can reduce some of the many risks inherent in producing fashion merchandise. One highly successful dress manufacturer estimates that more than half a season's business is in reorders, and that sometimes about 10 percent of the line accounts for the bulk of the season's business.[20]

Importance of Speed

The fashion industry in the United States is distinguished by the rapidity with which it produces and distributes accepted styles. In a business that must keep up with changing fashion, time and distance factors are surmounted by speed and flexibility in production. Timing is of paramount importance. As previously explained, designs for a coming season are prepared from six weeks to three months prior to the openings. Once orders have been received, the production process at the beginning of a season may take anywhere from three weeks to two months. Retailers start their selling season with broad assortments and relatively limited quantities of individual numbers, so that they may reorder quickly those numbers or features that are well received by their customers. To be able to fill these reorders quickly while demand is at its peak, the manufacturer must have speed and maneuverability. No matter how early the industry starts preparing its lines, and no matter how early the retailers place their initial orders, production becomes a race with the clock once the consumer has entered the picture and indicated the direction in which her preferences lie.

[20]Hy Derfler, Leslie Fay, Inc., in *Women's Wear Daily*, June 16, 1971, p. 33.

The need for speed does not apply quite so much to the more basic items of fashion merchandise, such as classic sweaters, denim jeans, and basic undergarments, for example. Items of this sort generally have predictably long fashion lives, and manufacturer and retailer alike can anticipate demand with minimum risk. But even among the classics, an occasional color, fabric, or detail of design may enjoy a sudden vogue and thus bring the beat-the-clock element into the picture. No branch of the fashion business—men's, children's, or women's—is immune to the need for speed.

MARKETING ACTIVITIES

Over the years, the marketing activities of the fashion industries have established a pattern of direct distribution to the retailer, heavy reliance upon personal contact between manufacturer's representative and retail buyer, and the use of advertising and publicity to supplement personal selling efforts. The development of foreign markets takes the form of establishing owned or franchised production facilities abroad.

Distribution Policies

Distribution in the fashion industries is generally directly from manufacturer to retailer. Only in such staple items as some hosiery, underwear, and children's wear does the wholesaler distribute appreciable amounts of merchandise. Since most fashions are relatively short lived, there is little time for the middleman to inject himself into the picture.

Distribution policies vary from firm to firm. Some manufacturers sell to retailers of any type or size; others prefer to limit their distribution to one or a few stores in each trading area or to specific kinds of stores, such as boutique, discount, specialty, or department stores. Deciding factors in the distribution policy of an individual firm are, for example, price lines, productive capacity, and the potential consumer market for its products.

Unlike such fields as men's clothing and the shoe industry, it is not common in the women's fashion field for a manufacturer to own retail outlets. In general, a fashion manufacturer needs all the time, energy, and capital he has for his own part of the job; he does not have enough of any of these for forays into retailing. A potent deterrent, too, is the reaction the manufacturer can expect from his present retail outlets if they find him in competition with them for the consumer's trade. His retail customers are quite likely to drop him completely. This has not been the case, however, when retail stores and apparel producers are under common ownership but operated as entirely separate divisions—a situation that can develop when a financial conglomerate buys up both manufacturing and retail companies.

Reliance upon Salesmen

By and large, apparel producers rely on their own salesmen to bring their products to the attention of the retail trade. Most firms maintain selling staffs in their showrooms to wait on retailers who come to the markets and to build up a following among professional buyers. Firms also employ "road" salesmen who travel with samples and whose duty it is to call on retailers in assigned territories. In addition, the larger firms supplement their sales forces with regional sales offices to provide better service to retail buyers. This regional office system is old hat in other major industries but relatively new and almost revolutionary for the fashion industry. For those manufacturers who do not have sales staffs of their own, or who seek continuous representation in areas not covered by their own salesmen, there are independent selling organizations that maintain permanent showrooms and represent several noncompeting lines. Examples are to be found both among out-of-town producers who are represented in New York City, and among New York producers who hire manufacturers' representatives in other major fashion centers, such as Los Angeles.

Advertising and Promotion

The emphasis on personal selling, however, does not stop the fashion manufacturer from advertising nationally to the consumer if he can afford it, or from seeking publicity in the consumer press. Some manufacturers invite representatives of the fashion press to their openings each season and follow through with a barrage of press releases about their lines and their activities. Many of the photographs and stories about fashion that appear on the women's pages of newspapers actually originate in press releases from the publicity departments of manufacturers.

Other promotional techniques include providing the retailer with selling aids: counter cards, display materials, customer mailing pieces, newspaper advertising mats, and photographs for use in store ads. Still other aids offered to retailers are training talks to store salespeople and help in staging fashion shows for customers by supplying scripts and sometimes commentators. Widespread use is made of cooperative advertising, an arrangement under which manufacturer and retailer share the cost of newspaper advertising run in the store's name to promote the manufacturer's goods. The retailer enjoys more advertising space than he pays for out of his own pocket; the manufacturer enjoys advertising that is run in conjunction with the name of a locally known and respected retail store, and that is usually backed up by the store with a substantial stock of that maker's goods. The retailer, moreover, as a large and consistent purchaser of space in his local papers, earns a much lower rate than the manufacturer could obtain for his occasional insertions; "co-op" money buys the garment producer more space for less cost.

In addition to the efforts they make to reach consumers directly or through the retailer, fashion manufacturers also use trade publications to advertise their merchandise to the retailer. The small, often highly specialized circulation of these publications brings their advertising rates far below those of consumer magazines, and a fashion manufacturer does not have to be very large to make good use of them.

Brand Names

The rise of giant apparel firms in the 1950s opened the door to the use of national advertising and marketing campaigns in support of manufacturers' brand and firm names. This development was encouraged by the substantial amounts of promotional funds made available by large producers of man-made fibers, such as Allied Chemical, Celanese, DuPont, and Monsanto.

Before World War II, the names of American designers and garment manufacturers were not generally well known to consumers; apparel was purchased by a combination of approval of a garment's appearance and confidence in the retail seller. The source of a dress or coat was considered the retailer's trade secret.

During World War II, merchandise shortages encouraged retailers to go along with the idea of featuring a maker's name if that was how he wanted it and if that would help secure salable merchandise for their stores. Later, when merchandise was again plentiful, other advantages of featuring makers' names and brands demonstrated themselves: opportunities for subsidized advertising and promotional tie-ins with fiber and fabric sources; editorial mentions of producers' names and sometimes of store names by consumer magazines; and opportunities for giant concerns to cultivate nationwide markets for their brand-name products by means of national advertising that they could now afford.

The amount of brand-name advertising done by apparel makers today is impressive in comparison with the almost nonexistent industry advertising of the days before World War II, but it is still small in comparison with what is spent by other major industries, such as automobiles, drugs, cigarettes, and foods. In fact, the apparel industry spends less than 1 percent of its sales for advertising as compared to an average of 1.4 percent of sales for all major manufacturing industries combined; 2.4 percent of sales for the food industry; 4.0 percent for the chemical industry; and 5.4 percent for tobacco, for example.[21]

There is a point of view in the apparel industry that advertising is something that can be overdone. David Schwartz, who headed the largest dress corporation in the world—Jonathan Logan, Inc.—once said that "in the fashion industry, it may be dangerous to over-advertise. If a particular design is seen too much, the woman who wants to be different will not buy it."[22] Another reason may be that the average woman is much more concerned with style and becomingness of garments than with the name that appears on them.

This last element, especially, gives a newcomer to the fashion business as good a

[21]*Advertising Age*, July 16, 1973, p. 34.
[22]"Big Business Comes to the Fashion Industry" in *Challenge, the Magazine of Economic Affairs*, April 1962.

chance to succeed as a more widely advertised maker, if he is able to offer a better-styled line. The premium is still on ingenuity in producing clothes that find consumer acceptance.

Cultivation of Foreign Markets

The fashion industry exports relatively little of its merchandise, but some of the larger manufacturers have found a way to develop markets abroad in spite of high tariff barriers and transportation costs. They do this by franchising foreign producers—that is, exporting their know-how instead of the actual merchandise. A typical arrangement is for the American producer to provide the designs, patterns, and technical manufacturing help to a foreign licensee who produces and markets the merchandise in his own country. Bobbie Brooks, the American sportswear producer, has such an arrangement with a Japanese firm. Jonathan Logan has a similar arrangement—covering women's knitwear—with another Japanese producer. Blue Bell has franchises all over the world for its Wrangler jeans.

Direct exporting is done, however, by a few individual firms whose brand names have been long and widely known. Often these are firms whose product requires skills that remain uniquely American, such as the mass production of garments in which precise fit is a critical element. Notable in this area is Maidenform, whose brassieres and related garments have virtually worldwide distribution. They are shipped not only to the entire Western hemisphere but also to Europe (including Russia) and to Japan. Other firms, like Kayser-Roth, cultivate foreign markets both ways. For some products and in some countries, they make licensing arrangements; for other products and countries, they export American-made goods.

FASHION DESIGN ACTIVITIES

The development of American design creativity was inhibited considerably by the undisputed position of the Paris couturiers as fashion originators. Most styles produced in the early years of the fashion business were adaptations or copies of Paris fashions. The fashion press, moreover, concentrated its attention on Paris offerings. Not until France fell to the Germans in the 1940s, and America was cut off from the French influence, did our own country's designers receive their long overdue recognition. Today, American designers include among their number many who are trend setters in their own right and whose names are well known to the public. Even so, the vast majority of the industry's designers remain completely unknown to the general public. Publicity tends to center on the designers whose output is newsmaking, forward looking—and usually so high priced that it represents only a small fraction of the industry's total output.

Diversity of Design Arrangements

The relationships between manufacturers and designers on Seventh Avenue are diverse and individual. Some companies hire one, two, or even a large staff of designers; others may hire none and rely on free lances or even a patternmaker with a good fashion sense. In most cases, the name of the house is featured and the designer remains behind the scenes—even if the designer is well known within the industry and has contributed mightily toward building acceptance for the company's name. Unless there is some assurance of a permanent relationship, the manufacturer seldom sees any advantage in building up the designer's name instead of his own.

Some of the best known designers, like Pauline Trigère, Mollie Parnis, and Adele Simpson, own their own firms. Others, like Bonnie Cashin and John Weitz, have their own free-lance design studios and do collections for manufacturers. A new trend is for designers to be backed by outside financial interests, under arrangements like those described in a reading that follows, explaining how Ben Shaw financed the design firms of Donald Brooks and Geoffrey Beene. In a similar arrangement, the Kenton Corporation backed the well-known designers, Oscar de la Renta and Halston, in their firms.

The output of "name" designers such as these is not relatively great in terms of units produced or volume of sales, but they do produce the major part of the industry's fashion news and secure the major part of its publicity.

"Couture" Ready-to-Wear

To differentiate the output of such high-priced firms as these from its more commonplace products, Seventh Avenue has perpetrated a semantic contradiction: "couture ready-to-wear." The designers themselves, moreover, have organized themselves into an association known as the New York Couture Business Council. Actually, however, these firms are not couture houses in the literal sense, no matter how high priced their garments are. As a subsequent chapter explains, a couture house is one that produces individually made versions of its own designs, each garment made precisely to the measurements of the individual customer. In America, however, the market for custom-made clothes has reached the vanishing point. The clothes of all our great designers are factory produced and distributed through retail stores. If adjustments are needed to make a garment fit the customer more accurately than a standard size happens to fit her, the required alterations are made in the store's workroom.

Prevalence of Style Piracy

Design and styling are such important competitive weapons in the fashion industry that style piracy, against which U.S. laws provide no protection, is considered a way of life in the garment trades. Copying the work of creative designers is standard operating procedure for many firms, especially the smaller ones and those dealing in cheaper lines. In the language of the industry, however, a design is never "stolen." It is copied, adapted, translated, or even pirated but never considered as having been stolen. This is not hypocrisy but simply the garment trade's way of acknowledging that copying dominates the industry; it is done openly and without apology. The late Norman Norell, considered the dean of American designers, expressed his philosophy about style piracy: "I don't mind if the knock-off houses give me a season with my dress. What I mind is if they bring out their copies faster than I get my own dresses to the stores."[23]

There are several reasons for this copying practice. Plunging into a fast-selling style, regardless of whose design it was originally, is one way to make a modest capital work to the limit. Another reason why style piracy is rife arises from the highly specialized nature of the firms themselves. If, for example, a dress intended to retail at $100 has features that would make it a fast seller at a lower price, the originator of the style is in no position to produce or market inexpensive versions. On the other hand, a maker specializing in garments to retail at $30 quite definitely is in such a position. And if the style can be copied still lower down the price scale, to perhaps $18 retail, a maker specializing in that level steps in.

Occasionally, the copying process is reversed, and a style that originates in the lower-priced lines will have features that make it desirable for higher-priced manufacturers to adapt. Normally, however, the procedure is for a style that originally retailed for hundreds of dollars to be "knocked off" at successively lower prices, if it shows signs of popular acceptance by customers. So common is style pirating that the industry even has a special term for a style produced by many different manufacturers at many different prices. They refer to it as a "ford."

Designers and Mass Production

Although it is often hard to pinpoint where original designing ends and copying begins, the creative expression of their designers or stylists is still the foundation of any apparel firm, and a vital element in its success. The economics of mass production, however, imposes tremendous pressures on the creative process. Whether the designer is an employer or employee, he must be practical and know what his firm is capable of and willing to produce. He must know what the customer has accepted in the past and will accept in the future. He must be original notwithstanding the fact that it is a great struggle to get huge textile concerns to produce, in small yardage, new textures and colors with which to experiment. His new style creations must be acceptable to many retail buyers, or they will never be produced.

Fashion designing may be an art but, in the final analysis, fashion is a business. As one design authority expressed it: "All successful designers eventually have to

[23]"He's a Fashion Purist with the Golden Touch" in *Business Week,* Sept. 12, 1964, pp. 64ff.

come to grips with the hard facts of fashion: that every design must be judged by whether or not it will sell, and that a style that's new and exciting is not necessarily salable. The designer must learn to take the commercial view of her own work."[24]

DIVIDING THE GARMENT DOLLAR

How Each Dollar Spent for Women's Garments is Divided among Wages of Production Workers, Material Costs, Manufactures' Overhead and Profit and Retailers' Markup

		Wages	Material	Mfrs'. Overhead and Profit	Retail Markup
Coats, Suits, Skirts	1961	14¢	31¢	18¢	37¢
	1969	12¢	28¢	20¢	40¢
Dresses	1961	17¢	27¢	20¢	36¢
	1969	14¢	24¢	21¢	41¢
Blouses	1961	15¢	29¢	18¢	38¢
	1969	13¢	26¢	20¢	41¢
Children's Outerwear	1961	16¢	29¢	18¢	37¢
	1969	14¢	27¢	20¢	39¢
Underwear	1961	13¢	32¢	16¢	39¢
	1969	12¢	28¢	17¢	43¢
Corsets and Brassieres	1961	12¢	21¢	22¢	45¢
	1969	10¢	23¢	21¢	46¢

Source: Research Department, ILGWU.

FASHION ACCESSORIES

Accessories, like the clothes with which they are worn, are for the most part mass-produced in this country. The industries that manufacture these goods are as diverse in size and nature as the merchandise itself. Some, like shoes and hosiery, are large and dominated by huge producers; others, like gloves, handbags, and millinery, are made up of small firms. Some are highly mechanized; others still use hand operations not much changed from those that prevailed 50 or even 100 years ago. Some have their plants in or near New York City; others are hundreds of miles from that center and merely have showrooms there.

The accessories industries do have several elements in common, however. All are

[24]Rosalie Kolodny, *Fashion Design for Moderns*, Fairchild Publications, New York, 1968, p. 43.

extremely responsive to fashion and are very quick to interpret incoming trends. Often consumer reaction to accessories fashions is the signal for a coming change in apparel fashions. For example, belts became popular in 1968 and 1969, even though it took a few years more for the silhouette itself to move closer to the body and place emphasis on waistlines. Extra long scarfs, emphasizing a long, lean look were worn in 1969 and 1970, while women were clinging to miniskirts and debating whether or not to try long skirt lengths. The growing popularity of over-the-shoulder bags in the early 1970s heralded the importance of those on-the-go clothes that *Women's Wear Daily* christened "sportive."

Also characteristic of most of the accessories industries is that they create two lines a year—one for spring and one for fall—timed to coincide as closely as possible with major apparel showings. This practice makes it easier for merchants to coordinate the apparel and accesories they purchase and to make sure that the assortments in their various departments reflect the look or looks that they believe their customers will accept.

In this section, we briefly examine representative industries in the fashion accessories field.

Costume Jewelry

Jewelry producers are divided into two separate and distinct industries. One industry works only with precious metals and gem stones and is referred to as the fine jewelry industry. The other is called the costume or fashion jewelry industry, and it works with whatever materials suit its needs and fancy: base metals, plastics, wood, ceramics, simulated pearls, and beads, for instance.

There are more than 750 firms in the costume jewelry field employing over 20,000 people and with a combined annual output above $500 million at wholesale. The industry has its giants, notably Coro in Providence, R.I., but small firms predominate. Three out of every four companies employ fewer than 20 people each. New York has almost half the country's plants; Rhode Island has most of the rest. In all, the New England and Middle Atlantic states account for nearly 90 percent of the plants in the country, and for more than 90 percent of the output.[25] Lines are shown in New York City, but without the fanfare of formal market weeks. Many of the producers have showrooms in the Marbridge Building, on New York's Herald Square, and a retail buyer can tour the various floors and review a number of lines on a visit.

Costume jewelry is one of the few industries in which both mass producers and tiny, handicraft operators can prosper. Women dearly love a touch of individuality in their dress, and this can be provided easily by a piece of distinctive costume jewelry. Thus a clever and creative craftsman can produce unusual pieces and sell them directly to the public or through a few nearby stores. If he has a true feeling for fashion and for jewelry, he may expand his operation. Most of those who enter the

[25]U.S. Department of Commerce: *Census of Manufactures, 1967; U.S. Industrial Outlook, 1973.*

Annual Factory Shipments of Shoes and Selected Accessories

PRODUCT	FACTORY VALUE OF 1972 SALES[a]
	(millions)
Shoes[b]	$3,200
Jewelry, precious metal[b]	1,030
Jewelry, costume[b]	506
Handbags, billfolds, and small leather goods[b]	530
Millinery	40
Furs	200
Apparel belts[b]	175
Artificial flowers	65
Hosiery	900

Source: U.S. Department of Commerce, *U.S. Industrial Outlook, 1973*, plus authors' estimates based on 1967 Census of Manufacturers and Annual Survey of Manufactures 1971.
[a] Retail values, allowing for transportation and markup would be roughly 1.6 times the value of shipments.
[b] Includes men's, women's, and children's.

industry by the handicraft route, however, are dedicated to a single material or single type of jewelry. When fashion favors it, they ride with the tide. When the vogue for their specialty dies, handicraft workers subside into hobby activity instead of venturing into other materials and techniques.

Gloves

The glove industry in the United States produces about $300 million worth of gloves at wholesale values; in addition, we import about $45 million more. The leather glove industry is located principally in the Northeast, with many of its plants in the city of Gloversville, New York. Fabric gloves are made in plants more widely distributed throughout the country but, nevertheless, with more than one-third in the Northeast. The two sections of the industry employ a total of 22,000 people in 320 plants. In the leather glove industry, where many hand-guided operations are required, fewer than half the plants employ as many as 20 people each; in the fabric glove industry, a majority of plants have 20 or more employees each.

Imports are a serious threat to the market of the leather branch of the glove industry. In 1972, about one-quarter of the leather gloves available to consumers in the United States were imported. A considerable portion of the imports were actually designed and cut in the United States, but shipped to the Philippine Islands for sewing and brought back into the country at a more favorable tariff rate than if they had originated abroad.[26]

The major market center for gloves—leather or fabric, domestic or imported—is, of course, New York City where many of the principal firms maintain permanent showrooms. These are usually in the East 30s, where many lingerie firms have their offices. Gloves, especially fabric gloves, are often produced by divisions of companies that also own foundation and lingerie companies—Kayser-Roth and Van Raalte, for instance. Leather gloves are usually produced by firms that are glove specialists, such as Meyers Make, Grandoe, and Dawnelle, to name a few. Some of the leather glove firms also produce fabric gloves, but that is about as far as they have gone in the line of diversification. They are glovers, first and foremost, and they flourish or suffer according to whether fashion smiles on or ignores the glove.

Handbags

Factory production of handbags in the United States takes place in 500 plants, of which 2 in every 3 are located in the New York area. Years ago, leather was the principal material from which bags were made, and this meant a large amount of hand-guided work. In recent years, plastics have displaced leather to the extent that four-fifths of the industry's output today is of that material. Leather, being a natural product, requires inspection, care, and resourcefulness in the cutting. Plastic sheeting, being man-made, can be cut as simply as fabrics from bolts of standard-width material.

The handbag industry remains an industry that is composed of small firms; half its plants employ fewer than 20 people each. Total output of the industry, at wholesale, is under $300 million a year. In addition, over $60 million a year in handbags is imported. Leather bags come from Europe; inexpensive plastic types from the Far East. Both types have been coming into the country at an increasing rate ever since 1960; by 1972, imports represented more than one-fifth of the total value of handbags available to the U.S. consumer.[27]

For the most part, handbag production remains in the hands of specialists; diversification is not yet the order of the day. In fact, even such accessories for handbags as wallets and key cases are made in a separate industry known as the personal leather goods industry, whose output is $250 million a year.

Hosiery

The hosiery industry is made up primarily of large firms, many of which are divisions of huge textile conglomerates. For example, Burlington Mills, Cannon Mills, and the

---

[26]U.S. Department of Commerce: *Annual Survey of Manufactures, 1971; Census of Manufactures, 1967; U.S. Industrial Outlook, 1973.*

[27]U.S. Department of Commerce: *Census of Manufactures, 1967; U.S. Industrial Outlook, 1973.*

J.P. Stevens Company have divisions that produce hosiery. Apparel conglomerates, notably Kayser-Roth, are also in the hosiery business. The industry is highly mechanized and does not offer a foothold to the craftsman with nothing but creativity to offer; a substantial investment in machinery is necessary.

Unlike other accessories industries, the hosiery field operates somewhat in the pattern described in connection with textile converters. Stockings are knitted in the *greige* and then can be dyed in whatever color is desired. This makes it possible for a wholesaler (or retailer or group of retailers) to initiate a private brand, specifying the colors and grade desired, and arranging to have the finished hose labeled and boxed with the brand name that has been chosen, instead of with the mill's own name.

More than 800 mills produce hosiery in the United States, most of them employing more than 20 people per plant. Industry employees total more than 100,000, about two-thirds of whom are engaged in the women's branch. Output of the industry, at wholesale, is approaching $2 billion; the women's branch alone is $900 million, nearly half the total. More than half the plants are located in North Carolina, and their combined output represents three-quarters of the value of the industry's output.[28] New York City, however, is the market center where the various companies maintain their showrooms. It is there that retail buyers come twice a year to select spring and fall styles, to learn about the national advertising programs of the big producers, and to arrange, if possible, for manufacturer cooperative participation in their own local advertising.

Millinery

The millinery industry in the United States is quite small, having been desperately hurt by the fashion for hatlessness that was widespread during the 1950s and 1960s. Annual output is considerably less than $50 million at wholesale, and total industry employment is not much above 7000 people. There are nearly 500 plants in the industry, almost all of them in the New York City area, and the vast majority of them are small.[29] Operations in the industry are mostly hand guided, and limited capital is no great bar to entry into the field. The industry has had its share of gifted designers, but these usually cater to the custom trade or move on into apparel, where the opportunities and rewards are much greater. Instead of a designer like an Adolfo or a Halston, the typical millinery house is likely to have a copyist and to devote its productive capacity to inexpensive versions of currently successful styles.

An unusual and important factor in the industry is the millinery syndicate. Such a firm operates leased millinery departments in retail stores across the country and provides these stores with a continuing supply of new styles. In order to obtain such styles, the syndicates have their buyers in the market constantly, not only to seek out actual merchandise but also to find and develop talented new producers. Help,

[28]U.S. Department of Commerce, *Census of Manufactures, 1967*; and *Annual Survey of Manufactures, 1971*.
[29]*Ibid.*

advice, and sometimes even operating capital will be made available by the syndicates to potentially creative resources.

Unlike other accessories, millinery does not function on two lines a year. Seasonality has its influence, of course, but in millinery the important element is an unending procession of new styles or new versions of currently accepted styles. Whether millinery itself is declining or growing in fashion importance, retail millinery shops and departments constantly require something new. At one time, when millinery was in its heyday, retailers sought to have completely new assortments every three or four weeks, and the term "millinery turnover" was used in retail circles to describe extremely fast-moving merchandise.

The millinery industry is primarily one of specialists and has been untouched by the drives toward bigness and diversification that most other fashion industries have experienced. Smallness is no handicap in a field like millinery, where there is little opportunity to mechanize, automate, or develop techniques for producing huge runs of individual numbers. If anything, smallness and the ability to "turn on a dime" are advantages. The life of the usual style number is short, and the faster a firm gets into and out of a good number, the better the operation, as a rule.

Shoes

The American public spends more than $9 billion a year on shoes for men, women, and children. The major portion of this merchandise comes from domestic producers, but imports, nevertheless, account for a substantial portion—over 20 percent of the value of the total supply. The U.S. shoe industry produces more than 500 million pairs of shoes and slippers a year, half of which are for women. The 560 firms in the field operate nearly 1000 plants in at least 40 of the 50 States. The Northeast is the major production area, with the states of Pennsylvania and Massachusetts alone accounting for one-quarter of the nation's output. Most of the plants in the industry are large, employing more than 20 people each.[30] The shoe industry, however, has not yet made great strides toward automation since much of its output uses leather, a natural product that requires hand-guided operations. Quick response to fashion is difficult, since each style number must be made up in a huge range of sizes. The problem is further complicated by the need to invest in lasts—the forms over which shoes are shaped—whenever a new style requires this. If a new style number means merely changes in color, trim, and detail this is not necessary, but if the whole shape of a shoe is to be changed, the old lasts will no longer suit. Despite these problems, the shoe industry has been able to speed its productive methods, simplify its size ranges, and keep in step with fashion.

Mergers, diversification, and conglomerates are a familiar story in the shoe business. One of the best known conglomerates in the fashion field, Genesco, was the General Shoe Company before it acquired its present roster of apparel

---

[30]U.S. Department of Commerce: *Census of Manufactures, 1967; Industrial Outlook, 1973;* and *Survey of Current Business,* July, 1973, p. 29.

producing firms and retail stores. The present trend in mergers in the shoe industry is for large firms to acquire small- and medium-sized companies that specialize in types or price lines that the acquiring companies do not themselves produce. Another trend is for large shoe producers to diversify into related lines, like luggage. Diversification into the shoe business by those unfamiliar with it, however, has not been notably successful. Apparel manufacturers have attempted it, in recent years, only to sell off or discontinue their shoe divisions thankfully after exposure to the problems of an industry entirely different from their own.

The shoe industry, unlike most others in the fashion field, has a considerable portion of its business concentrated in the hands of a few large firms. The eight largest shoe companies provide 34 percent of the industry's total output. By contrast, it requires the combined output of the 50 largest producers in the dress business to provide even 24 percent of that industry's total. In the fashion field, only the cosmetics industry has a higher degree of concentration in the hands of large companies than the shoe industry. In cosmetics, the eight largest firms account for 52 percent of the industry's volume.[31]

Other Accessories Industries

The roster of fashion accessories industries includes also such tiny industries as belts, neckwear, scarves, and handkerchiefs, whose combined output totals little more than $300 million a year at wholesale. The fortunes of these and other accessories industries wax and wane according to the direction taken by fashion. When skirts are short, shoes, boots, and hosiery have their day. When fashions move close to the body, belts and bodystockings gain in importance. With ladylike, romantic fashions, elegant neckwear and gloves flourish. A gypsy influence brings beads, bracelets, and earrings into strong demand. And so it goes.

The Designer's Role

"Name" designers were rare in the accessories field until the late 1960s. Many accessories producers, in fact, managed quite well with free-lance designers who would come in twice a year to "style" the line. Others maintained designing staffs who did their work unrecognized by retailers or consumers. To make capital of a designer's name was the exception rather than the rule, even among really creative houses.

In the 1960s, however, the total "look" became important in fashion and consumers began putting together outfits in which the accessories were quite as essential as the apparel items. For example, a jumper might be combined with a bodystocking, vest, scarf, cap, boots, gloves, and shoulder bag to achieve the

[31]U.S. Department of Commerce: *Statistical Abstract of the United States, 1972,* p. 705.

precise degree of casual smartness the customer wished to achieve. Without the right accessories, the "look" is not possible.

This trend has broadened the designer's field and has brought apparel creators into accessories. European couture greats, like St. Laurent, Cardin, and Valentino, have moved into accessories to complete the look that their apparel is intended to achieve. Among other items, they design scarves on which their signatures appear—to provide status as well as fashion satisfaction to the wearer. Other apparel designers have moved into various accessories fields, usually working with a different manufacturing company for each type of product and usually limiting their involvement to the creative function. Hosiery, scarves, patterns, watches, and luggage—all by Bill Blass—are a notable example of this movement.

There are few barriers today to the designer who understands what the fashion consumer wants. The importance of the total look has developed a need for total design and for a unified presentation of accepted fashion ideas throughout every branch of the fashion industry. By bringing great designing names into accessories, this trend is also encouraging accessories manufacturers to develop and publicize their own potentially great design talent.

READINGS

The articles and talks selected for inclusion in this section are concerned with the growth and development of the women's apparel manufacturing business in twentieth century America. Some readings provide an overall view of the industry; others deal with individuals and individual firms. Together, they show how the industry's growth has been nurtured by developing creativity, marketing skill, and financial strength. Further development in these three areas will undoubtedly contribute to future growth.

THE DEVELOPMENT OF AMERICAN CREATIVITY IN FASHION

Virginia Pope

You've often heard the expression "from rags to riches." Creativity, as applied to the garment industry, might well be referred to as "from the tailored skirt to billions." It has all happened in a comparatively short space of time, as human events go. It has taken about three-quarters of a century to move from the cutting table to the design room and the most beautiful and luxurious of creations by highly trained artists.

In the late 1800's, there existed only men's suit factories and makers of underwear. The former graduated into the making of ladies' skirts, the latter produced shirtwaists. Such was the market in those days. Fine ladies were costumed by dressmakers. Women went out and sewed by the day; small dressmaking houses had plates as their guides. Then there were the extravagant salons where costly costumes were confectioned. I question that the word designer was used, certainly not with frequency. The caterers to the wealthy went to Paris for their fashions.

You will find it hard to believe, when I tell you that it was not until 1908 that some bright fellow had the brilliant idea of joining a bodice to a skirt and calling it a dress. Houses manufacturing them were later to become well known in better brackets.

It was just before World War I that manufacturers became aware of Paris. They learned that the Miss Carrolls, Thurns, Farquahrson & Wheelock, and similar houses, went to Paris and brought back

SOURCE: As fashion editor of The New York Times for 25 years, Miss Pope "eye-witnessed" and also influenced many developments in the apparel industry. She delivered this address to a Retail Workshop in Fashion Merchandising on February 3, 1964, at the Fashion Institute of Technology, New York, N.Y.

fabulous clothes for their private clientele. Awesome names were Worth, Paquin, Cheruit, and Callot. These were creators in a real sense. The boys got wise: they hopped on fast French liners, taking a showroom girl or model with them. Off they went to the races—it was at Longchamps that they saw the styles worn by the flashing demimondaines who set the pace. They went, they saw, they bought. From the costumes they brought back they learned the intricacies of French cut. They were apt at translating them to their need, and applying their technique to their purpose.

Creators of fashion were in the making. Some of the young women pioneers were later to grow famous in their own right. Outstanding was Louise Barnes Gallagher, designer and manufacturer of suits. She was perhaps best known for a fabric she developed, Gallagher mesh, forerunner of our present-day knitted fabrics. Another smart gal was Jo Copeland, whose name is known from coast to coast for her high-style fashions.

Merchants caught the Paris fever. In the summer of 1914, John Wanamaker sent his top buyer and stylist, Mary Walls (her name is legend), to bring back a collection. The Germans were advancing on Compiègne. In the course of being shipped out, her trunks were lost. Nothing daunted, Irish Mary dashed behind the lines, the atmosphere blue around her (she could swear like the best of troopers), and found her treasures. She returned to New York triumphant. Mr. Wanamaker turned on the works. He notified Mr. Hearst, of journalistic fame; the papers carried banner headlines; and crowds rushed into the store. Paris fashions had their first volley of publicity.

The couture furore spread. Fabric houses found a means of bringing Paris to the manufacturers. They bought sizeable groups of originals, and invited the cutters to see and copy them, provided they signed a guaranty to purchase $250 worth of fabrics with which to manufacture them.

The industry was struggling to its feet. Embryonic creators were getting their first experience. A new element was entering the scene. The leaders had been tailors. Edwin Goodman, Eddy Meyer, and Harry Frechtel knew the intricacies of cutting and fitting, bringing perfection to their trade. Young designers, artists in the matter of coloring and detail, added embellishments to the severity of the tailored costume.

In 1918, the wholesale price of a dress ranged from $16 to $39. The $10 dress was born over the weekend in the May 1919 depression. The bottom fell out of the fabric market: raw silk dropped from $20 to $7; silk fell from $2.75 a yard to $1.50. John Wanamaker jumped into the situation, and marked down his prices by 25 per cent. With such a drop in values, the manufacturer could afford to cheapen his product. By the end of 1919, the $10 dress was firmly established, and has held its own ever since.

Unions were few and far between in those days, and lacked organization. Price adjustments were easily made. It was all week work: those who were paid $12 then receive $125 now. Bundles went to the factories, dresses were individually draped. Mass production was in full sway.

Let us remember that, immediately after the war, fabric types were limited. Dresses were of cotton, wool, or silk. Textures were not known as they are today. Among the woolens, broadcloth was high style; gabardine and serge were utilitarian. Designers had less to work with. It was not until some time later that nubby fabrics came into being. Textures and weights changed. Man-made fibers were soon to revolutionize the fabric field. Creativity was at work in chemistry, as well as in fashion.

The art of fashion was beginning to bloom when the industry moved uptown into the garment center. Young women who had been trained in the skills of French dressmaking used their ability to devise the soft suit. In Paris, they had outstanding leaders: Chanel and Molyneux were revolutionary. The severely tailored suit yielded its place to the newcomer. Jane Derby is mentioned as one of the first to skillfully adopt the theme. From her dressmaking establishment on upper Broadway came Nettie Rosenstein, whose little black dresses made

fashion history. Another name in the twenties and thirties was Anna Smithlein, sister of Adele Simpson. Not only were these women able designers, they were, and still are, successful business executives.

It was about this time that creativity in fashion branched out in another direction. A new and exciting influence came out of Hollywood and the movies. The pictures called forth talent—American talent. The most brilliant was Adrian: he influenced a generation. I hear young designers speak of him with bated breath. Other men who dressed the stars were Travis Banton and Omar Kyam. The glamorous actresses whose charms they enhanced cast their aura over the country; in every hamlet, women aimed to copy them.

In the thirties, we had good designers in New York, but so great was the enthusiasm over Paris that they went unsung. Their names were rarely mentioned in the press or by the stores. It took another war to bring about a change in creativity. Complying with the limitations on the use of materials imposed by the government, the designers performed brilliantly. With Paris blacked out and no couturiers to play up, we discovered our own. A great woman and an outstanding merchant, Dorothy Shaver (later president of Lord & Taylor), recognized America's young designers and brought them to the fore. She promoted and advertised them, gave shows, and invited press and public. Among them were: Elizabeth Hawes, Helen Cookman, Clare Potter, Claire McCardell, and Vera Maxwell. What an incentive to creativity!

Fashion was reaching out in many directions. The urge of youth was strong. Ours is a country of sport-loving people; nature offers us vast playgrounds. Responding, young talents turned to sportswear. They created brilliantly with freedom and color. Once again, California, with its enthusiasm for open-air fun, came to the fore. Throughout the world, America took the lead in playclothes. An enormous market was developed.

American democracy and know-how gave creativity another opportunity to show its ingenuity and strength. Ready-to-wear opened a broad vista—clothes for everybody, short and tall, thick and thin, young and old. Sizing and styling for age groups were the next steps. In the "dark ages," there had been 10's to 14's and mamma house dresses (32, 34, 36, 38, 40). Children's clothes were very simple. A whole army of young things was crying out for styles of their own. Along came Jack Horwitz with the gayest of junior togs, styled by college-age kids who understood their own needs. Emily Wilkens took teenagers out of the little-girl class and offered them sophistication. There followed designers for subteens. Soon, tiny tots' clothes were inspired by Paris.

Then statistics forced on makers the fact that 75 per cent of the women in the country were 5'4" and under. Designers faced another challenge. Came fashions for the short-waisted, the petites, the "Troy" figure—everyone has a different name for them.

With each new phase, there was fresh talent to meet its call. The young element was better equipped than its forerunners had been. Far-thinking spirits in industry and education recognized the need for training young people eager to enter the fashion world. Schools and colleges started courses in design and merchandising. Three great institutions were founded in New York—Pratt, Parsons, and the Fashion Institute of Technology, the last-named the outgrowth of the Needle Trades High School.

All of this puts us on the threshold of a fabulous era, for as in the other arts such as science and industry, fashion is living up to the American tradition of productivity and progress. But, it is not all whipped cream. Our artists face many stumbling blocks, and they are not easy to hurdle. This Niagara of talent that we have in our midst is sometimes dammed—I use the word without the "n." It is restrained because of the constrictions and restrictions of the business world.

Once again, I look back to earlier days when New York's stores were under the guidance of giant merchants, men of authority and individual taste. They had a personal interest in all that went into their businesses. Such were John Wanamaker, Paul Bonwit, Franklin Simon, Edwin Goodman. They were in close contact with their buyers, they knew the manufacturers and their products, and they were well informed about the customers who came into their stores. An amazing example was S. Klein of 14th Street, who invited the most fashionable social registerites to luncheon at Sherry's. Mr. Edwin Goodman, I am told, was a frequent visitor to the garment center houses from whom he

bought. He checked fabrics, and made certain that production came up to standard. He was often seen throughout the store. No one was a better judge of furs. Owner-controlled shops were more individual in their buying. Men of the type I refer to gave wide latitude to their buyers, who were the Napoleons of their departments.

True, business was not conducted on the same volume basis as it has been in the last quarter of a century. Management and policies have changed. In 1963, figures count—we are in the impersonal IBM stage. The mechanical mind, rather than individual thinking, is in control. Banks are at the helm. Statistical information is the guiding power of the chain-store empire. The buyer is no longer as close to the customer. She is directly responsible to her merchandise manager. The bugbear of her existence is the markdown. With corporation control, banks care more about figures than style and individuality.

Buyers, prone to stick with the best sellers of last season, resist experimental new styles—a dampening effect on creativity. The manufacturer, seeing a bold innovation on the part of his designer, removes it from the line or never cuts it. Young designers, and older ones as well, who aim to put America abreast if not ahead of Paris, are discouraged by these hindrances. . . .

My friends in the market, who have lived through several decades of expanding creativity, point out other changes. For example, in the twenties and thirties, it was not the custom to show large collections. Limited groups were presented for not more than six or seven weeks. Buyers came to the showrooms frequently, and placed their orders promptly. All of this has altered. Collections are larger and more comprehensive, ranging from daytime to cocktail and evening dresses. As about 50 per cent of the average collection is put into production, it is almost impossible for the manufacturer to place the orders for his fabrics far in advance. Deliveries are frequently from eight to ten weeks.

The designer has greater stature. Much more is demanded of him. The scope of his creativity has broadened. The dress house makes suits, the suit house makes dresses. Contrary to the practices of yesterday, the designer's name is promoted by stores and press; his clothes carry his signature as unmistakably as a canvas does a painter's. The customer, aware of this identity, seeks the creations of a favorite. The manufacturer, on his part, has developed customers with whose buying habits he is familiar, and which he is partially responsible for molding.

SEVENTH AVENUE'S NEW, CORPORATE LOOK

Isadore Barmash

Giantism is becoming Seventh Avenue's hottest number as consolidation and diversification toughen the warp and woof of America's apparel industry

In vivid contrast to the traditionally amorphous outlines of the women's apparel industry, a new shape has been emerging on Seventh Avenue. The new shape represents the consolidation of companies into multi-product manufacturers, their lines either closely related or diverse.

Spreading giantism, the result of the consolidation trend, has brought sweeping changes to both the scene and image of Seventh Avenue. The reality of apparel makers transacting $200 million a year, as Jonathan Logan hopes to do this year, or $125 million, as Bobbie Brooks expects in 1966, has caused not only retailers, but bankers, investors, and economists to radically revise their concept of the garment industry.

Economists are discovering that it is hardly the highly-fragmentized industry it was only a few years ago. "Seventh Avenue" is no longer dominated by small producers with little concept of marketing and maximum annual sales of $30 million.

Either Logan or Brooks today represents a corporate consolidation which is the equivalent of 15 to 25 separate companies. And each of its entities, or divisions, has its own marketing plan, closely tied in with retail growth objectives. . . .

SOURCE: Reprinted from *Stores* magazine, September 1966. Permission granted. Isadore Barmash is a business writer for *The New York Times.*

Consolidation, strangely enough, flowers both in good and bad times.

During bad times, for example, liquidations, curtailments of operations and other depression symptoms tend to reduce the number of active companies.

However, growth among the giants in recent years clearly denotes an attempt to capitalize on good times, to seize opportunites, and to use the financial and administrative benefits of the corporate umbrella to capture a greater share of the market.

On Seventh Avenue, the expansionary forces in the past decade have seen a 50 per cent gain in consumer apparel spending, improved retail and merchandising patterns, public ownership of companies, improved profitability via multi-line operations, and a beckoning foreign market.

Within the past year, apparel industry leaders have taken their most ambitious steps toward greater diversification through acquisition.

I. PROS AND CONS

Retailers and labor union officials have welcomed the advent of new, large companies and the ever-increasing size of Seventh Avenue leaders.

Giantism also means more advertising, more efficient service—mainly due to use of electronic data processing for inventory systems—more knowledgeable and sophisticated salesmen, with consequent benefits in helping to train salespeople, and a better break in the fabric market.

But the giant aspect has some drawbacks for stores. The giants are demanding. They want large orders, and they want them early.

As the head of one major specialty store, who thought it wiser not to be identified, put it:

"It's good dealing with the big manufacturers because they come with ideas, with selling and marketing plans, and they back it all up with top skill in manufacturing. It has taken a lot of the guesswork out of the merchandising picture. But the rub is that many of them are geared to big, forward commitments. They're impatient with you unless you come across in a big way in the beginning—they want you to extend yourself—and all through the season. The pitch of these boys is that they're partners in business with you. But that, for obvious reasons, just can't be the case."

Before his retirement last June after 34 years in his post, David Dubinsky, president of the powerful International Ladies' Garment Workers Union, commented:

"We'd rather deal with the big boys. They're tougher for us to bargain with—but because of their size, their commitments, their greater responsibility, they have to be industry-minded. The trouble with the small manufacturer is he doesn't have this feeling about the whole industry, only about himself. The new trend today is to assume part of the responsibility for all."

Louis Stulberg, successor to Dubinsky, feels the same way. He was, for many years, head of the union's organizing drive. He was also instrumental in the I.L.G.W.U.'s signing "national labor agreements" with the Logans, the Brooks, and other king-sized firms.

In addition to the last-mentioned companies, which dominate the field of producers making outerwear, dresses, sportswear, and knits, there are more than a dozen public and private producers whose annual sales are in the neighborhood of $20 million a year and up.

II. THE BOSSES

Many started in a tiny loft, with two sewing machines, one pressing machine, and a salesman who knew how to hustle.

Today, most of them, such as David Schwartz, chairman of Jonathan Logan, or Fred Pomerantz, chairman of Leslie Fay, spend as much time studying possible acquisitions as they do in routine, company business.

Maurice Saltzman, the tiny, bustling president of Bobbie Brooks, is a production expert. Often he can decide if a potential merger partner would be compatible merely from looking at the equipment in one of his factories.

In fact, like many a store president who finds his time monopolized by matters of real estate, finance and pending legislation, rather than by merchandising, the big men on Seventh Avenue today are more administrators, entrepreneurs and followers of the corporate "wheeler-dealer" life than the salesmen and production men they used to be.

This is feasible because these principals can now attract new management talent to assume duties they no longer want to handle themselves. Giantism has attracted highly-qualified executives to the apparel industry.

As a result, companies that were formerly operated by a man or a family, now have cost accountants, marketing directors, fashion or design coordinators, time study men, etc. They also use the latest factory-automation techniques, market research and electronic data processing.

III. MANAGEMENT-TO-MANAGEMENT PLANNING

The surge toward giantism was in great part impelled by the proliferation of multi-store operations. Large and concentrated demands created opportunities for broad-scale suppliers.

An inevitable development was management-to-management planning. The buyer was not necessarily being circumvented. But when a retailer with several branch stores purchased almost $1 million worth of merchandise from one supplier in one year, the heads of both firms naturally gravitated toward one another, in mutual gratitude and in an attempt to safeguard and capitalize on their mutual investment.

This has hardly pleased the buyers. And not all the giants are sold on management-to-management planning.

Planning a merchandising approach with stores is becoming an industry trend, but its practice varies widely. Some Seventh Avenue companies believe the planning should be carried out at the top level. Others leave it to their divisions.

Jonathan Logan, for example, prefers to let each of its 12 divisions stand on their own as far as contact with retail accounts is concerned, according to Richard J. Schwartz, the 27-year old president.

"Of course," he said, "we maintain management-to-management contact in an informal way, to meet with top store people to discuss and plan our mutual growth, to learn what their strengths and weaknesses are and also to improve each of our divisions."

But Richard Schwartz thinks it is impractical to make a practice of selling a store, or a store group, through its top management. Logan divisions have differing styling and marketing impact, as well as varying arrangements on granting retailers exclusivity.

Also, the company's divisions have diverse price lines. These points militate against constant, top-level relations which look mainly to buying and selling, he insisted.

"Besides, being utterly candid about it," Schwartz added, "the store president is in no position to deliver his buyers to us. And we as manufacturers are not in a position to commit all our divisions to any one store."

However, Susan Thomas, Inc., a leading producer of coordinated sportswear, has effectively achieved management support on at least two of its lines, the Susan Thomas coordinated ensembles and the Adele Martin casual clothes lines.

"We have had some real progress in selling these two lines as a combination," reports William B. Thomas, president. "Now, we are switching to a combination of Susan Thomas and Vivo, our new line of knitwear. One element that helps in this approach is that the two separate lines or divisions normally come under the same merchandise manager in a store."

"Partners-in-Profit" is a concept employed by Russ Togs, Inc., diversified sportswear and apparel maker.

According to Eli Rousso, president: "When management will take the opportunity to sit down with us, we can show them how we can become a top-profit line for them. This works to our mutual benefit, but it requires an open mind."

The discussions seek to identify which of Russ Togs' divisions are suitable for the store. Selection of fabrics in choosing a line receives close attention in such talks, Rousso said. . . .

Leslie Fay, a diversified producer which has grown dramatically through acquisitions, has prepared an elaborate program which it calls "P.E.P., or Profits Every Period."

Participating stores set up a separate open to buy and agree to work with Leslie Fay in virtually every promotional area. Stores distribute mailers on Leslie Fay merchandise, allocate window and in-store display space, use Leslie Fay's "magazine feature service" on fashion editorials, stage fashion shows, and grant Leslie Fay participation in store training programs.

Says Zachary Buchalter, Leslie Fay's president: "We will supply the merchandise, suggest mannequin and 'T' stand displays, supply store mailers, engage in national advertising, supply editorial coverage, train store personnel, supply advertising mats, print fashion show invitations and programs and supply customer address books for salesgirls."

Like Jonathan Logan's president, Mr. Buchalter wants each of his nine divisions operating autonomously, selling different buyers in the same store. Loyalty to any Leslie Fay line will depend more upon the service each provides than on the strength its management might attain with store brass, he believes.

Companies such as Puritan Fashions Corporation shoot for an arrangement whereby one retailer would more or less guarantee a large, set amount of purchases in order to obtain preferred services. . . .

IV. BRUSHFIRES

There's a potential brushfire in criticisms a cross-section of apparel producers suggest permeates management thinking and injures retailer-vendor relations.

The producers charge retailers with:

- Vague buying plans and confusion as to what to carry as initial stock.
- Permitting long delays between the time lines are seen in New York and the time orders are placed.

This practice, which often stretches into weeks during strategic market periods, allows the producer little time to plan and tends to hurt the retailer because production time is wasted.

- Inadequate training programs for sales personnel. Giants complain that many stores are lackadaisical about training new help.
- Overworking executives. "People just can't get to people," one producer charged. "Getting decisions becomes a matter of real frustration."
- Poor communication with branches. Vendors say that multiunit department stores and chains often do not get sales information from branch stores for as long as two weeks. As a result, sales are lost through "walkouts".
- Lack of top management interest in merchandising. Some giants charge that policy, real estate, finance and community interests preoccupy store heads, and that this is beginning to spread to general merchandise managers as well. One veteran producer who estimates that a year and two years ago, store presidents were equally divided in their interest between policy and merchandising says the ratio is increasing toward the former.
- Penny-pinching with shipments to the stores. Routing through lowcost motor or air carrier and through consolidated motor carriers is responsible for many late deliveries, manufacturers claim. One producer summed it up: "The fastest carrier in the fashion business usually turns out to be the most economical."

V. SMALL PRODUCERS

Despite its trend toward giantism, the women's and children's apparel industry is still largely made up of small companies. But the ability of the big company to venture not only into more and more segments, but into either higher or lower price lines, has created an even more stringent competitive climate for the small producers.

However, big producers such as Russ Togs' Eli Rousso firmly believe that there will always be small houses. "They can turn faster," he said. "They can knock off a style today and deliver it in 48 hours. For all our size and scope, the big outfit has to have planned production and can't move that quickly."

The small firm can exist on one good season out of two or three, William Thomas of Susan Thomas points out. "The large company has to ensure year-round employment," he added. "And that's one big reason why the industry's consolidation has provided a new stability to the apparel market."

Most industry sources predict that an even greater share of the market will be taken over by fewer companies. But that will scarcely happen overnight. Bobbie Brooks, the second largest firm in the industry, still accounts for only three percent of the women's apparel market. The small producer who is "geared to turn on a dime" will continue to have a place for some time to come.

By the same token, the nation's retailers are in a fortunate position. At least for the next five to ten years—when some observers foresee the big slice of the pie going to possibly half-a-dozen supergiants, each with annual sales of $500 million or more—merchants can accept the blandishments of the big, multi-division suppliers, and work with a variety of small producers who can offer some services their bemuscled competitors cannot.

"GOING PUBLIC". . .

Henry Bach

New Fashion in Financing for the Fashion Industry

For several years now, a significant new trend has been apparent in the apparel industry: the fashion world seems to be moving into the securities market. During 1959 and 1960 a number of sportswear issues enjoyed the popularity of the market. And now another wave of new apparel issues appears to be readying itself for sale to investors.

Such group movements are phenomena long noted and studied by securities analysts. Issues do have a tendency to rise and fall in industry groups, as seen in electronics, missiles, optics, fiberglass boats, bowling, aircraft, printing and publishing, and discount stores. The vogue for a particular business sets off a chain reaction which, in turn, is stimulated by the feverish search by stock analysts for issues of a popular industry which have not risen with their peers. This searching out and recommending of overlooked issues in itself serves to heighten the tendency of industry groups to advance "by the numbers."

Participating in the excellent market which characterized most of 1959–1960, a number of relatively recent apparel issues have given admirable accounts of themselves. Some scored spectacular gains. Bobbie Brooks common stock ranged from a low of 5¾ in 1959 to a high of 50⅞. The Majestic Specialties Inc. issue jumped from an 11½ low in 1960 to 44¼. Colonial Corporation rose from an 8⅛ low in 1959 to a high of 44. Some of the more seasoned apparel equities which have been on the market for many years also turned in excellent

records during this period. Hart, Schaffner and Marx common, for example, ranged from a low of 17 to a 33½ high. Munsingwear rose from 12⅜ to 27, Reliance Manufacturing from 16⅜ to 47, and so on.

WHY GO PUBLIC?

Why do companies go public? Why do businessmen who are doing well on their own go out of their way to take on a few hundred partners?

Undoubtedly, the biggest bull market in the history of this country has proven to be an irresistible lure. This attraction has been highlighted by the vigor of the new-issue market. Constantly repeated oversubscription of new issues by the investing public has made "going public" seem easy.

But what are the advantages of a public issue? There are a number, and they are compelling—if you measure up.

1. *To Raise Capital.* This may be required to enable the company to launch a new sales program, to produce a new product, or just for working capital purposes. Some have sought to escape the factor's relatively high rates by resorting to public funds. Needless to say, if this is the company's sole reason for going public, caution is wise counsel. A thorough study should be undertaken to determine the urgency of the need for new money. And, equally important, the availability of alternate sources should be explored.

2. *To Become Liquid.* Often, having spent most of his adult life building a business, the entrepreneur finds himself tied to his company. It becomes virtually impossible to convert the years of sweat, worry, and creativity into ready cash. A

SOURCE: Reprinted from *Apparel Manufacturer*, October 1961. Permission granted. Henry Bach heads Henry Bach Associates, Inc., a leading advertising and public relations agency, with offices at 245 Fifth Avenue, New York City.

public issue is the simplest and best way of withdrawing cash while retaining control. While most responsible underwriters will cast a jaundiced eye on a "bail-out" for insiders, liquidity may be attained in a number of ways. Some stock may be sold by the insiders at the public offering. In addition, a small amount may be sold every six months without resort to expensive registration procedures. Eventually, if the issue flourishes, a sizeable secondary issue may be floated in which the principals can sell a substantial part of their holdings to the public.

3. *To Expand.* Business these days must grow or perish. Utilization of internal capital resources for expansion purposes is a long, slow and difficult process. The fastest way to expand is to acquire companies in allied fields, with needed sales coverage or other desirable features. However, selling out for cash presents many tax and other problems. By far the most preferable way, for most companies, is through the exchange of stock, with perhaps some cash involved. There is little inducement to accept the shares of a privately owned company. The lure is great, however, if the purchasing firm's stock is traded publicly.

Further, in many fields of activity it becomes necessary to attract outside talent in order to grow. Really competent personnel look for stock options rather than salary as an inducement to make a change.

4. *To Improve Public Relations.* The publicity which going public imparts to a company can be important. Aside from hundreds or thousands of new stockholders who become company boosters, repeated references to a company in the financial pages of newspapers or investment journals offer priceless opportunities for free publicity. Often the glamour which may surround an issue favored by the stock market carries over to the products manufactured or sold by that company.

5. *To Minimize Inheritance Litigation.* The successful businessman is naturally concerned about his family's future. He may be adequately insured; his children may even have their own incomes; his wife may be well provided for. But his most important earthly possession is the business he leaves behind him. If the company is sizeable, the estate may be tied up for years in negotiation

and litigation with the Internal Revenue Service while the true value of the business for tax purposes is determined. In a publicly owned company this problem does not exist. Market price determines the value.

BUT, BEFORE YOU RUSH TO THE UNDERWRITERS . . .

Going public requires a good deal more than a company's mere desire to take this step. A company must justify this move by meeting certain criteria of suitability. Accounting and profitability requirements aside, there must be an intrinsic quality about the company and its products which would make its shares an attractive investment. There must be a combination of factors present which serve to excite the imagination and interest.

In this age of electronics, space flight, matter and anti-matter, an out-of-this-world product list or program serves as the only vital ingredient for many investors. A prospectus needs something to embellish it. Obviously, no matter how hard the imagination is worked, it is no simple matter to find "Buck Rogers" products or talents in the apparel industry; even space suits have been pre-empted by the rubber and electronics companies.

It is possible, however, for an apparel company to justify its public status the old-fashioned way— by being a well-run, profitable business. A five-year history of rising sales helps. Good earnings, of course, are the real clincher. Rising sales and earnings curves on the charts provide the sex appeal to which Wall Street responds.

Such a record, maintained over a period of time and with some indication that it will continue in the future, carries with it the designation, "growth company." This is the "open sesame" to successful financing in today's market. Of course, it also helps if the balance sheet shows substantial stockholder equity.

Then, there is the question of leadership. Management, as a factor in underwriting, is seldom underestimated. Investment bankers pay particular attention to the qualities of top company management. They also look for second-echelon understudies to provide depth of leadership. Unless you can take the underwriter to your leaders, they will probably not take to you.

Remember, there are literally thousands of stock issues traded on the various exchanges and over-the-counter. Among these are a large number of apparel issues, some with years of seasoning behind them. It is a humbling experience to ask yourself what your company has to offer an inves-tor which cannot be found in one or a number of equities already in the market. If the answer is not a record of above-average growth or the possibility of a superior, safe return on investment, perhaps "going public" may not be the answer to your problems.

JONATHAN LOGAN, King of the Jungle

Nobody is quite certain how the epithet "jungle" first came to be applied to New York's garment center. One story, undoubtedly apocryphal, has it that two tigers once escaped from the circus up at Madison Square Garden and became lost in the noon-hour maze that spreads over Seventh Avenue when workers and bosses pour out of the buildings to take in the few shafts of sunlight that break through the canyons and to philosophize about life, liberty and the pursuit of business. The two tigers, like almost everyone else, became entangled in the ferment of human traffic and were almost run over by one of the hundreds of hand-trucks that scoot in between trucks, taxis and peo-ple. Finally one tiger turned to the other, shook his head, and said, "Cat, this is what I call a jungle."

There are other stories, equally preposterous, which range from partners hurling themselves out of windows with Tarzan-like agility because of a coming Chapter XI, to the ferocious man-eating quality of the men who run the businesses along Seventh Avenue and Broadway.

Yet, as in all jokes and exaggerations, there is a core of truth from which these stories emanate. The reality of the situation is that there is no other industry anywhere in the world quite like the gar-ment center with its thousands upon thousands of firms concentrated in an area five blocks long and three avenues wide struggling side by side to per-form a seemingly impossible task—to stimulate 100 million American women into parting with their money because of fashion.

SOURCE: Reprinted from *Clothes* magazine, July 15, 1967. Permission granted.

CHANGES IN THE JUNGLE

In the more than four decades which have elapsed since ready-to-wear became an industry in New York, literally tens of thousands of firms have stubbed their toes over the word *fashion* and in the process have either disappeared from the scene or have reorganized to take another whack at the pot of gold which lies in wait for those able to interpret the whims of the American female.

If, however, the world of Seventh Avenue seems remarkably different from that of other industries, (it is, after all, the only one where the buyer goes to the seller for his merchandise) changes were taking place even in the heart of the jungle which would affect not only its way of doing business but would bring the industry more into line with other business. Moreover, the changes that were being wrought stemmed largely from factors outside the industry itself—or to be more precise, from the growth of the economy and the major retailers who dispensed the goods to the consumer.

Starting 15 years ago, the department and lead-ing specialty stores throughout the country began to open branch stores in the suburban areas which not only changed the face of retailing but also that of wholesaling. A better-organized jungle was now in order if the ready-to-wear manufacturers were to service these growing outlets. The word "com-puter" might have seemed light years away at that time but the problem of shipping to branch stores as well as to the downtown plant was becoming a reality for the women's wear trade.

The result of this was not to lessen the competi-tion within the framework of the jungle but rather to hasten the growth of the leading firms and to mark the beginnings of a strange new word for ready-to-wear—national brands.

Where previously any firm doing a volume of business of $5 to $10 million had been considered a colossus, by 1959 this figure was becoming if not a commonplace then certainly no longer a rarity. Furthermore, with the growth in dollar volume there were men in the garment center who were prepared to do the impossible—go public and be listed on the stock exchanges along with other industries.

It was indeed a strange world. Fashion was now to be on an equal footing with other industries in the sense that the public—people outside of the entrepreneurs and factors—would invest in the discernment of a few individuals who could fathom out what vast numbers of American females wanted to wear this year.

ALWAYS KNOCK IT OFF

Going public was a great new idea. But like any good idea on Seventh Avenue it didn't take long for the competition to knock it off. Within a few years one firm after another had taken this route and many of those who didn't were soon destined to become subsidiaries of those who did.

The jungle was still there but clearings had been made within it and all of a sudden, eight years later, there were garment center firms doing $100 million and more and taking it all for granted. The great leap forward had been made by Seventh Avenue and where formerly talk had been restricted to "cut velvet" and the like, conversation now centered on what was said at the security analysts' meeting down on Wall Street.

The jungle was still there, the handtrucks were as evident as ever but a new breed of cat had suddenly come into existence—a cat whose claws were as sharp as before but a cat which in less than a decade had become quite sophisticated, moving with the rag business into the world of big business.

THE KING GOES PUBLIC

And along the canyons of the garment center there

is little doubt which cat is now king of the jungle. It is Jonathan Logan, a firm which, in 1967—just eight years after going public—did in excess of $200 million in volume and brought home a net profit of better than $10 million after taxes.[1] And the man who heads this giant operation is not the tough old veteran commonly associated with the garment center but a 28 year old young man, Richard J. Schwartz, who assumed presidency of the firm three years ago, and since occupying the office has brought its volume up from some $97 million to its present figure.

For the Logan of today is not only the largest women's wear manufacturer in the world; it is also the largest branded manufacturer of soft goods, exceeding in volume even the big branded names in men's wear which have been around far longer than the 30 odd years that Logan has been in existence.

The Jonathan Logan story can be divided into two parts. The beginning—is the history of Jonathan Logan as the leading firm in the junior dress market and that story belongs entirely to David Schwartz, chairman of the board of Jonathan Logan, Inc. and still the active head of the Jonathan Logan dress division. The second part begins in 1959 when Logan went public, launched Butte Knit, and started out on a trail of building and acquiring subsidiaries which enabled it to become the leading firm in the garment center.

---

[1]Jonathan Logan's admission to the New York Stock Exchange in 1960 was accomplished through the purchase of all assets (except mining assets which were sold off to Anaconda Copper) of the Butte Copper and Zinc Co., which had been listed on the big board for years. In the transaction the more than 3,000 stockholders of Butte in effect became stockholders of Jonathan Logan and even today two members of the original family which founded the mining company sit on the board of directors of the fashion industry giant.

Through the acquisition Logan, although then doing a volume of only $26 million, was able to have its stock traded side by side with the giants of American industry. It also acquired a brand name for its new knit division, Butte, which proves that in the garment center one name is as good as another provided the product is right. The American consumer still doesn't know how to pronounce Butte. Who could imagine fashions being related to a mining town in Montana?

But the Logan of the second part is more than merely an amalgamation of such diverse firms as Rose Marie Reid and R-K Originals. The Logan of today is in reality the General Motors of the women's wear business—with one exception. Unlike the automotive giant this is still the rag business with all the limitations imposed upon it by tradition and the nature of the fashion beast. While all of the subsidiaries may sit under the Logan umbrella and draw upon the parent firm for financing and advice, each one operates differently in accordance with the way that is demanded by that part of the fashion business in which it finds itself.

For example, one salesman carries two of the firm's three major lines, Jonathan Logan and Butte Knit, and is paid by salary. Some of the smaller divisions, such as Youth Guild and Junior Accent, have separate and small sales divisions and these men work on commission. R&K Originals and its half-size offshoot, Amy Adams, sell only from showrooms strategically located throughout the country. No road men are required to sell these lines.

There are just no set formulas for the operation of a garment center General Motors other than that each division operates autonomously. But even here the tables of organization are different. Jonathan Logan and R&K are headed by one man with a staff under him. Butte Knit, Misty Harbor and Junior Accent are each headed by two man teams while Youth Guild and Modern Juniors are each one man operations.

Even in its approach to manufacturing there are wide variations between the member corporations. Butte Knit is a wholly integrated operation engaging in spinning, knitting, dyeing and sewing of its own garments—working from the fiber to the finished product. Misty Harbor and Harbor Master have their own plants for producing rainwear but R&K Originals uses nothing but contractors and the Jonathan Logan dress division uses a mixture of the two.

And basically it has been this flexible approach to the fashion business which has, more than anything else, been responsible for the enormous success racked up by Logan these past eight years.

Only two criteria seemingly determine whether Jonathan Logan is to acquire a firm or create its own. One—the firm should have a volume potential of at least $10 million. Two—it should be so structured as to make a profit of at least 10 per cent before taxes.

It is because of these two considerations that Jonathan Logan's growth pattern over the past four years has seemed, at times, to be without a specific direction. For Logan has not only added to its roster of firms by acquisition and from scratch, it has also disbanded or sold some divisions which could not measure up to these potentials.

THE MERCHANDISE MIX

What is the merchandise mix that Logan has put together these past eight years? There is Jonathan Logan Dresses—still the leading junior dress manufacturer in the country with a volume in excess of $30 million. Its counterpart is R&K in the misses dress field which, in the three years it has been in the Logan organization, has gone from a volume of some $22 million to amost $40 million and in the process added a line of half-sizes, Amy Adams, which became one of the largest half-size dress houses in the country, doing $8½ million.

The last member of the "big three" which, together, account for better than 60 per cent of the Logan volume, is the baby of the group and also its largest firm, Butte Knit. Launched in 1959 to open a market for popular price knit dresses, its growth has been literally phenomenal and today, with its volume of more than $40 million, it has become one of the leading dress manufacturers in the country.

Following the big three in order of importance are three firms whose merchandise mix is outside the dress field—Modern Juniors, Misty Harbor and the latest acquisition, Davis Sportswear.

Modern Juniors is subdivided into three areas—the parent company which follows the whims of the sportswear market so that it is presently in the bonded knit dress field; Beach Party, highly successful junior bathing suit division which accounts for 20 per cent of the volume and perhaps 50 per cent of the profits, and Weeds, which concentrates on coordinates built around jeans.

Misty Harbor is the Logan rainwear firm which was started from scratch some three years ago and which expects to hit a volume of $17 million in 1967. But Misty Harbor is also Harbor Master, the only Logan concern involved in the malewear industry and which is now in its third season. Harbor Master, of course, is an anomaly. Thus far the management at Logan has, apparently, been uninterested in acquiring any men's wear concerns and the basic reason for the launching of Harbor Master in the men's raincoat field must be attributed to the fact that Misty Harbor's management team, Ed Kraus and Lou Rothstein, both came out of the men's rainwear industry. Since the quality level at Misty is said to be on a par with the better men's branded rainwear concerns, it was felt that with no change in production facilities a successful men's rainwear concern could be launched.

If Harbor Master should prove to be successful it could be the catalyst which would expand the Logan interests deep into the men's wear business.

Davis Sportswear is one of the larger car coat manufacturers in the United States but, although it has generated a large volume, its profits have been something less than desirable. Furthermore, the car coat business is too dependent on the whims of fashion so that Logan is now moving this organization into the volume rainwear field.

Next in order of importance among the Logan subsidiaries are the two quality dress firms, Junior Accent and Youth Guild. The former, which previously had been in the top end of the junior market, has like many of its peers, moved over to the better misses market so that, despite the label almost 90 per cent of its dresses are now sold in misses areas. It is reputed to do a volume of some $10 million and is said to be among the most profitable members of the Logan team. Youth Guild, on the other hand, concentrates on selling the medium to better junior dress market and its growth has now taken it to the point where it does some $7 million.

The remaining Logan divisions consist of Act III, a better misses knit sportswear division, which is sold in conjunction with Rose Marie Reid, the better bathing suit house whose name Logan acquired three years ago; Bleecker Street, formerly a popular priced junior dress line sold under the Betty Barclay name and now converted into a popular price misses dress house; Alice Stuart, a blouse division which is gradually expanding into shirtwaists, and Turtle Bay, a children's sportswear house which Logan launched two years ago and which specializes in preteen sizes.

All these, of course, do not take into account the Logan foreign operations in Canada, the United Kingdom and Venezuela, all of which contribute to the total Logan sales and profit picture.

Taking all this into account, what is the relationship of Jonathan Logan to the ready-to-wear market? In dresses it is far and away the dominant firm in the business from the viewpoint of volume, both in misses and junior medium priced and better lines. In bathing suits, it has two powerful lines covering both the junior and misses markets, although the latter, Rose Marie Reid, has a long way to go to catch up with its previous high in volume of some $17 million. It has an outstanding misses rainwear division in Misty Harbor and strong possibilities for opening up the volume rainwear market with Davis Sportswear.

BUT NOT IN SPORTSWEAR

The one area of outerwear where it does not seem to be the dominant factor is sportswear which, while it is seemingly in the doldrums today, still holds the greatest potential because its eclectic nature causes it to move freely into all other areas of apparel.

What makes Logan unique is not that it has encompassed all areas of women's wear so that it can fill the entire needs of a store but rather that it has built its horizontal layer of individual firms to dominate that particular area of a store. It has accomplished this by allowing the executives of each division to pioneer within the framework of their markets.

Perhaps none of this would have come about were it not for the success story of Butte Knit which resulted from the decision by David Schwartz, then president and chairman of the board, to let his son, Richard, merchandise the new line as he saw fit albeit he was just out of college.

The idea and timing for the launching of Butte Knit could not have been better. By 1959 there was no doubt that double knits, up to that time imported largely from Europe, had found a strong place in the better dress market.

The idea that David Schwartz had was that by moving quickly into the medium price knit goods range, from $25 to $50 at retail, Logan could carve out a huge market. The important factor for the knits, however, was to buy the machinery and set up a plant. To run it he found a brilliant young man, Andrew Teszler, who excelled in knit goods production.

For a sales force he relied on the pros of his own Jonathan Logan dress division which had built up a $25 million volume over a period of 22 years. The big question was the market for these new knit dresses. Where the Logan dresses retailed from $15 to $25, the new knits started where the top end of the Logan line left off. But, since an investment had been made in plant and machinery, the main job at hand was to sell. And the Logan men, being no different than any other salesmen, took the garments to that department where it would be easiest to sell—the junior dress area where they had an entree because of their success with the parent line. In a few instances they also sold them in misses departments.

PROVIDING DIRECTION

Basically, of course, the new knits were too high priced for the junior dress areas of those days and most of the better knit dress departments in stores were reluctant to bring in the new garments for fear they would jeopardize the sale of the higher priced imports. So that when Richard Schwartz arrived on the scene in 1960 Butte Knit was going nowhere. Yes, it had the plant and the machinery and the sales force but of marketing direction it had none. Richard was to make trips around the country to various key stores to see why Butte was not as successful as it should be in light of the potential market.

The answer was obvious. Butte, because of its price range, belonged either in the misses dress area or in a separate knit department. It had no business being in the junior area.

What Richard did was to turn the business completely around at the time it was just coming off the ground. The risk for the company just turned public was large. The Logan sales force would have to pull Butte out of the junior departments and set them in misses areas even though almost all of the

business for the fledgling concern was concentrated in juniors.

But David Schwartz allowed his son to take the gamble and the rest is history. Once in the proper store location Butte began to take off. Furthermore, Richard made another basic move to broaden the market. Rather than take a long markup the firm would gain volume by keeping the top end of its price range at $40 rather than $50. In addition the firm would insist on quality to the point where the Butte dresses could sell side by side with the European imports. And lastly, the salesmen would insist on the store bringing in a minimum of 10 styles for each season so that there would be enough Butte merchandise on view to keep it from getting lost in the pack.

To back up the quality end, Logan was to expand the plant again and again to become a completely integrated operation so that, up to the present, the parent organization has poured in more than $10 million in investment—an investment, incidentally, which has more than paid off.

Here was a new phase for the garment business. First, a two-man team operating a business—one for production and manufacturing—Andrew Teszler, the other for marketing and merchandising —Richard Schwartz. Secondly not only did the team produce a sales miracle—a $40 million volume in less than seven years—it also showed that the garment industry could make major investments in plant and machinery in like manner to the hard goods industry. For not only does the plant at Butte produce knits for itself, it also sells them to the other Logan divisions.

By 1964, with Butte a success, David Schwartz was to take a second gamble. He would turn the presidency of Jonathan Logan, Inc. over to his 25 year old son, Richard, who had proved himself on a level that the father understood—creating a successful business in a brief period of time.

To the garment industry the idea of a 25 year-old heading up 15 domestic and foreign divisions doing a volume in excess of $100 million was a difficult thing to comprehend. How could one man with only four years experience in the jungle watch the store at so many places at the same time? The answer, of course, was that each division was watching its own store and that the job of management was solely to coordinate the activities of the divisions to see that they brought in the projected sales and profits.

THE R&K STORY

One of the best examples is R&K Originals. Brought into the Logan organization in the middle of 1963 for a cash outlay, this misses dress firm was the most successful in the industry and had been so for years. When Logan acquired R&K it was doing a volume of some $22 million. Heading it up was Manny Eagle, who had worked his way up from production to become the chief upon the sale of the firm.

The success of this firm was actually based upon a decision made in 1936 by the two partners, Rosenthal and Kalman, not to sell every dress shop in America. Instead, they would build up certain customers in every trading area. Although this would limit distribution, it would enable the firm to insist on certain requisites for carrying the line.

A BUSINESS OF FRANCHISES

The plan was simple. In order for a store to hold an R&K franchise it was obligated to buy at least 10 numbers from each of the four lines that the firm put out during a year. There was to be no deviation. If a firm decided to bypass the line for any season it dropped its franchise. Since the firm's line was extensive (today it numbers about 160 styles a season) management felt that there was no reason why a store could not find the 10 numbers it wanted from within the framework of what was offered.

The retailer was invited to become a partner in the fashion judgment of the manufacturer. As the firm grew in size the requirements stepped up to 25 numbers a season but the merchant had the knowledge that R&K would not flood his particular trading area with his garments.

Using only contractors, but guaranteeing them work 52 weeks a year, the misses dress firm soon established itself because of the quantity of its offerings and the quality control invested in its medium price misses dresses.

But a man can only eat three meals a day and wear one suit at a time. Being an enormously profitable operation there seemed no reason for pre-Logan management to make moves in further directions albeit the opportunity was there.

When Logan acquired it in 1963, Manny Eagle expressed his long pent-up desire to enter the half-size field. Given the manufacturing know-how and distribution of the R&K line, he felt there would be no problem in establishing a highly successful half-size division. The go-ahead was given, a distribution center constructed and four years later Amy Adams was one of the dominant lines in its field doing a volume of $8½ million. Nor has R&K lagged behind. It, too, has grown considerably since flying the Logan banner. Now, it will take a further step in the misses dress market by entering the after-five dress field.

But perhaps the greatest coup of the Logan organization outside of Butte Knit was its rainwear division, Misty Harbor, which in the short space of three years has become one of the important better rainwear lines in the country.

In entering the rainwear market, Logan was again showing its perspicacity in sensing future developments just as it had in medium price knit dresses. Since the new division would be literally starting from scratch and in an area that had yet to begin to bloom, Logan went to the outside for its personnel. To head the company and supervise production it hired Ed Kraus from Gleneagles of Baltimore. For a marketing man it lured Lou Rothstein away from the giant of the men's rainwear producers, London Fog. As was the case with Butte Knit this was to be a team operation.

Since both men had been associated with the better men's rainwear market it was obvious that the new line would not pursue the high fashion field but, rather, would concentrate on basic styles with a quality control and reorder business which would enable department and specialty stores to operate their women's rainwear departments in a manner similar to that of men's wear retailers.

Today Misty Harbor, along with its malewear subsidiary, Harbor Master, will do an estimated $17 million. The guess by the Logan organization that the trend to casual living which had built up the men's rainwear industry would do likewise in women's wear, had paid off.

But perhaps there is a better insight into the way the Logan management thinks in the story of Harbor Master. This has been and is the only venture by the parent corporation into the malewear field, and it was done despite the misgivings of management which has based its growth and success on the area it knows best—women's wear.

MAN AND WOMAN

There is good reason for this thinking as well as good reasoning on the part of the management team at Misty Harbor. Women's wear, being largely a consumer oriented business based on fashion, is much quicker to pick up new concepts and lines particularly when there are any number of success stories already linked to other members of the parent corporation.

Men's wear on the other hand is, by and large, dominated by the retailer, and he can see little if any reason to switch resources or take on a new one particularly when he is doing well with the old resource in that category.

Thus, where a women's department might welcome a new source in the hope that it would produce additional revenue, a men's buyer would generally remark, "Let's wait and see."

But Kraus and Rothstein, both out of the men's wear field, analyzed their potential market differently. The firm which dominated the better rainwear market was London Fog, with sales estimated at $30 million. The number two firm, Gleneagles, had sales of only $8 million. And the remainder of the competition was obviously doing less business than that.

Given a quality men's rainwear production, the two executives felt that the possibility of becoming number two was not that difficult. So, despite the hesitancy of management, Misty Harbor was allowed to plunge into the men's rainwear market.

ALWAYS A GAMBLE

And this, in substance, is the reason why Jonathan Logan is king of the jungle. It has the capacity and nerve to gamble on the judgments of its executives even if it isn't fully in accord with their thinking. It is willing to take risks provided the potential market is there. It has stumbled in the process but on an overall basis it is one of the most progressive and aggressive firms in the industry.

Make no mistake about one thing—the women's wear business is still a gamble. There are checkpoints for it and Logan has learned them well, such as testing styles first in the southwest and later in San Francisco and the Pacific northwest before cutting on a major scale. But it is still ready-to-wear and when a sportswear market goes into a national nose dive there is nothing anyone can do about it except to cut back on production and keep losses to a minimum. It is a business that requires constant attention and the executives of the various Logan divisions have learned this lesson well. They have learned that early checkouts mean nothing unless a good many numbers have been shipped because there are always consumers who will buy anything that's new if there's nothing else around—thus giving a false picture of consumer demands.

They have learned to watch merchandise checkouts at key stores so as to avoid heavy markdowns. When the famous three-piece knit suit of Butte Knit did not show its strength at the early southwest exposure last year but dresses and costumes did, Butte despite the fact that it had based its growth largely on this number, switched to dresses and costumes. The result was the best year in the history of the knit division.

But the gambler is always there and certainly David Schwartz is one of the best or how else do you explain the Venezuelan company, Texfin, C.A., which today does better than $11 million a year and nets better than $1 million?

Texfin is one of those ventures that just happened to come along. David Schwartz happened to know a man named Ghetel P. Kahan, who had a hosiery mill in South America and then retired. But Kahan was dissatisfied with retirement and instead wanted to launch a mill in Venezuela which would produce fabrics for the local population. Schwartz was game to the idea and for his investment obtained a 51 per cent interest.

As Texfin expanded and became a fully integrated operation—spinning, weaving, finishing and printing its own textiles for the Venezuelan market—it was absorbed into the Logan corporation.

Today, it produces cottons and polyester/cottons for its local market. And it has integrated itself to such a degree that it even produces its own polyester.

This, then, is Jonathan Logan. A Venezuelan subsidiary, Canadian subsidiaries which market Jonathan Logan, R&K and Butte Knit as well as manufacturing other apparel, and all its domestic divisions.

THE FUTURE

It is a company which shortly expects to hit $250 million in sales and in a 10 year projection perhaps a half a billion dollars. It has five major divisions, Jonathan Logan, R&K, Butte Knit, Misty Harbor and Modern Juniors, each of which it expects will eventually be able to produce $50 million or more in sales. Davis Sportswear may or may not reach this total but it represents, in management's mind, the next largest division.

As for the other divisions, most of them are expected to grow in line with the expansion of Logan's customers and the potential consumer audience.

What does the future bode for Jonathan Logan and the other large concerns which now dominate Seventh Avenue? In the old days when a jungle was a jungle, each season saw only the fittest surviving as the retailers cracked the whip.

Today, with most major retailers facing the problem of stocking multi-branches and with manufacturers now as large or larger than their best customers, the mood is becoming less jungle-oriented and more computer-oriented.

But as long as the gauge remains fashion with all that word connotes in terms of risk, such fruits as the jungle offers will still belong to the successful gambler and the perspicacious business man. Jonathan Logan has proven over the last eight years that it has no shortage of either of these qualities—and for that reason the King's crown fits easily upon its head. . . .

FASHION—A VERY HOT TIN ROOF

Harry Serwer

Fashion Creators Woo American Womanhood with a Few Guesses and Lots of Aspirin

'Twas said yon Cassius was a cloak-and-suiter because he had a lean and hungry look; and that's the first thing you note about his modern counterpart—the harassed countenance so symbolic of his trade.

You can never tell when your number is up in the ready-to-wear business. Today store buyers break down your doors to get at your fashions. Tomorrow you're on the cafeteria-line scrounging for a cup of Java.

SOURCE: Reprinted from a "Picture of a Union," May 17, 1959, by special permission. Harry Serwer was a well-known fashion merchandising consultant.

Who is responsible for this scary situation? The Union? No! The Union provides seasoned workmen who will make good merchandise if you tell them how you want it made.

Are the suppliers responsible? No! They confine themselves to providing the fabrics and findings out of which your fashions are made.

Are the store buyers responsible? In all fairness, No! They are only human too.

Well, who *is* responsible? With the utmost directness we must blame the American Woman, the lady known as the arbiter of fashions. Why is she responsible? Because she has no loyalty to particular versions of smartness since Fashion begets no loyalty. Thus, the American Woman contracts a thousand love affairs with Fashion, but never a marriage; and because she flaunts her waywardness in the market place she is responsible for the turbulence and volatility of the ready-to-wear industry.

That is the reason for the constant gripe: "How-ya gonna figure a woman out? Offer her red and she hollers for green. Give her lace trimming and she wants buttons. Make her a high waistline, like it says in fashion pages and suddenly she wants it around her knees. Everything she asked for two months ago, when nobody had it, she don't want it now when everybody's got it."

Now you understand why the lean and hungry look and the nitroglycerine tablets. And if you are in the explosive business you must agree with the Seventh Avenue philosopher who said, "Verily, Fashion is like ice cream melting on a hot tin roof."

The apparel manufacturer loves the American Woman but he has no delusions about her. He has her pegged as the real Czar of the industry from whose dictum there is no appeal.

But he is constantly confronted with the inevitable realities and deadlines of his business, and so he constantly reminds buyers that "Making women's apparel takes time; it ain't no Mickey Mouse climbing on a ceiling with the flick of an artist's brush."

Creating a new fashion collection for the coming season has all the frightening aspects of a nightmare. Shall he buy wools, silks, cottons, synthetics? And what percentage of each? Shall he buy solid colors, checks, stripes, plaids? Shall he mix fibers? All this is important because his styling is influenced—and often limited—by the fabrics he adopts. So he goes into the fabric markets with his designers and piece goods buyers. He buys a thousand sample cuts—half of which will never see the cutting table, and thus are destined for the rag bins. He listens to a thousand conflicting prophecies most of which are not only valueless but dangerous. He sends his designers to foreign markets, his copyists to the new plays, the Opera, the smart restaurants, to see the new ideas the women are wearing.

The very great fashions are usually the divinations of the gifted. The rest are rehashes. The number of "new styles" created every year are legion to the few that really succeed. The cost of all this

"creation" is like a millstone around the neck of the industry. Ironically, in Fashion as in Politics and Social Structures, the good is not always new, and the new is not always good.

It doesn't have to make sense. There is only one yard measure; if your styles walk out of the stores at a profit you're okay; if they have to be marked down you're dead—and it makes no difference how hot you were last year, that was last year!

So the race against the crazy clock runs something like this. The designing staff works at white heat for about six weeks living on benzedrine, coffee, and quarrels. The collection is finally finished: some of it is original creation; some is downright plagiarism; some models are ingenious copies so trickily conceived that no one can tell exactly whose swipe it was and where the swipe started. Then the whole sales staff is brought in, including the resident salesmen from far-flung cities. The collection is paraded by the appetizing models like a first night dress rehearsal. The salesmen sit around, looking very wise; and instead of confessing they couldn't pick the winners in a hundred years, they handicap the collection like professional touts at a race track.

So what happens when the season opens?

Some of the styles become sensational sellers —to the stores, that is. And in the stores many of these die. Why? American Womanhood gave them the Bronx Razoo. Don't ask her why.

Many of these pre-season "flops" have become sensations. One, in particular, had an eight-year run, and more than a million and a half dresses were sold in a single color! But as a rule, nobody knows what's going to sell—except the liars, and they don't know either.

Isn't Fashion ever influenced by events? Of course it is! Look how terrifically the migration from the city to the suburbs has influenced Fashion. Suburban living has sparked gigantic markets in play, sports, and classic clothes. The garden needs special clothes. So does the school pool. So do the beach and the woods. And what about the automobile journey called shopping?

But what about the manufacturer's nightmare and his seeming inability to divine the Fashion needs of the distaff public? Is this shrinking the overall volume? It is not! This nervous and perpetual need to keep on one's toes has spiraled the volume to fantastic figures. More women are wearing more clothes in America than in any country in the world. Our stenographers are better dressed than the upper crust in Europe or elsewhere. A great compliment can be paid to the apparel manufacturer of this country: he is always on his toes, but never on those of the Fashion Consumers.

THE WORLD OF THE DESIGNER

Evelyn Portrait

Fashion's backstage drama

"The show must go on" may mean Broadway to most people, but the drama backstage and on-stage on Seventh Avenue is equally exciting. The similarity is insistent in the talents that put together the collection—the designer-star creating, backed up by manufacturer and production room; the coordinating teamwork of accessory talents; and finally the models, the performers, if you will. Lights up; the audience is in, the dress rehearsal over. On with the show! Here we go, behind the curtain on Seventh Avenue to chat with the people involved; to define how the show goes on, how it looks, how it reaches you.

When I view a collection these days I see a total-look show. Geoffrey Beene explained why to me: "It takes almost three months to put together a collection, and since a great deal of design must be experimental, sometimes the line doesn't show itself until midway through. Just two weeks before showtime the Chinese influence clarified itself for my recent summer collection." Since Geoffrey feels strongly that "the accessories pull a collection together" and his preference is for "an exaggerated statement," the next steps toward coordinating the look followed logically.

House model Kathy Collins had let her hair grow in, and they worked together on a pulled-back, loose-pigtail, "Oriental Coolie" hairdo. Geoffrey asked designer Beth Levine to make up a group of

SOURCE: Reprinted by permission of *Cue* magazine, March 11, 1967.

25 clogs, colored specifically to match the clothes; he coordinated 15 different-color stockings with Hudson. Kenneth Jay Lane provided 40 pairs of brightly colored "golf ball baubles" that were mix-matched at the ear and in the hair. Finally, Geoffrey added color names—demonstration blue, riot red—and he put his thoughts into words, explaining that the Chinese influence evolved from his political interest in the recent rift and revolution. Incidentally, the "exaggerated statement" doesn't mean he wants all women to dress that way; rather, "It's to make my point loud and clear."

In spite of a growing tendency on Seventh Avenue to include private clients at shows, Geoffrey says, "No. I don't encourage it—I think it's distracting with buyers and press present." On the subject of store showings, he limits his participation severely, because "putting together the collection is too much work." For you, the ultimate audience, the show goes on for Geoffrey Beene at Saks, Bergdorf's, Bendel's, Bonwit's, Lord & Taylor.

Bill Blass reacts in an almost opposite way. Bill feels that his models should not be exaggerated, wants them as close to natural as possible, is always on the lookout for fresh faces. Viewers at all but his most recent collections learned to enjoy the natural, outdoorsy look of his house model, Kit Gill, whom he discovered and trained over a three-year period. (Kit is now a professional free-lance show model.) He told me that he hires model Barbara Brown to help execute the models' make-up.

"When the girls wore heavy eye make-up, it took them an hour. Now they're natural and that make-up takes two hours." As for the clients, Bill continues: "About five years ago, I thought they ought to see our collections as they saw Paris—a total look. It's impossible for the stores to do." Some 50 clients are invited to Maurice Rentner's (Bill's house) the day of the press showing, when prices are not quoted. Then difficult and tiring as they are, Bill does as many out-of-town personal appearances as he can because he feels that "women who spend $300 and up for clothes want to relate." He consults with customers on the right shoe, will even dissuade one from buying "the wrong dress." Bill's last S.R.O. show included David Evins shoes, KJL jewlry, Adolfo millinery. You don't need a ticket to see his clothes at Bergdorf, Bonwit's, Saks, Lord & Taylor, Martha's.

And now the show model. What does she contribute? I talked with Gillis MacGil, an elegant show model who also owns the Mannequin Agency—home to New York's top show models. To begin with there are only 40 such gals in New York. Gillis explained the difference between the photographer's model whom you see in the magazines and ads and the gal on the runway. "The photographer's model doesn't really have to know what she's wearing. She can be made-up, pinned in by a stylist, and the photographer can make her look any way he wants. But the show model must be knowledgeable about clothes; she has to have style, an attitude. No, I can't teach it, no one can. The model has to learn it, usually as a house model. She's responsible for how her hair looks, her own make-up, for her lingerie and shoes. She's responsible, that's the key." In case you've an interested daughter in your household, Gillis goes on: "A high-fashion model today is about five-feet-seven or five-seven-and-a half inches tall. Years ago she had to be about five-nine. Her approximate measurements of 34-24-34 are most important, because all good show models are interchangeable; the designer can whip a dress off one and transfer to another. She weighs about 118 pounds, is never as lean as the photographic gal. Top models earn $30,000 to $35,000 a year and enjoy the peripheral benefits of traveling the world for special shows and being able to buy designers' clothes at lowest costs."

Barbara Brown, one of fashion's most popular, If somewhat a-typical, show models continues on the "performer's" obligation. I was unprepared for the information that, in her book, the most delightful part of showing is the camaraderie. "Models are thrown together for a long period of time. A show is not any one girl but a group of models; it's a combined effort for the clothes. No model would ever let another walk out on the runway if her bra strap were showing." Barbara said that it's tough for a new gal to break in, but if she really wants to learn, every model will pitch in to help a novice grow into a professional. (Stars, watch out!) I discovered that there's little time for the stuff we equate with beauty. "Busy models just haven't time for exercise classes, facials—their hair (and hair-pieces) are most important, so it's the hairdresser once a week—but the slim, healthy figures are the result of hard work." Period. Though Barbara feels that the model is "a commodity" on the runway, off the runway "a good model is a woman first, a model second." Barbara and her husband and teen-age daughter relax together in their country house weekends. Along with model-partner Clare Morrow, she's a recognized decorator; she's also a consultant on skin care.

Another a-typical typical model is Claudia, who was for nine years as familiar to audiences at Norman Norell's shows as "the master" himself. Claudia enjoyed the enviable position of being Norell's friend, and a kind of number-one assistant. "I think I was his sounding board. We'd look at fabrics together, consider a silhouette. He always consults a model; to him she's not just a body, she's a woman—and he likes the opinion of a woman." Claudia agrees completely with Barbara: "Being a model is like belonging to a non-union union, built on friendship." The peripheral benefits? "I was well-paid for a house model," she said. "I traveled all over the world with him, and I own 100 Norells." But probably more important, the knowledge, the elegant taste that is Claudia today is used to different advantage. Now Claudia is number-one assistant to her designer-husband, George Halley. Once again she helps select fabrics, models for his shows, and books other models.

Once the show is open, the analogy to theatre continues. Favorable press notices from the daily newspaper reporters, from fashion-magazine editors, are almost as important to the designers as to Broadway. The buyers are as important as any enthusiastic audience; if the buyer doesn't applaud and buy, you won't see—and buy.

But I spoke also of you, most important of all, the customer—what if you're not privileged to visit showrooms? Many designers appear throughout the country, but it is difficult to see a collection in New York. First of all, there are many conflicts in a city that boasts the largest number of fashion salons in America. Secondly, spokesman for Lord & Taylor, for Bendel, Bergdorf, and Saks, all said they simply didn't have the facilities for public fashion shows. Saks does have daily informal showings in their Park Avenue Room and, on special occasion, designers Donald Brooks, Jacques Tiffeau, Oscar de la Renta, Geoffrey Beene, or Bill Blass might appear. Mildred Custin, Bonwit's President *extraordinaire*, recently launched a group of public designers showings in the store, with the designer present. "We feel more strongly than ever," she said,"that the designing talent of this nation is unsurpassed and we believe that American designers have taken their rightful places alongside the great couturiers of the world. Their

creative thinking is abundant and their production know-how is unbeatable." This reporter can only shout "Bravo, Miss Custin!" Keep your eyes open to ads of the future, because hopefully Bonwit's success will repeat itself, and you'll be able to visit with Trigère, Teal Traina, Zuckerman, John Moore, Mollie Parnis. Chester Weinberg, Hannah Troy, Chuck Howard recently appeared. Adele Simpson arrives late-April. Though limited to by-invitaion only, Ohrbach's *couture* line-for-line showings mean run-don't-walk to some 2,500 women, a sizable group. And, of course, you are always welcome at store-sponsored charity shows. Most of our large department stores participate in a few a year. Alexander's underwrites a charity effort twice a year to introduce their *haute couture* copies to some 3,000 women.

Sure, it's theatre—the glamour, the excitement, the uncertainties. No matter how successful, a designer is never sure he has a hit on his hands, but like the Broadway producer, once he has a hit, he has to repeat it. But for him, there are always four seasons. It's one show that never really closes.

AMERICAN COUTURE: Toujours Trigère

What is American couture? To the consumer it is either a trunk showing with models moving gracefully across the carpeted floor while the commentator sings out the numbers or it is the confined cubicle of retail—a fitting room bedecked only by fresh flowers and that special sales girl who coos, oohs and aahs while dragging the dresses out of the stockroom. Finally, it is that particular party or afternoon tea when, with all the insouciance in the world, madame drops the word—"yes,my dear, it's just a little Norell or Galanos or Rentner or Trigère."

SOURCE: Reprinted from *Clothes* magazine, July 1, 1968. Permission granted.

What is American couture to the retailer? He, too, watches the models float by with the latest creations either at the fashion showing or individually in that sequestered almost laboratory-like atmosphere of the couture showroom where again, only fresh flowers are allowed to compete with the garments being shown. But the fashions he finally selects represent more than mere garments—they are the escutcheons that he flies over his retail emporium to tell the world that his is a high fashion store featuring the best in American fashions in terms of design, fabric and make. In other words, American couture is as much of a charisma to the retailer who buys it to enhance his stature as to his customers who also like to drop names.

Couture Sets The Trends

But if American couture's importance was restricted only to specific sales made to retailers and consumers this would be but a shadow of what its true import is to the fashion industry. For American couture is the trendsetter for the entire apparel field—whether in terms of knock-offs or scale downs, or silhouette or fabric.

Finally, because the bulk of the couture firms are located in the heart of the garment center they have given an aura to all the firms doing business there in that they, too, are drinking from the fount of fashion so that even the volume producers can share in the mystique of fashion if not in fact then at least in spirit.

But, while all the foregoing may represent couture to the trade and public at large, to the few who practice the art of creating new designs it is quite different. For one thing, as a business it is far from profitable as witness the decline in the number of firms still in existence. For another, despite the accolades and the publicity these few firms are showered with by the fashion and consumer press, not one can lay claim to being starred in its own boutique within a store. Yet in men's apparel, a newcomer to the field of designer names, the stores have not only found the space to create designer boutiques but also the dollars to set up a decent inventory. In other words, American couture owns all the palmiers but one—the green stuff in the palm.

On a Par with Paris

But if American couture is ill-rewarded financially for its efforts it can at least take comfort in the fact that, over the last 20 years, it has produced three or four great names which could, tomorrow, open in Paris and compete with the best of French couture. Among the most famous of these names is a dynamic French woman who, in a period of 25 years, has not only established herself as one of the top two or three designers in America but has, in addition, built the largest American couture business. The woman is Pauline Trigère and the firm is Trigère—which this year will do better than $3 million in dresses, coats, costumes and evening wear that retail from $200 to $3000.

How do you get to be a Pauline Trigère with an audience of thousands of the best dressed women in this country who swear by your taste—and more importantly how do you maintain this position over a period of 20 years despite the vicissitudes of fashion?

The success story of Trigère is not the usual saga of the garment center where a man starts with two sewing machines and 20 years later winds up a millionaire. To start with, Miss Trigère is not a millionaire and, as for sewing machines, there are still only two since that is all that is required for making up the samples.

To better understand the success story of Trigère one has to go back to the beginnings of American couture and in fact define the term, couture, itself.

For one thing, American couture is not French couture. French couture is based not only on design but on a series of individualized fittings where the garment is shaped to the wearer's body so that it is truly custom-made. To undergo the discomfort of these fittings required a class of women who had the time to go back for each session as darts were adjusted, seams let in or out and details carefully brought into line to make the gown a work of art for that particular body. Before the war there were a dozen or so couturiers in New York who performed this kind of labor but as times changed one by one they either switched to ready-to-wear or gave up the ghost.

Obviously, with labor costs going up and the source of talented labor shrinking from the working scene, American couture as it was then did not have much chance for survival. Even in France where the leading couturier houses are subsidized either by fabric or perfume concerns, the number of couturieres has been dwindling over the years as the necessities of economics take precedence over artistic creativity.

But back in 1942 there was still a healthy number of couture houses in New York. Pauline Trigère was then working for one of the leading houses in New York, Hattie Carnegie. One day, shorly after Pearl Harbor, one of Hattie Carnegie's most important customers from the West Coast arrived in town. "Hattie," he said, "the Japanese are coming—it is time to get out of the business." Hattie Carnegie, affected by the contagious fear of her friend concluded that if it wasn't time to get out of business entirely, it was certainly the moment to substantially reduce her operations. And so Pauline Trigère found herself out on the street, with two young sons to support and no visible means of income.

A Business Is Born

Hocking a ring and borrowing some money she came up with the munificent sum of $2,000 and thus launched herself on the road to success. For quarters she leased part of the space formerly occupied by her boss. And she had her two sewing machines.

At the same time this was taking place, the late Dorothy Shaver, then president of Lord & Taylor, felt that there was an enormous vacuum in the better dress area now that the French designs and designers were cut off because of the war. To compensate for their absence, Miss Shaver decided to promote American designers by name in the windows of Lord & Taylor.

With this move by Lord & Taylor, couture, as it is known in America to day, had its birth. Only one other ingredient was necessary to catapult it to fame and importance—that was an official award.

And in 1947, instigated by Eleanor Lambert, the Coty awards for excellence in design were created. Two years later, Pauline Trigère won the first of her Coty awards and she was on her way to success.

In reality, of course, recognition and success did not come solely from the awards. What was necessary was to create a climate in the department and specialty stores for better merchandise and, in particular, for the wares of Miss Trigère.

Using trunk shows and generally scouring the hinterland, Miss Trigère and her brother Robert, who is her partner, gradually broke down the resistance of stores and somehow a Trigère dress or coat would appear in still another store in still another city.

But perhaps one of the major reasons for the success of Pauline Trigère outside of her innate talent is her common sense as a business woman. Trigère, unlike some of her contemporaries, tends to keep certain price lines which she knows can sell in volume. In addition, there are certain so-called basics in the Trigère line, particularly in jersey dresses, which sell year in and year out. Colors may change or a neckline may be altered,

but by and large large there are the old reliables to be depended upon.

Who is the customer for the Trigère garment? According to Pauline it is the active woman between the ages of 25 and 50 who is involved in what is going on around her but still wants to dress like a woman.

The key to Trigère's designs are her fabrics. As a matter of fact, in creating a new silhouette Pauline will work not from a design—she admits her drawing skill goes no further than a croquis—but from the fabric. Starting with a pair of scissors she will begin to cut according to the way she sees the fabric in light of its weight, pattern, color and hand. From there it is a question of pinning and draping and details here and there. While a dress must not be a work of art it could be a thing of beauty given the proper balance and proportion for the type of fabric. And it is these intangibles which make the designer and, in particluar, Pauline Trigère, a winner.

Fitting Mrs. America

Once the garment is cut and pinned on the model a sample is made. It is on this first sample, a size 12, that corrections are made by Miss Trigère. Seams might be ripped, a collar could be altered, new darts put into place to raise or lower the bustline. But it is only when the decision is made to put the garment into the next collection, that the true skill and genius of American couture and of Miss Trigère come to the fore.

For from this model's garment must come the duplicate sample which is made to fit Mrs. America and Mrs. America who buys Trigère is not shaped quite like the models on the ramp.

In reproducing this garment on the duplicate model with all the nuances that have gone into the design based on a fashion model's figure, there is only one skill that counts—that of the fitter. And in this Miss Trigère has no peer. For the essence of American couture as opposed to European is that there will be no multiplicity of fittings. The design may be as complicated as that of the great French couturiers but the size 12 must fit a great number of size 12's with a minimum of alterations particularly in view of today's absence of trained fitters from most stores.

Once the duplicate model is approved it is time to cut the pattern. Now a cutting in couture has nothing to do with a cutting in any other business. For example, 110 pieces of a number is an excellent cutting. If you can cut 250 garments at a time you have a real winner. Nor are all the garments cut on the premises. At Trigère, only the coats and costumes are cut in their own workrooms and all manufacturing is by contractors.

Does each couturiere work continuously with only its own contractor? Generally speaking, yes, but there are times when merchandise is shipped to other shops.

Since Trigère comes out with four or five collections each year it means that this process is repeated about 400 times which, in part, explains why the profitability of a couture business leaves much to be desired.

Fall—The Major Season

The major season for couture is generally fall. This involves two collection—a capsule one of about 50 garments in mid-April for delivery in August, and the full collections during the mid-weeks of June in which the capsule collection is combined with the remainder of the line—bringing the total to about 110 garments. For the bigger line delivery calls for completion on or before the end of September.

Following fall come the resort and holiday lines and these are followed by spring and then summer—the latter being a season couture does not like to discuss since it is found to be inordinately difficult to sell lightweight dresses for $200 and above. Summer, of course, is the briefest of all the lines with about 40 pieces in the collection.

Couture, of course, is by and large a reorder business. Although Trigère will book as much as two-thirds of a season's production by the end of June it is the reorders or special orders which make for the success of the season.

The reason for this is that for most stores, particularly the large department stores, couture is a luxury and is bought with an eyedropper. Thus, stores do not buy a range of sizes but generally purchase garments either for specific customers or in the size range in which they do the bulk of their business. Since it takes approximately three weeks to manufacture a garment and since not all num-

bers are reordered equally, Trigère, like the other couturieres, finds herself cutting one of a size of a color—but just one size. This is not the way to riches. And yet, this is the nature of the business.

What is Pauline Trigère's business? It is about 50 per cent daytime and cocktail dresses, 25 per cent coats and the balance in costumes and evening wear. Her merchandise is sold in better coat and dress departments and in the so-called French Rooms of the nation's leading stores. Her business is divided about 50-50 between the specialty and department stores.

About 20 per cent of the business is done in New York and the bulk of the remainder in the major markets of America. Yet, the firm has good cusomers in such unlikely places as Jacksonville, Fla. and Wichita, Kansas, which is to say there is no guessing where elegance in taste may turn up.

Branch store business is generally out of the question. Even in the main store it is remarkable to get an order for a full range of sizes which run from 6 to 16.

Less Markup at Retail

As for retail markup there is less of it in the couture business than in most departments. The stores generally average about 44 per cent with terms and the Trigère firm averages about 45 per cent.

One of the major expenses for both Trigère and the stores is the trunk show which generally kicks off the couture season for that particular store. While the store hires the models and pays for the transportation of the garments, either Robert Trigère or one of the key sales personnel journey out to that city to give the commentary and to help with the selling. This fall, for example, Trigère will have 14 trunk showings starting out in Colorado Springs where May D & F is opening a new store and winding up in Atlanta sometime in September. Then—back to New York in preparation for the next openings and the rat race goes on.

If, from the point of view of dollars and cents, couture is truly an impossible operation, why, then do people stay with the business? Certainly Pauline Trigère could license her designing ability and name for a percentage of the price as she has already done in hosiery, shoes and, most recently, in precious and semi-precious jewelry.

The Power of a Name

But even the best of licensing agreements can only be successful if the star's name is still on the marquee, which is to say, if she is actively engaged in the metier. And this holds true whether the subject is couture or golf or men's fashions. A name is only as good as its current performance in the market place which means that Trigère must continually create new lines and new numbers—about 400 of these each year—whether or not they prove profitable.

In other words, American couture has taken on an impossible job. Without being subsidized, as is the case with most of the French houses, it must function as a business within the framework of a market which is generally using it— not as a money maker—but as a show piece for its own everyday fashions.

Is there, then, any future for couture which hangs on to its old-fashioned methods because of the limitiation of its market? Some people feel that American couture, like French couture, will be dead within the next decade because of this limited distribution and because so few people are willing to invest in a high fashion business where the return is at best limited. Furthermore, with the focal point of the fashion industry concentrated more and more on the youth syndrome which demands change for the sake of change, what chance does a name designer have to compete with the swingers and beautiful people, particularly when they are interested basically in inexpensive ready-to-wear?

Finally, there is not only a shortage of talented young designers but, more importantly, there is a very serious shortage of competent and trained production people to turn out the subtleties of couture work on a uniform and quality level.

Thus it is that American couture, the flagship of all ready-to-wear . . . .the area of the fashion business which gives it its glamour in the eyes of the consumer and the consumer press, is enjoying little if any of the prosperity which the bulk of the fashion business does, now that this country has a mass affluent society. . . .

Tomorrow's Trigères

The genius of Trigère as a designer is now taken for granted. What is important for the fashion industry is to have more Trigères to follow in her footsteps. For without American couture and without the Trigères Seventh Avenue will become a much smaller and less meaningful street . . . .

ONE CORNERSTONE OF AMERICAN COUTURE IS A MAN NAMED BEN SHAW

A series of partnerships combining design talent, production know-how, and money helps build our leadership in fashion from "RTW couture" on up

Ben Shaw retired in 1952 after 35 years in the garment industry—20 of them as the head of his own firm. Retire to a life of travel, golf, and keeping a watchful eye on real estate and stock investments as might be expected of man who made a considerable amount of money on Seventh Avenue? No. Ben Shaw "retired" to his favorite hobby, talented people—a hobby he parlayed into a fashion manufacturing empire expected to produce over $20 million sales volume in 1967.

SOURCE: Reprinted from *Stores Magazine*, October 1967. Permission granted.

This combination genius-genie is the business mastermind behind some of the most potent labels in American fashion one-upmanship—Geoffrey Beene, Donald Brooks, Lotte Hoffman, and Leo Narducci. He has been likened to Sol Hurok, David Merrick, and the Wizard of Oz—but Shaw avoids parallels between the fashion business and the theatre. "In the garment industry, unlike the theatre, a smash collection doesn't mean a run of several years, road companies, and movie rights. It means you are expected to come up with an equally good collection the next season."

Shaw's assurance of successive, critically acclaimed, money-producing collections rests in the hands of five designers—"all gifted with their own talent"—whom he backs to the hilt and for whom he provides the business-attuned wherewithal that lets them design. His unique understanding of "his" designers is the dream of every creator who yearns for the name-on-the-label and it leads to an average of two "partnership approaches" per day.

Ben Shaw has purposely avoided the centralized control of a Jonathan Logan, say, or Leslie Fay. He is in partnership with each of his own designers and, while other members of his interlocking organizations may have an interest in more than one firm, there is no overall superstructure.

There isn't even an office—or a telephone number. Things might be easier under one roof, Shaw concedes, but he's afraid he'd get bogged down by organizational detail. "The way I work now, I keep in touch with the daily pulse of the firms," he explains.

Even to find Ben Shaw requires ingenuity, perseverance, resilience. Telephoning his firms is frequently futile as he collects a wad of telephone messages at each stop, stuffing them into a breast pocket already bulging with checkbooks and various memoranda—the closest thing to a filing cabinet in Shaw's non-office. The best way to get in touch with him is to hang out in front of 530 and 550 Seventh Avenue, the garment industry's "status" buildings, in which all his firms occupy showrooms.

But don't look for a slicked-down Seventh Avenue sharpie to emerge from his sleek chauffeur-driven limousine. Shaw is a tall, fatherly man in his sixties who looks as if he takes a genuine, personal interest in every facet of his business—not just the money-counting. And he does.

This doesn't mean, however, that Shaw separates himself from the ritual of Seventh Avenue. Quite the contrary. In fact, you might say that to spend one day with Ben Shaw would be sufficient to learn what makes the fashion industry tick—from biggest deal to smallest detail. And when the invariable question arises as to how he maintains a pace that can leave even his youngest associates panting to keep up, he replies simply, "I love it."

Loves the frenetic pace

Shaw loves the frenetic pace of Seventh Avenue far more than a life of leisure and travel, apparently, as he tried the latter barely a year. He returned to the fashion mainstream as a partner of Jane Derby, where he later brought in Oscar de La Renta, who acquired Mrs. Derby's interest—and his name on the label—shortly after her death. During this time, Shaw was also an overall administrator to Sarmi.

In 1963 he went into partnership with Geoffrey Beene, who was opening his own business, at Beene's invitation. Two years later a similar invitation arrived from Donald Brooks. Then, after a lapse of two years, he took a double plunge this year—backing Lotte Hoffman, a well-known designer in the knitdress industry, and Leo Narducci, who had already gained a formidable reputation for young, moderately priced clothes.

Shaw is hesitant to discuss the images, personalities, or design approach of his designers —tactfully insistent on "equal time" for all. "The look, the feel is different . . . women who wear the clothes know." Individual differences do crop up in conversation . . . the "seamless" shaping of Geoffrey Beene's designs that require a master pattern-maker, the tenacity of Lotte, who will go to all ends in pursuit of a new knit effect, the indefatigability of Donald Brooks, who can put together a gem of a collection in the mad rush of designing costumes for a movie, the merchandising sense of Leo Narducci.

"I find it's talent I'm looking for rather than an existing organization," Shaw answers when asked why he doesn't go around buying going businesses. "I offer business partnership—and personal independence." He also offers valuable advice on staffing, since the talent he's looking for isn't exclusively in the area of design.

The production man is also a partner in each of the organizations—a fact arising from Shaw's contention that the most important ingredients in any garment manufacturing setup are fit and quality. "But the production man can only convey, carry out a designer's ideas," he's quick to add.

Shaw is also instrumental in finding other outlets for his formidable supply of design talent". Status" signature scarfs are a big thing with Geoffrey Beene and Donald Brooks. Expanding the accessory bit, Brooks designs a collection of shoes, Beene is involved with stockings. . . . "The license has to fit in with the total designer picture," Shaw maintains.

This feeling of maintaining a consistent designer identity also extends to matters such as fabric purchases, fiber tie-ins, store promotions. "I could order a hundred cuts of fabric, and if the designer didn't like one of them he could reject the whole batch—and I would go along," he says. He also pays meticulous attention to how the clothes are shown and sold—has been known to go so far as to insist that a dress with a slightly pulled hemline be removed from a store window and replaced with a perfect example.

The next move is to open in Europe—first, most likely, with Geoffrey Beene. "There's a big demand for these clothes in Europe . . . and we'll definitely go it alone, show a complete collection and manufacture there, rather than participate in any of these composite export showings. I already have an agent looking for appropriate manufacturing locations."

Why hasn't Shaw become financially involved in the European couture? "I could have gone with any of them—the best—but, somehow, it just wasn't right at the time."

The couture concept of a "collection," however—embracing a wide variety of clothes, all bearing an individual designer stamp, rather than limited to sportswear, or dresses, or coats and suits—is consistent in Shaw's fashion thinking. It is not surprising, then, that he feels the only way to buy designer clothes is by collection. And he finds the majority of important stores—importance having nothing to do with size—are buying this way, even for branch units.

Couture ready-to-wear, a semantically contradictory concept spawned by Seventh Avenue, raises the caliber of the entire store, Shaw feels. He goes so far as to say it could be the salvation of downtown units experiencing the inroads being made by suburban shopping. And it isn't limited to the uppermost reaches of the price scale. Leo Narducci, whose clothes rarely go over $100 retail, designs in the same "collection" train of thought as Beene and Brooks, whose whose clothes inch up to, and sometimes beyond, $2,000.

Collection buying requires flexibility of the part of a buyer—and, most important, on the part of store management. It also requires a store and department image as consistent as an individual designer image.

Allowing customers to see a designer's collection in toto is great, Shaw says, but economically unfeasible in other than a very limited way. The alternative is to show everything available from one designer together, not parceled out into various departments. On the other hand, Shaw is quick to add, there are stores—usually big ones—that carry portions from a given line in more than one department, and with great success. The key to the matter, he feels, is to have a wide enough representation in one place to get the message across.

Shaw gets his message from the designers. "I learned everything from them," he says. "They deserve all the prestige." And prestige has been lavished upon them—Coty Awards and virtually every other accolade known to fashion. Yet they attribute much of their success as designers—designers left free to design—to Shaw's magic touch.

This magic touch enables Shaw to select the superstar from the more than one hundred designers who approach him annually. Granted, his close association with store presidents, buyers, press, fabric and fibers people keeps him tuned in to available talent—but it is his own personal reaction that counts. And the decision to go into another partnership is often instantaneous.

Ben Shaw forsees a greater personalization of American fashion—away from the anonymous-designer-in-the-backroom sort of operation to a strong designer identity. There are many manufacturers who shy away from the overpowering designer image for fear that if and when the designer goes, the business goes with him. Shaw has solved this with his close partnership arrangements and his unusual understanding of the designer—as a person and personality.

A DANIEL BOONE ON SEVENTH AVENUE

Eugenia Sheppard

The great American Designer, Claire McCardell, and manufacturer Adolph Klein, who died Saturday, were a great team.

"We had a kind of Daniel Boone life together. We were pioneers," Adolph Klein told the Costume Institute of the Metropolitan Museum when he gave them a group of McCardell dresses after Claire died 10 years ago.

The two of them came into each other's lives at just about the beginning of World War II. Adolph, who had the reputation of a terrific salesman, joined forces with Henry Geiss, who already owned an S.A. firm called Townley. They were looking for a designer with new and different ideas and hired Claire in spite of dire predictions from other manufacturers.

"We knew we had to be either basic or exciting," Adolph Klein once said. "We were too small to be basic so we had to be exciting."

At the time the name Claire McCardell didn't mean a thing. Claire had graduated from the Parsons School in 1928, in the same class with Mildred Orrick and Joset Walker. She walked up and down S.A. looking for a designing job, painted roses on lampshades for a while and finally went to work for Hattie Carnegie. Her ideas were all too simple to make Hattie happy.

One of the first customers for the new setup at Townley was Majorie Griswold of Lord & Taylor.

"I remember Adolph called me and told me he had something new and exciting to show," Miss Griswold says. "That's what they all say, of course, so I went over expecting nothing. When the first dress came in, I sat up straight. It was a real surprise."

Marjorie Griswold became one of the earliest and most enthusiastic backers for what most people now recognize as this country's most completely indigenous, independent and avant-garde fashion talent.

It was Claire McCardell who first thought of turning the stretch bandages of World War II into strapless tops for dresses. It was Claire who took out the foam rubber pads and cut slinky black swimsuits on the bias. It was she who first used brass hardware, forgot about waistlines, glorified camel's hair and started many things that were innovations then and have now become just normal chic for contemporary clothers.

Adolph Klein backed his designer every step of the way. Whatever she wanted, he gave her. Whatever she designed, he produced. "These women —you never know where they get their inspiration from. It may be a crack in the wall," he once said, loving every minute of it.

Though he sometimes complained mildly ("We don't make much money but we have a lot of fun") the business was far from unprofitable.

With his encouragement, Claire McCardell designed the famous wartime, wrap-around popover dress, and later the Empire dress with little puffed sleeves. Her monastic dress that fell straight from the shoulders but could be fitted to any figure in the world with tiny string ties must have sold into the thousands before it was knocked off and became a world classic.

The partnership (she became full partner in the firm) lasted until Claire McCardell died in 1958. After that, though he tried with Mildred Orrick, Donald Brooks and Chuck Howard and helped Mollie Parnis start over after her husband died, things were never the same for Adolph Klein.

"Claire was it. She was the only one for me," he once said to Life's Sally Kirkland.

Besides the dresses to the Metropolitan Museum, Adolph Klein gathered all of Claire's rough sketches together and gave them to the Parsons School of Design. By special grant, the school has

SOURCE: Reprinted with permission from *Women's Wear Daily*, August 13, 1968.

had them bound into a year-by-year set of volumes.

"It wouldn't be fair to tell you the name of some of the designers who have consulted them," says Mrs. Anne Keagy, "but I can tell you there are still McCardell knock-offs in every big sportswear collection in the country."

Students all love the croquis because they have some of the designer's own dry wit. "They are funny and human, not just beautiful sketches," Anne Keagy says.

McCardell has become a cult with many women who still cherish a single dress or a whole wardrobe, like Kay Kerr of Neiman-Marcus.

Young designers like Nan Herzlinger frankly worship her. At the Fashion Group show of rtw last June, it was a McCardell dress under a long camel's hair coat that rated the big applause.

Adolph Klein was a soft-spoken, friendly man with a shrewd business head, but that's not why a group of friends will soon start to raise funds for scholarship in his name at the Parsons School.

His great gift to fashion was to sense a talent and, without drama, to make the clothes come true. It happens all too rarely along Seventh Avenue.

RESEARCH SPEARS LEVI STRAUSS' FASHIONABLE MARCH INTO EUROPE

It may be a wild projection but perhaps one of the prime movers toward a truly Common Market will be the youth of Europe.

If that be the case, Levi Strauss & Co.—Europe S.A. is well seated here in Brussels to lead the way. Fashion is one of the first areas where youthful trends appear, and now that the look has become almost universally informal, it's a happy day for Levi's—a name that is almost synonymous with casual pants.

Many of the women in offices across Europe, just as in the U.S., have traded in their dresses and mini-skirts for the more casual slacks, but nowhere was this more evident than in Levi's Brussels headquarters. Gals in every style of pants, from low-slung hip-huggers to button-decorated bell bottoms, whisked through the hallways as they went about their work. And even the attractive secretary who led the way to the office of Peter L. Thigpen, general manager of Levi-Europe, was wearing a snappy pair of Levi's.

Mr. Thigpen, a tall, youthfully handsome American, is responsible for Europe, Africa and the Middle East. He explained that Levi's are now sold in over 100 countries. It's come a long way. The company traces it origin back to 1850, when an enterprising Bavarian immigrant named, of course, Levi Strauss, followed the Gold Rush to California where he started a dry goods business and made canvas pants for prospectors.

Strong evidence of the company's rapid growth in Europe, Mr. Thigpen observes, is that as recently as 1968 it had only one plant in Europe, whereas now it has eight more, of various sizes and various stages of development. The company has set up its plants in Europe in such a way that none is more than two or three hours away by car. The point is: Plants were set up for convenience of operations, rather than sites to exploit tax advantages or cheap labor. "We have higher priorities than that," he said.

Other than certain policies, guidelines and standards emanating from Levi's headquarters in San Francisco, the European operation has a relatively free reign over its product line. In the men's line, only two items are exactly the same as in the U.S., and both are blue jeans, Mr. Thigpen told AA. "The rest of our product line has been tailored uniquely for what we consider European taste."

SOURCE: *Advertising Age,* July 31, 1972. Reprint permission granted.

For example, he said "corduroy has been a very popular fabric here, whereas in the States I think it peaks and troughs. While in the U.S. they may run six to ten colors in corduroy, we'll run 25 to 30 colors. The theory is that the power of the line will be in the depth of the color range. In other words, we would prefer to run one style in one fabric in 25 to 30 colors, rather than, say three styles in four fabrics in five colors each. We try to make sure we have a Pan-European color line. There are times when we find that we have to have a color for a certain market, but we try to steer clear of this, partly because of manufacturing efficiencies."

Levi has ten subsidiaries in various countries of Western Europe, and they're responsible for "being our eyes and ears," as far as getting information from the market is concerned, Mr. Thigpen said. "When we start getting feedback from our best merchandisers, we listen to them harder than to others," he stressed.

"We've missed a few times—no question about it—we've had some colors we didn't need to have."

One sees some interesting trends across Europe, he said, while cautioning against drawing "too strong a psycho-socio-economic conclusion from them." One might anticipate that in Sweden, being so far north and so cold, more somber colors might be preferred, but Levi has been selling some of its brightest colors there, precisely because of the rather drab climate. Sweden also has many similar characteristics to the U.S. "Colors in the U.S.—particularly in men's wear—are far more flamboyant than in Europe. Over here, you can spot an American male miles away."

Levi's for girls are called Miss Levi's in Europe, representing an entirely different line from that in the U.S. Mr. Thigpen admitted that Levi's was late in getting into the women's line in Europe because "research led us to believe that we were selling a very high proportion of our regular products to women, and we were afraid of getting into switch business." So when Levi's introduced its women's line in Europe, it made a conscious effort to aim it at a different market segment.

"Our market segment in the men's line was, say, the 15-to-25 age group, male and female," he said. "So we determined with Miss Levi's to go after the 20-to-35 group. We priced the line up a bit, while adding more fashion and high quality fabrics. It sells in different retail outlets than our men's line, and it has been extremely well received.

"We were into bell bottoms probably a bit sooner than the U.S. because of the demand for them here." And when corduroy jeans became the rage, Levi-Europe tried to service the market for both men and women by widening the hips a bit and dropping the rise so the garment would ride on the hips, whether the wearer be male or female.

Levi Strauss has probably done as much as anyone to promote the unisex look. Ads for its men's line are keyed to both men and women. "We show people in boy-girl type situations," Mr. Thigpen said. Levi's agency in Europe is Young & Rubicam, with the exception of France where Levi has an exclusive distributor who uses Dupuy Compton. Levi uses a wide range of media and spends between 2% and 3% of sales for advertising.

Levi's creative efforts are Pan-European—but it wasn't always that way, Mr. Thigpen confessed. "We came from anarchy, really. We came from every country doing whatever it wanted to do. But we tried to centralize our creative efforts for a number of reasons: (1) To standardize the images, (2) to get certain economies of scale in print work, etc., and (3) we felt there was a much greater mobility among our target market, moving across borders all the time. We wanted to make sure that the young German vacationing in another country would see the same type of advertising he'd seen in Germany."

The market is getting more and more difficult all the time, Mr. Thigpen admitted. Five years ago, a pair of jeans labeled, "Made in U.S.A.," could be delivered three or four months late, and perhaps even be in the wrong style or color, but it would be bought, nonetheless. That has changed. "Now you've got to be in the right place with the right product at the right time and the right price—or you're not going to make it." Levi is finding a tremendous amount of competition, not so much from Pan-European companies, but from the small locals who can "beat our heads in" because of their great flexibility.

"We have a tremendous problem with Hong Kong imports," he commented. There are a lot of people, he explained, who distribute low-priced, unbranded Hong Kong-made garments that "particularly hurt us in the low end of our price range." He also is a bit apprehensive that the Hong Kong imports may hurt Levi in a new line it plans to introduce for boys aged between four and 12 or 14.

Mr. Thigpen doesn't think that the expanded Common Market will make the competition any tougher. "I think the expansion of the Market will help us. First of all, it means we can source our fabrics any place within the expanded Common Market and still get the tariff advantages. Secondly, it means we can make our products any place we want to and still get the tarriff advantages. Now, if we want to be as profitable as possible, we buy EEC fabric, manufacture in the EEC and sell to an EEC customer."

Mr. Thigpen isn't looking to expand production facilities immediately. "At this point, we're happy with the number of plants we have here," he said. "We'll continue to import goods from the U.S." The company makes its fashion items in Europe, while importing its "basics" from the U.S., since it isn't as critical if they arrive a bit late.

What Mr. Thigpen seeks is an effective transition from a production oriented company to a marketing oriented one. It used to be a case of "make more and you'll sell more, but now the market's getting tough."

Asked if he felt there could be a move to "buy European goods" or "buy EEC goods," Mr. Thigpen shook his head. He felt, however, that on a grandiose scale, the only disadvantage of an expanded Common Market is that it might divide the world into blocs. A threat is that the U.S. administration and U.S. business might feel that they had better form a bloc themselves because the EEC "of the ten is going to be a tremendous force. The six already is." He said the Market represents a "tremendous amount of economic power, especially with its ties to the less developed countries, and with its general preference schemes. The Community seems to be just starting to forge ahead now." He would hate to see the advantages of the enlarged Community marred by tariff barriers among the major trading blocs.

BIBLIOGRAPHY

American Apparel Manufacturers Association. *Impact Apparel–A View to 1980.* Washington, D.C., AAMA, 1969.

Arnold, Pauline and Percival White. *Clothes and Cloth.* New York, Holiday House, 1961.

Ballard, Bettina. *In My Fashion.* Philadelphia, McKay, 1960.

Bender, Marilyn. *The Beautiful People.* New York, Coward-McCann, 1967.

Brockman, Helen. *The Theory of Fashion Design.* New York, Wiley, 1965.

Chambers, Helen A. and Vera Moulton. *Clothing Selection.* Philadelphia, Pa., J.B. Lippincott Co., 1965.

Cone, Walter E. *Modern Footwear Materials and Processes.* New York, Fairchild, 1969.

Daves, Jessica. *Ready-Made Miracle: the American Story of Fashion for the Millions.* New York, Putnam, 1967.

Disher, M.L. *American Factory Production of Women's Clothing.* London, Devereaux, 1947.

Fashion Group. *The Making and Makers of Fashion.* New York, The Fashion Group, Inc., 1959.

Fashion Group. *Your Future in Fashion Design.* New York, Richards Rosen Press, 1966.

Frank, Bertrand R. *Progressive Apparel Production.* New York, Fairchild Publications, 1970.

Fried, Eleanor. *Is The Fashion Business Your Business?* 3rd Edition. New York, Fairchild Publications, 1970.

Fuchs, Victor Robert. *The Economics of the Fur Industry.* New York, Columbia University Press, 1957.

Glove Life, National Association of Glove Manufacturers, Inc., Gloversville, N.Y.

Glover, John George and William Cornell. *The Development of American Industries.* New York, Prentice-Hall, 1955.

Gold, Annalee. *How to Sell Fashion.* New York, Fairchild Publications, 1968.

Hall, Max. *Made in New York.* Cambridge, Mass., Harvard University Press, 1959.

Hawes, Elizabeth. *Fashion is Spinach.* New York, Random House, 1938.

Hawes, Elizabeth. *It's Still Spinach.* Boston, Little Brown, 1954.

Kolodny, Rosalie. *Fashion Design for Moderns.* New York, Fairchild, 1968.

McCardell, Claire. *What Shall I Wear?* New York, Simon and Schuster, 1956.

Richards, Florence. *The Ready-to-Wear Industry.* New York, Fairchild, 1951.

Roshko, Bernard. *The Rag Race.* New York, Funk and Wagnalls, 1962.

Sices, Murray. *Seventh Avenue.* New York, Fairchild, 1953.

Solinger, Jacob. *Apparel Manufacturing Analysis.* New York, Textile Book Publishers, 1961.

Stuart, Jessie. *The American Fashion Industry.* Boston, Simmons College, 1951.

Strum, Mary M. *Guide to Modern Clothing,* 2nd edition. New York, McGraw-Hill, 1968.

Vance, Stanley. *American Industries.* Englewood Cliffs, N.J., Prentice-Hall, 1957.

Vecchio, Walter and Robert Riley. *The Fashion Makers, a Photographic Record.* New York, Crown Publishers, 1968.

Weitz, John. *The Value of Nothing.* New York, Stein and Day, 1970.

TRADE PUBLICATIONS

Apparel Manufacturer, 1075 Post Rd., Riverside, Conn. 06878

Beauty Fashion, 60 East 42nd St., New York, N.Y. 10017

Body Fashion, 757 Third Ave., New York, N.Y. 10017

Boot & Shoe Recorder, Bala Cynwyd, Pa. 19004

Boutique Fashions, 1300 Broadway, New York, N.Y. 10001

California Apparel News, 1011 Los Angeles St., Los Angeles, Calif. 90015

Clothes Magazine, 380 Madison Ave., New York, N.Y. 10017

Corset, Brassieres & Lingerie Magazine, 95 Madison Ave., New York, N.Y. 10002

Fashion Calendar, 8 East 77th St., New York, N.Y. 10021

Footwear News, 7 East 12th St., New York, N.Y. 10003
Fur Age Weekly, 127 West 30th St., New York, N.Y. 10001
Handbags & Accessories, 1133 Broadway, New York, N.Y. 10010
Hosiery & Underwear Review, 757 Third Ave., New York, N.Y. 10017
Intimate Apparel-Underfashions, 757 Third Ave., New York, N.Y. 10017
Jewelers Circular-Keystone, Bala Cynwyd, Pa. 19004
Leather and Shoes, 30 Church St., New York, N.Y. 10013
Women's Wear Daily, 7 East 12th St., New York, N.Y. 10003

APPAREL–ACCESSORIES TRADE ASSOCIATIONS

American Apparel Manufacturers Association, 2000 K St., N.W., Washington, D.C. 20006
American Cloak and Suit Manufacturers Association, 450 Seventh Ave., New York, N.Y. 10001
American Footwear Manufacturers Association, 342 Madison Ave., New York, N.Y. 10017
Corset & Brassiere Association of America, 220 Fifth Ave., New York, N.Y. 10001
Greater Clothing Contractors Association, 100 Fifth Ave., New York, N.Y. 10011
Jewelry Industry Council, 608 Fifth Ave., New York, N.Y. 10020
Lingerie Manufacturers Association, 41 East 42nd St., New York, N.Y. 10017
Luggage & Leather Goods Manufacturers of America, Inc., 220 Fifth Ave., New York, N.Y. 10001
National Association of Glove Manufacturers, Gloversville, N.Y. 12078
National Association of Hosiery Manufacturers, Charlotte, N.C. 28202
National Dress Manufacturers Association, 570 Seventh Ave., New York, N.Y. 10018
National Handbag Association, 347 Fifth Ave., New York, N.Y. 10016
National Knitwear Manufacturers Institute, 350 Fifth Ave., New York, N.Y. 10001
National Millinery Planning Board, Inc., 10 East 40th St., New York, N.Y. 10016
New York Couture Business Council, 141 West 41st St., New York, N.Y. 10036

SECTION REVIEW AND ACTIVITIES

FASHION BUSINESS TERMINOLOGY

Define, identify, or briefly explain the following:
Cutting-up trades
Seventh Avenue
Contractor
Market weeks
ILGWU
Couture ready-to-wear
Accessory
Publicly-owned firm
Style piracy
A "line"

QUESTIONS FOR REVIEW

1. What factors contributed to the history and development of the U.S. apparel industry? When, how, and why did the industry develop?

2. Explain the economic importance of the apparel industry.

3. Why is New York the wholesale fashion center of the United States? Explain New York's development as a center. Name three other women's apparel centers.

4. Compare the sales volume of the garment giants with the sales volume of the largest firms in other major U.S. industries. How can you explain the differences?

5. How does an "outside shop" differ from an "inside shop"?

6. The apparel industry has been described as one of the "last refuges of the small independent manufacturer." Do you agree? Defend your answer with facts and figures.

7. Explain the steps that an apparel producer takes in "creating a line."

8. Why should apparel producers have to wait for buyers' reactions before putting their new styles into production? Why shouldn't their designers have the final say about what designs should or should not be produced?

9. Are manufacturers' brand names or designer names as meaningful to customers when they are buying apparel as names or brands are to the same customers when they buy foods, cosmetics, or appliances? Why?

10. Name five different categories of accessories and name one to three producers in each category. Where are these producers located?

11. Why do apparel firms "go public"? Name five apparel or accessory firms that are listed on the New York Stock Exchange.

12. Do fashions in accessories change more or less rapidly than fashions in apparel? Why?

13. Do you agree that the "American customer is the real Czar of the (fashion) industry from whose dictum there is no appeal"? (See reading, "Fashion–A Very Hot Tin Roof") Explain.

APPLICATIONS WITH EXAMPLES

1. Analyze and then prove or disprove the following statement from the July 1, 1964 issue of *Forbes Magazine:* "The apparel industry is suffering from a form of schizophrenia because, although it manufactures clothing, it doesn't sell clothing. What it sells is fashion."

2. Discuss and/or show visually the relationship between current fashions in accessories and in clothing.

3. Discuss and/or illustrate with examples the apparel industry's common practice of featuring the name of the manufacturing concern instead of the name of the designer of the garment or accessory. Draw conclusions on the pros and cons of the anonymous-designer-in-the-backroom type of operation in terms of the customer, the producer, and the designer.

SECTION 4
FOREIGN FASHION PRODUCERS— COUTURE AND READY-TO-WEAR

Since importing, copying, and adapting European styles is a multimillion dollar activity of the American fashion business, no book about U.S. fashion industries should omit a discussion of foreign producers in general and Paris in particular.

Paris is considered to be fashion's capital. It is the center of an industrial area (in many ways the most remarkable in the world), devoted to the production of textiles, apparel, and accessories for women.

This section of text and readings deals with the reasons for Paris's fashion leadership, the workings of the *haute couture*, and the increasing variety and volume of ready-to-wear and accessories imported by the United States from Europe and other fashion-producing areas.

PARIS

The influence of Paris on this country's fashion business dates back to colonial days, when the wealthier ladies copied the latest French fashions with the help of seamstresses. From the early years of our own fashion industry, manufacturers have looked to Paris to set the styles. An exhibit of French dress models at the Chicago World's Fair of 1893 increased popular interest in French styles, and a number of American stores began to send their buyers regularly to Paris to buy original creations for resale or copying. The emergence and growth of fashion publications, such as *Vogue* and *Harper's Bazaar*, which did much to publicize Paris fashions, kept France in the forefront as the authority on fashion. When many French design houses were forced to close down during World War I, and again during World War II, the American fashion industries had to look closer to home for design inspiration. Nonetheless, Paris returned to favor stronger than ever following both wars.

Reasons for French Fashion Leadership

The importance of Paris as a source of fashion creativity is often ascribed by the disciples of French fashion to something intangible in the air of Paris that is conducive to originality and creativity. The reasons, however, are much more mundane and derive from a complex blend of history and economics.

Brilliance in fashion designing is not exclusively a French talent; in fact, many of the great houses have been headed by people of other nationalities who were drawn there by the advantages that the city offers for fashion designers. For example, we have had Balenciaga, a Spaniard; Crahey of Lanvin, a Belgian; Jean Dessès, a Greek; Mainbocher, born in Chicago; Molyneux, an Englishman; Schiaparelli, an Italian; and, of course, the man who is considered the father of modern French couture—Charles Frederick Worth, an Englishman.

A major attraction for talented designers has been the availability of skilled seamstresses, a condition that makes possible the tremendous amount of experimentation that is essential to the development of new clothing ideas. These dedicated perfectionists, to whom designers can safely entrust the steps from drawing board to finished garments, are the spiritual and, possibly, even the physical descendants of the seamstresses who stitched garments for the French nobility hundreds of years ago.

Moreover, in Paris, designers have a magnificent French textile industry upon which to draw. Unlike American textile firms, the French producers are ready and able to turn out small runs of new fabrics. The Paris couture houses, therefore, are not limited to mass-produced materials.

Also of great importance is the fact that Paris is an international market patronized by women of wealth from all over the world. These women live the full social life that makes fashionable dress a matter of first importance; they also have the means, the time, and the desire to have their clothes custom-made in the workshops of the world's greatest designers.

Another great help and attraction to designers has been the presence of auxiliary industries that use hand labor to produce trimmings and similar materials of great individuality and on a small scale. Almost anything a designer needs to carry out his ideas for a sample garment is available in Paris.

Another factor has been the existence of French laws that protect the work of creative designers from unauthorized copying and do much to encourage originality. In the United States, by contrast, efforts to protect original apparel styles have generally fallen afoul of our antitrust laws.

Of major importance in the development of the French fashion industry has been the historic encouragement and support of the French government. This support dates back to the fifteenth century, when the silk industry in France came under the direct patronage of its kings. Jean Baptiste Colbert, who was an adviser to Louis XIV in the seventeenth century, believed that "French fashions are to France what the mines of Peru are to Spain" and supported them accordingly.[1] Top-ranking designers have long been recognized by the French government as artists and important contributors to the national economy. For example, Rose Bertin, who was Marie Antoinette's dressmaker, was given the title of "Minister of Fashion" for services rendered to this unfortunate French queen; it was also not too many years ago that Christian Dior was awarded the Legion of Honor for designing the New Look that swept the fashion world in 1947.

A noted American designer once explained what it was like to work in Paris:

"Everything is arranged for couturiers in Paris. . . . when you design in Paris, you know that everyone understands what you are trying to do, and wants to help. . . . The handicraft background provides hand weavers as well as hand sewers. . . . Machines could do it, yes; but no machine can work out the first bit of a new design. . . . Any time you want a special buckle in France, someone will run it up for you. They don't have to make a die and cast a thousand of them."[2]

[1]Anny Latour, *Kings of Fashion*, Coward-McCann, Inc., New York, 1958, p. 63.
[2]Elizabeth Hawes, *Fashion Is Spinach*, Random House, New York, 1938, p. 16.

Since so many important style trends have been born in Paris, it sometimes looks to the outsider as if nothing more is needed to start a fashion than a Paris address and a designer's caprice. Actually, the meaning behind an expression such as "Paris decrees" is simply that, with so many inspired and encouraged talents at work there, coupled with its historic prestige, Paris has become synonymous with fashion.

Paris Haute Couture

The focal point of the French fashion industry is a small group of creative *couturiers* (the French word for dressmakers), whose establishments are known in the trade as *haute couture* houses. The term *haute couture*, literally translated, means the finest needlework but, as used in the fashion business, it describes a firm whose designer periodically creates sample collections of original styles that are then reproduced individually on a custom-made basis. To qualify as a *haute couture* house, a concern must present two collections a year that express the designer's own ideas (instead of executing styles specified by customers); it must show a minimum of 50 models on living mannequins; it must show original styles created by the firm's own designer without recourse to designs bought from outsiders; and it must produce the samples and the made-to-order reproductions in its own custom workrooms.[3]

There are hundreds of dressmakers in Paris but there are usually fewer than 30 at any given time who merit the title of *haute couturier*. In 1970, 20 firms were listed as couture creation houses by the Chambre Syndicale de la Couture Parisienne.[4] In addition, there were such firms as Cardin, Chanel, and Courrèges that functioned outside the Chambre Syndicale. Of all the Paris houses, only about 10 at any one time achieve worldwide fashion reputations. In the early 1970s, for example, the names best known to the ordinary consumer included the late Balenciaga, Cardin, Chanel (who died just before her January 1971 collection was presented), Courrèges, Dior, Givenchy, St. Laurent, and Ungaro.

The couture approach to the fashion business is very different from the American approach. Ours is based on quantity production by factory methods of fashion apparel for the many; theirs is predicated on producing individually measured and made-to-order garments for the few. Most of our output is at relatively modest prices; the couture's is very costly. Our garments are produced to standardized sizes and are cut from uniform measurements; theirs are created to the measurements of the live models, who will show them, or the customers who order them. Our producers cut and sew thousands of one style at the same time; their workrooms cut and sew each garment individually. Their garment production involves several fittings on living models; our production involves measuring on dress forms. Although we do have a group of American producers of high-priced

---

[3]Press Attachée, English speaking countries, Chambre Syndicale de la Couture Parisienne, Paris, France, letter dated November 24, 1964. Also Celia Bertin, *Paris à la Mode*, translated from the French by Marjorie Deans, Harper, New York, 1957, pp. 76–77.

[4]Chambre Syndicale de la Couture Parisienne, *Calendrier des Collections Automne-Hiver, 1970*, a listing of 20 couture creation houses.

ready-to-wear who refer to themselves as couture houses, they are not couture operations in the French sense, since they produce in factories for resale through stores, and do not do custom work. The American operations most similar to French couture are those few retailers, such as I. Magnin, that still maintain custom workrooms.

Other major differences are the French practice of selling original designs to professional buyers for copying and the dominant role assigned to the head designer in a French house. American fashion producers do not sell their designs for copying; neither do they, with few exceptions, regard the designer as anything other than a hired employee. Nevertheless, there is a small but growing number of designer-entrepreneurs in the United States who head their firms or are partners in them: Bill Blass, Galanos, Adele Simpson, and Pauline Trigère, for example.

Founded by Charles Worth.   The founder of modern *haute couture* is acknowledged to be Charles Frederick Worth, who was a brilliant young English designer with a flair for business. In 1854, about the time that Elias Howe was perfecting his sewing machine in the United States, Worth was busy putting Paris "high fashion" on the map. After working in that city as a draper in a retail shop, he opened his own business with the idea of designing luxurious custom-made clothing for wealthy patrons. He soon attracted the attention of the Empress Eugénie, was appointed dressmaker to the queen, and won the patronage of other great ladies of the time.

Worth is credited with being the first dressmaker to show collections of made-up samples of his own design instead of working to specifications of individual customers. He is given credit also for conceiving the idea of showing collections of garments on living models. Prior to his time, dressmakers had usually suggested new styles to customers by means of sketches accompanied by bolts of materials; if a complete dress was produced, it was shown on a wooden dummy, not a live woman. Some dressmakers followed a practice, believed to have originated with Rose Bertin, of sending to customers at other European courts or in America fashion dolls or "fashion babies," as they were then called. These dolls were small figures, dressed by a Paris house in miniature versions of its latest styles.

Worth also instituted the practice of selling to foreign trade buyers, along with his private clients, and began the wholesale relationship between France and the United States. At the height of his career, Worth employed as many as 1200 people—a big fashion business, even by today's standards.[5]

Organization and Operation of a Couture House.   The working organization and operation of typical couture firms are fairly uniform. Each firm is known as a house because its operations are housed in a residential building instead of a commercial factory. Generally, an elegant old home or palace in a good residential neighborhood is renovated for this purpose.

The head of the house is generally the chief designer, who will have several personal assistants, such as a fabric specialist and a sketching specialist (who interprets and sketches the designer's ideas). There will be a number of production

[5]Madge Garland, *Fashion*, Penguin Books, Ltd., Middlesex, England, 1962, p. 36. Also Edith Saunders, *The Age of Worth*, Bloomington, Indiana University Press, 1955.

workrooms, depending on the size of the house, each headed up by a *première* who is responsible for reproducing the work of the designing department. The *premières* are in charge of the *midinettes* who do the sewing and stitching. For example, Chanel, as long ago as 1930, had as many as 26 workrooms, and employed over 2000 people.[6] The live mannequins on whom the original samples are made and shown are supervised by a house *directrice*, who is also in charge of the selling showrooms and the saleswomen, called *vendeuses*. The largest couture house of them all, the House of Dior, also has a complex business office, which includes a public-relations department, a publicity department, and the like.

Although there are exceptions, the name of a couture house is generally that of its head designer, and its reputation is essentially a one-man or one-woman affair. Occasionally, however, as in the case of Chanel and Dior, a well-known name is retained after the founder's death, with a hired designer or changing series of designers. As in America, different houses earn their reputation for different things: some, like St. Laurent, become known for their originality as trend setters; others, like Balenciaga, for their outstanding workmanship; some, like Chanel, for their suits; still others, for their dresses.

The couturiers prepare major collections of new designs twice a year for showings which customarily take place in the latter parts of January and July. These collections are first shown to American and European manufacturers and store buyers, who buy styles with the express license to reproduce them in their own countries. A few weeks later the French designers show their collections to their private clientele, for whom they make garments to measure. At most houses, trade buyers are charged a deposit or required to purchase a specified minimum number of models, the cost of which must be guaranteed before they can enter. The deposit, called *caution* (the French word for deposit or surety), is deducted from the amount of any purchases made; if no purchases are made (or if purchases do not equal the amount of the *caution*), it is considered an admission fee and is not refundable. The amount of the *caution* may be as low as $500 in some houses; in others, it may reach $3000. Where the *caution* takes the form of requiring a minimum purchase, the house usually specifies either one or two models as a minimum.[7]

The trade buyer who purchases a garment for copying usually pays $800 to $1400 for a dress, $1000 to $1500 for a suit, and $1200 to $1600 for a coat. The price, of course, varies with the garment, the house concerned, and the value of the dollar on the foreign exchange, but it is higher than would be paid for the same garment if a private customer bought it for her own use. The higher price is explained partly by the fact that the commercial customer is also buying copying rights to the model, and partly by an attitude expressed by Christian Dior, who said that the commercial buyer has a photographic eye and, when he buys one model, he carries 10 more home in his head.[8]

---

[6]Garland, *op. cit.*, p. 40.

[7]*Women's Wear Daily*, July 2, 1973, p. 22.

[8]Christian Dior, *Talking about Fashion*, as told to Elie Rabourdin and Alice Chavane, translated by Eugenia Sheppard, G.P. Putnam Sons, New York, 1954, p. 84.

The Price of Paris

The Minimums

CHANEL: one model.
DIOR: See cautions.
FERAUD: Four toiles ($1,000).
  One model ($1,000).
GIVENCHY: See cautions.
GRES: $1,200 for one model (if this model is an evening dress, it cannot be embroidered because this is more expensive)
LANVIN: See cautions.
LAROCHE: See cautions.
PATOU: See cautions.
ST. LAURENT: $1,500.
UNGARO: One dress ($1,200).
  One suit ($1,400).
  One coat ($1,600).
VENET: One dress ($800)
  One suit ($1,000).

The Cautions

CHANEL: One model.
DIOR: $2,500 for two people.
FERAUD: $500 for two people; $150 for each extra person.
GIVENCHY: For U.S.A., two models.
  For Europe, two paper patterns worth 5,000 francs.
GRES: $1,200.

LANVIN: For U.S.A., two models or $1,500; no sale of paper patterns to the U.S.A.
  For Europe, one or two persons 3,000 francs giving the right to two paper patterns; three or four persons 4,000 francs giving the right to three paper patterns; 1,000 francs for each supplementary pattern.
LAROCHE: For U.S.A., two persons $1,500, one model or two paper patterns; for two persons not buying $1,000, $600 for each additional person; for department stores, three persons $1,000 for one model or two paper patterns.
  For Europe, 3,000 francs for two persons (two paper patterns); 2,000 francs for two persons not buying, 800 francs for each additional person.
PATOU: For U.S.A., two persons to see the collection one time $1,000 for two models or three toiles.
  For Europe, two persons to see the collection one time 2,800 francs, three persons 3,500 francs; two and three people to see the collection and buy two paper patterns 4,000 francs; four persons to see the collection and buy three paper patterns 4,800 francs.
ST. LAURENT: $1,500.
UNGARO: $1,800 per person, $800 for each additional person from the same store.
VENET: For U.S.A., one model. For Europe, one paper pattern worth 1,500 francs.

Source: *Women's Wear Daily*, January 4, 1973.

Dollar sales figures are not publicly reported but, in 1972, it was estimated that sales of *haute couture* models to private customers amounted to about 75 percent of total couture purchases.[9] Some authorities say that leading couturiers could not survive financially on private customers alone. The preparation of each new collection is a very costly affair and as one leading couturier himself stated: "We must depend on commercial buyers to recoup our initial outlays. Private customers cannot do so."[10] The trade sales are more profitable than those to private clientele because of the higher prices paid, and also because there is none of the fittings and fuss that is necessary with private customers. On the other hand, couturiers believe

[9]Jacques Rouet, Director of Dior, "Couture is Alive and Well," in *Women's Wear Daily*, June 26, 1972, p. 4.
[10]Pierre Cardin, speaking in "Paris, a Story of High Fashion," presented on NBC-TV, New York, February 16, 1964.

that "For the houses of *haute couture* to be creative, continuing contact with the fashionable women of the world is essential to the creation of collections. We cannot afford to have the prices for our private customers go so high that we will lose them."[11]

Couture Openings.   The content of every major collection is a closely kept secret, representing weeks and months of preparation and creative work. There is intense rivalry among the couturiers, and their creations are as jealously guarded until opening day as are the new automobiles in this country. Although the designers do have mutual agreements as to dates of openings and deliveries, there is no collusion among members on color or silhouette. It will often happen, however, that when one designer develops a new line that meets with the approbation of both his private clients and the foreign copyists, many of the other designers will pick up that trend for the next collection, and may develop it even further.

Before showing collections to trade buyers, it has been the custom to hold press previews for fashion reporters who come to Paris from all over the world to cover and report on the openings. The press, however, must pledge not to publish sketches or photos before a specified release date—approximately six weeks after the collections are first presented. This time lag gives the professional buyers time to copy the costly garments they have purchased before all and sundry can see what has been shown.

Opinion among the couturiers is divided as to the value and importance of press showings. Pierre Cardin, for example, has been quoted as saying that a press showing is "A day that may mean fabulous success or failure . . . for it is through the eyes of these reporters that women of the world see the couturiers' offerings. It is the fashion reporters who pick things to be photographed that they think are right . . . who edit the collections and report on styles they like."[12] Others, however, hold fashion reporters less highly in regard. Balenciaga, for example, in his day closed his doors to the press, and expressed himself publicly as "fed up with fashion editors who know nothing about fashions, telling buyers what and where to buy."[13]

The atmosphere of a couture house prior to the openings has often been compared to that of a theatre during rehearsals; as with any premiere, it is not until the collection is shown and the orders placed that the principals know whether they have been successful. In addition, success in any one season is ephemeral, and, six months later, the couturier will have to prove himself all over again.

Sources of Income Other than Couture Apparel.   Most leading houses have sources of income, other than couture apparel, that are often more profitable than couture itself.

1.   SALES OF OTHER PRODUCTS. In addition to apparel, most houses market other

---

[11]Robert Ricci, president of the House of Nina Ricci, in an interview reported in *The New York Times*, June 5, 1962, p. 46, "French See Revolution in Couture."
[12]Cardin, *op. cit.*
[13]*Women's Wear Daily*, June 29, 1960, "The State of the Paris Couture Today."

products, of which perfumes bearing the name of the house are perhaps the best known and most profitable. Many houses also run boutique shops on the ground floors of their establishments in which they sell jewelry, lingerie, handbags, and other accessories, along with some ready-to-wear.

2. OUTSIDE LICENSEES. Some designers, in addition to marketing other products themselves, license the use of their well-known names on merchandise ranging from hosiery to social stationery; this merchandise is manufactured and marketed by other, more specialized producers who, of course, pay for the use of the designer's name. For example, Christian Dior men's suits are licensed by Fashion Park, hats by the Hat Corporation of America, gloves by Crescendoe-Superb, Inc., shirts by Embassy Shirtmakers Ltd., and so on.

3. OUTSIDE FINANCIAL BACKING. Some leading houses have the financial backing of outsiders who support them for various reasons of prestige or profit. For example, the collections of a couturier can give superlative exposure to the products of textile interests. An illustration of such an arrangement was the launching of the House of Dior by the Cotton Industry Board, headed by Marcel Boussac, as a means of stimulating demand for French fabrics.[14] Couturiers and their textile suppliers are mutually dependent; thus it is understandable that textile firms should finance individual couture houses. Textile firms, regardless of whether they have a financial interest in a house, are not averse to supplying, free of charge, dress lengths from which the house's initial samples are made or to carrying, without advance payment, the stock that is required for the made-to-order reproductions.

4. READY-TO-WEAR. To an increasing extent, most of the major couture houses are involving themselves with ready-to-wear. This development, which is discussed in detail later in this section, has become a source of far greater direct revenue than couture clothes.

Chambre Syndicale de la Couture Parisienne.   Most of the *haute couture* houses are members of an association known as the Chambre Syndicale de la Couture Parisienne. This is a trade association that was founded in 1868 to represent the different branches of the French fashion industries and to deal with the administrative and labor problems of its membership. Its major activities on behalf of the couture are to perform the following duties.

1. COORDINATE THE OPENING SCHEDULES. Days, dates, and hours during the week of openings are coordinated so that trade buyers and reporters may be able to see the work of several houses in one day.

2. REGULATE SHIPPING AND RELEASE DATES. All orders placed by professional buyers during opening week are shipped on a uniform date, approximately 30 days after the initial showings. The release date for publication of press photographs or sketches is set for approximately six weeks after showings. This press release date is arranged so that buyers of expensive models will have time to get copies made before the news of what has been shown is disseminated.

---

[14]Dwight E. Robinson, "The Importance of Fashions in Taste to Business History," *The Business History Review,* Vol. XXXVII, Spring/Summer, 1963, p. 30.

3.   REGULATE CONDITIONS FOR COPYING. The right to offer copies is granted to a purchaser only in his own country, and only in fabrics; the making of paper patterns for resale purposes is forbidden. Manufacturers are also asked to sign an agreement not to sell or sublet the model to an unauthorized producer. These rules for copying are legally unenforceable in the United States, and there have been many violations, as well as some lawsuits; any person or firm suspected of infringing on these regulations, however, is never again allowed in an *haute couture* house.

4.   REGISTER NEW DESIGNS OF ITS MEMBERS. If an unauthorized copy of a registered design is found in France, the style pirate is subject to prosecution under French law.

5.   ISSUE PRESS CARDS FOR THE OPENINGS. Press representatives can obtain the *cartes d'entrée* to the collections only through the Chambre.

The Chambre also represents its members in its relations with the French government, arbitrates disputes, regulates uniform wage arrangements and working hours, and sponsors a school for the education of apprentices. There is also a Chambre Syndicale des Paruriers that represents accessory firms, and other different divisions represent milliners, ready-to-wear manufacturers, and the like.

The Economics of Couture.   Parisian *haute couture* is more than its talented designers, original creations and glamorous mannequins. It is also a business, and one which is of major importance to the economy of France. It may not be large in comparison with the American industry but it does provide employment for many thousands of French workers. The top 20 houses alone are said to employ about 8000 workers at the peak of a season.[15] Even more important is the great prestige, the publicity value, and the luxury image that couture showings lend to other French fashion products and to the perfume and licensee business ventures of the couture houses themselves. The fact is that most of the couture houses make enough profit on perfume alone to cover the costly couture presentations. As Jacques Rouet, Director of Dior, explained it: "The couture is the motor pulling everything we do. It is indispensable."[16]

Figures on the sales of individual houses or on couture as a whole are not publicly reported; neither are authoritative statistics available. The Chambre Syndicale, to which most (but not all) couture houses belong, estimates that its members in 1969 sold *haute couture* merchandise, exclusive of perfumes and accessories, amounting to the equivalent of $32 million. Of this amount, exports were believed to account for one-third and sales to private clients accounted for the balance.[17] The House of Dior, as a result of its subsidiary activities, is generally reported to have the largest sales volume of any of the couture houses and has been listed among the top 300 French exporters. Of its estimated $60-million-a-year business, excluding perfume sales, only 4½ percent is attributed to sales of couture apparel; the balance is accounted for by a wide range of American and European licensing arrangements.[18]

[15]Chambre Syndicale de la Couture Parisienne, *loc. cit.*

[16]*Women's Wear Daily*, February 3, 1972, p. 1.

[17]Daniel Garin, President of Chambre Syndicale de la Couture Parisienne, letter dated October 16, 1970.

[18]G.Y. Dryansky, *Women's Wear Daily*, January 26, 1973, pp. 1 and 8, "The Couture: Not What It Was, but Still a Power."

For the *haute couture* as a whole, trade estimates—educated guesses—in the 1970s were that private customers would account for about 75 percent of merchandise sales. American professional buyers are believed to spend about $1 million yearly on couture models for copying purposes, a sum that is surpassed by trade buyers from other countries. Germany is reputed to be the leading nation in terms of purchases of couture models.

Haute couture houses are in good shape creatively but have been facing many financial and operational problems. One of the problems is the ups and downs of the business. For example, the nine Dior workrooms are so rushed after a new collection that they have difficulty filling their orders; during other months there is not enough work to keep the 350 employees in the workrooms busy. Another major problem is that custom-made clothes, despite their high selling prices, are not very profitable because of the steadily mounting costs of labor, material, and taxes. Even as far back as 1965, the pinch was being felt. As always, behind the artists are the accountants.

> *"And this is how they count: in a collection of 174 models (such as Dior showed in 1965) $200,000 is invested in labor and in materials. Then, each model is reproduced, one by one, to a client's measurements, with three fittings according to haute couture traditions. Each dress represents an average of 135 working hours—$470 just in labor costs—plus the material, $80—plus general overhead.*
>
> *"The seamstresses must work in the same building where the dresses are sold. Necessarily, a haute couture house is located in one of the most expensive districts of Paris and at the cost of a square foot in these areas, the rent and taxes are wildly extravagant. If an American manufacturer had to house his entire labor force in the building where his products are sold, his prices would be more than double."[19]*

Despite the low profit margins on custom-made originals, the couturiers carry on. Their dresses serve as a facade of publicity for the famous names that sell such quite different goods as shoes, lingerie, men's ties and suits, hosiery, and above all perfume, which alone brings in an annual sales contribution of close to $400 million.[20] As Pierre Cardin explained it: "The dresses we make are like sails on a sailboat. They help to sail the boat, but all fishing goes on from the boat itself."[21]

American Copies and Adaptations of Couture. The American fashion industries look to the Paris couture for several reasons. One is prestige. Another is for new ideas and trends in silhouettes, trimmings, fabrics, and other style details. Although declining in number, a few retailers, such as Ohrbach's and Lord & Taylor in New York, buy couturier styles to reproduce and promote exact "line-for-line" copies on a semi-annual basis. Most retailers, however, use the couture models they purchase in order to make adaptations or to study even a single significant new element of the design for possible copying or adaptation. This kind of copying is legitimate and is

[19]Françoise Giraud, "After Courrèges, What Future for the Haute Couture," *The New York Times Magazine*, September 12, 1965, p. 50.
[20]*Ibid.*
[21]Cardin, *op. cit.*

not to be confused with style piracy, the *stealing* of designs. It must be remembered that French and other European couturiers sell their designs for this express purpose, and trade buyers pay well for this privilege.

The copying operations begin with the January and July showings in Paris, which are attended by two major categories of professional buyers: those who represent the manufacturers, and those who represent and buy for retail stores. In many cases, store buyers and manufacturers work together; the retail buyers will select the styles to be carried and share the cost of the original garments with the manufacturers who make the copies for them. Even though many professionals purchase only a few models, the new ideas that they see are often more valuable than those that they buy.

There is a great variation among the professional buyers in the number of houses that they shop, the number of styles that they buy, and the factors that influence their selection. The tastes of the clientele to whom their particular firm caters must be taken into consideration, as well as the prices at which they plan to sell the garments. Another important consideration is their advertising and promotion plans. Some styles will be purchased for prestige purposes; others for their volume possibilities; and still others for their newness and trend-setting aspects. Firms whose copies and adaptations are geared to a volume ready-to-wear market must consider the practicality of reproducing certain cuts and details by mass-production methods, in which hundreds of garments must be cut at one time. All buyers, however, look for styles that will create fashion news and stimulate customer interest. Indeed, some retailers admit that they buy Paris models to copy purely for prestige purposes. They have no expectation of profiting from the sale of copies, even expensive ones, but they do hope that some of the Paris glamour will rub off on their other ready-to-wear lines.

Since the garments shown in the collections are for sample purposes only, each buyer can specify the color and size of the reproduction that will be made up to his order. French models, despite their high price tags, are not sold on an exclusive basis and, unless there is a special understanding, the couture house will take as many orders as it can get on a given number. It frequently happens, therefore, that the same styles will be sold to many buyers, each one representing a different type of firm, and each copying or adapting them to sell at different prices.

All orders placed during the initial showings are delivered on a uniform date, approximately four weeks after the opening. Although the actual copying or adapting process must wait until models are received, preliminary work on the copies begins as soon as the buyers return. Most firms try to have their line-for-line copies ready for sale two to three weeks after the originals arrive in the States. This means that much preparatory work must be done prior to the arrival of their orders. Appropriate fabrics and trimmings must be selected and readied for quick production; store buyers must make arrangements with manufacturers to whom they will give the models to be copied; advertising, window displays, fashion shows, and other promotional devices must be preplanned and scheduled. Since speed is vital, many people wonder why it is necessary to wait for the actual garment itself. The reason is that, for good copies, the manufacturers must be able to examine the original, inch by inch, and seam by seam to determine exactly how it is made in order to make a pattern. This is the only way to be sure that its shape and fit will be what its creator intended.

Since the majority of Paris designs are purchased simply for copying or adapting, buyers have no permanent use for the original models. The garments, therefore, are generally brought into the United States under bond. This is an import arrangement with the United States Customs, which means that American firms have agreed not to resell the original garments within the confines of the United States, and therefore do not have to pay duty (which could amount to almost half as much again as the original cost of the garments). After one year, the United States importer must dispose of the original. Many firms sell the "used" samples to Canadian firms who specialize in the buying and selling of second-hand Paris models.

The majority of buyers deal through foreign commissionaires, for whose services they pay a fee. The commissionaire handles language barriers; translates prices into United States dollar values; follows up on shipping, packing, and customs arrangements; and also acts as the banker, adviser, and buyer's representative until the merchandise is shipped and received.

The actual extent of the influence exerted by the Paris couture on the American fashion industries is indeed debatable. Since couture creations are as noteworthy for their exquisite workmanship and fit as their styling, if not more so, there is a question of how much Paris can be injected into the mass-produced apparel of this country. Furthermore, in recent years, the growing prestige of American designers and the emergence of couturiers in other countries have loosened the hold of Paris to some extent, but its *dicta* are still respected by American manufacturers and designers. As one American designer explained it: "There is no question that the Paris establishment does have the benefit of the mystique even though the mystique is just a hangover."[22] The long history of Paris as the capital city of fashion has developed such a habit of thinking among American trade buyers that many of them have been accused of buying styles to which they would not have given a moment's notice if the styles had come from any other city in the world. There have been seasons, indeed, when buyers returned from Paris, bubbling over with enthusiasm for a "new" idea that already had been born on Seventh Avenue. Although American buying of Paris originals has decreased in recent years, there remains an enormous respect for the drama and authority with which the French couture conveys its fashion message.

Future of Couture.   Despite frequent predictions of its imminent demise, the Paris couture seems destined to remain active in the foreseeable future for the following reasons.

1.   PRESTIGE AND PUBLICITY VALUE. Although revenue may be lost because of narrowing profit margins on custom business, many houses consider the loss of a few hundred thousand dollars a year a small price for the prestigious reputation that couture bestows on a name. Couture showings, with their attendant worldwide

---

[22]Luba of Elite, "Paris Grip on Fashion Unraveling," in *Women's Wear Daily*, February 19, 1969, p. 28.

publicity, give the luxury image that is essential in promoting the more lucrative businesses of perfumes, licenses, and growing ready-to-wear activities.

2. CONTINUING TRADE BUSINESS. Trade buyers from all over the world, regardless of whether they actually purchase garments for copying, continue to attend showings and pay their *cautions* for the inspiration they get from viewing a creative collection. Typical is the attitude of Alexander's in New York. When that store discontinued its line-for-line copying operation in 1970, its fashion director, Francine Farkas, was quoted as saying: "We went to Paris to view, not to buy."[23]

3. CONTINUING PRIVATE CLIENTELE. The fit, the workmanship, and the distinction of a custom-made couture garment continue to remain important to an international group of wealthy women. Their purchases, although not as great as the volume of business that their grandmothers placed with some houses in the past, still account for a sizable majority of total couture sales. Even though the private customers of the couture houses may use ready-to-wear for such informal occasions as sports, travel, luncheons, and shopping, they do not wear mass-produced garments for occasions that call for elegant dress, spectacular jewels, or luxurious furs. Moreover, the chore of custom fittings becomes minimal when a woman is a regular customer. She makes her selections, lets the fitter confirm her measurements from her previous fittings, and is on her way, arranging for the finished garments to follow her by air to whatever country or continent is next on her itinerary.

4. CREATIVE CLIMATE. The couturier, whatever his national origin, functions best in Paris for many valid reasons. Paris still provides thousands of gifted seamstresses who have sewing skill in their fingertips. The city can also supply, in small quantities, the accessories, belts, and embroideries that the couturiers need. Then, too, there is no other place where one can find such an appreciative audience—men as well as women—to love fashion and to honor with respect and fame a successful designer. The advantage of Paris as a creative fashion center was admirably summed up by Yves St. Laurent, when a reporter from *Women's Wear Daily* asked him if he could design in the United States: "I could design anywhere in the world," he replied. "But in Paris, all is possible. . . . Without those thousands of artisans I could not realize my ideas so well. . . . All is in Paris."[24]

Among the people who view the future of the couture darkly, the recurring comment is that the couture and its custom approach do not relate to modern life. The argument is that women do not want to waste time on fittings and that they prefer to have many inexpensive clothes instead of cherishing a $2000 dress for 10 years. Also cited are the high costs of custom-made clothing and the rapid pace of change that tends to make a large collection out of date almost before it has been shown. The risks and costs of assembling a couture collection are enormous, and the demands on the design staff's creative talent are great. The pace is particularly rugged if the house interests itself also in ready-to-wear, boutiques, men's wear, and related activities that require supplementary collections to be created each

[23]*Women's Wear Daily*, August 5, 1970, p. 23.
[24]*Women's Wear Daily*, November 1, 1965, p. 2.

season. Cardin's answer to the problem was to announce in 1970 that he would show but one collection a year—in March. Other Paris houses, however, continue with their usual schedules and apparently thrive on the multiple challenges that their obligations present.

At the very least, all observers agree that the fashion influence of the couture is not what it once was and that *haute couture*, as it used to be, is fading away. What seems most likely is that *haute couture* houses will be content to maintain their less-profitable couture operations for the publicity and prestige value that these operations give to the other, more lucrative business ventures to which they are turning to an increasing degree.

From Couture to Ready-to-Wear

Factory-made ready-to-wear has been produced in France throughout the twentieth century; the firm of Mendès France is credited with having started the industry in 1903. The industry was small, however, and was made up primarily of small firms—until the 1960s when couture houses moved strongly into the field. By 1970, the involvement of the couture houses of Paris (and the houses of other major fashion centers) in *prêt à porter* (French for ready-to-wear) had reached proportions that would have been unthinkable even in the early 1960s. Most houses are interested in ready-to-wear as a source of far greater volume and more profitable revenue than made-to-order couture clothes.

Produced by Outside Factories.   Ready-to-wear is not entirely new to couture houses. Many of them have long had boutiques on their premises. There they sold factory-produced, less-expensive versions of their own custom designs, made for them by outside manufacturers specializing in ready-to-wear. These manufacturing specialists usually arranged also for broader distribution of this ready-to-wear, not limiting themselves to the designs of a single couturier.

More and more couturiers have been going into the ready-to-wear business on an increasingly larger scale. Production arrangements vary for the different houses. The manufacturing firm of Didier Grumbach, a grandson of Mendès France, produces and distributes the ready-to-wear collections of such well-known designers as Yves St. Laurent, Givenchy, Castillo, Lanvin, Jean Louis Scherrer, and Guy La Roche, for example. All the collections are marketed together and distributed not only in France but also in other countries, including the United States, but each collection bears the name of the designer who creates it. The showings take place in October and in April.

Some couturiers maintain manufacturing divisions for their ready-to-wear in France and in other countries as well. Dior, for example, has a manufacturing firm right in the heart of Seventh Avenue in New York City; Patou has one in Angers, France. Other couturiers have contracted with manufacturers of ready-to-wear and with pattern companies, in the United States and elsewhere, to design styles exclusively for them. Several houses make contracts with major retailers to design limited collections for them each season, leaving production arrangements and promotion to the stores. In these relationships, personal appearances by the designer to stimulate consumer interest and sales are often part of the bargain.

OCTOBER 21 TO 26
1972

24° salon du prêt-à-porter féminin

INTERNATIONAL
BOUTIQUE
DE LUXE

paris

PORTE
DE VERSAILLES

FOR MEMBERS OF THE TRADE ONLY

éditions Léonard

Source: As advertised in *Women's Wear Daily,* 1972.

Others of the couture simply sell their ready-to-wear boutique clothes to Paris department stores for resale—a practice that began in the mid-1960s.

Ready-to-Wear Boutiques.   Ready-to-wear boutiques, operated by couture houses under their own names but at locations apart from the custom operations, made their appearance in the late 1960s and opened a whole new market to these firms. Especially noteworthy is the separate boutique operation of Yves St. Laurent who, in 1966, launched his first Rive Gauche Boutique on the Left Bank in Paris with such enormous success that a franchised chain of boutiques has been established throughout France, in other European countries, and in the United States. The original Left Bank store is the only boutique owned outright by St. Laurent Rive Gauche; the others are franchised. All shops are uniform in decor and carry only merchandise designed by St. Laurent. Didier Grumbach manufactures the apparel in Europe; American firms are licensed to produce the jewelry, belts, and shoes.

Encouraged by the success of the St. Laurent boutiques, other couturiers are following in his footsteps. There is a Givenchy Nouvelle Boutique in Bergdorf Goodman, Inc. in New York, along with about 40 others in leading stores throughout the United States and Europe. Patou has boutiques in Japan and Europe. The Italian couturier, Valentino, opened a division, called Boutiques Valentino, to license boutiques in U.S. stores. These stores carry accessories and apparel of his design, the accessories being manufactured in Italy, but the apparel being produced in the United States. Cardin, after his boutique met with great success in Bonwit Teller, New York, arranged for similar tie-ups with retail stores in other parts of the country.

French Ready-to-Wear Industry.   Fashion and mass production have combined to build a French ready-to-wear industry of about 2000 enterprises. The 30 largest account for 25 percent of the business. The total output is estimated at approximately $500 million, with one quarter of the output, in terms of value, exported principally to countries in the European Common Market.[25] West Germany is reportedly the biggest user, taking one quarter of the output; the United States uses less than 10 percent. Although the French industry has a number of outstanding and successful firms, some of the best-known names in the ready-to-wear field belong to the couturiers who have joined the mass market.

Along with the possibilities that a sizable ready-to-wear business offers to creative couturiers to capitalize on their fashion talents, the French industry's ready-to-wear growth also represents a social revolution. Until recently, French factory-made clothes consisted mainly of cheap, poorly styled merchandise intended almost exclusively for working-class consumption. Today, through its ready-to-wear, the couture is keeping pace with a new aspect of fashion demand among the wealthy women who traditionally constitute its custom clientele. At the same time, its ready-to-wear price lines and distribution methods bring well-styled Paris clothes to women who could not possibly afford to shop Paris's custom salons. To the extent that it serves women who are not spectacularly affluent and who shop in their home

[25]Fédération Française des Industries du Vêtement Féminin, letter dated May 10, 1971. Also *The New York Times*, April 18, 1971, p. 16, "Buyers' Paris Trek."

areas, the couture is broadening its market—and putting itself into direct competition with producers of better-grade fashion merchandise in the United States.

OTHER FOREIGN FASHION CENTERS

The decades following World War II have seen the accelerating growth of fashion markets in countries other than France. Although other centers have never matched the importance of Paris, cities such as London, Berlin, Florence, and Rome have had long-standing couturier traditions of their own. Today, Italy, Spain, England, Sweden, Israel, Canada, and the Far East are among countries that make their bids for a share of the ready-to-wear and accessory fashion pie. The various governments concerned, each eager for export trade, have nursed their fashion industries along by means of subsidies and other aids. Although these other foreign fashion centers do not match Paris in reputation, they have amply demonstrated their ability to attract the custom clientele, trade buyers, or both. Their attraction is enhanced by the fact that travel is so fast today that even if a city has only one really creative house, a single lively fashion talent, the idea-hungry producers, retailers, and custom clientele will go there.

The key word in *all* countries is "export" and, although the methods of government support vary, foreign fashion designers are being given every opportunity to develop their businesses, provided, of course, that they utilize the natural resources of their respective countries. Although foreign apparel manufacturers are not yet geared for the sizable volume of the American ready-to-wear industry, there is every indication that history in fashionable ready-made clothing and accessories is a worldwide happening today.

Italy

The Italian couture differs from the Paris couture in that there are not many houses, and they are not concentrated in any one city. Their impact is especially strong in sportswear, knitwear, and accessories—notably shoes. Each season, a different city is host to buyers attending the collections, and few major buyers visit Paris without making a quick trip to the designated Italian city in search of fresh, exciting fashions.

There are designers in the Italian couture who acquired their skills during World War II and thus developed without the benefit of Paris influence or tradition. Many of the houses are headed by members of Italy's nobility, whose businesses flourish in their ancestral palaces. Perhaps the best-known couturiers are Emilio Pucci, who has been called the father of couture sportswear, and Valentino, whose house has become part of the American conglomerate, Kenton Corporation. Other familiar names include de Berentzen, Fabiani, Fontana, Galitzine, Mila Schoen, Simonetta, and Veniziana of Milan.

As a member of the European Common Market, Italy does not offer government subsidies and special tax exemptions to encourage exports. However, textile firms that wish to add prestige to their fabrics are completely free to associate with high-fashion designers after the pattern of the French textile industry. The government's assistance takes the form of facilitating showings. The historically famous Pitti Palace in Florence has been made available for ready-to-wear showings, and the Strozzi Palace in that city has been provided as a meeting place for the actual buying and selling transactions. A Center for Promotion of Italian Fashions and Textiles has been established at Milan's Mitam, and models purchased for the purpose are shown there.

Recent experience of the Italian couture has run parallel to that of the Paris houses. Rising costs have threatened the profitability of custom operations; boutiques have gained favor as a source of revenue; and couture houses have been attracted to the income possibilities in perfumes, accessories, and licensing fees. Valentino ventured into the ready-to-wear field in the beginning of the 1970s, and there were indications that other houses were considering similar moves.

England

British efforts to nurture the fashion industry were so unremitting that one observer characterized Britain's Board of Trade as the "fairy godmother to whom is due the survival of their couture and the rapid development of their now large and excellent ready-to-wear trade."[26] The couture's efforts, led by Molyneux, took the form of producing collections and showing them to American buyers just before the Paris openings. This effort was not very productive and, by 1970, the membership of the Incorporated Society of London Fashion Designers had dwindled to five houses.

Couture for women and Savile Row tailoring for men did not draw the fashion dollars into postwar England that were so desperately needed. It was only when that country made itself felt as an interpreter of the young spirit of the times that its influence on the course of fashion reached significant proportions. Especially notable was the contribution of a young newcomer, Mary Quant, who functioned in ready-to-wear instead of in the field of *haute couture*.

Mary Quant understood early what many couturiers in her country and on the Continent were quite late in recognizing: "Once only the rich, the Establishment, set the fashion. Now it is the inexpensive little dress seen on the girls in the High Street. . . . Snobbery has gone out of fashion, and in our shops you will find duchesses jostling with typists to buy the same dresses."[27] It was Mary Quant whose miniskirts gave expression to the free young spirit of the late 1950s and the 1960s and sent feminine hemlines soaring from their safe below-the-knee location all the way up to midthigh. Paralleling the Quant influence on women's fashions was the effect of the group of men's shops on Carnaby Street, where new and uninhibited fashions were launched.

[26]Garland, *op. cit.*, p. 73.
[27]Mary Quant, *Quant by Quant*, G.P. Putnam Sons, New York, 1966, p. 75.

London Fashion Fair
April 20 21 22 1972
Presented by the
Clothing Export Council
of Great Britain

Associated Fashion Designers
and
Bloomsbury Pret-a-Porter
and
Kings Road Club
and
Knitwear Fashion Group
and
London Designer Collection
and
London's Leading Collections
and
all under one roof in
The Great Room,
Grosvenor House, Park Lane

and
The London Look for Autumn 1972
An Authoritative Fashion Presentation
sponsored by The International Wool
Secretariat

Advance information and tickets from:
Clothing Export Council of Great Britain,
54 Grosvenor Street, London W1X 0DB
Telephone: 01-493 8882

Source: *Women's Wear Daily*, January 25, 1972, p. 17.

The British are not content, however, with exporting solely the genius of their designers. In addition to whatever their designers may earn abroad in the form of fees or licensing arrangements, the government also seeks solid sales of British-made clothes in the American market. With this end in view, the Board of Trade's Export Service Division maintains fashion market experts in major cities of the United States to report on the size and nature of the market in various localities and on the competitive situation with respect to British goods. Among other duties, these resident experts arrange for British producers to stage joint showings of their fashion wares at centers where sufficient retail interest exists to make this worthwhile. For example, as part of a sustained drive to sell fashion merchandise in California, arrangements are made for a British Week in San Francisco, to which West Coast merchants can come in order to view British lines conveniently. The public is not ignored in these efforts. In the 1971 British Week, Princess Alexandra visited San Francisco; a replica of a British pub was set up in the city; and the Lord Mayor of London exchanged greetings with the city's mayor. Through pageantry, press agentry, and the business approach, the consumer and the retailer alike are invited to consider British apparel offerings.

Spain

Madrid's *Alta Costura (haute couture)* has been heavily subsidized by the government in a variety of ways: large-scale advertising campaigns; renovation and development of modeling schools; development of sketching talent; entertainment of visiting buyers and press; and drawings among potentially large customers for free trips to Spain. All this plus some very talented designers! Of the 14 members of the *Alta Costura*, perhaps the best known is Pertegaz; others include Elio Berhanyer, Carmen Mir, Pedro Rovira, and Herrera y Ollero.

Other Countries

Almost any country with any fashion capability is in competition for a share of the world's fashion business. The race is not limited to countries with couture capacity, nor even to those with creative ready-to-wear designers. Countries with only sewing skills to offer have been acquiring the know-how to work their way into the world fashion market.

Europe.   In addition to the countries discussed earlier in this section, the Scandinavian countries, the Low Countries, Scotland, Ireland, Switzerland, Austria, and West Germany all produce ready-to-wear. Many group efforts are made to attract buyers from the United States and other parts of the world. The most impressive attempt, undoubtedly, is the international exhibit of European ready-to-wear held each season at Dusseldorf, Germany. There, 1400 firms from 14 countries show their lines to 25,000 buyers from all over the world. There are also smaller ventures. Scandinavian producers stage a show in Copenhagen and also send a group showing to the United States regularly. Ireland, too, sends a group regularly.

Israel.   Patterning its apparel industry on that of the United States, Israel has set up a school along the lines of New York's Fashion Institute of Technology to prepare students for careers in the fashion trades. The government also supports ATID, a marketing organization in New York for Israeli products and provides substantial subsidies for apparel exports.

Far East.   Japan, Hong Kong, Korea, the Philippines, Taiwan, and other countries in the Orient are not so much fashion centers as producers of garments for the low-end market. Much of their export trade to the United States consists of merchandise ordered well in advance by American producers or large-scale retailers who specify the desired styling and sizing to insure acceptability in the home market. Under such arrangements, planning and ordering are usually done far in advance—a factor that more or less rules out styles with a high degree of fashion innovation and fashion risk. Nevertheless, considerable quantities of knitwear, blouses, and undergarments are imported into the United States from the Far East each year.

AMERICAN IMPORTS OF READY-TO-WEAR AND ACCESSORIES

Until 1950, imports of ready-to-wear and accessories were not of significant size in volume or value; almost all apparel purchased ready-made by Americans was supplied by our domestic industry. Beginning in the mid-1950s, however, and continuing at an accelerating pace, imports of apparel grew, passing the $1 billion mark in wholesale value before the 1960s ended. In 1960, imports of clothing of all types amounted to $304 million at wholesale value; in 1970, the figure had reached $1267 million, a fourfold increase, during a period in which the total imports of the United States increased two and one-half times in value.[28]

American ready-to-wear producers, however, have been unable to match their exports to the rising tide of imports. High tariffs and a wide range of such nontariff barriers as value-added taxes and exchange controls, imposed by the same foreign countries who enjoy a large U.S. market, make our domestically produced apparel almost prohibitive in price within their borders.

The Rationale of Imports.   American wholesalers and retailers purchase imported ready-to-wear and accessories for several reasons.

1.   PRICE. On the price front, the simple fact is that foreign countries, particularly those in the Far East, pay their employees considerably less than garment workers are paid in the United States. Often a completed garment can be purchased

[28]U.S. Department of Commerce, *Statistical Abstract of the United States, 1971*, pp. 777–778.

in the Orient and brought into this country at a cost lower than the production costs alone in an American factory. To obtain salable, attractive merchandise, however, it is often necessary for the American wholesaler or mass retailer to style the producer's line, and sometimes to supervise production every step of the way from raw fiber to finished product. Even so, the price advantage is often considerable. A further price advantage accrues in many countries because of government subsidies and other aids to the export trade.

2. EXCLUSIVITY.   American retailers are always in search of new and different merchandise to which they can get exclusive rights without the massive purchases required by large, volume-minded American producers. This is one of the ways in which merchants can generate storewide sales excitement and also obtain a higher markup percentage. It is also one of the ways in which domestic producers can overcome any inadequacies they may encounter in the American market when there is fashion demand for materials of specific types, qualities, quantities, or price, or when they seek exclusivity and uniqueness in fabric without having to commit themselves to the purchase of huge runs far in advance of the season.

3. FASHION AUTHORITY.   There are many foreign fashion designers whose names are familiar to American shoppers and whose labels almost presell their products. In the case of franchised designer boutiques, moreover, the store that operates a boutique has the additional advantage of exclusivity with respect to the designs it offers for sale—a trump card for retailers, insofar as merchandising and promotion are concerned.

Imports of Selected Women's and Children's Garments (in thousands of units)

PRODUCT	1961	1968	1969	1970	1971	1972
Coats	558[b]	9,311	12,088	14,041	16,626	19,235
Suits	75[b]	166	219	662	879	992
Dresses	3,323[b]	17,378	21,986	25,227	30,327	26,917
Blouses	29,426[b]	53,812	78,432	102,777	129,296	103,209
Skirts	504[b]	6,625	7,318	7,916	9,517	7,178
Sweaters	7,201[b]	87,369	108,201	92,724	116,745	116,535
Slacks and shorts	31,146[b]	62,781	81,029	93,110	138,323	145,677
Playsuits	10,988[b]	10,336	14,429	19,167	20,215	22,087
Raincoats[a]	1,337[b]	6,323	6,967	6,326	6,579	10,681
Dressing gowns and robes	476[b]	4,535	4,306	4,012	3,214	3,176
Nightwear and pajamas	4,492[b]	10,249	14,728	17,079	18,245	10,872
Underwear	1,650[b]	4,974	6,939	10,170	22,941	24,870
Brassieres	31,523[b]	44,515	43,786	51,021	59,938	71,594

Source: International Ladies' Garment Workers' Union, New York, *Conditions in the Women's Garment Industry*, February 28, 1973.
[a]Men's, women's and children's.
[b]Estimated by ILGWU Research Department.

Impact of Imports upon the Economy. The rise of imports has created an economic problem for American textile and apparel producers. When ideas are imported, we import only the inspiration that keeps our own industry working. When we import ready-to-wear clothing for resale, we are usually providing work for lower-paid labor in other countries and, at times, displacing our own labor and idling some part of our production equipment.

At the 34th ILGWU Convention in May 1971, deep concern was expressed over imports; the General Executive Board reported that in 1966 imports accounted for 12 percent of the garments sold in the United States and that, by 1969, the figure had grown to 18 percent. The prospect that 20 percent of the market would be preempted by clothes of foreign origin appeared obvious.[29]

Although it is generally agreed that the increasing of international trade is in the long-range interest of our country and of the world, the prospect of dislocations caused by further penetration of the American market by imports is not pleasant for the industry. The ILGWU continues to work toward effective control of the flow of fashion goods from other countries. The union's president suggested: "A legislative solution to this problem is a measure of last resort. It is still the hope of all concerned in this country that voluntary agreements can be reached with individual countries."[30]

Our government has recently worked out agreements with major apparel exporting nations that put a ceiling on the rate of growth of apparel imports into this country. The first slowdown in the rate of increase of apparel imports was noted by the ILGWU in 1972, when the square yards equivalent of imported apparel and accessories for women and children rose only 2.4 percent. By contrast, the rate of increase for 1971 over 1970 was 29.3 percent.[31]

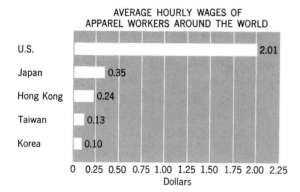

AVERAGE HOURLY WAGES OF
APPAREL WORKERS AROUND THE WORLD

U.S.	2.01
Japan	0.35
Hong Kong	0.24
Taiwan	0.13
Korea	0.10

0   0.25 0.50 0.75 1.00 1.25 1.50 1.75 2.00 2.25
Dollars

Source: U.S. Department of Labor and *Apparel Manufacturer.*

[29]International Ladies' Garment Workers' Union, *Trends and Prospects in the Women's Garment Industry*, May 1971, p. 15.

[30]Louis J. Stulberg, letter to editor, *The New York Times*, April 27, 1970.

[31]Research Department, International Ladies' Garment Workers' Union, *Conditions in the Women's Garment Industry*, February 28, 1973, pp. 5 and 6.

READINGS

Famous Paris designers have been discussed in many books that are available in most libraries. We, therefore, have avoided this aspect of the subject in our selection of readings, except for the concluding reading, which sums up the careers and contributions of famous designers—including three Americans.

The articles in this section focus on the excitement of a couture opening and on the changing importance of the couture itself. They discuss copying, imports, and the leadership that Paris exerts or, at times, fails to exert. Other subjects explored are the value of the United States as a market for fashions produced abroad, and the reasons why stores and consumers in this country turn to foreign sources for fashion goods. As several of the readings show, imports and copies have a place at all points along the price scale, from exclusive specialty shop merchandise to goods intended for the bargain racks of discount merchants.

BACKSTAGE AT PARIS' FASHION DRAMA

Françoise Giroud

If Women Await the Spring Modes Breathlessly, the Designers Are Pretty Out of Breath, Too

The invitations are printed. The chairs have been rented. The new clothes are almost completed. France's couturiers are ready for the opening of the greatest show on earth tomorrow—the show they put on twice a year, now and in August, at which they launch some 2000 new designs in six hectic days.

Naturally, just before the opening, Christian Dior will contemplate suicide. Cristobal Balenciaga will murmur about entering holy orders. Hubert de Givenchy will sob. Coco Chanel will cry, "Why did I ever get back into this ridiculous business!"—and destroy twenty costumes out of forty. But when has there ever been a great spectacle without stars, or a star without majestic opening-night temperament? It's all part of the show, like the chronic outrage of the London press, which biannually proclaims, "We are *not* going to get ourselves up according to Monsieur Dior's dictates."

The fact is, this Monsieur Dior—51 years old, shy, bald, a roly-poly trencherman—has in the last ten years busily transformed women into tulips, cupolas, H's, A's, string beans and arrows; and, moreover, without the slightest serious resistance.*

Dior himself, who sets the best table in Paris, fats up. But his mannequins get thinner and thinner, straighter and straighter, flatter and flatter—except when it occurs to one of them to have a baby. At the first Dior collection in 1947, the one that was to

revolutionize fashion, the mannequin Tania fainted twice. "It's emotion," people said. It was, in fact, a baby, protesting the New Look in its own way.

Men, however, were the ones to protest the Flat Look, three years back. Women accepted it almost unanimously. Christian Dior is a man who does nothing without consulting his fortune-teller.

At 40 he was a well-bred, penniless member of the middle class with no discernible future, demurely designing clothes. Today he reigns over an empire that includes Dior branches in London and Caracas, Christian Dior-New York, a wholesale dress operation, and a perfume business. His house in Paris has twenty workrooms and 1200 employes, who make and sell 8000 garments a year—the cheapest of which costs 120,000 francs, or three times a secretary's weekly wage. Nonetheless, when Coco Chanel has lunch with him she tells him, "I adore you, but you dress women like armchairs."

Chanel was already world famous and had sold 20,000 dresses a year when Dior was still a schoolboy. She had exalted fake jewelry and that humble material, jersey, to the height of fashion; she had launched the famous Chanel No. 5 perfume. She reigned over Paris for twenty years, vanished for fifteen years, then reappeared because she was bored. And this winter everyone is imitating her designs.

Dior thinks above all about foreigners; Chanel thinks above all about Parisiennes. Dior shows 200 designs; Chanel shows forty. Dior fears being copied, and fashion buyers must deposit a *"caution"* of 100,000 francs if they are European, 350,000 if American, to see his collection. Chanel on the other hand likes to be copied and lets the press

SOURCE: Reprinted from the January 27, 1957, issue of *The New York Times Magazine* by permission of *The New York Times.*

---

*Dior, deceased, is replaced now by Marc Bohan.

reproduce all her designs as early as she feels like it, because, she says, "discoveries are made to be lost." Dior loves lavishness, the million-dollar look; Chanel loves the impudent, the seemingly inexpensive. These two great couturiers, however, have one thing in common. Neither knows how to sew.

Contrariwise, Balenciaga—dark, gaunt, distinguished, and of indeterminate age—made his first design with his own hands when he was 10. It was a jewelled collar for his cat. And in all his collections there is, according to superstition, one dress he has sewn entirely himself.

Balenciaga never shows himself, never goes out in society. His establishment is not a shop; it is a temple, in which 350 seamstresses and twenty saleswomen officiate. His dozen mannequins are not beautiful willowy girls, they are high priestesses of a sacred cult. His clients? They are a sect. When one of them requested an admission card for a friend a while ago, Balenciaga's assistant, the terrible Mademoiselle Renée, replied, "No, madame. Curious women do not interest us."

If Dior's ideal client is an elegant millionairess and Chanel's a witty, knowing Parisienne, Balenciaga's ideal is a tragic young widowed queen, always dressed in dramatic tones—black, white, red. Balenciaga is the couturier of night.

As for Marquis Hubert Taffin de Givenchy's ideal type, she embodies the notion of an American a Frenchwoman gleans from the American fashion magazines at her hairdresser's. Givenchy, the greatest of all dressmakers so far as height is concerned (he stands over 6 foot 6 inches and, since he is only 29 years old, may grow taller) uses clashing colors with an audacity that amounts to genius. That is why his spring collections are always bigger hits than his winter ones.

For all their dissimilarities, these four—and a few others, equally gifted—create twice a year a homogeneous commodity, one that is universally recognizable. They create Paris fashion.

The first hint of what this week's openings would be like came last November, when eighty cloth manufacturers displayed some 12,000 different fabrics here. Dior ordered 600 samples to experiment with; Castillo of Lanvin-Castillo, 400. Since then, these bundles of material have been stacked up in all the various designers' studios.

But it is in December and June that the creators create. And everybody with an ambition to become a couturier creates, too, in the hope of selling his ideas to an established house. Thirteen years ago, two young chaps were doing just that for Lucien Lelong; a third young man was an apprentice *chez* Jacques Fath. Their names were Dior, Balmain, and Givenchy.

This season's Dior collection began with 600 designs sketched by the master. These *croquis* Dior turned over to his two assistants, Madame Marguerite and Madame Raymonde, to be made up experimentally in muslin. Of the 600 "dry run" samples in muslin, Dior by now will have weeded out 400—after hot discussions with his staff. Two hundred remain. They have been modified, rectified, wrenched apart: the muslin model of a not particularly complicated tailored suit may require about 375 work-hours before it is considered finished.

Many different kinds of skill will have gone into the suit before that stage is reached. In the workroom, the *première main*, or "first hand," supervises the translation from sketch to muslin reality. She herself is a former seamstress who has climbed the ladder of the *haute couture*'s rigid hierarchy, step by step, since her debut as an apprentice. (Apprentices currently start their careers at a salary of 550 francs a week, or $1.57.) By now, the *première main* is a woman whose back aches from kneeling at fittings, who has bad nerves from years of putting up with a couturier's creative anguish on the one hand and with clients' unreasonable ways on the other. "Dressmaking," says one such veteran, "would be a marvelous profession without the customers!"

To make up a muslin model, or *toile*, is infinitely more amusing than to endure the bad temper of some clients. First, the cloth is draped on a mannequin whose looks best correspond to the spirit of the design. Every couturier has a mannequin who represents the *jeune fille*, or "junior miss"; one who personifies the fair lady; one who is languidly distinguished; another, fresh-faced and piquant.

A spirit of collaboration develops spontaneously between the mannequin and the workroom *première*; commonly, they use the intimate *tu* instead of *vous* in speaking to each other. Summoned to the boss's studio, the one adorned in the muslin draped on her by the other, they are just as unnerved as pupils of Michelangelo might have been when called before the master. The *première* is entitled to utter an opinion if she is asked for it; the mannequin can only be silent and obey.

"Turn around. . . ." "Walk. . . ." "Come forward. . . ." "Raise your arm. . . ."

By the time the *toiles* have finally been perfected, the establishment will have been rocked to its foundations by a noteworthy number of "scenes," with resignations offered and withdrawn. And still the ideal fabric for each design must be chosen from among stored-up samples. The right button, ribbon, belt, and flower must be found.

At this point, the couturier is really living; he is a little boy again, playing at dressing his doll. All the great dressmakers of our day preferred dolls to electric trains when they were children. This is what makes them so different in their behavior and their creations from the great prewar leaders of Paris fashion. In those days, many designers were women (Jeanne Lanvin, Madeleine Vionnet, Chanel) who knew that women, first of all, strive to please. Or they were men (Poiret, Patou, Lelong, Rochas) who, in designing clothes, gave a talented expression to their taste for women.

As the new designs begin to shape up, the mannequins step forth to present them to their creator. He picks out the hat, the gloves; burrows into great cardboard boxes to find the appropriate earrings, a necklace. He tries one, another, a third, goes back to the first. Oh, what fun!

Then, all of a sudden, everything crumbles. On the evening of the pre-opening run-through, it all seems hideous, spoiled, unbalanced, boring. What has he done that's *new*?

Pretty dresses are not enough to keep the couture alive. Pretty dresses are everywhere—in every shop in America, Italy, Spain; maybe even in England. No. What the Paris designer must regularly provide, must indeed *impose*, is the stinging flick of the whip that keeps fashion in line, even though it cries with rage, each time it seems about to slip off into the soft, the seductive, the easy way. The lash that disciplines each time fashion, after having been first disturbing, then beautiful, becomes merely pretty.

Rare, indeed, is the couturier who doesn't panic at the eleventh hour. To be sure, he can still transform one dress, throw out another, whip up a third. But a collection always revolves around three

or four basic themes: the set of the sleeves, the width of the shoulders, the location of the waistline, the architecture of the skirt. Last minute-changes can be rung in; but it's impossible to create a whole new production overnight.

Meanwhile, other problems are rearing their heads. How to seat 500 people in a salon with a capacity of 100? How to make room for 100 in a front row that allows for fifty? Any executive who can't settle this problem had better get out of the business. But then, this is the reason so many retired diplomats' wives finish their careers attached to couturiers' establishments. Balenciaga and Givenchy, of course, have eased the problem in their own way, by banning the press from their premises for a month after the opening.

There is an eloquent contrast between the greetings and chatter "out front"—as each guest finds the chair that bears his name, and thus serves as an index to his importance—and the atmosphere backstage.

Trembling in every limb, the couturier takes refuge in *la cabine*, the mannequins' dressing room; he makes the sign of the cross, and in general behaves like a playwright at curtain time. The *cabine* has in fact the atmosphere, the lighting and the disorder of a theatrical dressing room. The mannequins, five at least, fifteen at most, have arrived early. Being harrowed with fear, they have eaten nothing. Each perfects her make-up before her mirror. Silence reigns, as before some great tragedy, while the guests in the salon read the printed manifesto in which the couturier sets forth his program, like a candidate for election.

A saleswoman announces the first number to the audience, in French and in English. The mannequins in the *cabine*, each wearing the first costume she is to show, rise and compose their features. Passing before the couturier, they gently incline their heads with a sort of grace that comes from the heart, and that seems to say, "Look, here I am just as you wished me, perhaps beautiful but perhaps ridiculous—and I go forth under fire, for you."

The spectacle begins. The mannequins walk the length of the salon, turning and whirling ceaselessly, a special skill which makes it virtually impossible to memorize the architecture of a dress and later copy it. Once they have swept offstage, they appear to disintegrate. The corners of their mouths fall, and if their bosoms do not also, it's because they are so firmly sewed into the dresses.

The couturier has begun to breathe again. And now, he tosses his bombshell—and listens. Where did it drop? Did it make a bang? Silence is not so good. Chatter is even worse.

There is a certain sound, recognizable among all others—the murmuring that accompanies satisfaction. Then, four times, five times (if this is an extremely successful collection), applause breaks out. And the manikin who has called it forth flounces backstage, prouder than Duse. Who remembers any more, either in the *cabine* or in the salon, that all this is only about dresses? The spectators and the actors are taking part in a kind of ceremony among initiates.

An hour passes; two hours. At last, the wedding dress appears that signals "The End." All 500 people present stampede to the *cabine*, gasping, "Marvelous! Divine! Where is he? I've got to kiss him!"

He (or she), on the verge of tears, is now scarred with a hundred lipsticks and bombarded with compliments, some of them sincere.

Slowly, the manikins take off their finery, shuck their jewels, and wearily find themselves with their own worries and their own little jersey dresses again. The seamstresses pour in through every door, asking, "So, was it O.K.?"

It is not always O.K.

Since World War II, three major houses have opened, but eleven have had to close. Each year there are fewer private customers, as the older ladies and the huge fortunes die out. The principle of *haute couture* itself is anachronistic: if a mattress manufacturer made his product today under the conditions of a century ago, he could not survive either. And that is possibly what gives this unique spectacle its truly emotional, dramatic character—it is like a fantastic circus act in which every year some acrobat will break his neck.

Beginning tomorrow, the acrobats of French high fashion will be leaping into space and displaying their new twists. Immediately, their designs will be flown out to foreign parts—some just as they were shown, others in muslin or as paper patterns—for the buyers who have paid for the right to reproduce them commercially. In two months, copies of them will be in every shop window in America.

But they will not be seen in the shop windows or on the streets of Paris. Here, copying is forbidden; and there are not ten thousand Frenchwomen with the means to dress at a couturier's. That is why Paris has two kinds of fashion: the high fashion, set by the couturiers, and another, wholly spontaneous, which one sees all around the streets. The couture inspires it, but every woman invents her own variations—and thereby makes it inimitable.

STYLE PIRACY

Kenneth Collins

As everybody knows, the latest Paris openings were marred by bitter charges of style piracy. No

SOURCE: Reprinted by permission of *Women's Wear Daily* from "Today and Yesterday in Retailing," September 25, 1958. Copyright 1958, Fairchild Publications, Inc. After a long and successful career in retailing, Kenneth Collins became a columnist in *Women's Wear Daily*, commenting on the fashion scene.

one claimed there was anything new about the situation except the speed with which the fashion thieves worked. That seems stepping up in tempo. And it appears that this practice of "lifting" styles is becoming more widespread than ever before.

On the above statements, I believe most people will agree. I offer no solution. Nor do I pretend to know the tricks of the trade. But the Paris bureau

of *Women's Wear Daily*, certainly the most knowledgeable group in the fashion capital, knows the
venal methods employed and has repeatedly commented on them. Still, the old game goes merrily
and sordidly on.

Now let me turn to a different aspect of this
subject. Every store in America, which appeals to
the masses knows that when European women of
limited means come to this country, the one thing
that flabbergasts them is the miracle of relatively
high style garments at modest prices. Sure, they
admire our gadgets, our cars, our major appliances—but these they can take or leave. But the
clothes! These visitors simply cannot believe what
they see. Nicely styled garments at $10, $15, $25.
Accessories at prices which seem peanuts. These
are the articles these women are bewitched by—
and they are the ones they take home.

Why are such lovely things available at so little
money? Well, much of the answer lies in mass
production and in rapid distribution. But behind
these factors is this custom of style piracy. And this
piracy is a large element in the success of volume

merchandising and of what foreigners call the "miracle" of good clothes at low prices.

Now with these remarks (including the unquestioned prevalence of stealing), let me turn to one
final consideration. In 1947, Allen Raymond, a veteran newspaper reporter, worked abroad for the
Herald-Tribune. I was then associated with the paper's European edition. Mr. Raymond made a
study of the financial history of the *Haute Couture;*
one fact astounded us. Before World War II, the
complete industry, from buttons to whole collections, was, by American standards, trivial in the
amount of money involved. But now the dressmaking business in Paris has become big business.

I draw no conclusions. I make no apologies for
robbery. "Thou Shalt Not Steal" remains in the
Decalogue. Yet I wish someone would try explaining why this entire sequence, from creation, to
pilfering, to wholesale copying, seems (at least to
an outsider) a case where both the thief (a con-
temptible fellow) and his victim are ultimate gain-
ers. Or is this all wrong?

MEET MANHATTAN

Marilyn Hoffman

The real "Miracle on 34th Street" these days is
Ohrbach's twice-a-year fashion "spectacular" of
Paris originals, along with its own copies. One
really has to see it to believe it.

More than 2000 women beat through the doors
on March 16—some arrived when the doors
opened at 9 A.M. to await the 1 P.M. showing.

The crowd included celebrities (we sat across

SOURCE: Reprinted from the March 24, 1964, issue of
The Christian Science Monitor. Permission granted. One
of the many ways in which Ohrbach's has made fashion
history is its success in attracting wealthy and socially
prominent women to the store for its line-for-line copies
of Paris originals.

from Eva Gabor, Ava Gardner, and Lauren Bacall),
socialites, salesgirls, Bronx housewives, and am-
bassadors' wives, from thirty countries. Many arrived in chauffeur-driven limousines.

Some, of course, have shopped the couture
houses in Paris. For others, these fabulous Ohrbach openings are as close as they'll ever get to a
Paris fashion showing. That's pretty close—only
the Atlantic Ocean is between. For Ohrbach's not
only shows line-for-line copies of the originals
they have purchased, down to the last seam,
button, and pleat—and 92 per cent of the time in
the same fabric—but also often the same hats,
bags, gloves, jewelry, and shoes which were

shown with the models in Paris are shown here.

This semi-annual fashion phenomenon has been going on at Ohrbach's since 1947, although only in recent years has it produced such excitement and near-hysteria. It has been likened to a Broadway first night and to a "Seventh Avenue convention." But Sydney Gittler, who is known as the coat and suit "king" of Ohrbach's, said the store worked a long time to get this kind of overjoyous response to its efforts.

Mr. Gittler is one of the most highly esteemed American buyers in Paris where he is much respected for his business acumen and intuition about which Paris styles will appeal most to American women. He is also known in France as an American professional buyer who is "one of the last of the big spenders." He and the store's vice-president, Rose Wells* (who buys accessories in Paris), and Margaret Kennedy, dress buyer, descend on Paris each season with a very sizable budget.

The Ohrbach team is said to be the biggest single purchaser in the Paris couture today. Once this trio has made its selections, the importing is arranged and the manufacturers are lined up here for the reproductions.

They use about thirty top Seventh Avenue houses to make the line-for-line copies, though which manufacturers are never announced. The copies must be completed on split-second timing. For instance, this time, the bulk of the models

---

*Irene Satz has replaced Rose Wells.

arrived from Paris by air on February 24 and February 27. They were put into the works, with Mr. Gittler and Miss Kennedy advising steadily with the manufacturers, checking first muslins, then patterns, then models.

Scarcely ever is the first finished copy accepted by the meticulous painstaking buyers. Last season Mr. Gittler had a Givenchy coat remade five times before he would accept the copy and allow it to go into production. Still, by March 12 the collection was complete, and by March 16, store stocks were ready to go.

Each seasonal show progresses with the original Paris model followed by the Ohrbach copy. It is difficult to tell one from the other. The price tag gives away the difference. An original violet and black printed silk dress was purchased from Balenciaga for $1250, while its counterpart made here is sold at $59.99 for the dress and $20 for the stole.

A St. Laurent two-piece navy blue dress was purchased in Paris for $1316, but reproduced for sale at Ohrbach's for $139.

How does a store do it? "Volume," said an official. "We'll probably sell more top-quality French copies this season than any other store in the country."

After the customer showing, the socialites and celebrities flocked to the Gray Room and the Oval Room to buy their favorite numbers. It's all cash-and-carry at Ohrbach's, but some leave the store with six and seven copies, which may range from a $59.99 linen copy of a Givenchy dress to a $350 copy of a Balenciaga double silk taffeta evening coat. . . .

FIRST DE GAULLE—Now Couture

Refusing to note the fact that Paris once again has completed her spring rituals—best known as the

SOURCE: *Clothes* magazine, February 15, 1970. Reprint permission granted.

Couture Openings—would be akin to refusing to recognize the presence of Red China. However, while the People's Republic controls about one quarter of the world's population, what does Paris control?

Of course, a good number of American manufacturers were still indulging in a bit of fantasy—hoping that the old fortune teller (or fortune maker) still had some remnant of her former powers. But, alas, spring cinched it, and the final notes of the requiem sounded loud and clear: if a light were to be found on the cloudy fashion horizon, it certainly wasn't over the skies of Lutecia.

True, there were dominant looks in the Parisian *printemps:* softer and longer— but even couched in the new terms, *doucette* and *longuette,* these silhouettes hardly constitute a new fashion direction. After all, the soft look, especially in clingy prints, has enjoyed success on both sides of the Atlantic for the past year. And, as for the midi: well, it was being sold in the Galerie Lafayette last fall—and that's like pirating fashion from Macy's (which, by the way, also has midis on the racks).

Actually, analyzing the length issue brings the entire Paris picture into focus—because the question of lengths remains as hazy as a Monet. Talk in the international consumer press, on Seventh Avenue, and even in the streets during the past few seasons has been lowering the hemline (where else could it go?)—so French Couture houses just took the cue and followed suit. But, longer lengths in Paris were anywhere from two inches above the knee to two inches above the floor—which is certainly not much of an answer. And, day-wear hovered around the knee for the most part—which is really where the majority of the Great Silent Majority of Middle America has been wearing hemlines anyway.

The problem is that Paris Couture at the height of its power accounted for less than 1% of the market—with, albeit, some of its influence trickling down. But, today, the information glut supplied by mass media not only permits the masses the questionable joy of voyeurism into the lives of the Beautiful People, but forces the jet set to be aware of what the more common and less affluent man is doing. Let's face it: The Beatles carried much more fashion impact than Bohan in the '60s,

and the public today is much more interested in the costumes and contrivances of Grand Funk Railroad than in the couture wardrobe of the Great Dowager Dinkle.

LITTLE COVERAGE

And, obviously, that's the way the press sees it, for this spring there was a notable lack of news coverage and lineage on the Paris openings—replaced by features on traditional Seminole patchwork garments or the origins of tie-dye in San Francisco. What has really happened is that those who have previously subsidized European couture are tired of backing losers who no longer reflect life.

While, once, money was synonymous with happiness (probably because of the freedom of travel and leisure it could buy), 'tis no longer so—partially because these freedoms are available to many more people today, and partially because the young have found that these freedoms don't necessarily mean happiness. So, as the mystique of money has disappeared, so has the mystique of Paris couture.

And, the Paris spring openings seem to indicate that the European designers are aware that their era is witnessing its dying gasps, for they simply reflected the trends already set by the masses—as if in capitulation. American manufacturers and retailers who might still be looking on the death of the oracle in disbelief can easily test the fact: How much influence can and will the Paris openings have on your fall merchandise? Doesn't it really come down to that?

Even if, by some miracle, the so-called midi turns out to be the greatest thing since Chevalier's "Little Girls," will it really account for more than five percent of the market? Seventh Avenue, wake up! Retailers, wake up! Mysticism can cost you more business than all the dogs you cut and markdowns you *intentionally* buy.

PARIS COUTURE: MORE RTW

Bernardine Morris

The old cliché that the Paris couture is for publicity and perfume has a new dimension these days. The perfume is still there, of course, and the somewhat faded magic of the couture showings still draws the biggest press contingent of any fashion event in the world. But the new push is for ready-to-wear.

The couture has been dabbling in ready-to-wear for years, but it is no longer acting like a dilettante about it. It's a serious business.

Some houses, like Pierre Cardin, prefer licensing arrangements with manufacturers around the world. For his women's wear alone, Cardin has such arrangements in Italy, England, Japan, Mexico, Argentina and Germany. His United States operation, headed by Gunther Oppenheim and Sandy Smith (who also own Modelia, the coat and suit house), booked more than $3-million worth of business in its first year. One hundred and eighty stores carry the made-in-America Cardins.

The designer is serious enough about the operation to send his assistant, André Oliver, to Seventh Avenue a couple of times a year to adapt the clothes to American taste.

NO PASSING FAD, THIS!

"He's interested in building an institution, not making a killing one year and getting out," Mr. Oppenheimer points out.

SOURCE: *Stores* magazine, September 1970. Copyrighted by National Retail Merchants Association.

Bernadine Morris is a well known commentator on various aspects of the fashion field. She is on the staff of The New York Times, *in which capacity she covered the recent showings in Paris, and she contributes to many publications as a free-lance writer.*

Louis Feraud, who designs rather gimmicky clothes for the young, and Lanvin, whose approach is more sophisticated, have both recently concluded contractual arrangements with Andrew Arkin to produce their clothes in this country. The Feraud styles will sell for $50 to $100 and the Lanvin things from $125 to $250 and both collections will be keyed to buying patterns here in terms of delivery schedules as well as styling, according to Mr. Arkin.

Yves Saint Laurent, who is probably the most swinging as well as the most-talked-about designer in Paris, has his own ideas about ready-to-wear.

He doesn't care to do a "collection" that is planned to include something to appeal to almost everyone, as most Seventh Avenue houses do.

ODD SIZES LOSE OUT

"He makes clothes for the young woman who wears size 6, 8, or 10—he doesn't care about 12s and 14s, he doesn't care about older women, and he doesn't want fat ones," explains Richard Salomon, Chairman of the Board of Lanvin-Charles of the Ritz, who holds the dominant financial interest in the company.

Saint Laurent's ready-to-wear is made in France under his supervision and sold in separate boutiques that are replicas of his Rive Gauche shop in Paris. By September, there will be seven of them in this country. There are 27 in the rest of the world. . . .

André Courrèges has still another approach to the ready-to-wear situation and his may be the most prophetic of all. He shows his ready-to-wear clothes along with his couture styles in Paris, right there, on the spot, to take advantage of all the hoopla and publicity the couture showings generate.

"The woman who reads about the showing almost anywhere in the world will be able to buy the clothes in a store in her city the same day," says Courrèges triumphantly. He'll take pains to ship the ready-to-wear earlier so that it's available.

Among the cities in which women can conceivably shop for a Courrèges the day they read about it are Milan, London, Brussels, Tokyo, Mexico City, Caracas, Los Angeles (I. Magnin), Houston (Sakowitz), and New York (Bonwit Teller).

PEOPLE ARE BASICALLY ALIKE

What is he doing to take care of the difference in figures and tastes in cities around the world? Not a thing, says Courrèges, adding, "More and more, what pleases people in Paris also pleases them in New York or Caracas."

To insure pleasing many people, the designer has added a new ready-to-wear group to the Couture Future line he has shown for a couple of years. It's called Hyperbole and it is priced starting at $90. The other Couture Future things are about twice as much.

Courrèges feels he's on to a good thing, and he's not interested in sharing the wealth. About five years ago, when his designs swept across the world, few manufacturers paid him any royalties. In fact, few bothered to buy the originals of the styles they adapted.

So for the last three years, Courrèges has invited no manufacturers (he produces his own styles in his own factories) and only buyers from stores that carry his ready-to-wear to see his collections.

This is a pity, especially for the fall collection, which was by far the most stimulating in Paris. His tiny, surgical white salon was filled mostly with press representatives—and this too is the wave of the future.

Cardin follows a similar pattern of only inviting those stores who carry his ready-to-wear to see his collection. It is expected that other couturiers will

follow suit as their ready-to-wear operations gain in importance.

This is not meant to suggest that Paris as the world's fashion hub is losing ground. It is simply developing a new stance.

THE PRESS EN MASSE

More than 900 press representatives from TV, newspapers, and magazines all over the world took up residence in Paris during the week of fall showings. As everybody was quick to observe, the companies that spent the money to send them there are not going to stint on the space for their dispatches. So, as far away as Australia and Japan, the fashion message from Paris will be disseminated to the people—in depth.

The main objective is not, as it used to be, to draw women of means to the couture salons. It is to lay the groundwork for the ready-to-wear. A woman who hears the name "Cardin" or "Courrèges" often enough is likely to be to some extent pre-sold when she finds Cardin or Courrèges dresses in her neighborhood store.

Well aware of this, the couture has lifted some of the restrictions and much of the secrecy that has traditionally surrounded the fashion showings. Photographing and even sketching the styles is permitted. Publicity directors, or often enough the designer himself, are increasingly available.

The mystery may be departing, but the opportunities for news coverage are increasing. Though it is likely in the next few years that buyers and manufacturers are going to be increasingly scarce at the couture showings, their seats will be taken by a growing number of press representatives sent to cover the world's hottest fashion story.

And while they may not turn up at the couture showings, the buyers and manufacturers are likely to continue to go to Paris, to look at the ready-to-wear collections, to shop the boutiques, to gaze at the women in the streets with their traditional chic.

SUBJECT: BUY AMERICAN

Dorothy Coleman Seeman

In 1968, President Johnson exhorted American business to help reduce our unfavorable balance of trade through a voluntary restraint on imports. For some of our stores a positive response to this appeal would involve drastic changes in merchandising. We have chosen two such stores as participants in this dialogue, Henri Bendel and Alexander's, going you might say from the sublime to the incredible. Both stores, though for very different reasons and in very different ways, depend heavily on imports. They represent two distinct approaches to the question.

HENRI BENDEL

After Maxey Jarman bought Henri Bendel a little over ten years ago, Geraldine Stutz proceeded to turn a store that was ready for the last rites into "the last word." She created a jewel box on 57th Street that retailers flocked to from all over the country and then went home hating their own stores. The "street of shops," subsequently copied with greater or lesser fidelity from Worcester to Pasadena, was Miss Stutz's original concept and exquisitely executed under her direction. Her merchandising concept, also original and not without risk, of catering to timeless chic women in the limited range of sizes 6 to 12, became the basis of the new Bendel image. The result, in the face of all superstitions about jinxed locations and dying streets, proved that there is nothing you cannot do with unlimited taste, a strong image, new and imaginative ideas about decor, and wall-to-wall money.

Jean Rosenberg, who describes herself as Vice President-in-charge-of-anything-that-happens-to-come-up ("That's the kind of store we are, you see."), is very much the personification of the Bendel image—petite, chic with a total absence of contrivance, and exuding the quiet confidence of a woman who knows her mind as well as her worth.

SOURCE: *McCall's Sportswear & Press Merchandiser,* September-October, 1968. Reprint permission granted.

On the question of imports, Miss Rosenberg expressed Bendel's point of view and explored the problems involved:

"European merchandise is important to our survival. For us, fashion itself is the most important aspect of importing. Exclusivity would be a secondary factor, and markup would be third.

"On the question of fashion, we do no couture, no copies, no reproductions. We do only ready-to-wear, sportswear and accessories, and we buy strictly for re-sale and reorder. It is very hard to find better-priced merchandise that's young in the American market. We have no resistance to a great shirt at $35 retail and just can't find it here. When we bring it in from Europe, we have no interest in having it copied—we want to sell it and reorder it. And, by the same token, the young fashion-y people in Europe have found that there are not many stores in the United States that can really sell young fashions at better prices, so they have come to value our business and work closely with us. They have a whole different approach there. They offer a marvelous choice of fabrics and colors in whatever you happen to be buying, so you can do one body in twelve colors or five fabrics. This gives us a diversity that is very important to us, in addition to the fashion itself. They also have a certain cut—a narrowness through the armhole, an approach to fit—that is very much our look, our customer.

"Going back to the subject of exclusivity, we do

like it, of course, but it's not something we have to work at very hard. Our image is so individual—almost personal—that we never feel obliged to do what is 'hot' in the market or in other stores. It's a strong boutique feeling that stems directly from Miss Stutz and is instilled in everyone in the store. Our stock reflects what we react to and our customers, therefore, always find the image they expect regardless of what others are showing. We are able to do many things simply because we are not enormous and don't have to make plans a year in advance. We keep our structure as flexible as possible and, when we do latch onto something, our needs are not so great that our makers would find it impossible to supply them.

"As for markup, it is generally accepted that a higher markup is required to cover the added risks of the one-way street of importing. This was true for us, as well, but by now we have established relationships with resources where fit and make are assured and with whom we have worked long and closely enough so that the risk is minimal. Therefore, we do benefit positively from the higher markup, but this is not a major consideration in our approach to imports.

"We find the middle-priced market best in European ready-to-wear, but our ready-to-wear imports have not been increasing. We are not interested in status labels or status prices and neither are our customers. They have other, more compelling interests even if it's only that they would rather buy a plane than have a half-dozen thousand-dollar dresses carefully hung in the closet.

"In sportswear, on the other hand, our imports are constantly increasing. It is difficult to say whether the percentage of imports has increased because sportswear business has increased so much overall in the past few years. The categories in which our imports have risen most are leathers, pants, shirts, skirts, knits, sweaters and swimsuits. Sportswear is terrific in all price ranges in Europe. There is something about France you can't get away from, and we do quite a lot in Italy, but very interesting things are being done in Sweden and Denmark. We also have one resource in England that we work with closely.

"We did wonder, after the President's speech, whether there would be any change in our customers' attitudes, but there has been no reaction against imports on their part whatsoever. Our own feeling is that our total imports, though sizable for our operation, are so infinitesimal compared, for instance, with the cost of the war, that even a complete reversal of our policy could have no effect on the balance of trade. We are not contemplating any change in our future import plans."

ALEXANDER'S

Since its brave beginning in the depressed '30's, Alexander's has come up—come all the way—from its rather modest early image typified by the Avis-type slogan "Uptown It's Alexander's." Those words still blink legibly above the original Fordham Road store which is still the best unit in the eight (soon-to-be-nine) store group. But the slogan bears little resemblance to the store's current image which yields place to no one in any part of town. The policy of offering the hottest fashions of the day at "incredible" prices has earned Alexander's the status of Number-One-Thorn-in-the-Side of the fashion stores in the New York metropolitan area.

Francine Farkas—vivid, dynamic and very *au courant*—gave up a four-and-a-half-year career of trading on the stock exchange to become fashion director of the giant enterprise that belongs to her husband's family. A mother of two (and, just among us 18,000, there is a third on the way), Mrs. Farkas indicated that her husband's only complaint since she's been in the store is that he hasn't been making as much money in the stock market.

Mrs. Farkas commented animatedly on the question of imports and Alexander's:

"The non-couture aspects of our import program are both for copying and for stock. The world is so much smaller today—London is right next door—and people want fashion ideas from all over. They're doing great styling in men's shirts in England which we've reproduced here for both men and women. Sweden is very important to us in menswear right now. Their styling is advanced and their workmanship is beautiful, which is very important. The knits we get from Italy and Hong Kong we could never produce here for the price, and the same is true for women's sweaters and men's shirts from Hong Kong. Because of our imports, we are able to offer values that other stores cannot. It wouldn't make sense to stop offering value.

"Exclusivity does not concern us—in fact, on the contrary, we prefer it when the customer can see the same merchandise in other stores and compare the value. Nor do problems with the American market force us to look abroad—there are very few doors that are closed to us here. As for markup, since we apply the same formula to everything, we don't use our imports to raise our overall mark-on precent. Our import policy is based simply on the fact that we do so much better abroad in quality and value. As for styling, generally speaking you can't beat America for ladies' sportswear, but we can still learn something from Europe in menswear.

"People like imports. If there has been any reaction against them on the part of our customers, it's a political and not an economic one. Of course, if some financial disaster occurred and we could help our country by discontinuing our imports, we would. So would everybody. But we don't feel we've been asked in a business way to limit our import program. We will continue to try to bring our customers the best fashions and values from wherever they are available."

APPAREL FIRMS RING BELL IN BIG HONG KONG YEAR

J.W. Cohn

HONG KONG.—The sweet smell of success is everywhere in Hong Kong.

This is the biggest and best year the Crown Colony has ever had in practically every field of business. It is by far the biggest year for the apparel industry. It is the biggest year since the Korean War for piece goods. . . .

Exports to the United States have been skyrocketing at a rate of about 40 percent above last year. The Macy-May buying office here reports purchases up 65 per cent this year. Every American buying office in town is enjoying its biggest volume year. And everyone is making money, money, money.

The increases this year are being highlighted by apparel, piece goods, electronics, plastics, wigs and toys.

The demand for Hong Kong knitwear is fantastic. Double knits are going big. The quality of sweaters has improved greatly and is approaching Italian standards while retailing in the United States at half the price of Italian merchandise. . . .

The colony currently has 33,200 worsted spindles

in place. To this will be added 14,400 new spindles during the coming months, increasing the monthly spinning capacity from 2,490,000 pounds to 3,570,000 pounds. The situation in woolen spindles is 9,300 in place with 5,600 additional to be installed, increasing the monthly production capacity from 400,000 to 630,000 pounds. Again most of the increased spinning capacity is earmarked for the knitwear trade with some going to carpets.

Exports of men's shirts are limited only by the supply of fabrics from Japan. Japanese producers cannot keep pace with the orders pouring into Hong Kong dress shirt manufacturers. This is particularly true for yarn-dyed piece goods.

Low-end men's dress shirts from Hong Kong are landing in the U.S. at from $16 to $16.50 a dozen and retailing at $1.99. American mills would be hard pressed to produce comparable merchandise at cost to retail at that figure, it is said here. The $2.99 retail shirts land in the United States at $22 a dozen, giving both the Hong Kong manufacturer and American importer a better break on profit margins.

The Textile Alliance, one of the giant cotton goods combines of Hong Kong, is currently launching a three-year $HK15 million ($2.5 million)

SOURCE: Reprinted by permission of *Women's Wear Daily*, copyright Fairchild Publications, October 22, 1968.

modernization program in its plants here. Manufacturers throughout the colony are reequipping with new labor-saving machinery.

Increased efficiency and wider use of modern, labor-saving machinery is enabling Hong Kong manufacturers to maintain a remarkably stable price structure for exports despite wage increases averaging 15 per cent during the past year and a rise of nine points in the consumer goods index. It is also helping them to maintain their quality lead over cheaper wage countries like Taiwan and Korea. . . .

Knitwear manufacturers are asking six-months deliveries instead of three to four months. Men's wear buyers who normally came into the market in January are now visiting here in October or November to cover themselves for the following fall. Sweater manufacturers are more receptive to orders for men's wear than formerly and substantial orders are being placed by American men's wear buyers for everything from fine gauge turtlenecks to ski sweaters. The "slubby look" in sweaters made of cotton and ramie is proving popular.

There are some clouds in the fair autumn skies over Hong Kong. The labor market is getting tight in trades that require special skills. Finishers in the higher-priced dress fields, for example, are at a premium. . . .

All this sweet smell of honey is, of course, attractive to the busy bees of the American apparel industry. Large numbers of manufacturers of women's dresses, men's clothing, shirts and raincoats have been in and out of Hong Kong, looking at factories, asking questions, acting mysterious.

One unconfirmed rumor is that four or five more Seventh Avenue manufacturers will be operating in Hong Kong before the end of 1969. Names are freely mentioned like Fred Perlberg, Harvey Berin and Jerry Silverman. But no one really knows anything. No contracts have been signed.

One local wag told this correspondent: "If it weren't for the unions in America and the Communists in China, Seventh Avenue would look like a deserted village. The manufacturers would all be over here."

THE IMPORT APPAREL WONDERLAND—A GUIDE FOR DISCOUNTERS

Aeta Salba

The import apparel business is scheduled for even greater growth than at present as more and more discounters upgrade. How are retailers profiting from this trend? What can discounters do who still haven't taken the buying tour through foreign lands? Here's a look at what's happening and the implications.

Recently, Robert Hall, in a move to enhance its fashion image, employed an Italian noblewoman as designer for its better range of apparel, retailing

SOURCE: *The Discount Merchandiser*, October-November, 1969. Reprint permission granted. Aeta Salba is a *DM* feature writer.

up to $100. The president of the company made it clear that it was not deserting its lower price lines. It was simply enlarging is fashion coverage to offer styles and values comparable to those offered by department stores except at prices that were still much lower.

This is an indication of a trend that more and

more discount stores are involved with—climbing a few more rungs up the fashion ladder. In achieving this goal, the discounters have reached the point where they need more imported merchandise now than ever before. And for two main reasons: To get the fashion impact of styles from Europe and Asia, and to deliver them at a price that is competitive with the better stores. The challenge is made more difficult, because the traditional stores have been bringing in imported high quality goods and selling them at prices that now compete with domestic goods on the racks in discount stores.

Of course, traditional stores and the larger discount stores have for years been sending teams of buyers abroad, and a number have their own buying offices, staffed with their own personnel, in almost every corner of the globe. Others use foreign agents, or trading companies as they are known in the Orient. All of them are seeking something new, something different, something better for less. For the higher-priced department and specialty stores, the original impetus was not price but exclusive merchandise. If the group was large enough, it dictated its own terms, ordinary margins of mark-up could be thrown to the winds, and were. But the two major essentials were a fine label and the snob appeal, largely from Europe.

The discounters, in the meantime, were concentrating on low-end goods from cheap-labor markets, mainly the Orient. The giants among them also established their own foreign offices, but the smaller discounters had to depend upon importers. Such goods were entirely basics or cheaper fashion accessories like gloves and straw bags. The lists gradually increased to include children's knits, later simple sportswear and eventually knit goods in the women's areas, raincoats, and car coats.

In all this one should recognize that the older importers were the original pioneers, staking their fortunes in an uncertain exploration. And whatever the acceleration in direct buying, these importers will always have a place in the market—for the smaller customer, for many of the larger ones also, seeking to supplement their own selections (To give an example, there is the Avon Glove Company, which carries one thousand different styles of cotton gloves, with a stock of 700,000 dozens in warehouses in various points of the country.) While the landed price and the importer's mark-up

have to be totalled to make the real price, and it is bound to be higher than the combine's own direct imports, the far greater selection makes up for the price differential.

A 40 PER CENT GAIN IN SPENDING

As an index of what has been happening in the import market of consumers' goods, one must look to the figures. In 1968, there was a 40 per cent rise in spending on consumer imports over the previous year; and that year showed almost a 20 per cent gain over 1966. Wearing apparel from Asia with some from Europe, rose about one-third from its previous figure. Shoe imports now constitute 45 per cent of all the shoes sold in this country. Hong Kong imports increased by 20 per cent, Israel by 13 per cent, Korea by 38 per cent, Taiwan by 42 per cent, Thailand by 26 per cent. About 40 per cent of all our wool-knit apparel is imported, across all price ranges. While consumer expenditures rose by 7 per cent in apparel and allied lines in 1968, imports rose by an over-all 32 per cent in those same categories, with a 62 per cent rise in man-made fibers and end-goods. That differential between the 7 per cent and 32 per cent must have come from domestically manufactured lines. And it is all just in its infancy.

J.W. May's, New York, advised that in 1966 they bought well over one million dollars in apparel at base cost, from both the Orient and Europe. That figure will surely increase as those markets become more sophisticated. Penney's spends at least 3 per cent of its volume on imported apparel. In a speech before the Textile Mfrs's. Association, its president said that it bought imports because that activity fell well within the firm's purpose for existence: to meet the needs and wants of the consumer profitably and competitively.

WHAT DISCOUNTERS SAY

A number of discounters will state, off the record, that they import from 5 per cent to 10 per cent of their apparel, with varying proportions from department to department. In one discount firm, more than fifty per cent of its sweaters were imported. One argued his case before a House Ways and Means Committee hearing on free trade. He stated that it gives a retailer a bargaining tool to keep prices down, enables him to shop the world to stock his shelves, and that curtailing low-price imports would hit the low-income consumers hardest of all.

While the witness was speaking for the low-income consumer, he should not have precluded all consumers, low-income or otherwise. The traditional stores, for instance, are relying on the higher mark-up realized from imported merchandise to help maintain earnings. The high-fashion stores will still visit European showings, pay enormous "cautions" for the privilege of sitting on uncomfortable little gold chairs, and watching the designs made by little golden boys for all the golden women. Although, that, too, is changing! France now is depending far more on her *prêt-à-porter* (ready-to-wear) for revenue, and French designers are taking their styles to be made in Hong Kong, for their own home consumption and for world trade.

The conventional store now works on an average 45 per cent mark-up and for an imported item must get at least 55 per cent to make it worthwhile. There is a great deal more work and wait involved in importing apparel from ten-thousand miles than from fifty miles, despite the improved travel and shipping conditions. If with all that, the store can still land merchandise that will allow at least 10 per cent more profit than domestically made goods, the answer is clear. For the discounter trying to offer comparable goods for less, once he gets into the fashion trade seriously, the same cheap-labor markets must be sought to retain the advantage. In fact, they have been utilized for a long time.

The bigger discounters for years have been sending teams to England to work with large knitwear mills an hour's ride out of London, and within easy access to many of the knit-fabric factories. There they choose their own confined fabric patterns, style their own range, and lay down their orders in January for early fall selling. While the same knitwear mills work with the better stores (so-called) and do not publicize their connections with discount chains, they refuse to be dictated to, as to whom and how they sell. For the same effort is made by conventional groups to shut out the discounters from sources of supply as were made in the domestic market, and in some cases are still being made. But the giants can well look after

themselves, particularly since they were in on the ground floor of the low-to-middle price import and certainly the Orient where they were the orginators.

WHAT NOW SMALL DISCOUNTER?

All this poses a problem for the smaller discounters, those who have either been buying from import distributors or confining themselves to domestic merchandise. Whatever their excellence, and variety in the familiar categories, discounters will be the first to acknowledge that their fashions were strictly utilitarian, if good value. Now many more resources are open to them, probably because of the very upsurge of imported apparel. If even the better department stores and specialty shops are beginning to bring in medium-priced goods from abroad, cutting into their production, these suppliers found discretion the better part of valor. More and more of them began to court the discount trade. Some branded lines made special unlabelled goods for discounters, but labels make little or no difference in low to moderate-priced apparel, and the garments were the same make and value.

Important as it may be to utilize whatever local resources are now made available, the smaller discounters must evaluate their position in this changing order. The traditional stores are looking after themselves, with increasing shipments from abroad. These days the newspapers are full of ads boasting imports: cotton dresses from Romania; cotton dresses from Taiwan retailing for as low as $10.00; evening gowns from Hong Kong; shoes from Italy and knit dresses from England with the dresses retailing for $26.00, a price now well within the range of most discount stores; ready-to-wear made in France with some items retailing as low as $25.00; knit costumes from Italy at $26.00 at a large discount store. What does all this add up to?

If merchandise is now being imported by conventional stores that will compare more than favorably in price with the domestic goods now being offered even the smaller discounters, the latter will not hold their own in the fashion areas. They do not have the buying power nor the past experience of dealing direct in foreign markets—the method which will be competitive. If the small discounter is content to go back to the old concentration on hard goods and low end soft goods he may manage.

But in the retail field, as in every other, there is no standing still. Just as the traditional stores changed many of their own methods to meet the discount threat, their new excursions into the cheap labor-markets of the world where they are now experimenting with lower-priced apparel, may negate whatever domestic gains the discounter has made in buying his apparel locally.

What good will it do him to have all these amenable firms open to him now, when the traditional stores will begin to import better for less? All this does presuppose a continuance of the cheap labor-markets, where prices have already risen somewhat in the past several years. But the odds are that it will be years before these foreign prices rise to the level that will make importing uneconomical.

In the meantime, traditional stores are helping style foreign collections in price ranges for their budget and moderate-priced sections. These will compete with the discounter's local goods to his disadvantage.

WHAT IMPORTERS CHARGE

They too, must enlarge their sphere of retailing to cover all the needs of their consumers, and that means all the fashion areas with goods from all markets. And if they must import, then they too must find some new methods of operating in foreign markets. The difference between direct buying abroad (with the essential foreign buying agent or office) and buying through an importer, may amount to ten to thirty per cent, depending on the items purchased locally and the size of the orders. Importers who stock large supplies and take all the risks, must work on a reasonable margin. One unusual firm of long standing, Paul Sernau, acts as buyer for domestic jobbers and chains on notion and gift items, for a fee of 7½ per cent, but they are not direct importers, nor do they touch the fashion fields which are now the important consideration.

Several myths should be dispelled at this point. One is that a foreign label carries some stigma. After the Second World War the "Made in Japan" label was a hindrance only for a short time. Low-income groups were the first to drop the pre-

judice. In that connection, the discount stores played an important role, as they were buying large quantities of low-priced goods through local importers. Middle-income groups retained their aversion longer, but with the improvement in the quality of such imports, they, too, began to look for bargains. Last year 35 per cent of all textile imports came here from Japan. In the same atmosphere of shifting values, "Made in England" and "Made in France" no longer means quality, necessarily. We have had enough badly-made garments from England, enough shoddy goods from France, to demonstrate otherwise.

With the increased foreign travel to all corners of the globe, clerks touring Bangkok, mid-Western housewives inspecting Shinto temples, little old ladies from Dubuque riding on camels, it would be hard to maintain the old preconceptions about Oriental goods.

WHAT IS "FASHION"?

The second myth that should be shot down has to do with the whole problem of fashion. Fashions are for those very customers upon whom any apparel business must depend, the bulk of the solid citizens. They may not be listed among the Beautiful People, but they make the cash registers ring. The fear is that fashion, being a fickle jade, one dare not go too far afield, lest she suddenly change her mind and leave one with a batch of minis when the style has suddenly switched to mid-calf. The other argument is that styles in general change too fast and too often for any long-range planning or ordering in the dress departments, or coats and suits, for that matter.

The giants place their orders almost a year in advance. As a rule, the teams leave in November for the bulk of their next year's fall seasons. With knit apparel, that time span has been narrowed, and many place their orders in January and February, as the teams and their foreign suppliers have established rapport and good working relations. Separates are not the same risk that dresses present; but the type of dress that has become almost the standard uniform of the past few years can hardly be called a design of such definite dating that could not be worn in a succeding season, especially in cottons and knits, and especially now when our seasons have become so blurred with one running into another, and datelines being shifted back and forth.

There is always a margin for the "faddy" bits that crop up each year, but for the most part styles do not change drastically from one year to another, except for the inevitable and necessary change of trim and touch to justify the new range each season. Few women, even the wealthiest, scrap their entire wardrobes every few months. In fact, they boast of wearing something precious for eight or nine years.

So good styles contracted in either the Orient or Europe have the same chance of reasonable tenure as those ordered in the domestic market . . . and can still be had at far better prices. While Robert Hall is hiring its Italian designer to style a range here, others are sending their local people to style ranges abroad. Most of them, especially for low-to-moderate prices, do not bother to send their own stylists abroad. They take with them a number of the current season's best sellers for copying—and with few alterations.

It is futile to argue origins and inspirations and ultimate sources in the ready-to-wear market. Some copyists go to Paris for refresher courses, and are willing to pay the "cautions" just to get the assurance they are drinking from the fonts; others feel it is a waste of time and money; a larger and larger group of the younger designers here just laugh at the whole bit. But all of them copy, copy and copy madly. They copy themselves, their earlier designs, their teachers, they filch from each other, from stores, from hints, early Chanel, early Worth, early Etruscan, early Greek ewers, early fig-leaf. After reading several fashion authorities, one may be left with the certainty that they do not know what they are talking about. To cull a few of the choice ones:

"The polyester cotton shirt is dead . . . it will sell as a basic, but it's no longer fashion." Since most of every store's sales depends on basics, how dead is dead?

"Frills are out—but they may be all right for the main floor." Since the main floors are supposed to be the drawing-forces, why should the frills be relegated to the most traveled parts of the store?

"The skinny look will generate volume . . . it calls for small sleeves and tight armholes . . ." but some buyers see full sleeves as capturing a good part of the market.

Thus, one argument levelled against the first group of dresses from the Orient was that the styles were uninspired. It so happened that the range had been designed specially by a name-designer, incognito, who was to have lent his flair to the experiment. Without the usual blurbs that surrounded his regular publicized ranges, the output was considered dull. Opposed to that are the goods offered regularly by a knitwear importer, consistently colorful and saleable, made in the Holland factory into which he has invested heavily, so that he could control the styling and production. Nobody could ever accuse the Dutch of being either very chic or colorful in their apparel, but what they turn out for him to sell here is both. So what is fashion, and who makes and who decides when it is good fashion and when not?

NO MORE GAMBLE IN IMPORTS

The larger chains and affiliated buying groups plan well in advance, and for the most part have forecast so well that the occasional dud can be absorbed without loss of faith in the over-all import operation. One chain found itself committed to a purchase of bulky sweaters, due the following year when suddenly and for no reason anybody could figure out, the bottom dropped out of bulkies. They had to mark down their goods before even having landed the lot. However, that has not stopped them buying abroad, and gambling on their own forecasts when they place their orders. Now that they have narrowed the delivery gap from almost a year to five and six months, there is less danger of that disaster. Particularly where knits are concerned, our own manufacturers are now showing foreign-made apparel in their own seasonal ranges; just as they use contractors in Connecticut, Pennsylvania, New Jersey, they use contractors in Italy, England, Hong Kong, Japan.

Many of them have invested in these foreign factories, as did the importer in his Dutch factory, so that they can have some control over the styling and production. We have several manufacturers who make all their apparel in their Far East factories, others who make part, others who count on foreign plants to offer them their knitwear styles the while they concentrate on the woven goods. There must be great advantages in this sort of operation, for surely they are not sending manufacturing business abroad to create good-will.

DISCOUNTERS CAN SET TRENDS, TOO

In the final analysis, whatever the Olympiads do up in their rarified regions, the regional retailer with his normal advertising through newspaper media, is the one who makes the trend, whoever has made the garments. One ad asked, "Aren't you glad that saddle-stitching is back?" Perhaps nobody had ever known saddle-stitching had gone, but with this announcement that it was back, the store's customers would surely be there to welcome it again. Their store had told them. With the strong position discounters now hold, and the increasing strength in the fashion area which, with all due acknowledgement to Sears and Robert Hall, they should realize if they exploit the opening markets wisely, they too can issue such ukases and launch their own fashions.

If the smaller discounters want to share in this development, but are too small to risk direct importing individually, they must think of that sort of group action which will give them the required volume for meaningful standing with foreign resources. All the good foreign factories are very much like our own: they want large orders as they are now geared to mass production. It is in this mass production the discounters will find their staying power. How small is small, and when is he too small? That is a moot question. But it would hardly avail any discounter to try buying direct, nor repay him for the time and trouble, unless he can spend at least several weeks abroad and spend one hundred thousand dollars at first cost.

One of the discount chains, S. E. Nichols, New York, has not yet embarked on direct importations, although the stores grow steadily. It may well expand its operations in this direction. As its apparel merchandise manager A. Mittelman explained it, its buyers must know all the relevant foreign imports through the old-time importing firms. They visit them regularly and are called on regularly, and they know comparative values to the penny. All things being equal, they are inclined to buy domestic-made merchandise for several reasons: easier and quicker delivery, a chance to place orders nearer to desired selling season, so not tying up their money. But where the importer can show a better value, and the delivery stretch is not onerous, it is free to buy there. As a privately owned little giant, Nichols prides itself on adhering to the true discounters' mark-up of 30/31 per cent, while still maintaining a healthy earnings growth pattern.

Mittelman indicated that many discounters and foreign sales representatives have been overlooked by importers. The price level of many upper quality goods are now well within the discounters' top range, somewhere near the good department store's lower range. Few of the visiting apparel people approach the discounters, all aiming for the same big departmental store groups and finer specialty shops. It may be pride that keeps them from approaching discounters, or fear that they may lose their department-store customers. Yet the upper level of the mass market is part of the largest retail segment in the country, and can absorb still many more hundreds of foreign lines.

Both Mittelman, typical of a group that has not yet bought direct in foreign markets, and John Shea, general merchandise manager for softlines at Arlan's whose teams go abroad regularly, indicated that whatever their foreign activities, they would always combine them with purchases from importers. The reasons are: the huge stocks carried by most large importing houses, the point of diminishing returns when direct buying is not economical, the ability to buy close to the selling season, the quick repeats, the novelties they can gamble on in small quantities.

Shea had further pointers for those retailers starting out on such a trip for the first time:

1. Start planning and studying at least four to six months in advance, to acquaint yourself with every requirement so far as possible, while still on home ground. 2. Whoever goes should be so expert in his field that he can know whether it will compete with a domestic item already available to him. 3. No visitor should attempt to work a foreign market without a good agent.

At the beginning of this gold-rush, many men were badly burned trying to avoid the expense of a foreign-based agent, whose charges vary from 5 per cent to 8 per cent as a rule, depending on the work and amount of buying involved. They fell into the hands of unscrupulous fringe firms, and the disasters were numerous: cartons half-filled with scrap instead of sportswear, garments with one sleeve missing, goods quite different from what had been ordered and always inferior. A good agent is well worth his fee, and supervises the making, packing and shipping of an order from placement to final lift onto steamer or plane. Firms like Sears, Ward's, A.M.C., have their own foreign offices; others like Arlan's use established agents or trading companies of repute.

START THE TRIP IN AMERICA

In that connection, the American offices of the various foreign trade commissions, should be the first step for anyone planning a trip abroad. These are all staffed by experts, men and women of encyclopedic knowledge of their home countries, with lists of good agents, good buying offices, good manufacturers in every category, complete knowledge of our own duties so they can advise on probable landing costs. Some have a large suite of showrooms where fascinating sample ranges can be inspected such as ATID (American Trade and Industrial Development with Israel). Hong Kong Trade Development Council has among its top management one of the most knowledgeable information officers one could find, Mr. Robert Sun. These are but two of the scores operating in the States, all of whom can offer a visitor an education in their countries' commercial and manufacturing operations. (The Hong Kong office also offers a visitor the best cup of coffee obtainable in New York!)

The Scandinavian countries, and the Netherlands, tend to favor higher-priced merchandise for their exports to the States. They do not have the physical capacity to supply a mass market, and in fact import most of their own very low-priced requirements, mainly from the Orient. However, even among these people there is a growing interest in improving coverage of the better known discount stores. One Dutch manufacturer was selling an appreciable and increasing number of car coats to a discount group, under a label designed specially for them, so it would not interfere with his business with the traditional stores.

There is a Scandinavian Fashion Fair twice yearly, held in Copenhagen, March and September, when every conceivable fashion type is represented. Discounters may want to investigate that for

their marginal requirements. Holland is building a huge central fashion merchandise mart in Utrecht, which will be ready later this year, where all price lines and all types of fashions and fashion accessories will be permanently displayed.

While low-priced goods are coming from all the countries of the world, the leaders of interest to the discounter would still be the countries of the Far East: Japan, Hong Kong, Thailand, Taiwan, the Philippines, Korea. Some low-priced goods can be found in Spain, Italy and Greece. In any one of these countries a group could work out its own arrangements for lines of apparel: sports and swimwear, cotton and knit dresses and costumes, raincoats, carcoats, blouses, pants, and, of course, men's and boy's wear and the older lines of cotton knit shirts, work clothes, handbags, scarves, slippers, robes and so on. While Hong Kong can be the discounters' paradise, it also supplies one of the finest high-fashion chain of specialty shops with much of its better lingerie, with slips retailing for $35 to $50.

COTTONS AND KNITS ARE SAFE

For the newcomer, there are two reasonably "safe" areas that could be explored for the start: cotton dresses, and knits in one, two and three piece outfits. While the latter at one time came largely from Italy, of late Hong Kong seems to have gotten the better part of the discounters' orders. One advantage in starting the apparel adventure with knitwear, is that extreme styles do not lend themselves well to the double-knit fabric, and while all colors and combinations are tried to create new effects, the basic lines cannot change too much from season to season, so there is less danger in long-range planning.

Cottons offer another territory that could well repay investigation. The hot-weather season is always a tricky one for domestic suppliers, and year after year their production gets smaller and smaller. Retailers, too, add to the problem, by starting their summer sales almost as soon as the true summer starts, so that by the time the weather is at its worst, one can hardly find a decent cotton dress in the market, all sad-looking odds and ends. Yet today, when holidays are taken all during the year to all climates, summer styles should be available at least through August, with smaller stocks for the cruise season.

With a bow to that fine Fifth Avenue shop that has been advertising cottons from Taiwan retailing for $12.00, the same store that used to retail Liberty Lawns from England for $40.00 and $50.00, the discounter might well gamble on a trial of cotton summer dresses from a contractor from one of the low-cost countries. He could retail the same value for less than $12.00. Some of these Far East countries are free ports, so they can obtain without duties fabrics from all over the world, and offer fascinating colorful prints and interesting weaves. Since the average summer cotton is little more than two oblongs of fabric seamed up the sides, the colors and weaves are the important features that make the diversity, and these can make the season.

GET A GOOD AGENT

That there will be problems is as certain as that there will be great advantages. The first problem is the proper agent, without whom it would be suicidal to attempt any program. There are problems of strikes, delivery delays, sudden increases in freight rates, even possible changes in duty which may affect the entire import program so carefully laid out. But the average retailer faces many if not all these same problems at home, without the cushion of the price savings. A good agent or export company will see that the orders are filled to the letter. He will keep in touch with the factory regularly, inspect the goods coming off the machines, inspect while being packed, adhere to all the numerous requirements of proper invoicing.

There is an international inspection organization, with headquarters in Geneva, which will, for a set fee, examine goods before packing in various markets of the world. But from a practical point of view, anybody planning to use the foreign markets extensively should appoint agents to represent him. In the long run, this may work out better than having inspection of every separate order by this international organization, and paying a separate fee for each inspection.

THESE DESIGNERS MADE FIFTY YEARS OF FASHION HISTORY

As the pace of fashion quickened during the past 50 years, an increasing number of dressmakers all over the world emerged from anonymity. Leaders emerged in the wholesale ranks in America as well as in the traditional couture center, Paris. A few designers have stood head and shoulders above the rest. These have captured in their designs the spirit of the times, and their influence has set a trend for a period, not just a season. The ten creators discussed on these pages have helped establish the look of the past half-century.

Gabrielle Chanel's signature and look was as well known at the end of the 1950s as it was in the 1920s when she made the first short dresses in "humble" fabrics, like tweeds and jerseys.

Setting her stamp on a way of dressing, as well as exerting a strong influence on other designers, Chanel is as responsible as any other individual for

SOURCE: Reprinted by permission of *Women's Wear Daily*, July 13, 1960. Copyright 1960, Fairchild Publications, Inc.

Gabrielle Chanel

died down, and the underplayed "poor look" that she catapulted into high fashion had become an accepted way of dressing.

While she has put her stamp on the loose-jacket suit and the jersey sports dress, Chanel has also always done evening fashions. Lace dresses are her perennial favorites.

Fashion is not always synonymous with change. It sometimes has a timely quality that defies change.

Prominent exponent of this kind of fashion was **Captain Edward Henry Molyneux.** Born in London in 1894, he scored an immediate success when he opened his own salon in Paris in 1919, drawing an international clientele. His reputation was based on the fact that he "designs clothes for ladies."

Captain
Edward Henry Molyneux

the look of the 1920s, and the movement away from corsets, ankle-length skirts, heavy hats, and long suit jackets. Her revolutionary simple short skirts, low waistlines, and loose jackets were easy to wear and to move in.

Chanel started her fashion career as a milliner, setting up shop shortly before World War I in the Rue Cambon, where she is still located. Her special look came in after the war, continuing until World War II, when she closed her house. The Chanel look was noticeably absent from the fashions of the 1940s, to return with strength in the mid-1950s. At 71, she reopened her couture house in 1954. By 1957, the open jacket suit and loose overblouse that she has consistantly endorsed was the big fashion everywhere.

The fake pearls, elaborate costume jewelry and sweaters that she put into fashion orbit had never

Fond of horses, dogs, and sports, he entertained extensively, knew the life a "lady" lived.

He explained that he designed by visualizing a particular woman in a special environment, engaged in a definite activity. He then selected the appropriate materials and color, making sure that "the modern note was present."

Disapproving of "costumy" clothes, he felt that the woman should stand out, not the dress. Result was a classic style, simple and direct. Lots of pleats, supple jackets, slender dinner gowns were his forte.

He constantly gained prestige during the 1920s, and during the early 1930s was rivaled by Patou for the greatest volume in the French couture; by the end of that decade, he was ahead.

An art student, he learned the dressmaking business from Lady Duff Gordon who had an enormous vogue as Lucille just before World War I with her delicate chiffons, elaborated with ribbons, laces, and embroideries. Returning after the war, he found his emphasis on simplicity in conflict with hers, and decided to branch out on his own. His house closed in 1940; reopened in 1946, and closed again in 1951.

A modernist, not awed by tradition, **Elsa Schiaparelli** was delighted to try anything new, which ranged from original closures on suit jackets (dog-leash hooks, leather love-bird links) to knickers for ski wear (in 1937, anticipating a fashion which made an impression during the 1959 season, and promises to be increasingly important in 1960–1961).

One year younger than the century, Schiaparelli launched her fashion career with her hand-knit sweaters in modern designs in the 1920s. A big success among women with a flair for fashion, they inspired her to branch out to sports clothes in 1927. She added evening styles in 1930.

She would try her hand at designing anything, and in the 1950s made arrangements for wholesale production in America of lingerie, scarfs, stockings, and gloves bearing her name.

Her boutique in Paris carried accessories, perfume, beach and sportswear, lingerie—and table linen.

As a result of her daring, she left her mark in many areas of fashion: Jewelry (a bracelet carrying perfume was one of her ideas), fabrics (she was known for her exciting prints and use of tweeds),

Elsa Schiaparelli

and sportswear. A jersey maillot for swimming in 1931, long stockings worn with pale corduroy shorts in 1937 (a precursor of tights and Bermuda shorts), and knee breeches for after-ski in 1952 were some of her off-beat ideas which clicked.

Gilbert Adrian boosted California as a fashion center, first with the glamour clothes of the film siren, and then with top-priced wholesale fashions.

He is associated with the silhouette that dominated the 1940s—broad, padded shoulders balancing a tapered hipline. In defense of this silhouette, he became involved in a tremendous controversy over the Dior-inspired New Look.

Sloping shoulders and padded hiplines brought forth his strongest attack, as he defended the "trim, square-shoulder suit."

His geometric handling and mitering of stripes,

Gilbert
Adrian

dresses, shirtwaist dinner dresses and one-sided drapery were some of his contributions.

Adrian retired in 1952, and died in September, 1959, at 56.

A spokesman for American designers, he was one of the first Americans to be copied by other native designers.

The first note of freedom for the feminine figure was struck by **Paul Poiret.** He emerged from the nineteenth century ateliers of Maison Doucet and Worth, to open his own shop in Paris in 1904. His daring approach to fashion made him a dominant influence during the years preceding and immediately following World War I. Some of the wild iconoclasm that was shaking the fine arts was

Paul Poiret

collarless jackets, slot seams, and waistline tie closings were other characteristics of his suit styling which were widely influential.

Born in Naugatuck, Conn. in 1903, Adrian served no long, tiresome fashion apprenticeship. A costume he designed for a fellow art student to wear at the Grand Prix Ball in Paris won praise from Irving Berlin, and was followed by commissions to do costumes for Berlin's Music Box Revues. Soon afterward, he went to California, where he spent sixteen years with Metro-Goldwyn-Mayer.

Among the stars for whom he designed were Joan Crawford, whose clothes in "Letty Linton" in 1932 were widely copied, Greta Garbo, Katharine Hepburn, Rosalind Russell, and Norma Shearer.

He left films in 1939, and showed his first custom and wholesale collection in 1942. Cotton evening translated into fashion terms, resulting in clothes with a new sense of drama, a fresh point of view.

The brash, clash colors of the Fauves (violent reds, greens, violets, oranges, and citrus yellows); exotic influences (primitive sculpture and painting, lavish Oriental motifs, the Russian ballet) and a new silhouette turned fashion to uncharted roads.

Trouser dresses and puffy harem skirts were some of the Eastern themes that Poiret adapted for the Western world.

His major contribution to the silhouette was that he freed women from their corsets. Though he eased the silhouette in some areas, he shackled it in another, namely hobbling the skirt at the hemline.

His spectacular personal life, sometimes rivaling the luxury-living of the Oriental potentates who served as a source of fashion inspiration, presaged the press agentry that characterizes certain aspects of fashion today.

Especially identified with pre-World War I fashions is his high-waisted drapery that marked one of the many Empire revivals, his tiered lampshade-skirt sheer dresses and his dinner dresses with bat sleeve capelike wraps known internationally as dolmans. Today, his name is invoked most frequently in relation to boldly colored, primary print motifs.

By 1924, his influence was definitely waning. When everything tended to simplicity, as Chanel led the way to the little boy look after World War I, he continued his Oriental lavishness.

Mme Vionnet

Mme. Vionnet introduced not only a new silhouette, but a new technique to the fashion world. Her big contribution: The dress cut on the bias. This dressmaking technique continues prominent today in the work of such Vionnet pupils as Mme. Gres, Mad Carpentier, and Jacques Griffe. When it was introduced in the 1920s, it helped revolutionize and modernize the entire concept of dressing.

The effect was of overwhelming simplicity based on the bias principle.

On a wooden mannequin, two and a half feet high, which she later bequeathed to Jacques Griffe, she worked out her simple-looking cuts, which were translated by her associates into full-scale clothes.

When the fashion silhouette was flat, she worked in the round, so that her styles reflected the curves of a woman's body. Her bias construction permitted the elimination of foundation garments and fastenings, and freed the silhouette.

Among the styles with which she was associated: The chiffon handkerchief dress, halter and cowl necklines, the hemstitched blouse. She also liked long, fitted evening coats.

Eighty-three years old today, Mme. Vionnet started her fashion career with Callot Soeurs in London, was "premiere" at Doucet, where she was known as Mme. Madeleine, and opened her own shop just before the war. Closing during World War I, she reopened in 1919, and proceeded to be a dominant fashion influence during the 1920s.

Among her nonfashion contributions was the provision of advanced social services for her workers, along with medical clinics and a gymnasium.

She also organized the couturiers into an association against copying.

Toward the end of the 1930s, her influence dwindled, and she closed her house in 1939, at the beginning of World War II.

Informal in her manner and her approach to fashion, **Claire McCardell** brought fresh individuality and prestige to the characteristically American fashion field, sportswear.

Credited with starting the "casual American look," she concentrated on comfort and function, with the result that she established a special style.

She always claimed that she designed for herself, and always wore her own clothes. Her tastes and demands happened to coincide with those of many other American women who were as proud of their

Claire McCardell

wholesale "McCardells" as other women were of their Paris couture styles. The fact that a "McCardell" endured for years was part of its appeal. And though widely copied, the original retained its individual stamp.

Her first big success was the monastic dress, a loose, flowing style which the wearer belted-in herself. This flooded the wholesale market in 1938. Characteristics of a McCardell dress were: surplice bodice, Empire waistline, hook and eye closing, halter neckline, little ties which could be varied, unpressed pleats. The dirndl for town-wear, the "Popover," an easy-to-get-into wrap dress evolved during the war as an aid to the hostess when she had to do without servants, and ballet shoes were some of her other inspirations. She liked wrapped waistlines, usable pockets, the kind of stitching associated with blue jeans. She made the shirtwaist dress her special province.

She gave a new lift to fabrics, especially cottons, which she used in distinctive colors and patterns.

Born in 1905 in Frederick, Md., McCardell joined the staff of Robert Tuck in 1929, and went with him to Townley two years later. Except for a stint at Hattie Carnegie, she continued there until her death in 1958.

The symmetry of **Christian Dior's** career as the head of the couture house that carried his name circled the decade from 1947 to 1957, during which period practically every collection was front page news.

His first collection, in February, 1947 put the term "New Look" into the general vocabulary. The designer, who had worked for Lelong since 1941, and with Piguet before that, was unknown to the general public. That first collection made his name a household word. It also made fashion a fighting word, as housewives organized clubs to defend the lingering short skirts, and men protested the descent of the hemline.

Nevertheless, the look took, and natural shoulder lines, flared full skirts, fitted waistlines, and suit jackets that were snug above stiff peplums became the prevailing fashion. This curving figure line, with echoes of the hour-glass shape of the past, provided a dramatic change from the skimpy, short, broad-shouldered look that had endured with few changes since the beginning of the decade. Wartime fabric economies were erased by

Christian Dior

A designer's designer, **Cristobal Balenciaga** de Eisequirre, while aggressively shunning the spotlight, has turned out to be a strong influence on some of the world's most smartly dressed women as well as on other designers. In 1951, his fitted front, loose back coats and suits set the ball rolling for an easier silhouette after the tautness of the New Look. This move, developed in subsequent collections, eventually changed the suit look all over the world.

In that same year, Balenciaga's famous brown lace dress, a two-piece style that bypassed the waistline, broke with a shock on the fashion world, and was the direct ancestor of the numerous unwaisted styles that succeeded it.

Balenciaga started his couture house in Paris in

Cristobal Balenciaga
de Eisequirre

lavish yardage—and Paris was again established as the world's fashion hub.

Subsequent collections continued to make news, and to help change the shape of the silhouette everywhere. Dark stockings were introduced in the August 1947, line. Scissors panels appeared the following year, and the "ligne verticale," pleated, straight dresses, were the newsmakers in February 1950, showing that the master was experimenting with a straighter silhouette. The counter revolution in 1953, when Dior shortened skirts, also made news, as did his 1954 H line.

A major contribution of Dior to the fashion world was the use of elaborate inner constructions. His wide skirts inspired petticoats and his small waistlines, belts. He also influenced blouses.

1937; previously, with houses in Madrid and San Sebastian, he had been a heavy purchaser of Paris models. His Spanish background still lingers in his rich embroideries, heavy passementeries, braids, fringes, and laces.

One sign of his mastery of dressmaking is that his line develops from season to season.

In the mid-1940s, Balenciaga was a proponent of the curvy, fitted suit that Dior popularized. In 1947, he introduced the barrel coat silhouette, which he worked over in ensuing years. In 1948, his contribution was the high-waisted coat; two years later, he introduced back blousing. All-around bodice blousing was the news in 1952, and hipline belts appeared the following year. By 1954, the loose jacket suit had crystallized, and "demi-fit" was accepted internationally.

Spare, unwaisted tunics appeared in 1955, and bloused tunics the next year. The straight line, with no waistline demarcation, was the rule by 1957, the year of the chemise.

Recently, "the master" has shown some tendency to closer fit.

Acknowledged dean of American designers, **Norman Norell** generated the same kind of enthusiasm with his first collection bearing his own name in June of this year as he did with his first collection with Traina-Norell in 1941, when he was said to have exploded on the season "like an electrical storm."

The thunderbolt this time was his divided skirts for town wear, substituting a type of pants for skirts.

Some of his enthusiasms, which turn up repeatedly in his collections: Slinky, beaded long evening dresses, easy-waisted fashions (he had a middy dress as early as 1944), tunics, Empire waistlines (with no indentation at the normal waist), shirtwaist dresses, and fabrics that cling to the figure, like jerseys and crepes.

As a true style leader, Norell is often seasons ahead of his time, appealing to the woman with fashion daring. He also is watched closely by other designers.

Long known as one of the top-priced wholesale designers, Norell designs clothes that are "so simple only the initiated can see in them justification for their altitudinous prices."

Norman Norell

While he has been established for two decades in the wholesale field, Norell has had diverse experience. Born in 1900, he came to New York from Noblesville, Indiana, in 1919 to attend art schools.

In the early 1920s, he designed costumes for Valentino and Gloria Swanson films, then worked with the Brooks Costume Company. After a few years with Charles Armour, he spent twelve years with Hattie Carnegie, where his name became known.

An articulate observer of the social scene, he considered the chemise a characteristic mid-twentieth century fashion, has had one in his collections for years. In his newest collections, he continues an exponent of the loosened line.

BIBLIOGRAPHY

Bender, Marilyn. *The Beautiful People*. New York, Coward-McCann, 1967.

Bertin, Celia. *Paris A La Mode*. New York, Harper, 1957.

Dior, Christian. *Christian Dior & I*. New York, Dutton, 1957.

Dior, Christian. *Talking about Fashion*. New York, Putnam, 1954.

Fairchild, John. *The Fashionable Savages*. Garden City, N.Y., Doubleday & Co., 1965.

Garland, Madge. *Fashion*. England, Penguin, 1962.

Latour, Amy. *Kings of Fashion*. New York, Coward-McCann, 1956.

Perkins, Alice K. *Paris Couturiers and Milliners*. New York, Fairchild, 1949.

Pickens, Mary Brooks and Dora L. Miller. *Dressmakers of France*. New York, Harper, 1956.

Poiret, Paul. *Kings of Fashion*. Philadelphia, J. Lippincott Co., 1931.

Quant, Mary. *Quant by Quant*. New York, Putnam, 1966.

Saunders, Edith. *The Age of Worth*. Bloomington, Indiana University Press, 1955.

Schiaparelli, Elsa. *Shocking Life*. New York, E.P. Dutton, 1954.

Spanier, Ginette. *It Isn't All Mink*. New York, Random House, 1959.

Vecchio, Walter and Robert Riley. *The Fashion Makers, a Photographic Record*. New York, Crown Publishers, 1968.

TRADE ASSOCIATIONS

Board of Trade, Export Services Division, Hillgate House, 35 Old Bailey, London EC4 (England)

Camera Nazionale della Moda Italiana, 00187 Roma, Via Lombardia, 44 (Italy)

Centro Di Firenze Per La Moda Italiana, Viale Gramsci 9/A, Florence, (Italy)

Chambre Syndicale de la Couture Parisienne, 100, Rue Du Fg St-Honoré, Paris 8 (France)

Clothing Export Council of Great Britain, 54 Grosvenor Street, London WIX ODB (England)

Comision Organizadora de la Presentacion de las Colecciones de Alta Costura, Palacio Nacional de Congresos Y Exposiciones Generalisimo, 29-Madrid 16 (Spain)

Fédération Française des Industries du Vêtement Féminin, 69 Rue de Richelieu, Paris 2 (France)

ADDITIONAL SOURCES OF INFORMATION

U.S. Department of Commerce, Washington, D.C., or any of its field offices in major cities. Also the consulates of the foreign countries concerned; usually in Washington, New York, and other major seaport cities.

SECTION REVIEW AND ACTIVITIES

FASHION BUSINESS TERMINOLOGY

Define, identify, or briefly explain the following.
> *Couturier*
> *Prêt-à-porter*
> *Haute couture*
> *Caution*
> Chambre Syndicale
> Line-for-line copy
> Adaptation
> Charles Frederick Worth
> Exclusives

QUESTIONS FOR REVIEW

1. Do you agree with the statement: "We have some great creative fashion talent in the United States but our industrial climate is not as favorable as Paris's to the growth and flowering of such talent"? Give reasons for your answer.

2. How does a typical Paris *haute couture* house differ from a typical Seventh Avenue firm?

3. Why do *couturiers* charge trade buyers a higher price for their merchandise than they charge private clients?

4. Does the practice of line-for-line Paris copies differ from that of style piracy? How?

5. Do you think that the ready-to-wear operations of the *haute couture* houses will eventually replace their *haute couture*? Cite the reasons given in the text for the probable continuance of *haute couture* in the foreseeable future. Do you agree with them? Why?

6. Why are foreign governments so eager to develop the apparel industry in their respective countries? Is the U.S. government as active as foreign governments in its support of our domestic industry? Why?

7. Why do the couture openings get as much publicity as they do in the United States?

8. Why do U.S. retailers buy imported merchandise often in preference to domestically made merchandise? Do you think that imported merchandise enhances a store's reputation as a fashion leader? Why?

9. Do you think that the United States should restrict apparel imports completely? Why?

10. What are the requirements that a couture house must meet to qualify for membership in the Chambre Syndicale de la Couture Parisienne?

11. Do you believe that the names of Paris designers are as meaningful to American customers as they appear to be to the American fashion industry? Give reasons for your answer.

APPLICATIONS WITH EXAMPLES

1. Examine your own wardrobe for apparel or accessories that were made in foreign countries. What countries are represented and why did you buy these imports instead of domestically made merchandise? Discuss and/or present with examples. Draw a conclusion about imported merchandise.

2. Analyze the imported apparel and accessories in one or more large retail stores. Discuss the countries that are represented and the type of merchandise in which each country seems to specialize.

3. Make a comparison of imported ready-to-wear and accessory items with domestically produced items that retail at the same price. Consider styling, fit, workmanship, and value, among other things. What are your conclusions?

SECTION 5
THE RETAILERS
OF FASHION

Retailing is the final step along the road that fashion merchandise travels on its way to the ultimate consumer. It is also the process that gives economic significance to the work of the talented designers and efficient producers who have contributed to the creation of fashion products.

In the United States there are 1.8 million business establishments devoted to retailing of all types: stores, mail-order firms, and door-to-door sellers. Available information about these establishments does not permit an exact count of how many of the total number or how much of their total volume should be considered as part of the fashion business. Information can, however, be narrowed down to retailers who deal exclusively in apparel and accessories, and to stores that deal in general merchandise and do a substantial amount of their business in the fashion field. When this is done, we find (1) that retail establishments that have at least a significant interest in fashion merchandise account for more than 10 percent of the 1.8 million retail outlets; (2) that they employ the services of more than one-fifth of the 11.7 million men and women engaged in retailing; and (3) that their combined sales of fashion and other merchandise constitute one-seventh of the $444 billion total annual retail sales in the United States.[1]

This section discusses the development of fashion retailing in America and the different kinds of retail outlets that distribute apparel and accessories for men, women, and children. The readings illustrate the fashion appeal and merchandising policies of different types of retailers and of individual, well-known firms.

FASHION RETAILING IN THE PAST

Retailing is as old as recorded history, if not older. Forerunners of many of our modern types of stores existed in the days of the Greeks and Romans. There have always been traders and peddlers traveling by ship, in caravans, and on foot; there were shopkeepers in the earliest towns.[2]

Many of America's great fashion retailers, especially those that have already celebrated their hundredth anniversaries, trace their origins back to a peddler, a small shopkeeper, or a custom tailor.

Peddlers and Small Shopkeepers

It was a traveling peddler who founded the retail dynasty that now owns the Saks Fifth Avenue stores. The peddler was Adam Gimbel, who opened a store in Vincennes, Indiana in 1842, and whose descendants built the Gimbel organization

---

[1]Authors' estimates based on U. S. Department of Commerce, *1967 Census of Business*, and *U. S. Industrial Outlook 1973*.

[2]Paul H. Nystrom, *Encyclopedia of the Social Sciences*, Vol. 12, The Macmillan Company, New York, 1934, pp. 346ff.

of which Saks Fifth Avenue is a part. Among the small shops that grew into major fashion stores, Lord & Taylor is an excellent example; it began in New York City in 1826 as a general dry goods store. In 1825 Arnold Constable, the New York specialty store, had opened as a shop devoted to the sale of imported goods, mostly textiles. Even earlier, in 1818, Brooks Brothers began operations as a men's tailoring shop.[3]

As towns and cities grew in America, and as factories began to produce goods in quantity, a countrywide network of retail merchants developed and assumed the role of getting goods from the producers to the ultimate consumers. By the late nineteenth century, many of our modern forms of retailing and most of this country's large volume retailers were well on their way. There were specialty stores like Filene's of Boston, established in 1873; department stores like Macy's in New York, founded in 1858; and mail-order houses like Sears Roebuck and Co., which began in Minneapolis in 1886 with a watch and jewelry mail-order catalogue.[4] There were also variety store chains such as Woolworth's (featuring small wares at 5¢ and 10¢), whose first unit opened in Utica, N.Y. in 1879—and was a failure. There were food chains, too, like the A & P, which began as a tea chain in 1859.[5] It was not until well into the twentieth century, however, that supermarkets, discount stores, and suburban branches of department and specialty stores made their appearance along with suburban shopping centers.

Custom Salons in the Nineteenth Century

The merchandise offerings of this country's early retailers could hardly be classified as "fashion goods," since they consisted mainly of staple and utilitarian products. The production of fashionable apparel was still largely in the hands of European couture houses and of American tailoring and dressmaking firms who bought the sketches or originals of Paris models along with the French fabrics from which they would make the reproductions for well-to-do customers.[6] Toward the end of the nineteenth century, a few exclusive big-city stores such as Marshall Field in Chicago and John Wanamaker and B. Altman in New York got into custom-dressmaking and began to send their own buyers abroad to purchase the latest French fashions.[7] Some of the stores whose names today are synonymous with fashion built the foundation of their fame in this manner—through their custom salons where people of means could order fashionable garments of good quality and workmanship. The retailing of ready-to-wear, however, awaited the development of textile and apparel production and it was not until late in the nineteenth century that significant amounts of manufactured apparel were even available for sale in stores. Department and specialty stores began to experiment with the new "store clothes" and, as the wholesale fashion industry developed, so did retail ready-to-wear departments.

Custom-made clothing remained important for many years, however, although it

[3]J. W. Ferry, *A History of the Department Stores*, The Macmillan Company, New York, 1960, pp. 35–74.
[4]Tom Mahoney, *The Great Merchants*, Harper, New York, 1965. Also Ferry, *op. cit.*
[5]*Ibid.*
[6]Ethel Traphagen, "Fifty Years of Keeping Step with Fashion," *Department Store Economist*, January 1961.
[7]John B. Swinney, *Merchandising of Fashions*, The Ronald Press, New York, 1942, p. 5.

steadily gave way before the growing and constantly improving ready-to-wear industry. By the second half of the twentieth century, most major fashion stores had discontinued their custom operations. By 1970, I. Magnin & Co. of Los Angeles was the last of the country's great stores to preserve its custom department and, even so, it did not extend its custom service to its San Francisco operation.

Reasons for the closing down of custom operations in retail stores were spelled out by Andrew Goodman in 1969, when his store—Bergdorf Goodman, New York—abandoned custom activity after 70 uninterrupted years in that field. Goodman cited (1) the rising cost of fabrics, (2) the shortage of skilled help to work on a garment, (3) dwindling customer demand for custom service, and (4) the fact that custom-made clothing had become so out of step with the times that to offer this service did nothing to enhance a store's fashion image. Said Goodman: "Custom-made clothes are of another era, another world, and have no relevancy to today's times. They are anachronistic where opulence and self-indulgence are giving way to greater social awareness and consciousness."[8]

Early Ready-To-Wear Retailing

The early years of ready-to-wear retailing were difficult ones for dry goods merchants who, up to that time, had had little or no experience with the vagaries of fashion. Apparel departments generally showed a financial loss which had to be made up by profits in other more staple lines. Apparel producers themselves were newcomers to the fashion business and could not offer much help. Together the retailers and manufacturers learned by trial and error. Custom-made clothing was still important but it was steadily giving way before the growing and constantly improving ready-to-wear clothing industry. By 1920, however, ready-made apparel departments were firmly established in all big-city department and specialty stores and in most general stores in smaller communities.

During the twenties, many department stores leased their apparel departments to ready-to-wear specialists who would install and manage an apparel operation in return for from 10 to 15 percent of the sales. Some of these leasing concerns operated in as many as 50 stores, mainly in the Middle West.[9] During the 1929 depression, most of them went out of business. Decades later, in the late 1950s and early 1960s, leased ready-to-wear departments enjoyed a brief resurgence of importance. This occurred when discount houses, formerly exclusively sellers of household goods, first ventured into apparel lines. Many of them turned the operation over to lessees initially. After the first few years, owner operation of apparel departments became the usual procedure in such stores, also. Today, leased departments prevail only where the problems and procedures are so different from those of ordinary apparel or accessories departments that merchants—exclusive or popular priced; department-store; specialty-store; or discount—find it desirable to let competent lessees run them. Typical of such

[8]"Bergdorf Shuts Custom Shop," *Women's Wear Daily*, May 13, 1969, p. 31.
[9]Swinney, *op. cit.*, p. 7.

departments are millinery, ladies' shoes, and the beauty salon, which are more commonly leased than owner operated.[10]

Fashion Authority of Early Retailers

In the beginning of ready-to-wear retailing, the owners of great fashion stores would work with the manufacturers to produce their ready-to-wear designs to meet the styling needs of individual stores.[11] Many retailers helped manufacturers to get started by bringing them Paris models to copy and starting them off with substantial orders.[12] Although this is still a practice in the industry today, with production on so large a scale it is the exception rather than the rule. In those days, also, the retailer was the main source of fashion information for customers, as well as manufacturers; there were few movies, few telephones, no television, and only a few publications to keep people up-to-date on what should be produced or worn. Long before the fashion show, the bridal counselor, and the college shop advisors were commonplace, great department stores were publishing fashion magazines that they mailed to customers. John Wanamaker began publication of a magazine in 1909; Marshall Field and Company in 1914.[13] As fashion traveled its long, slow route from Paris to Podunk, customers looked to their favorite retail stores to bring it into their towns when the time was right for it.

DIVERSITY OF FASHION RETAILING TODAY

The history of fashion retailing up to the mid-1900s involved primarily department stores and fine specialty shops. The years between 1950 and 1960, however, witnessed what many people refer to as a revolution in retailing—a revolution that left many changes in its wake. One change is that, today, retailers of every conceivable type pour a steady stream of fashion goods into American homes.

In terms of their merchandise assortments, the retail stores that sell fashion merchandise today divide into two classes: specialty shops and general merchandise stores. In terms of the quality of goods they carry and the degree of service they render to the customer, the variety is infinite. There is everything from the bargain-basement type, in which the customers must scrabble through piles of merchandise to find what they want, to the salons where customers are seated and waited upon by expert salespeople. There are cash-and-carry stores, in which the relationship between customer and retailer begins and ends at the cash register;

---

[10]"Leased Departments, A Report to Management," *Stores, the NRMA Magazine*, July-August 1964, p. 34.
[11]Lew Hahn, *Stores, Merchants and Customers: A Philosophy of Retailing*, Fairchild Publications, New York, 1952, pp. 177–182.
[12]Swinney, *op. cit.* p. 5.
[13]J. Appel, *Business Biography of John Wanamaker*, The Macmillan Company, New York, 1930, pp. 114ff. and L. Wendt and H. Kogan, *Give the Lady What She Wants*, Rand McNally Co., Chicago, 1952, p. 293.

and stores that deliver, charge, and send on approval. There are also nonstore retailers, who do their selling by catalogue or door-to-door solicitation; and there are facilities in many stores for buying by mail or telephone.

There are little "mom-and-pop" stores that sell $100 or less a day and there are large-scale retailers who employ thousands of people and sell as much as $1 million worth of goods on some days. There are retail stores owned and operated by manufacturers, particularly in the men's wear field. In fact, there are almost as many different types of fashion retailers as there are different kinds of people.

The fashion industry's close watch on the consumer is made easier as a direct result of the buying and selling activities of fashion's retailers. These retailers, large and small alike, while seeking goods that are acceptable to their particular customers, act as a sounding board for producers—a series of listening posts on the consumer front. At the same time, in the course of their selling activities, they serve as a medium for educating and informing the public about fashion and, by the very nature of their business, do much to stimulate consumer demand for fashion products.

Department Stores

The department store is a descendant of the trading post and general stores of pioneer days. Many of the large and well-known department stores in the United

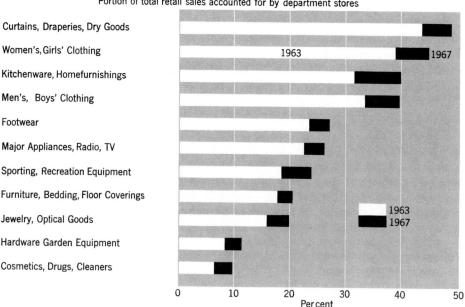

THE DEPARTMENT STORE'S MARKET SHARES BY MERCHANDISE LINE
Portion of total retail sales accounted for by department stores

Source: *A Guide to Consumer Markets 1972/1973*, The Conference Board, Inc., New York. Published annually.

States today came into being between 1840 and 1880 when the growth of cities and the increase in mass production created a need for this type of retailing.[14] One of its basic appeals to the consumer was that she could purchase under one roof merchandise for herself, her family, and her home.

By definition, a department store employs at least 25 people, and handles a wide variety of merchandise lines including home furnishings, apparel for the family, and household linens or dry goods.[15] Establishments that meet these criteria except as to number of employees, are classified as general merchandise stores. Department store executives add several points to this bare description: that the merchandise is offered for sale in separate departments, each of which is administered by a buyer or department manager; that sales service is provided; that credit, return, and delivery privileges are offered; that the customer may shop in person, by telephone, or by mail; and that the store participates in community affairs.

Department stores may be independently owned or parts of ownership groups. Whatever their ownership, they offer the full complement of customer services. If they do not, the department store community refers to them as discount stores, mass merchandisers, or by any name except department stores. Manufacturers, too, tend to avoid attaching the department store label to stores that do not meet the criteria laid down above.

Having thus delineated the department store, we shall describe its function in the fashion business. The typical department store chooses as its target group of customers people in the middle- to upper-income brackets, with fairly large discretionary income. The fashion appeal of department stores stems from the breadth of assortment in middle- to upper-middle prices, in styles, and in brand names that they present to their customers. Browsing among its broad stocks, and guided by its advertising and displays, the customer can develop her own ideas of what she wants to buy. When she has made her choice, she is able to buy with confidence because of the store's refund policies. The offer of money back if the merchandise is unsatisfactory, or if it merely fails to please the family at home, has been a cornerstone of department store policy for more than a century.

In the fashion industries, the department store represents a large volume of sales and accounts for half the total retail business in women's and children's apparel and accessories.[16] It also offers producers an opportunity to expose their merchandise, often with considerable drama, to the public. It is not uncommon for department stores to have auditoriums or other facilities for staging fashion shows, or for them to stage shows outside the store for clubs and charities. They advertise, they display, and they bring customer traffic into the store. Since department stores cover so many fields of merchandise, they can generate more traffic than a specialized clothing store; a woman who comes in to buy shoes for her child or a lamp for her living room may see and buy on impulse some fashion item that was not on her

---

[14]Ferry, *op. cit.*

[15]The retail definitions in this section are those of the Bureau of the Census unless otherwise indicated.

[16]*Conditions in the Women's Garment Industry, February 28, 1973,* Research Department, International Ladies' Garment Workers' Union, p. 3.

nal shopping list. Department stores cater chiefly to women and typically do
ly 40 percent of their business in apparel and accessories.[17] Even in the
artments that handle men's furnishings, women do a huge part of the
rchasing.

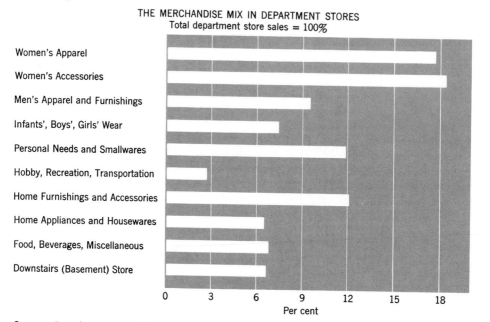

THE MERCHANDISE MIX IN DEPARTMENT STORES
Total department store sales = 100%

Source: Based upon annual reports, *Department Store and Specialty Store Merchandising and Operating Results,* published by Controllers' Congress, National Retail Merchants Association, New York, N.Y.

Specialty Stores—Large and Small

In contrast to the department store's wide range of merchandise and broad appeal, the specialty store is a retail organization dealing in a category of merchandise such as jewelry, shoes, lingerie, or blouses. It may also specialize in several related categories of merchandise such as women's apparel and accessories, or men's clothing and furnishings. For census purposes, these are classified as apparel shops; in the fashion business they are referred to as specialty shops or stores. Among consumers, the larger versions are frequently miscalled department stores because they are departmentized, offer extensive customer services, and carry wide assortments of the merchandise in which they specialize. To qualify as department stores, however, they would have to carry home furnishings as well as apparel.

Specialty stores (or apparel shops) may be individually owned or units of chains. They may even be apparel discounters. They may range in size from a small

[17]Authors' estimates, based on *Departmental Merchandising and Operating Results,* an annual publication of the Controllers' Congress, National Retail Merchants Association, New York.

Sales Size: Apparel Stores, 1967

ANNUAL SALES VOLUME	APPAREL, ACCESSORIES, TOTAL		WOMEN'S CLOTHING, SPECIALTY		MEN'S, BOYS' CLOTHING[a]	
	ESTAB-LISHMENTS	SALES	ESTAB-LISHMENTS	SALES	ESTAB-LISHMENTS	SALES
All establishments[a]	110.2	16,672	44.5	6,517	16.7	3,385
Number operated all year[b]	106.5	16,280	42.8	6,369	16.4	3,300
Percent distribution[c]	100.0	100.0	100.0	100.0	100.0	100.0
Under $30,000	23.7	2.5	28.0	3.0	10.7	1.1
$ 30,000- 50,000	13.3	3.3	14.4	3.6	10.6	1.9
50,000-100,000	23.2	10.9	23.2	11.1	22.0	8.0
100,000-300,000	28.9	31.9	24.2	27.3	39.9	34.3
300,000-500,000	5.7	14.3	5.0	13.0	9.3	17.5
500,000-1,000,000	3.5	15.4	3.3	15.2	5.4	17.9
1,000,000 or more	1.6	21.6	1.8	26.8	2.1	19.1

Sources. *A Guide to Consumer Markets 1972/1973,* The Conference Board, Inc., N.Y., Report #569.
[a] Refers only to establishments with payroll.
[b] Establishments in thousands; sales in millions of dollars.
[c] Based on establishments operated entire year.

neighborhood or rural shop to such large, universally known fashion retailers as Bergdorf Goodman in New York or Neiman-Marcus in Dallas. Great or small, apparel specialty stores usually cater to a restricted clientele—the woman of great wealth and discrimination, the suburban housewife, the outsize woman, the young woman on a small budget, the tall girl, the maternity customer. Atmosphere, displays, selling effort, and the actual merchandise are all pointed strongly toward the particular customer who is the store's target. Salesmanship, if only because it is specialized as to merchandise and clientele, is likely to be of a higher order than what the customer encounters in stores aimed at a broader market.

The small stores specializing in apparel for men or women play a very dominant role in the fashion business. Despite the competition of larger stores, their collective share of the total volume of fashion merchandise sales is substantial. Among women's apparel shops, for instance, units with annual sales of less than $500,000 constitute 95 percent of the total number of such stores in the United States and constitute 58 percent of the volume of such sales.[18] A large percentage of these small shops are independently owned and there is no small town or big city where they do not exist. Their attrition rate is high, of course, but so is the replacement rate. Figures released by the Credit Clearing House, a division of Dun & Bradstreet Inc., show more than 250 failures among womens' ready-to-wear stores in a typical year—and over 1200 new stores in the same category opening that

[18] *A Guide to Consumer Markets 1972/1973.* The Conference Board, Inc., New York, 1972, p. 222.

year, with an average starting capital of barely $13,000 each.[19] It is from modest beginnings such as these that most of today's great fashion retailers have evolved.

From the consumer's point of view, much of the staying power of small fashion retailers can be attributed to the individuality of their operations, the convenience of their locations, and their intimate knowledge of their customers' needs and tastes. Their owners know the way of dressing in the communities in which they are located and many times will take the trouble to buy with individual customers in mind. Their importance to the fashion industry is best expressed in the words of an executive of the industry's largest volume producer of apparel who said:

"In our company we see the different role played by the various classes of retailers very clearly. Our nationally advertised brands have won their place in the sun, and maintain their leadership, primarily through the cooperation and good will of the independent retailers, most of whom are, relatively speaking, small retailers. . . . The independent retailer is highly important to our economy as well as providing valuable services to the customer. It is the existence of the smaller independent that really makes national distribution possible."[20]

Mail-Order Houses

Mail-order houses have their roots far back in the past, having developed to meet the needs of rural and small town customers in the days before the automobile. The isolation of farm life, the inadequacy of country stores, and the introduction of free rural mail delivery all combined to create a favorable business climate for the early mail-order enterprises. By census definition, a mail-order firm is one that makes the bulk of its sales and deliveries by mail—as distinguished from retail stores that do most of their business with the customer in person—yet also provide mail order service to supplement their over-the-counter selling. Mail-order establishments may specialize in the type of merchandise they sell, or they may feature full lines of general merchandise. An example of the former is Spiegel's, Inc., a Chicago firm specializing in apparel, whose annual volume in 1972 was almost $400 million. In the latter category are Montgomery Ward & Co., founded in 1872, and Sears Roebuck and Co., founded in 1886. Sears Roebuck is the world's largest general merchandise retailer, with total annual sales of almost $11 billion in 1972. The catalog division's sales are estimated to be 22 percent of that total, the balance originating in its retail stores.

The catalogs of both these general merchandise giants, along with the catalogs of their smaller competitors, were the standbys of rural customers for generations. Although the fashions offered were not exciting, the prices and assortments surpassed those available in rural stores, and they were a delight to the country clientele that they were intended to serve. In the eyes of these women, the catalog

[19]From 1972 and 1973 press releases of Dun & Bradstreet, Inc. New York.

[20]Norman A. Jackson, Financial Vice-President, Kayser-Roth Corporation, in a presentation to the National Association of Credit and Financial Management, Los Angeles, California, May 19, 1964. Excerpts reprinted in *The Apparel Outlook*, June-July, 1964.

indeed earned the name that came to be applied to it: the "wish book." So well, in fact, did the mail-order houses meet the needs and broadening interests of the rural customer that by 1895 the Sears catalog consisted of 507 pages, and the company's annual sales exceeded $750,000.[21]

As rural families acquired mobility, thanks to improvements in transportation, retail stores became more accessible to them and their tastes became more sophisticated. Increasing awareness of fashion also came through developments in communication such as publications, movies, and radio. Rural families' fashion awareness and shopping patterns broadened—and so did the mail-order houses'. In the 1920s, mail-order houses opened chains of retail stores. In the 1930s they initiated catalog sales offices to which customers could come and have the help of skilled salespeople in filling out orders for merchandise listed in the catalog. During the 1950s, they began to give considerable space to ready-to-wear and to upgrade all their fashion lines, to the point that they were commissioning European couturiers to create special collections for them.

To the customer, the mail-order catalog offers the convenience of ordering her merchandise at home, by mail or telephone, whenever it suits her—a convenience that has attracted a share of city and suburban customers who find themselves either house-bound or daunted by traffic congestion and thus unwilling to face the rigors of shopping in person. Such customers, of course, also buy from catalogs published at intervals by retail stores and sent to their charge customers—for example, catalogs sent out at Christmas, back-to-school, and other peak shopping seasons. But although a store's catalog may reach thousands or even tens of thousands of customers, a mail-order house's catalog reaches millions of households. As far back as 1905, Sears was distributing more than 2 million copies of a single issue of its spring catalog. By the 1960s, the total number distributed in the course of a year by Sears had reached 50 million—with Montgomery Ward just a step behind that figure.[22] By the 1960s, too, another retailing giant had entered the mail-order field; the J.C. Penney Co., with its strongly established chain of stores serving middle-income customers, set up a catalog operation.

The mail-order houses represent a huge market for the fashion industry's products. When a style is purchased by their buyers, and placed in a catalog that goes into millions of homes, the prospects of selling many, many garments of that one style are excellent. In their relationship with manufacturers, the mail-order companies exercise a great deal of leadership. Their testing laboratories check apparel for fit, workmanship, wearing qualities, fabric strength, stability, and color fastness. Their sales records provide them with a vast storehouse of information on the public's preferences. Their purchasing power and prestige make it possible for them to specify the thread count wanted in a fabric, or the number of stitches per inch in the seams of a garment, to make sure their customers get the wearing qualities they expect. More recently, their immense buying power has been used to bring smarter, more fashionable garments to their customers by the device of

[21]*Merchant to the Millions*, Sears Roebuck and Co., Publication Service, Department 703, 925 S. Homan Avenue, Chicago, Ill.
[22]"Putting Out the Wish Book Is a Complex All-Year Production at Sears," *The New York Times*, May 19, 1963, Section 3, p. 14.

employing leading designers, both here and abroad, to design garments especially for them. Current catalogs of leading mail-order houses list well-known designer names and many higher-priced apparel items without, however, neglecting the traditional, popular-priced, mass-market merchandise that is still the largest part of their business.

Chain Store Retailers

In the retail trade, the term "chain" is applied to a group of four or more specialized or general merchandise stores when they are centrally owned; when the units are very similar in physical appearance and in lines of merchandise carried; and when the individual stores are managed from the chain's central or regional headquarters where the buying, selling, and other operating policies are formulated. A department or specialty store that has several branches, or becomes part of a centrally owned group of other stores, is not usually described as a chain—it is called an ownership group, a parent store with branches, or a group of sister stores. In part, this bit of semantics harks back to the 1920s and 1930s when most department and specialty stores were individually owned and when most chains granted little or no autonomy to their local managers.[23] The situation has changed sharply since then. The chains have decentralized more and more; department and specialty stores have sprouted branches and affiliated with units in other cities and even in other parts of the country. But the semantics remain. To retail professionals, chain store retailing continues to mean standardized stores and merchandise and remote central management.

From the point of view of the popular-priced fashion business, the years from 1920 to 1929 may well be called "the chain store era." During the preceding decade, the manufacturing and retailing of blouses, or waists as they were then called, was at a peak. Blouses were fashionable and blouses were also moderately priced in comparison with the ready-to-wear dresses which were then being retailed in department stores from $50 upwards. Induced by the demand of lower-income customers for lower-priced ready-made apparel, chains of "waist stores" made their appearance in the form of small specialized shops in the trading areas of large cities.[24] About 1919, blouses went out of fashion and the waist manufacturers turned to making dresses which could retail from $16.95 to $25.00 and which were lower in price than those being featured by the department and large specialty stores.[25] It seemed quite natural that the waist chains should add these popular-priced dresses to their merchandise assortments; with department stores catering to middle-income families, there was little competition for chains in the popular-priced apparel field. This period saw the start of many apparel chains that emphasized lower-priced ready-to-wear and catered to the class of new "working

[23]Godfrey M. Lebhar, *Chain Stores in America*, Chain Store Publishing Corp., New York, 1959, p. 287.
[24]Swinney, *op cit*. p. 25.
[25]*Ibid*. Authors' note: many of the most successful dress manufacturers of the 1920s and 1930s evolved from these early waist producers.

THE CHAIN STORES' SHARE OF RETAIL SALES

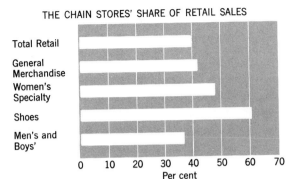

Total Retail

General
Merchandise

Women's
Specialty

Shoes

Men's and
Boys'

0 10 20 30 40 50 60 70
Per cent

Source: Authors' estimates based upon reports of the U.S. Bureau of the Census.

women" who had entered business during the manpower shortage of World War I. A notable example of an early waist chain is the Lerner Shops, which got its start during these years and which is one of today's largest apparel chains; its 428 stores had sales of $435 million in 1972, primarily in lower-priced fashions for girls and women.[26]

Conditions in the 1920s favored the growth of chain organizations, encouraging the entry into the field not only of apparel chains but also of other types: shoe chains, millinery chains, men's hat chains, men's clothing chains, variety chains, and family clothing chains. During the 1920s, communications were improving, and the rural customer had periodicals, movies, and radio to whet her appetite for fashions. Moreover, thanks to Henry Ford's much laughed-at but eminently practical "Tin Lizzie," transportation to stores in nearby towns became cheap and readily available for the farm wife. The mail-order catalog and the country store were no longer her only sources of supply. At the same time, the country as a whole was swinging over from predominantly rural to predominantly urban population; in 1920, the census figures showed a majority of the U.S. population living in rural areas but, in 1930, the majority was in urban areas. Opportunities in trade and industry were drawing people to towns and cities and creating a burgeoning market of customers who were available to shop in person for merchandise at low and moderate prices. The chains jumped in to meet this need, and by 1930 there were an estimated 150,000 chain stores in the United States.[27]

The same period witnessed the beginning of the general merchandise chain-store operations of the giant Sears Roebuck and Co. For one thing, chain stores were beginning to blanket the country and cut into Sears's mail-order business. In addition, American cities were growing up and Sears's rural customers were abandoning the farm for the factory. City dwellers, reasoned Sears, were not good catalog customers. Beginning in 1925 with one store located in the Chicago mail-order plant, their retail operation grew to 324 stores in 1929 to more than 800 stores by 1972. Today their retail stores account for more than three-quarters of

---

[26]*Women's Wear Daily*, March 20, 1973, p. 38.
[27]*Merchant to the Millions*, Sears Roebuck and Co., Chicago, Ill. p. 10.

Sears's total sales.[28] The mail-order house of Montgomery Ward and Co. followed in Sears's footsteps albeit on a smaller scale.

After World War II, chain organizations of many types began broadening their merchandise assortments and extending their price ranges upward in response to the increased affluence and greater fashion awareness of their customers. An outstanding example of a chain that recognized the sharpened fashion sense of consumers of modest income was the introduction by the J. C. Penney Co. of Mary Quant styles in the 1950s. Mail-order houses, like Sears and Ward's in their retail chains, have given prime locations to women's apparel and accessory departments and have traded up (sold higher quality) their fashion offerings in their stores and catalogs. Chains such as the F. W. Woolworth Co. and the W. T. Grant Co., which were once known as five-and-ten-cent stores or limited-price variety stores, today carry a complete range of fashion merchandise in low and moderate price lines and constitute an impressive mass outlet for the fashion industry's products: undergarments, foundations, hosiery, sleepwear, gloves, handbags, costume jewelry, dresses, and sportswear, among other categories. Their combined retail sales of such goods are reported to have passed the $1 billion mark by 1969.[29] Supermarket and drug chains also move substantial amounts of the more staple apparel and accessories items.

Most chain-store retailers of women's apparel, with very few exceptions, feature styles in popular-priced apparel and accessories that are at the peak of fashion demand. Fashion leadership is not their objective and their displays emphasize their assortments and low prices rather than fashion alone. A large chain's buying power is enormous and it can give manufacturers large enough orders to have merchandise made to its own specifications and labeled with its own private brand name. In this manner, large chain operators are able to obtain at low prices merchandise that is made and styled exclusively for them.

Chain stores may not have the fashion authority of department and specialized stores, but they can and do move a great deal of merchandise. Their role, as the industry views it, is a dominant one in the fashion business: selling very large quantities of moderate priced apparel to the sizable customer audience of relatively modest income.

Discount Stores

Discount stores are not easily defined; some are department stores in every sense but for the intangible attributes described earlier in this chapter. The editors of the magazine, *The Discount Merchandiser*, have developed this accepted definition: "A departmentalized retail establishment utilizing many self-service techniques to sell hard goods, health-and-beauty aids, apparel and other soft goods, and other general merchandise. It operates at uniquely low margins. It has a minimum annual

---

[28]*Ibid.*

[29]"Variety Department Store General Merchandise and Discount Market," *Variety Department Store Merchandiser*, 37th Annual Report, p. 10 M.

volume of $500,000 and it is at least 10,000 square feet in size."[30] Most of these stores are open to the public; a few are of the "closed door" variety, restricted to member customers, who pay a token annual fee to belong. Memberships are usually solicited among people of nearly identical social and economic positions, whose merchandise needs will be similar.

Discount retailers, featuring nationally advertised brands of home appliances at less than "list" price, came into their own during the late 1940s. Their development and growth was sparked by the Fair Trade statutes enacted during the 1930s, that made it possible for wholesale suppliers to set resale "list" price minimums. At the beginning, these stores provided no customer services of any kind, relied largely on word of mouth advertising and confined their operations primarily to the sale of well-known brands of hard goods. During the latter part of the 1950s, however, the situation changed rapidly. Discounters began to open additional stores in the burgeoning suburban communities and to broaden their merchandise assortments to include apparel. Many new discount stores came into being in cities and suburbs alike.

Although underselling remained and still remains their major appeal, alert discount merchants, aware of the higher profit margins and potential sales volume of ready-to-wear, began to trade up apparel offerings and stress fashion as well as price. As volume increased, discount stores began to carry larger quantities of clothing. Also, they began to upgrade their displays, advertising, and even their locations. E.J. Korvette's Fifth Avenue store, in the heart of New York City's most fashionable shopping area, was an early and notable example of changes such as these.

Today, many discount operations call themselves mass merchandisers or promotional department stores, de-emphasizing the term "discount." Nevertheless, their appeal to the customer is still on the basis of bargains; their role in the fashion business is that of moving lower-priced merchandise rapidly and in large quantities. They can be enormous buyers in the wholesale markets because some of them are chains with many outlets. Others turn over their ready-to-wear to leased department operators who specialize in apparel concessions in retail stores. These lessees, serving many stores or store groups, have great buying power also.

Some apparel manufacturers, who are concerned about the retail prices at which their goods are sold, or who are fearful of antagonizing the traditional stores among their customers, refrain from selling to discount retailers. Other firms, however, are glad to manufacture secondary brands for such stores or to produce lines of lower-priced merchandise to be sold under a discount store's own label. There are also manufacturers who specialize in producing goods for discounters, and there are still others who sell them only their discontinued or marked-down garments. In an industry containing thousands of apparel producers, there is no shortage of merchandise or suppliers for discount buyers.

In one sense, the apparel-discounting developments of the 1950s and 1960s are not new; apparel stores that specialized in cut-price merchandise have been in existence since the 1920s—notably Ohrbach's and Alexander's. What is new,

[30]"The True Look of the Discount Industry," *The Discount Merchandiser*, June, 1970.

Selected Discount Store Sales, 1972

	SALES VOLUME (add 000)
Alexander's	$318,074
Daylin	481,138
Goldblatt Bros. Inc.	246,794
Harzfeld-Zody	269,000
Interstate Stores	571,000
Unishops	235,000
Vornado	793,000
Zayre	939,710

Source: Annual company reports.

however, is the multiplicity of discount operators in the United States and their growing importance as distributors of popular-priced fashion apparel. The publication, *The Discount Merchandiser*, estimates that the number of such stores in the early 1970s was 5000, that their combined retail sales of women's and girls' apparel was nearly $2.5 billion, and that there were at least 39 companies in the field whose individual annual volume figures reached or exceeded $100 million.[31]

Direct-Selling Establishments

Direct-selling establishments are in the retail business but they do not have stores. Instead, they employ salespeople on a commission basis to approach the customer in her home. Selling is done either through door-to-door canvassing or some form of party plan. Both methods have been used successfully in the fashion field. Although the role of the direct-selling operations may not be a dominant one in fashion retailing, it bears watching.

Door-to-door canvassing usually involves only a single line of merchandise and requires good salesmanship on the part of the canvasser to gain entrance into the home and to put the customer in a buying frame of mind without the aid of displays and the contagious excitement of being involved in an in-store shopping situation. The quality of the merchandise is usually excellent, since the house-to-house seller has no adjustment or exchange clerk to deal with the customer if the products fail to give complete satisfaction. In the fashion-related field, Avon cosmetics is perhaps the best-known operation of this type. Door-to-door selling is not new in the fashion field. In the period before World War II, silk hosiery and custom-made foundation garments were successfully sold this way.

The party plan of selling depends on encouraging one woman in an area to invite a number of her friends and neighbors to her home for refreshments and the presentation of merchandise. Each hostess receives a gift for her efforts, even though the refreshments are usually provided by the salesperson. At a gathering of

[31]*Ibid.*

Retail Sales of Women's and Children's Clothing and Accessories by Type of Outlet (in millions of dollars)

PERIOD	TOTAL SALES	DEPART-MENT STORES	WOMEN'S READY-TO-WEAR STORES	FAMILY CLOTHING STORES	OTHER RETAIL OUTLETS
1966	$18,377	$ 8,051	$5,799	$1,317	$3,210
1967	18,794	8,358	5,726	1,377	3,333
1968	20,329	9,325	6,039	1,434	3,531
1969	21,583	10,213	6,128	1,436	3,805
1970	22,192	10,600	6,196	1,426	3,970
1971	24,261	11,853	6,696	1,596	4,116
1972	25,736	13,047	6,850	1,595	4,244

SOURCE: ILGWU Research Department (benchmarked to 1963 and 1967 Census of Business and adjusted in line with revisions in Census retail trade statistics). From *Conditions in the Women's Garment Industry*, ILGWU, February 1973.
[a]Data include traditional products of the women's garment industry as well as millinery, furs, hosiery, gloves, and other accessories.

this kind, the salesperson can present a fairly extensive line, take orders on the spot, arrange for later delivery to the purchasers' homes, and sound out prospective hostesses for future parties. This is the method associated with such names as Tupperware and Stanley Home Products in the home-goods field. It has also been used effectively for costume jewelry and other fashion merchandise.

An outstanding party-plan success story is that of Beeline, a seller of moderately priced dresses, sportswear separates, and similar items, including some staples for men and children. Although the company did not come into being until after World War II, its volume is catching up with the figures of Fuller Brush and Avon, those giants in the direct-selling arena. Beeline's clothes are modestly priced and are carefully chosen to be squarely in the center of current fashion demand, and also to be styled so that fitting is not a crucial problem. No fads, no extremes—just wearable fashions susceptible to wide sale. Beeline's range of styles is relatively narrow, but their sales per style have been known to reach 10,000 dozen or more in a season.

Still another direct-selling method used successfully for fashion goods is exemplified by the operation of Doncaster, a maker of fairly high priced, fairly classic women's apparel, made to the customer's measure from a selection of styles and fabrics. Each season, the company's representative in a certain area receives, on loan, the company's new line of samples. She then invites prospective customers to her home by appointment to view and select. When she takes an order, she also takes an elaborate set of body measurements for accurate fit. Later, the garments are shipped to her for delivery to customers, collection of the sales price, and any adjustments in fit that may be needed.

Direct-selling operations, in all their variations, lean heavily on the enterprising housewife to carry the fashion and selling message to other women in a relaxed, social atmosphere. Where the sales representatives are well motivated and trained, fashion firms seem to prosper. This is one of the many ways in which women like to buy apparel and accessories.

CURRENT TRENDS IN RETAILING

The retailer, as an intermediary between the fashion industry and the fashion customer, has to respond to changes on both sides. If he must deal with giantism in industry, for example, he must become a giant himself through mergers, acquisitions, and sheer growth. If customers, surfeited with the output of mass producers, yearn for the unusual and the exotic, the retailer has to find it for them and present it in a boutique environment. If the lines that distinguish one social stratum from another grow blurred, then the lines between stores that serve customers of different classes and types become less sharp.

Giant Combines

Preceding sections of this book have mentioned the trend to giantism in the textile and apparel industries. The same trend exists in the retail field, although it is not always apparent to the layman. One is aware, it is true, of the size of an individual store that reaches giant size, such as a Macy's in New York and a Hudson's in Detroit, or of the size of a chain when all of its units bear the same name, such as Sears Roebuck and J. C. Penney. But sometimes one chain is a subsidiary of another, or one company owns two or more chains. And sometimes a store becomes part of an ownership group but retains its old name. Occasionally, a store or group of stores of one type develops or acquires stores of quite a different type.

For example, in the chain field, Lerner Stores are owned by Rapid-American, which also owns the McCrory chain of variety stores. In the department and specialty store field, the Broadway-Hale Company, whose stores are largely in southern California, has acquired the Emporium in San Francisco, Neiman-Marcus in Dallas, and Bergdorf Goodman in New York. In the discount field, the Fedway stores were established by Federated Stores, which owns such department stores as the F. & R. Lazarus store in Columbus, Ohio and the Bloomingdale store in New York. The J. L. Hudson Company of Detroit, the second largest department store in the country, has become part of the Dayton-Hudson Company, an organization of discount and department stores.

ADVANTAGES OF GIANTISM.   When a department store group—such as Federated Stores, Allied Stores, or the May Department Stores—exceeds $1 billion in annual sales, its purchasing power in the fashion markets is enormous. Like the chains, and like some of the remaining large, many-branched independent department and specialty stores, it is in a position to encourage producers to manufacture fashions in which it has confidence. It is in a position to develop brand

Sales of Selected Store Ownership Groups, 1972
(combined store totals)

GROUP	SALES (add 000)
Allied Stores Corp.	$1,482,955
Associated Dry Goods	1,130,004
Broadway-Hale Stores	931,000
Dayton-Hudson	1,297,386
Federated Department Stores	2,665,147
Gimbel Bros.	812,184
Macy, R.H., and Co.	1,041,122
May Department Stores	1,468,000

Source: Annual company reports.

names of its own in fashion merchandise or in other lines. It is also in a position to send its buyers abroad to seek out desirable merchandise that may not be available in the United States.

These benefits of bigness are not always for the giants alone. Small, independent department and specialty stores can enjoy some of the same advantages by pooling their purchasing power through their resident buying offices. Just about every department and specialty store beyond the mom-and-pop size has a buying office to serve it in the fashion markets. By marshaling the buying power of its subscribing stores, the buying office can create a private brand that each of its stores can use in its own trading area, can seek out unusual items in foreign markets, or can supply needed encouragement to a fashion producer in order to have him manufacture wanted styles.

PROBLEMS OF GIANTISM.　The path of giantism is not always smooth. There have been retail organizations that bought or built so many stores in a particular area that the Federal Trade Commission regarded this as stifling competition and ordered a cessation to expansion. There have been retail organizations that bought up other stores and chains and then found that they were unable to operate their acquisitions successfully because of insufficient capital, management talent, or other reasons. It requires a broad spectrum of assets and skills to operate a giant retail organization successfully, whether that organization is a single enormous store, a chain, or an ownership group of department or specialty stores.

THE FRANCHISE ROUTE.　One method of expansion familiar in other fields, but relatively new in fashion retailing, is franchising. This is a business relationship familiar in fields such as gasoline service stations, ice cream stands, and fast food service. Essentially, the franchiser offers a known name and pattern of operation, expert guidance, and the merchandise or supplies that the franchisee will require to conduct his business. The franchisee makes a substantial investment, pays the parent company a percentage of sales, usually obligates himself to buy from the franchiser, and invests his time and energies in the project. The store presents itself to the public as if it were one of a chain, such as the Mode O'Day apparel stores, some units of the House of Nine (specialists in small sizes in apparel), and the Rive Gauche franchised stores of Yves St. Laurent. Actually, the person whose position corresponds to that of the chain store manager is the owner. Insofar as the customer is concerned, she is dealing with a warmly interested local owner; insofar as the market is concerned, it is dealing with a large buyer serving many stores; and insofar as financing and costs of operation are concerned, the burden is shared by the central organization and the various local units. Success depends upon two intangibles: the ability of the franchiser to select and guide suitable franchisees, and the ability of the franchisee to respond creatively to the guidance of the franchiser. There have been failures and successes in the field.

Boutiques and Small Shops

Paralleling the growth of giant retailing combines has been the emergence of multitudes of small boutique operations, functioning as independently owned shops or as departments in large stores.

The term *boutique* is the French word for shop. As used in France, it has long been associated with the little, intimate departments within the Paris couture houses that sold perfumes, accessories, and gifts that were selected or designed by the couturier and that carried the label of the house. In the United States, however, and in London, when the boutique boom started in the early 1960s, it was used to designate a small shop that carries a collection of highly individualized and specialized merchandise presented in a nontraditional manner. The customer segment that an individual boutique attempts to attract is narrow but well defined. Some boutiques cater to the *avant-garde* young; others cater to the old. Some feature merchandise tagged at astronomical prices; others carry merchandise that sells for pennies. Some deal in couture clothes, others in space-age fashions; still others specialize in a wide variety of offbeat accessories. In all boutiques, merchandise categories are freely mixed—with blouses, skirts, scarves, belts, ash trays, and household items on display, side by side.

The independently owned fashion boutiques of the type that emerged and proliferated in the 1960s are small shops, usually established by a creative fashion enthusiast eager to sell merchandise that satisfies her own taste to people who share that taste. Some boutiques of this kind design all or part of their merchandise; others have workrooms for custom or semi-custom production; others simply buy and sell. Boutiques usually offer only a few pieces of each design that they carry. Often the merchandise is too new and different, too limited in appeal, for a large store or department to stock it; only a boutique can handle it successfully. Decor and fixturing in the boutique are generally improvised and uninhibited. Garments are likely to be hung from walls or draped on furniture; accessories may be placed in apparently careless confusion on tables instead of in showcases or on a rack.

DESIGNER BOUTIQUES

PIERRE CARDIN HIMSELF IS COMING TO BONWIT'S FROM PARIS! Incroyable! The fabulous Pierre Cardin himself, as well as his famed associate Andre Oliver and Mme. Herve Alphand, directrice of the house of Cardin, are coming to Bonwit's in person to celebrate the opening of the new Cardin Boutique on our Designer Sixth Floor! Meet them and see the entire new Cardin collection at a formal fashion show tomorrow, Tuesday, at 11:00 a.m. Informal modeling Tuesday till 4:00, Wednesday 12.00 to 4:00. Come revel in the Paris visionary's new coats, suits, sportswear, dresses and evening dresses, all of it sizzling with Cardin inspiration and housed in the fabulous module that is our new Sixth Floor Cardin Boutique! Collection from 40.00 to 575.00. It has, sans dire, The Bonwit Teller Touch! We honor the American Express Money Card. Fifth Ave. at 56th Street, N. Y. A selection in all stores (and soon in Beverly Hills)

Source: Advertisement by Bonwit Teller in *The New York Times*, September 25, 1972.

Often the tables, chairs, or other furnishings that have been pressed into service for display purposes are available for sale if a customer fancies them.

SMALL SHOPS IN LARGE STORES.   Independently owned boutiques made such an important place for themselves in fashion retailing in the mid-1960s that large stores began studying the problem of how to create special boutique nooks for the fashion customers to whom they obviously appealed. Many stores established a series of small, highly specialized shops featuring merchandise assortments keyed to a particular "total look" in apparel and accessories. In 1968, *Business Week* cited Bonwit Teller's experience as an indication of how boutiques within large stores were increasing in importance. Although Bonwit's had no boutiques before 1965, it was reported in 1968 to be doing 20 percent of its total volume through its little shops, with prospects for that percentage to increase.[32]

DESIGNER BOUTIQUES.   The boutique idea gained further impetus as designers in the European couture ventured into ready-to-wear and franchised carefully chosen stores in the United States to set up boutiques for their apparel and accessories. The combined attraction of a designer name and the "total look" type of merchandising proved great, indeed. Boutiques sprang up for the merchandise of Cardin, Givenchy, Courrèges, Adolfo, and Valentino; for the Rive Gauche collections of Yves St. Laurent; and for the fashions of American designers like Anne Klein, Luba, Donald Brooks, Bill Blass, Oscar de la Renta, and other greats. By 1970, the "name" boutique had become so important in fashion retailing that Saks Fifth Avenue, in its New York store, converted its fifth floor into a "Street of Shops" to present each designer's collection in an environment compatible with that designer's fashion thinking.

[32]"Boutiques Rack Up Big Sales," *Business Week*, October 12, 1968, p. 91.

Whether a boutique is individually owned or part of a large retail organization, it brings fun, individuality, and discovery to fashion shopping for the consumer. For the fashion producer, it provides an outlet for the original, the offbeat, and the experimental—the frosting on the cake of the really creative designer.

Suburban Operations

Before World War II, a few city department and specialty stores had opened branches in the surrounding suburbs for the convenience of the relatively limited number of customers, usually well-to-do, who lived in these outlying areas. These early branches were small stores, generally located within the confines of suburban communities. Following World War II, the suburban operations of big city stores proliferated mightily, in response to the vast migration of well-to-do and young city families.

SHOPPING CENTERS.   A major retail phenomenon growing out of the postwar migration to suburbia was the development and proliferation of shopping centers—groups of stores located where there is easy access and ample parking for the suburban shopper. These centers were usually (and still are) developed by real estate interests and, occasionally, by very large retailers. They have their own management, promotional activities, and merchants' associations to weld their stores into a cohesive group.

Developers of early centers usually sought out one branch unit of a major downtown store and one unit of a well-known chain to act as "anchor" stores or principal drawing cards. Around the key retailers were located a variety of independently owned small shops, each of which specialized in different categories of merchandise. The early centers were generally located on the outskirts of suburban communities that were populous enough to support them. Each center attempted to assemble stores and services geared to the carefully defined needs of its particular community.

As the suburbs grew, so did the shopping centers. They have become more regional than local, however, and their tenants have expanded in number, size, and variety. The early centers each contained only one major downtown store branch; today they each contain branch units of several competitive downtown stores. Where formerly discount stores were barred from shopping centers, they now stand side by side with prestigious department and specialty stores. New multi-leveled centers with covered malls, serviced by multi-storied parking facilities, are now the rule instead of the exception. Children's playgrounds, restaurants, and movie theatres are being included, as are medical and banking facilities.

The importance of shopping centers today is evidenced by the fact that by 1971 they reportedly accounted for more than one-third of all retail store sales in this country.[33]

LARGER SUBURBAN STORES.   Most downtown store branches and chain units in the suburbs are in shopping centers, and as shopping centers have grown in size

[33]U. S. Department of Commerce, *U. S. Industrial Outlook 1972.*

Examples of Branches Outproducing Parent Store, 1971

STORE	PARENT STORE EST. VOLUME (add 000)	BRANCHES EST. VOLUME (add 000)	BRANCH STORE APPROX. % OF TOTAL VOLUME
Bon Marche, Seattle	$30,000	$ 80,000	73
Broadway, Los Angeles	11,000	267,000	96
Carson-Pirie-Scott, Chicago	65,400	117,600	65
Davison's, Atlanta	23,000	31,000	57
Gimbels, Phila.	31,500	91,500	75
Sanger-Harris, Dallas	25,900	55,100	68
Stix, Baer & Fuller, St. Louis	36,000	63,000	63

Source: *Stores* magazine, August 1972.

and breadth, so have the suburban store operations of urban retailers. Many major department and specialty stores today do more than half of their total store volume through their branches, and they continue to open more of these branch stores. The trend is for each new branch of a downtown store to be larger and more autonomous than its predecessors and in shopping centers that are more distant from its parent. To cite a few examples, Lord & Taylor of New York has branches in Massachusetts, Maryland, Connecticut, and New Jersey; I. Magnin of California has opened a branch in Chicago, Ill., and is planning new branches in other states; Neiman–Marcus of Texas now has a branch in Florida.

To keep fashion buyers who are located at the main store in intimate touch with individual demand at the branches, electronically processed data are usually required to provide prompt and detailed information on stocks and sales at each location. Branch personnel are also trained to be alert to indications of customer demand that their buyer cannot observe personally and to report these to the buyer promptly, along with any inadequacies in the stocks. When a main store buyer handles 5 , 10, or more branches, as is often the case with large stores, opportunities for personal contact with the stock or the customers are limited, indeed.

Variety, mail order, discount, and other chains have also moved out to meet the suburban customer at least halfway by opening units conveniently close to her home; they, too, are likely to use electronic methods to keep their central buying and merchandising operations apprised of what is selling and what is needed at each location. Many of the suburban units of chains (including mail-order chains) are larger, better laid out, and better equipped for the display and sale of fashion merchandise than the central city units of the same companies. They are newer, of course, and thoroughly modern in design and decor. They also reflect the efforts of the chains to upgrade their fashion image, as explained earlier in this section.

SUBURBAN FASHION CENTERS. Shopping center developers and stores with suburban branches have found, however, that women who are intent upon major fashion purchases or are in quest of high-priced fashion goods generally will bypass a conveniently located center and travel substantial distances, even into a traffic-choked city, in order to select from the assortments of well-stocked, prestigious stores or departments. In response to this behavior, a new type of center has developed: the fashion center. This is made up of large branches of city department and specialty stores with reputations for fashion leadership, possibly supplemented by local shops of the same nature. Typical is the fashion center near Ridgewood, N. J., only a few miles from the huge regional shopping center of conventional type at Paramus. The usual suburban family can buy virtually all its needs at Paramus, but the high-fashion consumer or the middle-income woman who is in quest of something special shops at Ridgewood.

Mass Fashion Merchandisers

When the giant chains of Sears Roebuck, Montgomery Ward, and J.C. Penney first entered the field of fashion distribution in earnest, they did so as mass outlets for low-priced, fairly staple clothing. Their *raison d'être* was price, and the impact of their fashion operations on the leaders of the industry was negligible. They catered to customers who either could not afford the merchandise of the fashionable department and specialty stores or were extremely conscious of price and value. Beginning in the mid-1960s, mass merchandising chains came of age as a major factor in the fashion business. Rising incomes, accompanied by a greater fashion awareness on the part of the mass customer audience to which they catered, encouraged the giant chains to put greater emphasis on higher price-lines, better quality goods, and more fashionable merchandise than they had featured up to that time.

Since large chains stock only their own private brands, which they buy in enormous quantities, they contract for merchandise that will be exclusive with them and on which they can specify colors, patterns, styles, fabrics and, occasionally,

Selected Chain Store Sales, 1972

CHAIN	APPROXIMATE SALES (add 000)	TYPE OF CHAIN
Gamble's	$ 1,350,000	General merchandise chain
W. T. Grant	1,950,000	General merchandise chain
Lane Bryant	277,500	Apparel chain
Lerner Stores	434,861	Apparel chain
McCrory Corp.	1,227,000	Variety chain
Mercantile Stores	458,328	Apparel chain
Montgomery Ward	2,640,122	Mail order chain
J. C. Penney Co.	5,530,000	General merchandise chain
Sears Roebuck & Co.	10,991,001	Mail order chain
F. W. Woolworth & Co.	3,148,108	Variety chain

Source: Annual company reports.

even the fibers. Large chains must, of necessity, place their orders well in advance of the department and specialty stores—often before these stores begin to shop the new season's collections.

THE "BIG 3."   Although relatively few in number, as compared to the multitude of department and specialty stores, chains control a large percentage of the apparel market. A textile marketing survey of their standing in various merchandise categories in 1969[34] revealed that the "Big 3" alone—Sears Roebuck, J.C. Penney, and Montgomery Ward—were then doing 18 percent of all women's sportswear business and almost 25 percent of all children's wear business. This is not surprising when we consider that the combined sales volume of Sears, Ward's, and Penney's is over $16 billion, which is more than double that of the eight biggest department and specialty store groups combined.[35] Intimate apparel producers credit Sears with having real fashion impact; hosiery firms are of the opinion that Sears leads in the early picking up and confirming of fashion trends.[36]

The buying power of the "Big 3" is so great that they have, in some ways, more influence on the industry than anyone else. The fiber companies, the mills, and the apparel manufacturers—and the chains deal with the best of them—cannot help but be influenced by the early fashion thinking and selections of these mass purveyors of fashion.

As one trade observer summed it up: "Chains—once just the tail of the fashion animal—are now showing every sign of doing a major part of the fashion wagging, too."[37]

RETAILING CHANGES WITH CUSTOMERS

The retailer's function in the fashion business is to serve the customer. As this section has indicated, this requires him to change as his customer's needs and interests change. Each generation, even each decade, sees changes, not only in the fashion merchandise that women buy but also in the manner in which significant numbers of them prefer to select and buy that merchandise. Customers, like fashion itself, are anything but static. Since the retailer's success depends on his ability to understand and serve the consumer, he changes as his customers change—or he falls by the wayside. The changes required of him are not merely in his fashion merchandising philosophy but also in the services he offers to his customers. For example, the buy-now-pay-later attitude that manifests itself in the purchase of homes, major appliances, and vacations on the installment plan has its fashion retailing echoes in the revolving credit plans that almost every department and specialty store encourages and in the credit plans that are offered by chains whose names were long synonymous with cash-and-carry selling. The willingness of

[34]Sam Feinberg, "From Where I Sit," *Women's Wear Daily,* January 10, 1971.
[35]"Annual Report on the 500 Largest American Corporations," *Fortune* magazine, May, 1973.
[36]Sam Feinberg, *op.cit.*
[37]"Fashion Is," *Clothes* magazine, January 15, 1970, p. 12.

the busy shopper to serve herself is reflected in the presence of self-selection fixtures and self-service devices in fashion stores up and down the price scale. The desire of house-bound and office-bound customers to shop by mail and telephone for at least part of their needs has led large city department and specialty stores to introduce improved telephone order techniques and to encourage mail orders by putting coupons in their newspaper advertising, enclosing special offers in their monthly statements, and issuing occasional catalogs. The eagerness of young adults and near-adults to express themselves in fashion has led to the development of special stores and shops within large stores for teen-agers, pre-teens, and young adults with a passion for clothes made of leather, denim, or whatever the current idea may be. Night openings, Sunday openings in some areas, discount stores and departments, and boutiques featuring designer names all came about in response to changes in customer demand.

The list of changes goes on and on. And there will always be more. Just as fashion changes to reflect the consumer's changing way of life, so does the retailer change his way of doing business to conform to his customer's changing preferences in the way she wants to buy.

READINGS

The readings in this section provide the student with an insight into the wide variety of operations, philosophies, and sizes that characterize fashion retailers. There is no single pattern.

Each of the first six articles describes the development of an individual store or type of store, showing how growth has resulted from the ability to serve a particular fashion customer. In each of the next four articles, the head of a major fashion retailing organization explains his store's philosophy of fashion merchandising.

LORD & TAYLOR: SERENDIPITY ON FIFTH AVENUE

Faye Hammel

If there is anything approaching a precise formula for creativity, Lord & Taylor, a store known throughout the world for an extraordinarily imaginative approach to merchandising, has come close to the heart of that subtle mathematics. "It's quite simple," a store executive explained. "You take people with flair, give them perfect freedom, and the result has to be creativity."

The creative streak started early at Lord & Taylor, even as far back as 1826, when Samuel Lord, a young Englishman newly migrated here, and his cousin-in-law, Mr. George Washington Taylor, refused to employ the everywhere-accepted "puller-in"—the not-so-gentle young men who helped customers make up their minds about purchases—in their Catherine Street dry-goods store. The merchandise had to stand on its own merits there, and in all the later stores—the first, on Grand and Chrystie Streets, described as one of the "architectural wonders" of Manhattan. In 1902 came a pioneering move to Fifth Avenue and the 20s ("Department Store Invades Fifth Avenue," a local paper headlined), and still later, in 1914, to the present 39th Street building (on a site where one of the battles of the American Revolution was fought) which set a standard for modern department store architecture that is still followed today.

Today at Lord & Taylor the creative spirit is expressed in a pioneering attitude that might best be characterized as the ability to anticipate a need and be the first to fill it. A current example is the Private Lives boutique, which was showing glamorous attire for at-home wear when most women thought long dresses were strictly for formal balls. The store pioneered, too, with non-crushable knits when the big travel boom was just a whisper. Back in the 30's it was the first to recognize the need for

a College Shop. Other firsts: a separate junior department (the famed Young New Yorker Shops), teen and pre-teen shops, and the first step—in the 5'4" shop—in acknowledging the fashion needs and problems of the petite woman.

Similarly, and all-importantly, the store was the first, back in the 30's, to give the American designer a place in the sun. "The door has always been open here and still is open for young creative talent," says Mr. Melvin Dawley, Lord & Taylor's president.* More than one budding design genius has walked into the store with a few sketches under his arm and found himself, in a short time, teamed with a manufacturer and being hailed and promoted by Lord & Taylor. Rose Marie Reid was a housewife in Canada, Bonnie Cashin a designer for the movies and Rudi Gernreich a dancer in Hollywood when they first came knocking at the Fifth Avenue door. A roster of the store's discoveries reads like an honor roll of American design: Ellen Brooke, Sally Victor, Anne Fogarty, Pauline Trigère, Sylvia Pedlar, Donald Brooks, Tina Leser, Claire McCardle, and Lilly Pulitzer—to name just a few. And all the discoveries express the Lord & Taylor feeling about clothes—in the words of one executive, "clothes that reflect the excitement of modern living and yet are so fundamentally right that they endure."

Nor has Lord & Taylor fallen behind in discovering European talent, either. It scored one of the great coups in recent fashion history by being the first to present Marchese Emilio Pucci, back in 1947, and it still has the largest collection of Puccis in town. Lydia de Roma, Dynasty of Hong Kong, and Ferragamo were other European "firsts." And the store-wide exposition of Ireland's taste and elegance, "The Pride of Ireland" in 1963, not only

SOURCE: *Cue* Magazine, July 17, 1965. Reprint permission granted.

*Mr. Dawley, then president, has retired.

helped push Ireland into the forefront of European fashion, but promoted a bevy of designers whose creations still abound in the store. Consider, for example, the handsome creations of Donald Davies and Kay Peterson in the Country Clothes Shop, coats and suits by Clodagh and Jack Clarke in the sportswear collection, Sybil Connolly's magnificent fantasies in the Designer's Salon, and even a bevy of cheery Irish clothes for children!

The hottest news from Europe, at the moment, according to President Dawley: Givenchy's designed and made-in-Paris collections just for Lord & Taylor, the brilliantly delicate leather work of Mitzou of Madrid, and the stunning Pertegaz couture collection made by the designer in his own workrooms in Barcelona. Prophesies Dawley: "Pertegaz is so talented that he may one day replace even Balenciaga as his country's leader in design."

The Lord & Taylor creative approach, however, is far from being limited to the world of women's fashion. Men have long admired the store's authentic sports clothes (the first floor Men's Shop is currently expanding); young marrieds scoop up the "Taste-Setters" collection of furniture, lamps and decorative fabrics; and everyone, from brides to dowagers, adores gifts from the Household Bazaar. Rug aficionados consider the Lord & Taylor collection—with its fabulous exclusives from Spain, Portugal, Morocco, Greece, Ireland and Sweden—outstanding. (Some Aubusson rugs, true beauties, are handstitched and completely created for the store in Bengal, India). And the brand-new Discovery Shop on the first floor brims with bibelots from every part of the store. You may find anything from an antique horse from India at $395 to a six-foot-high collapsible Japanese feather duster at $5, from elegant French crystal chandeliers and gorgeous Mexican pillows to a fat pink ceramic pig for your favorite youngster.

The Now and Then Shop, surely one of the most unique and amusing antique collections in the world, is one of the best examples of the Lord & Taylor creative genius in full flower. The import furniture buyer spends at least five months of the year traveling around the world, bringing back engaging surprises. There is no telling where and to what measures his "buying instinct" will lead him. In India, for example, he has no qualms about whisking antique, hammered and etched grain jars (which may later be converted into lamps) literally off a donkey's back—trading them for bright new ones cheerfully accepted by the drivers. Once, finding refuge in a chicken coop during a drenching rain storm in the French provinces, he discovered that the "drop board," piled with three inches of chicken droppings, was actually a handsome, early-19th-century table. The farmer refused to sell, until offered a shiny new table instead. The droppings had preserved the wood in its original condition, and one of Lord & Taylor's assiduous collectors was the happy beneficiary. Throughout the shop, whose thesis is that old and new things can work beautifully together in a room, you'll find both original antiques and reproductions in furniture and decorative accessories. All are one-of-a-kind, with a choice ranging from circular stairways from Italy to art nouveau pieces so homely they're attractive, from old cradles from Spain to collector's cabinets filled with shells or butterflies or even birds' eggs! (Buyer take all.) Be sure to see, too, the Far Eastern section of the shop, which has one of the most important collections of Oriental furnishings available for purchase. Should you happen to need a 19th-century Siamese red and gold throne (just $850) you'll find it here, as well as Japanese wall decor, screens, and copper-lined hibachis and braziers, planters, tables, and stunning mythological carvings from India.

The Lord & Taylor penchant for creativity finds an outlet beyond 39th Street as well. Firmly committed to the cultural and civic welfare of the city, the store is currently at work on a project to expand Gracie Mansion. Past beneficiaries have included the Museum of Modern Art, Carnegie Hall, the Municipal Art Society, and the Costume Institute of the Metropolitan Museum of Art, which the store considers an indispensable resource for the design and fashion world. "When the top French designers come to New York, they never miss a visit there," comments Dawley.

As for the future, Lord & Taylor is zooming ahead in a policy of expansion. There are already nine suburban stores, and four more—in Falls Church, Va., Ridgewood, N.J., Boston, and Stamford—are on the agenda within the next three years. Each is being planned not as a "branch store" but as a complete Lord & Taylor in itself. "In ten to fifteen years," Dawley predicts, "there may be as many as twenty Lord & Taylors." All of which may prove very confusing to people like the lady we know who always tells friends on shopping trips to "meet me at the store." Asked to be more specific, she replies: "Lord & Taylor, of course—*is there any other store?*"

BLOOMINGDALE'S: "FIRST THE IDEA, THEN THE MERCHANDISE"

Susan Margetts

Plum-and-walnut-with-brandy jam, an emerald and diamond ring, Limoges china bearing the inscription, "Handpainted in France especially for Bloomingdale's," and a shocking-pink knit dress priced at $26—all are part of a New York City happening called Bloomingdale's. Now a quality store catering to the whims of Manhattan's swinging East Side, the 95-year-old Federated division is a prime example of the city store that has radically altered its image to meet changing consumer demands.

The metamorphosis began at the end of World War II. Until then Bloomingdale's main business was supplying its surrounding tenement dwellers with low-priced, low-end merchandise. "But after the war," explains President Lawrence Lachman, "we realized the area would change. We saw it as a potential business and residential area."

Bloomingdale's set out to become a part of that change. The famous old Third Avenue El came down, and the store's quality went up. "The three ingredients we wanted," says Chairman Harold Krensky, "were quality, fashion and excitement. We wanted the high-income and career-girl markets."

Inevitably, the change was slow because it in-

volved every aspect of the store: merchandise, advertising, display and service. "First we had to convince the people of the idea," Lachman explains, "and then we had to translate that into merchandise."

Merchandise was upgraded in stages, department by department. When one department reached an acceptably higher level, attention was turned to the next. "The fun and excitement of this entire change," confesses Krensky, "is seeing each department reach the next plateau."

Once the quality of the merchandise had been upgraded, the next problem was to display it properly. Soon a maze of small shops-within-a-shop and special boutiques spread from one end of the store to the other, creating an atmosphere of exclusive specialty shops rather than the vast-sea-of-merchandise effect.

The toughest turnabout was in the basement. "It was a long, long haul," says Krensky. Run under separate management, the basement had long been famous for its next-to-nothing specials and, like other basements of its kind, was boycotted by suppliers of high-end goods. It was not until a year ago that the basement's management was integrated, and today every buyer does the purchasing for all the floors in her department, including the basement.

In any consumer-oriented business, a direct corollary to better-quality merchandise is better service. At Bloomingdale's the switch to the customer-is-always-right approach seems finally to have taken hold. Yet Lachman admits that the biggest headache in managing the staff of 25,000 is the "people problem—just getting them to be nice." In any case, a visitor waiting in the store's executive offices is more likely today than in the past to hear a soothing voice assure a customer that "Bloomingdale's was completely at fault."

In advertising, too, there has been a radical switch away from yesterday's incessant hard sell. Although there are now four suburban branches (Hackensack, New Rochelle, Stamford and the recently opened Short Hills), advertising for all the stores reflects what Krensky calls the "1967 New Yorky" image.

So far, at least, Bloomingdale's formula for change has proved successful in turning an old-line retailer of mass-produced cheap merchandise into a high-quality emporium catering to the latest trends in taste and fashion. While Federated does not give out division sales, an industry observer reports that sales at the New York store alone hit $97 million last year. How does Bloomingdale's itself assess its progress? Says Krensky: "We're not anywhere near where we would like to be, but we're getting there."

WE'D LIKE TO TELL YOU ABOUT LANE BRYANT

The story of Lane Bryant began in 1904, when an elegant woman approached the tiny apartment of a young seamstress, an immigrant from Lithuania, widowed shortly after the birth of her son.

The lady had often used Mrs. Bryant's services as a seamstress since the young widow began her work four years previously, but this time she was to make an unheard of request. Could Mrs. Lane Bryant design a dress for her to wear during pregnancy? The lady actually wanted to be *seen* while expecting!

Shocking as the first Lane Bryant creation was, more shocks were to follow. Though in that day it wasn't easy, even in gay, sophisticated New York, to overcome society's spinsterish attitude toward pregnancy, the need was great, and Mrs. Bryant's efforts wholehearted. By 1909, the famous Lane Bryant Number 5 maternity gown—unique in its elasticized waist and elegant style . . . suitable to the mother and the woman simultaneously—had itself given birth to many other maternity gowns. Shortly thereafter Mrs. Bryant married an engineer

named Albert Malsin, and soon began wearing her own creations.

MATERNITY MISERIES LIGHTENED

Though expectant mothers eagerly sought out Mrs. Bryant's designs, manufacturers were reluctant to take orders for her clothes, and had to be subsidized to make them in quantity. But in quantity they were needed, for in 1911, a large part of maternity miseries were dispelled forever. The *New York Herald* was induced to accept a Lane Bryant advertisement for maternity dresses. It read:

"It is no longer the fashion nor the practice for expectant mothers to stay in seclusion. Doctors, nurses and psychologists agree that at this time a woman should think and live as normally as possible. To do this, she must go about among other people, she must look like other people.

"Lane Bryant has originated maternity apparel in which the expectant mother may feel as other women feel because she looks as other women look."

SOURCE: Courtesy of Lane Bryant, Inc. Company booklet reprinted by permission.

The next day, the entire stock of street wear maternity dresses was sold by closing time. In 1917, Lane Bryant sales passed one million dollars.

Jumping ahead a bit, probably the greatest tribute to Lane Bryant's identification with the expectant mother came in a letter received some 15 years ago. It was addressed simply: "Maternity dress, size 32, Amerika." From a young woman in Poland, it was delivered promptly to the Fifth Avenue store.

A DREAM TAKES SHAPE

The story could have ended happily with a well-developed maternity line, but for Albert Malsin's dream of other specialties. One day, a chance letter gave direction to his thoughts, "Won't some ingenious man please take pity on us stout women?" the letter pleaded. And so, as a result of Mr. Malsin's mathematical training and his wife's creative designs, began another area of specialization unique in the retail industry—clothes for the fuller-figured woman.

Albert Malsin made a study of female figures, obtaining measurements of more than 200,000 women from a large insurance agency. He discovered that nearly 40 percent of them were larger than the "perfect 36," idealized by the era's artists and dressmakers. Lane Bryant, employing principles from such wildly divergent areas as Gothic architecture and the camouflage innovations of World War I, created garments to give the illusion of slenderness to the fuller feminine figure, while maintaining the elegance and grace of the latest fashions—curvacious camouflage.

LANE BRYANT EXPANDS

Through the years, Lane Bryant has grown and expanded. Today, the company houses a wide range of specialties. These include larger sizes as well as complete shops for tall women, for mothers-to-be and for chubby girls. Most recently, a new specialty—clothes for tall and large men—was added under the name of Lewis Bryant. Incorporated in 1916, Lane Bryant includes, in addition to its continuously growing mail order operation and retail stores, three other divisions: The Coward Shoe, the Newman-Benton division, and Town & Country Department stores.

Although Mrs. Lane Bryant died in 1951, she lived to see her firm develop into a nationally known company. Her son, Raphael, now guides the organization in the pioneering tradition formulated by his mother.

LERNER SHOPS—MORE THAN JUST WINDOW CHANGING

There probably is no greater testimonial to the power of advertising than the lofty budgets allotted by retailers to let their customers know that they need not be plagued by midriff bulge, that pants suits in fiber X will put the dry cleaners out of business, or that spectacular values will be available in their coat departments for one week only.

SOURCE: *Clothes* Magazine, March 1, 1971. Reprint permission granted.

Yes, indeed, the necessity to advertise in a highly competitive retail arena is as inevitable a fact of life as death and taxes are invariably visited upon the individual. And what began in the early twentieth century as a highly entertaining form of communication to consumers who were then unaccustomed to being assailed by the pictorial hard sell has developed into a highly sophisticated business. Or as McLuhan claims, no team of sociologists or anthropologists has quite so efficiently dissected the habits and desires of the public, hidden or otherwise, as those great "frogmen-of-the-mind"—the denizens of Madison Avenue.

Because of the constant cajolment through newspapers, radio and TV for the public to buy . . . buy . . . buy, it is rarely noticed that there are some retailers who eschew paying homage to either the printed or spoken word as a sales stimulator.

These are mostly women's (sometimes children's) wear stores that have made their mark in dollars and share of market without resorting to what is known as the common means of communication. Sometimes they are known as the Eighth Avenue group, but their stores are not limited to New York. They can be found everywhere— throughout the South, Midwest and along the West Coast. They may vary in size and shape but they all have one thing in common. They deliver, on a specialty store level, volume fashion to a volume audience, and despite the fact that they never promote their names to their trade, they are as easily recognized as any other famous specialty or department store retailer.

Among these is a company of 401 stores extending from coast to coast that has been in business 53 years and is well known to the average customer for volume fashion at a price—Lerner's.

There was no great intrigue or mischievous intent to set the Lerner wheels in motion by running counter to traditional retail policy concerning advertising. For Lerner's, it was merely more expedient at the inception of the business to refrain from this promotional push. In essence, it was ambition rather than audacity which told the founders of the chain that they had but one alternative. For when the objective of a young organization is no less lofty than to start with one unit and proceed to blanket the entire country with stores as quickly as possible, obviously the bulk of the available capital and profits must be put into new leases, store construction, fixtures and inventory to fill the proliferating shelves.

Consequently, advertising became an "also ran" in the list of priorities. More sales were produced by adding stores and square footage than by any attempt to increase business through advertising. It was as simple as that. And today, generally, it is

still company policy to refrain from advertising. An exception has been Lerner's participation in the events and promotions initiated by the shopping centers and malls in which they reside.

Actually, the advertising bug has taken a bite out of the Lerner philosophy from time to time. They did try some advertising in the past decade, but quickly dropped it once again. Lerner's plans for new stores still absorb a great deal of capital and energy. Besides, competing in the ad game today requires a much larger dollar outlay than it did years ago. Now there are 10-page supplements, catalogs, mailers, radio, TV, on ad infinitum.

And Lerner's doesn't do things half way. Either you advertise or you don't. Right now, and including management's assessment of future policy, Lerner's can live nicely without it.

There are many reasons why the company has been able to avoid the media and still grow at such a phenomenal rate. One of these is Lerner's insistence that every store occupy a 100 percent location. There has never been any scrimping on expensive property, even in the early stages of its growth. Each store was planned in a high traffic area surrounded by giant retailers—(who did, of course, advertise to build traffic and let their customers know just which fashions were *au courant* for that particular season). Lerner's merely put the items in its windows.

When a competitor chose to advertise let's say a junior coat at $55, it would not be unusual for the customer to proceed, ad in hand, to that store. But, en route, she would notice that Lerner's had the exact same style in the window for $35. This is known as a 100 percent location.

Furthermore, what Lerner's has perfected in lieu of advertising is a sort of powerful but "silent sales force"—a citizenry of mannequins (dummies, if you prefer), that number more than the population of many small towns. More than 26,000 strong, these mannequins, which are constantly changing their finery, from the Lerner windows project the image, attract the passing crowd and sell the goods. To the *cognoscenti* in the trade who are aware of the term, Lerner's is what is known as a "window changer store"—a store that lets its windows do the job of telling the customer just what the company stands for and exactly what she's going to find there in terms of style, price and color. And judging by the number of mannequins and the amount of merchandise displayed in the windows, a "window changer" operation is most definitely not in the business of selling carpets.

But the management team at Lerner's doesn't like to dwell solely upon windows and display. They consider these to be very important factors in their operation, but only one of the merchandising supports which they have developed along with the merchandising expertise itself that has enabled them to grow from one unit to a chain 401 strong. Lerner's management asserts that no amount of mannequins can supersede the strength of the people running a constantly growing organization that's already the largest chain of women's and children's apparel stores in terms of both volume and the number of units. And rightly so.

The Johnny Appleseed approach to new stores can be attributed to its founders—three Lerner brothers, Sam, Michael and Joseph, who were on the other side of the fence, manufacturing ladies' blouses, and Harold Lane, Sr., who was the blouse buyer for Filene's basement in Boston. To further the Lerner brothers' desire to expand into the retail blouse business, they sought the aid of the blouse "pro" at Filene's. In effect, since the Lerner brothers retained their manufacturing business for several years, the organization set a precedent early in the game by being one of the originators of dual distribution. The year was 1918.

But pace-setting policies were far from a rarity in the fledgling organization. Their objective from the outset was to open stores in most large cities throughout the country, and no natural boundaries were considered. Ocean to ocean was their goal.

Sam Lerner became the resident expert in real estate, and Lerner's moved fast. In 1918 their first store was opened in New York City. It was a small shop, but only a year later there were 18 others. All were less than 2,000 square feet with about a 15-foot front and an approximate 60-foot depth. But the important thing was that the Lerner logo was becoming a familiar one in New York City.

In 1919 five additional stores were opened, marking Lerner's first move across state lines and into the New England area with stores in Connecticut and Massachusetts.

According to Harold Lane, Sr., now chairman of the board of Lerner Shops, the big blouse numbers at the time were extremely dressy, but sheer. The popular fabrics of the day were crepe de chine and georgette, and due to their gossamer nature, the way was paved for the ascendency of the camisole. What the ladies needed was something attractive between their filmy blouses and their corsets, and the need precipitated Lerner's first expansion of merchandise categories with the entry of lingerie and underwear.

In the early '20s skirts were added along with a move south into Richmond, Baltimore and Washington. And by the late '20s geographic expansion extended as far west as Chicago and south into Florida.

At the same time, the Lerner team was getting its feet wet in the product lines that are now a major portion of their sales—dresses, coats, and sportswear (although sportswear then referred primarily to sport dresses). As these categories grew, so did the size of the new stores in order to house these expanding categories. Further, the Lerner brothers and Harold Lane discovered that major refixturing was needed in the earlier stores since they were constructed to house only short, "half-garments" such as the original mainstays of the business —blouses and camisoles—rather than full length coats and dresses.

In 1930 the owners realized their ambition to reach the West Coast and opened in Los Angeles. But the California achievement was at the top of the Depression decade. How did Lerner Shops fare? Fortunately, they had already established themselves in the community as specialists in fashion apparel at budget prices, and even the Depression didn't stop their rate of expansion, for during the 1930s "budget" became even more important to the upper-middle and many in the higher income brackets.

But Harold Lane, Sr. doesn't minimize the effects of the Depression. The heyday of the $10.75 dress that went for $14.99 retail was over, and $4.75 units selling for $6.99 came into demand. Down the line, by classification, it took more units to maintain the volume.

But Lerner Shops not only weathered those bad economy years, they grew. By the early 1940s they had achieved a network of more than 160 stores in prime downtown locations.

The new stores were larger, equaling 10,000 to 12,000 square feet, which, incidentally, is the same size as the stores being opened today. By 1945 a near-complete evolution of today's Lerner Shops had been accomplished. Hosiery, accessories, millinery, and children's wear were added for a greater merchandise mix and annual sales volume reached a new high that year with a total of $75 million. The basic Lerner concept of specializing in the latest fashion styles at popular prices, the detailed attention given to windows and display, and a sound executive and buying staff were already incorporated in the 160-store framework.

But in retrospect, as strong as the chain was in 1945, it was merely on the launching pad about to be hurtled into a more sophisticated era of development.

In contrast to the 1955 achievements, Lerner's now has 401 stores in operation with more on the drawing board. And by 1969, sales had reached better than $329 million for a 16.3 percent increase over the 1968 total. Of this increase 13 percent was due to the performance of existing stores even though the chain opened 13 units during the 1969 fiscal period. Earnings for 1969 increased by an even more impressive percentage of 37 percent, reaching $13.8 million. Further, this earnings figure represents the largest percentage of net profit for that year within the McCrory Corporation which acquired 60.6 percent of the Lerner stock in 1961.

Sales for 1970 were another record breaker at $354 million for a 7.7 percent increase over 1969.

Controlling 401 stores makes the 160-store bonanza of 1945 seem almost bucolic by comparison. Yes, the scope of the chain has changed radically, but then, so has the entire retail picture. In 1945 there were no discounters purveying soft goods, the mail-order chains had yet to direct their thrust into fashion apparel, and the country was just on the threshold of the great urban exodus that was to change the complexion of retail distribution in the decades to come. Thus, Lerner's competition was once merely the budget areas in department stores, primarily their basements, and the few other chains of their ilk that specialized in lower-priced apparel and a similar "up front" window policy.

Now competition is more extensive and intensive, and the fashion changes are more volatile than ever. Today it is incumbent upon Lerner's or any other retailer to strive to set itself apart from the competition.

One method that's working at Lerner's is its adherence to the original philosophy of constantly presenting the latest fashion styles geared to a discriminating 18-to 29-year-old customer and with a selection in these items that the lower-middle income bracket can afford. There is some merchandise designed for the older woman, but Lerner's feels that catering to the younger, fashion-conscious working girl or housewife provides the chain with more repeat traffic and a better turn. For that reason, approximately two-thirds of ready-to-wear and sportswear are now sold in junior sizes and in a closely-watched, tight price range.

Dresses and coats, which make up 28 percent of the volume, are sold in the $10 to $30 and $30 to $70 brackets respectively. Sportswear, representing another 28 percent of sales, ranges from $4 to $10 for sweaters and blouses and $6 to $12 for pants. Foundations and lingerie, another 15 percent of the business, are one of the few areas in which Lerner's uses brand name labels and these are in the budget price range. Hosiery and accessories create another 10 percent of the volume, with Lerner's own private label hosiery considered a strong factor in the entire hosiery market with their strength at the $1.59 price range.

Children's wear, which was the last addition to Lerner's merchandise categories, today represents a healthy 19 percent of total sales. Girls' wear, from toddler sizes through 14, represents 80 percent and boys' wear, from toddlers through size 16, provides the balance.

Why has children's wear become so important at Lerner's? First, the shop already had a captive audience among the young mothers. Second, a store that is so tuned to both fashion and price, and shows it, just can't miss in children's wear. At Lerner's, the very recent and more rapid acceleration of children's wear volume is attributed to the fact that fashion changes are becoming almost as frequent in children's apparel as they are in women's.

And the quicker the fashion changes in any category, the better they like it at Lerner's. For when the longevity of an item is decreased by style changes, the larger the audience grows for fashion at a lower price.

No, Lerner's does not claim to be the first in town with the latest paraphernalia that Seventh Avenue has a whim to dole out to retailers. But what this firm does insist upon is quick reaction to new fashion items and then stocking them in depth at precisely the time they can be sold in quantity. To accomplish this, Lerner's is constantly testing merchandise in several of its key "fashion sensitive" stores. When the item in question is purchased the store manager is immediately alerted, and upon receipt of the goods there is a quick change of one of the mannequins in a prime window spot. As a result, sometimes within as little as half an hour Lerner's knows whether or not there is volume potential there, and an order can be placed for the entire chain. At Lerner's, the windows can be quicker than the computers. (They have the computers too, but the sales information takes all of a week for the machine to complete.)

The tempo of Lerner's merchandise reactions is buttressed by the speed in which it is able to get the goods into the stores. As every retail chain would testify, when there are 401 pins on the map, the physical manipulation of merchandise and the fashion idiosyncrasies inherent with varying climatic conditions would, at best, be difficult to cope with. For these reasons Lerner's embarked upon an intricate system of decentralized management, a rather complex arrangement which belies the apparent simplicity of its basic merchandising philosophy. The objective was to establish a basis of operation similar in structure to the management core in New York which would make the organization more sensitive to the needs of the stores in each geographic sector and permit getting the goods to the stores in the shortest possible time.

The first of these regional offices was established in Los Angeles in 1941, followed by other set-ups in Denver, Chicago, Jacksonville, Atlanta and Pittsburgh. The home office in New York City is also the regional office servicing the stores in the New York and New England areas plus Puerto Rico and St. Croix in the Virgin Islands. It is, in fact, the office with control over the greatest number of stores with 120 units in its fold while other regional areas are made up of from 41 to 63 units.

The genealogy of the personnel in these offices begins with a senior vice-president of the company at the top of the chain of command. There is an operations manager and a senior merchandise manager who works with merchandise coordinators specializing in specific product categories and district managers whose responsibility it is to closely supervise the stores by visiting each one on a regularly scheduled basis. Display, credit, security, expense and inventory control personnel are also a part of the regional make-up. And each store within their jurisdiction has a store manager plus its own window trimmers.

Each regional office is an expansive 80,000 square feet with approximately 60,000 of that devoted to warehouse space and the remainder to offices. But this warehouse area must be multiplied seven times to obtain the true picture of the warehouse complex that serves the stores. And, in reality, while Lerner's refers to this area as a "warehouse," by the very definition of the word, the space really doesn't qualify. For nothing is stored there.

Occasionally merchandise arrives late in the day and the floor space provides an overnight billet. But this "warehouse" is really a receiving and shipping center which is so highly mechanized that merchandise is out and en route to the stores within 24 hours. Merchandise is shipped directly from the manufacturer to the regional "warehouses" where all shipments are given a not-so-standard receiving area treatment. Following a count of the merchandise, a merchandise coordinator is alerted to its arrival by means of a lightening-fast pneumatic tube system from the receiving area to the offices. Upon receipt of the information, the merchandise office checks each store's sales to see which ones are in most need of the merchandise and in what quantity. The item is then distributed according to the most up-to-date sales figures, not those which were available at the time the order was placed.

While the merchandise office is preparing for the dispersion of goods on paper, the receiving area continues processing the merchandise. Although Lerner's does not have laboratory testing equipment, 10 percent of each shipment is selected at random to undergo stringent quality inspection. By the time "warehouse" personnel have prepared the merchandise for packing, the rocket-like container has gone full circle in the tube system and instructions for individual store allocation are ready and waiting in the "warehouse" area.

There are no buyers in the regional offices. The 29 buyers for Lerner's are a part of the New York office with the exception of three in L.A. But this does not mean that the regional people are in any way excluded from the merchandising function.

Buying plans originate in the regional offices, and following their review in New York, the buyers place merchandise to coincide with the needs in each area.

Everybody gets into the act when it comes to the selection and allocation of merchandise because the management of Lerner's encourages it and stresses the importance of this function. According to Harold Lane, Jr., who was elected president of Lerner Shops in 1969, it's not at all unusual for him to get a call from one of the store managers who just "couldn't get any satisfaction from anyone else." And more often than not the reason for the call is that the store wants more merchandise or can't understand why they didn't have a particular new style in stock.

All voices are heard at Lerner's and the competitive spirit between stores and regional areas is keen. Aside from giving Lerner's the sensitivity to merchandise requirements, the regional breakdown and their "let's top Pittsburgh" or "we can do better than Atlanta" spirit is a factor in inducing bigger sales volume and better profitability in the chain. Furthermore, bonus incentives are prevalent throughout the chain, based upon company, regional or individual store performance, whichever is applicable to the employee.

Another key to Lerner's growth was their early realization that the population was going to the suburbs and that this shift presented an entirely new consumer market. Lerner's became one of the first to pioneer in suburban sites with its first unit outside of a downtown area opening in 1948. During the '50s Lerner's cut the tape for 84 suburban units, and in the past decade another 120 were put into operation. In 1970 another 15 stores were opened bringing the chain's total number of units to its present 401. Therefore, 220 or 56 percent of their units are located in shopping centers.

With the evolvement of the shopping centers into sophisticated enclosed "cool in summer and warm in winter" shopping malls, the facade of the shops has also been subjected to some alterations. Instead of a large glass-enclosed window area, the typical new Lerner's has switched to a more modern, totally open-front design. During business hours, the sliding glass doors are totally out of sight, and at closing, they are slid into a locked position. The mannequins are still there but they are reduced in number, and glassed-in show windows have been virtually eliminated.

It would seem that Lerner's would approach this new type of architecture with trepidation since it has always relied heavily upon window displays to bring in the traffic. But shopping centers are not downtown. They generate their own traffic of customers who are specifically there for shopping as opposed to the downtown throngs who might have any one of a dozen objectives in mind other than shopping. Besides, the open store front which eliminates any separation from the passer-by and the interior makes the customer feel that she's already inside the store.

Does this emphasis on new suburban stores mean that Lerner's is pessimistic about the future of its downtown units? Feelings run high here that as strong a force as suburban stores have been, there will also be a future trend toward urban renewal. Although the chain has dropped its leases on a few downtown stores upon their expiration, they are also remodeling or enlarging several urban units. But, at the moment, all new leases are being taken only for stores in suburban shopping centers . . . and for 100 percent locations within them—the same philosophy that was applied to downtown locations.

Lerner's goals for the future? Right now, management is talking only in terms of the next five-year period. And five is the magic number in more ways than one. By 1975, the chain expects to launch an additional 100 stores, bringing the total count to 501. And with each new store achieving in the neighborhood of $1 million, plus the sales growth of the existing stores, that brings expectations to $500 million total volume by 1975.

Diversification into other product lines or price ranges is not a part of the master plan. And why should it be? Lerner's has learned that by sticking to a specialty, its stores stand for something to a particular customer.

Many retailers with a fuller merchandise assortment and a wider price range than Lerner's are just at the portals of coming full circle to the Lerner philosophy and are embarking on a specialty store route of their own. For the efficacy of the Lerner philosophy is one that many other retailers are just beginning to grasp. That philosophy, of course, is that it's a pipedream to believe that volume of any significance can be achieved by attempting to be all things to all people with a merchandise latitude that is broad in price and fashion. But price alone is not the answer, and neither is a purist approach to fashion.

Within the framework of a limited amount of square footage (and everyone is really dealing with small square footage, using a department within a store as the frame of reference), the only way a retailer can provide a selection in depth is to concentrate his efforts in one direction for a specific customer audience.

This is the principle that has been successfully nurturing the growth of Lerner Shops over these past 53 years.

ALEXANDER'S—Underselling New York

Our scene opens at "Incredible Alexander's" flagship store on Manhattan's East 59th Street at noontime. Office girls who work in the neighborhood and residents of the tall apartment houses nearby crowd into the $20-million emporium to buy $1.49 bras on the main floor and $3,000 mink coats on the third. In the basement, sharp-eyed women elbow each other as they vie for the cotton print shifts that were put into stock that morning and then wait on long lines at central cashier stations to pay for their purchases.

The scene fades to the Alexander's buying office at 500 Seventh Avenue, where in tiny cubicles on the eighth floor, hard-nosed buyers examine the wares of anxious apparel salesmen during the morning hours. "What's your price?" says one of the 72 buyers to a vendor on the other side of a counter, hardly looking up as she consults her stock book. "It's $4 and I'll take take back what you have left," pleads the salesman as he empties his sample case. Meanwhile in the waiting room, another dozen hopefuls anxiously anticipate their precious ten-minute chance for an order or reorder.

Dissolve to a longshot of Paris in July, then pan to a showing of the new designs at the establishment of a top couturier, say Cardin, St. Laurent or Givenchy. In the audience sits an impassive Alex-

ander's merchandise manager or possibly someone from its top management, quietly recording numbers and searching out every design and fabric detail. . . .

EIGHT-STORE CHAIN

If a motion picture were ever made about the phenomenal rise of Alexander's Department Stores these would probably be a few of the scenes. For they tell, in brief, the story of an eight-store chain in the New York metropolitan area that has achieved an annual volume of some $245 million and a roster of 7,000 full and part-time employees through a marriage of low prices and high fashion, or as its executives prefer to say, style and value. In the most sophisticated city in the nation, Alexander's has made its mark largely by selling mass amounts of sophisticated clothing to a broad gamut of customers at "lower than retail" prices.

Perhaps the opening scene of this epic should be on Third Avenue in the Bronx 40 years ago in the first Alexander's store, a 1,500-square foot unit selling mostly closeouts and markdowns to price-conscious and style-conscious women. This original store is still in existence, although it has been enlarged 30 different times and now totals 160,000 square feet. The yearly dollar volume at this store has also increased about 100 times from $200,000 four decades ago to $20 million today. . . .

SOURCE: Condensed and reprinted from *Clothes* magazine, September 1, 1968. Permission granted.

THE UNDERSELLERS

In merchandise, Alexander's is one of a group of stores in the New York region known as "underselling" stores, a term that was in vogue long before the postwar emergence and proliferation of discount stores. Like such other underselling stores as Ohrbach's, S. Klein and J. W. Mays, Alexander's is soft goods oriented and grew on the principle of lower-than-average markups, higher-than-average turnover and the elimination of costly "frills" like charge accounts. . . .

The overwhelming bulk of the merchandise sold by Alexander's bears no manufacturer brand names, since right from the outset producers would not risk the loss of their traditional department store customers to sell anything, or at least the same styles to an outlet where suggested markups were not followed. However Alexander's often came into Seventh Avenue and other markets through the back door and a listing of the manufacturers whose unlabeled merchandise was and is sold in Alexander's stores would make a Who's Who of some of the most fervent advocates of nationally-branded goods.

STARTED WITH CLOSEOUTS

The initial Alexander's approach was to buy what a manufacturer had left at the end of a season: overcuttings, closeouts, samples and anything else remaining around the shop. These could be scavenged from a garment maker who needed cash badly at substantially below the wholesale cost and this savings was passed along to customers, after allowing for an adequate profit for Alexander's.

In the beginning when there was only one store, and even when the second big Bronx unit was opened on Fordham Road five years later, there was plenty of this closeout merchandise available to meet Alexander's needs. The Fordham store soon became known as the largest neighborhood store in the world and Alexander's told worried manufacturers whose styles could be identified even without the labels that the Bronx was a separate "city" and that its stores didn't compete with the department stores downtown.

But beginning in 1956 when a full-scale expansion program got underway, there were more and more stores to fill with merchandise and the closeouts started drying up. As one former Alexander's employee says, "No manufacturer makes a 5,000-piece error."

And so Alexander's has been moving steadily toward regular supply sources, to the extent that even certain branded products are sold at its stores. Today about 80 per cent of its merchandise is bought just like everyone buys—on a planned basis from regular supply channels. Closeouts represent about 15 per cent of the inventory and another 5 per cent is heavily-advertised promotional merchandise. Because of its huge size, Alexander's finds it necessary now to carry some fixed-price items but, says Sandy Farkas, "the department stores still complain to the manufacturers even when we charge the same prices they do." With its so-called regular goods, though, Alexander's policy is to sell a basic item sold in department stores for $3.00 at $2.69 or $2.79—and often have a better assortment.

This is not to say that Alexander's is unconcerned with upgrading its image, however. To build up its virtually non-existent fur department some years ago, it began selling all of its fur stoles at $50 above cost and its fur coats at $100 above cost. Today with its fur volume surpassing $4 million, Alexander's maintains the same mark-up policy as an additional lure to customers.

Loss leaders, in fact, abound throughout every Alexander's department on a consistent basis and regular shoppers at the eight stores pounce on them ferociously when the merchandise reaches the floor. Bargain ads appear in the New York papers for certain items one week and different ones in succeeding weeks, practically guaranteeing strong business in the particular departments the next day.

11 DRESS DEPARTMENTS

There are few retailers in the United States that sell more dresses than Alexander's, which has 11 separate dress departments in its stores. These range from two in the basement—located in all of its branches—where inexpensive styles are mixed together on the racks—to a dress boutique upstairs where couture fashions are sold in more elegant surroundings for as much as $500.

All ready-to-wear, including dresses, coats, suits and sportswear, represents 30 per cent of the goods at Alexander's, with fashion accessories—like hats, shoes, hosiery, jewelry and handbags—adding another 25 per cent. Men's and boys' wear comprises 20 per cent; infants', children's and pre-teens totals another 15 per cent, and hard goods are the remaining 10 per cent.

Maintained markups have been inching up at Alexander's as they have at other retailing organizations, but the company still manages to keep them at an average of around 30 per cent. Similarly, net profits have also been rising from 1 per cent to 1-1/2 per cent and now, in the fiscal year ended July 31, to about 2 per cent.

In the early 1950's, Alexander's discovered Paris and both have not been the same since. Whether the discovery came because the company felt a need to add to its low-price staple merchandise more higher-priced fashion garments (which it couldn't buy in the market here because of department store opposition to its merchandising policies) or whether it was stimulated primarily by G.F's love of travel and his desire to see the new collections depends upon who is telling the story. At any event, with many misgivings Alexander's launched its twice-a-year program of selling line-for-line copies of top designer stylings and was catapulted into the fashion headlines.

On a strict cost accounting basis, Alexander's doesn't earn profits on its line-for-line merchandise any more than the manufacturers and contractors who produce these goods for the big chain do. But both gain in other ways. For Alexander's, the whole costly hoopla gives it an early indication of seasonal fashion trends, a sharp fashion image and an opportunity to obtain reams of publicity as celebrities, socialites and fashion leaders flock to the charity openings to buy. For the manufacturers, the entire exercise is not only an opportunity to please a very large customer but also a chance to sample early and perhaps even to put some of the numbers in their own lines if they are well-received.*

---

*The line-for-line activity was discontinued in 1970.

NEW MEN'S WEAR EXCITEMENT

Nor do its other ultra-high fashion departments, like the well-touted Tomorrow Shop for men, bring down much black ink to the bottom of the Alexander's p-and-l statement. But here, as in women's wear, the excitement and attention garnered by the way-out merchandise, flashing lights and loud rock music make it all worthwhile. Alexander's is so enthused about what the Tomorrow Shop has accomplished for the image with younger men in the four months of its existence that it will open two other men's boutiques next month at its Manhattan store featuring the merchandise of designers Valentino of Rome and Michael Fish of London.

Men's apparel does make money, though, for Alexander's and its men's furnishings department is one of the most profitable in the chain. Another of its traditionally strong areas is the children's wear department, because socially-conscious mothers who would never drape a coat bearing an Alexander's label over a chair at a party have no such inhibitions about the lower-priced clothing worn by their young offspring. Hosiery is also a big money-maker at Alexander's, where the department is physically small but volume-wise tremendous.

Even the best departments, however, couldn't make money if the store locations were wrong and this is where Alexander's is also in the catbird seat. From the start, G. F. and his staff have selected sites that turned out to be big winners, resulting in a group of stores with an average sale per square foot level of $108. Moving into the suburbs conservatively and after many of its competitors, Alexander's has notched a record of finding a market for its merchandise wherever it went.

At each of its branches, Alexander's has managed to bring along its special charisma that attracts shoppers from all economic levels. Wherever its name is known—and that means the entire New York metropolitan area—Alexander's has customers and wherever enough of these customers are located, there is another possible site for a branch store.

For example, the Fordham Road store became the shopping hub of the entire Bronx all by its lonesome and has been so strong that it has one the highest—if not the highest—dollar volumes per square foot, $152, in the country. In White Plains, N.Y. a 160,000-square foot branch opened 12 years ago does almost as well. Alexander's Rego Park, Queens, store was so successful in bringing a department store to an untapped area that not only was its size practically doubled through an enlargement last year but it also attracted the attention of Macy's, which built a branch nearby.

Its Paramus, N.J. and Valley Stream, L.I. stores are in the midst of major shopping complexes that draw millions of people and dollars every year. In Manhattan, its newest store, across the street from Bloomingdale's on the East Side, is in an area that has become a mecca for affluent singles and couples who shop the store day and night—leading to a 10 per cent growth each year since the unit's opening in 1965. And its far different Third Avenue store in the East Bronx, located in and merchandised for what has become a ghetto area, is certain to benefit from the planned "Hub" redevelopment project there which will encompass the entire neighborhood. Only in the sparsely-populated area of Milford, Conn., is Alexander's volume at a low ebb and here an active community relations program is attempting to bring more customers to the store for such things as bridge, stock market, knitting and yoga classes in order to stimulate greater traffic.

LOOK TO THE CITY, TOO

Clearly, Alexander's likes the suburbs—but it is also loyal to the city. In 1970 both Alexander's and Macy's will open stores in Brooklyn in an enclosed shopping center along the Flatbush waterfront on a 23-acre property originally purchased by Alexander's more than three years ago. A unit will be opened after that in Yonkers, on a site bought by G. F. long ago across from the $70-million-a-year Cross County Shopping Center. The company is also making noises about another Manhattan store in an office building in the middle of the rejuvenated Pennsylvania Station-Madison Square Garden area and it has its eye on potentially-rich sites in New Jersey and Nassau and Suffolk Counties.

Within its stores, Alexander's is organized so that the merchandising and operating forces complement each other. The store director is the "boss" and is responsible for the 13 or so merchandising executives at each branch—whose functions correspond to those of the merchandise managers at the buying office and who handle in-store merchandising, selling and presentation. Another line on the organization chart, comprising department managers through salesclerks, reports to the store manager, who is responsible for everything but merchandising that is required to run a big department store.

On top of the pyramid—about as unstructured, incidentally, as any large store organization—sit three youthful but veteran vice-presidents: Jack Hirschhorn, in charge of merchandising; Roger Barrer, in charge of operations; and Walter Freedman, in charge of finance.

THE FAMILY OF FARKASES

And, of course, there are the Farkases. In addition to G.F. and Sandy, there's G.F's wife Ruth, an educator and the secretary of the company, and three other sons: Robin, Alexander's treasurer; Bruce, the general merchandise manager; and Jonathan, a college student who recently organized a high-styled boutique for young women at the Manhattan store called the Bridge Shop. Francine, Sandy's wife, recently rejoined Alexander's as fashion director after working for a few years as a stock broker. . . .

VALUE AT A PRICE

And this is what Alexander's is all about—value at a price. Yes, it will attempt to enhance its prestige by moving into couture merchandise, but the bread-and-butter items are on the main floor and in the basement. Yes, it will seek out the swingers and jet setters who are attracted to the British, French and Italian merchandise for women and men, but a big chunk of its profits will come from private-label shirts and suits cut and sewn by a contractor in the Far East. Yes, it will sell certain items below its own wholesale cost, but it will make this money back and more by the heavy traffic drawn into the stores which, in turn, buys from Alexander's regular stock. Yes, it will cut prices on auto rentals, but it business by advertising this service will be placed on a ~~~.

And as certain as anything is certain in the constantly changing world of retailing, Alexander's will remain in the New York area rather than taking the extremely hazardous step of spreading out nationally where its name does not ring that same surefire bell of recognition. Both G.F. and Sandy are well aware of what happened to its "partner" Korvette, which moved southward and westward at an irreparable cost. Alexander's belongs to New York and, if the Farkas family can retain its magic touch, a good piece of New York will belong to Alexander's in the decades to come just as it has since 1928.

THE DRUGSTORE OF THE 60s—Boutiques

Thomas Isbell

A year ago, Paraphernalia had just opened. Before, the word "boutique" had been loosely applied to a few stores scattered through mid-Manhattan—Act I, Splendiferous, Serendipity. Now, the boutique has multiplied by arithmetic progression and produced a sensibility of its own. In the meantime, Paraphernalia has become a nationwide chain. Soon: there will be a boutique on every corner—the Drugstore of the Sixties.

The boutique, American style, has a history somewhat different from its current English counterparts: Granny Takes a Trip, Tuffin and Foale and Carnaby Street. I rather think that the atmosphere of the the American boutique started, in a sense, with the Village coffee-houses which, in turn, evolved from the Beatnik nostalgia for junk. The coffeehouse was an easy extension of the pattern of Italian life on the old Lower East Side, which was transferred first to MacDougal Street. Cafe Reggio, filled with Victorian-Renaissance furniture, yellowed paintings and a monumental chrome Espresso machine is the prototype of a style readily reflected in the demimonde of Chicago's Old Town and San Francisco's North Beach, haunts of the long-haired bard. It was only another step to begin peddling the Art Nouveau *garbage* which the Fifties lovingly sought out in secondhand stores

SOURCE: *Harper's Bazaar*, May 1967. Reprint permission granted.

and incorporated in their paintings (l'Ecole Rauschenberg).

At the same time, however, Serendipity was more noticed for its sodas and ice cream parlor ambience. The *objets* were secondary. The Camp sensibility was, as yet, a minority position unidentified as an esthetic register. So much was happening in New York with Action Painting, the Off-Broadway implosion and the Beat personality cult surrounding folk singers and poets, that the emergence of a coffeehouse format was obscured. The atmosphere of the coffee-house, with its casual interior, its informal service, its simple arrangement along the walls, had an appeal which was readily adapted to the boutique.

Serendipity had moved the coffeehouse format uptown, cleaned it up and neutralized the elements of social protest inherent in the dingy Village interiors. The break with the respectable middle-class store had been made. It was a beginning and it was a Boutique. It was a shop which sold memorabilia and accessories mirroring the faggot interiors of midtown Manhattan. It had none of the wild dresses or ties now so familiar in boutiques. Its interior had white enameled Victoriana, ornate mirrors and a blurred distinction between merchandise and décor. But, most important, it was full—crammed with junk.

To interrupt this simple chronology and insert a comparison, we should now consider Tiger

Morse's Teeny-Weeny, also crammed, but inaugurated long after Serendipity and Paraphernalia. Here, junk has been replaced by gear. The clothes are the decoration. The boutique is boxlike in more than its scheme. Plastic panels conceal closets. The floor has as much meaning as décor as do the walls or ceiling. The window is only a thin partition which separates the store from the street. There is so little distance that someone looking at the buttons in the window is just as much in the store as someone inside looking at the red-white-and-blue-flag ties. Visiting Teeny-Weeny is like taking a space-encapsulated trip. The interior is part of the plastic inevitable scene with its patterns of hard, manufactured surfaces and dizzying destruction of up-and-down. The blinking lights and paranoic interior are a far cry from the easy nostalgia of Serendipity, but Teeny-Weeny in its plenitude is the same scene—in orbit.

Like so many trends, the boutique—a far more personal projection of image than the department store or shopping center—is a reflection of the extreme and eccentric atmosphere in the interior decoration of beauty shoppes, florists and Provincetown art galleries. What triggered the success of the boutique was not so much its rampant personalism as its amalgamation of a whole series of crazes: the need for a wider variety of costumes and poses, the rejection of Paris and the idea of high fashion, the demand for both unique and cheap à la mode designs (Betsey Johnson at twenty-three is already compared with Chanel), the apocalyptic boom of Third Avenue decorators, the Camp/Art Nouveau equation, the role of social indifference and the faded work shirt mentality, the confusion of sexes, the big campaign for sex-as-art; and, beyond, the freewheeling use of materials found in contemporary architecture. Is a Boutique Style recognizable? The tags may vary but there is always an emphasis on freshness, personalism and originality. If the purpose of a boutique interior is to entice the customer, the variety of interiors is part of the general competition. Inside a boutique, there is no question; Boutique Style is apparent.

A few categories do emerge. First is the purist style evident in Paraphernalia both up- and downtown (a style which is caught also in the Vidal Sassoon beauty parlor which joined Paraphernalia on Madison Avenue)—definite, clean and semiar-

chitect-designed. The most popular category, however, is the Gay Nineties motif with its dark, shabby interiors. Into this group fall most Village boutiques. The third category is the Psychedelic type where hookahs and mandalas are pushed. Tiger Morse's Teeny-Weeny falls into this category because it incorporates so much of the machinery of the Mixed Media, blow-your-mind school. In the fourth and loosest category are all the shops derivative of the three other styles, combining elements from the most original boutiques in an uneasy eclecticism.

The hotbed of this eclecticism is St. Marks Place, the Fifth Avenue of the East Village boom. There, the boutique has matched the down-and-out fancy of the new generation by mating high-laced boots and African prints with repetitious abandon. The source is not Mod, but an indigenous and childish affection for used clothing exploited by canny boutique keepers.

A rich lode of such fantasy is Khadejah, which began to use African fabrics at a moment when the city's race consciousness was increasing. The interior of the store, below street level, mixes the primitive and the *décadent*. Gigantic Gothic Revival chairs are covered in zebra prints—the ceiling by a long runner of African cotton. The lines of the dresses may be simple, but the fabrics are bold, part of the urbanized jungle.

A more ordinary example of the recherché is Fandango, a Thirties joint with a 78 jukebox humming "Sunny Side of the Street." Here, the junk includes *moderne* ashtrays, Shirley Temple mugs and mementos from the 1939 World's Fair. The mood is broken, however, by the clothes, which might well be from any other boutique, clashing colors, slick-finish fabrics and all.

Of all the New York boutiques, and for all the outrageous Good Humor of Tiger Morse's Teeny-Weeny, it is Paraphernalia—both uptown and downtown—that has some of the best things to be seen today in boutique décor. By chance, I got involved in a conversation with the carpenter who did the curved floorboards of the ceiling which pull the eye from the street into the shop. The carefully constructed ceiling described by the carpenter, the simplicity of the whitewashed interior, and the straightforward use of tubes to hold the racks of clothes, are all part of Paraphernalia's pure image. The tractor seats used as chairs and the simple display cases do not interfere with the clothes, which are seen with a minimum of distraction.

Boutique Style plugged itself into a segment of the American sensibility which has always been attracted to clutter—from dime stores to junkyards. The efflorescence of the boutique is more directly an extension of the drugstore with its inventory of trivia and vague aura of fantasy. Clothing, within the boutique format, is no longer handled as necessary apparel but as rapidly expendable decoration. Boutique Style is part of a way of life in which humor about one's person and appearance is supported by a continuous demand for change—throwaway fashion. The décor of the boutique serves the same function as packaging does—to motivate the customer, but further, it embodies a personalism which is all but absent in larger units of American architecture.

The Boutique Style is an extraordinary expression of a kind of lovable amateurism rampant in this country. As a manifestation of contemporary taste, nothing compares with its use of materials and imagination in unlikely situations—a far more exciting attempt at filling spaces, large and small, than diners, beauty shoppes and florists ever were.

FASHION, THE HEARTBEAT OF RETAILING

Hector Escobosa

Fashion had always been I. Magnin's act and it is fashion we want to discuss today.

1. Fashion is the Force behind All Discretionary Spending. . . . Fashion keeps the retailer in business, fashion keeps merchandise moving. Fashion is the most exciting, most creative, most dynamic force in one of the most competitive businesses in the world. Fashion produces obsolescence . . . an important factor in the American economy.

2. Fashion Is Our Most Effective Tool with Which to Meet Today's competition. . . . Our competitor is no longer just the merchant across the street. Competition today goes beyond our cities, our counties, our states and even our country. In our stores today we compete with the world at large.

SOURCE: Mr. Escobosa, now deceased, was president of I. Magnin, San Francisco, when he delivered this address at the Annual Convention of the National Retail Merchants Association, January 7, 1963 (Statler-Hilton Hotel, New York).

We have discount houses selling dresses and other soft goods, supermarkets selling such items as hosiery, more customers buying clothes in Paris and Rome, more customers shopping in Hong Kong and Bangkok, more shopping centers, more branches of well-established stores, more mail-order specialists and unscrupulous and short-sighted manufacturers selling to customers directly.

Competition is keen between retailers. It is also fierce between different businesses and services, all striving for a larger slice of the consumers' total income. Should she buy a coat or a car, should it be a dress or dryer, go on a safari, or buy a sofa? To meet this competition we must work for the elimination of all waste.

We must achieve greater efficiency. We must use every tool at our command. We must learn to think of fashion not as an unpredictable and mysterious process but as a tangible force which can be charted and graphed . . . which can be understood, explained, and projected. The more we know about fashion, the better we can use it.

3. Fashion Know-How Is the Extra Ingredient Every Store Must Have. . . . Fashion is the quality which adds luster, life, character, personality, and interest to a store. It is the difference between death and survival, between dullness and sparkle.

Fashion is the retailer's most productive ally . . . our assets and attractions may include . . . beautiful assortments, attractive stores, convenient parking areas, brighter advertising, but fashion is the catalytic agent which keeps customers coming.

Fashion is the final spark that gets everything moving and parts the customer from her cherished dollar . . . provided we understand it and also provided we teach our salespeople what it is and how to use it. But more about our salespeople later. Their importance is really my message today.

4. But What Is Fashion? . . . Fashion exists in all fields from dresses to diets, from furs to furniture, from cars to coats. It affects what we eat, the movies we see, the language we use, the way we think and vote and act. Fashion affects not only the way we dress, but almost every facet in our lives.

Fashion is a constantly evolving tide—seldom capricious—and generally orderly in its constant evolution. Fashion is a power stimulated by man's eternal desire to create something better or more beautiful—and praise the Lord for the designers, for the artists and for all the creative souls in this world.

Fashion feeds on new designs and new designs are created by a dynamic compulsion that keeps creators constantly experimenting . . . striving for something newer, more exciting, more beautiful.

5. And Where Does Fashion Come From? . . . Is it always and only from Paris? No, its sources today are many. To better understand it, fashion must be studied at all its sources.

Representatives from I. Magnin have been going to Europe regularly since 1906 and we try to keep up with what is going on in all the creative markets of the world.

Paris is no longer the only fashion fountainhead —but Paris still supplies the spirit, the mood, the essence, the overall direction that fashion follows. Paris is the best laboratory of fashion ideas, it is the place where many of the accepted styles are born. Perfect atmosphere for creation. Besides Paris we have: Italy—superb knits and exciting sportswear. Since World War II: exotic, far-away places such as Thailand—Siamese colors—textured silks. India—handwoven silks—exquisite saris. Japan—obi sashes—kimono sleeves—subtle, mysterious print designs. Hong Kong—Chinese brocades—tribute silks—frog fastenings. West Germany, Scotland, Spain all contributing to the eternal process of trial and error—of developing ideas with the hope that the customers will like them.

Many painters create purely for self-expression, but good fashion designers create to please the ultimate consumer as well as to express themselves.

6. In Discussing the World Influences on Fashion We Must Pay Tribute to America's Tremendous Contributions. . . . From the exclusive, expensive, and very fine designs of Norman Norell and Galanos down to the remarkable values of Jonathan Logan and Suzy Perette, the United States is very good at every price level. . . .The United States supplies the best values, most sizes (about 35 different sizes and proportions)—most scientifically cut—most quickly adapted—best mass-produced clothes in the world.

We have the greatest ability to interpret and adapt ideas from the world—we can and do deliver the Dior A line, the St. Laurent tunic, or the Balenciaga shape three weeks after Paris presents it.

We influence other countries as much or more than they influence us—often an American idea goes to Paris and returns with a French accent and rave notices. But as great as the New York market is. . . .

7. All Good American Fashion Does Not Come from Seventh Avenue. . . . Good American clothes are designed in New York, but also in Chicago, Florida, and other cities. I must mention the influence and development of California as an important fashion source. Swim suit—sportswear —casual dresses—couture—began with Adrian in the 40's, now include such greats as Galanos, Kilpatrick, Jean Louis. California makes a distinguished contribution to today's one world of fashion—by working on a realistic delivery schedule continues to increase the share of the market that it takes.

8. With Jets, Television, and Travel There Is Only One World of Fashion Today. It is hard to tell the women from Madrid apart from the one from

Montreal—more and more standards of what is good fashion have become international.

9. Choice Today, from the Whole World, Is So Varied That Each Store Has to Edit and Present What Best Fits Its Audience. . . . Its own interpretation of fashion or it ends by having assortments that confuse the customer. Fashion is not the same for every store—hot numbers in one store can fall flat in the competitor's.

Fashion is more democratic in the twentieth century than ever before in history—great similarity in appearance of people of all income levels—distinctions are subtle and often only apparent to the initiated. This democracy in fashion raises importance of status symbols—sable coats, square-cut diamonds, black alligator bags, understated simplicity and real quality.

Fashion acceptance in our materialistic society, travels down from the high to the lower income levels—startling exceptions such as denim play clothes or laminated fabrics sometimes begin at popular prices and by popular demand travel up to the better price lines. This reversal of the traditional process is strictly a twentieth century phenomenon.

10. Besides the Acquiring of More Fashion Understanding by Its Personnel, How Can a Store Strengthen Its Fashion Reputation and Presentation? . . . Each store must cultivate its own clientele. Must precisely interpret what its customers want—keep its eye on its own grandstand.

This is an important part of the philosophy of P.G. Winnett, Bullock's, Inc., Chairman of the Board—important cornerstone building the Bullock character and customer acceptance. Each Bullock store works on precisely reflecting its own individual clientele. The assortments in the new San Fernando Valley store are young, fresh, and keyed to the young families of the area—the Pasadena store reflects the wealthy conservatism of that community—Bullock's Wilshire is a fine sophisticated specialty shop. . . . They all follow the same quality and service standards, but each one develops its own flavor and personality.

Good fashion stores, like good sailors, choose their course and stay on it—I. Magnin's 86 years of devotion to the same objectives has resulted in a business producing enviable profits—a fine record of growth and development—an illustrious fashion name with worldwide recognition. This could not

have been accomplished by a course interrupted by detours and changes of policy. . . .

11. To Have Its Own Individual Appeal and to Succeed in Projecting a Clearly Defined Image- . . . . Each store must: (1) Develop its own buyers. (2) Train its buyers to lead—necessary to merchandise ahead not behind its consumers—to anticipate rather than to follow. (3) Guide its buyers first and its customers subsequently into investing in blue chip fashions—avoid fads. (4) Have a consistent fashion point of view (I. Magnin's is feminine, refined, lady-like, derived from Paris, rich). (5) Encourage good taste—a relative term- . . . which needs interpretation. (6) Cherish, respect, and guard its fashion integrity—sell, promote and present what it believes in. (7) Protect its customers from making fashion mistakes by selling them only that which is becoming and suitable. And to live for the pleasure and the satisfaction of its customers—for profit can be the result of a job well done, rather than the first objective.

12. We Must Never Underestimate our Customer. . . . She is more sophisticated, better educated, more traveled, better informed, more self-confident, and more independent in her choices than ever before in history. She is less loyal to one designer or to one store—more loyal to her convictions and to finding what she wants. She often knows more about competition than we know ourselves Customers are revolting against uniformity—trying to express her individuality in a society that is pressing for monotony and conformity. We must understand who our customers are and how they live—their demands result from their way of life.

At I. Magnin & Company we believe all our customers are stylish, young, sophisticated, and able to buy what they want—we visualize them that way when we buy for them and when we sell to them. We respect their convictions. Admire their taste and ideas and live to bring to them what will please them. And this brings me back to our salespeople.

13. The Research, the Analysis, the Planning, the Hard Work, the Imagination, the Advertising, the Merchandise Can Succeed or Fail by the Actions of Our Salespeople. . . . .salespeople can make us or break us.

14. Management Must Pamper, Love, Cultivate, and Over-pay Salespeople. . . . We must encourage salespeople to work for the customer more than they work for the stores. Salespeople can teach customers to buy fewer but better clothes . . . to practice the economy of good quality . . . good fashion cannot exist with poor quality.

We must teach salespeople to sell their customers better clothes than the customers can afford —to sell merchandise which will make customers happy—to understand the customers' needs and desires.

In the final analysis the significant projection of fashion is ultimately made in the fitting room. To repeat let us pamper, love, and cultivate, and over-

pay our salespoeple—in their effectiveness, rest our fates. Too many retail executives in the daily pressure of a demanding business fail to find time to work with, help, and train and inspire their staffs.

15. The Broadway Play Succeeds in Business by Really Trying. . . . Today—the retailer succeeds by living, eating, dreaming, understanding, and loving fashion. Fashion is the heartbeat of retailing, providing and *only* if our salespeople have been taught all about it and use it as the effective selling tool it is.

FASHION MERCHANDISING

Alfred H. Daniels

To make for a better visualization, let us picture a ready-to-wear floor. We see on it not only a lot of pretty women but an inventory, and this inventory is comprised of these variables: (1) categories, e.g., coats, suits, dresses, skirts, etc.; (2) classifications, e.g., fur-trimmed coats, untrimmed coats, print dresses, plain dresses, etc.; (3) style numbers; (4) prices; (5) sizes; (6) colors.

These are variables in terms of what a customer wants, it should be noted, so it should be clear that one of the chief jobs a fashion merchant has is to control his variables so as to come out with the right composite of inventory. He has three basic problems: (1) How *much* of each variable to have—the quantitative factor; (2) what *kind* to

have—the qualitative factor; and (3) *when* to have it—timing.

Quantitative Merchandising. Quantitative control of inventories, we know, is developed through dollar control and unit control. There is an overlap. Since the latter has even more to do with the qualitative factors, it will be discussed separately in a subsequent section.

A number of different procedures are useful in achieving dollar control. Under the Six Months Plan, each department plans its sales, stocks, and markdowns six months ahead in dollars, and markups in per cent, by month or period. Planned purchases are a matter of simple arithmetic. Many factors are taken into consideration in the development of these plans, including economic trends, commodity trends, comparative performances, and so on. It is this plan that becomes the framework of reference for dollar control by departments. Incidentally, the store has an overall plan which is a composite of the individual department plans.

SOURCE: Excerpted and reprinted with permission from *Harvard Business Review*, May 1951. Mr. Daniels, whose article has become a classic, has been vice-president of Abraham & Straus, Inc., of Brooklyn; Board Chairman of Burdine's, Miami; and Group President of Federated Department Stores and President of I. Magnin, California.

A second procedure is the Weekly Open-to-Buy Sheet. The control division releases weekly an open-to-buy sheet indicating by department current sales, stocks, markups, and markdowns as against plan and as against last year. Adjustments of the original plan are made periodically in view of the current trend. If customers show a preference for suits rather than dresses (as they have lately), the former departments will have a revision upward of their planned sales and/or stocks, giving them more spending power, and the latter will have revisions downward.

The Daily Sales Sheet is also useful in dollar control. Each morning in my company we receive such a "flash" sheet which summarizes, by departments, dollar sales yesterday and a year ago yesterday and sales month-to-date this year and last. This flash sheet is our ticker tape or box score. From it, sales trends are perceived that eventually are interpreted back into the open-to-buy market sheet. It is particularly helpful, even though the experience is not always merry, if you have a sister store with whom to compare daily departmental sales. By using another store as a measuring stick, you are in a better position to differentiate general trends from your own weaknesses. For example, your fur sales may begin to fall off. If this is likewise true of your sibling rival, a trend may be indicated—a switch into fur-trimmed coats, for example. If not, the trouble may lie in your sponsoring muskrats rather than persians, and capes rather than stoles.

Federal Reserve comparisons are a fourth method of dollar control. Monthly the Federal Reserve Banks collect and disseminate departmental sales figures for all stores in the various Reserve areas and in given cities. These statistics, like the store's own sales sheets, can be used to determine trends, weaknesses, and strengths. Much as baseball managers are judged by their standing in a pennant race, departmental managers are evaluated on the basis of their ranking in their district. "Going behind the district" is lèse-majesté in our business while "going ahead" makes one a Casey Stengel.

Basically, the foregoing discussion is merely an application of the retail method of inventory. Fashion merchandising is no different from any other kind of merchandising, save for one very important factor. "Controller thinking" should never determine money amount to fashion buyers. A fashion

inventory is worthless unless it is right; that is, unless the customers want it. Therefore, open-to-buy can never be completely mathematical. A department may have no money to spend according to its plan; but if the stock is comprised of fur-trimmed coats and customers want untrimmed coats, the buyer is what is known in our trade as "hooked," and he has to start all over, dollar mathematics notwithstanding.

One of our apparel departments recently had a sudden slump in sales, and its inventory was high. Rightfully concerned, several of us toured the department for an appraisal. The buyer reassuringly patted us on the back and said, "Don't worry at all. Prices in the market are going up. Further, this inventory is composed largely of 'classics' [a famous last word in the fashion business]. It's like money in the bank." The department's business fell off 40 per cent that day. Soon everyone in town broke with a sale on similar classics (sic!). The buyer had his money in the bank all right, but the bank had failed. This leads right into the problem of making qualitative decisions.

Qualitative Merchandising. Next to understanding the definition of fashion, qualitative merchandising is the most important aspect of this analysis. Once it is determined under dollar control that a department is going to spend a certain amount of money, the question is: Spend it on what? There are a myriad of possibilities. Should coats be trimmed or untrimmed, box or fitted? What kind of fur collars will sell best? What colors? What fabrics? Long coats or short coats? Ad infinitum.

The problem is not so complex as it appears, however, since there are two ways of determining what to buy qualitatively—or to put it another way, of determining what the customer is probably going to want. The first method is by talking to people; the second, by getting the facts together and talking to yourself, the soliloquy method you might call it.

One group of people worth talking to is the fashion advisory services—Tobé, Amos Parrish, and so on. These vary in type, quality, size, and fee. Let me use the Tobé office as an example because it happens to be one with which I am familiar (there are possibly others equally good). It is headed by Miss Tobé, a top fashion authority (and merchant). She has a relatively large staff of experts whose job it is to cover everything from what is being worn at the Opera and Dog Show to what is being shown on "Seventh Avenue" (i.e., the ready-to-wear markets). The office is jam-packed with information, some of which is published in a comprehensive weekly report. Tobé and her staff can tell you fashionwise what is considered *de rigueur* and *de trop* at Palm Beach or what is selling "like pancakes" on Fourteenth Street. They will offer opinions about skirt lengths next fall and why your sales were disappointing last Saturday.

Central buying offices—Associated Merchandising Corporation; Kirby, Block & Company; Mutual Buying Syndicate, Inc.—etc.—comprise a second group worth talking to. As a member of Federated Department Stores, my own particular organization is a participant in AMC, a voluntary group of 24 department stores which maintains a large buying office and sees to it that member stores keep their books alike and exchange information on operations continually. The AMC stores have a sales volume in excess of one billion dollars and, therefore, obviously have a substantial soft goods business. The AMC office has a full and complete fashion organization, including market supervisors, buyers, assistants, and even a specialized fashion office. In most instances, these persons do no direct buying for us, unlike certain other offices, but act as advisers to our merchandise staff. Their advice is based on a wealth of information. Save for the matter of direct buying, most buying offices are like that of AMC and do not vary much in terms of function.

The fashion merchant also profits from comparing notes with other merchandise managers, buyers, and assistant buyers. Many a constructive tip has developed thus from a phone call or over a cup of coffee. And don't forget the customers! The simplest, and most direct, and *best* method of finding what a customer wants is to ask her (or him). Salesgirls can be helpful, too. If the salesgirl in question has gone home, you can "talk" to her by reading her entry on what we term a "want slip."

Last but not least, it is important to talk to your resources, who are necessarily in the position of having to anticipate what stores are going to buy and whose opinions about the future are, therefore, particularly valuable. It is well to believe their sincerity when they proffer advice; they have backed it with their bankroll! Months ahead they have committed themselves to bold prints rather than subdued ones, to clan plaids rather than flannel, to no fabrics at all if perchance their belief is in Bikini swim suits. Consider, too, that they have been more often right than wrong.

In other words, there is no paucity of fashion information, all intelligible, if you like talking to people. And there is consensus more frequently than you might think.

The Unit Control Card. A second method of determining what to buy qualitatively is essentially a process of getting the facts together and talking to yourself. Here I would like to introduce the subject of unit controls, which, as I have mentioned earlier, has to do with quantitative as well as qualitative merchandising.

The unit is the style number. A style *number* is a designation given by a resource to a particular garment and to all identical garments from that resource. The number has its own attributes in terms of design, classification, price, colors, and size range. Following its history intelligently is as important in the merchandising business as following a patient's chart in the medical profession.

The mechanics of unit control are relatively simple. An individual style card is devoted to each style number carried. Daily someone enters on the card yesterday's sales, receipts, customer returns, then sales-to-date, and finally, by deduction, number on hand. This forms a perpetual inventory control in units. The various cards are arranged by classification, price, and resource. The summary information about price and classification is developed daily and weekly in different forms by different stores.

The panel (that is, the receptacle holding the cards) gives the complete running history of a fashion department. It is alive with information and clues of all kinds. When you want to see how your wool dresses are "going," you look at your wool cards. If they are not going well, you might reason it was too warm out or you had the wrong ones. If you wanted to see how you were doing with wools at $16.95, you would look at that particular section.

You might find none and remind yourself that several customers had asked for them at this price.

As far as the individual style number is concerned, obviously, you can learn exactly what to do by looking at the individual card and talking to yourself, even if you are unimaginative. If the number is not selling, you say to yourself, "I ought to reduce it." If it has sold pretty well, you say to yourself, "I ought to reorder a fair amount." If it has sold exceptionally well, you might muse that in fairness to all your other emulative customers, whom you do not wish to frustrate, you really should reorder a lot. After having done this with a hundred cards, you know how you want to spend your money qualitatively.

There will be a few question marks, of course. For instance, the classification summaries may have showed inadequate stocks of untrimmed coats. On the other hand, your cards show only slow sellers—what we call "pups." Therefore, you need to find, say, two new styles. You saw some new fur-trimmed coats at a favorite resource of yours, and he has told you to "check" (i.e., buy) a few. You do. He also whispered into your ear that they were selling at "better" prices (the fashion cycle!). So you earmark some money for this. Also, Tobé has indicated her complete disgust with you because you have no coats whose sleeve length shows the tip of the index finger. You have no confidence in the fashion, but feeling insecure about your job, you earmark a few dollars for it anyway.

It is difficult for me to overemphasize the importance of the unit control card. I know of a very successful department store buyer who used to boast that he never knew what a dress in his stock looked like (*not* that I recommend this, but it illustrates the point). He simply lived in, and made his living out of, his cards. Nine out of ten and he would reorder. None out of ten and he would try to return or "swap." Two out of ten and he would mark down; and so on. To refer again to my own experience, I used to pull the cards out of the panels and arrange them to see what common denominators I could detect. I might arrange them by resources, to see who was "hot" and who was "cold." Or I might take the ten best cards, get samples of the merchandise in the office, and see what they had in common. If it was dresses, it

might be a kind of print, or a lot of fabric in back (what we call "back interest"), or a stripe, or whatnot. The point is that I was able to find out what customers wanted even though I was neither a couturier nor a designer.

Let me give you an example, an instance where I supposedly showed fashion *flair*, fashion feeling, and heaven knows what else.

About two years ago, our Blouse Department got "very sick." It was serious because we were going into our big Christmas season, during which a continued slump of the same degree would have been disastrous. Not being too close to the facts, I went at the problem administratively. I talked to the buyer and divisional merchandise manager, both of whom were rightfully dejected; called a few friends, who had no suggestions; had our competition shopped and found there was "no activity"; and had a complete survey made, finding that we were "covered." The sum total of my administrative efforts, therefore was nothing.

As a last resort—it should have been the first—I requested the cards, together with samples, of the best sellers. Upon scrutiny, it was apparent that seven were wool jerseys. In desperation, we decided to run a wool jersey promotion. This decision, though, did not quite "hit home." Competitors had advertised wool jerseys, and our grapevine had indicated nothing startling. As our meeting was about to adjourn, I asked to see the two best sellers once more. Then the light came. Never did two necklines plunge so precipitously—and wickedly!

No time for modeling. We hurriedly reordered the two blouses in large amounts, bought three new styles with the same common denominator (sic!), and scooped—both literally and figuratively, I guess—the country with "Deep Plunging Wool Jersey Blouses." Our blouse business became enormous. Some even said that a new fashion had been started, for the "deep plunging" look was soon advertised in dresses, slips, and bras all over the country.

Had I "started" a fashion? Of course not! There had been a general, and obvious, fashion trend toward bareness—"The Bare Look"—for some time. Subconsciously, that is probably why I had asked to see the two blouses again. Had I started a specific style? Of course not. We *all* had some blouses of this kind—and they had been selling. In other words, to revert to our definition, the fashion was "currently appropriate." One merely had to look at the record to see it.

It will be seen that much of what I have been discussing here is scientific, if by scientific one means a logical interpretation of *merchandise* facts. Undoubtedly, for this reason, many engineers have been successful fashion merchants. Several of America's top-flight fashion divisional men not only went to engineering schools but taught in them. Many successful dress, coat, and millinery buyers are men whose forte is operation.

Certain stores, from Ohrbach's to Jane Engel, have gone much further than what has been indicated above, literally mechanizing much of their fashion merchandising. IBM machines can be "souped up" in such a way as to tell you how many two-piece as compared with one-piece dresses were sold yesterday, how many dotted swisses as against voiles, and even, for all I know, whether you have got the right ratio between red-headed salesgirls and black-haired shoe clerks.

Timing. Granting that the questions of how much and what kind are settled, the next question is: When? This actually refers to two different issues—(1) the timing of a specific fashion and (2) seasonal changes and demands. To illustrate the former, a thousand dollars may be exactly the right appropriation, and a hundred red print dresses at $10 the right components, but if they come in two weeks late, you may be just as badly behind the times as if you had a batch of late-Victorian bathing suits on your hands. (Incidentally, this is one reason for being precise about delivery dates in the fashion business.)

As an example of the problem of seasonal timing, at a recent meeting of my company's stores, it was pointed out that for the past several years most of the stores had been doing more spring coat business per week in April than in March. Yet our stocks had been peaked for March 1. The results were big markdowns and lost business; for, when our customers wanted spring coats, the stocks were neither fresh nor right. The moral was like the delayed buck in football, in which the ball carrier does not plunge until he sees the right opening. By waiting until March 15 instead of bringing in coats at the end of February, we could see what was "currently appropriate."

Timing is a big and important subject in our business. Timing a fashion is a matter of alertness to what is going on. One gets to know seasonal timing by intelligently looking at the record. The heartening fact on this score is that there is so little change from year to year.

ARTS OF FASHION MERCHANDISING

Some fellows in our business are big, others are medium size. They all seem to apply the same principles. What is the difference? It is a matter of degree of application. With a few exceptions, the arts of fashion merchandising boil down to the mechanics—only more so. There is very little about them that is mysterious or exotic. Let us take a look at three of the arts to see that this is so.

"Running Up and Down Stairs."   A prominent retailer, at a Fashion Group luncheon, recently said:

"Basic utility cannot be the foundation of a prosperous apparel industry (because nothing wears out). We in the soft lines business have a responsibility to accelerate obsolescence. It is our job to make women unhappy with what they have in the way of apparel. We must do so by offering them something more desirable. We must make these women so unhappy that their husbands can find no happiness or peace in their excessive savings."

To my mind this statement is impressive because of its understanding as well as misunderstanding of our business. First, a few words of background.

The soft goods or fashion business has been a little ill in this past period for a number of reasons. The gentleman in question was attempting a pep talk to rally the fashion girls to do something about it. Two years ago, he pointed out, the fashion business was enormous because of a change in silhouette; skirt lengths dropped. Every woman had to buy a new wardrobe or else look like something out of *Gentlemen Prefer Blondes*. He was recommending that it be done again.

Well, this is "nice work if you can get it." But if my earlier discussion has been convincing, it should be enough to point out that it cannot be done again—not on purpose. General fashion trends cannot be changed by masterminding on the part of any group. If they could be, the fashion business in total would always be enormous.

The retailer's remarks also had considerable insight. In effect, he said that our business is dependent on our being constantly able to seduce customers with something new—in other words, to get a lot of fashion cycles working within the general fashion trend. "New—different—fresh!" That is the vitality of our business. I think that the German poet, Heine, had something when he said that "When a woman begins to think, her first thought is of a new dress." The job of the fashion merchant is to keep her thinking.

When I was young in the business, I made it a point to make sure we brought in new things—anything new, just so long as they were in fair taste. In the trade this is called "running up and down stairs." I figured that, even though I did not know what I was doing, if the manufacturer could put half his savings into the production of a new idea, I could gamble Abraham & Straus money to the extent of 40 dresses. Naive? Perhaps yes, but my premise was a correct one.

Promotion. Every father has his favorite child, and promotion is mine. A psychiatrist might call the pleasure of promotion sadistic, for it involves torturing a competitor by selling quantities of something he usually has. Sadistic or not, it is fun. (Caution! Having the wanted fashions in stock at all times may be less fun, or more tedious, but it is more important. Thus, remembering the mechanics could well be labeled an art.)

To be a promoter requires certain technical knowledge. A promoter must know, first, how to make a plan—what the objective is and how to map out strategy. Just as important, he must know how and when to change a plan. Pity the poor persons in our business who compulsively stay with the blueprint. As football players change from cleats to sneakers when the field freezes, so must the fashion merchant change his strategy when the market changes.

He must also be able to differentiate between the values of different kinds of promotion: (1) sales promotion, which has to do with value events, typically in assortments; (2) item promotion, where the objective is to sell specific things (a butcher linen dress, for example); (3) idea promotion, where the goal is to sell quantities via an idea (e.g., pink shirts); (4) departmental promotion, where one attempts to establish the reputation of a department (e.g., the Junior Size Center); (5) brand promotion, where one plans a campaign to build a particular manufacturer's line (e.g., Carolyn Schnurer sportswear).

The promoter should have an understanding of media—how to reach his audience. Media problems are varied, ranging from which *kind* are appropriate (newspapers, direct mail, magazines, radio, TV) to which one (a certain paper, list, or station). Decisions are made, essentially, by knowing something about what persons are reached by a specific medium—where they live, how many there are, how they buy, what their age is, what they spend. As examples of how intricate this subject is, circulation *per se* can be meaningless, for some papers are read for their ads, in which case advertising receives high audience attention, and others are not; Sunday advertising in some communities receives more attention than comparable advertising midweek; morning papers may pull better than evening; and so on. This complexity does not deter store people. Everyone who ever entered our business felt he could be a self-labeled publicity expert after two weeks on the training squad. It is almost immoral not to feel that way. Incidentally, part of the fun of promotions is "kibitzing" the publicity director—which is sadistic, too.

Promotion problems are like so many others we have discussed. They should be kept as simple as possible, conclusions about them being reached through use of experience and direct judgment. For example, if you are planning a big mail- and phone-order response to a $7.95 fly-front gabardine dress, you use a paper with a geographically scattered circulation ("full-run") rather than a local one. If it is a floor promotion of high-price coats, you might consider a direct mail piece to your charge customers, who are your "best" customers; there is less dilution in this method than in using the typical newspaper. A "cutie pie" boxy sweater advertised in *Seventeen* should outpull the same item in *Charm* because of the different age composition of its readership, while a dress designed for the career girl might better be featured in *Charm*.

Aside from the technical aspects, the art of promotion requires several personal qualities which deserve comment here. The first is *alertness*. Now, it should be axiomatic that if his competitor does something successfully, the promoter should duplicate. Yet very few do. It should be obvious that if a sister store effects a coup, it is not unsporting to try to imitate. Again, however, not so many do. Finally, it should be clear that it pays off to be alert to the dictates of your own customers. For instance, the coat business was very poor last October. Like others, our store ran several coat sales in a row, all of which "flopped." Yet our buyer was alert enough to recognize that each time the lynx fox trimmed coats moved out. Therefore she contrived a promotion on *just* lynx coats—and really got results! As far as the first personal quality is concerned, in other words, it is not so much a matter of fashion as of glasses and a hearing aid.

A second vital quality is the *ability to reason inductively* (a phrase which appeals to me more than "imagination" because it puts it within the reach of ordinary businessmen). This has been mentioned earlier under the subject of qualitative merchandising, but let me present still another example. Several years ago, in going through the dress cards (here we are, back looking at the record, you see), it was found that virtually every black washable dress on our floor had been sold. Six out of eight, nine out of ten, and so on—all small quantities, but "sold out." We had our competitors shopped and found that they had no black dresses in stock either. According to our notes, there had been calls for such dresses a year ago at the identical time, namely, the end of May. On the basis of this and a few other facts, we bought 10,000 black summer dresses—the largest dress purchase in our history before or since.

I will never forget the weekend before the promotion; with no warning it had turned cold and wet. Before store opening on Monday morning, the stockroom was about as depressing a sight as possible: wave upon wave of dresses, each as black as the next. It looked like doomsday, and we braced for the worst. Then the store opened. Well, to cut the story short, the response was simply enormous—$150,000 of business in three days! Never underestimate the desire of a woman to be "appropriate."

The point is, this successful venture in fashion promotion came about as the result not of some great fashion imagination but of a little workaday logic. "Hunch" decisions are reminiscent of Mark Twain's comment that it had taken him three weeks to develop his extemporaneous remarks.

In the fashion business there are times when nothing succeeds like excess. This puts a premium on *courage* which is another quality the promoter needs. He gets courage, not through a devil-may-care attitude or by tremendous internal security or fortitude, but by being reasonably sure of his premises and facts. In the case of the black dress mentioned above, facts pointed in the one direction. The promotion could be as sure, no more, no less, as if it had tried to corner the canned tuna fish market because of evidence of a switch in demand from canned salmon. After all, there is a certain amount of unpredictability in anything.

A final quality that needs mentioning is *speed*. This refers not only to the fact that fashion changes quickly, as per our definition, and that seasonal demand changes, but also to the fact that fashion is a highly competitive field. The promoter has to get his facts quickly and act upon them quickly. Had we been two weeks later with the black dresses, the party would have been over; we would still be counting them.

Resource Relations. Resources can help the fashion merchant in many, many ways—from giving him good deliveries to pushing him to big ideas and concentrating his stocks. In this third art it is important for him to know how to work with his resources and how to get them to work for him. The Nettie Rosensteins, Howard Hodges, Adele Simpsons, Sally Victors, Barbizons, Harris Classics, Shagmoors, Winfields, McKettricks, Brimbergs, Sayburys, Betty Hartfords, Jerry Gildens, Young Viewpoints, Monarchs, and others can, by themselves, build a huge business for the store. If there is a quick short cut to success, this is it. It does not require fawning or frolicking; the fashion business has become more mature than that. It does require an ability to listen, and to say "yes" many times and "no" sometimes. Also it requires loyalty. This is one case where it is imaginative to be consistent.

The subject of resources has received more and more attention on the part of top-store management. An Associated Merchandising Corporation planning committee, comprised of several key store executives, spent a year developing a 150-page manual dedicated to "ideal resource relations."* It was presented to the AMC store principals at a meeting in White Sulphur Springs last fall and received a tremendous ovation. There was a recommendation that all merchandise persons in all the stores read it—and practically memorize it—as essential to their growth as merchants.

The great change which has occurred in the fashion field is in the development of strong brands and is, in my opinion, a stabilizing and salutary one. This development has been of such recent vintage that many persons are unaware of its existence, let alone its significance. The fact is, women are now developing as much preference for Red Cross shoes and Henry Rosenfeld dresses as for Uneeda Biscuits and Chevrolet cars. My company had for years an underdeveloped suit department. Analysis recently showed that we were missing perhaps the strongest brand, Handmacher, so we decided to concentrate on getting that line. I am sure our suit business will expand as a result. Needless to say, not only will we have the wanted merchandise (customers coming to us because of the reputation of the manufacturer), but we will also have at our command all of the know-how and genius of suit experts to help us build *our* department.

It is perhaps understandable why a store's relations with its key resources should be of such concern.

FEELING FOR FASHION

My final topic is that particularly mysterious piece of mumbo-jumbo called "fashion feeling."

Some bright fellow years ago, in order to get an increase, must have sold his boss on the idea that fashion feeling was like sex appeal—you either had

*Associated Merchandising Corporation, *Resource Relationship Manual* (New York, August 1950).

it or you did not. Blarney! All the discussion in the preceding pages is fashion feeling, from the application of logic to resource loyalty. However, two points deserve a little amplification:

(1).   We have discussed emulation as a prime drive in the purchase of fashion. How obvious, then, that it is important to keep in stock at all times merchandise that represents advance fashions, typically at higher prices than you ordinarily sell. The object is to be convincing to the people who buy a lot of your merchandise. We say that we carry "prophetic" fashions so that we can sell "accepted" fashions. Professor Copeland says "distinctive" fashions and "emulative" fashions. The customer says: "I am proud to wear that store's label."

How do you get advance fashions? You go to the name or couturier resources, and they do the work for you. A person who does this is known as a "fashion leader," which is the equivalent of 33rd degree Mason.

(2). We have indicated that women buy clothes to look glamorous, young, attractive. I think it was Lin Yutang who said that "all women's dresses are merely variations on the eternal struggle between the admitted desire to dress and the unadmitted desire to undress." How elemental that fashion merchandise be displayed, stocked, advertised, and sold attractively? We call this a "soft" approach, and without it we would have no fashion business. Much as you judge a housewife by the way she keeps her home, you can evaluate an apparel man by the appearance of his fitting rooms. If the fashion merchandise manager need not be a couturier, he must scrub himself daily and insist that his salesgirls do the same. In this sense, fashion feeling can be defined as cleanliness. You cannot sell fashion in a fish market.

Summary.   Let me summarize the main points about fashion merchandising that have been discussed above: There are three broad aspects of fashion merchandising. The first, the *mechanics* of fashion merchandising, concerns itself with how much to buy, what kind, and when. The merchant develops answers by looking at the facts and by talking to people, including himself.

The second aspect, the *art* of fashion merchandising, has to do with the know-how involved in getting bigger and better than your competitors.

This is done by bringing in new, irresistible merchandise, by promotion, and by developing close working relations with prime resources and new sources who look as if they are going places.

The nerve center of fashion merchandising is the unit control card. The fashion merchant should always be close to these cards—pulling them out, analyzing them, summarizing them. It is helpful to have actual samples of merchandise available. This is the unmysterious road to what is enviously termed "fashion flair."

The third aspect, *fashion feeling*, is a matter of good grooming. This applies to yourself, your staff, and your floor.

MERCHANDISING FASHION

Stanley Marcus

The problems of merchandising fashions for a profit are multitudinous, and differ from one type of store to another. . . . Fundamentally, a *store* must know at what point it wants to get on this fashion cycle, and when it wants to get off. Since fashion is not static, this process may involve some leaps and some occasional skinned shins, but severe falls are most unusual. In our particular store we must be in at the beginning of a fashion trend, or as close to the beginning as possible. Our trick is to recognize the new trends quickly, represent them in our stock in small quantities at first and larger quantities as the demand accelerates, continue with them until we reach or just pass the crest, and then jump off and mount a new trend.

If we had only one fashion at a time to contend with we wouldn't have too difficult a problem, but at any particular time there may be a number of trends in varying stages of development. Some of them may be reaching the peak; others may be just beginning; and still others may be in an ascending or descending stage. All of this may sound extremely complicated, and it is; but it *is* possible to learn the criteria upon which fashion understand-ing can be developed. Fashion forecasting is more complex and requires certain innate sensitivities. To get the proper understanding of these fashion movements, there is no substitute for the experience gained from an internship in selling and buying. *The customer* is the buyer's best teacher, just as she is a designer's best inspiration. . . .

The fashion magazines, such as *Vogue* and *Harper's Bazaar, Glamour,* and *Mademoiselle,* are extremely helpful monthly guides and are essential reading to keep up with fashion development. *Women's Wear,* a daily trade publication, does one of the most remarkable fashion news reporting jobs in the world and tells of fashion changes occurring around the world. It is vitally important for anyone in the fashion business to keep up with the news of the day, because the news exercises a great influence in setting the economic and psychological atmosphere which affects the trends of fashion.

To sell fashion we have to use a number of promotional devices. First of all we try to educate our sales people so that they understand the new fashions and believe in them. This takes great organizational effort, but we believe it is the foundation for a successful fashion business. After we have educated the sales person we then start to educate the customer by advertising the new fashions in the newspapers and magazines, by showing them in our windows and in our interior displays and in our fashion shows. We have found that the fashion

SOURCE: Excerpted from a lecture delivered by Stanley Marcus, President of Neiman-Marcus, Dallas, Texas, at Harvard Graduate School of Business, March 10, 1959. Reprinted by author's permission. A classic explanation of how a top fashion merchant functions.

show is an extremely important device for education, because it combines visual presentation with a convincing verbal commentary. We have found that the personal appearance of the designers at fashion shows and on the selling floors is another important promotional device. Women are interested in the personalities of designers just as ardent movie-goers are intrigued by the personal appearance of one of their favorite stars. Most important of all techniques in the development of a new fashion is getting the new fashion on the right women to start with, for we must never forget that emulation works only if the example is inspiring.

In our stores we have found that new fashions properly timed and properly priced will attract more people than a value promotional event. We don't believe in planned obsolescence as a means of selling merchandise, for we think that theory is economically unsound. We do think there comes a time, though, in the evolution of the clothes when the designers and the customers alike get tired of the uniformity that results from a successful dominant fashion. The human desire for self-individualization is so great that customer demand begins to make itself felt, and the designer, having the sensitive perceptions of the artist, frequently anticipates

his customer's requirements. Fashion merchandising has lots of hazards, for even small mistakes can prove to be tremendously expensive. As a business it is neither the easiest nor surest way of making a profit. There are few, if any, fashion merchants who will show the kind of net profit that merchants of more staple categories of goods, like Best & Company, or The May Company, will show. Profits they do make, as testified by the success of such as Bergdorf Goodman, I. Magnin, and Neiman-Marcus. Not long ago I was having luncheon with an oil man who turned to me and asked, "What sort of profit do you fellows make in the retail business?" I told him that the Controllers' Congress figures showed the average store made anywhere from 1 to 2-1/2 per cent on sales, after taxes, and that a few extremely well-operated stores might make as much as 3 to 3-1/2 per cent. He thought about that for a couple of minutes and then turned to me and said, "Hell, you are in the wrong business. We spill that much!" What the fashion business lacks in profits, though, it makes up in the excitement of a fast paced business, the interesting people one meets both as customers and designers, and in the opportunities of exercising the qualities of judgment and prophecy and decision at home and abroad.

THE CHANGING FACE OF RETAILING

Stanley J. Goodman

I have been asked to speak on the changing pace of retailing. I am going to ask your permission to make a typographical error and talk about the changing face of retailing. I will divide it into three parts: the effect on the customer, the effect on the store, and the effect on the merchant.

I feel that the most important changes affecting

SOURCE: Address by Stanley J. Goodman, President of the May Department Stores Company, before The Fashion Group, Americana Hotel, N.Y., April 18, 1969. Reprint permission granted.

us today come from the impact of science, and they are:

The superabundance of goods and services.
The shrinking of space and time.
The disappearance of security.
The population explosion.

These changes are shaping us in a number of interesting ways:

1.   The superabundance of goods has led to higher taste levels, to sophistication in choice mak-

ing and, therefore, to a more demanding, more easily bored customer.

2. We are in an eye-motivated age. The human eye has never before been subjected to the stimulation and to the powerful shapes and colors that are now our daily fare in magazines, art galleries, movies, television, and in the home; and a high percentage of this visual stimulation is two-dimensional instead of three-dimensional. All of this two-dimensional viewing leaves us hungry for three-dimensional visual excitement, eager to see the real thing instead of the picture on the page or the screen.

3. With the effective shrinking of space and time, people feel a growing impatience and expect things here and now that exist anywhere on the globe. Taste movements are worldwide and almost instantaneous.

4. As a reaction to the headlong rush of automation, there is a growing nostalgia for things of the past and for handwork.

5. The disappearance of security applies equally to individuals and to nations. People live today with the imminent possibility not only of their own death (for example, in air travel) but of massive annihilation. Fifty million of us can be wiped out by the pressing of a button, and that would be a population explosion indeed! And if the button is not pressed, we cannot seem to escape that other population explosion: the deadly overcrowding of this planet. All this erosion of peace of mind has no doubt had its effect in the deterioration of human relations, and the exploding anger of the young. Rejection of their elders by the young is perfectly normal, but the violence of this rejection today is unusual and disturbing.

6. Along with this has come a personal recklessness that expresses itself in apparel and in the arts. Men and women are less and less governed by conventional standards of behavior and dress. You see progressive nudity in women and more and more showy attire in men. What a long way we have come from the days when a lady was called "wanton" for the slightest overstepping of the mark in modesty of dress and a gentleman was called a "cad" for being at all conspicuous in appearance.

What does all this say to us in the department store business? Change is nothing new to us, but the violent acceleration of the rate of change is having its effect both on our customers and on us. Human life has existed on this planet for 2 million years, yet the geometric progression of change under the influence of science has brought more innovation in the last 100 years than in all the time before. America is the natural home of change because for 200 years we have lived off the unique stimulation of having been founded by people who left their homes, rejected their establishment, and journeyed to the other side of the world to find change.

Living organisms have a low tolerance for change. If you transplant a tree, you may kill it. If you try to make a dog sleep in a different place every night, he will become neurotic. But the American public, under the stimulation of all the things we have talked about, has developed the capacity to accept change and actually like it. Therefore, our job as merchants is to acquire increasing skill in handling change, and the only way to handle change is to become a part of it. Too much of the time we stand behind our customer—way behind. We have to rethink our jobs, restudy what has happened to the customer, catch up, and get out in front. Let's give it a name: people-merchandising.

The first step is to recognize the complexity of our audience. We do not have a customer, we have hundreds of kinds of customers. Stimulated by the abundance of goods and services pouring out of an innovative economy, the consuming public is dividing itself into more and smaller, sometimes overlapping, taste groupings. In every major community, the public can be put into scores of such groupings by age, size, shape, sex, income, neighborhood, type of school attended, cultural background, ethnic origin, personality type, and many other factors. These factors, to the merchant, are like the genes in our body cells that are invisibly nudging us into being what we are and pointing the way at every crossroad. And so what each of you is wearing today consciously or unconsciously reflects a whole complex of these influences, reinforced by the judgment of others in your group.

Therefore, our job as people-merchants is to be aware of and devote ourselves to the study of these taste-groupings. We must see that retailing is people-business and that understanding people in all their complexity is the mainspring of its whole process.

Meanwhile, back at the store, what is happening as a result of these changes? A great deal. If the store is to communicate to its audience, only a small specialty store can have one overall look. The department store must have many looks, as many as there are major taste-groups at which it is aimed. The wide-open floor is a thing of the past in the quality department store. It is better suited to the discount store in which the orderly arrangement of merchandise in a self-service environment best serves the convenience of the customer.

Ideally, the department store should be thought of as a walking theatre. When the store is planned, the layout of the main aisles and feeder aisles decides where the customer will walk. It is then up to us to see to it that as she walks through the store at a normal pace we are communicating with her and holding her attention with dramatic display statements at regular intervals. Almost the worst crime the store can commit is to bore the customer, and it must be remembered that with her increasing sophistication she bores easily.

In making merchandise statements to the customer in a store, we borrow from the arts of the theatre. The best presentation is the one that speaks to the customer's state of mind as she stands before it. Too often we sell the wrong thing—the item we bought—instead of the subjective value it will bring to the customer. What is she buying in the linen department, a tablecloth or the admiration of her friends at her next luncheon party? Well, then, show the party, not the tablecloth. The merchandise gains from presentation in a living setting—the table set to receive guests with linen, china, glass, silverware, and flowers. When the customer buys a piece of French tinware in the housewares department, isn't she really buying her admission to the status of gourmet cook, and so shouldn't we put this merchandise in a French kitchen setting? The fur coat draws psychic value from the antique table over which it is draped. The furniture in an irresistible room setting makes the customer want to live with it as she sees it. If the young are revolting (no pun intended!), shouldn't their merchandise be put in a setting that is violently different from the rest of the store?

And so, as the customers walk through the store

their eye should be caught by a procession of shops, boutiques, gazebos, armoires, stage settings, each designed with accessories, color, and light to present the merchandise in its exciting, living character to a taste-group of consumers. Is it any wonder that shopping has become a regular pastime, a major medium of entertainment and instruction for the American family?

All this means that the life span of a store interior has been greatly shortened. The faster rate of change must reflect itself in the store if it is to be in tune with the public. A new floor in a department store used to look fine for 15 years. Today the department we did last year may already look passé. We need more and more "now" shops planned for a season. There must be a shift from heavy store remodeling to the use of theatrical skills to create the scene easily and effectively, so that it can be shifted at will. In the past year 235 boutiques were opened in May stores, and the same is no doubt happening in other companies.

Along with this must go a new elasticity in allotting space to merchandise. For example, a store that has not, in the past year or two, tripled the lineal feet allotted to scarves or sunglasses is not fully responsive to its present market potential.

And now what about us, how do we have to change to fit this people-oriented store? The nature of the buying and merchandising job has changed. The old pro, loaded with experience, blinded by the successes of the past, the great trader of commanding presence, is often at a disadvantage today. Neither is "playing it safe" a safe procedure any more, since it carries with it the risk of missing the profitable early selling on a new look, then trying to buy it when deliveries are slow, perhaps settling in desperation for a second- or third-rate version, and finally winding up with quantity shipments in time for the markdowns.

The qualities needed today in buyers are qualities that make them at home in the changing life of the people they are trying to interpret: awareness, perceptiveness, taste, instinctive understanding of their people-groups, and a talent for showmanship. The role of the merchandise manager becomes one of developing the buyer's eye, sharpening her perceptiveness and taste, nudging her into a more courageous posture on new things, encouraging an early exit from the looks whose growth has begun to wane, curing markdown fears, and teaching markup-through-excitement.

There is room for a whole new recruiting and training program to bring out these skills for people-merchandising. For the buyer to be good at investing money in the things that will grow through the excitement they generate, she needs talent reinforced by training, perhaps along these new lines:

1. Visual arts training. Our whole business works through the eye, so should we not try to educate the eye of the buyer who has to select the stock? You are the last people to need convincing that good design is more and more the mainspring of consumer response. Therefore a buyer who has a grasp of the rudiments of good design, not only in her own field but in others, should be better at recognizing the new look with the future excitement. Along with this might go training in sharpness of perception, perhaps through the use of tests and puzzles.

2. People-training, that is knowledge of the people-groups to be served by her department. This might be backed up by research and consumer panels.

3. Permanent training through a continuing dialogue with customers with strong point-of-sale feedback, especially from the branch stores. The open mind, the open ear, the open eye.

4. Showmanship, bringing out the feminine talent for "playing house", presenting things dramatically in a living setting, helped by coaching from the professional staff.

5. Backbone building, developing the courage of the buyer's convictions. Since "safe" buying is too dangerous, she must be weaned away from the tyranny of last year and encouraged to make bold decisions based on conviction.

6. General awareness. The buyer should know what is going on in the world, particularly as it affects the lives of her customers. It would not be difficult to teach useful reading habits, supplemented by a flow of helpful capsule information and periodic quizzes. On the plane the other day I asked my wife to write down 10 things she would expect a buyer to be able to identify, just to be in touch with today. This is what she wrote: Bauhaus, Stonehenge, Art Nouveau, Hibachi, Biennale, Zen, Aries, Ken Scott, Ufizzi, and John Cage. I will not ask you to give me your own score. But I will say emphatically that the more you are aware of many-faceted life today, the better merchant you can be. The subconscious stores these things and influences your choice, as it does for the customer. In this business, therefore, what you know or don't know *will* hurt you.

My time is up and you have seen and heard a lot in less than an hour about what is happening to us in this windstorm of change. Where does all this leave us? Up in the air, I suppose.

But isn't that where we belong?

BIBLIOGRAPHY

Appel, Joseph H. *Business Biography of John Wanamaker*. New York, Macmillan, 1930.

Baker, H.G. *Rich's of Atlanta: The Story of A Store Since 1867*. Atlanta, Division of Research, University of Georgia, 1953.

Cahill, Jane. *The Backbone of Retailing*. New York, Fairchild, 1960.

Case, Margaret. *And The Price Is Right.* Cleveland, World, 1958.

Corinth, Kay. *Fashion Showmanship.* New York, Wiley, 1970.

Drew–Bear, Robert, *Mass Merchandising–Evolution and Revolution.* New York, Fairchild, 1969.

Duncan, Delbert J., and Charles F. Phillips. *Retailing Principles and Methods.* Homewood, Illinois, Richard D. Irwin, Inc., 1970.

Editors of *Women's Wear Daily. The Story of Sears Roebuck and Co.* New York, Fairchild, 1961.

Emmett, Jueck. *Catalogues and Counters.* Chicago, University of Chicago Press, 1950.

Feinberg, Sam, *What Makes Shopping Centers Tick.* New York, Fairchild, 1961.

Ferry, J.W. *A History of the Department Store.* New York, Macmillan, 1960.

Gold, Annalee. *How To Sell Fashion.* New York, Fairchild Publications, 1969.

Gold, Ed. *The Dynamics of Retailing.* New York, Fairchild, 1963.

Gore, Budd. *How to Sell The Whole Store as Fashion.* New York, N.R.M.A., 1969.

Hahn, Lew. *Stores, Merchants, Customers.* New York, Fairchild, 1952.

Herndon, Booton. *Bergdorf's On the Plaza.* New York, Knopf, 1956.

Jabenis, Elaine. *The Fashion Director–What She Does and How To Be One.* New York, Wiley, 1972.

Judelle, Beatrice. *The Fashion Buyer's Job.* New York, N.R.M.A., 1971.

Kimbrough, Emily. *Through Charly's Door.* New York, Harper, 1952.

Mahoney, Tom. *The Great Merchants.* New York, Harper, 1966.

Mayfield, Frank. *The Department Store Story.* New York, Fairchild, 1949.

Merchandising Problems in Opening the New Branch Store. New York, N.R.M.A., 1969.

Mersel, Randy and Jeanne Taylor. *Where the Boutiques Are.* New York, Simon and Schuster, 1967.

Nystrom, Paul H. *Fashion Merchandising.* New York, Ronald Press, 1932.

Ohrbach, Nathan. *Getting Ahead in Retailing.* New York, McGraw Hill, 1965.

Palmer, J.L. *The Origin, Growth and Transformation of Marshall, Field and Company.* New York, Newcomen Society in North America, 1963.

Projan, Ben. *Grass Roots Retailing.* New York, Fairchild, 1962.

Readings in Modern Retailing. New York, N.R.M.A., 1969.

Reilly, Phillip. *Old Masters of Retailing,* New York, Fairchild, 1967.

Scott, George A. *Your Future in Retailing.* New York, Richards Rosen Press, 1961.

Scull, Penrose, and Prescott Fuller. *From Peddlers to Merchant Princes.* New York, Fawcett Pub., 1967.

Tolbert, Frank X. *Neiman Marcus, Texas.* New York, Holt, 1953.

Troxell, Mary D. and Beatrice Judelle. *Fashion Merchandising.* New York, McGraw Hill, 1971.

Wendt, Lloyd and Herman Kogan. *Give the Lady What She Wants.* Chicago, Rand-McNally, 1952.

Wilinsky, Harriet. *Careers and Opportunities in Retailing.* New York, N.R.M.A., 1970.

TRADE PERIODICALS

Boutique Magazine, 1300 Broadway, New York, N.Y. 10010
Chain Store Age, 2 Park Ave, New York, N.Y. 10016
Department Store Management, 60 East 42nd St., New York, N.Y. 10017
Discount Merchandiser, 205 East 42nd St., New York, N.Y. 10017
Merchandiser, 419 Park Ave. South, New York, N.Y. 10022
Modern Retailer, 10 West 33rd St., New York, N.Y. 10001
Stores Magazine, 100 West 31st St., New York, N.Y. 10001
Women's Wear Daily, 7 East 12th St., New York, N.Y. 10003

TRADE ASSOCIATIONS

Association of General Merchandise Chains, 1441 Broadway, New York, N.Y. 10018
International Council of Shopping Centers, 445 Park Ave., New York, N.Y. 10022
Mail Order Association of America, 612 N. Michigan Ave., Chicago, Ill. 60611
Mass Merchandising Association, Inc., 100 Merrick Rd., Rockville Center, N.Y. 11570
National Association of Direct Selling Companies, 165 Center St., Winona, Minn.
National Retail Merchants Association, 100 West 31st Street, New York, N.Y. 10001
Shoe Retailers League, 60 West 32nd Street, New York, N.Y. 10001

SECTION REVIEW AND ACTIVITIES

FASHION BUSINESS TERMINOLOGY

Define, identify, or briefly explain the following:
    Retailer
    Department store
    Specialty store

Mail–order house
Chain-store retailer
Discount store
House-to-house retailer
Franchising
Boutique
Shopping center
Branch store

QUESTIONS FOR REVIEW

1. Is the retailer's primary function in the fashion business to serve as a distributing agent for producers or as a purchasing agent for customers? Explain.

2. Why have most fashion retailers discontinued the practice of making clothes to order?

3. Prove the following statement from the history and development of retailing in the United States: "Continuing social and economic changes bring about new forms of retailing." Explain the social and economic factors that led to the development of (a) department stores, (b) chain stores, (c) mail-order houses and (d) discount retailers.

4. How do present-day discount houses differ from early discounters?

5. Explain the statement that there are "different types of stores for different types of people."

6. Do you believe that small, independently owned fashion retailers will continue to play an important role in the fashion business? Why? How do small neighborhood apparel stores manage to survive the competition of giant retailers?

7. Explain the differences between any three different types of retailers. Cite examples of each in your local community.

8. What are some of the major appeals of the discount store, the chain store, the department store, and the small boutique to (a) customers and (b) producers?

9. Why do retailers develop their own private brands? Give examples of private brands in retail stores in your community. How do they compare with manufacturers' brands in terms of price, quality, and style, for example?

10. What, in your opinion, is the future of the fashion operations of the mass merchandisers? Explain your answer.

11. Are there new types or aspects of retailing currently emerging? What types are there and why?

12. Explain the statement made by Hector Escobosa in the reading, "Fashion, the Heartbeat of Retailing" that "fashion is not the same for every store."

13. Is there a large department or specialty store in your community that is owned by one of the big-store ownership group? Which store? What group owns it?

14. How does the shopping center nearest to your community compare with the new centers described in the text?

15. How can stores like an Alexander's (see the reading, "Alexander's–Underselling New York") "undersell" other equally large retail stores on the same or similar merchandise?

APPLICATIONS WITH EXAMPLES

1. Shop, for comparison purposes, the fashions being featured by a leading fashion store in your community and the fashions being featured by the Sears Roebuck, J.C. Penney, or Montgomery Ward store in your community. Discuss or present visually the similarities and/or differences that you find. Draw a conclusion.

2. Examine and compare the fashions featured in a current catalog of a large mail-order house with the fashions being featured by leading fashion stores in your community. Discuss or present visually the results of your comparison and come to a conclusion.

3. Research the history and growth of the largest store in your community and discuss the social and economic factors that influenced its history and growth. (*Note:* Check your local library for store histories or contact the public relations officer of the store itself for a printed brochure.)

SECTION 6
AUXILIARY FASHION ENTERPRISES

Of vital importance in the fashion business is the contribution of the many specialized services and advisory enterprises that operate in the field. Their activities
supplement and complement those of producers and retailers and aid materially in
giving direction and impetus to the movement of fashion. Such enterprises include
fashion consulting firms, consumer publications, trade publications, advertising
agencies, public relations firms, and other groups whose activities elude easy
classification. These auxiliary fashion enterprises are the subject of this section.
Some of the readings included here are written by professionals who are active in
these special areas.

FASHION IN PRINT

The amount of material that is printed about fashion and its workings staggers the
imagination. Aside from the paid advertising messages sponsored by makers and
sellers, there are editorial treatments in the daily papers, in news magazines, in the
women's magazines, in specialized fashion publications, and in segments of the
trade press that are in any way concerned with the fashion business. Fashion is
news, and news media cover it.

This printed material, along with what is done through broadcast media, serves as
a vital means of communication between related parts of the industry and between
the industry and the consumer.

Fashion Magazines

Fashion magazines, which have as their major activity the reporting and interpreting
of fashion news to the consumer, together with additional features for balanced
reading fare, have been functioning in this country for more than a century. *Godey's
Lady's Book,* which was started in 1830, carried pictures of the latest fashions, gave
advice on fabrics, contained other helpful hints and, of course, included
advertising. Its distinguished editor, Sara Josepha Hale, gave early proof that a
woman could have a successful career in the business world even in the days of
hoopskirts and cinched waists. Its masculine counterpart, *Burton's Gentleman's
Magazine,* also had an editor whose name acquired luster: Edgar Allan Poe. His
editorial career there was brief, however, from 1839 to 1840. The present-day roster
of fashion magazines consists of highly specialized publications, each appealing to
its own carefully delineated market. Examples include: *Harper's Bazaar* and *Vogue,*
in the high-priced field; *Gentlemen's Quarterly, Playboy,* and *Esquire,* their
masculine counterparts; *Mademoiselle* and *Glamour,* for college, career, and young
married women; *Seventeen,* for teen-aged girls; and *Ingenue,* for still-younger
girls.

The way in which fashion magazines made a place for themselves is illustrated in
the history of *Vogue.* Its initial issue, December 17, 1892, simply presented a gazette

of social activities. By 1915, however, it had developed into a fashion shopping guide for readers who had generous clothing budgets. As their editors conceived it, *Vogue* aimed to develop and influence the taste of its readers by showing what society's "Four Hundred" were wearing and what new styles were being offered by the fashionable New York stores, dressmakers, and milliners. The appeal to advertisers was based on the premise that high-priced merchandise "is better advertised in a periodical with readers of a special type: people of breeding, sophistication and means."[1] *Vogue* sponsored the first fashion show in America in November 1914, a "Fashion Fete" that presented gowns designed by New York houses and approved by a committee of women selected by the editors as "best dressed." Admission was charged and the proceeds were donated to French charity.

The role of fashion magazines is a many sided one. As fashion reporters, their editors shop the wholesale markets both here and abroad, to select and feature styles they consider newsworthy for their individual reading audiences. As fashion influentials, these editors sometimes take an active part in the production of merchandise by working closely with manufacturers to create merchandise that they consider acceptable to their readers. They participate in distribution by contacting retailers and urging them to carry and promote the designs they feature and to emphasize the trends endorsed editorially. Finally, they provide their readers with information not only about the styles they recommend but also about who produces them and who sells them at retail.

An important tool of their activities, and of other consumer magazines that cover fashions to a lesser extent, is the editorial *credit*. This is how it operates: the editors select garments and accessories that, to their minds, exemplify fashion news. They photograph and show these styles in their pages, identifying the makers and naming one or more retail stores in which the consumer can buy them, and usually citing the approximate price. The magazine's sponsorship and the editorial mention encourage the makers to produce the garments in good supply, the retailers to stock them, and the customer to buy. Even in stores that do not have editorial credits for it, a fashion item featured in a strong magazine may be given special attention. If the magazine concerned has a good following among the store's customers, the editorial sponsorship becomes a selling point of the garment not only to consumers but also to the merchant. The style is then stocked, advertised, and displayed and the magazine's name is usually featured in ads and displays. Hangtags on the garment and posters in the displays remind the customer that this is the style she saw in the publication. The magazine, of course, provides the tags and posters.

Like most publications, fashion magazines derive their principal revenue from the sale of advertising space. A single page in *Vogue, Seventeen,* or *Mademoiselle* costs many thousands of dollars. In general magazines like *Reader's Digest,* or in women's magazines like *McCall's,* the rates are about $50,000 a page in black and white. Color pages run higher.[2] Naturally a high ratio of advertising to editorial

[1]E. W. Chase and Ilka Chase, *Always in Vogue*, Doubleday & Co., New York, 1954, p. 66.

[2]Standard Rate and Data Service (a reference service for advertisers) provides information on rates and circulation and brings figures up to date at frequent intervals.

pages means a prosperous magazine. Although conditions vary from issue to issue and from year to year, advertising generally accounts for nearly half the total number of pages in a consumer fashion magazine.

Dependency on dollars from advertisers instead of dollars from subscribers is not always conducive to unbiased fashion reporting; it can result in a conflict between editorial comment and advertising interests. Editorial mentions of merchandise bring to producers highly desirable publicity and prestige, since the editorial pages tend to have more authority in the reader's eyes than do pages devoted to paid advertising. Thus, firms who buy space in a magazine and contribute toward keeping it profitable are likely to protest if they are not given adequate editorial attention. Such a clash of interests often makes objective fashion reportage difficult, if not impossible. On this subject, designer Luis Estevez once said: "Magazines give my clothes editorials on their merit once in a while, but mostly because of my advertising dollar. I admire them, I love them, I hate them."[3]

The money the advertiser spends for his page is, in simplest terms, spent to influence customers to buy his product. If a publication can show tangible evidence that it can move merchandise into the retail store and then out into the consumer's hands, its chances of selling advertising space improve. One magazine editor has stated that, in order to attract advertisers, "Nothing is more important to fashion magazines than their relation to stores. This fact accounts for the increasingly large staffs of departments almost unknown to their readers—promotion and merchandising."[4]

The promotion and merchandising editors act as the liaison between the fashion editors, the advertising staff, and the retail stores. Their job is to ensure that editorialized and advertised merchandise will be placed in retail stores where readers can buy it. They do this by telling the retailers what the magazine is featuring and why—and where to buy it. They then list for their readers' information the names of stores where the merchandise can be found. This service to the reader also helps to impress the advertisers with the magazine's selling power among retailers.

There are mishaps, of course. Editors can make unwise selections; manufacturers can accept credits and fail to produce in sufficient quantity; and retailers can accept credits and fail to stock, display, and advertise the style properly. One classic example, many years ago, involved a striking jacket featured on the cover of a fashion magazine. The editor was thoroughly justified in her confidence, and stores and consumers clamored for the garment. But the manufacturer did not share the editor's enthusiasm, and his production of the garment consisted of the one piece that was used for the photograph. Magazines try to circumvent such things by insisting upon firm promises of cooperation in return for credit.

The closer their relationship with both the producers and retailers, the easier it is for magazines to attract advertising. In order to cement these relationships, many free services are offered by fashion publications. Their staff members keep fabric and apparel producers informed on new trends, and advise them on ways and

[3]"Luis Says," *Women's Wear Daily*, March 13, 1964, p. 5.

[4]Bettina Ballard, "Eye on Advertising," *Women's Wear Daily*, June 6, 1961, p. 22.

means of selling merchandise. The fashion editors encourage them to manufacture items for which they anticipate a demand and, secure in the knowledge that the items will be featured by the editors, the producers will plunge ahead. The merchandising and promotion departments provide advertisers with "as advertised" posters to distribute to their retail accounts. In addition, most magazines that are active in fashion prepare, well in advance of each season, elaborate charts of their color predictions for the guidance of manufacturers and retailers alike. These charts show samples of the colors, lines, and fashion influences that they believe will do well in the months ahead. As described by one magazine: "The chart is a matter of inviting everyone out on a limb—but at least on a limb that the magazine feels is strong."[5]

In developing a close relationship with retail stores, the fashion magazines make themselves a source of information for them. In order to make their editorialized and advertised merchandise desirable to retailers and, ultimately, to their customers, the merchandising departments prepare elaborate retail store kits that, along with the list of sources for featured garments, contain suggestions for advertising, fashion shows, and display. The kits also include selling aids such as hangtags, signs, and other promotional materials. If an important retailer requests the service, the magazine will send a representative to commentate a fashion show. Occasionally a magazine will set up a seasonal showroom in the garment district and invite retail buyers to preview the merchandise that will be featured in the forthcoming issues. Many of them stage semi-annual fashion shows and clinics in which they preview their featured merchandise and analyze incoming style trends. Members of the magazine staff are also available in their offices at almost any time to show samples of merchandise to retailers who call, and thus encourage buyers to visit the producers of the apparel and accessories.

Most of the consumer magazines, including those primarily concerned with fashion, also maintain research departments. A function of these departments is to survey the readers of the magazine and compile information about their buying power, living patterns, and merchandise preferences. *Seventeen*, for example, surveys high-school girls and college freshmen annually and compiles reports for retailers and manufacturers about what these girls buy, how much they spend, and similar information. The fashion magazines, then, not only interpret fashion for their readers but also interpret their readers to the fashion industry. In the process, they serve as a clearing house for information in the fashion feild.

As compared with consumer magazines of general interest, such as *Time*, with a circulation of more than 4 million, or women's magazines like *McCall's*, with about 8.5 million in circulation, the fashion magazines have small circulation. *Vogue* and *Harper's Bazaar* have circulations of under a half million each; *Mademoiselle* has close to 700,000. *Seventeen* and *Glamour* are the largest, with a circulation of about 1.5 million each.[6] Their influence in the fashion business, individually and collectively, is great and far out of proportion to their actual circulation. Fashion editors ignore styles and designers in whom they have little faith, but give a great

---

[5]"Are You Cut Out for Seventh Avenue," *Mademoiselle*, March 1962, p. 119.

[6]1973 figures. See Standard Rate and Data Service for current figures.

amount of free publicity to those that they favor. Ordinarily, however, what they do is, as one editor describes it, "Try to pick the most dramatic, the most exciting—not always the most wearable fashions—but the ones that will really stir things up."[7]

Newspapers and General Magazines

As mentioned earlier, almost all newspapers devote space to fashion. Coverage varies, of course, both in amount and depth. A paper with the facilities of *The New York Times* may have its experts report the Paris openings and express opinions that are read by consumers and trade professionals alike. A small-town paper, on the other hand, may assign its society editor to fill out the woman's page with items about fashion, clipped from what the wire services send, what comes in by way of press releases, or what the local retailers supply. Papers of medium to large size usually send their editors to New York twice a year, to get a fresh, first-hand observation during the semi-annual Fashion Press Week, an event that is subsidized by the members of the New York Couture Business Council. An article in this section describes the activities of the Council and the history of Press Week.[8] Each paper's policy and the interests of its readers determine how much space the publication devotes to fashion news.

The "credit" operation of the fashion magazines does not exist for newspapers. But it is within the scope of newspaper fashion reporting to mention sources and shops for items illustrated, and even to cover the opening of new departments in local stores, the arrival of the new season's merchandise in retail stocks, or fashion shows and similar events that have news value.

Among the women's magazines not in the fashion-magazine category, there is also coverage of fashion, and it varies with the nature of the publication. Fashion editors of such media, looking at the fashion scene through the eyes of their average reader, will select for illustration and comment only the items of interest to the young mother, the middle-class housewife, the ageless city sophisticate, or whoever the particular audience may be. Usually these editors, like those of the fashion magazines, make direct contact with the markets.

Some of the women's magazines give credits. Some of the general magazines show merchandise; others, like the *New Yorker*, show no merchandise but discuss what the shops are showing. The activities of their fashion editors, as in the case of newspapers, vary according to the importance that each publication and its readers attach to fashion information.

Trade Publications

There is a special field of journalism known as trade or business publishing. Some business newspapers and magazines in the fashion field concern themselves with a

---

[7]Helen Valentine, then editor-in-chief of *Charm-Glamour,* and former editor-in-chief of *Seventeen,* in an address to The Fashion Group, reported in *The Making and Makers of Fashion,* The Fashion Group, New York, 1959.

[8]"How American Fashion Got There."

particular class of merchandise, from raw material to the sale of the finished product. These publications are not addressed to the ultimate consumer but to the fashion professionals concerned with the manufacture and distribution of that merchandise. Typical examples are *Body Fashions, Boot and Shoe Recorder,* and *Clothes.* Other business publications devote themselves to only one aspect of production or retailing and have a horizontal readership. Examples of these publications are such monthlies as *Stores* magazine, which goes to department store management, *Chain Store Age,* for chain store management, and *Modern Textiles,* which is concerned with mill problems. Fairchild's *Women's Wear Daily,* which is published five times a week, covers the fashion waterfront in the women's fashion business—raw materials, manufacturing, retailing, and how the trend-setters among the consuming public dress. Founded in 1890 by E. W. Fairchild, it has headquarters in New York City and maintains offices in cities throughout the United States and Europe—even in Asia. *Women's Wear Daily* reports collections, trade conventions, fashion events, new technical developments at all stages of production, personnel changes at the executive level, the formation of new fashion businesses—and the wardrobes and activities of prominent individuals. It is often called the industry's "bible" and no women's fashion enterprise is without its copy of *Women's Wear Daily.* The Fairchild counterpart for the men's wear industry is the *Daily News Record.*

Business publications are not aimed at the general public and are inclined to discourage subscriptions from people not active in the fields they serve. They seldom appear on newsstands, except for the Fairchild dailies in the garment district. Their circulations are quite small as compared with those of consumer magazines, and their advertising rates are correspondingly small, usually well under $1000 a page. *Women's Wear Daily,* with a circulation in excess of 80,000, is a giant in the field. The *Daily News Record* has a circulation of more than 25,000. *Boot and Shoe Recorder* serves the shoe industry with a circulation of a little above 10,000. *Stores Magazine,* which serves the department store field, has between 14,000 and 15,000 subscribers; *Body Fashions,* in the foundation garment field, has about 4000 subscribers.[9]

The capacity of trade papers for disseminating fashion information is out of all proportion to their size. Their readership, it should be kept in mind, is concentrated among people dealing in the merchandise they cover. They talk shop to such people. And, in terms of the amount of merchandise involved, when a manufacturer or merchant responds to information on fashion, that response moves a lot of merchandise.

Trade paper editors are usually in their markets every day of the business year, and they cover every nook and cranny of their fields. They analyze fashion trends for their readers and show sketches or photos of actual merchandise, identified as to source and style number, to assist buyers and store owners in keeping abreast of the flow of new products. In addition, trade publications discuss business conditions and contain articles on how to manufacture, promote, or sell the trade's products. They analyze and report on foreign markets, cover conventions and other meetings

[9]1973 figures. See Standard Rate and Data Service for current figures.

of interest to the trade, report on legislative developments of interest, and write up merchandising and promotion operations of retail stores.

Solid market research is also part of a trade publication's work. These magazines and papers make estimates of the size of their markets, survey subscribers on buying responsibilities and attitudes toward current problems, publish directories of manufacturers, help retailers and manufacturers find sources of supply, and report on seminars and conventions appropriate to their fields.

Within their particular fields, trade-paper editors and reporters are extremely well informed. Reading their articles is like listening to a group of experts indulging in shop talk.

ADVERTISING AND PUBLICITY AGENCIES

There are two ways in which producers and retailers use space in print media or time in broadcast media to get their message across to the trade or to the public. One way is paid advertising. The other is publicity—time or space given without charge by the medium because it considers the message newsworthy.

Advertising Agencies

An advertising agency is a service agency whose original function was simply to prepare and place ads in magazines or newspapers for its clients. Today its job encompasses much more: research of the client's consumer markets, advice on promotional needs, planning of promotional campaigns, preparation of print and broadcast advertising, preparation of selling manuals, creation of selling aids, labels, signs, and packaging—anything that helps to increase the sale of the client's product and makes the advertising itself more effective.

Advertising agencies in this country date back to the 1840s, but the pattern of operation that is common today did not begin to settle into its mold until the 1900s. The oldest of the agencies in existence today is N. W. Ayer & Son, which was founded in 1869 by Francis Ayer. Before this time, advertising agencies were more or less brokers of newspaper and, occasionally, magazine space. Ayer had the idea of acting as a buyer of space for his clients, the advertisers, and giving them every service that would make their advertising more effective, increase their sales, and thus make more funds available for future advertising.[10]

An advertising agency may consist of one talented, hard-working executive with a few small clients, or it may be an organization with a staff of thousands and clients with hundreds of millions of dollars to spend each year. Revenue is derived primarily from commissions. These are paid, not by the client, but by the media

[10]*Advertising Age,* December 7, 1964, Section 2, pp. 2–4.

from whom the agency purchases advertising space or time. Custom has fixed the rate at 15 percent. In recent years, there has been some effort to change the relationships, so that the client pays directly for the agency's services. Some agency services and a very few client-agency relationships are on that basis today, but this is not yet the prevailing pattern.

When an advertising agency bids for a client's account, it studies the firm's operation thoughtfully and draws up a presentation that outlines the campaign the agency suggests and the varied services that the agency performs. When awarded the account, the agency may delve into package design, market research, the creation of selling aids and sales training material—plus its original function of preparing and placing advertising in publications, in broadcast media and, in some cases, in transit and outdoor media.

In the fashion industries, it is usually only the largest producers of nationally distributed merchandise who make use of advertising agencies. These include some makers of finished apparel plus the giant fiber and fabric sources. Retailers, whose audience is local or regional, usually maintain their own complete advertising departments that handle their day-to-day newspaper advertisements. Ohrbach's Inc., whose institutional advertising pages have won several awards, employs Doyle Dane Bernbach Inc. to prepare and place its ads. Ohrbach's, however, is the exception rather than the rule in the retail field.

The agencies that specialize in fashion accounts are not among the largest in the

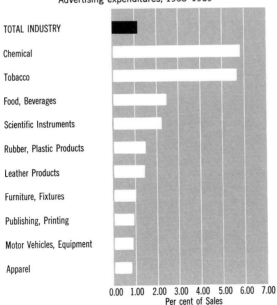

THE IMPORTANCE OF ADVERTISING BY INDUSTRY
Advertising expenditures, 1968–1969

TOTAL INDUSTRY

Chemical

Tobacco

Food, Beverages

Scientific Instruments

Rubber, Plastic Products

Leather Products

Furniture, Fixtures

Publishing, Printing

Motor Vehicles, Equipment

Apparel

0.00 1.00 2.00 3.00 4.00 5.00 6.00 7.00
Per cent of Sales

Source: *A Guide to Consumer Markets 1972/1973,* The Conference Board, New York, 1972.

field; national advertising expenditures by fashion producers are small compared to expenditures of other major industries. This is because the apparel industry is composed of thousands of small producers who have very limited advertising budgets. The entire men's, women's, misses', children's, and infants' outerwear and undergarment manufacturing group spends an average of 0.79 percent of its yearly sales on advertising—as compared, for instance, with 10.09 percent for soaps, cleaners, and toilet goods.[11]

The work of a fashion agency requires it to employ personnel who are expert in the language and background of the fashion business, account executives who work with clients and coordinate what is done, art directors who know how to visualize fashion, copywriters who are familiar with fashion appeals, and stylists or fashion coordinators who are responsible for the fashion slant of the ads.

People with similar talents are also found in the larger, more general agencies, of course. The work of the fashion expert in the agency is not necessarily limited to fashion accounts, however. If a woman's or man's figure appears in an ad for cigarettes, automobiles, or soft drinks, it is most likely that a fashion advisor in the agency that placed the advertisement has checked the model's outfit to make sure that it is in tune with the current fashion picture, and that the styles worn are in keeping with the occasion and the level of society that is being represented.

Many agencies also use outside fashion experts to assist them with advertisements in which fashions are shown—even though there is no reference to clothing or accessories in the copy, and even though the subject of the ad may be anything from a refrigerator to a savings bank. Typical are the Marschalk Company, an advertising agency that retained China Machado, a *Harper's Bazaar* fashion editor, to style its ads for Tab, a soft drink, and Grey Advertising, that employed designer Bill Blass to dress the models featured in a Haig & Haig Scotch whisky advertisement. The president of the Marschalk agency, F. William Free, explained: "Fashion is the quickest way of identifying things today. . . . There's a new kind of person whom we want to reach. This person is younger, better educated, richer, more sophisticated, and certainly more knowledgeable. We try to get a quick identification with this group by the way in which the woman in the ad is dressed."[12]

Thus the advertising agency, whether or not it has a fashion account on its roster of clients, becomes involved, indirectly and directly, with the business of fashion.

Publicity and Public Relations Firms

Publicity, unlike advertising, cannot be controlled in relation to where, when, and how a particular message will appear—if, indeed, it appears at all. The publicity practitioner's control over the fate of the story he wishes to place with a medium rests primarily in his ability to convince the particular editor that the material is truly news of interest to that medium's audience.

[11]*Advertising Age*, July 16, 1973, p. 34.

[12]"Advertising Heeds the Eloquent Call of Fashion," *The New York Times*, August 16, 1966, p. 30.

Publicity's purpose, like advertising's, is enhancing the client's sales appeal to his potential customers. The space or time supplied by the media, in this case, is free, but the public relations firm's services are not. Working on a fee basis, with provision for expenses, the publicity agency develops news stories around the client's product or activities and makes these stories available to editors and broadcasters.

The key word in effective publicity is "news." The publicity expert's first job is to find or "create" news value in the product, activity, or personality he wishes to publicize. Next, he considers the media that might conceivably find this news of interest to their readers and writes his story (called a press release) in a form appropriate to the media that constitute his target. If they are likely to use illustrations, he may attach a suitable photograph to his release.

Typical publicity activities include getting editorial mentions in consumer and trade publications, "plugs" on television and radio, school and college tie-ins, representation in fashion shows, feature articles in newspapers and magazines, and anything else that makes the products or the client's name better known and more readily accepted by the consumer—or by an industry, if that industry is the client's customer. An example of a simple publicity device is trying to place a photograph of maternity wear on women's pages of newspapers. The news angle might be the fabric, the occasion for which the garment is worn, the "unmaternity" appearance, or whatever seems most likely to win acceptance. Photographs, captions, and story are mailed to newspapers' women's pages. Alternatively, these items are made available to retail stores selling the line so that the stores can "place" the material locally. That is, the store's advertising and publicity department offers the item to the local papers in the store's name.

The publicity firm does more than merely use its contacts to place material for its client. It also prepares press releases, distributes photographs, writes radio and TV scripts, sometimes works out an elaborate fashion show, and hires and coaches professional actors to sing, dance, and model for the audience. If a medium, whether print or broadcast, is working on a special feature touching the client's field, the public relations people swing into action to provide the writer of the feature with facts, photos, and other help. Many fashion editors in smaller towns depend on press releases and photographs for the content of their fashion pages.

A broader term than publicity is *public relations*. A public relations firm does not limit its efforts to getting the client or his product mentioned in the media through press releases and similar efforts. It may supply expert advice on how to improve the client's public image and may develop some potent but less obvious ways of getting publicity for the client: suggesting him as a speaker at conventions of appropriate groups, having him give scholarships, and establish awards and foundations, for instance. Examples of firms that receive a great deal of publicity through award activities in the fashion industries are Coty, which gives the annual Coty Fashion Award to outstanding fashion designers, and Neiman-Marcus, the Dallas store that makes annual awards for contributions to the fashion field. An example of an educational award is the Chair of Fashion, at the Fashion Institute of Technology, given by Bergdorf Goodman.

There are many independent publicists and public relations agencies who specialize in Seventh Avenue publicity, including such leaders as Eleanor Lambert Inc., Rosemary Sheehan, and Ruth Hammer Associates. All three have their headquarters in New York City. As is the case with advertising agencies, their clients are generally fabric or apparel producers instead of retailers, since retailers usually maintain their own internal publicity staffs. Rosemary Sheehan has been described "as the closest thing Seventh Avenue has to Perle Mesta. . . . She is renowned for the parties she throws and the (fashion) shows she stages for fabric clients like Galey & Lord Cottons, Hartford Fibres and the like. Miss Hammer, on the other hand, sees publicity as 'an adjunct to selling,' wastes little time on frills that won't pay off . . . or on projecting any images of herself."[13]

Insofar as the fashion producers are concerned, the public relations and publicity fraternity performs the very useful function of feeding information about the industry to the news media and thus stimulates business by keeping fashion in the limelight.

FASHION CONSULTANTS

A fashion consultant is an independent individual or firm, hired by fashion producers or retailers, to help them in their fashion operation. Although all manufacturers and retailers of any size have experts of their own within their firms, many use outside consultants for objective viewpoints, against which to check their own analyses and conclusions.

One of the oldest and most widely respected consulting agencies is Tobé Associates whose founder, Mrs. Tobé Coller Davis, died in 1962 but whose firm continues to operate from its headquarters in New York City, serving practically all major retailers in the United States. Tobé, who had a background of experience in the retail field, established a retail fashion and consulting service in 1927. She hired a staff of reporters to survey the women's apparel and accessory markets and report on the trends, successes, and reorder numbers, as they were identified in stores across the nation. The staff also covered important social events, such as opera openings, charity balls run by celebrities, or college football games, and commented on the new fashions or the preponderance of a particular color, fabric, or headgear.

The firm sends to its clients an 80-page weekly mimeographed brochure with fashion illustrations, described by one retailer as a "fashion dopesheet complete with names and numbers of all the horses, jockeys, weights, and handicaps."[14] From these reports, retailers can get a confirmation of their own interpretations of fashion or they can get a viewpoint so different from their own that they reappraise their original thinking. Although there are other fashion consulting firms in the

---

[13]"Eye on Plugola," *Women's Wear Daily*, December 19, 1960, p. 1.

[14]Stanley Marcus, president of Neiman-Marcus, Dallas, in a presentation at the Harvard Graduate School of Business Administration, Cambridge, Mass., March 10, 1959.

industry today, no person or firm has yet attained the stature of Tobé herself, or even of the organization that she founded. Tobé personally won many awards, among them a Neiman-Marcus Fashion Award in 1941 and the Chevalier of the Legion of Honor award in 1953. Prominent retailers honored her by establishing the annual Tobé Lectures in Retail Distribution (now discontinued) at the Harvard Graduate School of Business Administration and by setting up the annual Tobé Retailing Award.

Consultants do not necessarily come up with the right answers all the time but, in the case of Tobé's firm, there is testimony to the worth of their services in the fact that retailers in this country and abroad pay annual fees that range as high as $25,000, depending on the volume of the store served.

The function of the fashion consultant was once summed up by Tobé as a form of journalism.

"We are the reporters and interpreters of the fashion world," she said, "speaking to the fashion-makers and the fashion sellers. . . . Our job is to tell the makers what the sellers are doing and vice versa. Most of all, we interpret and evaluate for each what is happening to fashion itself. . . . We make it our business to stay abreast of just those economic, social, and art trends which I maintain are the great formative currents of fashion. . . . From all these we try to pick the significant trends that will change our lives, and hence our fashions. . . . We keep an eye on what those in the fashion vanguard are wearing and doing and seeing. This not only means reporting on what smart people wear. . . . It also means keeping abreast of what plays, films, and TV presentations they are seeing, which are successful, where they travel, and what books they read. . . . All of this information flows into our offices, where it is digested, sorted out, evaluated, and then disseminated through a weekly report. . . . Our clients—department stores throughout America, specialty stores in Europe, a wool manufacturer in Finland, the Export Institute in Israel—they can all shop the Fifth Avenue stores, the Paris showings, the Seventh Avenue showings, without budging from their desks. They can keep track of resort life without going to Monaco or Florida or the Caribbean. They can read about the fads, as well as the foundations of fashion, without spending much time or effort in research.

"So it is our business as a whole to interpret the current scene to the makers and sellers of fashion wares."[15]

RESIDENT BUYING OFFICES

In strategic market centers, notably New York, there are hundreds of resident buying firms that act as market representatives for, and render other related services

[15]Address before Harvard Graduate School of Business Administration, Cambridge, Mass., April 25, 1957, reprinted with permission of the late Tobé Coller Davis in the 1965 edition of this book.

to, different groups of member stores.[16] Their major function is to scout the wholesale markets daily and keep their client stores informed of fashion, price, and supply conditions in the wholesale markets. Their work supplements but does not replace the work of the store buyers.

Fifty years ago the resident office was likely to consist of one employee who was stationed in the market to service a single store at a distance from the city. In those days, most of the retailers bought from traveling salesmen, or drummers, who called on them perhaps twice a year. The New York buyer "in residence" was in the market, however, to follow up on orders and see that they were shipped on time, to take care of special requests and additional needs, and to be alert for bargains. Today, the typical resident office serves many stores—from a handful to several hundred—of similar type and customer appeal, but each store is in a different trading area and thus not in direct competition with any other.

Types of Resident Offices

The majority of the resident buying firms are independently owned enterprises to which client stores pay a yearly fee. A few others are cooperative enterprises, owned and supported by the stores that they service. A third type is owned and financed by a parent corporation that also owns the stores for which they are run. There are also some firms, called merchandise brokers, that represent stores but collect a commission from the manufacturers with whom they place orders. Among the largest resident buyers of the independent type are firms like Kirby, Block and Co., Felix Lilienthal & Co., Inc., and Atlas Buying Office. An example of a cooperative office is the Associated Merchandising Corporation, which is supported by and serves 31 major department stores and their branches located throughout the United States; an example of the corporate type is Macy Corporate Buying Office, serving the stores that are owned by the parent R.H. Macy & Co., Inc. Typical of the fourth kind of office, the merchandise broker, is Apparel Alliance, Inc., which services several hundred small independent stores in all parts of the country.[17]

Many of the larger buying offices maintain branches in other market centers like Los Angeles or Chicago. A few of the biggest also have offices in foreign countries to assist their stores in foreign buying; some offices also have client stores abroad and export American goods to them. One example is the Associated Merchandising Corporation, which has branch offices in Chicago, Los Angeles, Paris, Florence, Madrid, and Tel Aviv, and also represents several stores located in foreign countries. Some buying offices serve only apparel specialty shops and report on fashion markets only—the Specialty Stores Association, for example. Others, like the Macy office and the A.M.C., cover the whole range of department store merchandise. Some are even more highly specialized and deal only in children's wear or millinery. All of them, however, perform similar services and serve the same function as representatives of their member stores in the wholesale markets.

---

[16]For a listing of resident offices and their member stores, see *Phelon's Resident Buyers*, an annual directory, Phelon-Sheldon Publications, Inc., 32 Union Square, New York, N.Y.
[17]*Ibid.*

RESIDENT BUYING OFFICE BULLETIN

IRs MARKET HIGHLIGHTS

INDEPENDENT RETAILERS SYNDICATE, INC.
33 WEST 34th STREET, NEW YORK, N.Y. 10001

DEPT. DRESS - WOMENS
$9.75

POLYESTER DRAMA

MISSY STYLING FOR THE

FASHION MINDED HALF SIZE

EXCELLENT VALUE

STYLE # 1441 -

Sleeveless solid polyester
long dress- drape bodice-
rhinestone strip- horseshoe
neckline.

COST:　　$9.75

SIZES:　　$14\frac{1}{2}$ to $24\frac{1}{2}$

COLORS:　Black, Purple

BUYER:　　　G. BIRNBAUM
DEPT. HEAD:　L. BRONSTEIN
NUMBER:　　0-3138-1-3
DATE:　　　9/5/72
TERMS:　　　8/10 EOM
DELIVERY:　A/R 2 Weeks
F.O.B.:　　NYC
RESOURCE:　CHALLENGE

Source: Reprinted by permission of Independent Retailers Syndicate, Inc., New York, N.Y.

Fashion Services of Buying Offices

At the start of each season, the resident buyers in the offices cover the market and present analyses of fashion and market conditions to their client stores. During the season, bulletins go out regularly—weekly, as a rule—in addition to whatever flash bulletins are needed to report new items and special developments such as manufacturers' fast selling styles, price changes, and new supply conditions. A typical bulletin may report on a tightening supply of a wanted fabric, an early demand for a certain type of swimsuit, or a new style trend in the wholesale markets. When buyers of client stores are in the market themselves, the resident buyers act as advisors and time savers; when the store buyers return home, the office buyers follow up on shipments of orders that store buyers have placed.

Most of the actual purchasing by the resident offices is done at the specific request of the individual store buyers and is ordered in their names. Some offices, however, have set up wholesale divisions that buy large quantities of reasonably staple products for resale to member stores at a close markup. Private brands are also developed by many buying offices, and the merchandise bought under the office label is available to client stores. An example of such a private brand operation is the A.M.C.'s Aimcee brand, which can be found on goods in many large department stores throughout the United States.

Some offices do centralized buying of lower and moderately priced ready-to-wear and accessories. This means that a resident buyer in the office makes the selection of styles for each store's stock within the framework of a budget set by the store. The office orders the merchandise and, guided by sales and stock reports from each store, reorders some styles and discontinues or replaces others. With the experience of many stores to draw on, the office has a national picture of fashion trends to guide its selections.

In addition to their buying and fashion advisory services, buying offices maintain departments that: prepare catalogs and other mailing pieces for use by the stores; supply advertising mats, suggested layouts, and copy; and offer assistance in finding merchandising personnel. Offices also hold special merchandise clinics for client stores during certain months of the year when the out-of-town store buyer influx into New York City is at its peak.

The degree and extent of services may vary from one office to another but, essentially, they all serve the same function in the fashion business: they keep the producers informed of what retail stores want, and they keep the retailers informed of what is happening in the wholesale fashion markets.

OTHER FASHION ENTERPRISES

There are enterprises of many other types that play important behind-the-scenes roles in the business of fashion. Their activities, however, are too varied and too highly specialized to be described in detail. A few examples and some well-known names in the business are briefly mentioned.

Specialized display consultants design and construct fashion display materials for manufacturers, retailers, and fashion magazines, for example. Among the pioneers in this field were Lester Gaba (whose visual merchandising activities also included the staging of fashion shows), Albert Bliss, and William Stensgaard. Specialized consultants in the fields of sales promotion or marketing are retained on a fee basis by manufacturers, retailers, and even magazines. Estelle Hamburger is an example of a retail marketing consultant; Estelle Ellis, president of Business Image, Inc., numbers *Glamour* magazine among her many fashion clients.

Market research agencies do consumer surveys for retail stores, publications, and manufacturers or retail surveys for producers. Among the research agencies who do work in the fashion field are the Eugene Gilbert organization, noted for their studies of the youth market, and Audits and Surveys, which has made some interesting studies of the buying patterns of retail store customers.

There are many trade associations that serve businesses and business executives with interests in common and that are set up for joint action or study of a common problem. Some examples are the National Retail Merchants Association (to which most major department and apparel specialty stores belong), the New York Couture Business Council, the National Association of Women's Clothing Salesmen, the New York Women Buyers Club, the National Association of Men's Sportswear Buyers, and so on. One reading in this section describes the history and activities of the Couture Council.

There are also associations of publicity and advertising specialists and associations of children's wear buyers, accessory buyers, and fashion designers. An association that encompasses fashion specialists of many different types is the Fashion Group, whose activities are described in another reading.

In short, there is a whole army of creative people who contribute to making the fashion business what it is today and who will undoubtedly contribute to its growth in the future.

READINGS

Behind-the-scenes views of professionals at work in the various auxiliary enterprises are offered in this group of readings. Here we hear from or about magazine editors, public relations experts, advertising agency executives, resident buyers, and the Fashion Group, a professional association. In some cases, practitioners in the particular field speak to us directly through their articles and speeches. In other cases, a research writer brings us the story and, in the process, demonstrates one of the many other skills that are at the service of the fashion business through its auxiliaries.

THE ROLE OF THE FASHION MAGAZINE IN THE BUSINESS OF FASHION

Edith Raymond Locke

We at *Mademoiselle*, as a fashion magazine for the most changeable of all consumers (a reader we identify by our slogan—Mademoiselle—not just one of the girls), must walk where angels, computers, and statistics fear to tread. We must have that crystal ball eye, that sensitive stomach, and that sense of history, of the immediate and of the next, that fingertip feeling about tomorrow's clothes. Indeed, at *Mademoiselle* we are concerned with and dedicated to the force that has rocked the business of fashion as much as the computer—the force of the youth market, the young adult market. Our publication has addressed itself exclusively to college-educated young women between the ages of 18 and 25 since its inception 35 years ago—when the demographics in that age group were not exactly awe-inspiring. The postwar-boom babies who are creating the tremendous under-30 population bulge in our world today had not yet been born. I am not even sure their parents were married. In fact, if we had had a good computer going for us in 1935, we probably would never have started the magazine, so unpromising were the prospects of the Youth Market. You might say we were a little ahead of our time; but we stuck with our specialty—and look at our market now!

You might wonder just what is our role as a fashion magazine for young adults in this business of fashion. You might call us the catalyst that makes possible the smooth blending of fashion and consumer. You might call us an experimentalist—a launcher of the "now" in fashion. You might call us an inventor—a creator of future fashion trends. You might call us the Linus's security blanket of young taste. To be useful to our readers, and

to the fashion manufacturers and retailers, we must be an accurate mirror of the total young way of life and dressing, from bikinis to midis and from pot to the pill. When you pick up a copy of *Mademoiselle* at the newsstand, you see only one-fifth of our fashion role exposed. We like to refer to the other four-fifths as "the iceberg" part of the magazine—equally vital to its function, purpose, and success as the copy you receive in the mail or buy on the newsstand. Designers, manufacturers, and retailers who really use and work with a fashion magazine look to us to predict the unpredictable months in advance of a season. We do it—not with a crystal ball but with a crystal-clear window on the whole world of fashion and all the peripheral influences. If we are clairvoyant, it is because our editorial staff is literally everywhere at the same time—reporting, interpreting, projecting, endorsing, and recommending—and, from all this, we are able to distill an informed and intuitive picture of what's new and what's next. Our seasonal predictions of things to come are edited into an advance report to retailers called "Young Fashion Futures." It is our unbiased—but by no means uncommitted—assessment of what lies ahead in young fashion.

Another part of our perceptiveness is a reflection of our activities in the fabric market. Six to twelve months before a new season begins to take shape, we are exploring, with fabric designers, mills and fiber companies, all the upcoming trends in colors, textures, patterns, prints, weights, fibers, blends, and every other facet, that influences that vast market. Our fabric editor consults with designers, stylists, manufacturing executives, and retailers, who regularly visit our fabric showroom to do a lot of "brain-picking," which we heartily encourage. We operate a direct line to hundreds of key retail stores throughout the country. We are a source of information to them and also a line of communica-

SOURCE: Excerpted from an address by Edith Raymond Locke, Editor of *Mademoiselle* magazine, before a Conference Board meeting, March 24, 1970. Reprint permission granted.

tion. Our showroom is open to them every working day of the year, and hardly a day goes by when there is not a buyer, a merchandise manager, a fashion display or promotion director, and a store president—or large groups of each—in there consulting our merchandising staff. They look to us for fashion guidance. We look to them for news, too. We want to know what is selling, what lines are selling, and what their thoughts are on fashion futures. We listen and they listen. We live and work together in our fashion business world, a world of change. To be geared for change is to grow—grow in the 1970s. We will not shave our heads or go naked—we will buy and wear a multitude of clothes and looks: long, short, bright, and muted. We will continue to be lured by fashion, to be under the spell of fashion—young fashion.

HOW AMERICAN FASHION GOT THERE

The New York Couture Press Week Was the Ladder

The New York Couture Business Council that, in January, 1971, celebrated 27 years of showings to the nation's fashion press, has been star-studded with personalities and highlights in its over 25 years of existence.

In spite of living in the shadow of the great French couture, until World War II blacked out all news from Paris, New York's clothing industry had grown to an awkward, sprawling, unorganized giant by 1941. Largely through efforts of the ILGWU to promote the "made in New York" label, manufacturers at last found a common meeting ground under the general title of the New York Dress Institute, organizing with admirable timing to take full advantage of the wartime blackout of fashion news from abroad.

Few of the 200-odd editors, usually in attendance for the presentations by the nation's top couturiers during the New York Couture National Press Weeks, remember the war-torn days that shrouded the birth of this organization.

Fifty-three fashion editors accepted the telegraphed invitation to attend the first Press Week in July, 1943. In awed wonder the New York Dress Institute (from which the Couture Business Council emerged) calculated at the week's conclusion that it had received more than 696,000 lines of publicity at an estimated space value of about a quarter of a million dollars. At the recent 55th Press Week in June, 1970, these figures were probably passed during the first day as daily newspaper reports were telephoned and cabled, as live TV went on the air, and as radio shows were taped—all through the Couture's well-organized press setup on the third floor of the Waldorf Astoria Hotel, the official headquarters each June and January.

From the original effort of assembling the national press came the continuity of semi-annual events that, more than any other single factor, has helped catapult American fashion to equal footing with Paris, projecting the "American Look" around the world for women the world over to admire and emulate.

Several women in the fashion world helped spark Press Week into existence, but it took a man with a keen business sense—Ben Reig—to dream up the idea and wrap it up in capsule form for fellow manufacturers to follow and understand. Reig, whose collection ranks every season with the top newsmakers, conceived the Press Week idea that has been fanned into semi-annual flames by the busy pens of the nation's press since July, 1943.

The organization prospered with Dorothy An-

SOURCE: Reprint permission granted by the New York Couture Business Council.

derson as its first director. Another feminine powerhouse who helped make it a going concern was Adelia Bird Ellis. A publicist, Eleanor Lambert, became director and held the post for about 12 years. Kittie Campbell, a fashion writer, left *Harper's Bazaar* in 1962 to become the fourth director of the Council until 1967.

The present and fifth director, Mildred Sullivan, was named to the post in October, 1967. Known as a "low key dynamo" throughout the fashion industry, this tall, willowy brunette of great charm and persuasion has moved forward to broaden the base of the Council, inviting California designers to show their designs under the Council's umbrella. "Fashion is no longer geographical," she believes, and to that end she has dedicated her energies.

The current president of the Council is nationally known, energetic Vincent Monte-Sano, formerly the owner of Monte-Sano & Pruzan, which during its reign was *the* "status" coat and suit house of the industry. Vincent retired and was elected to the presidency of the New York Couture by the Board of Directors in 1968. His forward thinking and knowledge of the fashion industry makes him a valued asset to the organization.

In 1952, a crisis developed for the New York Dress Institute. Manufacturers of lower-priced merchandise reexamined the advantages of participating in Press Week and felt that the top designers were getting the lion's share of the news coverage. At about the same time, the original union fund reached the bottom of the barrel. The result was reorganization on a "club basis," with a nucleus of high-quality houses forming the New York Couture and assuming the obligation of Press Week.

With Press Week the established success it is today, it frequently finds itself with new sets of problems. Although completely supported financially by the members of the New York Couture Business Council, Press Week plays host to affiliated businesses that are invited to be associates. Some associates are the Millinery Institute of America, Woll Industry, Denim Council, Coty, West Point Pepperell, After Six Men's Formals, and Sears Roebuck and Co. They pay a fee to be placed on the Press Week schedule so that members of the press can be presented with a well-organized plan of events without conflict and with a minimum of confusion.

The unique opportunity provided by the Couture Business Council, which arranges to have the valuable fashion press of the nation in one spot at one time, has proven to be an excellent promotional tool for the fashion manufacturers. Under the aegis of the New York Couture Business Council, the one organization in the world whose members know how to mass-produce quality, Press Weeks will continue to flourish for many years to come, acting as the official "spokesman" for the number one industry in New York City and New York State—and the second largest industry in the country.

THE FASHION ROLE OF AN AD AGENCY

Arthur A. Winters

SOURCE: Mr. Winters, President of Arthur Winters Advertising Agency, which specializes in fashion advertising, wrote this article especially for this book. He is professor of advertising at the Fashion Institute of Technology, New York, N.Y.

Calling an advertising agency by any other name may not be just as sweet—but it could be more accurate. The ad agency is now involved in so many marketing functions that the mere preparation and placement of ads in print media would severely limit its usefulness to most clients. This is especially true in the fashion industry where the agency helps primary and secondary level firms develop the right product in the right package at the right price and gets it the right distribution in the right markets. Merchandising becomes an agency function which helps a mill or a manufacturer stimulate his sales force, design sales presentations, train salesmen, plan sales conventions and exhibits, and organize sales drives. The agency can research markets or customer motivations and preferences. Dealer aids, cooperative advertising, tie-in promotions, and point-of-purchase materials are planned and produced. These functions are offered by agencies as a full service or a supplement to the firm's own staff. The agency role today is to assist a client in *marketing his product.* In the full sense of the meaning of marketing this includes merchandising and any of the direct sales promotion activities—advertising, display, publicity.

Most agencies who work for fashion producers are extremely retail-oriented They realize the vitality of selling activities that get their inspiration from consumer wants and needs. Those efforts that best supplement personal selling and coordinate sales promotion are the basis of ad agency service. The extent to which the agency gets involved is largely up to the client and his requirements. Many primary, and some secondary firms, have substantial staffs of their own which perform the aforementioned functions.

Ad agencies have generally found that regardless of how limited their original arrangement is—if they can really help a client—they are gradually asked to do more and more. A good agency is considered a staff element in the organizational structure of many firms in the fashion industry.

We haven't mentioned the retail level yet—and purposely. Here the story is quite different. It is difficult for the average ad agency to provide service for retailers. Agencies that have been most successful serving retail accounts found it necessary to institute "local" advertising departments that specialize in retail store advertising. These departments are specifically designed to handle daily newspaper advertising with its problems of quick deadlines and last-minute changes.

The advertising agency that equips itself for this service is prepared to plan and produce *all* of a store's advertising. This, however, is not as common as the case of agencies which undertake to prepare *special* advertising material and research, and offer counsel on planning and copy concepts. By limiting their service, they are not involved with the constant pressure caused by the day-in, day-out advertising and sales promotion in which retail stores must engage.

Several large stores, who have their own advertising departments, use outside agencies to prepare institutional advertising while they themselves prepare product advertising. Other stores may engage an agency to handle their radio advertising while handling all their newspaper advertising themselves.

The most successful example of a large store-advertising agency collaboration is the long-standing effort of Ohrbach's in New York City and their agency, Doyle Dane Bernbach, Inc. The institutional advertising produced by this combination had not only advanced the progress of the store, but is universally regarded as a classic in retail institutional advertising, and the series has been widely imitated and developed into an established and recognized style.

Agencies with clients such as fabric mills and garment manufacturers are now engaged in a full range of activities which serve to help originate, develop, package, distribute, and promote products. They also provide public relations programs which include research and publicity. The range of services which agencies render to retailers is much more limited. The number of agencies seeking business on the primary and secondary levels of the fashion industry grows daily. The problems of handling the promotion of retailers inhibit the agency's full-scale entry.

PROMOTING FASHION THROUGH EFFECTIVE FASHION ADVERTISING

What is fashion advertising and what does it take to create it effectively? In order to answer this question it is necessary to discuss what fashion is. But first, I would classify fashion advertising into two distinct categories: (a) exclusive fashion advertising, as exemplified in fashion magazines and in advertisements for exclusive stores, and (b) volume fashion advertising, as exemplified in volume selling in department and promotional-price stores.

The definition of what is and what is not fashion has confounded the so-called fashion practitioners for years. It has been analyzed and defined by poets, scholars, researchers, and advertising men, and no two explanations have been exactly in agreement. It seems that fashion is as elusive as it is illusive . . . and by nature a most capricious commodity. Therefore, rather than add to the long list of controversial definitions, I would choose to explain fashion in terms of the human motivation and desire which help shape it, applying these to a discussion of how they affect fashion advertising.

I am sure you have heard of the socioeconomic theory that wars, depressions, social and business environments determine the nature of fashion. I've never accepted this theory beyond the point or premise that all things affect fashion, which is *what people want*. Fashion is a personal affair, an individual's reaction to his own needs and desires. In women, the approach is so personal that it often takes a woman to sell a woman. A man might understand how important it is to a woman to wear a skirt that is shorter and tighter this season. But he is at a loss to explain how she actually feels in it. A woman can sell fashion because she knows the intimate feel of the sheath dress . . . she sells the feel of fashion, the tight skirt or flared skirt, the high waist or low waist, almost before she sells the particular garment. The basic difference in the salesmanship of fashion advertising is emotion. The appeals are emotional, the approach more imaginative. Effective fashion advertising will use a knowledge of the particular set of emotions concerned with the desire and need for individuality, romance, recognition, acceptance, compensation, career, etc. The partnership of illustration and copy must create in the customer the feel of fashion, and generate a specific satisfaction or emotion which can be attained with this fashion. Fashion advertising is extremely effective when it lets the woman know exactly how she will feel, and what will happen when she wears this black satin sheath on her next date.

Creating exciting fashion advertising must rely upon constant exposure to what makes people want and feel as they do. It requires comprehensive orientation on what is happening and what has happened in our world. And most important, it necessitates an understanding *of your customer* and *your store* and the particular appeals which it has for them.

We are now ready to discuss fashion advertising in terms of our original classifications, "the exclusive fashion customer," and the "volume fashion customer."

Exclusive fashion advertising can be formal or informal, but it must be authoritative and signify leadership. Fundamentally, this advertising is directed to women who want to *lead* in wearing a fashion and is designed to sell a concept rather than a specific garment in stock. Lord & Taylor's advertising is a good example of this most important characteristic. The approach is usually one of breathless excitement about what the fashion will do for you. The message is directed towards people who want to set the pace; the appeals are prestige and individuality. The atmosphere created is illusionary and full of mood. There is more concern with mood than details, and this type of advertising should try to convince the reader that she is influencing the fashion, rather than being influenced by it. Copy is usually brief, but dramatic and descriptive. Art work should be dynamic, fresh, dramatic.

The techniques in volume fashion advertising are designed to sell the woman who must keep up with fashion rather than be a leader. Here a knowledge of customer, product, and salesmanship are perhaps more exacting . . . for the advertising must be effective enough to influence much larger groups. Here, in a certain sense, an awareness of buying patterns, merchandising, and customer preferences are more important than writing ability. The style of volume fashion advertising must be forceful and emphatic and geared to attract attention, maintain interest, arouse desire, and prompt to action.

This customer wants to dress smartly, but she is also concerned with budget, keeping her family healthy, her home attractive, leisure activities, etc. Many other considerations and products are vying with fashion for this customer's attention, and a dozen other stores are competing to sell her the same garments. If the advertising is to work, it must say it better and be more compelling. The appeals here are somewhat different from the specialized appeals in exclusive fashion advertising. Here we try to convince the customer that she is buying and wearing what is new and smart, and infer that she has the good judgment to recognize smart fashion. We emphasize why it will be becoming to her and try to leave no doubt that she is well dressed due to the merchandising skill of our store—*her store.* The fashion is related to her activ-ities, her way of life. The copy gives details, wearability, washability, width of seams, fabrics, colors, sizes—and gives more importance to price as the type of store goes more promotional.

Selling fashion today relies upon a very accurate knowledge of what your customer wants and what you have to offer in the way of product and conditions of sale. It is the blend of this, plus the emotional excitement of buying "something strictly for one's self."

COSTUMERS' NIGHTMARE: MINIS, MIDIS, HOT PANTS!

Question: Which fashions will look upbeat and contemporary six months from now? Agency people who clothe models in ads must come up with answers

How vital a role fashion acumen can play in promoting a non-fashion product is called to mind by the hoopla advertising woman Mary Wells Lawrence created when she outfitted Braniff Airline stewardesses in costume-like uniforms by Italian designer Emilio Pucci.

Another recent and notable example of the use of fashion in advertising is the successful campaign created for Virginia Slims by the Leo Burnett Co. which employed various styles of dress to illustrate just how liberated women have become and thus helped to establish that brand's image.

Fashion coordination in advertising has always been a fundamental creative function, particularly so since the advent of color television. It is usually unsung and unnoticed; if its presence were singularly apparent, it could be a discordant element.

Given that last fact, consider the challenge of the year of the mini-midi-gaucho-hot pants phenomenon.

Gayle Carlisle heads the fashion department at J.

SOURCE: *Marketing-Communications,* May 1971. Reprint permission granted.

Walter Thompson. Last year that meant almost 300 jobs for which she and her six assistants had to advise art directors and copywriters as to what apparel would do best to convey their conceptions of real life; see that the clothing was on the set when needed, that it fitted properly and, above all, that one model's outfit did not clash with another's or with the set. "The importance and workings of color are something most people aren't aware of," says Miss Carlisle. "You can set so many moods just by the colors you use. . . .

"It takes a lot more time and thought than that. The coordination, for example. You even have to know what your set designer is doing. If you have four scenes and four different changes of costume, you have to think your way through the whole thing and coordinate the whole commercial so it works well together."

Getting the cooperation of Seventh Avenue fashion houses isn't always easy, even for a company with the leverage of Thompson, because ads almost never give a credit line.

Miss Carlisle has been involved with the midi-mini controversy as have others in and around the fashion business. "We've been wearing the midi in the office here for a while, but I know no men have accepted them, and there's a good deal of concern on the part of clients about how long the style will last. We've used some long skirts, but not many. I would say we've stuck pretty much to pants—either gauchos or knickers. Of course, on Singer and Ford and some of our other accounts we have used midis."

Fashion director Irene Beckmann at Doyle Dane Bernbach claimed not to be interested in the midi-mini controversy. She says it has been kicked to death. But, of course, she's involved.

"On the high fashion accounts , naturally there wouldn't be any problem," she adds. Burlington and Clairol get the largest share of catering-to from Doyle Dane's fashion department.

"But take a Polaroid commercial where you have the average American family. That's where you have a problem. You have to decide how average, and you work around it. You can show only waist-up shots or you can decide it's a mixed group and the young people have their own thing going while the older women wear shorter skirts. For outdoor at the moment I would show a midi-coat on the mother, I think for indoor I would probably try to avoid it, or show her in pants. . . ."

Who has the final say on styling? "The art director. That's the rule at Doyle Dane Bernbach."

The art director relies on the fashion department to understand the spirit he wants and how to achieve it in the ad, the DDB fashion director explains. "It's one thing to say, 'I want a girl who looks like she's hysterical and crying and she's coming from the woods with a chiffon thing. I see it. It's filmy,' It's one thing to say that and another to go out and find the girl and the right dress and make the whole thing work."

Doris Wilson, fashion coordinator at Foote, Cone & Belding in Chicago, exults over surveying the collections of the Seventh Avenue fashion houses. "It's always lots of fun to hop in and out of the houses and see exactly what the designers are predicting—to look at it in person rather than in magazines. In New York you get a much better chance to do that than we do here."

About the midi: "It creates problems in that so many of the clients are afraid to take a definite stand. We would recommend one thing, but they were kind of afraid and we ended up going with pants a lot.

"We just did a series of things for Kraft Foods. It's supposed to feature a very with-it young housewife, and the farthest the client would go was a midi raincoat with boots, while definitely showing she was wearing something short and more conservative underneath.

"The commercials are going to be running for quite a while, and the client was afraid to take a definite midi stand fearing that it might not be around that long. It was either that or pants and everybody is doing the pants thing these days or shooting above the waist. I think there's been a lot more above-the-waist shots. Just from what we've been doing, I think so."

With fashion-minded clients, Miss Wilson points out, there's the risk that she may not be current enough.

"Clients like Kimberly-Clark want to be very current as far as fashion goes, so there again you kind of have to put your foot in your mouth when you're shooting stuff in January that's going to run for the rest of the year. You simply hope that what you're showing is going to be in by next September or November. But that's the fun part of the whole business, I think. . . ."

Miss Beckmann, at DDB, didn't recall precisely which commercial had been the most expensive to costume, but she did say that she often does have to buy some very expensive things from Seventh Avenue only to have them destroyed. "We might have paid $500 for it and the art director says, 'That ruffle on the bottom—I'd like to see it off. And I'd like to see it as a cape.' So there you go. Or you just spent $700 for an Oscar de La Renta and there you are in the field and the art director says, 'I want to see her rolling along that wet grass. . . .'"

One reason Gayle Carlisle at J. Walter Thompson thinks it's important to have a staff fashion department in an advertising agency is because the department is familiar with clients and the kind of image they want to project in their promotion. It can visualize the entire situation. "Not only do you think of the commercial and what you're trying to do, but you must remember what your clients' likes and dislikes might be.

"We used to have a saying on Eastman Kodak that if you saw the clothes, you made a horrible mistake because what you're trying to show is the warmth of a personal relationship between a mother and child or something like that. So we never wanted far-out, high-fashion clothes on Kodak. It was always the kinds of things that would go into the background. But even that has changed."

Fashion coordinators, naturally enough, enjoy assignments which permit them the greatest range of creative expression—which in most cases means a high-fashion ad. "I like the ones that are more fashion-y, that allow you to get out and do whatever you want to do," says Foote, Cone & Belding's Doris Wilson. "I worked for about a year on the Sears account, which was kind of binding in that you had to use all Sears merchandise. You weren't able to go out and do wild things; but it was kind of a challenge on the other hand to make the Sears merchandise look *avant-garde* and up-to-date. That was done through accessorizing and things of that sort."

Freelancer Blanche Greenstein enjoys doing period costumes most of all. At Doyle Dane, Irene Beckmann says, "When a girl can create something and get involved in it, that's where her interets are. When we do something in Napoleon's time, she has to go to the library and get out all kinds of books and figure out just what was worn in those times and what the accessories were and then find them and put the whole thing together or work with a dressmaker or costume house and try to get the whole thing to look like it's right there in that time. . . ."

Just where fashion coordinators see fashion going appears to be anybody's guess at the moment. "Fashion is much more fun today," exclaims Miss Carlisle of J. Walter Thompson. "It's not so set. It's much more of an individual look, and it's much more fun to put together and work on."

A JAUNT WITH FASHION

Jean Cameron

A fashion publicist bases her work on the premise that a woman must be ill if she doesn't want to know the latest about clothes. We are, apparently, a remarkably healthy nation.

Eleanor Lambert of New York, fashion publicist of great skill, is a prime generator at this wild side of a multibillion dollar industry. In its more drab end, that of production, it gives fruitful, if sometimes shaky, employment to one million U.S. citizens.

Among Miss Lambert's clients who participate vicariously and fruitfully in the excitement she generates in the press, are a distinctive group of fashion designers, here and abroad. Manufacturers who pay her court and costs admire the high plateau to which she raises the newsworthy in their fashion.

With a quick mind for timing, she analyzes fashion in New York, then Paris, to determine what will, and what will not, make fashion news. At two yearly meetings with the press, and in a myriad of releases during the year, she feeds out news; she bolsters opinion—and she sways it.

A blonde dynamo, Eleanor Lambert travels regularly between New York and Paris, loved by many, envied by many. An associate says, "Anyone who has become a success has critics. Eleanor Lambert has hers certainly."

Her world is fashion, and fashion has been good to her. She is at home in these worlds—divergent as Paris and New York—and thanks to her ener-

SOURCE: *Realm*, October 1963. Abridged and reprinted by permission of Medalist Publications, Inc., Chicago, Illinois. Miss Lambert is one of the best known and most effective public relations experts in the fashion field.

gies, all her worlds are luxurious worlds.

Her energy is expended on behalf of—in America—names such as Anne Fogarty, Ceil Chapman, Adele Simpson, Coty, Jean Louis and Rudi Gernreich. In Europe, Simonetta et Fabiani, Roger Vivier, Sybil Connolly, Castillo, Ferraras.

Although she has a staff of 17 people (she hires more at busy times), she does all the writing for each of her accounts herself. "She works all the time," says one associate in New York. Her experienced hand and mind guide, influence, and direct much creative talent in fashion. Producer of large and lavish fashion shows, she has produced the gala March of Dimes show, originated the Cotton Fashion Awards shows. And the fashion extravaganza, the Cherry Blossom Festival Fashion Show, has been staged for two years with a Lambert touch.

For 20 years Miss Lambert directed the New York Couture Group's semi-annual Press Week showings of new fashion. This year she gathered her group of outstanding designers into an aggregation known as the American Designers Group, and held a press week showing. Fashion editors from all over the country were treated to nearly two weeks of new designs.

The most interesting fashion show she ever produced? In 1959 she selected American fashions shown in Moscow by the U.S. government. They caused a sensation among Soviet women and brought frowns of displeasure from the Soviet government. There was no acceptance by the Soviet that it was at all suitable for their women to think, look or dress as Eleanor Lambert thinks women should. (It was at this show that sample Coty lipsticks were snatched with glee by Kremlin belles.)

Scores of designers attribute their success to Eleanor. She "put Arnold Scaasi on the map," is now promoting Pepe Fernandez, the Cuban refugee designer. He arrived in the United States from Cuba with only the clothes on his back, and unlimited talent and ability.

Eleanor is always attracted to new, young, striving talent. In the beginning, her publicity for the struggling designer costs him practically nothing. She has a list of distinguished clients, true, but many of them are distinguished as a result of the Lambert flair.

She has great know-how, a keen sense of fashion. A friend says, "She has a fantastic memory. If she goes to the art gallery or the theater, she is able to mentally pigeonhole what she has seen, and sooner or later she will relate it to fashion. She relates *everything* to fashion." Another friend terms her a very "current" person, says she has a great sense of the past in relation to the present.

The pro's and con's of the *Ten Best Dressed* list, which Eleanor transplanted here from Paris in 1933, are debated hotly. Eleanor thinks it is important, mails 2500 ballots each year to qualified judges of these matters, such as society editors, columnists, and the like. She also thinks it important that the not-so-wealthy are dressed best. She worked out the uniforms for the women of the military as special consultant on publicity to WAC and U.S. Army Nurse Corps. She saw to it that Mainbocher, her client when he returned to America from Paris in 1940, designed a smart, feminine uniform for the WAVES.

"No matter what they're up to, women should look like women," maintains Eleanor.

"In America," she continues, "women have a tendency to either over-dress, or to be too conservative. That's why I try to spark the dull clothes, and eliminate all the fuss and nonsense from fussy clothes. If clothes are presented to the press as dramatically as possible, and properly, it's certain to get through to readers of women's pages. Because of all this vital fashion publicity, American women have become well dressed. It's a matter of fashion education."

POLKA DOTS ARE POISON IN GEORGIA

Sonia Arcone

The Work and Life of a Resident Office Buyer

Bounded on the north by Forty-first Street, on the south by Thirty-fifth, on the east by Broadway and on the west by Eighth Avenue, there is an island of industry known as the Garment Center and, to people in the business, more familiarly as Seventh Avenue or the Market. Here a group of people gets paid to know that there are towns in Georgia where polka dots are poison, that southern Alabama hates red, that the heat in San Diego comes in September, and that sleeveless, low-cut dresses are taboo in Mormon country. These people are called resident buyers.

A resident or buyers' buyer can spot a Midwest accent and often the exact state in which the accent was acquired. She can sometimes tell a home town from a dress or its color. And she knows, oddly enough, by the number of dresses she's to purchase for a town in Pennsylvania whether the coal miners are working, on strike, or have a three-day week. She also knows when the law has clamped down on a wide-open gambling town (requests for formals drop to nothing).

Sometimes she knows from the type of dress a store may request, or by the urgency of cancellations, or demands for off-priced goods to stimulate business. Sometimes her strange conglomeration of knowledge comes from a word, phrase, or paragraph in hastily written letters—the tip-off to news that will break into headlines a week later. Her job, buying (and planning) fashions for perhaps a hundred stores in a hundred cities, is part of a billion-dollar business—one that has played a large part in

influencing the growth of stores and the tastes of women all over the country. And her work and life have special interest for college women excited by the touch-it, try-it, own-it-temporarily glitter of a department store buyer's job. For the resident buyer, unlike her store counterpart, is not responsible for daily sales volume—the strain of making each day's profit figures equal or surpass those of a year ago. And she does not work on Saturdays. She may, however, have to travel more miles (breaking home ties) than the would-be store buyer to get her start and keep her power; resident buying is not any-city kind of work. There are a few resident buying firms in Chicago, some in Los Angeles. But most, well over two hundred, are in New York.

If it's hard for a regular department store buyer, say in Minneapolis, to anticipate the multifaceted needs and wants of her store's clientele, you can imagine what octopus-like vision is required of the resident buyer whose job it is to satisfy the needs and desires of customers shopping at stores all across the country, not to mention customers in Africa or Japan. Indeed, the resident buyer's business has such scope that if she longs to identify herself with something big she may gravitate to international dress-buying. Thus one buyer we know took her pattern-cutting knowledge to England to show an English coat and suit manufacturer how to style his garments for good United States sales; she advised Italian silk houses that Americans wanted to buy their silks but not in lingerie tints.

Supposing it were possible for you to pay a visit to one of these progress-and-prosperity-minded buyers. Her office is in a tall, tall building on Broadway among some shorter buildings where ribbons, hats, and leggings are sold wholesale. On the seventh floor of the building, after you've passed rows and rows of glassed-in, semiwalled offices teeming with busy women, you come to a separate semi-walled office of frosted glass and guarded by two secretaries. Inside you find a very, very busy woman who sits in quiet authority under a black hat of dignity and breadth reading a big book of reports. She nods for you to read a magazine until she's through. The secretaries whish in and out, the high heels echo briskly up and down outside the door, the buzzer buzzes. Finally: "And what is it I can tell you about resident office buying?"

She pauses. Then, "To begin with, our stores own us. We don't own the stores."

Actually, she might go on to explain, only a few (about six) of the New York buying offices are literally store property—they are owned cooperatively and operated by groups of major big-city stores. Other offices—about a hundred—are maintained by nation-wide or territorial chains. A hundred more are independent organizations commissioned by the stores and paid annual fees based on the volume of their services (another way of being owned). Our big-time buyer would point out, however, that all buyers in resident offices, even offices that live by commissions, are salaried and work on a year-round basis. Maybe this sounds secure. It isn't.

IN THE MARKET

For the resident buyer of dresses the New York market is a vast jungle of manufacturers, factories, and showrooms where merchandise is born, bought, and shipped out. From the catacombs of ancient buildings on Thirty-fifth Street (called Chinatown by the trade) where the cheaper dresses are manufactured by the thousands to the more modern edifices on Broadway and Seventh Avenue where more expensive clothes are made, the resident buyer knows her way around. Because there are over two thousand New York dress manufacturers plus many, many offices of out-of-town firms to be shopped, each dress buyer has to specialize in a particular size and price range. The budget dress buyer of misses sizes, for instance, knows of over two hundred makers of dresses that retail from $8.95 to $17.95. She shops as many as

are humanly possible, can recognize top value for the money, and may do business with thirty-five to fifty manufacturers within a season.

The manufacturers are the resident buyer's friends and often her problem children. They seek her advice and opinion on styles fresh from the designing room. She, in turn, tries to see and hear everything that goes on in factories and showrooms. To a bit of information about a color or a sample cut of fabric she gives serious consideration, storing it away against some future project. And each week she writes a long report (plus many shorter ones) telling her store buyers what's happening. Usually, she'll give advice on what to buy—from then on it's up to the store buyer.

The buyer's long, full day regularly starts at nine sharp with at least three long-distance calls from stores, a heavy pile of mail as well as a line of people impatiently waiting, requesting merchandise or information. And a buyer's morning usually starts off, too, with a series of headache calls from salesmen—salesmen on the phone or arriving with bulging sample cases. Either way, they must be put off until the special hours set aside for "looking"—usually in the late afternoon. It's important that a buyer get out into the market early if she's to make all the stops, often at least ten, necessary to fill that day's requests and to collect information from salesmen on what's "hot" at stores she doesn't buy for: How many stores bought item X? How fast was it reordered in three big stores? What colors were reordered in what quantity?

KEY SEASONS

. . . The resident buyer is both Midas and menace to the manufacturer since she is the guide for the store buyer, who, unless she's with a major Eastern department store, averages only two to four trips to the New York market a year. It is often the word of the resident buyer that influences a large purchase or none at all.

January and June are the months of the heavy buying weeks when the bulk of spring and fall purchasing is done—hectic weeks when every day is devoted to working along with one or a group of store buyers, guiding their steps, suggesting "resources" (manufacturers) in order of importance, demanding where possible that valuable time be saved by showing only preselected samples.

Sometimes the resident buyer is greeted by wariness and even a certain amount of hostility on the part of the store buyer who feels that he or she has been coming to New York's market long enough to know the score. Mostly, however, the store buyer is grateful—or learns to be—for the additional services of a buyer who scouts the market regularly and who, after all, is supplied by her own employers at a substantial cost. It's to the advantage of the resident buyer if she has the liking and confidence of a store buyer: it can mean the privilege of "open money" and the right to buy on her own, in small quantities, any new item that looks right for the store. This added power, sought after by resident buyers, turns every month into a rush month. More details mean more errors and more promises mean more broken. Even a good idea may backfire.

A recent purchase was made in New York for a California store. When the dresses arrived the store buyer turned pale. There were twelve dresses in the package, six blue and six brown. Brown is difficult enough to put over in California and this was the most monstrous shade she had ever seen. Furious, she sent the dresses back direct to the manufacturer without troubling to write a letter of explanation.

The package was refused and returned to the store because no explanation arrived. In great disgust and not wanting to be bothered any more, the buyer put the dresses in stock and muttered with heavy sarcasm to her assistant: "Lovely new color."

The dresses sold out in one day. Resident buying is full of these mysteries: the good guess gone wrong, the unspectacular style that suddenly becomes "hot."

Small wonder a myth has grown up that the successful buyer has a sixth sense. No one has devised an aptitude test for this, however. Key questions for beginners are rather "Can you write?" and "How's your health?" For many who make otherwise excellent buyers become bogged down with the constant and heavy writing of reports. And since every buyer runs a little business of her own, employers figure she'll manage it better if she knows the details of planning stock,

markups, gross margin, and bookkeeping to start with—learned perhaps in a department store selling or stock room job or from merchandising courses, or sometimes in the market itself.

The lowliest of lowly jobs (fate of the inexperienced) is that of a "follow-up." The follow-up girl does nothing but check on shipments of merchandise. She's slave to the assistant buyer she works for and at the mercy of the shipping clerks. Even an assistant buyer must go through months of following up orders, observing, note-taking, placing small orders. Then one day, she'll say to herself, I shouldn't be placing that reorder for wools now—by the time they reach San Francisco it will be late spring. Then maybe she's on her way—a girl who will one day sense the trend in colors, fabrics, styles, can advise her stores whether Dacron blends are more important than rayons or tell them what is the coming thing in shoe shapes. Most important is the ability to forecast a major market break—the frantic time when the sudden arrival of, say, the sheath demands fast reporting, buying, and promoting, when if a buyer misses she makes a million-dollar mistake.

Some say the excitement of the buyer's job lies right here: the power to make big decisions affecting big money. For the buyer who helps to earn dollars for other people doesn't always carry away a purseful for herself. A beginner's meager live-with-your-family wage can grow gradually until it reaches, in three to five years, an average of five thousand dollars—that's the pay that goes with the job of full buyer. A chosen few reach ten thousand. A handful even higher.

They say a buyer's work either becomes a passion with her—or that she can't stand it. All those faces. All those people—some she can trust, some she can't. Everything a crisis. Concessions. Cancellations. Lost packages. Sometimes the glamour of being a very special person. Sometimes the feeling she's just a letter carrier—"neither rain nor snow . . ."—with aching feet. And eventually, perhaps, a buyer meets with flattering reminders of her influence. Traveling across the country, she is startled to see it: in the skirt a Lancaster schoolgirl wears or the Saturday night date dress on a farm girl in Iowa. These were samples she took a flier on—all in a day's work.

HOW TO SELECT A RESIDENT BUYING OFFICE

Ernest A. Miller

A time comes in the growth of some small retail businesses when the buying function can no longer rely on the occasional visits of manufacturers' and wholesalers' salesmen and the sporadic trips to national or regional trade shows. When that time arrives, the owner-managers of these businesses, especially apparel and home furnishings, must "go into the market." While necessary, such trips are costly and become more and more frequent if these merchants wish to remain competitive and satisfy demands of their customers for new styles and current models.

One way of cutting the cost of going into the market is the independent resident buying office. Yet, some retailers are so used to doing things for themselves that they neglect the possibilities offered by these offices. Their do-it-yourself attitude deprives them of dollar savings over and above the cost of such offices. In addition, the resident buying organization sometimes offers assistance in merchandising, promotion, inventory control, and management which small stores could not provide on their own.

TYPES OF INDEPENDENT BUYING OFFICES

For the small store, there are two types of buying offices: the independent, operating on *fixed fees* paid by its client stores that usually are noncompetitive—that is, they are located in different cities; and the independent, working on *commissions* paid by the manufacturer or vendor. By buying through either of these types, the small store obtains, in varying degrees, the advantage of the large store that maintains its own buying office. Services of the commission office, of course, are usually more limited than those provided by the

SOURCE: Condensed & reproduced by permission of Small Business Administration, from Small Marketers Aids No. 116.

traditional, independent buying office. The commission office is confined to the resources that pay a commission on the orders the office brings.

The great majority of resident buying offices are located in New York City—the hub of the nation's apparel, soft goods, and related accessory indusries. Chicago has buying offices that specialize in furniture, home furnishing, and appliances. Los Angeles serves as a center for stores interested in West Coast fashions. A scattering of small local offices can be found in a few other major cities.

Of the several hundred buying offices in New York, some only represent large volume department stores. Some combine large and medium size department stores. Both give full coverage of both soft and hard lines. Some concentrate on women's wear, including children's wear and fashion accessories. Others are specialists in a single line of merchandise—furs, millinery, men's wear, or children's wear.

If your store retails a broad merchandise line for the entire family, together with some home furnishings, you will look for a buying office that has across-the-board merchandise coverage.

Buying offices are of all sizes. Some are literally one-man offices with a few store accounts. Others may revolve around a dominant person and yet have additional buyers—specialists in soft lines. Still others represent several hundred stores and maintain large staffs with separate divisions for various types of goods—women's and children's fashions, accessories, men's and boys' wear, piece goods and domestics, and housewares—each with specialist buyers in their fields. Such concentration gives the retailer client access to a team of buyers he could not possibly employ himself.

SCREENING THE POSSIBILITIES

Your task is to narrow the field and avoid buying offices which are not suitable to your store. You should be certain that your choice reflects your type of store.

Is the buying office known for its popular-priced and promotional merchandise? Or, is it a specialist in medium and higher-priced fashions? In a word, does its retail thinking agree basically with yours? Would your store be too small to be serviced properly? Do the principals and staff of the buying office strike you as the kind of people you can do business with on a close and continuing basis?

You have every right to be careful in your interviewing because the buying office becomes your market representative. It is important that a buying office "shop" all the important resources in each field rather than restricting itself to a few favorites. Speak frankly with the buying office's management. Examine its facilities. Ask for references. Check them. Check the office's list of clients. Are most of them retailers like yourself? Speak to some of their principals and get their opinion of the buying office. Speak also with manufacturers. They know which offices have competent staffs and give good service.

THE SERVICES TO EXPECT

As you search, you will find that a buying office is set up to save you time, to help you eliminate needless trips to the market city, and to offer professional retail assistance. It is your eyes and ears in the market.

You can expect a well-staffed buying office to furnish certain basic services, such as:

1. Advising on the best sources of merchandise.
2. Keeping constant contact with the market —particularly with the new styles, new products, price changes, and good buys.
3. Buying merchandise for you with your approval when you are unable to come to market.
4. Following up on orders so that you receive merchandise on time. (This in itself can be a major competitive advantage, justifying the fee in many cases.)
5. Handling adjustments—returns and cancellations.
6. Providing office space and clerical-secretarial services for you and your buyers when you are in the market city.

7. Notifying manufacturers that you plan to come to market.
8. Assigning buyers to accompany you on visits to manufacturers' showrooms.

Some resident buying offices also sponsor formal and informal meetings where you can discuss your operations with stores similar to your own. They organize fashion clinics to examine the market's offerings. They sometimes offer fashion coordination services.

They assist you in analyzing your various operational costs, help you plan a branch store opening, prepare Christmas and other holiday catalogs on a group-saving basis, and suggest ways to improve your advertising.

Original Information on Fashion. Many buying offices serving smaller stores have built strong reputations on their fashion and merchandising reports. Their buyers comb the markets for news about merchandise, fashion, styles, and price trends. This information is sent to you regularly in reports and newsletters, often far enough ahead to give you an advantage over competitors who do not use a buying office.

A fashion report may inform you, for example, of possible trends in fabrics to be featured in next season's dresses. Some reports may analyze management subjects, such as new developments in inventory control or how to use data processing in sales analysis.

Central Buying and Private Brands. To the conventional services of resident buying offices, which have already been described, some of the larger offices have added central and private brand buying. The use of these additional services enable the resident offices to obtain, exclusive lines of merchandise for their client stores.

Under central buying arrangements, the client stores turn over buying authority to the buying offices. Loss of this authority is offset by: (1) lower merchandise costs, (2) better selections of merchandise by full-time buyers, and (3) continuous flow of new merchandise.

This service is successful when the buying office knows enough about your needs and so adapts itself to your local situation.

Some buying offices sponsor private brands to

help their smaller stores compete with the private brand merchandise of large department and chain stores. Examples of lines that have been developed are domestics, hosiery, lingerie, blankets, men's shirts and underwear.

For small stores, private brands of selective merchandise help hold customers and lend themselves to special promotions. Other advantages are: lower wholesale cost, greater markon, increased profit, and distinctive merchandise often packaged with your store's name on it.

Some offices perform as wholesalers of staple goods, both national and private brands. The office buys in quantities and distributes to its client stores. . . .

WHAT WILL IT COST?

What will using a resident buying office cost? The standard retainer fee used by most leading, independent buying offices is one-half of one percent of a store's annual sales volume for the past year. It is payable in equal monthly installments.

If the annual volume is small, the office may require a minimum monthly fee. Most buying offices request a 1-year agreement, and there is usually some arrangement for cancelling it. This annual fee covers all normal market representation and allied services.

Most buying offices serve only a single store in any given city or trading area. Thus your store would be the only one in your locality with that office's services.

In addition to the annual fee, client stores of buying offices pay for postage, long-distance telephone calls, and miscellaneous expenses. All such additional costs should be noted during your discussion with a potential buying office. Postage, for example, covers the mailing of all fashion brochures, literature, and special reports. The cost of the enclosures, however, is included as part of the basic fee.

Stores that participate in certain voluntary programs, pay additional fees—for example, the fee for engaging the central buying service. This fee is for the extensive administration and additional buyers which are necessary for central buying. Typically, it is 3 percent of the retail cost of the merchandise which you purchase through the buy-

ing office. For example, if in a year, your store bought merchandise retailing for $50,000, the cost for central buying would be $1,500. This cost, of course, is offset by savings in time and travel expense and, in some instances, the salary of a full-time buyer.

The Commission Office. Commission or broker buying offices, as was said earlier, do not charge any fee to client stores. Manufacturers pay them commissions which range from 2 to 5 percent of the wholesale price.

Commission buying offices concentrate on buying. They provide few fashion, promotional or counseling services. Some smaller stores use commission offices solely because there is no charge. Many stores maintain that commission offices cannot be objective since they must generate orders to receive income.

In effect, they are the manufacturer's agent, not the retailer's. However, this type of buying office is noted for efficiency in getting merchandise delivered to stores.

WORKING TOGETHER

After you have picked the buying office which you feel is best for your store, you will need to see that a strong working relationship is developed between you and it.

In developing a profitable working relationship, you should take the people in your buying office into your confidence. Tell them your problems. Seek their advice. Adopt their suggestions.

You will want also to use the many services and programs that your buying office offers. Many of these are better and at a lower cost than if you bought them individually or prepared them yourself.

In building a good working relationship, it is important to notify the buying office of your plans well in advance of market trips. Then the buyers can prepare to make your visit a time-saving and productive one. Keep in mind also that often the value of a buying office to the retailer depends on the retailer. The rule "ask and you shall receive" is most applicable to building a relationship which can be your first link in assuring that your store remains competitive and independent.

WHAT IS "THE FASHION GROUP"?

Sarah Tomerlin Lee

THE FASHION GROUP IS:

The Fashion Group is an organization of over 4800 women executives in every phase of fashion manufacturing, communications, merchandising, advertising, editing and publishing. Within its scope, The Fashion Group includes fashions for the home as well as clothing, cosmetics, fabric, lingerie, sportswear, accessories, ready-to-wear and design the world over. Its membership meets for the consideration of new developments in all of these fields. The Fashion Group is a non-profit (in dollars and cents) organization of enormous profit and inspiration to its members.

PURPOSE:

The Fashion Group's founding and purpose was, and is, to improve the level of taste and knowledge throughout the fashion industries by example, education and dissemination of information. Its goal—equality of opportunity and remuneration; the maintaining of the highest standards of executive conduct; association with members who are active in the widely dispersed fields of fashion; to encourage and develop new interests in fashion through training courses, scholarships, civic and cultural projects; and to help women in business.

ORGANIZATIONS:

The 30 Groups are officered by Regional Directors, and their committees are manned by members who serve without remuneration. The Fashion Group's executives are an elected President and Board of Directors, Chairman, Treasurer, and Secretary. These board members represent the major committees, whose responsibility it is to cover their field and prepare and stage exhibitions,

SOURCE: Miss Lee is a Former President of the Fashion Group, Inc. Reproduced by permission of Eleanor McMillen, Executive Director of The Fashion Group.

fashion shows, reports and talks for the membership. All of these programs, as well as annual career training courses and all other activities of The Fashion Group (publishing fashion-career literature, scholarship-management, career-counseling, the reception of visitors, the booking of auditoriums and handling of reservations, the printing of Fashion Group bulletins, the voluminous correspondence with its member Fashion Groups) is conducted from the New York office, which has become the International Headquarters of The Fashion Group . . . in a very real sense, the Fashion Center.

BENEFITS:

Beyond the benefits derived from the Fashion Group meetings are the published speeches, the information in The Fashion Group Bulletin which is mailed to all members, the privilege of transferring membership to any Fashion Group city in the world, fashion shows and exhibits, the Fashion Training Courses throughout the United States, career counsel, professional and trade information, and the prestige that is naturally bestowed on its membership.

HISTORY:

The Fashion Group's first meeting was in 1928. An unofficial gathering in a tearoom, of women fashion executives who felt the need of an organization to give dignity and standing to fashion women and to supply them with a clearing house of information. From these early days the most distinguished women in the fashion industry have been its working members. The caliber of members—enthusiastic, unselfish, imaginative, thoughtful women who have flocked to The Fashion Group—is what has made it, from those early days, such an impressive factor in the fashion industry.

BIBLIOGRAPHY

Beaton, Cecil. *The Best of Beaton*. New York, Macmillan, 1968.

Brown, Russel A. and Charles M. Edwards. *Retail Advertising and Sales Promtion*. Englewood Cliffs, N.J., Prentice-Hall, Inc., 1959.

Chase, E. W., and Ilka Chase. *Always In Vogue*. Garden City, N.Y., Doubleday, 1954.

Donohue, Jody. *Your Career in Public Relations*. New York, Julian Messner, Inc., 1967.

Fitzgibbon, Bernice. *Macy, Gimbels and Me*. New York, Simon and Schuster, 1967.

Finley, Ruth E. *Lady of Godey's*. Philadelphia, J. B. Lippincott Co., 1938.

Gottlieb, Edward and Philip Klarnet. *Successful Publicity*. New York, Grosset and Dunlap, 1964.

Kelly, Katie. *The Wonderful World of Women's Wear Daily*. New York, Saturday Review Press, 1972.

Kleppner, Otto. *Advertising Procedure*. 5th Edition. Englewood Cliffs, N.J., Prentice-Hall, 1966.

Reynolds, Quentin. *The Fiction Factory*. New York, Random House, 1955.

Schwartz, James. *The Publicity Process*. Iowa City, Iowa, Iowa State University Press, 1969.

Snow, Carmel. *The World of Carmel Snow*. New York, McGraw-Hill, 1962.

Winters, Arthur and Stanley Goodman. *Fashion Sales Promotion Handbook*. Revised Edition. New York, Fashion Institute of Technology College Shop, 1972.

TRADE PERIODICALS

Advertising Age, 740 N. Rush St., Chicago, Ill. 60611

Display World, 407 Gilbert Ave., Cincinnati, Ohio 45202

Journal of Marketing, 230 N. Michigan Ave., Chicago, Ill. 60601

Public Relations Journal , 845 Third Ave., New York, N.Y. 10022

TRADE ASSOCIATIONS

American Association of Advertising Agencies, 200 Park Ave., New York, N.Y. 10017

American Business Press, Inc., 205 East 42nd Street, New York, N.Y. 10016

American Newspaper Publishers Association, 730 Third Ave. N.Y. 10017

Association of Buying Offices, 100 West 31st St., New York, N.Y. 10001

The Fashion Group, 9 Rockefeller Plaza, New York, N.Y. 10020 and also in major cities throughout the country

Magazine Publishers Association, Inc., 575 Lexington Ave., New York, N.Y. 10001

National Association of Broadcasters, 485 Madison Ave, New York, N.Y. 10022

National Retail Merchants Association, 100 West 31st Street, New York, N. Y. 10001

Public Relations Society of America, Inc., 845 Third Ave., New York, N.Y. 10022

Television Bureau of Advertising, 1 Rockefeller Plaza, New York, N.Y. 10020

SECTION REVIEW AND ACTIVITIES

FASHION BUSINESS TERMINOLOGY

Define, identify, or briefly explain each of the following:

Women's Wear Daily
Editorial credit
Press Week
Trade publication
The Fashion Group
Tobé Associates
Fashion magazine
Advertising agency
Publicity
Fashion consultant
Resident buying office

QUESTIONS FOR REVIEW

1. Explain the difference between a fashion magazine such as *Seventeen* and trade publications such as *Women's Wear Daily* or *Clothes* magazine.

2. Explain the difference between "editorialized" merchandise and advertised merchandise in a fashion magazine. Bring into class an example of each from the same magazine.

3. What is the role of a fashion magazine in the business of fashion, as described in your text and in the readings?

4. How great is the influence of fashion magazines and fashion pages in newspapers upon their readers' actual purchases of apparel and/or accessories? Explain.

5. Many large producers run advertisements in both fashion magazines and trade papers. Would they be likely to run the same type of advertisement in both these two media? How might their ads in each differ, and why?

6. Most of the advertisements run by large apparel and textile producers are handled by advertising agencies. Why do producers use outside agencies instead of employing their own advertising specialists?

7. Analyze the fashion pages of your newspapers or the television programs and see if you can "spot" a publicity message. What was it, and how do you think it got there?

8. Many large retailers who employ such fashion specialists as fashion directors and buyers in their own organizations also retain outside fashion consultants. Why?

9. Why do retail stores who employ their own specialized buyers utilize resident buying offices? Why would a New York store use a resident buying office that is located in New York?

10. How can you explain the free advice and help offered by fashion magazines to manufacturers and retailers as contrasted to the paid advice and help given by fashion consultants?

11. As compared to producers, very few large retailers use outside advertising agencies. They generally maintain complete advertising departments of their own. How can you explain this?

12. Do fashion editors and consultants predict fashion, or do they report fashion? Explain.

APPLICATIONS WITH EXAMPLES

1. Discuss and illustrate with examples the factors that might influence fashion editors of magazines in their selection of merchandise to be featured editorially. Compare them with the factors that might influence a retail buyer in his or her selection of merchandise to be purchased for stock. Explain the differences and/or similarities in their criteria for merchandise selection. Draw a conclusion.

2. Analyze a copy of one trade publication in the apparel or accessory field. Discuss the different types of information it contains and show examples of each. Explain to whom this information or this trade publication would be useful and why.

3. Analyze a fashion magazine for the following purposes: (a) the names of its different departments, (b) the content in the magazine for which each department is responsible, and (c) the number of pages or amount of space given to editorialized merchandise as compared to advertised merchandise.

SECTION 7
THE MEN'S WEAR INDUSTRY

The men's wear industry is an important segment of the economy in the United States. More than 3000 firms engage in the production of men's and boys' clothing and furnishings, and their 4100 plants have a combined output of about $8 billion a year at wholesale value. Well over a half million people are at work in this field, earning wages and salaries that total more than $2 billion a year. Unlike the women's apparel business, the men's wear industries are not concentrated in any one area; their plants are distributed throughout the country—from Maine to California and from Oregon to Texas.[1]

In the men's apparel business, until the late 1960s, fashion moved at a glacial pace. Although there were stirrings of consumer demand for bright plumage and style change in men's sportswear as early as the 1950s, the industry as a whole did not consider itself to be in the fast-changing business called *fashion*. It was accepted as a fact of life that a new style in men's wear would take 10 years to assert itself and 10 years more to run its course. New fashions evolved slowly and usually expressed themselves in little more than a variation in the width of a coat lapel, the number of buttons on the cuff of a jacket, the amount of fullness in the trouser leg, or in other small and fairly unobtrusive ways.

Men, in the 1960s, stimulated by the new life-styles introduced by young people, began to think along lines that were quite different from the industry's traditional, methodical, and often inflexible ways. They began to demand greater variety, faster change, and more opportunity to express their individuality in their manner of dress. Their changed attitude grew out of the socioeconomic changes that were taking place on the American scene: greater economic security, hours of new leisure time, suburban casualness in dress, faster communications, and more and faster travel for both business and pleasure. The men's wear industry (reluctantly and slowly in some segments) responded to the increased fashion interest evidenced by the American male and began to rethink and reshape its styling, its production, and its marketing.

Today, men's wear is as much a part of the fashion business as any segment of the women's apparel field. A modern study of the fashion business would not be complete without a discussion of the men's wear industry—the subject of this section and its readings. In these readings, the psychological aspects of the masculine response to fashion are examined, along with the industry's problems in meeting the changing demands of its customers.

HISTORY AND DEVELOPMENT

The men's apparel industry, as explained in an earlier section, began in the United States early in the nineteenth century in such port cities as New Bedford, Boston, New York, Philadelphia, and Baltimore. Sailors, who otherwise would have had to buy secondhand clothes to replenish their wardrobes during their brief stays

---

[1]U.S. Department of Commerce, *U.S. Industrial Outlook, 1973.*

ashore, were the industry's first customers. Seafaring men patronized "slop shops"—a term that aptly describes the fit and quality of the garments made up and offered for sale there.

From Retailers to Manufacturers

Since no firms then existed that produced clothing for others to sell, these early shops were both retailers and manufacturers. Some of the proprietors were custom tailors who produced ready-made garments from cheaper grades of cloth in addition to carrying on their primary business of made-to-measure clothing. Others cut the cloth on store premises and contracted to have the sewing done by tailors who worked at home.

As industrialization developed in the early nineteenth century, cities grew and a new mass market began to emerge among middle-class or white-collar city dwellers. To attract these customers, some of the more enterprising shop owners offered higher-priced and better-made garments. The quality of "store clothes" improved and their acceptance increased. By 1830, the market for "store bought" apparel had expanded so greatly that there were firms that specialized in the manufacture of garments for others to sell at retail. The first steps in the establishment of the men's clothing industry, as we know it today, had been taken. By 1835, some manufacturers in New York City, which had acquired the reputation of the nation's leading center for ready-made men's clothing, reportedly employed from 300 to 500 workers.[2] Boston, Philadelphia, Newark, and Baltimore also progressed rapidly as manufacturing centers, as did Rochester, Cincinnati, and St. Louis, toward the middle of the century. Impetus was gained when the sewing machine was perfected in 1846, and progress was further speeded when the Civil War created a great demand for ready-made clothing and also introduced standard sizing to conform to body measurements developed by the government. Until the 1860s, there had been no recognized standards, and sizing was haphazard.

Emergence of Wholesale Jobbers

As the country expanded geographically, many clothing manufacturers found that they had little means of distributing their output to the multitude of small, retail clothing shops that were being opened in all sections of the country. As a result, local jobbers, usually former store owners familiar with retail needs in their particular areas, came into existence and performed the distributive function for the manufacturers. It was more feasible for producers in distant clothing markets to sell to one jobber in an area instead of to a number of small stores. These wholesale jobbing firms bought from various producers of clothing and from other dry goods

[2] H.Cobrin, *The Men's Clothing Industry, Colonial Through Modern Times,* Fairchild Publications, New York, 1971.

resources and then resold the merchandise in smaller quantities and appropriate assortments to the retailers.

In the nineteenth century, it should be remembered, travel and transportation of merchandise were slow. A storekeeper could not readily leave his place of business for weeks while he journeyed to a major city and scoured the markets, examining the offerings of dozens of producers. Even if he did, he faced a problem in bringing many small shipments to his store, each from a different manufacturer. It was far more practical in those days to purchase virtually his entire stock of clothing and general merchandise from a single wholesaler, and to have a single large shipment of goods packed into wooden crates and sent to him by sea or overland freight.

The jobbing function diminished in importance as the twentieth century got under way. Some of the producers in the industry had grown to considerable size, and they could not only supply a retailer with a large portion of his inventory needs but could also carry his account if he required credit. In the early years of the twentieth century, the latter point was important. More than one-third of the labor force was engaged in farming, and farmers required credit. They ran up bills at the local store and paid at harvest time. Since the merchant had to sell on long-term credit, he was inclined to seek long-term credit in the market and to place business with producers who were substantial enough to offer him this assistance.

Also as the twentieth century moved along, transportation and travel were becoming swifter and easier. The auto, the truck, and the bus were coming into wide use. A producer's salesman, traveling by car, could visit not only major cities but also outlying hamlets that were not served by railroads. New methods of packing and shipping made it simpler and less expensive than it had been for a merchant to purchase from a number of producers rather than concentrate his buying with a wholesale house. Many of the retailers who sold men's clothing were also in the women's ready-to-wear business. The women's fashion business of that day was teaching merchants (if they had learned it nowhere else) the value of coming to market, seeing lines, observing what big city stores were showing, and returning home stimulated and refreshed. By the middle of the century, jobbers, as a factor in the industry, had practically disappeared.

Custom Tailors and Made-to-Measure Firms

Because men's apparel requires more expert tailoring than women's clothes, custom tailoring has remained important in the men's field longer than custom dressmaking has in women's wear. Most of the men's tailors who did custom work in this country had been trained in Europe under the apprentice system; they could design a suit, sponge the fabric to preshrink it, cut the garment, run up the seams, sew on buttons, make buttonholes by hand, and supply the fine stitching on lapels that, to this day, is the mark of good workmanship. Until the 1920s, a man could enjoy the excellent fit of a made-to-order suit at prices and in qualities that compared very favorably with ready-made clothing.

The supply of custom tailors, however, began to dwindle in the 1920s and 1930s. Immigration had been restricted and, as the older European-trained tailors died or retired, very few new ones crossed the Atlantic to take their place. Work in the factories of this country did not produce craftsmen capable of making complete garments; as in women's apparel, efficient methods of operation required some men to specialize in cutting, others in sewing, and still others in the hand finishing. Today, there are only about 1200 retail custom tailor shops in the United States and their combined sales do not total $100 million a year.[3]

In addition to the retail custom tailors, there are also tailors-to-the-trade or made-to-measure firms. These are factories that specialize in cutting individual garments according to the exact measurements of customers who place their orders through retail stores serviced by these firms. The customer selects style and fabric from fashion books and swatches that he consults in the retail store; the retailer relays his selection and his measurements to the factory; and, in due course, the garment is made up. Wholesale tailoring houses of this type, located in Chicago, Cincinnati, and Baltimore, at one time offered strong competition to manufacturers of ready-made clothing. As late as 1928, their output constituted 20 percent of the industry's total suit production. The dwindling supply of skilled tailors and the improvement in ready-made clothing, however, caused operations of this kind to diminish in importance. Although tailors-to-the-trade are still recognized as a branch of the industry and have special representation on the board of directors of the National Clothing Manufacturers Association, their output is less than 5 percent of the industry's total and is no longer separately reported in census figures.[4] Much of the made-to-measure business nowadays is handled by large producers of ready-made apparel who have set up separate divisions that handle this special-order business.

Unionization: "The Amalgamated"

Like the women's garment industry, the men's clothing industry presented a dismal labor picture at the beginning of this century, with sweat shops prevalent. Producers contracted to have the sewing of garments done outside their plants, either by individuals who did the work in their tenement homes or by contractors who gathered sewing hands together in equally uncomfortable and unsanitary lofts. A New York factory inspector's report in 1887, which also could have applied to clothing production centers elsewhere, described these workshops as:

" . . . *foul in the extreme. Noxious gasses emanate from all corners. The buildings are ill-smelling from cellar to garret. The water-closets are used alike by males and females and usually stand in the room where the work is done. The people are*

---

[3]Authors' estimates.
[4]Cobrin, *op. cit.*, pp. 152–153.

huddled together too closely for comfort, even if all other conditions were excellent. And when this state of affairs is taken into consideration, with the painfully long hours of toil which the poverty-stricken victims of contractors must endure, it seems wonderful that there exists a human being that could stand it for a month and live. We are not describing one or two places, for there is hardly an exception in this class of manufactories in all New York.''[5]

In 1910, a strike that started at the Hart Schaffner & Marx plant in Chicago spread and eventually drew 35,000 workers from their jobs. Settlement of the dispute brought improved working conditions, reduced working hours to 54 a week, and set up machinery for adjusting grievances. A few years later, in 1914, the craft union that formerly represented the men's clothing workers yielded its place to the Amalgamated Clothing Workers of America, an industry union, and one that has established a record of labor peace and pioneering effort.

"The Amalgamated" worked for arbitration and industry-wide bargaining; it sought stable labor relations with management as a means of keeping its people employed. It has encouraged scientific techniques in industry management, and it has provided extensive and innovative social welfare services to its members. The union points with pride to its relationship with that same Hart Schaffner & Marx, at whose Chicago factory a strike triggered the events that led to Amalgamated's birth. In more than 50 years, that plant, now the world's largest in the men's clothing field, has never had a strike.

GEOGRAPHICAL CENTERS

The men's wear industry is widely dispersed throughout the United States. The Amalgamated, whose jurisdiction extends to all items of male apparel, claims membership from Maine to the deep South and from Puerto Rico to the Pacific Coast. Principal centers for the production of suits, trousers, and coats are in the Northeast and Middle West. Production of shirts, jackets, and work clothing is distributed throughout the South, the Southwest, the Far West, as well as in the East. Because these garments do not demand a high degree of tailoring skill, they are sometimes made in small factories, located in tiny towns, remote from the urban centers in which the owning companies have their headquarters.

Importance of New York

New York City is not only an important production center for many types of men's wear, but it is also the hub of the industry's marketing efforts, and houses the sales offices of virtually every important producer. In a single building—1290 Avenue of

[5] *Ibid*, p. 67.

MEN'S WEAR INDUSTRY PRODUCTION

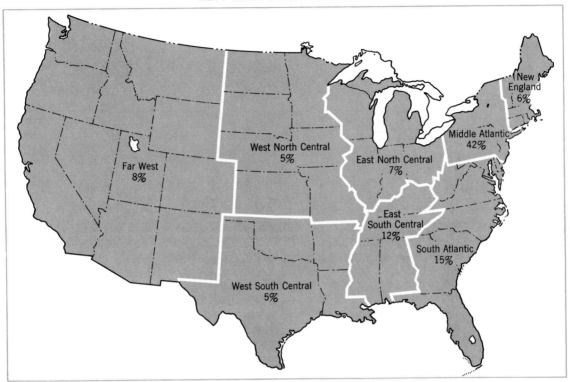

SOURCE: U.S. Department of Commerce, Census of Manufacturers.

the Americas—about 125 men's wear firms have their offices, and these firms represent an estimated 75 percent of the men's clothing produced in the United States.[6] In the Empire State Building, at Fifth Avenue and 34th Street, there are sales offices of many of the larger men's furnishings producers. Farther downtown on Fifth Avenue, and on Broadway below 23rd Street, is the area that was once the center of the men's clothing industry in the city. There, many of the smaller clothing firms still maintain their offices; they house both their production and their sales facilities in the loft buildings of that district.

The importance of New York City in men's wear is further underscored by the fact that an enormous share of the industry's total output originates in the three Middle Atlantic states—New York, New Jersey, and Pennsylvania. More than half the country's men's tailored-clothing plants are in this area, and they account for nearly 60 percent of the dollar volume of suit and coat production. When all major categories of men's wear are considered together, even including the categories that have their major production facilities in the South and Southwest, the Middle

[6] *Ibid.*

Atlantic states account for more than 40 percent of the plants in the country, and for one-third of the dollar value of the output.[7]

Other Centers of Production

Centers of production outside of New York City are usually associated with one or two categories of men's wear, instead of with the across-the-board production and selling that characterizes that city. Philadelphia, where the open shop prevailed in the men's clothing industry longer than in most other cities, has factories that are of medium size and produce suits and coats in the medium price range. Chicago has very large plants that produce men's clothing in higher grades. Specialists in producing separate trousers are located mainly in Texas, New York, Pennsylvania, Tennessee, and Mississippi. Plants specializing in work clothing (i.e., dungarees, jeans, and other articles of leisure wear as well as those intended to be worn at work in factories and shops) are among the largest in the industry and concentrate in the Southern states. Tennessee and Texas are the two largest states producing work clothing; they are larger in the number of plants, the number of employees, and the value of output. Undergarments are produced primarily in the South, with North Carolina alone accounting for one-quarter of the output. In the Middle Atlantic states are nearly half the plants that produce men's and boys' heavy outerwear coats and jackets, sweaters, swimsuits, and other miscellaneous items. The industry is truly national, and there is scarcely a state that does not participate in the production of men's wear.

NATURE OF THE INDUSTRY

The men's wear industry, which also serves boys and youths, resembles the women's wear industry in some ways and differs markedly in others. It resembles the women's field in the respect that manufacturers usually specialize in garments in some clearly definable category; in addition, its various branches produce seasonal lines for much of their merchandise. The industry differs from women's apparel, however, in the fact that it has many large producers whose collective share of the total volume is substantial. Manufacturers' brand names, moreover, are better established, more widely advertised, and better known to the consumer. And the men's wear industry differs very sharply from the women's branch in that dual distribution practices are found among the major producers. That is, they sell through retail stores of their own, in addition to selling to other retailers for resale to the consumer.

Specializations of Industry Divisions

The men's wear industry divides itself along product lines into several different divisions, each of which is highly specialized. Although it is not growing in volume

[7]U.S. Department of Commerce, *U.S. Industrial Outlook 1973* and the *Census of Manufactures.*

The Men's Wear Industry, 1971
Economic Profile of the Five Major Divisions of Men's Wear

MEN'S AND BOYS'...	NUMBER OF PLANTS	WHOLESALE VALUE OF SHIPMENTS	EMPLOYEES
		(in millions)	(in thousands)
Suits and coats	865	$1,876	109
Shirts and nightwear	692	1,816	119
Separate trousers	647	1,858	85
Work clothing[a]	457	1,237	86
Clothing not elsewhere classified[b]	547	735	41
Totals, these categories	3,208	$7,522	440

Source: U. S. Department of Commerce, *U. S. Industrial Outlook, 1973.*

[a]Includes such leisure items and jeans and dungarees.

[b]Includes heavy outerwear and sweaters.

of sales as rapidly as the industry as a whole, the largest division is the one that produces men's and boys' tailored coats and suits.

The fastest growing division in the industry has been the one that produces trousers and slacks intended to be sold separately rather than as parts of suits. (The sports jackets that men and boys wear with separate trousers are produced by the tailored coat and suit division.) From 1960 to 1969, when the value of the total annual output of the industry's five major divisions increased by 53 percent, the value of shipments in the division increased by 152 percent.[8] This section of the industry has benefited particularly from the trend toward casual dress and the preference for mixing rather than exactly matching jackets and trousers.

Second only to separate trousers and slacks in rate of growth has been the work-clothing division of the industry that produces such items as jeans and dungarees. From 1960 to 1969 this division increased the annual value of its output by 89 percent.[9]

The division that produces shirts (both dress and sport shirts) and nightwear is the second largest in the industry. Its annual shipments of over $1.6 billion at wholesale value represent more than one-fifth of the industry total.[10]

There are several smaller divisions in the men's wear industry, none of which contributes as much as $1 billion to the total annual output. The largest of these divisions is the one that produces heavy outerwear jackets, sweaters, swimsuits, knit jackets, and similar merchandise. Other divisions specialize in the production of underwear, neckwear, or hats and caps.

The various divisions described above constitute the men's wear industry. Men

[8]U.S. Department of Commerce, *Annual Survey of Manufactures, 1969; Census of Manufactures, 1967;* and *U.S. Industrial Outlook, 1973.*

[9]*Ibid.*

[10]*Ibid.*

also wear shoes, hosiery, gloves, belts, and sometimes furs, but these items are not considered in the trade to be part of the men's wear industry. Possibly this is because each of these other industries produces its goods for both men and women instead of primarily for one sex.

Dominance by Large Firms

Although 80 percent of the approximately 3300 firms in the men's wear industry are small and employ fewer than 250 people each, the large firms in this field do a greater percentage of the total business than is the case in the women's field. The top four firms in men's wear account for 22 percent of total shipments in the industry; the top eight account for 33 percent. The degree of concentration varies from one division of the industry to another. In coats and suits, the eight largest firms control 27 percent of the volume; at the opposite extreme, in the underwear division, the top eight firms control 60 percent of the volume. By way of contrast, in the women's apparel industry, the corresponding figures are 7 percent for the top four firms, and 17 percent for the top eight firms.[11]

Until the 1960s, publicly-owned firms were the exception rather than the rule in the industry. Most concerns were closely held corporations, partnerships, or individually owned. During the 1960s, many firms went public or became parts of conglomerates. Among the reasons were: the advancing ages of the owners, the absence of successors, the consideration of estate taxes likely to be levied on the death of the owner, and the need of capital for expansion.

One of the major publicly-owned firms in the field is Phillips-Van Heusen, with an annual volume that passed the $250 million mark in 1971, and with manufacturing operations in the men's shirt and clothing field plus 103 retail men's shops, including Kennedy's of Boston. Another firm is Cluett Peabody, whose sales exceeded half a billion dollars in 1972, divided about 75 percent in the manufacturing of men's shirts, suits, and sportswear, and the balance in 62 retail stores owned by the company. There is also Hart Schaffner & Marx, which did $423 million in 1972. About two-thirds of this total was done in its more than 200 retail stores and the balance in the manufacture of men's clothing. Manhattan Industries, principally in shirts and pajamas, reached $214 million in annual sales in 1972.[12]

Among the conglomerates that have entered the men's wear field is the giant Genesco, whose annual sales volume of over $1 billion is contributed to by companies producing men's suits and work clothes and whose retail department and specialty stores run the gamut of kinds and price levels. Another conglomerate in the field is Warnaco, which owns Hathaway Shirts in addition to its companies devoted to fabrics, packaging, sportswear, and women's intimate apparel.

[11]Carl Priestland, Associates, *Focus 1971, Economic Profile of the Apparel Industry*, and U.S. Department of Commerce, *U.S. Industrial Outlook, 1973*, p. 162.

[12]The Johnson Redbook Service of Prescott, Merrill, Turben & Co., Battery Park Plaza, New York, and annual statements of the firms concerned.

Pattern of Operation

The pattern of operation in men's wear varies from one branch of the industry to another but, in general, all phases of production are under the control of the manufacturer. The outside sewing contractor, so important in the women's apparel field, is not a factor.

In some branches of the industry, garment size ranges are enormous compared to the size ranges that prevail in women's wear. Whereas a dress producer may cut each style in five or six sizes for a single figure type, such as juniors or half-sizes, a men's suit producer is likely to cut each style in many chest-measurement sizes (such as 37, 38, and on into the 40s) and also to produce each style in three or four separate figure types: average, short, tall, and portly. This tremendous variety of sizes is important to the retailer, since he absorbs the cost of any alterations required by the customer, as a rule. He seeks, therefore, to have a stock that permits almost any size or figure type to be fitted with a minimum of adjustment.

Similarly, the men's dress-shirt industry copes with an elaborate range of sizes, since there are several sleeve lengths for each of the many neck sizes in which a shirt is cut. This means a considerable investment in inventory for each style number in a producer's line and for each style number in a retailer's stock.

With elaborate sizing systems such as these, production is necessarily cumbersome. Before cutting can begin, there must be the assurance of large orders, so that many layers of fabric can be cut at one time in the whole huge range of sizes. This procedure does not encourage the exploitation of best sellers that prevails in women's wear, nor does it encourage uninhibited copying of individual numbers. It is well adapted, however, to basic styles that do not change radically from one season to another. In men's suits and coats, and in dress shirts, styling does not so much involve numbers or items as it involves incoming or outgoing looks—narrowing or widening lapels, narrowing or widening trouser bottoms, and lengthening or shortening shirt collar points, for instance. Merchandising is by trend rather than by item or style number.

On the other hand, sports shirts are produced in a limited size range—three or four sizes only with no requirement for precise fit at the neckband and often with sleeves that stop above the elbow and present no length problem. Therefore, experimentation with new colors, new fabrics, and new ideas is much less of a risk in this merchandise. Similarly, the less-complicated size problem in sports jackets and in separate trousers and slacks encourages experimentation and response to fashion demand in those areas, too.

Improvements in production methods have not yet made it possible for the industry to respond as rapidly as it would like to changes in fashion demand. True, a powered cutting-knife moves through many layers of fabric rapidly—but there must be many layers, and thus a large run of a number before cutting can be done economically. Although electrically-powered sewing machines operate far more quickly than the foot-powered machines in use at the beginning of this century, the fabric can be stitched no faster than an operator can feed it under the needle. Experimentation with cutting by laser beam and stitching with electronically guided machines is going on and may, some day, make it possible for the industry to produce short runs and respond quickly to changes in fashion demand.

For the present, however, the industry continues its tradition of offering store buyers two lines a year: in February for fall selling and in August for spring selling. Thus, showings are held four to six months in advance of the selling season, or much further ahead than is the case with women's apparel.

Manufacturer-Retailer Combines

The men's wear field differs from the women's apparel industry in that many of the large manufacturing firms own retail stores as well. This close link between manufacturing and retailing goes back to the industry's infancy, as was explained earlier in this section. The conditions that led to the emergence of jobbers after the Civil War, however, caused these combinations of manufacturing and retailing to disappear. But in the 1920s the chain store movement in retailing had gained great momentum and sparked the return to manufacturer-retailer links that are so prevalent today. Men's retail clothing chains, such as Bond Stores, Crawford Clothes, and Richman Bros., developed or acquired their own manufacturing facilities. Manufacturers, meanwhile, either started their own stores or acquired some of the retail accounts they had been servicing. With the depression of the 1930s, many of these manufacturer-retailer combinations were dissolved, but in the years following World War II they again became a factor. The "big seven" men's wear producers (Botany, Cluett Peabody, Eagle, Genesco, Hart Schaffner & Marx, Manhattan, Phillips-Van Heusen) together own an estimated 600 stores. Nearly 250 of these stores are owned by Hart Schaffner & Marx alone—the Wallach's, Silverwood, Baskin, and Hastings chains among others. Against the overall total of stores selling men's wear, the producer-owned stores do not seem numerous, however. There are, in the United States, nearly 30,000 stores that specialize in men's apparel or family clothing, and more than 50,000 department and other general merchandise stores that would be likely to have men's apparel in their assortments.[13]

Link to Women's Wear

Through the establishment of separate divisions and also by the merger route, several men's wear producers have entered the women's apparel field. For example, when women were demonstrating an enormous appetite for shirt-type blouses in the 1960s, Manhattan Industries set up a Lady Manhattan division to produce these blouses, and Cluett Peabody set up a Lady Arrow division—each capitalizing on the acceptance of its name in the men's field. Cluett Peabody also owns Van Raalte, a long-established producer of women's intimate apparel and accessories. Women's wear producers have stepped into the men's wear field. Usually this is through

[13]U.S. Department of Commerce, *Census of Business.*

acquisitions and under names different from the brand or company names they control in the women's field. For example, Jonathan Logan, the country's largest producer of women's apparel, owns Harbor Master, a man's raincoat company. Warnaco, which was originally Warner Brothers, the country's oldest manufacturer of corsets, owns Hathaway men's shirts. And, of course, there is Genesco, which had its beginnings in men's shoes. It now produces men's and women's apparel, textiles, and other goods, and it owns such glamorous women's shops as Henri Bendel in New York and the Bonwit Teller group. It also owns such budget stores as the S.H. Kress & Co. chain.

MARKETING AND DISTRIBUTION

Since the decline of the jobber as a factor in the men's wear industry, in the early years of this century, distribution has been directly from manufacturer to retailer for most men's wear goods. Retailers come to market at least twice a year, as they do in the women's field, and they usually have resident buying offices to advise them of developments and to follow up on orders between market trips. Manufacturers send their salesmen on the road to visit retailers regularly, and they also have representatives or branch offices in major market centers outside of New York City, such as the Merchandise Mart in Chicago. In this respect, the distribution pattern in men's wear resembles the pattern in the women's field—with the exception that it is rare for a men's wear retail-store buyer to "live" in the market as is often the case with buyers for women's departments of stores that are fashion leaders.

Importance of Brands

Manufacturers' brand names are of greater importance and have been promoted longer in the men's wear field than in women's wear. There are many widely known producers' brands in all branches of the field, and there are also many firmly established private brands developed by men's specialty shops and chains, department stores, mail-order houses, and general merchandise chains. Advertising of both producers and retailers has traditionally stressed quality, workmanship, value, and fit. Fashion was not used as a selling tool to any noticeable extent until the end of the 1960s.

Some of the brand names prominent in men's wear date back to the beginning of this century, or earlier. Hart Schaffner & Marx began promoting their name through national advertising in 1890. In 1901, Joseph & Feiss (now owned by Phillips-Van Heusen) embarked on a national campaign to sell their "Clothescraft Clothes," retailing at $10 and upward, by telling their retail customers that "the wearer will be brought to you by judicious advertising. We pay for it."[14] This, of course, was an early and simple form of cooperative advertising.

[14]Cobrin op. cit., p. 317.

With some exceptions, men's wear manufacturers have not been notable users of national advertising; they leave much of their consumer advertising to retailers, sometimes with cooperative advertising allowances, and to their own retail stores. In recent years, fiber and fabric sources have provided encouragement and cooperative advertising dollars for national advertising, along the lines followed in the women's trades.

Dual Distribution

As has been mentioned earlier in this section, the men's apparel field has firms that engage in both manufacturing and retailing and that sell to other retail stores and through their own, thus achieving dual distribution. Stores that are owned by or are under common ownership with manufacturers, however, also buy from outside sources. For example, the stores owned by Hart Schaffner & Marx, such as Wallach's and Hastings, purchase sportswear, women's apparel and accessories, and other items from various other manufacturers. Similarly, Kennedy's of Boston, although owned by Phillips-Van Heusen, carries a full range of men's wear and necessarily patronizes producers other than the giant shirt company alone.

There are also retail men's wear chains that control their own production facilities, such as the Howard Stores and the Robert Hall chain. Stores of this kind, too, necessarily patronize other producers for categories and items of merchandise that their plants do not handle.

Dual distribution as practiced in the men's wear field has come under attack from several quarters. Manufacturers who do not engage in the practice contend that, when one of their retail store customers has been taken over by a competing manufacturer, they can scarcely look forward to flourishing business with that particular outlet; future orders can be expected to be reduced or eliminated entirely. Retailers object to the presence of manufacturer-owned stores in their trading areas on the grounds that they can find themselves purchasing from a resource that is in direct competition with them. The Justice Department of the United States has entered the picture, requiring Hart Schaffner & Marx to dispose of some of its stores on the grounds that they may substantially lessen competition in the manufacture and sale of clothing in the better-price ranges.[15]

Retail Channels of Distribution

The men's specialty shop is the major retail outlet for men's clothing. A 1966 study made by the National Credit Office found that 64 percent of the total volume was channeled through men's specialty stores, 21 percent through department stores, 11 percent through chain and mail-order houses, and 4 percent through discounters and others. The chains and mail-order companies are somewhat more important in the distribution of separate trousers than in the sale of suits and coats. There has

[15]"Sell 30 Stores by 1973, U.S. Tells Hart Schaffner & Marx," *Women's Wear Daily*, April 30, 1970, pp. 1, 30.

been no appreciable change in the relative importance of the various types of outlets since that time, although the volume of business has increased.

Several reasons are given for the dominance of the men's specialty shop in this field. One is that men hesitate to enter the predominantly feminine confines of the department store—a reluctance that even special entrances and special elevators for men's departments do not entirely break down. Another reason is that the men's specialty shop is usually so arranged that furnishings and clothing are displayed and sold together, and a single salesman can range through the entire stock with a customer. In department stores, this is not always the case.

Some items of men's clothing, however, are retailed energetically in stores patronized principally by women—sports shirts (which wives and girl-friends often select) and undergarments (which are usually replenished by wives for their husbands). But where try-on is required and a man has to shop in person, he seems to gravitate toward the more personalized service and masculine atmosphere of men's specialty shops.

FASHION REVOLUTION IN MEN'S WEAR

During the 1960s, the winds of fashion change began to blow up a storm in the men's wear industry. What had been considered a backward, overly traditional business began to acquire a lively fashion pace and to develop points of resemblance to the fast-moving women's apparel field. As men's interest in fashion quickened, the industry came up with an abundance of new style ideas, and both manufacturers and retailers showed themselves eager to exploit them. Press coverage of men's fashions increased, and male consumers found themselves reading about new fashions, talking about them, buying them, and wearing them. Fashion coordinators, who once functioned almost exclusively in the women's field, entered the men's wear field to tackle the problems of how new fashions should be merchandised, displayed, and promoted. Fashion shows ceased to be rarities in men's wear; department stores and other outlets that handled apparel for both sexes began to assign larger space, better locations, and more promotional activities to their men's departments.

Deemphasizing Seasonal Patterns

One effect of men's greater fashion awareness has been a degree of departure from the rigid, twice-a-year pattern of introducing new lines. Although this pattern continues to prevail, an occasional producer of clothing introduces an intermediate line, and some sport shirt producers introduce special groups for occasions like Father's Day and Christmas.

Regardless of the industry pattern, however, producers are learning to put a new idea into production whenever it develops, and to publicize it promptly through advertising and editorial mentions in men's fashion publications. There are more fashion publications for men these days than there were a decade or two ago, and they are eagerly read by a responsive group of young and not-so-young fashion-aware males.

There is also the impact of television, which can launch a new style with rocket speed and without regard to the seasonal merchandising patterns of producers or retailers. A classic case occurred in February 1968 when Johnny Carson, on his network *Tonight* show, appeared in a Nehru suit. Fashion-conscious men, unconcerned with the industry's calendar, liked the Nehru idea and wanted it at once. A single retail chain in New York, Weber & Heilbroner, reported over 1000 requests for the style the day after its exposure on television. A single producer, Andrew Pallack & Co., reported shipping more than 6000 Nehrus within two months after the Carson show.[16] The fashion took off, flourished, and in time died, but it demonstrated to the industry that its designers could no longer put their pencils down after a season's line was completed. Fashion innovations were becoming a year-round job.

Changing Pattern of Production Output

Unitl the 1950s the typical masculine wardrobe consisted largely of suits. Except for the relatively few men who participated actively in sports like golf and tennis and had special clothes for such occasions, and except for the blue-collar worker who wore work clothes all week, the average male's closet held suits almost exclusively.

Early indications of the changes that were in store for the industry came in the 1950s from the sportswear sector. The great exodus from cities to suburbs took place; leisure time increased; and the range of activities of the typical man broadened to include more sports, do-it-yourself pursuits, and other occasions for which casual dress was adequate and comfortable. A more relaxed way of dressing became popular and spilled over into city life.

Although tailored clothing and dress shirts remained essentially conservative, sportswear changed and developed rapidly. New colors and patterns followed one another in rapid succession; men bought sport shirts in (then) daring styles and paid more for them than their weekday whites; trunk shows (showings of a producer's or designer's complete collection of samples) by leading sportswear producers were tremendously successful in stores; and a national association of men's sportswear buyers was formed to encourage and direct fashion change. Thus, in the era of the gray flannel suit, male interest in fashion was awakening, and at least one segment of the industry was responding to it.

An analysis of the changes that took place in production between 1956 and 1965 demonstrates the dramatic shift from suits to separates and from dress shirts to sport shirts. In 1956, there were 8.9 million sports coats produced in this country; by 1965, production had reached 12.3 million—an increase of 38 percent. Production of

---

[16]*Business Week*, July 20, 1968, p. 69.

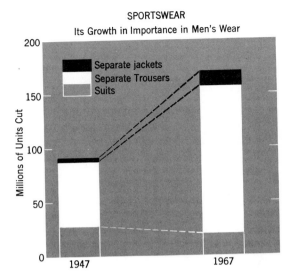

SPORTSWEAR
Its Growth in Importance in Men's Wear

Source: U.S. Department of Commerce, Census of Manufactures.

men's separate slacks more than doubled during this same period, and sports shirts increased by 19 percent. Dress shirts, by moving away from whites into a variety of colors and patterns, increased by 42 percent during this decade. In this same period, in spite of a constantly increasing number of adult males in the population, men's suit production remained static at 21 million units.[17]

Growing Importance of Designer Names

Until the 1960s, the men's wear industry was not in the habit of exploiting designer names. As in the case of the women's apparel industry before World War II, the men's wear designer, who was often simply a tailor, was a shadowy figure in the background, no better known to retailers and consumers than were the cutters and pattern makers in the plant. Moreover, there was no Paris couture to stimulate and publicize fashion directions.

In the course of the 1960s, however, the growing fashion awareness of the male and the entry into the men's apparel field of American and European designers, who had already achieved distinction in feminine apparel, helped to change the industry from a replacement business to a fashion business. Among the designers were Pierre Cardin of Paris; Hardy Amies, the English couturier and dressmaker to Queen Elizabeth II; Christian Dior and Yves St. Laurent of Paris; and Valentino of Rome. Among the Americans were Oleg Cassini, John Weitz, and Bill Blass. The usual arrangement under which these designers operated was to franchise or license a manufacturer to produce their designs. Unlike the designers directly employed by men's clothing manufacturers, the couturiers who entered the men's field did not

[17]Carl Priestland, "Evolution in the Men's Apparel Industry," *Apparel Manufacturer*, September 1967, p. 27.

FASHION SHOWS IN MEN'S WEAR

Leading New York newspapers say...

"smashing example of new kind of clothes"

"accent on elegance"

Now Alexander's invites you to the public
premier of the <u>show</u> hailed by the press!

" simply elegant"

MEN'S FALL '72 COUTURE

from the world's most prestigious
designers of menswear

London · Paris · Rome · New York

Wednesday, September 20th, 6 P.M.
on our 3rd floor

free admission

ALEXANDER'S

Source: As advertised in *The New York Times*, September 19, 1972.

have to become involved with the economics of factory production, nor did they have to confine themselves to any one segment of the industry or to any one producer. The couturiers made licensing agreements with a variety of different firms so that their suits and jackets could be manufactured by one producer, and so that the related ties, jewelry, scarfs, or even hats could be produced by other firms in the appropriate fields. The designers remained free to create and coordinate, to help publicize their lines, and to collect their share of the various producers' sales dollars.

The entry into the men's field by these famous designers has resulted in new methods of merchandising men's wear. Stores, large and small, have set up special shops or boutiques for their "name" collections. Some of these shops feature a single designer—for instance, the John Weitz "club" at Lord & Taylor, New York, the Oleg Cassini shop in John Wanamaker's, Philadelphia, and the Cardin boutique at Bonwit Teller's, New York. Other stores combine the merchandise of two or three designers in a single special shop.

Manufacturing companies that have signed agreements with these famous designers usually have established separate divisions and have allocated separate plant facilities for their "name" fashions while proceeding along their accustomed operational lines with their other merchandise.

Meantime, partly as a result of the interest in designer names generated by the entry of couturiers into the men's field and partly because men's wear itself has become a more exciting fashion area in which to work, men's wear producers are beginning to develop and feature design talent of their own. It is no longer necessary for a creative designer to turn to women's apparel in order to find challenge, satisfaction, and freedom of expression. Although designer "name" merchandise remains only a small percentage of the industry's total output, its very presence testifies to the vastly increased importance of fashion in men's wear and helps to attract top-notch creative talent to the industry.

READINGS

To understand the changes that have taken place in men's wear, we must first understand the changes in men themselves. Therefore, the readings in this section begin with a discussion of the "Peacock Revolution" by Dr. Ernest Dichter, the motivational researcher who taught businessmen to apply psychological insights to marketing and advertising. Other readings explore the slow decline of conservatism in masculine dress, the development of fashion marketing strategy in the men's field, and the growing importance of the designer's name in the creation and sale of men's wear.

THE PEACOCK REVOLUTION

Dr. Ernest Dichter

In the animal, bird and fish world the male is normally the most colorful and attractive of the sexes; this is particularly true of the peacock. In the human world men have for many years been the drab ones; women the colorful ones—at least in dress.

Yet something is happening. Young men want, need and intend to change this situation. In the future there will be peacocks in the human world because deep down inside, young men desire the same gratifications from wearing apparel that young women desire *and get*—the pleasure of using apparel as an outlet for expressing one's own uniqueness as a personality as well as one's varying day to day moods.

A SCHIZOPHRENIC INDUSTRY

The clothing industry has for years maintained a schizophrenic personality—with the vital, constantly changing women's apparel market in dramatic contrast to the lethargic men's apparel market. Apparel manufacturers featuring the "durable press," the "no iron shirt" and "drip dry suits" have often exclaimed, "Ah, this is it, this will put vitality into the men's apparel market." While interesting and sought after by men, these features have not created the hoped for reversal. The market as a whole still suffers from lack of vitality.

How did the men's clothing industry get into this dilemma? Men want to express themselves via their wearing apparel, yet society restricts them. The popular "whipping boys" today for society's ills—our educational system, suburbia and mass communications—cannot be considered the cause of the social dilemma about which we speak. The prime cause appears to be the emergence of a large and dominant business class in Western

society. Historically, as more men began to work in business, there was a gradual change from dressing for a role—ruler, scholar, man of God, court jester or leisure class gentleman—to dressing for the job.

BUREAUCRATIC CLOTHES

This business class simplified men's clothing as a reaction against court life as well as for practical reasons such as expense. A simple jacket replaced the doublet, trousers replaced breeches, plain fabrics replaced silks and velvets, and fit replaced cut. Today's man is a lawyer, executive or salesman first, when it comes to dress. He wants to look the part. He does not dress for his role as a man. He dresses for his job. A woman, by contrast, dresses to be a woman first.

At last, however, it appears as though the end of this social dilemma is in sight. Groups of men are emerging, not only in the USA, but everywhere in the western world, who reject the bureaucratic organization.

NEED FOR SELF-EXPRESSION

They refuse to dress for a job. They are dressing for a role as a man—a rebel, swinger, hot-rodder, surfer, beatnick, etc. They are expressing their own individuality. They are the peacocks of the future. This group, the youth market, particularly ages 17 to 25, is not only less respectful of traditions and less inhibited (just watching the Frug, Watusi or Jerk gives you that message) but is very verbal about its likes and dislikes in wearing apparel and is obviously exerting a major influence on the dressing styles of older men.

This market is growing by leaps and bounds. It is estimated that by 1975 there will be approximately 42% more young men in this age group, all with

SOURCE: Reprinted by permission of *American Fabrics* magazine, Issue 71, Spring-Summer 1966.

money to spend to express their own personal needs. Why shouldn't most of this self-expression evolve around clothes instead of cars? Our prognosis for the future is good. This youth market is bored with the clothing choice available to them.

HOW DIFFERENT IS YOUTH?

It has been generally acknowledged by everyone, particularly we parents, that today's youth is different. The big question is, "How are they different?" Essentially, they are different because they have little or no desire to conform to adult behaviors. They want their own life, their own individuality.

SECURITY AS A MAN

First, they are more secure as men; more sure of their masculinity. Witness the tremendous growth of the men's fragrance industry, directly attributable to the influence of the younger men. *Only* a man who feels completely secure as a man can allow himself to wear anything with feminine overtones, for he is not threatened by it.

DESIRE FOR NEW EXPERIENCES

Secondly, young men are not simply looking for a niche in the world. An increasing majority—starting with the most influential group of trend setters—want to experience many more facets of life than did their fathers. They may be part of the bureaucratic machinery from 9 to 5, playing the role of the jobs they fill, displaying the proper decorum, saying the right things to the right people. After all, they have to eat.

But, on their own time they do not want to be typical job holders. Life has too much to offer, as television has so effectively convinced them during all of their young lives. The young people travel more, further and at a younger age than we did. With an automobile at their disposal, they not only see more and do more, but they meet a greater variety of other young people than in the days when they were solely confined to neighborhood contacts. Resultingly, they experiment with a variety of interests. They cultivate the new, the unique

and have an unquenchable thirst for new roles and experiences.

THE ADONIS COMPLEX

The Greeks fervently believed that a young man's body was a thing of beauty. The most beautiful of all bodies in mythology was that of Adonis. Today's youth has revived that spirit with the help of our present day worship of the youthful look. Resultingly, a young man imagines himself an Adonis, a possessor of a young and beautiful body. He wears his clothes so as to show off that young body. He does not want his clothes to modify his body shape as the A-line dress does for a woman. Rather he wants clothes to adhere to his body, to show it off in all its young splendor. Not only is he an exhibitionist when he wears tight-fitting clothes, but he is creating the illusion that he, the wearer, is the master—the clothing yields to him. Young men need to feel and to make others feel that they are in command of life, for unless they're lucky enough to be successful 16-year-old recording stars, they have not yet made their mark in life. Resultingly, for all their assured facade, deep down they are not only unsure of how they will make out in the world but unsure of who they are; what they are really like as people. In fact they are even unsure of what they are intended to look like, inasmuch as their bodies have never ceased their rather unpredictable growth. To the young man, tight-fitting or tailored-to-the body contoured clothing gives him a feeling of security—he can feel his body and this feeling gives him the security of knowing that he is intact.

A TREND TO HEDONISM

Perhaps, the most important development in the total men's apparel market that we will witness in the future is that apparel of all types will become more important in the lives of men than has ever been true before. The peacock will emerge. And, the purchasing and wearing of clothing will drastically change. It will become more hedonistic —pleasure-seeking.

Buying of clothes used to be a traumatic experience financially and emotionally. As we come to have increasingly more money disposable for wearing apparel we shall buy more often and we shall make less fuss about each purchase. The future holds great promise for increased diversity in the apparel market. Men will want to express their individuality by playing a variety of roles through the clothes they wear.

The apparel industry has a tremendous opportunity. It can benefit by this trend towards apparel-hedonism—the buying of clothes because it is fun to do so and not only because of need. The Peacock Revolution! This opportunity, however, requires more dramatic communication via product development and advertising message with the young man market. We must relieve his frustration that no one is listening to him. Convince him otherwise and he will respond eagerly.

THE TERRIBLE TROUBLE WITH MEN

They're conservative. They think last year's clothing style is good enough for the next five years. That's why the men's clothing industry doesn't have even half the volume of the women's clothing industry. That's also why it's more stable.

The men's clothing industry is one of the last strongholds of cautious, conservative management in our dynamic, affluent society. One result is that, while there are nearly as many men as women in the U.S., the men's clothing industry does less than half the dollar volume of the women's clothing industry. . . .

The average cutter (as the manufacturers of women's clothing are called) stays in business for only seven years. In the men's clothing industry, manufacturers who have been in business for 75 years are commonplace; companies a century old are far from rare; and there is one company, J. Capps & Sons Ltd. of Jacksonville, Ill., that started in 1839 by carding wool, went into the manufacture of blankets and fabrics and wound up making men's clothes. Robert Capps is the fifth generation of his family to run the firm. That, incidentally, also illustrates another fact about the men's clothing business: To a startling extent it's a family-owned industry, with companies handed down from grandfather to father to son, though in recent years

there has been a growing tendency for the families to sell out to such diversified corporations as Genesco Inc., Cluett, Peabody & Co., B.V.D. Co. and Phillips-Van Heusen Corp. The companies that sell out retain their identities, and, quite frequently, the family remains the overseers. For example, although H. Daroff & Sons is now a part of Botany Industries, Michael Daroff still runs it.

FEW PUBLICLY HELD

In the women's clothing industry they have a saying: "He didn't go bankrupt; he went public." Possibly because they don't go bankrupt, very few men's wear makers are publicly held corporations. And these few are not strictly men's wear makers. Howard Stores Corp. and Bond Stores, Inc., for example, are retailers as well as manufacturers. United Merchants & Manufacturers, Inc. not only turns out Robert Hall clothes, it also produces textiles, including fabrics of glass and plastic. B.V.D. Co. is better known for its underwear, foundation garments and lingerie, than for its men's clothing.

Far and away the biggest and widest-ranging

SOURCE: Condensed from *Forbes* Magazine, July 1, 1967. Reprinted by permission of *Forbes* magazine.

company in the business is Genesco Inc. This high-ly diversified company is a $760-million-a-year (fiscal 1966 sales) fashion-and-apparel outfit: men's wear accounts for probably 15% of its over-all volume. Genesco is certainly the only company in the business that can bring a broadly integrated corporate and merchandising outlook to bear on the men's wear business. . . .

Even those companies that own retail stores are fairly small by the standards of any other industry. Bond stores, for example, which owns more than 140 outlets, did $97.7 million worth of business last year; Richman Brothers Co., with 281 outlets, only $75.9 million. Among manufacturers that do not have retail outlets, a company that does between $25 million and $50 million worth of business a year is considered a large company; between $5 million and $25 million, a medium-sized company.

Although no men's wear maker is really hurting, even here good management helps and poor man-agement hurts. Howard Stores, for example, has shown almost no recent growth in sales and was recently delisted by the New York Stock Exchange. In 1962, Howard's sales amounted to $49 million. Last year sales were $51.9 million, a rise of a mere 5.9%. Even Richman Brothers and Bond Stores, two rather lackluster performers, have done better than Howard. In the same period, Richman's sales have increased by 24% and Bond's by 10%.

All three companies look pale when compared with Hart Schaffner & Marx. Like others, Hart Schaffner & Marx is both a manufacturer and a retailer. Since 1962, it sales have risen from $97.8 million to $183.8 million, 88%, and its earnings have risen even more, from $2.9 million to $10 million, 244.8%. The other companies manufac-ture relatively lowpriced clothing, but Hart Schaffner & Marx has been quick to capitalize on today's affluence; it specializes in high-quality suits, ranging from $95 all the way to the $255 Hickey-Freeman line.

SUCCESS & ITS INGREDIENTS

Statistics for privately held companies are impossi-ble to come by, but within the industry there is general agreement that Michaels Stern & Co. of Rochester, N.Y. has slipped. Michaels Stern was once a leading manufacturer of medium-priced suits. In recent years, according to industry sources, it has been passed by L. Greif & Bro., a subsidiary of Genesco; J. Shoeneman. Inc. of Bal-timore, a subsidiary of Cluett, Peabody & Co.; and Botany's H. Daroff & Sons. But such is the nature of the men's wear industry that Michaels Stern re-mains a highly profitable company. . . .

What makes one manufacturer do better than another? Dependability of deliveries is one very important factor. When a retailer orders a new line, he wants the first deliveries to cover a balanced variety of sizes, with emphasis naturally on the sizes most of his customers wear. If this doesn't happen, he will lose sales. In that case, he's likely to cancel his order.

The manufacturers of women's clothing are con-centrated in a few blocks of mid-Manahattan's Sev-enth Avenue and the streets radiating from it. ("Seventh Avenue" is a synonym for the industry; another synonym: "the rag business.") There's no such concentration in the men's-wear industry. New York is the center, but from New York it spreads out to Philadelphia. Baltimore, Rochester, Chicago, Cincinnati, Los Angeles, San Francisco and scores of towns and cities in between. Slacks manufacturing, a real growth sector in the indus-try, is located mostly in the South. . . .

Slacks and sport coats are the fastest-growing part of the industry because the growth of sub-urbia has led men to dress more informally. In 1940, the industry turned out about 13 million pairs of slacks; in 1965, 151.4 million. The output of sport coats reflects the same trend. In 1965, 12.3 million sport coats were produced; in 1940, sport coats were so rare they didn't even rate their own category.

NO HOT NUMBERS

The basic reason that the men's and women's clothing industries are so different is that one sells clothes, while the other sells fashion. Men's clothes do change from year to year, but so imper-ceptibly that not one man in a hundred notices it, and not one man in a thousand cares. If the manu-facturers are featuring two-button suits this year, that doesn't make last year's three-button suit out-moded. The result is that if a man likes a suit, he'll keep wearing it until it wears out. A woman wouldn't think of wearing that perfectly stunning gown she bought last year because *nobody* is wearing ruffles this year. The man couldn't care less if half a dozen other men at the country club dance are wearing tuxedos exactly like his. The woman will die a thousand deaths if "that dreadful Janie Smith, that old bag who thinks she's still 20," wears a dress like hers.

Of course, as Hardy Amies, a London designer of both men's and women's clothes who recently went to work for Genesco, points out, women's clothes really don't change as much from year to year as women think. However, women are acutely conscious of the changes. Every newspaper in the U.S. of any consequence has a women's editor to bring them news of the changes: almost none prints men's fashion news regularly. Every women's magazine from *McCall's* and the *Ladies' Home Journal* to *Seventeen* and *Mademoiselle*, to say nothing of *Vogue* and *Harper's Bazaar*, devotes a great deal of attention to women's fashion. By comparison, even *Esquire* and *Playboy* among the men's magazines pay much less attention to men's fashion, although they occasionally show what the well-dressed duck hunter will wear.

CAN MEN CHANGE?

There are those who say that if newspapers and magazines did pay more attention to men's fashions, men would become just as fashion-conscious as women. "Never underestimate the power of advertising." they declaim. "Men can be *brainwashed* into becoming fashion-conscious. How do you think women got that way?" Chip Tolbert, fashion editor of *Esquire*, says: "I think the industry has to try to create obsolescence just as the women's manufacturers have been doing. Anyone who is bringing in changes is helping the industry. People who say that men don't want to change are just not in touch with current thinking." In the industry, this is a minority view. Even so interested a person as John D. Gray. president of Hart Schaffner & Marx, the largest U.S. producer and retailer of men's clothing, will admit: "It's hard to get men to think about clothing. They just aren't interested."

Some manufacturers insist, moreover, that even if men could be made fashion-conscious, the industry would have to continue to sell clothes, not fashion. The cutters can sell fashion, they say, because many dresses are made of print goods; men's wear makers can't because suits are made of woven goods.

To understand this argument, one must understand how the women's clothing industry works: The fashions originate with a handful of designers in Paris, Rome, New York and Hollywood. Manufacturers of high-priced dresses in the U.S. decide which of them will go and instantly copy both the fabric and the design, with modifications. Then, manufacturers of dresses selling at slightly lower prices decide which of *them* will go and copy *those*, again with modifications. And that's how the industry operates right down the line, from manufacturers of dresses selling for $900 to manufacturers of copies of copies of copies of copies of copies selling for $10.

The reason the women's clothing industry can operate in this manner is that print goods are so easy to manufacture. If women suddenly go wild over a particular fabric, the U.S. textile industry can turn it out by the mile almost overnight. The problem of the cutter is simply to make the right guess on what to steal—and to steal it and start producing it before any of his competitors. If obtaining the fabric were a problem too, he obviously couldn't do this; and the whole process whereby a copy of a dress shown in Paris can be worn by a matron in Wichita, Kansas, three months later would become impossible.

TIME LAG

Unlike print goods, woven goods are difficult to produce. They must be ordered at least eight months in advance, preferably ten. Most manufacturers of men's wear already have ordered for 1968. If blue becomes a popular color in 1968, there's nothing a manufacturer can do unless he's already ordered blue. "We can't run to the mills and say "blues are hot, what have you got?" says Harvey Weinstein of West Mill Clothes.

The situation is aggravated by the fact that, by

and large, the mills don't give the manufacturers a very wide choice. Chester Kessler, president of William B. Kessler, cites an example: Some years ago, several manufacturers introduced a new color, burgundy, but "about the time burgundy came along green was also becoming popular. The mills decided they couldn't push both so they chose green." Why didn't the manufacturers put pressure on the mills to produce burgundy as well as green? "I don't know," answers Kessler. "I guess it's just the thinking of our industry."

This attitude seems to extend even to technology. Men's suits in the U.S. are made exactly the way they were 50 years ago, with about 150 steps needed to make a jacket. In England, manufacturers have been experimenting with pasting, rather than sewing, seams, a much faster and less costly process. All through Western Europe, there are machines that can cut trousers along the contours of the body, instead of merely in a straight line. Not in the U.S.

The manufacturers do envy the larger volume of business in the women's clothing industry, but they know that if they were to attempt to sell fashion in the manner of women's clothing manufacturers, they would put an element of risk in the business. They might get stuck with a line men wouldn't buy. The retailers feel the same way. They like the present system whereby if they can't sell a suit this fall, they can sell it next fall: nobody will know the difference. Says Amies; "Whenever I talk with retailers about making changes, they get a little panicky. They ask. "How soon?" I reassure them by saying, "It depends on inventory size.""

The industry actually is organized to prevent change. When it comes to style, for example, the CMA has committees; on sport clothes, on conventional business clothes, on the male equivalent of women's "high style." They meet and decide what the prevailing styles will be. Above them is what the CMA calls "the editorial committee." Once the editorial committee approves the decisions, that's it: that's what all but a handful of mavericks will make. The CMA then puts out a book for distribution to retailers, showing them how next year's clothes will look.

Twice a year, the CMA holds what it calls "clothing market actions." One action is held during the last week in February and the first week in March. There, the manufacturers show their fall and winter clothes. The other action is held the last week in August and the first week in September; that is the spring and summer showing.

The mavericks like designers Pierre Cardin of Paris and John Weitz of New York, who attempt to buck this system, cause some in the industry to erupt in four-letter words. Says Michael Daroff: "Most Americans wouldn't be caught dead in that stuff."

MOD STRIKES OUT

In criticizing European styles, the manufacturers like to dwell on the swift demise of Mod, the style introduced by Carnaby Street in London. There is one manufacturer, however, who insists the industry itself was responsible for the failure of Mod to catch on. Preferring to remain anonymous for obvious reasons, he says: "The mistake was not trying to adapt the style, which was for young kids, to older men. The industry isn't smart enough to realize that instead of getting men to wear Mod, they should have adopted some of its elements —colors, small style features. Seventh Avenue learned this a long time ago, and our industry may eventually catch on." Indeed, the women's clothing manufacturers put women through a conditioning process. They don't spring an extreme fashion like the miniskirt on women all at once. They get women used to wearing shorter and shorter skirts, and then, at the right psychological moment, come out with the miniskirt, obsoleting last year's dresses because they cannot be shortened to miniskirts without ruining the lines.

There *are* pressures on the industry to change. They come mostly from those still-few retailers who believe that more and more men are tired of wearing the same dull clothes year after year. One of them is Fred Pressman of Barney's in New York, the nation's largest single independent men's specialty store. Pressman, son of the founder of Barney's, sells more than 250,000 garments a year. "Our industry doesn't realize that the important thing is creating excitement," he says. "Even if fashion doesn't sell any suits, it gets people interested in clothes." Pressman believes the industry should attempt to get at the men through their wives and girl friends: "Most men want something a bit different, but they need their wife or girl friend to persuade them to buy."

Will the industry ever change? Genesco has just placed a small bet that it will. That is why it recently joined with Amies to establish a new division, Hardy Amies-USA. The company is not abandoning its conventional operations, like Phoenix Clothes, L. Greif & Bro., and English American Tailoring, of course, but with Hardy Amies-USA it will attempt to inject fashion into men's clothes. The changes will come gradually. "I think in terms of five years. I don't want the men's trade ever to develop the built-in hysteria of the women's trade," says Amies.

Amies believes that American men can be made fashion-conscious. He points out that Englishmen are. "Every major English newspaper now has a men's editor, reporting every style change," he says. "Even the financial press—*The Financial Times*, for example—follows men's fashions very closely."

Amies admits that injecting fashion into the men's wear business will also inject an element of risk. "But," he says, "the biggest risk is just going along the way we have been." On this, B.H. Willingham, president of Genesco, agrees. "I don't think that we're heading toward the seasonal changes we have in the women's industry," he says, "but I feel it's wrong to think this year's inventories will be just as good next season. Too much is happening, subtle changes such as lighter clothing, different lengths, new colors. . . . We felt the real big risk was to do nothing."

Summing up for the industry, Kuppenheimer's Harry Roth says "Our big problem is that we don't let men get their kicks in our industry. So they spend their extra dollars other places, color television, sporting goods and Mustangs."

A LITTLE CHANGE?

Can the men's wear manufacturers persuade more Americans to get their kicks out of the way they dress? There was, after all, a time when men did pay as much attention to style as women do; when men were popinjays. Perhaps they will become popinjays again. Meanwhile, however, the best bet for the men's wear industry appears to lie in getting men to buy clothes of higher quality. Hart Schaffner & Marx has been doing this, putting out ever-more-expensive clothes. So has Botany Industries. Even pants manufacturers have been doing it. Henry I. Siegel, for example, originally made private-label slacks for mass retailers like Montgomery Ward and J.C. Penney. It switched to manufacturing higher-quality slacks under its own labels, "h.i.s." and "h.i.s. for her," and promoted them heavily. Since 1957, Siegel's sales have risen from $19 million to $63.8 million, but, even more significantly, profit margins have increased from 1.8% to 5.06%.

The men's wear makers today are enjoying prosperity by doing almost exactly what their grandfathers did in almost exactly the same way. However, this obviously cannot continue forever. The world keeps changing. The population is getting younger. Perhaps the younger generation will demand style. Certainly, it will become more affluent. Whether it's style or quality the coming generation demands—or both—the companies that survive, as always, will be those that anticipate the demand.

MALE PLUMAGE '68

The once securely-buttoned-down fortress of male fashion is clearly under heavy siege. From New York to San Francisco, men are breaking loose from sartorial regimentation and wandering off into a bizarre world in which yesterday's heresies are rapidly becoming today's orthodoxy.

Just ten years ago, a man who dared challenge the supremacy of the three-button sack suit was promptly dressed down by his peers, often at the expense of his "masculine image." Rather than buck the status quo, the male simply remained safely hidden behing the drab anonymity of his "uniform" and dutifully paid the bills for his wife's shopping flings.

But a new dawn was soon to break over the soft, shapeless waistland of male attire. It came—among other things—with the Beatles, the hippies and the student revolts. In short, when a new era of social expression was born in the United States, the dark ages of male fashion began to die. Now, no longer afraid of criticism, the American male is submitting his body to perfumes and his hair to stylists; wrapping himself in form-fitting suits of every shade and fabric; hanging pendants and beads from his neck; adorning his feet with bright-buckled shoes, and generally carrying on like a dandy straight out of the days of Beau Brummell.

"Today it's the great idea of liberty," says Yves St. Laurent, the distinguished Parisian designer who is now branching into male fashion. In London, where Carnaby Street has become an international center for flamboyant styles, young Britons deck themselves in baby blue corduroy slacks and matching mini-Shetland sweaters. The French students, clad in shocking-pink velvet pants and tight flowered shirts, are doing their thing. So is many a way-out Roman, who favors a bejeweled white crepe Mandarin shirt and a jaunty foulard scarf.

SOURCE: Copyright *Newsweek* November 25, 1968. Reprinted by permission.

FRESH LINEN

Fashion, of course, always changes. George Bryan Brummell, an early nineteenth-century sartorial rebel, took the play away from the British aristocracy—who wore musty and crusty old court uniforms—by stressing faultless line, skillful tailoring, starched cravats and a profusion of fresh linen. Later, the Edwardian dandy revolted against staid Victorian clothes, and more recently, as the working class got its hands on extra cash, rebellious styles popped up all over the place. The U.S. offered the zoot suit, and England had its Teddy boys, while the mod look—hip-huggers and gaudy shirts—bounced back and forth across the Atlantic.

But seldom has male fashion switched, twitched and disported itself with the urgency of today. Money and leisure are part of the reason; the suburban man wants—and can afford—bright togs to fit his weekend fun. A more energetic and pervasive influence is youth. Hipped on color and cacophony, whether it's psychedelic art *or* discothèques, young people dress to fit their milieu—and their elders are picking up the beat. "It used to be that the son sneaked in to borrow his father's tie," says James K. Wilson Jr. president of Hart Schaffner and Marx Clothes. " Now the father is sneaking in to borrow his son's turtleneck."

Certainly the media have provided plenty of the sales message. In the decade between 1955 and 1965, the number of newspapers regularly covering men's wear has jumped from 100 to more than 800. Color television has encouraged entertainers—and even golfers—to seek the brightest apparel. Equal thrust has come from such TV personalities as Johnny Carson, whose show presents an almost nightly dialogue on the latest radical male fashions. After Carson modeled an Oleg Cassini Nehru suit last February, NBC got 1,000 phone calls from viewers asking where the suit could be bought.

"Media is the key reason for the spurt," says Everett Mattlin, editor of Gentlemen's Quarterly.

"On his way to the sports pages, a man can't help but see what's on the women's pages—and it's very likely to be men's fashion."

FLEUR-DE-LIS

Indeed, once a no man's land, the women's pages are chuck full of male paraphernalia. Covering a Southampton wedding this summer, The New York Times burbled more excitedly about the men's widly flowered trousers than about the female frocks. Just as typical is the syndicated society column "Suzy Says," whose author went to the opening of "Hair" in Munich last month and spent most of her raves on male dress, including producer Michael Butler's black velvet jacket encrusted with a gold fleur-de-lis pattern and gold-braid borders. Wrote Suzy: "Who cares what the girls were wearing?"

The new plumage spreads well beyond the jet-set scene. West Coast financier Bart Lytton, 55, who wears a midnight blue Nehru suit with white turtleneck and Byzantine medallion, marched six of his top executives into Sy Devore's Hollywood boutique and bought each two natty, slim-cut suits. "They were sitting around making million-dollar deals in nondescript clothes," says Devore, "and Lytton thought that was inappropriate." Side-burned auto king Henry Ford II wears turtlenecks on formal occasions, and Canada's colorful Prime Minister Pierre Trudeau is apt to appear at the doors of Parliament in his custom-made otter fur coat. Even diplomats are getting into the act. Recently, Ambassador-at-Large Averell Harriman, representing the U.S. in the Vietnam peace talks, received from home a pair of snug-fitting Pultizer pants sporting a turquoise-and-white bulldog pattern.

Professional athletes are flamboyant, too. Boston Red Sox slugger Ken Harrelson favors powder blue Nehrus; New York Jets quarterback Joe Namath recently purchased a $5,000 double-breasted mink coat; former Yankee catcher Yogi Berra endorses hair spray on television. And Detroit pitcher Denny McLain ambled onto the stage of a Detroit nightclub last week to perform at the electric organ and show off his $3,000 Russian white broadtail Nehru jacket, complete with medallion.

Leading the way in the revolt are the scores of boutiques that have sprouted across the country. So rapidly do styles change that each city has its own hot items. In Houston, the demand for leather jackets and overcoats seems to harken back to the days of the cowpoke, while in New York, the accent on frilled shirts, velvet Regency suits and bellbottom pants recalls the city's English heritage. In southern California—where the male fashion revolt is most widespread—wide-lapelled Edwardian long jackets and flared pants have stolen the thunder from the Nehrus and beads. In San Francisco, a cotton chambray shirt with voluminous sleeves called the "Billy Budd" is the current rage.

To stay ahead of the customers' mercurial tastes, designers are working overtime to come up with new styles. Sometimes the effort produces zany results. "So many bad things are being done now," says David Platt, editor of Men's Bazaar. "We're getting a fanfare of bad taste, extremes and excesses." Such bizarre creations as male handbags, his-'n'-her Dracula capes, miniskirts for men and see-through blouses and pants have been tried on the public with little success—as yet. "What will be left from all this," nonetheless admits Platt, "is at least more knowledge about clothes."

SALES PITCH

Beyond the frills and laces, satins and bows displayed in the boutiques, the Peacock Revolution has ruffled the feathers of the traditional manufacturers. The American consumer—who will spend about $750 million in 1968 on such "forward" styles—is forcing significant changes. For one thing, big houses such as H. Freeman & Son and After Six are stressing designer names (as in the couturier trade, names apparently provide a more appealing sales pitch). For another, manufacturers offer a much wider variety of styles in their basic suits; H. Daroff & Sons (Botany 500), for one, has increased models in one typical line from two to twelve.

Retailers have also had to retailor their approach. For example, they can no longer afford to order so much of their stock six months ahead: tastes change too quickly. This season many a big department store—after placing huge advance orders

—found itself stuck with a glut of Nehru jackets when the style suddenly began to wither. One answer to this problem comes from Barney's, largest men's store in the world, whose sales motto is "Select, Don't Settle." It is now planning a new, six-story Manhattan store; five floors will be devoted exclusively to boutiques, each specializing in different trends. "All kinds of ideas should be shown," says Fred Pressman, president of Barney's, "because there's no one right way in men's clothes any more."

Not every retailer has responded to the new trends so eagerly. Brooks Brothers, the prime bastion of conservatism, only recently introduced its first two-button, shaped suit. "It incorporates," murmurs the genteel Brooks catalogue "slightly squarer shoulders, definite waist suppression, a flare to the skirt and a deeper center vent." Even this minor compromise is too much for many old-school London tailors. "A well-dressed man should not be observed," sniffs a spokesman from Benson, Perry and Whitley, a dignified shop just off Savile Row, More practically, he notes that his well padded customers simply wouldn't wear the new creations: "There is no sense designing an Edwardian suit for a man with a 52-inch chest, 52-inch waist and 52-inch seat, now is there?"

Such seditious talk is rare, however. The new wave is fully and truly rolling—and no one is riding it with more aplomb than Parisian Pierre Cardin. Today, at 46, the fragile, green-eyed couturier is generally credited with doing for male fashion what Pablo Picasso did for modern art. His empire sprawls over five continents; his 1967 gross sales hit $22 million. Two-thirds of that sales total came from his male line which, in addition to suits, shirts and ties, includes gloves, sari-silk lounging pajamas, shoes, jewelry, fur coats, leather suits and even attaché cases. This year, Cardin expects his sales to jump 25 per cent—despite last spring's general strikes that brought French manufacturing to a halt. Says leading American designer Bill Blass. "He's the most stimulating influence in the last decade—perhaps even in the last century."

Like nearly every well-known men's designer, Cardin originally designed only for women. After World War II, friendless and unsure of his talents, he got his first job in the Paris workroom of Paquin. "Within a few days," he says, "I realized that I knew as much as anyone." Cardin opened a modest-fashion women's salon in 1949. Soon, the prestige of his name rivaled even that of Coco Chanel. "I believed in myself," he says. "I walked straight ahead with strength and will power."

Such positivism led the designer into the static world of men's attire. And, in 1954, Cardin started a men's shop on Paris's posh Faubourg-St. Honoré, featuring tapered shirts and gaudy ties. "We made 10,000 ties," he recalls. "People said they were vulgar—that only homosexuals would wear them." Actually, few men of any kind wore them—until six years later when the Beatles and Rolling Stones began sporting similar versions, and Cardin cravats boomed.

LUMPS

Far more influential was the classic Cardin suit. "I was bored with those awful square men," recalls Cardin. "All that padding, with their pants floating around their thighs, with great lumps in the pockets on their rumps, with trouser cuffs slopping around their shoes. It was monstrous. I am happy to have been responsible for destroying all that." The result was a slimmed-down waist-hugging style with longer jacket and cleaner, more youthful lines. First put on the market in 1959, Cardin's new silhouette has since been imitated throughout the world. In the U.S. alone, his label is sold in 92 stores, including New York's Bonwit Teller, which has a Cardin boutique featuring suits priced from $210 to $300.

Cardin continues to look ahead. "The job of fashion," he declares with almost evangelical fervor, "is not just to make pretty suits or dresses. It is to change the face of the world by cut and line. It is to make another aspect of man evident." Cardin's most exotic gesture in this direction is the "cosmonaut suit"—a two-piece affair with zippered pockets and sleeveless top. Asked if he thinks the world is ready for the cosmonaut suit, Cardin grins and says: "Ten years ago, people laughed at my fitted shirts and said I was crazy. Ten years from now, people who wear the 1968 Cardin suits will look like outmoded old men."

Sharing some of the limelight with Cardin is a handful of other designers. Among the most prosperous, powerful and provocative:

• John Weitz. After gaining a reputation in the United States for his comfortable functional women's sportswear, Weitz began resenting the fact that he was not recognized internationally. "Every year," he says, "the American press went to Paris, copied them, paid them a lot of money. No one looked at our designers. Meanwhile, men's wear went untouched." Thus, in 1965, Weitz was the first major designer to open a men's shop in the U.S.—at Lord & Taylor in New York City. The functionalism that Weitz brought to women's clothes, he also brought to men's. "I design for the international businessman," he says. "The men who rush for cabs, carry suitcases and sit on jets." He suits are of soft fabrics, no padding and a single button at the waist. His whole line—including everything from raincoats and watches to a toiletries selection called "International Club"—is sold in 33 U S. stores and ten foreign outlets. Last year, domestic sales hit $10 million. Weitz, 45, born in Germany and educated in England, insists he doesn't really design clothes but creates an ambiance. "One has to design mores, manners and moods," he says. "Clothes are not art—they must be worn. Art hangs on a wall—clothes must live."

• Oleg Cassini. While most designers are adept at cutting and sewing fabrics, the dapper, silver-haired Cassini never bothered to learn. "I create the concept," says the 52-year-old jet setter. "Call me the quarterback—I pass to my catchers and move the ball." Cassini's biggest score was being chosen to design Jackie Kennedy's White House wardrobe. Claiming about $25 million annual sales from men's fashions alone, Cassini says what really has made him a success is "my personal life. . . . I'm better known than any other designer in this country. I'm an outdoor man with an indoor look. I look like a villain, a bird of prey . . . I was probably the first hippie." As a designer, he's currently hipped on the Western look in accessories—loafers with brass hardware, belts with bold buckles and silk neckerchiefs.

• Bill Blass. "I am convinced that, other than speech, there is no better way to express yourself than through clothes," says the 41-year-old couturier whose bright checks and bold plaids are his masculine hallmark. Winner of the first Coty award for men's fashion, Blass is particularly adept at leisure wear—including explosively hued slacks

accented with sashes around the waist. Some of the Indiana-born designer's line shown recently at Chicago's Bonwit Teller (where Blass shares the spotlight with Cardin) was deliberately calculated to shock. A skintight terry-cloth "beach suit," for instance, was close to a total revelation to the audience. Since his debut collection a year ago, Blass had sold $2 million worth of clothes—and expects to double that figure in 1969. "At first," he says, "most men found it impossible to identify with the new fashions because many of the innovations were pioneered by the Negro and the homosexuals. Then along came the young. That made the difference."

• Hardy Amies. Recalling the explosion of mod fashion in London, the leading British men's designer says: "Let's face it. The men's clothing industry—especially Savile Row—was caught napping. They were still thinking like eminent Victorians when all around them young men were in revolt." Amies trained British spies and saboteurs during World War II ("The atmosphere was heavy with intrigue—which was valuable training for the clothing business"), then he opened a London salon. Before long, his list of female customers read like Debrett's Peerage; it was headed by Queen Elizabeth II. In 1957, Amies branched out into men's fashion, developing longer, shaped jackets and trousers with diagonally cut, cuffless bottoms. One-third of the Amies empire, which produced $70 million in sales last year, is owned by Hepworth's, Ltd., a British chain of some 300 men's shops. Says the 59-year-old Amies: "Men are more concerned about their looks these days then women."

While the big-name designers justifiably receive the major accolades, it is usually the little boutique that is one wild twist ahead. In Los Angeles, The Great Linoleum Clothing Experiment is pitching old shirts decorated with new swatches of doilies and shawls (average price: $40). In Southampton and Palm Beach, Lilly Pulitzer will soon offer silkscreen designs on corduroy trousers; she is also experimenting with boldly flowered underwear. In London, an American public-relations consultant named Larry Thaw only recently opened Sids—a boutique devoted wholly to red, green, tan, dark blue, gray and tortoise-shell $30 shoes, most of them crafted out of patent leather. In New

York, The Zoo ("Attire for the Male Animal") specializes in vinyl jackets and suits. Sample Zoo fare: a $90 yellow vinyl see-through bush jacket to be worn over a jumpsuit.

QUEST

Often enough the birth of a boutique is the result of a personal quest by the owners for more exotic attire. "We started off just for fun," says Dr. Joseph B. Santo, who opened Europhilia last spring in New York City. "We wanted a shop where we could get different clothes." But after raking in $100,000 in sales over the first three months, former dentist Santo figured he had struck a nerve; he has since become all business.

Part of the business, to be sure, is show biz. At Experiment One in New York's Greenwich Village, sputniks and moons hang from the ceilings while slides of planets and stars are projected on the walls. Also in Manhattan, Alexander's Tomorrow Shop uses flashing strobe lights, crashing music and dazzling silver décor to benumb the customer. Incense, sitar melodies, deer heads strung with love beads, glass fragment sculpture, psychedelic posters, even free champagne—anything to stir the buyer to do his thing is used. It is, in a sense, a matter of fun and personal fulfillment. "Clothes should not reflect how 'They' or 'I' think you should look," says Michael Fish of London's Mr. Fish. "Clothes should reflect how you want to look."

Of course, the way today's more unconventional male wants to look is still psychologically unsettling to many men. At worst, such critics dimly see such clothing as a homosexual conspiracy. At best, they fob it off as sophomoric high jinks—a kind of post-adolescent costume party better kept in the fraternity house. "It's the fear of not being taken seriously that influences a man's choice of clothes," says John Weitz. "He doesn't want his attire to prejudice his credibility."

Certainly, bright, eccentric fashions are not necessarily effete. Recalling the wild Edwardian caricatures of the Teddy boys, British fashion historian James Laver insists that such "new looks" are an assertion of masculinity. In the animal kingdom, as Laver and many other observers endlessly point out, it is the male that is resplendent in order to attract his mate.

CONFUSION

Yet a few psychologists still worry about today's flamboyant plumage. Dr. Charles Winick, who devotes an entire chapter to the subject in his book "The New People," puts forth the thesis that there is a definite desexualization in American life. "As the polarities in our national life become more visible," he says, "people tend toward the middle in things they control. . . . Men's clothes have become an approximation of women's, and women's clothes copy men's. When clothes express such confused roles—then society is in trouble."

Most social commentators, however, take a far less serious view. "It's been long overdue," says author Marya Mannes. "I love full heads of hair, beards. I love the turtleneck; I love fitted jackets; I love tight pants—all the things which emphasize a good figure and a good head are just fine."

Whatever its implications may be, the male fashion revolution appears to have only begun. For instance, two leading designers—Weitz and Cardin—predict men will wear fewer and fewer clothes —whatever their design. And more likely than not, the new clothes-conscious man will continue to experiment—frequenting boutiques, reading fashion magazines—and maybe even hiring a carpenter to enlarge his closet. It's what's happening.

THE LAST CONVERT TO MARKETING

Ralph Leezenbaum

Inside the Sperry Rand building in Manhattan, where most of the major marketers of men's tailored clothing (suits, sport and top coats) house their showrooms, salesmen with big cigars and enormous cuff links mix with young men in modern pinch-waist suits and brightly colored shirts. The young men, the sons and grandsons, the nephews and sons-in-law of the founders of large clothing companies, set the style. And some of the older men, kicked up stairs, look a little out of place trying to keep pace with their fashionable offspring.

They're easy to recognize, these stiff-lipped old-timers. As the elevator pings its way down the 40-story building, they greet each other as long time competitors will—polite, but familiar. They eye each other's suits appreciatively with the eyes of connoisseurs. The piece goods, the cut, the make, they know a good suit when they see it.

Sometimes they give voice to their appreciation. As a matter of fact, the only thing that gets more compliments than their clothing in these elevators is their advertising. Which is surprising, because those who should know, the agencies who work with these clothing companies, say their ads are some of the dullest and most uninspired around.

"Ninety-nine percent of men's clothing advertising is dull, moronic, imbecilic, appeals to idiots and is wasted money. And you can quote me on it," blasts Robert J. Cohen, executive vice-president of Waterman Advertising which handles several men's apparel accounts.

The problem, says Louis Emmanuele, BBDO vice-president and creative supervisor, whose major account is Du Pont fibers for apparel, "is that a lot of them are doing the ads themselves, or using a brother-in-law who's in the business, or a smart

kid, a nephew in college who majored in advertising, or just fly-by-night agencies."

Undoubtedly it is just this personal touch which explains all the inter-industry compliments. The man who says, "Izzy, I liked your ad," knows what a compliment he is really paying him. After all, it couldn't be any more Izzy's ad. His wife picked the suit, Izzy wrote the copy telling how many stitches in the lapel, and his nephew placed the ad.

Men's clothing advertising, even in consumer media, has traditionally been directed at the retailer. Mark-ups are low in the business and ad budgets reflect this. There are only a handful of nationally advertised brands. And some of the largest branded clothing makers do no consumer advertising at all.

Clothing marketers have relied on retailers to push the merchandise through to the consumer and promote their brand names. The largest national ad investments among clothing marketers last year amounted to only about $1.5-million.

There are definite signs, however, that things are changing. The look of men's clothing has changed almost overnight and this has forced the once conservative men's clothing industry to thoroughly re-examine its traditional ways of doing business. Clothing makers are increasingly becoming clothing marketers.

Says Cohen at Waterman: "They believe in advertising today. A few years ago the clothing industry didn't really believe in advertising."

Franchellie Cadwell, president of Cadwell Davis, which handles the Palm Beach account, backs him up. "Advertising by these big companies has become a real tool. They don't question it every season. Palm Beach has had a regular advertising program now every season for the last three years, I'd say. Before that they decided every season whether they were going to advertise or not."

One reason clothing brands can now afford to advertise more is because fiber companies along

SOURCE: *Marketing/Communications, December 1969. Reprinted by permission.*

with the Wool Bureau, among others, have determined it's good business to back these investments. But also, with retailers relying less on conventional branded sources for the kinds of fashion merchandise they need to stay on top of what the industry calls the "peacock revolution," brands are having to offer their retail outlets more cooperative ad dollars and the opportunities to use more media. Comments Stanley Voice, vice-president of advertising for H. Daroff & Sons, makers of Botany 500 clothing: "I think the retailer is too intelligent these days to have a manufacturer show him an ad he's going to run in Gentleman's Quarterly with an 80,000 circulation or The New York Times Magazine with a million circulation and make a federal case out of it."

Traditionally marketing communications have been product oriented. Individual items of apparel have received more attention than brand image because newspapers, the medium conventionally used most by retailers, are ideal for featuring individual retail promotions.

When clothing marketers began producing TV commercials last year to offer to retailers on a cooperative basis, they stayed with this approach, according to Miss Cadwell, because "the commercials were done to replace newspaper advertising which was item advertising, and this appealed to the retailer."

But clothing advertisers are finding this strategy works less satisfactorily on TV, where the suit or sport coat is seen only briefly. They are finding the medium better geared to creating and further developing brand recognition, a topic of much discussion among clothing marketers these days. A recent Gallup survey showed only two manufacturers' brands with recognition much above 51%. The top manufacturer's brand was recognized by only 69% of the men interviewed.

"Your're not going to sell a suit on television. It just doesn't seem to happen. But you can sell an idea," observes Michael I. Rosen, vice-president of marketing at Leonard Sacks, account executive for Cricketeer and Tempo-Internationale and former marketing director for Joseph & Feiss. "We're selling strictly a brand name concept to young guys. The commercials this year are very swinging, modern and fast-moving, and hopefully they get over the idea that Cricketeer is with it."

Print advertising for Cricketeer develops the theme of the TV commercials: 17 sure-fire opening lines for guys on the make such as, "I just bet a fellow over there $25,000 you'd come to dinner with me." Cricketeer ran a contest in Playboy and Esquire this year offering a complete Cricketeer wardrobe for the best opening lines.

Michaels/Stern is also using TV to emphasize brand identity more in its 1970 commercials. The clothing marketer, which has offered commercials on a regional basis before, moved out of its limited print schedule this year to become what is believed to be the first men's clothing advertiser on network TV. William B. Pattison, vice-president and account supervisor for the brand at Ogilvy & Mather, says, "We have a new campaign starting next year, which I think will get the name across even better than what we're doing now.

"It's been more of an item by item thing in the past. What we're going to do is build a whole campaign around the theme, 'The Master Tailors of Rochester.'" The brand theme will also run in print advertising which the company plans to revive next year.

Strengthening brand identity becomes increasingly crucial for the top brand advertisers, postulates Frankie Cadwell, because, "what's happened is that men's wear has moved into more fashion and so there are a lot of different looks and the looks change more quickly. Today if the look is right and it seems to be relatively well made, men will buy it. The big brand is going to come on increasingly hard times because the label is going to become less meaningful."

Palm Beach, which has carried its "Looked at— not stared at," message only in The New York Times Magazine, will make it national this spring in Sports Illustrated. Palm Beach agency head Cadwell explains the "looked at" strategy this way: "It started because a big-volume company like Palm Beach can't compete fashion-wise with all the little makers who come along; so it's good for them to take a position where we say, 'Yes, we're fashionable, but we don't make you look odd or jerky.'"

Palm Beach, which ranks third among recognized men's clothing brands (excluding chain labels like Sears, Robert Hall and J.C. Penney) upped its television investment substantially this year. Robert Ward, Palm Beach executive vice-president of advertising and merchandising, reveals, "We were in TV in a minor way this past year. This year a fair portion of our cooperative dollar will go into TV. Until now it has been pretty much four-color newspaper advertising." Palm Beach's cooperative dollar is considerable for the industry, reportedly almost $1-million this year and expected to exceed that figure next year.

The most sophisticated marketing methods in the industry, insiders agree, are employed by Hart Schaffner & Marx. HS&M also consistently puts the most money into advertising of all the major brands—nearly $1.5-million in measured media last year for its three suit brands and Gleneagles rainwear. The basis of Hart's strategy is that it gears its enormous advertising and marketing leverage—from window displays in retail outlets to national advertising—to bi-monthly pre-packed promotions at retail.

This marketing scheme, conceived by now president James K. Wilson six years ago as a way of selling retailers "a collection of ideas rather than a collection of swatches," makes available to the retailer a promotional package each two weeks of the retail selling season.

"The promotion could be based on a color theme, fabric, model or an idea," says marketing group vice-president Bill M. Sansing.

The majority of the promotions are backed up with national advertising. The clothing giant then generates funds from outside sources such as fiber companies for the retailer to run a full color regional ad. The company also provides at cost, mailing pieces, display windows, local newspaper ads, and a salesman incentive contest, as well as television commercials for those retailers who wish to place them. The key to the program, says Sansing, is that, "the suits are timed to be delivered with the running of the national ad."

In the lexicon of the men's apparel industry, tailored clothing refers to suits, sport coats and top coats. In the past this segment of the industry, as distinct from sportswear and furnishings, has often been the most conservative.

Today's emphasis on fashion has considerably complicated the lives of clothing marketers. Says Murray Harris, sales manager of William B. Kessler, makers of Hammonton Park and Calvert Clothes,

"If a few years ago we made 15 models, we did business on three. Today we make 30 and do business on maybe 28."

To illustrate the rapidity of the change, he emphasizes that only two years ago Hammonton Park's shaped model represented only a little more than 10% of orders. "Today the figure is 58%. A decade ago it would have taken a decade to bring that change about."

It has meant, according to Arnold Cohen, vice-president of the Horatio Alger division of Joseph H. Cohen, that, "while retail sales of men's apparel were really up substantially, month after month this year, the traditional and staple and conservative aspects of clothing have actually gone behind,"

Cohen attributes the turnabout from a basic to a fashion business to what he calls the leisure age. Others say it's affluence. All clothing marketers agree whatever else accounts for the volatile tastes of today's consumer, it has everything to do with youth. Sansing at HS&M observes along with some others, "When I grew up I wore what my father wore. Today it's the other way around. Fathers are dressing like their sons." The effect, he indicates, is that "where manufacturers used to decide what clothing would look like, today the influence is in the hands of the consumer."

The most immediate result of this has been to make clothing a risky business. Clothing manufacturers are no longer able to be just something more than order fillers, they are now having to gamble on the changing tastes of the consumer.

The clothing buyer for one of the largest department stores in the world reports, "When it became apparent a year and a half ago there was going to be a rather marked change in men's interest in fashion clothing, the established manufacturers, in particular those with brand names, did not shift with the speed they might have, and therefore newer, smaller, fringe resources got a foothold in many places, simply because the things wanted by the buyer were not available at his traditional resources."

With the consumer demanding more fashion and the retailer becoming increasingly unwilling to gamble on merchandise six months in advance, as the traditional two wholesale selling seasons require, the clothing advertiser is suddenly living in a new, less certain world. Though most retail buyers didn't purchase less than 50% of their open-to-buy this past season, they didn't place the 80% to 90% of their requirements as in years past.

Clothing marketers, large and small, are having to accommodate their operations to this new way of life. Some marketers, like L. Greif and Joseph & Feiss have moved into three selling seasons, giving retailers two cracks at fall.

Says B. G. Cox, vice-president of marketing for Joseph & Feiss, "We're going to have to adjust the way we market our product. We can't continue to market clothing on long cycles or even the two-season basis we operated on for many years. This industry is well on its way to a three-season cycle and we'll probably go to a fourth and who knows maybe a fifth and a sixth."

The rapidly changing look in men's clothing in an industry that didn't substantially change its models for years and demands by retailers for a faster turn-over and fresher merchandise more often has given rise to a debate within the industry: whether or not the men's wear business will become like women's wear—with all the ulcers that brings.

On one side stand the major brand marketers who lagged behind in getting into the fashion business in the first place. Voice at Daroff speaks for most of these when he says, "The men's wear market won't approach women's wear for many reasons. Sure we would love to make clothing obsolete every year, but it will never happen or it won't happen for a long time. Men don't want to change their styles that quickly and they won't be blackjacked into doing it.

"There is some obsolescence now, but the question is what percentage of men notice it. What percent react to it? And then in the women's business, when something gets hot, they call the mill and get an extra 10,000 yards, cut it and ship it. We can't do that."

On the other side of the fence is Franklin Bober, designer/merchandiser for Clinton Swan. Clinton Swan is one of those fringe resources which had the foresight to make the switch to fashion clothing, and in three years it has tripled its volume. Sales have gone from $1.6-million to $5-million.

Compared with major brand marketers, the dollar volume isn't great, but there are others in Clinton Swan's category and the major brands are feeling the pressure.

Comments Bober, "Actually it is getting to be, and it already is, the way I see it, like the ladies' business, not so much for the big manufacturers, but it's becoming that way for the retailers." A major retail buyer backs him up. "The retailer is buying cautiously, more frequently and from more resources because there is a much faster change in what the consumer wants."

Small marketers like Clinton Swan which don't market clothing on the traditional wait-and-see basis are beginning to have their effect on the industry. Says Bober, "A manufacturer like us can twist and turn a little bit because we project ahead. We don't just wait for a guy to give us an order and then go ahead and cut it. When he walks in here, in many instances, we've cut the merchandise already. So our risk is naturally greater than the basic manufacturer."

Joseph H. Cohen & Sons, a subsidiary of Rapid-American Corp., and reputed to do upwards of $40-million a year in men's clothing, is one major marketer which has decided the big money is to be made in the fashion business. Observes Arnold Cohen, divisional vice-president of Joseph H. Cohen, "The leisure age and the exodus to the suburbs has made the need for tailored clothing minimal." The figures bear him out. Suit volume has fluctuated around 21-million units for a decade.

Continues Cohen, "Men are going into alternatives for suits, sport coats and slacks, sportswear and pants of various types. This includes a good deal of sophisticated people, such as executives, who are looking to have more of an element of fun in their dress."

What Cohen has done is to change the name of the Horatio Alger division to Palladium Department and offer fashion merchandise on a monthly basis, something heretofore unheard of in the industry.

Says Cohen, "I operate today under the concept that people in their non-business hours want to dress in 'costumes.' " If his brainchild works, it could have far reaching effects on the industry, among them, to give the marketing rather than the production men top billing in the industry.

Cohen puts together two lines a year in the same traditional way as other manufacturers. But he explains, "I call it a collection and presentation, but somewhat tongue and cheek, meaning I no longer expect to sell more than token orders when offered six months in advance. My purpose is not really to get anything more than an indication of interest on the part of the retailer. Then I see what items look good and I start to change the models themselves, even if they sold.

"For example, I had a single-breasted cardigan for spring which I felt would be much stronger if I made it a double-breasted cardigan. I not only changed the copies of orders and raised the price, but I'm about to cut a stock of about five times my advanced orders because I'm that confident."

In addition to modifying and cutting models far closer to the retail selling season, Cohen also decides what merchandise to offer as an item-of-the-month through a monthly mailer which he sends to the trade four weeks or less before the article is ready for delivery.

For six months after Johnny Carson wore one on his nightly show, retailers were calling resources night and day asking for Nehru jackets. The Nehru hit the industry by storm and most marketers were unprepared for it. Outfits like Clinton Swan were turning them out by the hundreds, but by the time the established basic resources had them, the item was dead. One giant marketer reportedly gave a warehouseful to the Salvation Army.

What everybody in the men's clothing business is worried about these days is what they call "another Nehru."

Voice at Botany expresses the large brand-maker's concern with fads: "We had the Nehru and we had the mod look, both of which dropped dead. And we had the Edwardian look which has only lasted six months or a year." Some in the industry now feel more confident about distinguishing between a fad and a genuine trend. But Bober at Clinton Swan is skeptical. "Two years ago you might have thought double-breasteds were a fad."

Sansing at Hart Schaffner & Marx is confident the industry is learning to market trends. He says, "The clothing industry has accepted change and we're mastering the art of managing it."

Palm Beach's Ward predicts, "Designer clothing will work its way into the regular clothing department."

Clothing marketers are not unmindful of the impact the media have had on their business in the last few years. For clothing obsolescence to work requires that men care about fashion and be constantly exposed to new fashion ideas. A highly visible crop of men's clothing designers, formerly exclusive to the women's wear field, have generated tremendous publicity for men's clothing; though their own lines account for only a small percentage of sales.

Some of the brand names are getting into the act by supplying clothing to TV personalities. Says Voice at Botany, "The greatest influence of all has been TV, expecially color TV. Whoever wears it, whether it's Gene Barry, who we provide with ward-robes, or Joey Bishop or Johnny Carson, more men see fashion on these men in one night than see it in a national ad in a year."

Sansing at HS&M acknowledges, "Johnny Carson has been the biggest influence on fashion today. He created the Nehru all by himself."

THE IACD DESIGNER STATES HIS CASE

With the excitement over fashion, a factional dispute emerges over the relative value of the name designer versus the traditional designer. In this issue, we give publicity to the traditional designer.

"The traditional designer thinks about his design—he creates it—and after he creates it, the company puts it in its line.

"About 99 per cent of what the IACD designer has put into the garment goes into the actual product."

In a sense, this was a summation of the case for the traditional designer —the member of the International Association of Clothing Designers—in the controversy between the *name designer*, whose work often receives the publicity, and the IACD designer.

The speaker was Guido Fusaro, head designer of Louis Goldsmith, Inc. of Philadelphia, manufacturers of a number two plus suit sold in Rogers Peet, Saks 5th Avenue, Jacobs Reeds, John Wanamaker.

"Pincus Brothers Maxwell, for example, has a Bill Blass line," Mr. Fusaro noted. "But they have designers to make the line up from the Blass designs. And when it's done, the sales amount to approximately five—or, at most, ten—per cent of the company's total production."

Most of the IACD designers, Mr. Fusaro pointed out, are very close to the top management of their companies. "The designer's ideas are essential to the company's way of manufacturing and selling."

"Remember," he said, "the designer is also responsible for creating the regular output of the company . . . in addition to the more advanced—the boutique—styles, and the creations that are far ahead of the season.

"Our new ideas are usually a few years ahead —perhaps three years ahead of what is acceptable. Our thinking is about that much ahead of what is actually being worn.

SOURCE: *Apparel Manufacturer*, April 1969. Reprinted by permission.

"But we are very much aware that our companies are in this business to sell their goods."

Guido Fusaro is a wiry, intense man—the traditional men's clothing designer of Italian extraction—whose nephew, Dino Fusaro, shares an adjoining office. Designing is a family tradition.

As one member of the IACD, in Philadelphia, said, "The name designers—you know their names —they *suggest* styles. They are not designers. They must have a designer to create what they have in mind.

"We have no axe to grind. If we were in the same position as they, we would probably do the same thing.

"We would create an exciting idea which may or may not be part of a complete idea—a style which a company can manufacture and sell.

"All name designers have staff designers—the men who can interpret drawings into patterns and workable designs."

We asked Dino Fusaro about the accusation that the IACD designer is overly concerned with minute alterations of older models—a sixteenth of an inch difference in lapel or length.

"We do design in a quiet way," he answered. "But our designs are acceptable to the consumer and the retailer.

"The Edwardian look with us is old.

"And our companies are making a dollar. In fact, we've sold so much goods here this year—at Louis Goldsmith—that we won't be able to make them.

"What you see in the big fashion shows—the chalk-line suit, the bell bottom pants—these are all designs we've made. In our versions they are selling.

"In the IACD you get the thoughts of many designers together."

Dino Fusaro said, "The designer is the factotum

of the clothing business. We are bound by the manufacturer not to go too far out.

"And yet, today, the designers have much more freedom.

"The young generation has broken away from the regimentation. It wants a different expression. The young designer today wants self-expression."

The designer's partnership with the entire manufacturing operation was stated by Guido Fusaro. "We must even be careful, for example, about how a piece of goods must be sponged. We do the whole thing, from putting the patterns on the floor, after making the masters, to making the pattern sizes.

"The designer is often the quality control man of the company, in a sense. Quality—of the finished garment—becomes his baby."

A spokesman for the IACD stated recently, "Often the company designer doesn't get a chance to go too far out. Sometimes the manufacturer holds the designs back, claiming that they are too drastic.

"Sometimes the retailer is responsible for a company's more moderate approach. An extravagant design will obsolete all the other clothes on his rack, he'll claim."

On Guido Fusaro's desk was a report containing sales figures. "Looking at figures is an important part of our business.

"If a designer doesn't do a good job with his company, he won't even have a job."

THE AMERICAN DESIGNER: The New Face of Malewear

Newness, like beauty, is in the eye of the beholder. And from that stance, men's raiments are, indeed, becoming quite revolutionary as the fashion bugles sound the latest attack on all fronts.

Through the centuries, though, man has regularly alternated from the uniform simplicity of a Roman toga to the foppery of a courtesan at Versailles, resplendent with color, pattern, hair (real *and* artificial) and, yes, even cosmetics and perfumes.

But, it seems, the cycle has once again run the course. Since the days of Versailles, garb had again progressively become less resplendent until men reclaimed the simple uniform—this time the grey flannel suit. And, since this side of the cycle dictated a very pristine approach to life, hair—in almost any form—naturally was out (crew, or ivy league haircuts required—beards and/or mustaches very gauche) . . . cosmetics and perfumes high foppery or high faggot.

Grey flannel suits, though, did not last as long as togas did. And the built-up compression for men

SOURCE: *Clothes* magazine, January 15, 1970. Reprinted by permission.

to let their hair down (ha!) and start living a little *has* caused an explosion that is ripping across the country.

At the moment, though, that explosion is one of color, pattern and attitude rather than any basic change of style to date.

Man's still in the same pair of pants—regularly widened, then narrowed in a predictable cycle. He's still in the same constricted suit coat—ditto on the cycle whether you're talking about lapels or shape or length. Ditto separate shirts. Ditto the tie. And back to boots.

A BRAND NEW CYCLE

On the new swing of the cycle, however, things might really be different. Certainly the right atmosphere is developing to allow new *style* directions. The individuality thing . . . the desire for comfort . . . the money . . . the youth thing . . . the wish to pamper one's self—all combine to set a proper stage for something really new.

But you've got to start somewhere.

And when the new moods and desires (circa 1970) started reading through to some men's wear manufacturers with enough nerve to try doing something about it, they went to their design rooms.

But, unfortunately, all they could find were uniform makers. In their crank'em out, grade 2, grade 4, grade 6 zeal, they'd forgotten to develop much *real* design talent—or, for that matter, to let much *real* design talent develop. In clothing, in particular, the escutcheon of the manufacturer is the only thing that has counted.

Yet the message was coming through louder and clearer all the time—*some* of the kooky stuff will sell, and if you call it a designer line you can get an extra buck or two. So where are the designers?

Where else?

Long gone to Seventh Avenue and beyond where they at least have a running chance at doing some designing. And if, at times, women might seem to be in *their* uniform (hems up, hems down, skirts in, pants out) at least the designers could change the uniform regularly and put some individuality into it through color and pattern.

In luring some of the designers over to do their thing for men's dull old duds, the inevitable happened—the competition began for who was going to have the biggest designer *name*. 'Cause where there are designers, someone *has* to come up leader of the parade.

And men's wear people just don't really understand that.

To most of them, the move toward latching on to a designer was just to get someone who might help them get a piece of that new "funny" business. Not only could the designer transform wild ideas into clothes that some men would buy, but he sort of gave the stitch-to-the-inch guys an excuse for getting into this nervous craziness.

If Mr. Proprietor didn't understand the newest upside-down spinach suit or didn't know what to say about it, he could just pass it off as so-and so's latest creation (designer, ya know). Or if the left-hand Bengal Charger's shirt flopped, *there* was the culprit—right over there at the design table.

WHAT'S IN A NAME?

But actually promoting a name to the public, *that* was something else—at least in the beginning

—because it was honestly just beyond the comprehension and experience of men's people.

The women's people—that's different. The history of women's wear was with the dressmaker who did the designing for madame. And brands never have meant a whole lot in fashion ready-to-wear, even in this day of corporate gargantuans.

Men's wear, though, started with the tailors. And with them, the gentleman usually specified what was wanted. There was so little variation in men's things, it was easy.

So little variation, in fact, that is was natural for the big branded giants to develop quickly as ready-made came into the picture. With lack of style variety, lack of color variety and lack of pattern variety, all that was left were the minor differences in cut.

So the brand has been the man's designer all these years (or, sometimes, even the store label a la Brooks Brothers), because between the few manufacturers and the most specialized of the store specialists all the little variations could be covered and it was just a matter of picking your favorite from among the few.

But now—tragedies of life—things so unheard of as pattern and color have come along to compound those few basic variations on the uniform into what is already being called, far and wide, a radical change in the industry.

You ain't seen nuttin yet.

But the manufacturers have already seen enough of what they don't understand to have them looking at those people from the netherworld—the designers—with a hint (just a hint, mind you) of respect starting to show.

Some are even starting to think that *maybe* there are men around who could identify with other than Arnold Palmer or Joe Namath. If they didn't already know the names of the top designers, maybe they could be taught. And, certainly, their wives already know the names as being the epitome of fashion and taste (and who buys all the gifts, most of hubby's furnishings and goes along to "help" pick out a new suit?).

Surely no better example exists of the big time women's designers that are now also doing men's wear than Bill Blass. As one of those sought early in the game to inject some life into the no-longer-quite-bleak men's garment landscape, he has done just that with both color and pattern.

At the same time he has exercised the common sense that is inherent with top designers in not going hog wild. Recognizing that the honest revolution is yet to come in men's clothing, he has not been seduced too early by the temptation to do radical things in *both* coloring and shape.

Men must be led slowly into this strange land of fashion. They may like a lot of what they see in clothing but be too attached to the security of their grey flannel suit. They might like deep-tone or patterned shirts on others but not know how to put it all together. (It *is*, after all, totally outside their experience.) They may accept the fact that cosmetics and perfumes are a fact of men's future, but they don't *yet* have the courage to walk in and ask a sales clerk for more than a bottle of after shave. They may even like the new look of long hair, but not many will go beyond letting their sideburns drop an inch or so.

Mr. Blass, therefore, leaves them the security of familiar things while introducing them also to fashion. If a suit is going to be unusual in its cut, the fabric may stay grey flannel or a similar tame type. If, on the other hand, unusual color or bold pattern is used, the cut stays very conservative. The same holds true for the furnishings side of his business, too.

This is particularly important because the Blass price lines—clothing $185 to $250—are intended to be within the reach of more than just the super-fashionable wealthy (and, in fact, are substantially less expensive than his women's line).

Extreme fashion—or that which now *looks* like extreme fashion and is likely to for a while, anyway—is left to the fringe manufacturers and fringe stores. Instead, he is trying to relax the look of men's dress by introducing a more casual country look that is acceptable for city wear.

Having moved past mere shape and deep-tone shirts which are now part of the uniform (the *new* uniform, but a uniform, nevertheless), he is starting to introduce minor details such as countrified pockets or unusual button placement.

COLOR AND PATTERN

His major talent, though, still remains in his use of color, bold patterns and mixes that are beginning

to give the uniform a look of individual and offhand fashion (or absolute chaos if the new initiate doesn't know how to get it all together yet).

But that's all, for the moment, that *really* is in the new clarion call for men's fashion anyway—at least in any meaningful volume areas. What's unusual in today's uniform except color and pattern and the mix (not to be confused, please, with the old clothing cum piece goods business)?

There's only one thing that's new—the larger and larger segment of men who are willing to experiment and be a little adventuresome in color and pattern and putting the mixes together. (Not for a minute to forget that it's becoming fashionable to have with-it husbands—causing a little more sweet encouragement from with-it wives.)

But the creeping sideburns and bold patterns and deep, *deep* skin bronzer are certainly symptoms of what's to come—the outlook and attitude—rather than any *actual* fashion fait accompli.

Bill Blass, though, is already getting ready for the further opening of that fashion door that's been opened a crack in men's minds. Sure, the same casual look will continue—with the patterns and with the colors and with the mix. But now variations in cut and silhouette are about to start creeping into his line in a meaningful way, too. His fall line will see higher armholes and yet much wider lapels and a small variety of shape.

And the important thing is not that the lapels couldn't really get narrower—at least not yet. It's that variation has *got* to come to every men's wear line, within the *same* line (and without making a line that has every possible variation so you're safe in the midst of the "fashion" frenzy). Neither is the important thing that the really new silhouettes will only constitute a minor part of any substantial line, it's that the cut, the shape, the construction and the complete look of men's clothing has got to change and is going to change.

MANY LOOKS FOR MANY LINES

With the accelerating demand for change and newness, the old two-lines-a-year approach is going to hear its death knell. Just as in the women's market the movement is toward a continual year-round feed of new items—and the Blass line is already heading rapidly in that direction.

Of course, Blass was only tempted into the men's business a little better than a couple of years ago and is still learning with each step of the way. Yet he has already achieved a volume approaching $2.5 million in men's goods (as against $4-plus million in his long-established women's business) while being represented in only 50 stores.

In about 30 of those, the Blass goods are shown together, boutique-style, in their own area. That, in itself, is a major accomplishment these days. For some reason stores that wouldn't think of operating junior or misses departments except on a total-look skin-out basis anymore, don't think the principle applies to men's operations.

Perhaps it's because his designs are shown together in so many stores, or perhaps it's just because he's taken a reasonably conservative approach in his ideas in order to lead the man into new ways, but Bill Blass maintains almost a normal percentage of his business in clothing by comparison to other designers who come up with such heavy furnishings figures.

But names can be valuable properties whether you're talking about clothing, lending it to a cosmetics line or designing a watch. The so-called "outside" design activities are done under license, bringing in—in the case of Bill Blass—from five up to eighteen per cent of the wholesale price depending on the volume and price structure of the product.

At this point, *all* of the Blass men's apparel is done under licensing agreements. (This in contrast to the fact that Blass makes his own women's line—owning, personally, a third of the company.) With so much of his focus now on the men's field, it will be interesting to see whether Mr. Blass is content to let it remain a pure licensing operation.

Licensing, though, certainly seems to be the norm for designers in men's wear—perhaps because there's such diversity in the products necessary to achieve a look and because of the historic lack of experience of name designers in the men's field.

The name with probably more experience in male wear than anyone else is John Weitz. And, not coincidentally, he probably is the licensing champ of them all with sales of his name products

running in excess of $10 million annually. (Like the others, he makes none of his own things.)

A UNIQUE APPROACH

True to form, Mr. Weitz also started out designing women's fashions. But he made a complete transition to the men's area long before it became the in thing to have a men's designer line. And his approach to designing for men has been quite different in many ways. In fact, it is radically different in some.

Perhaps the greatest point of departure is that Weitz is the only designer on this or any other apparel scene that doesn't stress how a garment looks. To him, looks are secondary to function and performance.

In clothing his approach is twofold. First, to get rid of as much construction as is possible while using fabrics that will allow packability and resistance to creasing; second, to design for functionality by using such things as this now-standard sloped pocket on a jacket so that a man can reach into it naturally.

To him, a *properly* designed garment will—like a swept wing jet—come out smooth and naturally good looking. He feels that the majority of the new men's fashion move is overdone and foppish and really only distracts from the individual.

So it is that his suit coats have no canvas or shoulder pads and are, indeed, capable of being rolled up into a tight ball without creasing which is true of few garments in today's market. But then John Weitz has been attempting to sell the emerging man of the future ever since he jumped the fence to men's wear.

The customer he wants is the man who travels—and packs—frequently and is always on the go. This, obviously, should have a broad appeal since everyone is doing more and more getting around as the world shrinks.

Whether or not Weitz actually sells the man because of these features is really a moot point. His garments—with their lack of construction—are certainly ahead of their time. For as fashion variation—in whatever form—comes about to take us away from the rigidity of the standardized jacket, as labor costs continue to spiral and as modern machine methods come to the fore, over-construction must go by the boards.

Aside from just construction though, Mr. Weitz also has a very advanced concern for the weight and performance of individual fabrics that far transcends that of the industry as a whole.

He is designing for a comfortable, consistent year-round temperature. Today, men go from temperature-controlled homes to temperature-controlled cars to temperature-controlled offices, and so on. He just isn't exposed to the rigors of harsh winter weather anymore. So John Weitz is concentrating on the lightest weight goods he can find consistent with performance.

With his concern for the man on the go, these lighter weight fabrics are generally styled with a freer moving action type of feel to them. Not only do the pockets slope, but the lapels aren't so wide, the jacket's a little shorter and it's cut away a little in the front (often with a single button).

Of course, a great deal of the construction used by the rest of the industry is dictated by the heavier weight goods that it has used for so long. It needs all the reinforcement and all those stitches just to support the bulk. Conversely, there's never been any demand for change, and the industry has had to go to the heavyweights for most of the textures and patterns it has been using.

NEW TECHNOLOGY

Now, however, the new fashion razmataz is pushing the mills—but fast—into colors and patterns aplenty in all of their goods, including the lighter weights. This fashion push is also forcing the technology of piece goods ahead at a faster clip than ever before as the industry learns to get the patterns into ever-lighter and better-performing goods. The knit crunch, too, demands goods with more and more patterns (not to mention finer and finer cut so the male timids will accept them as wovens to get started).

But, of course, Weitz does not just design clothing. In doing that kind of licensing volume, he gets into nearly every phase of men's apparel. The entire approach to the practical, functional man, though, follows through. . . .

There isn't just diversification in the products that John Weitz designs, there's also diversification in the price lines. At the outset, he does not try to hold himself above the crowd price-wise. The most expensive of his products are no higher than moderate to better non-designer goods.

But it doesn't stop there. He has been able, also, to put out less expensive lines in the same product categories as well. You can pay $150 for a John Weitz designed suit, or you can pay $75. All of this, of course, tends to indicate that his manufacturers are more interested in the design than in just marketing his name.

And this would tend to be proven out in the stores where the Weitz designs generally have no particular department of their own (which would be a little difficult, anyway, since there are so many from so many different manufacturers), but are mixed right in with the other merchandise.

So where's this fashion trail leading in men's wear? What's it mean to the plain old cutter when two examples of the new-found phenomenon—the men's designer—are at almost diametrically opposed poles about what's going on? One says the look's the thing, the other that the function and comfort are the things.

Well they're really not totally opposites. In fact, they've got a lot in common.

Both of them realize that nothing approaching a fashion revolution has even started yet. It's only a minor incident so far compared to what's coming—like comparing the Boston Tea Party to the Declaration of Independence.

But, like the Boston Tea Party, it's a sure indication of the mood that's in the air and if you go around calling this a revolution, what are you going to call what's yet to come . . .

Man's natural vanity is starting to surface—but fast.

As it does, and men and the men's wear manufacturer come face to face with the *real* fashion revolution, more designers—be they big names from women's wear or these who are still submerged in men's wear anonymity—will surface. And they will surface not as gimmicks or necessities of the moment, but as fashion leaders to guide the male out of the wilderness of uniforms.

THE DESIGNER SHOP

The fashion revolution in men's wear during the 1960's produced new methods of department store merchandising. The Designer Shop, which is springing up in small as well as large communities, is examined closely in this DSM survey of key stores around the country.

Men's wear designer shops in the 1970's will concentrate on the look rather than the designer, will feature fewer signed names and more private labels, and will seek the general consumer through more moderate pricing.

These are the views of representative department stores in a DSM nationwide survey and reflect sales patterns in more than 200 individual designer shops.

Department store executives agree that the excitement generated by designer name clothing has been the catalyst in helping move men's wear from a replacement to a fashion business. While designer shops have been the major force in boosting overall men's wear sales, retailers have mixed emotions over their financial success. Therefore, they do not think designer lines will grow in relation to the predicted boom for fashion merchandise. Almost all the retailers surveyed thought the shop was worth the investment in the prestige it created, but they were split on the question of its profitability. Retailers see the current flock of designers reduced to a few key names while they plan to build their own private label designer image.

PERCENTAGE OF SALES

Designer shops now account for under two percent of the total men's wear volume in 58 percent of the stores surveyed, from five to ten percent in 29 percent of the stores and over ten percent in 13 percent of the department stores.

SOURCE: Excerpts reprinted from *Department Store Management,* February 1970. Permission granted.

That designer-type apparel volume is growing is evident from the more than 97 percent of the stores reporting sales gains last year. Of those, 50 percent had five to ten percent increases, 33 percent enjoyed 20 to 25 percent growth and 17 percent reported more than 25 percent gains. It is significant, however, that private labels and off-brand designer names accounted for as much as 50 percent of the sales in stores where they were featured. It is in this direction that major retailers are looking for future growth.

PRICE IMPORTANT

Retailers point out that designer names have not had the same influence on their male customers as on ready-to-wear. Price is still the major factor in the buying decision of most men and the garment with the designer look selling for less will get the sale regardless of the label.

For this reason, 93 percent of the stores surveyed have combination designer shops featuring several names under one banner. The other stores carry only one designer but have indicated plans to broaden their designer programs into combination merchandising.

Combined shops usually feature two or three major designers. Names most frequently mentioned include Pierre Cardin, Hardy Amies, Oleg Cassini, Bill Blass, John Weitz, and Christian Dior.

Retailers explain that designer names have the greatest impact during the inaugural year of the shop. For example, Higbee's of Cleveland used designer names in its Signature Shop "to set the entire tone and image of the men's wear department." The shop was heavily advertised in newspapers and over television. Merchandise manager Michael Wynn explains that Higbee's new designer image paved the way for volume profit when it introduced its own Signature designer label.

Neal Fox, merchandise manager at Neiman-Marcus in Texas, citing the designer influence, points out that "designer merchandise makes fashion merchandise in other departments more palatable." He believes the acceptance of new styles is due to their contrast with the forward looks in his One-Up Shop. "A five-inch tie in a designer shop helps sell a four-incher elsewhere."

Richard Ford, vice president for men's wear of J. W. Robinson in Los Angeles, likens his designer shops to "a small generator in our men's department that generates fashion excitement." He says that volume in his shop which features only one major designer is moving slower than high fashion volume outside the shop. However, Ford sees the shop as a permanent addition to Robinson's and disagrees with retailers who think the big name influence is depleting and the designer shop is a transient and temporary means of merchandising. Most retailers agree the designer bin is an extension of the general trend toward shop or boutique merchandising. . . .

DESCRIPTION OF CUSTOMER

According to the survey, the average customer of the designer shop is a man between 30 and 40 years old who earns around $20,000 a year and is a swinging executive who's looking for elegant, not kooky styling. He's in the shop at least twice a month and his average purchase is well over $50. He's basically a tailored clothing customer though he is buying sportswear more frequently. Most stores report their design shops are clothing oriented but that sportswear is inching toward 50 percent of the volume.

Retailers running successful shops say that it is essential that the designer bin be adjacent to the clothing area because that is where the volume comes. Minimum departments need at least a $25,000 inventory to provide adequate depth in preferably several hundred square feet.

Introducing the department to the customer usually involves a full-scale party in which pros-

pects are invited to meet one or more designers represented in the shop. Halle Bros., Cleveland, used its women's designer customers to develop its prospect list. Merchandise manager William A. Hefner explains that it's usually the fashion-oriented woman who understands the concept and persuades her husband to be a more daring dresser. The list was later expanded to other boutique customers such as ski enthusiasts.

Great importance is stressed on selling the total, coordinated, head-to-toe look. According to Gerald Fillmore of J. L. Hudson's New Direction Shop in Detroit, the total look of merchandising starts with the buying. Go-togethers are not just displayed together in the shop, they are actually bought that way—suits and coats, shirts and ties, slacks and sports coats or sport shirts.

Apparel is coordinated in terms of patterns and colors, says Fillmore, who also purchases the alternative ways of wearing an outfit.

At Hudson's, sales personnel are trained to promote the multiple sale. They don't let the customer out of the store without the total garment, including accessories. They are trained to suggest alternative ways of wearing outfits. Fillmore points out that it's the store's responsibility to have a customer who purchases a $200 suit, a $15 shirt and a $10 tie look right and not waste his money.

Knowledgeable salespeople are considered vital to the success of the design shop and stores should give them special training and orientation. The chief criteria retailers recommend in selecting help is that they look the part and are interested in fashion themselves. Few stores, however, give their salespeople special price breaks to help them purchase designer clothes. Halle's, in fact, thinks that appearance is so important that it has arranged for its salespeople to order wholesale direct from the resources.

QUALITY, DELIVERY PROBLEMS

Quality and delivery problems coupled with price are considered the major barriers to increased designer volume.

While 84 percent of the stores labeled designer quality as fair to good, only 16 percent thought the quality excellent. Retailers say designers have deserted the traditional men's wear credo that value received in quality should equal the price paid. One Midwest retailer who is highly critical of designer merchandise, takes "a dim view of the future of designer influence" and sees "a short life for them if the quality of the merchandise is not upgraded."

A northern California retailer cited the "lack of control" in the licensing and contractor program. He charged that too many designers "let their package go out from too many different outlets and will fail because their poor quality dilutes the design statement they are making."

Neal Fox says that he has always "believed in inherent value for dollar received," but that value should be considered within the shorter life span of the garment. "We want the best of both worlds —fashion plus a degree of quality."

Retailers view the trend of established apparel manufacturers moving into the designer business as an ultimate cure to the quality control problem. In fact, merchandise managers privately say they have fewer quality problems from these resources. The hookup of these manufacturers with major designers also may be the answer to delivery problems. Of the 69 percent of the retailers who complained about late deliveries, 44 percent said they were late enough to hurt business and accused multiple resources used by designers as the cause. . . .

STORES WANT SHORTER CYCLES

If designers want more liberal open-to-buy policies, stores say "show me new lines more often." Design lines presently have four basic seasons for clothing with more showings for sportswear and furnishings.

According to Neal Fox, the men's high fashion industry is "still in the embryonic stage." He says that it has yet to learn the r-t-w approach and hasn't the ability to "beat an item to death."

Fox would like to whet the customer's appetite week-to-week while being able to re-order fast moving items. Not the specific item, he points out, but if stripes are selling, he wants a comparable stripe with which to fill in.

"People who want to be in the fashion business have to be more gutsy—put the knife to the fabric before the order is written," he says. "Men's wear is a marginal industry in relation to women's wear because it's been so stable and inflexible. Despite all the influence of design merchandise, we haven't solved the problem of cutting down on the cycle with the result that there is no basic difference in buying designer clothing than buying regular clothing."

SOME WANT SLOWER CHANGE

The overall pressures have been for designers to move more slowly. Actually, their greatest success is being achieved by creating a general forward fashion look which is shared in some degree by all designers. Buyers are looking for greater individuality from furnishings and sportswear.

One merchandise manager in a New York store expresses the feelings of many surveyed when he still smarts from the Nehru and Mod failures. He's not against planned obsolescence but thinks that a man should expect to wear a suit two years and not feel foolish. While he favors changes in fabrics and construction, he hopes that designers will not seek to shift too quickly from the current wide lapels, body contour shaping. He's upset over reports of a possible new narrow lapel and stresses that men's wear is not ready for the gyrations of r-t-w.

And so the designers are entrusted with the future of the fashion revolution—make changes but keep the balance of taste which is essential to their continued success.

BIBLIOGRAPHY

Bennet–England, Rodney. *Dress Optional; the Revolution in Menswear.* Chester Springs, Pa., Dufour, 1968.

Cobrin Harry. *Men's Clothing Industry: Colonial Through Modern Times.* New York, Fairchild Publications, 1970.

Editors of *Menswear* Magazine. *75 Years of Men's Wear Fashion 1890–1965.* New York, Fairchild Publications, 1965.

Fahy, Neal. *265 Tested Promotion Ideas for Men's Wear Retailers.* New York, Fairchild Publications, 1959.

Feldman, Egal. *FIT For Men.* Washington, D.C., Public Affairs Press, 1960.

Laver, James. *Dandies.* London, Weidenfeld and Nicholson, Ltd. 1968.

Saltz, S. Thomas. *Creative Men's Wear Retailing.* New York, Fairchild Publications, 1961.

Shapiro, H.T. *Man, Culture and Society.* London, Oxford University Press, 1956.

Taylor, John. *It's a Small, Medium and Outsize World.* London, Hugh Evelyn Publications, 1966.

Winnick, Charles. *The New People: Desexualization in American Life.* New York, Pegasus, 1968.

TRADE PUBLICATIONS

Apparel Manufacturer (monthly), 1075 Post Rd., Riverside, Conn. 06878.

California Men's and Boys' Stylist (monthly), 1020 S. Main Street, Los Angeles, Calif. 90015

Clothes Magazine (semimonthly), 380 Madison Ave., New York, N.Y. 10017

Daily News Record (daily), 7 East 13th St., New York, N.Y. 10003

Men's Wear (semimonthly), 7 East 13th St., New York, N.Y. 10003

Style for Men (weekly, Calif.), 1011 South Los Angeles St., Los Angeles, Calif. 90015

TRADE ASSOCIATIONS

American Apparel Manufacturers Association, 2000 K St., N.W., Washington, D.C. 20006

Boys' and Young Men's Apparel Manufacturers Association, 10 West 33rd St., New York, N.Y. 10001

Clothing Manufacturers Association of the United States, 135 West 50th St., New York, N.Y. 10020

International Association of Clothing Designers, 12 South 12th St., Philadelphia, Pa. 19107

Men's Fashion Guild, 353 5th Ave., New York, N.Y. 10019

Menswear Retailers of America, 1290 Avenue of the Americas, New York, N.Y. 10019

National Association of Men's Sportswear Buyers, 185 Madison Ave., New York, N.Y. 10016

National Outerwear & Sportswear Association, 347 5th Avenue, New York, N.Y. 10016

SECTION REVIEW AND ACTIVITIES

Fashion Business Terminology

Define, identify, or briefly explain the following:

Jobber
Made-to-measure firm
Amalgamated
Dual distribution
The Peacock Revolution
Designer name
Custom tailor
Cluett Peabody
Designer shop

Questions for Review

1. Briefly trace the history and development of the men's wear industry and explain the economic and social factors that contributed to its growth.

2. Why are custom tailors still more important in men's wear than in women's wear?

3. Do you think that working conditions in the men's wear industry and other industries would have improved without the help of labor unions?

4. Compare the men's wear industry with the women's wear industry. How does it differ? What similarities are there?

5. Which is the largest division in the men's wear industry? What has slowed down the growth of this division as compared to other divisions of the industry?

6. Explain why brands in the men's wear industry are of greater importance than brands in the women's wear industry.

7. Why do men prefer to shop in specialty stores instead of department stores?

8. Explain the increased importance of fashion in the men's wear industry.

9. Compare the sales volume of the men's wear industries with the women's wear industries and explain why men's wear does much less volume than women's wear.

10. In your opinion, are designers' names of equal importance to male and female customers? Explain.

APPLICATIONS WITH EXAMPLES

1. Research the history of men's fashions. Discuss and/or illustrate with examples the historical periods in which men's fashions have been equally as elaborate, if not more so, than women's fashions. Explain why.

2. For purposes of analysis, shop men's clothing stores or men's wear departments in large retail stores. Notice any designer names that are featured on men's clothing or accessories and try to determine whether these designers also design women's clothing and/or accessories. Form a conclusion about the relative importance of designer names in men's and women's clothing and accessories.

3. Discuss and/or illustrate with examples the relationship, if any, between men's and women's current fashions, fads, and fashion trends. Come to conclusions as to (a) whether there is a relationship, (b) what it is, if any, (c) why there is or isn't a relationship, and (d) which sex's dress tends to precede the other's in response to fashion change.

SECTION 8
DIRECTIONS IN THE FASHION BUSINESS

The increasing awareness of fashion and the enormous growth of the fashion business in the United States in the twentieth century reflect the vast socioeconomic changes that have taken place during that period. A review of these changes, and their effect on the fashion industry, is a necessary preliminary to any evaluation of future changes and their possible effect on the fashion field. This section, therefore, deals with social and economic conditions—past and projected—to point out their significance from the viewpoint of the fashion business.

DEVELOPING MARKETS FOR FASHION

Industrialized production of apparel in the United States started long before the twentieth century, as we have seen. Enterprise, technological developments such as the sewing machine, and substantial supplies of labor were all present. What was still absent in the early 1900s was the magical growth vitamin, *fashion*—or, more precisely, the democratization of fashion.

Democratization of Fashion

In the early years of the twentieth century, growth of the apparel industries was slow. Not many people were exposed to fashion or were in a position to enjoy fashionable dress. A majority of the population lived in rural areas. City dwellers included many immigrants with little or no funds, skills, or knowledge of the English language. Not much more than one-sixth of the labor force was engaged in white collar occupations. Women constituted less than one-fifth of the labor force, and nearly half the working women held miserably paid domestic or farm jobs. To dress fashionably was the privilege primarily of well-to-do men and their wives and daughters.

In such an environment, fashion could not spread fast or far. Too few people were exposed to new ideas in dress, and still fewer had the means to adopt them. By contrast, today the majority of Americans are comfortably middle class and are living in urban areas. They are exposed to and can afford changing fashions. Even rural areas are no longer remote from fashion news, thanks to newspapers, magazines, television, and motion pictures—to say nothing of the immensely improved private and public transportation facilities that bring rural and suburban dwellers into town quickly or that carry city and rural residents alike to distant areas for pleasure or business travel. The present environment is, indeed, a different one from the environment in which the apparel industries began their existence; it is one that democratizes fashion and fosters fashion growth. Max Lerner said, in his analysis of American civilization, that "few societies in history have been as fashion conscious as the American, and there have been few in which styles and clothes changed so often. Students of human society know that changing fashions are an index of social change within a society."[1]

The Demographics of Fashion Demand

Fashion thrives in countries that are well developed economically. History shows that static national costumes yielded to fashion earliest in the countries that were first to develop economically, and were retained longest in those that were slowest.[2] History also shows that fashion grows best where there is a growing and prosperous middle class and in societies that are changing.[3]

Changing social and economic conditions in the United States created new wants, new needs, and different mores. New wants caused changes that required the fashion industries to revise their products, methods of production, and distribution. In the old days of the women's apparel industry, for example, expectant mothers went into seclusion; today, they remain active and buy maternity apparel. The emancipation of women when, in the years between 1910–1920, they won the right to vote and to attend some of the same colleges as men, pointed the way for less unwieldy dresses, giving them greater freedom of movement. World War I gave many women their first view of an occupation outside the confines of the home and accelerated the need for ready-made clothing. Rising incomes opened markets for goods previously considered to be luxuries for the "idle rich." Shorter working hours and a wider choice of recreational activities increased the need for special purpose garments for a variety of occasions. The tremendous growth of the suburbs, or what one industry professional has called "the backyard way of life," brought about a revolution in dress for suburbanites and city dwellers alike. Casual clothes and sportswear separates gained widespread acceptance among both sexes and cut back the demand for more conventional outfits. The educational level of the population rose. At the beginning of this century, the typical adult had only a grade school education; by the 1970s, half the adult population had at least a high school diploma. The working wife (a rarity in the early 1900s) became more commonplace; by the 1970s, two out of every five married women were in the labor market. They enjoyed money of their own with which to buy fashions for themselves; their earnings also augmented the family income so that their husbands and children, too, could afford more fashion than might otherwise have been possible.

These influences, among others, have affected the fashion industries and have encouraged producers to bring forth new styles in response to actual or anticipated changes in consumer demand. In their totality, the socioeconomic changes just outlined have created a mass market for fashionable apparel and a broadening of the fashion field, such as was impossible to conceive in the days when the

[1]Max Lerner, *America As a Civilization*, Simon & Schuster, New York, 1957, pp. 646–647; also Rom Markin, *The Psychology of Human Behavior*, Prentice-Hall, Inc., New York, 1969, p. 2.

[2]Quentin Bell, *On Human Finery*, The Hogarth Press, Ltd., London, 1947, p. 72.

[3]*Ibid.* p. 70.

well-to-do had their garments custom-made, when women of moderate income did what they could on the home sewing machine, and when poorer women had so pitifully little to spend that a woolen shawl was likely to serve as hat, coat, scarf and gloves for all occasions. The same influences have made themselves felt in other parts of the world, but it is in the United States that the trend has been most marked. It is here that the development of mass markets, mass production methods, and mass distribution of fashion merchandise has been most rapid. In the process, American design talent has been developed; fashion schools have been established to teach design; schools and colleges have been established to teach the many other attributes required to produce, publicize, and distribute fashion merchandise in quantity. It is to this country that manufacturers and retailers of other countries turn for the know-how of making and selling fashionable ready-to-wear merchandise.[4]

CHANGING DIMENSIONS OF THE FASHION MARKET

The dimensions and character of the fashion market change from year to year, responding to changes in consumers. Several ways of measuring these changes are available and help to indicate the direction of growth in the past and the foreseeable future.

Consumer Spending for Fashion

The total amount of money spent for various purposes is estimated annually by the U.S. Department of Commerce.[5] The amount spent on apparel and accessories for men, women, and children, including shoes was $62 billion in 1972—more than double the $27.3 billion spent in 1960 and more than three times the $19.6 billion spent for the same purpose in 1950.

For years, however, the fashion industry has been faced with the fact that as disposable consumer income expanded following World War II, apparel expenditures tended to account for declining shares of both purchasing power and total spending for all purposes. For example, apparel expenditures that were 9.4 percent of disposable income in 1946 declined to only 6.3 percent in 1965.[6] Many theories have been advanced to explain this development: a rising percentage

[4]Madge Garland, (in *Fashion*, Penguin Books, Ltd., Harmondsworth, Middlesex, England, 1962, p. 67ff) tells how a delegation of French businessmen came to the United States to study ready-to-wear clothing manufacturing methods in 1947. In that same year, M.L. Disher published an elaborate study of American methods in *American Factory Production of Women's Clothing* (Devereux Publications, Ltd., London) for British readers.

[5]These annual estimates are published in the July issues of the *Survey of Current Business*, a publication of the U.S. Department of Commerce.

[6]U.S. Department of Commerce annual reports of consumption expenditures.

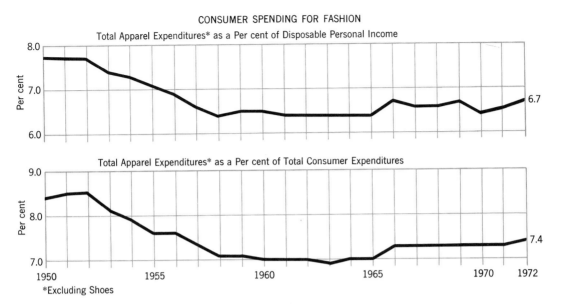

CONSUMER SPENDING FOR FASHION

Total Apparel Expenditures* as a Per cent of Disposable Personal Income

Source: U. S. Department of Commerce, annual reports of personal consumption expenditures.

going to housing, recreation, automobiles, and personal services; a decline in the prestige status of clothing; and the trend toward sportswear separates that encourages the purchase of less-expensive clothing units.

In the past few years there has been a reversal of the declining apparel spending pattern and the beginning of an increase in the share of spendable income that consumers are devoting to clothing. The 1972 outlay for apparel was 6.7 percent of disposable personal income. There are several demographic factors that favor this turn for the better. One is the changing population mix that is running in apparel's favor; the young adult group, which has the highest per capita apparel consumption, has been growing faster than the rest of the population. A second factor is the continued rise in average family income; as family incomes rise, so do family expenditures for clothing. A third contributing factor is the fact that women have been accounting for a steadily larger percentage of our labor force, and these working women tend to spend a larger share of their income on apparel than do their stay-at-home counterparts.

Leveling of Seasonal Demand

A major dimension of the fashion business is correct "timing." Determining when people want to buy fashion merchandise is of great significance to all segments of the fashion industries. For many articles of apparel and accessories, the change of seasons establishes traditional shopping periods: early fall for winter clothes, late

Seasonality in Consumer Spending:
Typical Percentage of Total Year's Sales to
Consumers Made by Stores in Each Month of Year

| MONTH | WOMEN'S, MISSES', JUNIORS' | | MEN'S APPAREL AND FURNISHINGS | INFANTS' AND CHILDREN'S WEAR |
	APPAREL	ACCESSORIES		
January	5.4%	5.6%	4.9%	4.6%
February	6.6	6.4	5.4	6.0
March	8.1	7.4	5.7	8.1
April	8.1	7.2	5.9	5.9
May	9.0	8.9	7.9	6.3
June	7.1	7.2	8.5	5.5
July	6.2	6.2	5.9	6.5
August	8.3	6.7	7.5	12.2
September	8.4	7.1	6.4	8.5
October	8.8	6.9	7.7	8.1
November	10.1	10.4	12.1	11.0
December	13.5	18.8	21.8	14.9
Year's Total	100.0%	100.0%	100.0%	100.0%

Source: Estimates by the authors based upon annual reports, *Department Store and Specialty Store Merchandising and Operating Results*, published by NRMA Controllers Congress, New York, N. Y.

spring for summer wear, and so on. In recent years, however, consumer shopping tends to ignore weather as a factor. People leaving cold climates for winter vacations in the sun are likely to buy summerweight clothes in January. People flying or motoring on business or pleasure trips at any time of year are likely to encounter warmer or cooler weather than they would find at home. Moreover, with air conditioning in summer and central heating in winter, there is less need to dress for the outdoor temperature.

Habit and tradition, nevertheless, still influence consumers to shop for new spring clothes before Easter, even in climates where Easter weather requires wool and fur. Similarly, the advent of fall starts consumers shopping for winter clothes, or at least a winter "look," even where the winters are balmy. Late summer brings a peak demand for young people's clothes, for back-to-school stocking up. Merchants and producers are aware of these consumer buying habits and seek to adapt their schedules to demand. When they succeed, consumers find a wide selection of seasonal goods in the stores from which to choose. When either the retailer or the manufacturer is out of step with the consumer as to timing, business suffers. If consumer demand is cut off earlier than the fashion industry anticipates, there are unsold stocks to be disposed of at drastic reductions. If the industry cuts off production before demand slows down, sales opportunities are lost because the consumer is frustrated in his efforts to buy.

Until the 1930s, consumers tended to outfit themselves for an entire season at one time. Retailers stocked and manufacturers produced in accordance with that pattern of demand—a pattern of sharp seasonal peaks and deep between-seasons valleys. More and more, however, consumers tend to shop throughout the year for their immediate needs instead of at periodic intervals and for an entire season. Stores and producers, therefore, have provided a steady flow of fashions. There are still peaks and valleys in demand, of course, but far less pronounced than before. In the women's coat industry, for example, the biggest month of the year in terms of units cut is October, and that month, in a typical year, accounted for 10.6 percent of the year's total. In the same year, March was the biggest month for cutting in women's dresses, accounting for 10.4 percent of the year's total. In men's dress shirts, October was the biggest month, accounting for 9.5 percent of the year's cutting; in separate jackets, October, the biggest month, accounted for 11 percent of the year's total.[7] These figures are a far cry from the pattern of layoffs and overtime that characterized the fashion industry a few decades earlier, when each year had its "frantic peaks" and its "fifth season"—the slow season when production virtually died.

Consumerism

For all its enthusiasm for fashion, the American public is nevertheless concerned about getting its money's worth, and is quick to indicate dissatisfaction if prices seem unnecessarily high or quality is not as represented. In the normal course of events, competition keeps prices under control, and the liberal return policies of major stores permit the fashion customer to demand and receive satisfaction if quality is the bone of contention. There have been times, however, when consumer dissatisfaction has become so general that individual stores and manufacturers could not handle the entire problem. Instead, a wave of consumerism developed, with consumer groups and consumer spokesmen reciting their complaints to the press and to legislators, demanding legislative controls.

Inevitably, consumer movements bring up the question of fashion itself and imply that it is a device of industry to render present wardrobes obsolete, thus forcing the purchase of new clothes but, as we have seen, fashion comes from the consumer, not from the producer or seller. When the public resents ostentation or is concerned with practical, long-wearing clothes, then the fashion is for utilitarian dress—and that is what the industry produces, as was demonstrated in the early 1970s, when jeans (in a broad spectrum of prices) became a widely accepted fashion for both sexes.

There have been times when the general fashion in apparel was for the lavish and the extravagant, and there have been times when the reverse was true. In the late 1960s and early 1970s, while the consumer movement was gathering momentum, fashion was moving toward the understated and the unostentatious. Similarly the late 1930s, an earlier period of consumerism, saw widespread acceptance of the

[7]U.S. Department of Commerce, *Men's and Women's Selected Monthly Apparel Cuttings, 1970 to 1972 (Revised)*.

simple shirtwaist dress, acceptance of the late Claire McCardell's almost
monastically simple styles, and acceptance of Elizabeth Hawes's very functional
clothes.

The obvious point here is: although some industries may need consumer
advocates to apprise them of the consumer's wants, the fashion industries, with
their long-established habit of observing currents in consumer wants and
preferences, are usually right in step with the changing values of their customers.
What the consumer wants, the consumer gets.

Price Controls

A gradual rise in prices has been characteristic of the American economy since its
inception. Except in periods of depression, the value of the dollar in terms of
consumer purchasing power is lower in each decade than in the previous one.
When the rise becomes especially rapid, the sharp increase in prices alerts
consumer and government to the need for action. After World War I, there were
consumer strikes and federal investigations into possible profiteering. During
World War II, there were rigid price controls, coupled with the rationing of scarce
commodities, to prevent people from bidding against one another and sending the

Rising Prices

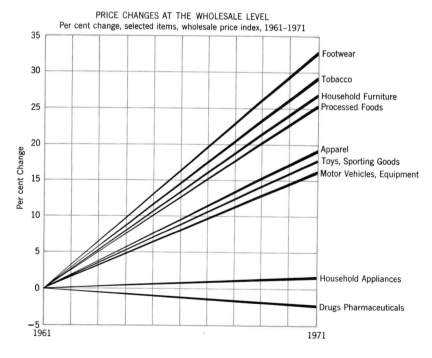

PRICE CHANGES AT THE WHOLESALE LEVEL
Per cent change, selected items, wholesale price index, 1961–1971

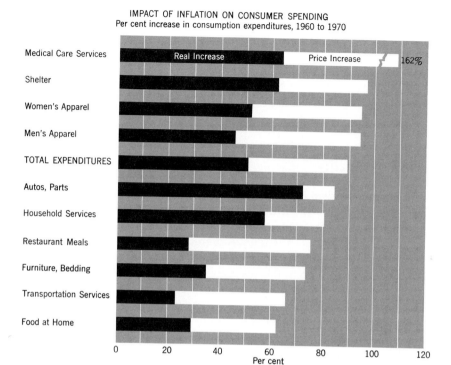

IMPACT OF INFLATION ON CONSUMER SPENDING
Per cent increase in consumption expenditures, 1960 to 1970

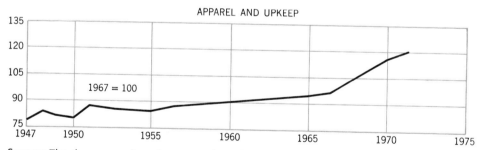

APPAREL AND UPKEEP

1967 = 100

Source: The three preceding charts are adapted from *A Guide to Consumer Markets 1972/1973,* published annually by The Conference Board. Reprint permission granted.

prices of inadequate consumer goods sky-high. In 1971, even without scarcities to drive them, prices showed such an inclination to climb that a "freeze" was put into effect by President Nixon, making excessive increases in prices or wages illegal.

Under normal conditions, the consumer's willingness or unwillingness to spend controls prices. If an individual producer or retailer prices goods too high, the market for the goods narrows, and the retailer realizes he has priced himself out of his market and had better move down to price levels that his customers are patronizing more freely. If prices in one branch of the industry go too high, the consumer may turn his back on its product and find less-expensive substitutes. A wardrobe of sportswear separates, for instance, can be kept looking fresh and varied by the addition of a few new pieces each season, at much less of an outlay than would be required for a woman's wardrobe of dresses or a man's supply of suits.

Federal Regulation of Quality

In the 1930s, a wave of consumerism led to the development of federal regulations in the labeling of wool products, textile products generally, and fur products. Until laws were placed on the books, a term like "taffeta" could be applied without modification to fibers that looked like (but actually were not) silk; terms like "Hudson seal" could be applied without explanation to dyed muskrat fur; and terms like "all wool" could be applied to fabrics made of reworked wool instead of virgin wool.

Not all such regulations are an outgrowth of consumerism. Some of them now on the books were initiated by industry and retailing, in the interests of fair competitive practices and in the interests of consumer protection. Careless or unscrupulous labeling of consumer goods and careless or unscrupulous use of comparative pricing in advertising, for example, cause the honest manufacturer or retailer to suffer a competitive disadvantage, in addition to the harm such practices work on the consumer.

The thrust of the 1970s consumer movement has been toward protecting the consumer against faulty and potentially dangerous automobiles, toys, and home appliances; against flammable fabrics; against potentially or actually deceptive statements of credit terms; and against potentially or actually deceptive packaging. In the fashion field, there has also been a movement toward permanently attached labels that spell out the care required for fabrics.

The Battle for Equal Rights

Some of the country's most spectacular battles for equal rights for all citizens took place in the 1950s and 1960s and continued on into the 1970s. Fair employment practices, equal educational opportunities, and equal pay for equal work—these ideals were applied not only to minorities in race or creed but also to the sexes. Women demanded and won the right to enter schools, occupations, and clubs that previously had been entirely male; men appeared on women's campuses; and enterprising males got into the news by demanding the right to work at such traditionally feminine jobs as switchboard operator and airline "stewardesses."

The equal rights turmoil promptly reflected itself in the dress of both sexes. In the late 1960s, there was a flurry of what *Women's Wear Daily* named "Unisex" fashions—nearly identical clothes for him and for her, sold in stores or departments serving both sexes. By the 1970s, this trend was expressing itself in a resistance among women to clothes that were constricting in any way, and by a much wider acceptance among men of colorful, comfortable clothes. A man's ruffled shirt was no more startling on a dress-up occasion than a woman's pants suit; a woman's wearing of a T-shirt on a casual occasion was no more startling than a man's wearing of a similar shirt. The men's branch of the fashion industry realized that its customers were becoming less inhibited, not necessarily less masculine in their apparel preferences. The women's branch realized that its customers were seeking a natural look in their dress. Women welcomed panty hose, relieving them of the necessity for girdles and garter belts, and body stockings, providing a complete and comfortable first layer of clothing. Men accepted slacks that were made for wear without belt or suspenders and that could be comfortably teamed up with sports shirts, T-shirts, or no shirts, according to climate and occasion.

Similarly, the fashion industries were alert to the new pride that black people were feeling in their own background, and "Afro" clothes, wigs, cosmetics, and jewelry made a place for themselves on the fashion scene.

Like any other strong social or economic current, the movement for equal rights has left its imprint on the fashions of its day, just as past movements have done and as future movements will do.

THE MARKETING CONCEPT

In its absorption with the problem of finding out what the consumer wants almost before he is aware of his own preferences, the fashion business presents an excellent example of the application of the *marketing concept*. This concept simply means that the fashion industry recognizes that its ultimate objective is to meet consumer demand. It orients itself toward the consumer and his demands instead of toward its own preferences and capabilities in production.

In the United States today, most consumer goods industries have productive capacity far beyond what the public actually needs. At the same time, most consumers have incomes in excess of what their households require for such absolute necessities as food and shelter. This combination of ample productive capacity and ample discretionary spending power means that the consumer has a wide choice of what he will buy. He not only is selective in the styles or items that he chooses from among those offered by a particular industry but he also is able to choose which of many industries he will patronize when he spends for anything other than the basic necessities of life. A woman, for example, does not merely choose between one dress and another; she also may choose between a new dress and a fresh idea in household linens. A man may choose between one jacket and another, or he may choose between a jacket and some new golf clubs. A family may decide to ignore the appeal of new clothes for a time and spend, instead, on a new car, a boat, a vacation trip, or whatever it chooses.

Consumer Orientation

Faced with the fact that consumers buy more often from choice than from necessity, wise producers in almost every industry seek to observe and adjust to consumer demand as accurately as they can. This was not always the case. In the early 1900s, manufacturers in many industries simply produced what they could most easily make, without consulting consumer preferences. Retailers selected from what was offered them in the wholesale markets and then sought to push upon their customers the goods they had bought. In time, these industries, too, began to understand the marketing concept and to realize, as the fashion industry did, that the consumer was king and consumer preference was law. As the president of General Foods explained the difference:

"Instead of trying to market what it is easiest for us to make, we must find out much more about what the customer is willing to buy. In other words, we must apply our creativeness more intelligently to people, and their wants and needs, rather than to products."[8]

Styles, as explained in an earlier section, do not become fashions unless they win acceptance among consumers. No producer, no seller, and no government has successfully imposed on the modern public any fashion that it was not ready and willing to accept. If the industry had any doubts about this, the disastrous outcome of their attempts in 1970 to dictate longer lengths in lieu of the then popular mini-skirts converted most people in the business to this view. While the much-touted midcalf length did find its way into many a wardrobe, it did so along with the mini, the maxi, the knee-length skirts, the pants suit, and assorted other looks expressing moods from poor peasant to well-heeled hippie. As well-known designer Bill Blass said: "One thing we learned is that never again will a particular fashion be forced on women. They're going to end up wearing whatever they want."[9]

Neither has it been possible to withhold from the public for long a fashion that it wanted. A classic case in the 1960s was the small, uncluttered automobile, which Americans bought from foreign makers in increasing quantities in preference to the larger cars that domestic makers were offering them at that time. Similarly, when the pants suit for women first came on the scene in 1967 and 1968, some of the more prestigious restaurants refused to admit women who wore them. And some of the same restaurants made similar objection to the then-new turtleneck shirts for men, worn without the traditional tie. Yet these were wanted fashions, and the demand for them persisted. Producers, if not restaurateurs, got the message, and within a year or two after their daring debut, both styles were quite commonplace.

Analyzing consumer demand and seeking ways to serve it constitute the very life principle of the fashion industry. On the relatively few occasions when fashion

[8]Charles G. Mortimer, "The Creative Factor in Marketing," 15th Annual Parlin Memorial Lecture, Philadelphia Chapter, American Marketing Association, May 13, 1959.

[9]"The Industry Still Wins," *Business Week*, February 27, 1971, p. 112.

producers or retailers have allowed their vision of the consumer to become blurred, progress has been slow. When the industry is in its usual good form, however, few other industries can match its ability to apply the marketing concept to every phase of its operations.

Computerizing the Details of Fashion Demand

Knowing the specifics of customer preferences—colors, prices, sizes, classifications, and other details of the merchandise—and getting the information quickly are the keys to survival in the fashion business. The systems that

COMPUTERIZING FASHION DEMAND

Print-punch ticket (courtesy of B. Altman & Co.), showing manufacturer, style number, color, size, classification and price, has four parts. The first two parts are used to record sales and returns; other parts are used to record resales and returns. Electronic data processing "reads" the punched holes and records the data contained in them on print-out reports.

manufacturers and retailers have for this purpose are now extremely rapid and sophisticated, thanks to the development of the computer. In retail stores, price tickets for fashion merchandise are often print-punched, which means that the merchandise information that is printed on the stub for the benefit of customers, salespeople, and store buyers is also repeated in computer language through tiny perforations. Stubs removed from sold garments are fed into a computer (at the store or through a service organization), and the retailer sees promptly what his customers have been buying. Manufacturers also process their own orders by computer and learn quickly and accurately of any shifts in demand that are surfacing. Information of this type, in stores and in factories, was formerly compiled by hand, and still is in some organizations. The computer, however, does it rapidly and can do it in great detail, with whatever cross analyses may be wanted—for example, the colors and sizes bought and/or sold in each price line.

Patterns of Apparel Spending

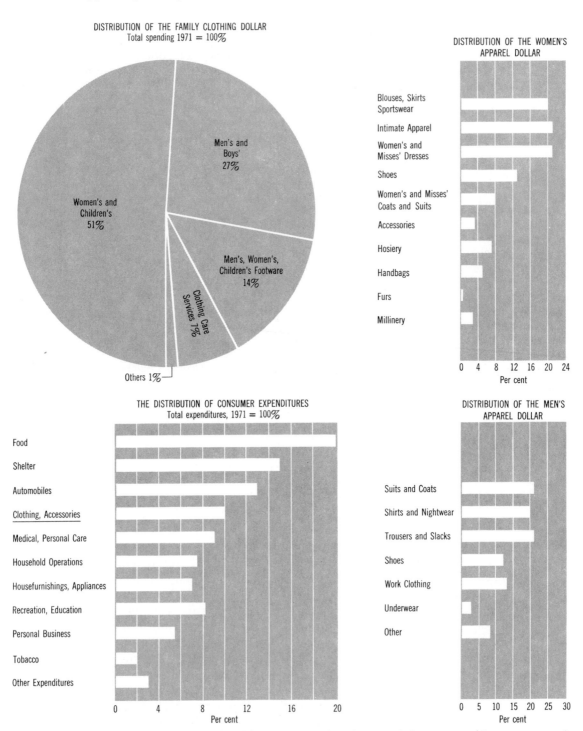

DISTRIBUTION OF THE FAMILY CLOTHING DOLLAR
Total spending 1971 = 100%

- Men's and Boys' 27%
- Women's and Children's 51%
- Men's, Women's, Children's Footware 14%
- Clothing Care Services 7%
- Others 1%

DISTRIBUTION OF THE WOMEN'S APPAREL DOLLAR

- Blouses, Skirts Sportswear
- Intimate Apparel
- Women's and Misses' Dresses
- Shoes
- Women's and Misses' Coats and Suits
- Accessories
- Hosiery
- Handbags
- Furs
- Millinery

Per cent (0 4 8 12 16 20 24)

THE DISTRIBUTION OF CONSUMER EXPENDITURES
Total expenditures, 1971 = 100%

- Food
- Shelter
- Automobiles
- Clothing, Accessories
- Medical, Personal Care
- Household Operations
- Housefurnishings, Appliances
- Recreation, Education
- Personal Business
- Tobacco
- Other Expenditures

Per cent (0 4 8 12 16 20)

DISTRIBUTION OF THE MEN'S APPAREL DOLLAR

- Suits and Coats
- Shirts and Nightwear
- Trousers and Slacks
- Shoes
- Work Clothing
- Underwear
- Other

Per cent (0 5 10 15 20 25 30)

Source: The figures on this page represent the authors' estimates, based upon U.S. Department of Commerce annual estimates of personal consumption expenditures, the *Census of Manufacturers*, the annual *Apparel Survey*, and *Department Store and Specialty Store Departmental Merchandising and Operating Results* published annually by the Controllers Congress, National Retail Merchants Association, New York.

A recent development is for the producer of fashion goods, such as gloves, blouses, and intimate apparel, for example, to attach print-punch cards to his merchandise for the retailer at the factory. In some instances, the retailer sends his ticket stubs to the manufacturer as his merchandise is sold, and the manufacturer is then in a position to observe fluctuations in customer demand almost at the moment that they occur, instead of having to wait for the retailer to report them on his next buying trip. Companies that have been experimenting with such procedures say that their designers can tell almost as soon as goods have been shipped which numbers are "hot" and which are out of tune with customer demand.

Cumbersome production methods and the quickening pace of fashion demand simply do not go hand in hand. That is one of the reasons for the keen interest shown by the industry in computer-guided cutting and sewing operations. Computers are being tested for such diverse manufacturing activities as designing textiles, making markers for cutting, doing the actual cutting, and guiding the needle in the sewing operation. Among the potential advantages of computer cutting are accuracy and the ability to cut small runs of a number with speed equal to or better than what has been accomplished by mass-production methods applicable only to huge quantities.

If big business in the fashion field finds it possible to produce small runs economically, then we may see large producers, as well as boutiques, answering the consumer's request for individuality by turning out limited editions of some of their style numbers. The United States may be a mass market, but the desire for individuality within the accepted fashion remains strong. In time, the fashion industry, by finding speedier ways to produce, may answer this element of consumer demand, too, even though it remains essentially geared to mass production.

THE BUSINESS OF FASHION IS CHANGE

What lies ahead in the fashion business? To answer that question, we must look to the ultimate consumers of the industry's products because as they change, so will fashions and the operations of the industry change. The business of fashion is a dynamic process requiring an understanding of consumers and constant adjustment to their changing needs and desires. This is a responsibility of makers, buyers, and sellers alike.

Guideposts

Where does one look for guideposts to fashion's directions? There was a time when one simply watched, measured, or read the reports of what the wealthy were wearing on Fifth Avenue and at Palm Beach, what the Paris couturiers were showing, and what was being featured in *Vogue* and *Harper's Bazaar*. Today, such sources of information represent only a drop in the bucket. The couples at the supermarket, the girl with a job, the men and women who attend colleges, concerts, athletic events, political rallies and the theatre, and the people in the streets—all these and more are part of the fashion scene. But it is not enough simply to observe what they wear. Also important is what they are thinking, saying, and feeling. The daily paper, the financial and political news, the television programs, and the Census reports all merit study. The guideposts to fashion are all around us if we look, listen, and try to interpret.

The Statistics of Change *

The development of the fashion business reflects the vast changes that have taken place in people's lives during the period of its growth. The tables and charts that follow provide some of the statistics of change, past and projected, that have significance for everyone in the industry. They show, among other pertinent facts, the gains in population, employment, and income. The final reading in this book discusses some of their many implications for the fashion business and takes a look into the future.

If the business of fashion is change, it is always unfinished business. You, with the thrust of an idea, can play a part in changing it—if you but keep your eye on the consumer.

Profile of Change, 1910 to 1970

	1910	1970
Total population	92.4 million	205 million
Gross national product	$35.3 billion	$976.5 billion
Disposable personal income	$26 billion	$688 billion
Civilian labor force	34.6 million	82.7 million
Weekly hours per employee on factory payroll	52.1 hours	39.8 hours
Factory workers' average pay per hour	$0.586	$3.36
Median years of education completed, age 25 and over	8.1 years	12.1 years
Percent of population in rural areas	54.3%	26.5%

Source: U.S. Department of Commerce, Bureau of the Census, *Long Term Economic Growth, 1880–1965, Survey of Current Business*, September 1971, and *Statistical Abstract, 1971*.

*Unless otherwise noted, all charts are adapted from *A Guide to Consumer Markets 1972/1973*, published annually by The Conference Board. Reprint permission granted. Source of figures: U.S. Department of Commerce and Labor annual reports.

Growing Population: More Consumers

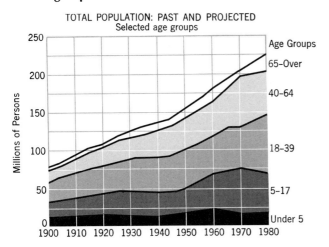

TOTAL POPULATION: PAST AND PROJECTED
Selected age groups

Age Groups
65-Over
40-64
18-39
5-17
Under 5

Millions of Persons

1900 1910 1920 1930 1940 1950 1960 1970 1980

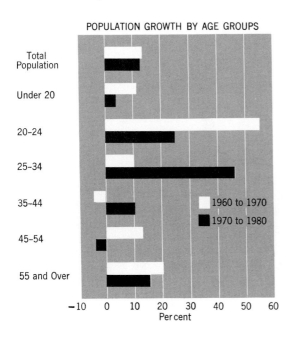

POPULATION GROWTH BY AGE GROUPS

Total Population
Under 20
20-24
25-34
35-44
45-54
55 and Over

1960 to 1970
1970 to 1980

Percent

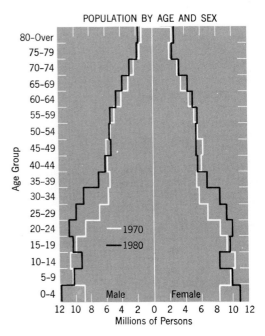

POPULATION BY AGE AND SEX

80-Over
75-79
70-74
65-69
60-64
55-59
50-54
45-49
40-44
35-39
30-34
25-29
20-24
15-19
10-14
5-9
0-4

Age Group

1970
1980

Male   Female

12 10 8 6 4 2 0 2 4 6 8 10 12
Millions of Persons

Increasing Affluence of Consumers

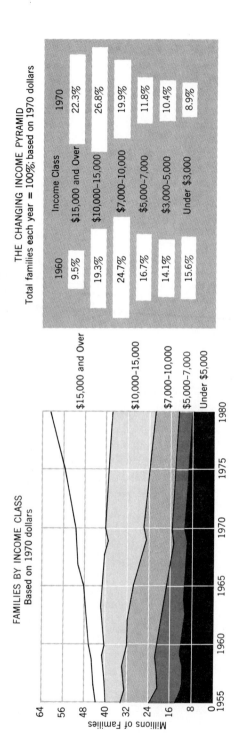

THE CHANGING INCOME PYRAMID
Total families each year = 100%; based on 1970 dollars

Income Class	1960	1970
$15,000 and Over	9.5%	22.3%
$10,000–15,000	19.3%	26.8%
$7,000–10,000	24.7%	19.9%
$5,000–7,000	16.7%	11.8%
$3,000–5,000	14.1%	10.4%
Under $3,000	15.6%	8.9%

FAMILIES BY INCOME CLASS
Based on 1970 dollars

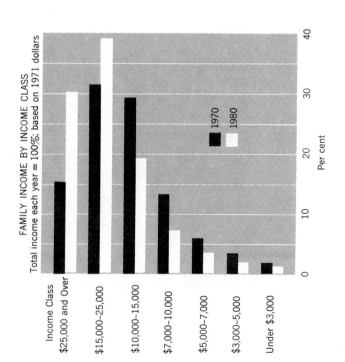

FAMILY INCOME BY INCOME CLASS
Total income each year = 100%; based on 1971 dollars

Income Class
$25,000 and Over
$15,000–25,000
$10,000–15,000
$7,000–10,000
$5,000–7,000
$3,000–5,000
Under $3,000

1970
1980

Per cent

Higher Educational Attainment

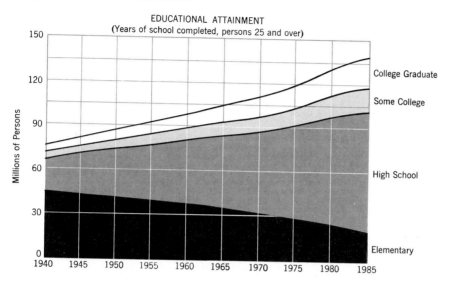

EDUCATIONAL ATTAINMENT
(Years of school completed, persons 25 and over)

College Graduate
Some College
High School
Elementary

Millions of Persons

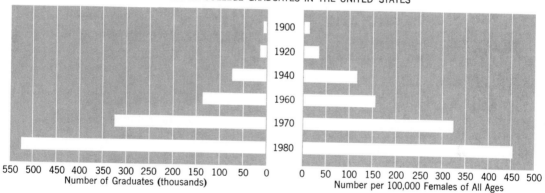

FEMALE COLLEGE GRADUATES IN THE UNITED STATES

1900
1920
1940
1960
1970
1980

Number of Graduates (thousands)

Number per 100,000 Females of All Ages

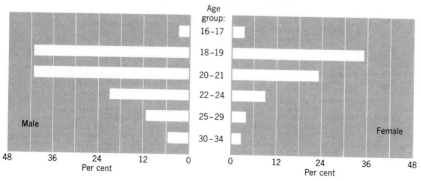

COLLEGE ENROLLMENT BY AGE AND SEX
Per cent of each age group enrolled, 1970

Age group:
16–17
18–19
20–21
22–24
25–29
30–34

Male

Female

Per cent

Per cent

More Women at Work

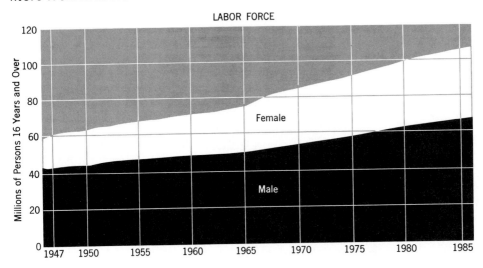

LABOR FORCE

Millions of Persons 16 Years and Over

Female

Male

1947 1950 1955 1960 1965 1970 1975 1980 1985

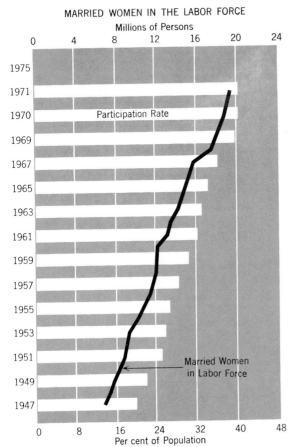

MARRIED WOMEN IN THE LABOR FORCE

Millions of Persons

0   4   8   12   16   20   24

1975
1971
1970   Participation Rate
1969
1967
1965
1963
1961
1959
1957
1955
1953
1951
1949   Married Women
1947   in Labor Force

0   8   16   24   32   40   48

Per cent of Population

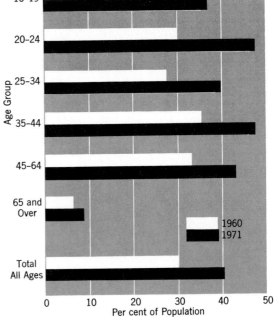

THE PROPORTION OF MARRIED WOMEN WORKING BY AGE

Age Group

16–19
20–24
25–34
35–44
45–64
65 and Over

1960
1971

Total All Ages

0   10   20   30   40   50

Per cent of Population

Changing Consumer Expenditures

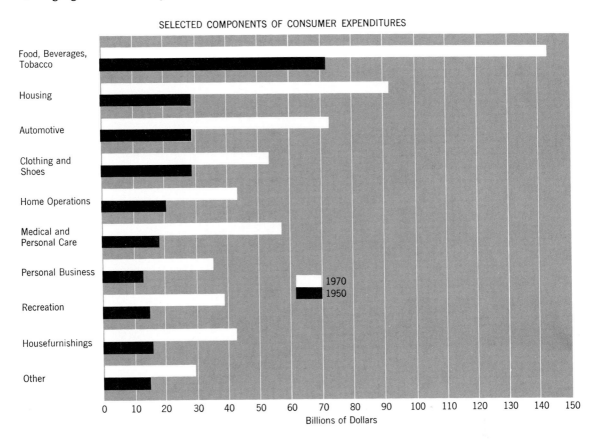

SELECTED COMPONENTS OF CONSUMER EXPENDITURES

Selected Components of Consumer Apparel Spending in Millions of Dollars

| YEAR | TOTAL | CLOTHING, ACCESSORIES | | SHOES, OTHER FOOTWEAR | CLOTHING CARE SERVICES | JEWELRY AND WATCHES |
		MEN'S, BOYS'	WOMEN'S, CHILDREN'S			
1950	23,709	6.026	10,002	3,347	2,744	1,318
1955	27,982	6,971	12,444	3,623	3,149	1,743
1960	33,032	7,976	14,769	4,516	3,629	2,094
1965	43,318	10,687	19,742	5,372	4,586	2,855
1970	62,278	15,539	28,794	8,063	5,730	3,994
1971	68,961	16,797	31,723	8,406	5,625	4,292
1972	72,676	18,553	34,454	9,157	5,857	4,576

Source: U.S. Department of Commerce.

READINGS

Only one reading is offered in this section—a talk by the ever-provocative E.B. Weiss. In it he makes clear the importance of keeping one's mind from getting into a rut, of breaking habitual molds of thought, and of looking around and looking ahead. And this is the key to understanding the consumer and thus anticipating the direction that fashion will take in future years.

LOOKING AHEAD IN FASHION

E.B. Weiss

Almost nine years ago, a talk I delivered before the fashion industry was correctly titled, "A Fashion *Ignoramus* Takes a Look at Fashion."

I'm *still* a fashion ignoramus—perhaps *even more* so than in 1960.

I really should not tempt a Fate that treated kindly several of my fashion predictions of nine years ago. However, I have been asked to do *precisely* that. I doubt you will *ever* extend that invitation again—but here goes:

In 1980, the composition of the audience at meetings of this kind will be *totally* different. And for two reasons:

1. Fashion—style—design— creative innovation will dominate practically *all* merchandise lines—*and* will become thoroughly *integrated*.

2. Creators in *unrelated* merchandise classifications will influence ready-to-wear fashion as often as vice versa. Moreover, they will all work with creative scientists, with creative architects, with creative engineers, and with creative sociologists. And those scientists and professionals are as creative as the apparel fashion creators. They simply are not as erratic.

Did you know that the May Department Stores recently acquired control of a *think tank* called Systems Science, Inc. that includes even theoretical physicists? Said Chairman Morton D. May: "Since May is in the people business we see potential benefits from these scientific minds who will use computer technology to learn more about the people who are our customers."

There will be more communication—more *formalized* communication—between *all* of those

who are involved in responding creatively to our total environment. A small clique will not be able to impose its eccentric will on apparel—or on *anything else*.

Paris may not be burning—but in *total environment creativity, it is dying*. And *that* will be precisely the name of the creative game tomorrow.

Did you know that about 4000 scientists, technicians and *artists* have organized into formal discussion groups premised on the conclusion that there is a close *creative* relationship among all three?

Did you know that mathematicians have published mathematical models scientifically constructed to plot fashion trends, predict peaks, and evaluate oscillations?

Did you know that several ready-to-wear houses are furnishing a large university with the total number of orders they filled each season for each number? The analysis technique being used is closely related to the techniques used (of all things) in biological taxonomy.

Did you know that biological taxonomy is the concept on which the NRMA's early work in standard classification was built?

Too many people in this audience *confine* flighty attention to fashion in apparel and in accessories. Too few are deeply interested in or involved in the great social and technological trends. Yet surely it is now obvious that creative inspiration must take off from the impact of these vast trends on our total society—*our total environment*.

When Dame Fashion could be the total dictator, the fashion designer could ignore society and environment—and bend society to his eccentric will.

But a sophisticated public will, more and more, exercise *individual taste*. That individual taste will stem from our new social concepts and our total environment. It will not tolerate dictation by anyone.

SOURCE: Talk delivered before The Fashion Group, April 18, 1969. E.B. Weiss is Vice-President and Director of Special Merchandising Service of Doyle Dane Bernbach, Inc. Reprint permission granted.

Ours is to become a *creative society*. Creativity will be dispersed—fractionated. You see ample evidence in the current hunger for self-expression in crafts—in self-decorated lunch boxes and waste baskets.

Even the unisex trend, for example, is by no means strictly ready-to-wear apparel and accessories. It is becoming a major factor in apartments for single people. That means that the home-furnishings industry is affected.

Traditionally, *Paris* dictated. Now the *total environment* will dictate. Rebellious youth is part of the environmental scene. Clearly rebellious youth has dominated fashion creativity for the last several years. The 20,000 hippies who marched up Sixth Avenue provided a better insight into the future of fashion than you will get from *Vogue* or *Harper's*.

The total environment concept for creative design suggests the following:

1. That *multi*-industry, *multi*-professional, *multi*-technological, and *multi*-talent creative design meetings will become *major* events.

2. That ready-to-wear fashion trends will respond to design innovations in remote merchandise categories—even by lamps where brilliant design is finally coming in.

3. That the regular treks to Paris will become less important except as *junkets*—which, to a large extent, is *precisely* what they are right now.

4. That the *same* designers will, in multiplying instances, apply their talents to pots and pans as well as to pantyhose and to furniture as well as to foundations.

5. That inspiration will become *extraordinarily* fractionated geographically. There *never* was scientific validity backing the theory that creative design talent is nurtured by geography. Primitive art by primitives everywhere continues an inspiration—they did not learn creative art in Paris. Paris surely borrowed from them.

6. That the grand old names in fashion creation may never die but they will surely fade away. That era is gone—passé—kaput.

7. That creativity will become a more *rational*, a more *intelligent*, and a more *socially-conscious* function—a *means to an end* rather than an end itself.

8. That the end will be a *better* life—a fuller

life—a more *cultured* life. The fashion freaks will freak out!

9. That fashion change that is simply an artificially created style obsolescence will wither. A more sophisticated society will not tolerate it.

10. Even the term "fashion designer" will disappear. Perhaps *environmental creator* will become the label.

11. Fashion and design staffs will include specialists in psychology, sociology, architecture, and even systems engineers. A giant ready-to-wear house is now working with systems engineers from Hughes Aircraft; as aerospace techniques come into the *production* of ready-to-wear, do you suppose these giant firms will knuckle down to creative eccentrics?

Yours is too much of a *restricted* club. You talk the same purposely vague language and you talk essentially to each other.

12. Fashion manufacturers will develop technological centers—staffed with scientists, technologists, and with fashion and design talent. In that atmosphere, the dilettante will not be welcome.

13. The role of staples in practically all merchandise classifications will continue to decline sharply; it is happening even in food. You have seen it happen in terry cloth, corduroy, and leather.

14. Universality of fashion and design creativity will mean still more diversity in manufacturing. The ready-to-wear manufacturers are invading each other's product lines. More to the point: Kayser-Roth plans to acquire rug, drapery, and home-furnishings manufacturers. This fact dramatically underscores the fundamental point I am making about the interrelationships in fashion and design in presumably unrelated lines. Burlington is deepening its penetration of furniture and home furnishings.

15. Apparel producers will move into still more remote merchandise classifications. Manufacturers of remote classifications will move into apparel. Fashion coordination and fashion ensembling encourage this trend.

16. There will also be an invasion into apparel and accessories by the conglomerates. It is entirely probable that, in an expanding number of

apparel classifications, over 75 percent of the total apparel production will be controlled by the following:

(a) Giant corporations that formerly produced apparel exclusively but have since diversified.

(b) Giant manufacturers of *other* fashion classifications—footwear, hosiery, foundations, and so on.

(c) Giant conglomerates.

These giants did not get where they are—and they will not get where they intend to go—by meekly surrendering to irresponsible prima donnas.

If these prophecies do not curl your hair, be patient. Here are some more:

1. The fantastic, new communication technology will revolutionize our society and, therefore, fashion and design creation. How many of you are adequately informed about the coming impact on society of the communications revolution?

2. Then there is the *next* generation of young people who are now 15 to 18. About one million of their immediate predecessors—just one million of the talented youngsters now on campus—radically changed our society. The next two million talented youngsters on campus will alter society even *more* significantly. They will have fewer children (our birth rate has already hit an all-time low). They will have children later in life. They will live for today, not for a rainy day. They will be wonderfully educated by computers. They will be still more cynical of the establishment, still more cynical of business, and still more cynical of traditional style obsolescence. They will lead the next phase of the great tide of rising expectations.

They will dictate to *you*—not vice versa. And they may stage riots aimed at *your* eccentricities, *your* lack of social understanding, and your *shallow* social involvements.

If you have not read the underground high school papers, I suggest you do so. *This is your future.*

3. New concepts in the custom-made will proliferate. Each of the Big Three in Detroit now makes available over one million options. Yet autos are mass-produced. The science of logistics made this feasible. Individual taste forced Detroit in this direction; it will do the same in fashion. This is inevitable as society insists that creative innovation must *enrich* society, not *enslave* it. *That* is the great new ingredient.

As an example of the extremes to which the custom-made concept may go, I note that custom-made molded chairs are being manufactured in West Germany. A customer is placed in a special chair—plastic foam is used to make a mold of his body—and a foam rubber chair is prepared from that mold.

4. Will it become fashionable to aspire to be unfashionable—to do your own thing? Is not that *precisely* the warning conveyed by the hippies?

5. Individual taste, affluence, etc., means that we are coming into an area of *think small*. Product line extension will *accelerate*. Product life will continue to *shorten*. Overstaying a fashion or design concept will invite still greater hazards. Computer information technology *must* provide instant feedback of item movement at the point of sale.

6. The specialty store, the boutique, will continue its strong comeback. The era is gone in which one store, under one roof, can hope to be *all* things to *all* people.

My conclusion is that higher education for more millions, higher discretionary purchasing power for more millions, more leisure time for more millions, and more sophistication among more millions will bring about a cultural explosion that may rival the one achieved by Greece. We face a future in which *millions* will participate in *and contribute* to the vast cultural and creative advances.

That's your future—and I doubt that *Vogue* and/or *Harpers' Bazaar* will lead you there!

BIBLIOGRAPHY

In place of a formal bibliography, the authors list here publications that aid the student or practitioner of fashion in keeping current and in measuring the present against the past and thus projecting the future.

The Conference Board, New York, *Guide to Consumer Markets*, prepared annually.
Editors of *Fortune, Markets of the Seventies*, New York, Viking Press, 1968. Similar studies are anticipated for each future decade.
U.S. Department of Commerce, Washington, D.C.:

> *Current Population Reports*, especially Series P-20, on population changes and projections, and Series P-60, on income. Issued at varying intervals.
> *Survey of Current Business*, monthly.
> *U.S. Industrial Outlook*, annual, issued near the close of each year to cover the upcoming year.
> *We, the Americans*, a series of reports from the 1970 Census of Population, of which the first, *Who We Are*, was announced in September 1972.

SECTION REVIEW AND ACTIVITIES

FASHION BUSINESS TERMINOLOGY

Define, identify, or briefly explain each of the following:
  Demographics
  Disposable personal income
  Consumerism
  Marketing concept
  Discretionary spending
  Consumer orientation
  Consumer expenditures

QUESTIONS FOR REVIEW

1. What socioeconomic changes in the past 20 years created today's mass market for fashionable apparel and accessories?

2. Do you agree that people tend to shop for apparel throughout the year instead of at periodic intervals for an entire season? Why? Give examples of items that experience a seasonal demand and examples of items that enjoy a year-round demand.

3. How important is consumerism today, and how is it being expressed, if at all (for instance, consumer movements and the like)?

4. Some people believe that changes in fashion are a device of industry to render present wardrobes obsolete. Do you agree? Why?

5. Do you believe that the fashion industries can control the amount of consumer expenditures for apparel? Defend your answer.

6. Do you believe that customers have better taste today than they had 10 years ago? Why?

7. What percentage of the family clothing dollar is spent on women's and children's clothing? What percentage is spent on men's and boys' clothing? How can you explain the difference in these percentages?

8. Does an increasing number of working women affect fashions? Why and how?

9. Summarize the major socioeconomic changes that are occurring in the consumer market, and suggest how these changes might affect fashion demand.

10. Suggest ways in which apparel retailers have adapted or may adapt to the changes taking place in the consumer market. Consider methods of selling, store hours, store locations, services, and assortments, for example.

APPLICATIONS WITH EXAMPLES

1. Discuss and/or visually illustrate with one or more current fashions the role that each of the following may have played in the development of this fashion.

     (a) Customer
     (b) Retailer
     (c) Apparel producer
     (d) Textile producer
     (e) Fashion magazine
     (f) Trade publication
     (g) Apparel designer
     (h) Textile designer
     (i) Accessory designer

2. The reading, "Looking Ahead in Fashion," was written in 1969. Which if any, of Mr. Weiss's predictions have already materialized? Cite or show examples to prove your answers. Are there any of his other predictions with which you disagree? Why?

APPENDIX
FASHION INDUSTRY LANGUAGE GUIDE

Accessories. All articles ranging from hosiery to shoes, bags, gloves, belts, scarves, jewelry, and hats, for example, worn to complete or enhance an outfit of apparel.

Accessorizing. The process of adding accessory items to apparel for display, for models in fashion shows, or for customers' clothes on request.

Adaptation. A design that reflects the outstanding features of another design but is not an exact copy.

Advertising. A nonpersonal method of influencing sales through a paid message by an identified sponsor. Advertising appears in media such as newspapers, magazines, television, and radio.

Amalgamated. Amalgamated Clothing Workers of America, the men's wear union.

Apparel. An all-embracing term applied to men's, women's, and children's clothing.

Avant Garde. In any art, the most daring of the experimentalists; innovation of original and unconventional designs, ideas, or techniques during a particular period.

Boutique. A free-standing shop or an area within a retail store, devoted to specialized merchandise for a special-interest customer.

Branch. In retailing, an extension (usually suburban) of the parent or flagship store, operated under the same name and ownership.

Caution. French term for admission or entrance fee charged to trade customers by *haute couture* houses.

Chain Organization. A group of retail stores that are centrally owned, each handling similar merchandise and that are usually similar in appearance. Chain stores are merchandised from a national or regional central office.

Chambre Syndicale De La Couture Parisienne. The French trade association that represents the *haute couture* houses of Paris.

Checked Out. A style number that sells rapidly; generally refers to retail selling.

Classic. A particular style that continues as an accepted fashion over an extended period of time.

Collection. A manufacturer's or designer's group of style and/or design creations for a specific season. The season's total number of styles of designs, accumulated for presentation to buyers, comprises a collection.

Confined. A line or label that is sold to one retailer in a trading area on an exclusive basis.

Contractor. A manufacturing concern that does the sewing for other producers (so-called because this work is done on a contractual arrangement).

Converter. A textile firm that buys or handles the "greige goods" or unfinished fabric from mills and gives the goods its finish—print, color, and any other treatment.

Cost Price. The price at which goods are billed to a store, exclusive of any cash discounts that may apply to the purchase.

Coty Fashion Award. Annual awards bestowed on outstanding designers.

Couturier. French word for (male) designer, usually one who has his own couture house. Couturière (female).

Craze. A fad or fashion characterized by much crowd excitement or emotion.

Custom Made. Apparel made to the order of individual customers; cut and fitted to individual measurements as opposed to apparel that is mass-produced.

Cutting-Up Trade. The segment of the fashion industries that produces apparel by cutting and sewing garments together (i.e., apparel producers).

Design. An arrangement of parts, form, color, fabric, and line, for instance, of a style.

Designer. A person who manipulates and arranges fabric, color, and line, for example, to create a version of a style.

Display. A visual presentation of merchandise or ideas.

Fad. A minor or short-lived fashion.

A Fashion (or Fashions). The prevailing style(s) at any particular time. When a style is followed or accepted by many people, it is a fashion.

Fashion. A continuing process of change in the styles of dress that are accepted and followed by a large segment of the public at any particular time.

Fashion Bulletin. Written report on significant fashions prepared by fashion specialists.

Fashion Clinic. Meeting of a group of persons interested in fashion (under the direction of a fashion specialist) for the purpose of presenting and/or discussing significant fashion trends; clinics are usually held at the beginning of new fashion seasons.

Fashion Consultant. A person who gives professional fashion advice or services.

Fashion Coordinator (or Director). A person charged with the responsibility for keeping abreast of fashion trends and developments, and acting as a source of fashion information to others in his or her organization. Other responsibilities vary from place to place, as do job titles.

Fashion Cycle. A term that refers to the rise, popularization, and decline of a fashion. It is usually represented visually by a wave-like curve

Fashion Forecast. A prediction as to which fashions and/or styles will be popular during a future period.

Fashion Group. A national noncommercial association of women engaged in the fashion business.

Fashion Image. The impression the consumer has of a retailer's position on fashion leadership, quality, selection, prices, and personality.

(The) Fashion Press. Reporters of fashion news for magazines, newspapers, broadcast media, etc.

Fashion Reporter. A person who specializes in reporting fashion news for magazines and/or newspapers.

Fashion Show or Showing. Formal presentation of a group of styles, often in connection with showing the season's new merchandise.

Fashion Trend. The direction in which fashion is moving.

Ford. A particular style or design that is produced by many different manufacturers at many different price lines simultaneously.

Garment Industry. Synonym for the apparel industry.

High Fashion. A fashion that is in the stage of limited acceptance.

Hot Number. A style number that sells quickly and in sizable quantities.

Haute Couture. The most important high fashion design houses in Paris.

I.L.G.W.U. International Ladies' Garment Workers' Union.

Inside Shop. An apparel concern that performs all the manufacturing processes on its own premises or in its own plant (as opposed to an outside shop).

Knock-Off. A design that is a copy of a higher-priced garment.

Line. A collection of styles shown by a producer in a given season.

Line-for Line Copy. Exact copy of a style originated by a foreign couturier.

Market. Potential customers for a product or service. A store's trading area. A city in which the showrooms of producers are concentrated. The period during which lines are first presented.

Markup (or Mark-on). The difference between the billed cost price and the original retail price of merchandise.

Mass Fashions (Volume Fashions). Styles or designs that are widely accepted and that can therefore be produced and sold in large quantities.

Mass Production. Production of goods in quantity—many at a time as opposed to one at a time.

Mode. Synonym for a fashion.

N.R.M.A. (National Retail Merchants Association). A trade association of the leading department, specialty, and chain stores in the United States.

Openings. Fashion showings of new collections by apparel producers at the beginning of a season.

Open-to-Buy. The amount of money that a buyer may spend on merchandise to be delivered in a given month.

Outside Shop. An apparel concern that utilizes contractors to do the sewing and finishing of its garments.

Prêt-à-Porter. (French term meaning literally ready-to-carry). French ready-to-wear apparel, as distinguished from couture clothes, which are custom-made.

Primary Market. Producers of the raw materials of fashion such as leathers and fabrics, for instance.

Private Brand. A trademark or brand name owned by a store or group of stores or a jobber, as contrasted to a producer-owned brand name.

Publicity A nonpaid message—verbal or written—in a public-information medium about a company's merchandise, activities, or services.

Ready-to-Wear. Apparel that is mass produced, as opposed to apparel made to a customer's special order (custom-made).

Reorder Number. A style number that continues to be ordered by sellers and consumers.

Resource. A retailer's term for a wholesale supplier.

Runner. A style number that continues to sell quickly over a period of time and that is reordered frequently.

Sample. The model or trial garment (may be original in design, a copy, or an adaptation) to be shown to the trade.

Secondary Market. Producers of finished consumer fashion products (dresses, coats, suits, and the like); the cutting-up trade.

Seventh Avenue. An expression used as a synonym for New York City's apparel industry. (Actually, a street on which are located the showrooms of many garment manufacturers.)

Showing. See **Fashion Showing.**

Smart. Having a fashionable appearance.

Style (noun). A type of product with specific characteristics that distinguish it from another type of the same product.

Style (verb). To give fashion features to an article or group of articles (as to style a line of coats and suits, for example.)

Style Number. An identification number given to a design or style by a manufacturer. The retailer uses the number when ordering the item and for stock identification.

Stylist. One who advises concerning styles in clothes, furnishings and the like.

Style Piracy. A term used to describe the use of a design without the consent of the originator.

Triangle Fire. A fire that occurred in the Triangle Shirtwaist factory in 1911 and took 146 lives. The tragedy was the turning point in the "sweat shop" era because it awoke the public conscience to the labor conditions in the garment industry.

Trunk Show. A producer's or designer's complete collection of samples brought into the store for a limited time to show customers the selection from which style numbers can be ordered in their size and color.

Vendeuse. French term meaning saleswoman.

Vendor. One who sells; resource from which a retailer buys goods.

Volume. Amount of dollar sales done in a given period by a retail store or other mercantile establishment.

Women's Wear Daily. Trade publication of the women's fashion industries.

CREDIT LIST

PAGE 52

Top "Signature of 450,000." Courtesy of the International Ladies' Garment Workers' Union. Union Label Department. (Solow/Wexton Advertising.)

Bottom Burlington Industries, Inc.

PAGE 102

Courtesy of the International Ladies' Garment Workers' Union. Union Label Department. (Solow/Wexton Advertising.)

PAGE 174

Top Photograph by Rhoda Roth.

Bottom Photograph of Givenchy Boutique. Courtesy of Bergdorf Goodman.

PAGE 230

Top Catherine Street store 1826. Courtesy of Lord & Taylor.

Bottom Modern branch at Falls Church, Va., 1965. Courtesy of Lord & Taylor.

PAGE 294

Left 1892 Vogue Magazine cover. Courtesy of Vogue Magazine.

Right 1972 Vogue Magazine cover. Courtesy of Vogue Magazine.

PAGE 334

Left Courtesy of Seidman family.

Right Delton Formal Wear, Inc., New York, N.Y.

PAGE 386

Left Courtesy of the International Ladies' Garment Workers' Union. Union Label Department. (Solow/Wexton Advertising.)

Right Courtesy of Ohrbach's Inc. (Doyle Dane Bernbach, Inc., Advertising.)

Pictures researched by **Linda Rosenthal** and **Carol Fogel.**

INDEX

Acceptance, customer, 3, 11
Accessories, cycles, 7
  industries, 129-136
  industry shipments, 131
  retail sales, 245
Acetate, 96
Adaptations, 185
Adrian, Gilbert, 32, 221-222
Advertising, apparel industry, 124
  cooperative, 124, 347
  fashion type, 317
  fiber producers', 87-88, 90-93
  magazine, 297
  men's wear, 347, 368
  percentage by industry, 303
  textile producers', 63
  use of fashion in, 319
Advertising Age, 166
Advertising agencies, 302, 316-318
Advisory services, 278
Affluence, 404
"Afro" fashion, 397
Agencies, advertising and publicity, 302, 316-318
Agent, import, 217, 219
Alexander's, 188, 210-211, 246, 268, 352
Alta Costura, 195
Altman, B., & Co., 399
Amalgamated (union), 339-340
American Fabrics, 88, 89
American Textile Manufacturers Institute, 55, 59
Amies, Hardy, 360-362, 366
Apparel industry, men's, 106, 335-384
  women's, 103-172
Apparel firms, giant, 108
Apparel Manufacturer, 373
Apparel sales, retail, 247
Apparel spending, 400, 407
Arcone, Sonia, 323
Associations, trade, 311; *see also listings in each section*

Auxiliary enterprises, 296-333
Avon, 247
Awards, 305
Ayer, N. W., & Son, 302

Bach, Henry, 145
Back-to-school, 392
Balenciaga, 225-226
Barmash, Isidor, 141
Barney's, 361, 365
Beckman, Irene, 320
Beeline, 247
Belt industry, 130
Bendel, Henri, 209
Bergdorf Goodman, 234
Bergdorf Goodman Chair of Fashion, 305
Bertin, Rose, 177, 179
Best sellers, 122
Blacks, influence of, 11, 397
Blass, Bill, 365, 366, 375, 377, 398
Bloomingdale's, 260
Bober, Franklin, 371-372
Bond Stores, 359
Bonwit Teller boutiques, 251
Bottom-up fashion theory, 10
Boutiques, 250-252, 277, 412
  couture, 189, 191
  design, 159
  men's wear, 353
Branch stores, 253
Brands, manufacturers', fiber, 90-94
  men's wear, 342, 347, 369, 375
  textile, 62
  women's wear, 125, 148
Brands, private, 310, 327, 347, 379
Britt, Steuart Henderson, 13
Brokers, merchandise, 308, 328
Brooks Brothers, 106, 233, 365
Brummel, Beau, 363
Bryant, Lane, 261-262
Bulletin, buying office, 309
Burlington Industries, 58, 61, 67, 76-81

Burton's Gentleman's Magazine, 296
Business publications, 300; *see also listings in
     each section*
Butte Knit, 148, 150
Buyer, resident, 323
   retail, 289
Buyers, resident, 279, 307, 323, 326, 347
   trade, 179, 180, 181
Buying, centralized, 310, 327
Buying offices, 279, 307, 323, 326, 347
Buying power, consumer, 64, 404

Cadwell, Franchellie, 368, 369
Cameron, Jean, 321
Capps, J., & Sons, Ltd., 358
Cardin, 182, 185, 189, 365
   boutique, 251
Carlisle, Gayle, 319
Carnaby Street, 173, 361
Carson, Johnny, 350, 363, 372
Cassini, Oleg, 366
Casual clothes, 15, 33, 46, 389
Catalogs, mail-order, 240
Cautions, couture, 180, 181
Celanese Corporation of America, 58, 68, 90-94
Celanese House, 93
Centers, fashion, 112, 113
Centers, production, accessories, 130-135
   men's wear, 340-342
   women's wear, 107-113
Centers, shopping, 252-254
Chains, growth of, 242
   mail-order stores, 241
   men's wear, 346
   sales, selected firms, 254
   share of market, 243
Chambre Syndicale de la Couture Parisienne,
     183
Chanel, 8, 95, 180, 219-220
Change, as element in fashion, 4
   statistics of, 402-407
Chinatown, 111
Civil War's effect, men's wear industry, 106,
     337
   textile industry, 57
Classics, 7, 123

Clinics, fashion, 299, 310, 328
Clothes Magazine, 76, 147, 158, 205, 262, 268,
     374
Clothing, family spending, 400
Cluett-Peabody, 344
CMA, 361
"Coffee house" boutiques, 272
Cohen, Arnold, 370-372
Cohen, Robert J., 368
Cohn-Hall-Marx, 58, 61
Cohn, J. W., 211
Colbert, Jean Baptiste, 177
Collins, Kenneth, 24, 203
Commission office, 328
Commissionaires, 187
Computer, 399-401
Conference Board, 402
Constable, Arnold, 233
Consultants, fashion, 19, 278, 306-307
Consultants, various, 311
Consumer, changing characteristics, 402-427
   marketing to, 397
   power of, 13-14
   role in fashion, 12-17
   spending for fashion, 15-16, 390-391, 400,
     407
Consumerism, 393
Contractors, men's wear, 339, 345
   women's wear, 114-115, 121
Controls, price, 394-396
Converter, hosiery, 133
   textile, 61
Copeland, Melvin, 6, 284
Copenhagen exhibit, 196
Copying, 127, 133, 177, 179, 184, 185, 203,
     216
Costumers, advertising, 319
Costumes, national, 389
Cotton, Maid of, 63
Cotton Industry Board, French, 183
Courrèges, André, 207
Couture, American, 127, 158-162, 162-165
   press week, 315-316
Couture, foreign, 176-226
   England, 193
   Europe, 195

Far East, 196
Israel, 196
Italy, 192
Paris, 176-192, 205-208
Spain, 195
Couture ready-to-wear, 127, 189-192, 193, 207
Couturiers in men's wear, 351
Cox, B. G., 371
Creativity, American, 138
Credit, editorial, 297, 300
Custom-made, 412
Custom salons, 233
Cutting, computer-guided, 401
Cutting-up trades, 54
Cycles, fashion, 6-8, 24

Daily New Record, 301
Daily sales sheet, 278
Daniels, Alfred H., 22-23, 277
Davis, Mrs. Tobé Coller, *see* Tobé Associates
Dawley, Melvin, 258
Deering-Milliken, 68
Demand, seasonal, 391
Demographics, 389, 397, 402
Department Store Management, 379
Department stores, 236-238
Design, 3
Design activities, apparel, 126
Designer boutiques, 251, 350
Designers, accessories, 135
   American, 107, 127, 156-158, 162-166, 258
   fabric, 66-67, 86-87, 92
   financing of, 162
   history-making, 219-226
   influence of, 411
   mass production, 128-129
   men's wear, 351-353, 373, 374-381
   millinery, 133
   stimuli for, 11
Designing process, apparel, 119
Dichter, Dr. Ernest, 356
Dimensions of market, 390
Dior, Christian, 6, 29, 33, 177, 180, 189, 224
Direct-selling establishments, 246-248
Discount Merchandiser, The, 244, 246
Discount stores, 212, 244-246

Display consultants, 311
Distribution, dual, 123-126, 264, 342, 347-349
Diversification, 58, 108, 138, 344, 346
Dixie Yarn Co., 66
Doncaster Clothes, 247
Door-to-door selling, 247
Doyle Dane Bernbach, Inc. 317, 320, 323
Dressmaking, custom, 233
Dual distribution, 123-126, 264, 342, 347-349
duPont, E. I., de Nemours & Company, Inc.,
   58, 67
Düsseldorf exhibit, 195

Eastern countries, 196
Education, effect on fashion, 389
Education, levels of, 405
Emmanuele, Louis, 368
Employment, apparel industry, 18, 104, 107,
   108
   costume jewelry, 130
   gloves, 131
   handbags, 132
   hosiery, 133
   labor force, 402, 406
   men's wear, 343
   retailing, 232
   shoes, 134
   women, 389, 406
England, fashion industry in, 193
Equal rights, 396
Escobosa, Hector, 274
Estevez, Luis, 298
Esthetics in fashion, 8
Europe, fashion industry in, 195
Events, news, 10
Everfast, 61
Excess, rule of, 27
Expenditures, consumer, 104, 400, 407

Fabrics, history, 95-97
Fad, 3
Failures, apparel industry, 116
Farkas family, 271
Farkas, Francine, 188, 210
Fashion, as promotional tool, 67-68
   business of, 17-19, 401, 388-415

centers, foreign, 192-198
consumer's role in, 12-14
definition, 3, 5, 22, 27
democratization of, 388
determination of, 8-12
forecasting, 14-17
high, 3
materials of, 54-100
meaning of, 2-5, 27
merchandising of, 277-285
movement, 5-8
nature, 22-23
prediction, 14-17
pre-planning, 89
retailers of, 232-293
role in U. S. economy, 184
schools of, 140
socioeconomics of, 1-50
terminology, 3
theories of, 9-10
trend, definition, 3
see also individual industries
Fashion accessories, 129-136
  value of shipments, 131
Fashion advertising, 317
Fashion babies, 179
Fashion business, 17-19, 401
  directions in, 388-415
Fashion enterprises, auxiliary, 296-333
Fashion Fair, London, 194
Fashion Group, The, 49, 329, 410
Fashion Institute of Technology, 140
Fashion Press Week, 300
Fashions, by decade, 30-34
  golden mean, 29
  post-crisis, 26
  prophetic, 284
Federal Trade Commission, 85-86
Fibers, man-made, 58, 62, 88-94
"Fifth season," 393
Filene's, 233
Fillmore, Gerald, 380
"Filter-up" theory, 9
Fish, Michael, 367
Flow chart, fashion industry, 19
Flow chart, textile industry, 59

Foley, Caroline R., 9
Foote, Cone & Belding, 320
Forbes Magazine, 85, 358
"Ford," 128
Ford, Richard, 380
Forecasting of fashion, 16-17, 42-44
Fox, Neal, 380, 381
France, fashion industry in, 176-192, 205-208
France, Mendès, 189
Franchise stores, 249
Franchising, couture, 191
Fur industry, 72-74
Fur Information and Fashion Council, 73
Fusaro, Dino, 373-374
Fusaro, Guido, 373-374

Galey & Lord, 79, 80
Garment dollar, chart, 129
Garmentown, 70
Genesco, 344, 359
Gernreich, Rudi, 9
Giantism, 412
  apparel industry, 108, 141, 145
  men's wear, 344, 358-359
  retailing, 248-250
  shoes, 135
  textile industry, 61-63, 96
Gimbel, Adam, 232
Giroud, Françoise, 200
Glove industry, 131
Glynn, Mary Joan, 10
Godey's Lady's Book, 296
Golden mean, 29
Goldsmith, Daisy, 35
Goodman, Andrew, 234
Goodman, Stanley J., 286
Grading, 121
Gray, John D., 360
Greenberg, Allan, 10
Greenstein, Blanche, 321
Grumbach, Didier, 189
Guideposts, fashion, 401

Hale, Sara Josepha, 296
Hamburger, Estelle, 37
Hammel, Faye, 258

Hammer, Ruth, 306
Handbag industry, 132
Harris, Murray, 370
Hart, Schaffner & Marx, 340, 344, 347, 359, 370
Hathaway Shirts, 344
Haute couture, 178
    see also Couture
Hawes, Elizabeth, 394
Hedonism, 357
Hefner, William A., 380
High fashion, 3
Hoffman, Marilyn, 204
Hong Kong, 211-212
Hosiery industry, 132
Hotpants, 39
Howard Stores, 359
Howe, Elias, 106

IACD, 373
ILGWU, 109, 198, 315
Imitation, 8
Immigrants, 110
Imports, 196-198, 209-219
Incorporated Society of London Fashion Designers, 193
Independent Retailers Syndicate, Inc., 309
Individuality, 401, 410
Industries, accessories, 129-136
    fur, 72-74
    leather, 70-72
    men's wear, 335-384
    women's wear, 103-172
Inflation, 395
"Inside" shops, 114
Integration, textile industry, 58, 85-86
Isbell, Thomas, 272
Israeli fashion industry, 196
Italian fashion industry, 192

Jewelry industry, 130
Jobbers, men's wear, 337-338
Jobbers, women's wear, 114-115

King, Charles W., 9
Klein, Adolph, 165

Klopman Mills, 67, 77, 78, 80
"Knock-off," 128
Korvette, E. J., 246
Krensky, Harold, 260

Labor force, 406
Lachman, Lawrence, 260
Lambert, Eleanor, 306, 321
Lane, Harold, Sr., 264
Lane Bryant, 261
Laser, cutting by, 345
Laun, Louis F., 90
Laver, James, 25-27, 367
Leaders, fashion, 7
Leased departments, 234
Leather industry, 70-72
Lee, Sarah Tomerlin, 329
Leezenbaum, Ralph, 368
Lerner, Max, 388
Lerner, Sam, 264
Lerner Shops, 243, 262-268
Levi-Strauss & Co., 166-168
Libraries, fabric, 68, 93
Licensing, Celanese, 93
Licensing arrangements, couture, 183, 191, 193
Life-styles, 11-12, 45-47
Line, creating, 117, 155, 346, 381
Line-for-line copies, 185, 204
Locke, Edith Raymond, 314
Lodge, Francis Cabot, 56
Logan, Jonathan, 147-154
Longuette, 37, 206
Lord & Taylor, 233, 258, 366
Lowenstein, M., 61

McCardell, Claire, 165, 224, 394
Made-to-measure men's wear, 338
Mademoiselle Magazine, 68-69, 314
Magazines, business, 300-302
    fashion, 235, 296, 300, 314
    general, 300
Magnin, I., & Co., 179, 234
Mail-order houses, 240-242
Malsin, Albert, 261
Malsin, Ralph, 262
Mannes, Marya, 367

Manufacturers, giant, *see* Giantism
Marcus, Stanley, 285
Margetts, Susan, 260
Market, mass, 389
Market weeks, 118
Marketing, men's wear, 347-349, 368-372
    textiles, 87, 88, 89-94
    women's wear, 123-129
Marketing/Communications, 319
Marketing concept, 397
Markets, fashion, 388, 390-391
    foreign, 126
    primary, 54
Mass merchandisers, 254
Mattlin, Everett, 363
Men's wear, 106, 335-384
Merchandising, fashion, 277, 285
Mergers, textile, 58, 85-86, 96
Michaels/Stern, 369
Miller, Ernest A., 326
Millinery industry, 133
Miniskirts, 193
Mittelman, A., 217
Mod fashions, 361, 372
Model, fashion, 157, 202
Molyneux, 193, 220-221
Monte-Sano, Vincent, 316
Morris, Bernadine, 207
Mortimer, Charles G., 398
Motivation in buying, 12

National Clothing Manufacturers Association, 339
National Recovery Act, 96
Needle trades, 54
Nehru jacket, 350, 363, 372
New Look of 1947, 6, 33, 177, 224
New York, 109, 110, 340
New York Couture Business Council, 300
New York Couture Press Week, 315
New York Dress Institute, 315
Newspapers, 300
Newsweek, 363
Norell, 17, 95, 128, 226
Nystrom, Dr. Paul H., 3, 7, 12

Offices, resident buying, 279, 307, 310, 323-326, 347
Ohrbach's, 204, 205, 303, 317
Open-to-buy, 278
Openings, couture, 182, 200
Openings, New York Couture, 118
"Outside" shops, 114
Ownership groups, sales of, 249

Pallack, Andrew & Co., 350
Palm Beach, 368, 369
Pants suit, 398
Paris, 107, 127, 176-192, 205-208, 233, 410
Party-plan retailing, 247
Pattern making, 120
Pattison, William B., 369
Peacock revolution, 349, 356, 364, 369
Peddlers, 232
Penney, J. C., 241, 244, 255
Perna, Rita A., 42
Personal leather goods industry, 132
Personalities influencing fashion, 11
Phillips-Van Heusen, 344, 347
Piracy, style, 127, 177, 183, 185, 203
Places influencing fashion, 5
Planning, retail, 277
Platt, David, 364
Poe, Edgar Allan, 296
Poiret, Paul, 14, 27, 95, 222-223
Pope, Virginia, 138
Population growth, 403
Portrait, Evelyn, 156
Post-crisis fashions, 26
Press, *see* Magazines; Newspapers; and Publications
Press in Paris, 208
Press release, 305
Press Week, New York Couture, 315
Pressman, Fred, 361, 365
Prêt-à-porter, 189, 190
Price ranges, women's wear, 120
Price, relation to fashion, 3, 7
Prices, 394-396
Priestland, Carl, 45-47
Primary markets, 54-102
Print-punch tickets, 399

Production centers, accessories, 130-135
 men's wear, 340-342
 women's wear, 109-113
Production systems, 121-123, 345-346
Profile, economic, men's wear, 343
Profile of change, 402
Promotion, men's wear, 347-348
 retail, 282-283
 textile industry, 63, 67-68, 93
 women's wear, 124-126
"Prophetic" fashions, 284
Public corporations, *see* Giantism
Public relations, 304
Publications, 296-302, 314-315, 350; *see also*
 listings in each section
Publicist, fashion, 321
Publicity, 124, 302, 304-305
Publicly owned, *see* Giantism

Qiana, 67
Quality regulation, 93-94, 396
Quant, Mary, 193, 244

Rayon, first mill, 95
Ready-to-wear, American, 103-172
 couture, 127, 164, 189-192, 193, 207
 foreign, 183-198
Reig, Ben, 315
Release, press, 305
Reorder numbers, 122
Research, market, 311
Resident buying offices, 279, 307, 310, 323-
 326, 347
Resources, fashion, 283
Retailers, fashion, 232-293
Retailing, changes in, 255, 286
Retail stores of producers, 346
Revolution in men's fashions, 349, 356, 364,
 369
Richman Brothers Co., 359
Rights, equal, 396
Rive Gauche shops, 207, 250
Robinson, Dwight E., 27
Rodier, Paul, 87, 95
Roe, John, 9
Rosen, Michael I., 369

Rosenberg, Jean, 209
Roth, Harry, 362
"Runners," 116, 121, 122

St. Laurent, Yves, 188, 207, 363
Saks Fifth Avenue, 232
Salba, Aeta, 212
Salesmen, producers', 124, 347
Salespeople, fashion, 276, 380
Salomon, Richard, 207
Salons, custom, 233
Sansing, Bill M., 370-372
Santo, Dr. Joseph, 361
Sapir, Edward, 12
Savile Row, 193, 365, 366
Schiaparelli, Elsa, 95, 221
Schwartz, David, 148, 151, 153
Schwartz, Richard J., 148, 151
Sears Roebuck & Co., 240, 243, 255
Seasonality, 391, 392
Seasons, accessories, 130
 apparel, 117
 men's wear, 349, 370, 381
Seeman, Dorothy Coleman, 209
Self-assertion, 13
Separates, men's, 350, 351
Sernau, Paul, 215
Serwer, Harry, 154
Seventh Avenue, 70, 111, 141
Sewing, computer guided, 401
Sewing machine, 106, 337
Shaw, Ben, 162-164
Sheehan, Rosemary, 306
Sheppard, Eugenia, 165
Shirtwaist style, 394
Shoe industry, 134
Shopping centers, 252
Shops, apparel, 238, 239
Shops, designer, for men, 353, 379
Shops, small, 250
Siegel, Henry I., 362
Silhouette cycles, 7
Six-months plan, 277
Size ranges, men's 345
Size standards, 106, 337
Slater, Samuel, 56

Slop shops, 337

Sloping of patterns, 121

Small firms, retail, 232, 239, 250-251
   textile, 60
   women's wear, 115

Socioeconomic causes of fashion change, 4

Spain, fashion industry, 195

Specialization in manufacturing, 116, 342

Specialty stores, 238, 348, 412

Species, endangered, 74

Speed, need for, 122

Spiegel's, 240

Sportswear, men's 350, 359, 380, 389

Statistics of change, 402-407

Status, 12

Stevens, J. P., & Co., 58, 61, 81-85

Stores, see Retailers; also category of
   store

Stores Magazine, 162

Stout, Pola, 86

Stutz, Geraldine, 209

Style, definition of, 3

Stylist, work of, 65-66, 69, 90

Suburbs, 11, 350, 359, 389

Suburbs, retailing in, 252

Sullivan, Mildred, 316

Syndicate, millinery, 133

Tailors, custom, 338

Tailors-to-the-trade, 339

Technology, effect on fashion, 10, 65

Television, effect on men's wear, 369-372

Textile Alliance, 211

Textile industry, 54-70, 75-100
   flow chart, 59

Thigpen, Peter L., 166-168

Thompson, J. Walter, 319

Thoreau, Henry, 13

Times, effect of, 10-11

Timing, 281, 391

Tobé Associates, 306

Toile, 201

Tolbert, Chip, 360

Trade associations, 311; see also listings in each
   section

Trade publications, 300; see also listings in each
   section

Trend, fashion, definition, 3

Trends, current, in retailing, 248

"Trickle-across" theory, 9

"Trickle-down" theory, 9

Trigère, Pauline, 111, 158-162

Trunk show, 161, 350

Turtleneck shirt, 398

"Underselling stores", 269

Union, Amalgamated (men's), 339-340

Union, ILGWU (women's), 109

Unisex, 35, 167, 396, 411

Unit control card, 279

Valentino, 193

Veblen, Thorstein, 4, 8, 9, 13

Vionnet, 95, 223

Vogue, history of, 296

Voice, Stanley, 362, 369, 371

Volume advertising, 318

Wages, apparel, 198

Ward, Montgomery, & Co., 240, 255

Ward, Robert, 369, 372

Weber & Heilbroner, 350

Weiss, E. B., 410

Weitz, John, 366, 367, 377-378

Whalen, Richard J., 81

Wilson, Doris, 320

Wilson, James K., Jr., 363, 370

"Window changer store," 263

Winick, Dr. Charles, 367

Winters, Arthur A., 316

Women, emancipation of, 389

Women, working, 406

Women's apparel and accessories, 103-172

Women's Wear Daily, 30, 95, 219, 301, 396

World War I and fashion, 126, 383

World War II and fabrics, 96

Worth, Charles Frederick, 179

Worth Street, 58, 70

Wynn, Michael, 380

Yarn, 60, 65, 90-94

Youth, influence on fashion, 35, 39, 411, 412